# THE RENAISSANCE
# THE PROTESTANT REVOLUTION
# AND
# THE CATHOLIC REFORMATION
# IN CONTINENTAL EUROPE

# THE RENAISSANCE
# THE PROTESTANT REVOLUTION
## AND
# THE CATHOLIC REFORMATION
## IN CONTINENTAL EUROPE

BY

## EDWARD MASLIN HULME
PROFESSOR OF HISTORY IN STANFORD UNIVERSITY

*46*

## Revised Edition

NEW YORK
THE CENTURY CO.

TO
GEORGE LINCOLN BURR,
BEST OF TEACHERS AND BEST OF FRIENDS,
THIS BOOK, SO DEEPLY INDEBTED TO HIM,
IS DEDICATED

# PREFATORY NOTE

This book is based upon the *Outlines of the Renaissance and the Reformation* by Professor George Lincoln Burr, printed, but not published, for the use of his students at Cornell. Here and there I have ventured to change the outlines, but the framework of the book remains his in every essential respect. To his list of references I am also indebted for guidance in my reading and for aid in compiling the list of books published for the first time in the second printing of my book. In the course of our long correspondence other books than those mentioned in his *Outlines* have been called to my attention by my former teacher, and for this aid, too, I wish to make public acknowledgment. Another debt to my master is for his " enthusiasm of humanity," which is so highly contagious, and which I hope pervades in some degree every page I have written.

For the subject-matter of the book I am particularly indebted to Gebhart, Berger, Dilthey, Gothein, and Beard, whose works are mentioned in the lists of references for the various chapters to which they relate.

E. M. H.

# TABLE OF CONTENTS

## THE RENAISSANCE

## THE PROTESTANT REVOLUTION

## THE CATHOLIC REFORMATION

# TABLE OF CONTENTS

# LIST OF MAPS

# THE RENAISSANCE

# THE RENAISSANCE

## CHAPTER I

### THE PAPACY

WE shall begin the study of the Renaissance with the last quarter of the thirteenth century. Not that the Middle Ages ended at this time and that then the Renaissance, in all its aspects, began. One cannot say when the Middle Ages gave place to the Renaissance. Indeed, in some respects, the Middle Ages are not over yet. They still subsist, stealing in silent currents along the subterranean ways of the world. It is impossible to date the bounds of an era with any degree of accuracy. Eras are not initiated with single dramatic events. In the great development of civilization there is nothing sudden, but rather is the change like that which takes place in a forest — birth, growth, and death go on almost unnoticed side by side. There are always many foreshadowings of any intellectual movement. So, one must not expect to find the Renaissance, or any other important era, inaugurated by a striking event or a violent revolution. Only very gradually did the new dispensation take form and shape. It was not announced to a startled world by the blast of a sudden trumpet.

Let us first of all make a brief survey of the Europe of that day from Sicily to Scotland, and from Cape Finisterre to the frontiers of Muscovy. At the dawn of the Renaissance, Christendom could claim only a small part of the world. The Mohammedan conquests had greatly diminished its extent since the seventh century. Christianity, as the ruling power, had been expelled from her most glorious seats — from Palestine, Syria, Asia Minor, Egypt, North Africa, and from a considerable part of the Spanish peninsula. The Greek and Italian peninsulas

3

were hers, the German Empire, France, the northern part of the Spanish peninsula, the British Isles, the Scandinavian kingdom, and in a rather dubious way the outlying Slavic and Danubian kingdoms. In exchange for her old and illustrious strongholds she had fallen back upon the northern countries, and all along her frontiers she maintained a spirit of incessant watchfulness and sometimes of actual aggression.

**The Divisions of Christendom**

But Christendom was divided within itself into two parts. There were the Greek Church and the Latin Church. In the Greek peninsula, and in Asia Minor, were to be found the adherents of the former, surrounded and submerged by the conquering Moslem; and here and there, too, in the turbulent Danubian and Slavic lands. To the Latin Church belonged the remainder and by far the greater part of Christendom.

**The Neighbors of Christendom**

To the East and the South there lay the Soldan's country. When the Moslems were defeated by Charles the Hammer, in 732, the tide of their conquest in the West was checked; but in the East it continued to flow onward, slowly yet steadily, until even Constantinople itself was subject to the age-long threat of capture. Beyond Islam was the far Orient, of which little definite information was possessed by the Europeans.

The schism that had divided Christendom into its Greek and Latin Churches took place in the tenth century; and so bitter had become the controversy between the two churches that in Constantinople the opinion was freely expressed that the Turkish turban would pollute St. Sophia less than the hat of the cardinal.

**The Greek Church**

The Greek Church had been reduced to a fatal though oftentimes mutinous subjection to the State; and it had little contact with Western life. Not only doctrinal and ritualistic differences had separated it from the Latin Church, but also political and racial. The elements that went to make up the Greek Church were very composite; and this is to be accounted for, in part, by the fact that there was a large Asiatic admixture.

**The Pope**

At the head of Latin Christendom was the Pope who claimed both spiritual and temporal supremacy, a claim which received its fullest expression at the hands of Innocent III and Boniface VIII. No Roman Emperor ever wielded such power. He it was who launched the Crusades against the infidel, the heathen, and the heretic. He alone could call a general council of the Church, and he alone could confirm its decisions. He could pronounce an interdict against an entire country; and he could create and depose kings. All Western Europe professed obedience to the Roman pontiff. The same splendid ritual was performed

in the same sonorous language, the same incomparable traditions were held in reverence, and the same doctrines received
universal assent. Within this vast fold were to be found the
most diverse peoples and kingdoms antagonistic one to the other.
This great Church was exceedingly well organized and immensely
rich. The Pope had his curia at Rome, the supreme appellate
tribunal of the Church with great power and many functions.
Indeed, the twelfth century had witnessed the final change of
the pastoral character of the Roman see into the juristic and
political character of the Roman curia, its moral and theological activity superseded by its worldly interests. Law had replaced theology as the basis of the papal power.

The cardinals were the advisers of the Pope, and it was they
who elected his successor. Eventually they were to be found
in all the principal countries, but as yet the non-resident cardinalate was only beginning and so the large majority of them were
Italians. Beneath the Pope were the archbishops, who could **The Clergy**
exercise their power only after having received the pallium from **of the**
him, and each of whom was the overseer of a number of bishops. **Church**
Under the bishops were the priests who administered the services of the Church to the people in town and country. The
regular clergy consisted of monks, and nuns, and friars. They
were grouped into different orders, the more recently organized
of which acknowledged obedience to a general. They were more
directly under the control of the Pope than were the secular
priests, who owed obedience to their bishops; the Pope could
give them direct orders through the generals, or other officers,
so they could be used as a sort of papal militia. The monks
remained in their monasteries and left the care of men's souls
to the secular clergy. But the friars, fortified with the privileges given them by the Pope, traversed the world. Everywhere they preached and heard confessions. They were itinerant priests. Through the friars especially the papal power was
felt directly in every part of the continent.

The Latin Church had gradually built up a most comprehensive and, with regard to its fundamental dogmas, a well-articulated system of belief; though one must not think that all its **Creeds and**
various elements had been completely harmonized, because there **Practices**
were many cross-currents, many conflicts of theory with prac- **Latin**
tice, and not a little that was confusing. For her creed she **Church**
claimed in the most outspoken of terms indefeasible authority.
She alone was the interpreter to man of the will and the word of
God. Seven sacraments had been instituted for the salvation
of man; they were indispensable to his spiritual life, and they

could be administered, with the exception of baptism under certain conditions, only by a regularly ordained priest. So the laity were absolutely dependent upon the priesthood for the nourishment of their religious life. Outside the pale of the Church it was hopeless to seek an approach to God. In temporal matters, also, the Church was omnipresent. Her penetrating power touched every worldly subject. She had come to be not only a religious guide, but also a great juristic, economic, and financial institution. Over the temporal as well as the spiritual personalities of men she exercised control in an extraordinary degree. Nor was her power confined to this world. She had been given authority to bind and loose in purgatory as well as upon earth.

There were two empires, both of them "imperial shadows that represented the majesty of Constantine and Charlemagne," yet both of them claiming the inheritance of the ancient authority of Rome. For centuries the Greek Empire had been essentially a static not a dynamic State. Its history is that of a government, not that of a nation. Its story is that of administration and law, rather than that of literature or of liberty. Yet it must not be forgotten that through the Middle Ages it held in its keeping the treasures of Greek learning. Out of hordes of barbarians it had created the kingdoms of Servia, Croatia, and Bulgaria. To Slavs and to Goths it had given ideas and institutions of government; and its missionaries were to be found from the shores of the Baltic to Abyssinia. Yet now it was in its last agonies of servile decrepitude, awaiting inevitable extinction at the hands of the Turk.

**The Greek Empire**

The Holy Roman Empire extended from the Baltic Sea to the Mediterranean and from France to Hungary. Nominally this vast territory was ruled over by an Emperor with supreme authority, but except in his own personal dominions his power was but a shadowy thing. Under strong and able successors of Charles the Great the imperial power had been made something more than symbolical, but under weak and irresolute ones it had diminished again to the vanishing-point. There were many reasons for this,—geographical, social, and political. The Holy Roman Empire had for its basis only an idea, that of cosmopolitan dominion, or world-monarchy; but feudalism established itself in Germany as elsewhere, and before the fact of feudalism the idea of imperialism gave way. Every decade saw the centrifugal force increase and the common bond of union grow weaker. The imperial office was not hereditary but elective; and the election lay in the hands of great feudatories who were generally

**The Holy Roman Empire**

unwilling to place in power any one who would be likely to check the gradual growth of their own independence. Imperial taxation and an imperial army, two things indispensable to the exercise of imperial authority, had never been acquired. So the Empire remained a congeries of some 362 principalities, ecclesiastical and secular; many of them composed of patches lying separate from each other; and many of them too infinitesimal to be represented on any ordinary map. Among the more important of the Germanic secular States were Saxony, Brandenburg, Bavaria, Lorraine, and Bohemia.

And now, having glanced briefly at the empires, let us look at the kingdoms. In Germany the most striking fact of the time is the election of Rudolf I of Hapsburg to the imperial throne. The territorial possessions of that secondary prince were insignificant, but in a few years he acquired Austria and Styria and so a new dominion was created, destined to assume great importance among the principalities that made up the Holy Roman Empire. Bohemia, which lies in the very heart of Europe, almost equally distant from each of the great seas, a distinct physical unit by virtue of its encircling and forested mountains, became a kingdom in the middle of the twelfth century, but it remained within the Empire. In France the principle of consolidation had been at work for a long time, and was continuing when the age of the Renaissance opened. Nowhere else was there to be found so highly centralized a government. These things were made possible by the sense of nationality which the French people had acquired, and by the existence of a national army and national taxation. In England the long reign of Edward I, a vigorous, able, and truly national king, had just begun. It was an era in which the English came into their own, a time of political, economic, and social development, and of territorial aggrandizement. In the land won back from the Moslem invaders in the Spanish peninsula there were four Christian kingdoms,— Aragon, Castile, Navarre, and Portugal. At times there had been more than three Spanish kingdoms. Their unions and divisions had been frequent, and such changes were to continue until at last but two kingdoms, Spain and Portugal, should share the territory south of the Pyrénées. In the far North there were three Scandinavian kingdoms, Norway, Sweden, and Denmark, whose relations to each other had constantly shifted. To the North and East three Slavic kingdoms were to be found. Bohemia, the land of the Czechs, was, as we have seen, a member of the German Empire. Poland had grown up from a collection of small States into a powerful kingdom. Lithuania, the last of the heathen States in Europe, which had led a troubled career, witnessed at the close of the Middle Ages a great outburst of vigor and became one of the most far-extended of the European countries.   In the territory drained by the Danube there was Hungary, the land of the Magyars, who with the Ottoman Turks, were the only Turanian people who succeeded in establishing permanent States in the continent of Europe.   The two other Danubian kingdoms, Servia and Bulgaria, were both Slavonic powers, and the chief of them was Servia, whose people made a brave resistance to the Turk.

Italy was made up of innumerable little republics and despotisms, petty commonwealths that were constantly at war with each other.   In that Southern peninsula it was the cities that

**The Cities**

were of chief importance.   In Italy and in Germany territorial disintegration had favored the rise and growth of cities that became centers first of commerce and then of culture.   Venice, Milan, Florence, Rome, Padua, Siena, and Naples were among the principal Italian cities.   In other countries, too, cities had achieved importance.   They were to be seats of the new secular culture that was to work so great a change in the world.   In Germany there were Augsburg and Nuremberg, and in the far North, Lübec, Hamburg, and Bremen.   In the Low Countries, Bruges, Ghent, Amsterdam, and Antwerp were all busy hives of commerce.

In this brief survey of Europe the universities must not be overlooked.   Until the rise of secular culture made the cities of chief importance in the social life of Europe the universities were the most potent of the intellectual forces.   In them were to be

**The Universities**

found the acutest minds of the time drawn from every country and from every class.   Far to the South lay Salerno, then as always chiefly a medical school.   The great law school at Bologna gathered to itself vast numbers of students from every land and by its inculcation of the principles of Roman Law became a force in the decline of feudalism and the rise of the modern nations.   The mother university, the one that served as a model for others, was Paris, and there scholasticism made for itself a stronghold.   In England there were Oxford and Cambridge.   In Spain there was Salamanca, devoted especially to law, and quite aloof from its sister institutions of other countries.   At the beginning of the Renaissance period Germany did not possess a single university.   Prague was founded in 1348, and the same century witnessed the establishment of Vienna, Erfurt, Heidelberg, and Cologne.   There were other schools of lesser importance such as Padua, Toulouse, and Montpellier; but altogether there were not many universities. The new age was to make

important additions to their number.

Such was the general condition of Europe when, on Christmas
Eve, 1294, Benedetto Gaetani was elected Pope and assumed the
title of Boniface VIII. He was a scholar learned in the civil
and the canon law, handsome, eloquent, and arrogant, and filled
with the lust of worldly power. Although he was an old man
his vigor, as he proceeded to assert the most extreme claims of
the Papacy, soon became apparent. Nine years previously there
had succeeded to the French throne Philip IV, a man bent upon
continuing the work of welding France into a compact monarchy.
He was ably assisted in his government of the country by men of
the sword and men of the law. Between the Papacy and France
there was soon precipitated a quarrel. In the great struggle
with the Empire the Papacy had triumphed, very largely because
the world-wide dominion to which the Empire aspired was opposed to the tendencies of the time. In its struggle with France
it was destined to fail, because it had come into conflict with one
of the rising forces of the time, that of national development.

Philip the Fair was the representative of the growing feeling
of nationality. The French and the English kings were at war
with each other over the possession of Guienne. The Pope required them to submit to his arbitration, and when they refused,
he issued the bull *Clericis laicos* which forbade the clergy to pay
taxes or to make gifts to laymen without the papal consent, and
summoned the French prelates to confer with him in Rome.
This bull, one of the most important pronunciamentos of the
temporal power of the papacy, is also the keynote of its decline.
Both Philip and Edward I replied with retaliatory measures.
The former, by prohibiting the exportation of money from France
without the royal consent, cut off French contributions to Rome.
In 1300, while this struggle between the medieval Papacy and
the rising tide of nationality was still in its first stages, Boniface
proclaimed the famous year of Jubilee. Remission of sins was
granted to all who should visit the Holy City in that year. Vast
throngs of pilgrims from many countries came flocking to the
" threshold of the apostles," filled with the desire to see the holy
places with their bodily eyes, and leaving large sums of money
as a token of their devotion. Boniface was seemingly triumphant. He had crushed the Colonna, his personal enemies in
Rome, and he had proclaimed that the Pope was set over the
kingdoms of the world, to aid or to destroy. But he could not
read the signs of the times. He was misled by the outburst of
feverish religious enthusiasm, and he failed to estimate the grow-

ing sense of nationality in Europe. He strained the bow too hard and it broke in his hands. The breach between the Papacy and France went on widening. The people of France, including the lawyers whom the recent development of legal studies had created, and even the clergy, were gathered about Philip, for they saw in him the champion of French nationality. In the course of the controversy the papal legate was imprisoned and brought to trial. In reply, Boniface, on December 5, 1301, issued the bull *Ausculta fili* in which he reasserted the papal power over kings and kingdoms, denied the right of all laymen to exercise any power over ecclesiastics, and repeated the summons of the French prelates to his presence. Philip caused the bull to be burned in public; the legate was banished, and the clergy forbidden to attend the papal conference. On November 18, 1302, Boniface issued the bull *Unam sanctam* in which he declared that the Pope holds both the temporal and the spiritual sword, of which he delegates the former to secular princes; and that it is absolutely necessary to salvation that every human creature should be subject to the head of the Church. Both sides began the final attack. At a meeting of the States-General in June 1303, in which every class of the nation, except the peasantry who were unrepresented, voiced its protest against the demands of the pontiff, the Pope was accused of heresy, tyranny, and unchastity, and an appeal was made from him to a general council of the Church. Boniface, who had gone to the little mountain town of Anagni, pronounced excommunication against Philip and was preparing to declare the French throne vacant, when he was seized by an emissary of the French king aided by Italians who had suffered injury at the hands of the Pope. It had been planned to capture the Pope and bring him before a Council in Lyons, but one of the cardinals persuaded the repentant populace of the town, who had abandoned the Pope to his enemies, to avenge the outrage upon the pontiff. The conspirators were driven from the town and the Pope released. A few weeks later, greatly weakened, if not mad with rage and terror, Boniface died. The outrage of Anagni has been called a " generative fact." With it the political supremacy of the Papacy comes to an end, and its ecclesiastical supremacy is threatened. Even the great Innocent III had failed to secure for the political claims of the Papacy more than a temporary success, and since his time the new force of nationality had made their success more hopeless than ever. So, when those claims were asserted at this time by a pontiff of inferior power, in words more haughty than those of the most powerful of his predecessors, it is scarcely a matter of surprise that the struggle ended with their defeat. Henceforth if we would find the medieval Papacy we must descend with Dante to visit the regions of the dead.

Boniface was succeeded by Benedict XI, a mild and conciliatory Dominican friar, who died within a year after his accession to the papal throne. The next Pope, Clement V, elected after an interregnum of nine months, was the nominee of Philip IV. He was a Frenchman, and after his coronation at Lyons he never set foot in Italy. For some time he wandered over Gascony and Guienne, stopping wherever he found reverence and entertainment. Then he took up his residence in the town of Avignon, which, in 1348, became the property of the pontiffs. With the election of Clement there began the long foreign residence of the Papacy. Seven successive pontiffs resided in Avignon, surrounded by French influence and, in the opinion of contemporary Europe, dominated by French interests. It is true that Clement V and his immediate successor bowed to the will of the French monarchy, but the other Avignonese popes were more independent of French control than has been commonly supposed. Clement, at the instigation of Philip, revoked the obnoxious bulls of Boniface VIII, and concurred in the suppression of the Templars whose property the king desired and whose power and privileges he wished to take away. The next Pope, John XXII, quarreled with Louis of Bavaria who had succeeded to the Germanic Empire; and when he pronounced heretical the doctrine of the Spiritual Franciscans that the Church and the clergy should follow the example of Christ and his apostles and hold no corporate or individual property he alienated a large part of that powerful body and also great numbers of the German peasantry. Benedict XII was a modest and feeble Cistercian who remained a monk under the purple robes of the pontifical office. Clement VI was an amiable man, luxurious and lettered, fond of the society of scholars and artists, and self-indulgent to the point of laxity. Under Innocent VI, a born ascetic and something of a reformer, the license of the papal court which had become notorious was somewhat checked. Urban V displayed no little sagacity in carrying out the reforms to which he was earnestly devoted. He returned to Rome but deemed himself too insecure there and so went back to France. The last of the Avignonese popes, Gregory XI, was also an able man of high character, sincerely though not very aggressively active in the work of ecclesiastical reform.

What had transpired in Rome, the erstwhile capital of Latin Christendom, during all these years of the " Babylonish Captivity "? Even under the ablest of the popes who lived in Rome before the Captivity the Papal States had never been effectively governed. Every city of importance was either a self-governing community or subject to a despot. In Rome itself the popes had exercised very little direct authority. Indeed, in turbulent times popes had been obliged to seek safety in flight. It was a difficult city to govern. Its rabble had been demoralized ever since the days of *panem et circenses*. Its streets were narrow and tortuous.

**Rome during the Captivity**

It was perpetually crowded with thousands of foreigners, many of whom doubtless discarded their own code of morals when they visited a city of alien manners, a fact frequently true of travellers today. But the chief cause of disorder was perhaps the fact that the great feudal families, particularly the Orsini and the Colonna, who had made the city a cluster of fortified camps, carried on warfare with each other within the city walls. It was seldom that the popes when they were in Rome had been able to quell the disturbances; and now that they were absent, the lawlessness and the license went on without restraint; the squalid populace was the prey of first one baronial family and then another; and brigands came up to the very gates of the city. At last Cola di Rienzi (1313?–54), a man of humble birth, took it upon himself to restore Rome to her greatness. He persuaded her people to resist the oppression of the nobles. On May 20, 1347, a self-governing community was established. But it was only for a brief time that the pale shadow of the great republic had been evoked from the ruins of the Campagna, for Rienzi was essentially a weak man. The new government fell at the end of seven months, and Rome relapsed into anarchy.

Despite the fact that the removal of the papal residence could be justified, in part at least, by the prolonged state of political anarchy that had prevailed in Italy, the residence of the popes in Avignon had the most deleterious effects upon the Church.

**The Church during the Captivity**

When the Papacy became to all outward seeming the mere vassal of France, it lost in a large measure the respect and the allegiance of other countries. Its revenues diminished. To offset this it resorted to increased taxation and to irregular practices. Bishoprics and abbacies were handed over to laymen in consideration of payments to the Papacy, that they might enjoy the incomes. Plurality of benefices was allowed for the same reason. The meshes of the whole network of the deplorable fiscal system were drawn ever tighter. At the head of monastic establishments were men better fitted to wear the helmet than the miter, and on the episcopal thrones were men who would have made better bankers than bishops. Increased fees were demanded for induction into the episcopal office and for the trial of cases in the ecclesiastical courts. This financial system contributed with the Avignonese residence to a great loss in the prestige of the Papacy. No longer did the Papacy derive any support from the fact of living outside the jurisdiction of any one of the conflicting European nations. No longer did it obtain additional reverence by residence at the shrine of the two great apostles, in a city universally deemed sacred and sonorous with the voice of many centuries.

Upon the religious life of the time the effect of the captivity was no less undesirable. It is true that several of the Avignonese popes were not unworthy men themselves, and that they initiated that patronage of the Renaissance which the papacy generally maintained until the Council of Trent; but their court was only too often a center of scandal. As the seat of the Papacy, Avignon was a cosmopolitan city and the center of European politics. Artists, scholars, statesmen, and adventurers flocked thither. It was a city given up very largely to worldly affairs, to pleasures and to gaieties. Its corrupt politics and foul immorality provoked the wrath of Dante, the mockery of Petrarch, and the censure of all who had the welfare of the Church at heart. The moral state of Latin Christendom matched that of its temporary capital. Everywhere immorality was increasing. The Franciscan revival was a thing forgotten; and the preaching friars of St. Dominic had themselves fallen into the most deplorable degeneration. Among the monastic and secular clergy alike, monks and nuns, prelates and priests, moral corruption was rampant. The quarrel with the Spiritual Franciscans had produced a profound division within the Church. Lollardy in England had alienated the sympathy of thousands. And everywhere mysticism was making for less dependence upon the Church and her sacraments. But while there was much corruption within the Church and incipient revolt against the Papacy there were many devout men who desired the return of the pope to Rome and an internal reform that should sweep away the crying evils of the time. It was St. Catherine of Siena, a dreamy and mystic girl, who in a state of ecstasy, so she believed, saw Christ and received the Host from the hand of an angel, that gave supreme expression to this spirit of religious enthusiasm. From her convent cell she had closely watched the politics of Italy, and had become aware of the wide-spread corruption that prevailed. She determined to restore the Papacy to Rome and to initiate a moral reform. There floated before her eyes "the vision of a purified Church, of which the restoration of the papacy to its original

Effects of the Captivity upon the Religious Life of the Time seat was to be at once the symbol and the beginning." Displaying the diplomatic finesse of the Italians in the highest degree she corresponded with popes and princes. From city to city she went pleading for peace in the distracted peninsula. She braved the perils of the sea, and at last stood at the foot of the papal throne. What passed between the pontiff and Catherine in their final interview at Avignon we do not know, but on September 13, 1376, Gregory, stepping over the prostrate body of his aged father, took the road to Marseilles where the galleys had secretly been made ready to take him to Rome. It was destined that Gregory and Catherine should meet only once more, but that was on Italian soil. She died on April 29, 1380, having proved herself to be the leading statesman in Italy in the fourteenth century. Had she lived, her purity and her perspicacity, her ardor and her persistence, and the feminine grace of her policy, would doubtless have profoundly modified the course of events.

Gregory died fourteen months after his triumphant entry into the Eternal City. Then it was felt that a great crisis was at hand. Only by the election of an Italian pope could papal residence at Rome be assured. The election to the Papacy of a French prelate would involve a return to Avignon. The conclave resulted in the election of Urban VI, an Italian, who at once began measures for the reform of the curia and the Church. But so tactless was he, and even brutal, that he soon offended a large number of the cardinals. Still more important than their personal dislike of Urban were the deep-seated motives of political interest that made the French cardinals view with disfavor the new Italian pope. Six months later, declaring that the pressure of the Roman populace, in its demand for an Italian pontiff, had prevented the free action of the conclave, some of the cardinals elected Roger of Geneva who assumed the name of Clement VII, and who before long took up his residence at Avignon. It is impossible to learn the absolute truth of the circumstances that brought about the great schism in the Church. The witnesses of one side take sharp issue with those of the other. But the schism was an indisputable fact. Motives that for the most part were purely political began to group the various nations and principalities about each of the rival popes. The German Emperor declared for Urban, but he did not carry all the Germanic principalities with him, for Bavaria, Luxemburg, Lorraine, Mainz, and other German States lent their sanction to Clement. Italy also was divided. Naples, Savoy, Piedmont, and Monferrato adhered to Clement, while the remainder of the peninsula acknowledged obedience to Urban. Scotland held for Clement.

England supported the Roman pontiff, as also did Flanders,
Hungary, and Poland. France, too, was divided; the English
possessions followed the leadership of their ruler, while the
French king recognized Clement. For a time Castile, Aragon,
and Navarre remained neutral, but eventually they gave their
support to Clement, while Portugal gave hers to Urban. Everywhere the prelates followed the princes in their allegiance, and
the people followed their pastors. The Schism was complete.

Very early there was broached for the settlement of the Schism
the plan of a general council of the Church. But great difficulties
were in the way. It would not be easy amid the conflicting
interests of Europe to decide upon a place of meeting. The
two popes were opposed to it. Who, therefore, should convoke
it? Then, too, the question as to who should be summoned was
a disputed one. And, should these difficulties be overcome, how
could the decrees of the council be enforced? While the question of a general council was being debated, three popes of the
Roman line died — Urban VI in 1389, Boniface IX in 1404, and
Innocent VII in 1406. The Roman pontiff was now Gregory
XII. In 1394 the Avignonese pope, Clement VII, had died.
His successor was Benedict XIII. Some of the cardinals of
both popes issued an invitation to all bishops to attend a council
at Pisa. An imposing number of prelates was present at the
council which met in 1409. The two popes, having failed to
answer the summons to appear at the council, were solemnly
deposed, and Alexander V was elected in their stead. The new
pope was acclaimed by the majority of the countries. But
neither of the deposed popes acknowledged the action of the
council; and as Naples, Poland, and parts of Germany continued
to obey Gregory, and the Spanish kingdom and Scotland persisted in their allegiance to Benedict, the council instead of les-
sening the number of popes simply added a third one. And in
the matter of the reformation of morals the council did nothing.
The new pope, Alexander V, proved to be altogether too feeble
and ineffective to meet the crisis. His pontificate was a short
one, lasting only a little over ten months. He was succeeded by
John XXIII who was more of a politician than a priest, more of
a condottiere than a Churchman.

A second council was inevitable. It was opened at Constance
in 1414, and continued for four years. John XXIII, the pope
elected by the council of Pisa, was deposed and submitted with
little opposition. The Roman pope, Gregory XII, resigned.
Benedict XIII of Avignon, was also deposed, but he stubbornly
refused to yield. When he died in 1424 three of his cardinals

elected one successor, and one cardinal elected another. But eventually these "phantom popes" disappeared. Then there was left only the Pope who had been elected by the council of Constance, Martin V. Thus the council had accomplished one of the tasks that had confronted it. The Schism had been healed. In its attempt to check the spread of heresy it committed John Hus and Jerome of Prague to the flames. But as for the moral reformation, for which the very stones in all Christendom were crying out, it did practically nothing. Europe was hopelessly distracted, and the council failed in its most important work very largely because it had reflected only too faithfully the national dissensions and antagonisms of the time.

The results of the long Captivity and the Schism had been most deplorable. At Avignon the papal retinue had gradually become larger and more luxurious, and the immorality of the city on the Rhone, despite its thousand belfries, had become a
*Results of Captivity and Schism*
byword throughout Europe. And when the Schism had occurred the nations had taken the side of one or the other of the rival pontiffs as best suited their own interests. Finally, when the high office of the successor of St. Peter was contested like a temporal throne by unworthy disputants, who were continually fulminating excommunications against each other, it had fallen into greater disrespect than ever. The papal administration had become demoralized. Among clergy and laity alike, immorality had spread like a plague. Corruption in every rank of the hierarchy is the constant theme of St. Catherine of Siena; and the reform measures considered by the Council of Constance "are eloquent as to the evils which they were designed to remove." Very largely the Church had ceased to answer to the spiritual needs of the people, and so heresy had been fostered and increased, and eventually the Protestant Revolution was to result. A not undesirable impulse was given to European thought. Within the Church the anti-papal theory of the supremacy of general councils over popes had gained adherents and had become entrenched in the University of Paris, hitherto the champion of orthodoxy. This discussion of the basis of papal power was not without result. The "old unquestioning confidence in the vice-gerent of God was gone."

The Schism had ended; but the position of Martin V was beset with difficulty. In the midst of the conflicting interests of na-
*The Rivalry of Papacy and Council*
tions and of individuals he had to regain the lost power and prestige of the Papacy, and to effect a satisfactory reformation throughout the entire Church. Something of the first part of this great task he had accomplished when he died in 1431, and

he had also made a beginning with reform. The Council of Constance had provided for the periodical summoning of a general council; and so it came about that a council was convoked at Basel in 1431. Three questions confronted it — that of reform; that of the spread of heresy, especially in Bohemia; and that of union with the Greek Church, the ever-increasing pressure of the Turkish conquest upon the Eastern Empire having brought this last question to the surface. The new Pope, Eugene IV, though "self-opinionated like all Venetians," was a man of culture, skilled and aggressive. He viewed with disfavor the independent spirit of the council, and the cynical politicians of the curia smiled at its enthusiasm. So, another struggle began between papal absolutism and the aristocracy of the prelates. The long-continued differences between the pope and council broke out into open war. On September 13, 1437, Eugene declared the council to be dissolved and then, as a foil, he summoned another one to meet at Ferrara, which duly acknowledged the primacy of the papal power. He desired to effect a reconciliation between the Greek and the Latin Churches, and the dire extremities to which the activity of the Turks had reduced the Eastern Empire seemed to furnish a fair prospect of success. For several reasons the Pope's council was removed from Ferrara to Florence. Thither came the Byzantine Emperor, John Palæologus VI, in company with a number of eminent prelates and scholars. It was argued that if a reunion of the two Churches could be brought about, men and arms could be obtained with the papal influence from the Western powers to thrust back the infidel Turk. The chief doctrinal differences between the two Churches were that the Greeks held that the Holy Ghost proceeds directly from the Father and not from the Father and the Son, and that the Pope does not possess supreme authority over the Church. Beneath these differences in dogma were deep-seated differences in temperament, in history, and in political interests. But so dark was the despair to which they had been reduced, that at length the Greeks acknowledged that the Holy Ghost proceeds from the Father and the Son, and that the Pope is the vicar of Christ upon earth and the supreme head of the entire Church. The Council of Florence, however, did not result in the union of the two Churches, for the action of the Greek envoys was repudiated by the Greek people.

In the meantime the Council of Basel, which had denied the right of the Pope to dissolve it, was pursuing its own way, and for some time it was not without support. In 1438 a synod of French prelates at Bourges resolved that general councils were to be summoned every ten years, recognized the authority of the Council of Basel, and provided for a number of ecclesiastical reforms in France.  This was the assertion by a national church of the right to determine for itself the details of its administration.  These things the king of France made binding as a Pragmatic Sanction.  The Sanction was obnoxious to the Pope because it gave countenance to the conciliar movement, and because it served as an example of national opposition to the universal authority of the Papacy.  True, the Sanction was abolished twenty-three years later, but it was another indication of the gathering force of nationality.  The Council of Basel ventured to depose Eugene for summoning a new council, and in his place it elected the Duke of Savoy, who assumed the title of Felix V.  By this time the council had lost greatly in numbers and in influence.  It had degenerated from a body earnestly committed to moral reform to a mere " engine of political attack upon the papacy," and afterwards it had resolved itself into a mere collection of political cliques.  So, gradually, it lost support.  Eugene was succeeded upon his death by Nicholas V, a man of high character, whose pacific diplomacy enabled him to win over Germany from the Council to the papacy.  Then Felix laid aside his office and, in 1449, the Council, having decreed its own dissolution, came to an end.  The Captivity was concluded, the Schism was at an end, and the Papacy, though not restored to its former power and prestige, was at least unmistakably reinvigorated.  But although the storm was past and a period of comparative calm was at hand, there loomed on the far horizon the ominous clouds of the Protestant Revolution.

the Italian publicist lies in the fact that he boldly carried the theory over into the ecclesiastical field. He asserted that the Church consists of all the faithful and that in their hands rests the ultimate legislative and elective powers. The faithful make known their will through the instrument of a general council, consisting of laymen as well as ecclesiastics, which is the highest delegated authority in the Church. The pope can impose upon the people only the things decreed by the council. The members of each parish have power to elect their parish priest. The power of the priesthood is equal in all priests. It comes directly from God; it does not require the intervention of a bishop; and it can be conferred by any priest upon any person who has been duly elected by the members of his parish. No man can be punished or even tried for heresy, for each is responsible for his religious beliefs to God alone. The clergy are entitled only to those exemptions and privileges directly necessitated by their spiritual activity, and they have the right to hold only as much property as is necessary to maintain them. The relations are clear. The pope, as a priest, has no greater religious power than any other priest, for all priests are equal. Whatever governmental authority he may possess arises out of expediency, and not out of any faith essential to salvation. This executive authority is derived solely from a general council and requires confirmation by the State. The pope, then, is merely an administrative official. In so far as spiritual matters are concerned, the Church has no visible head and requires none. All the property of the Church rightfully belongs to the emperor, the supreme representative of the people, who can punish any ecclesiastic. Such was the most audacious of all the attacks yet made upon the Church, an attack that went far beyond the positions that were to be assumed by Luther and Calvin, an attack that had to wait for a partial realization until the days of the French Revolution. The papal controversialists were equally bold. Agostino Trionfo and Alvaro Pelayo claimed for the pope absolute authority over the entire world.

Among the Spiritual Franciscans who flocked to the support of Louis was William of Occam (?–1349?), an Englishman who at Paris, where he was a distinguished lecturer, had been closely associated with Marsilio by whom he had been greatly influenced in his political thought. Taking as his point of departure the distinction between the temporal and the ecclesiastical authorities he asserted that to the temporal power belongs the control of all the secular things of life and that to the ecclesiastical power there is entrusted only the care of faith derived from revelation.

Influence of Marsilio and Occam

The Church has no coercive authority; she can exercise no jurisdiction. There is only one authority, the secular, in legislative
and judicial matters alike. The power that makes the law is the
only power that can interpret and apply it. So the cognizance
of what is just or unjust belongs exclusively to the secular authority. The influence of Marsilio and Occam upon their time
was not very wide-spread, for they were too far in advance of it.
Yet they did much to help the legal theory of the inalienable
and imprescriptible sovereignty of the State to displace the medieval conception of the subordination of the State to the Church,
and their influence seems clearly traceable in the thought of the
leaders of the Protestant Revolution.

In the flaring up of a national sentiment in Germany, due very
largely to the French residence of the Papacy, Louis enjoyed an
important advantage not possessed by his imperial predecessors
in their great struggle with the popes. But his personal unfitness rendered him unable to profit by the situation. He threw
away the opportunity to build up a strong central government in
Germany, spent his energy in pursuing the Italian will-o'-the-
wisp, alienated many of the German princes by his policy of
adding to the territorial possessions of his family, and finally, in
1346, saw himself displaced from the imperial office by the election of Charles IV. The new ruler, the first of the Bohemian

emperors, a member of the house of Luxemburg and a grandson
of Henry VII, was a diplomat, a peace-maker above all things
else, well fitted to cope with the serious difficulties that confronted him. In four years all opposition to his election had
been smoothed away and then, practically renouncing the imperial
claims to Italy, he found himself free to devote his attention to
creating an effective central government. Foremost of all the
problems to be settled was that of the imperial elections. The
solution to this was found in the famous *Golden Bull* of 1356
which restricted the right to vote in the imperial elections to
seven princes — the archbishops of Mainz, Cologne, and Trier,
the king of Bohemia, the count Palatine of the Rhine, the duke
of Saxony, and the margrave of Brandenburg. The new law
resulted in peaceful elections, but it increased the prestige and
power of the electors, whose territories were never to be divided
and whose succession was to be determined by the law of primogeniture, and it stamped Germany as a confederation rather than
a nation. At his death in 1378 Charles was succeeded by his son
Wenceslaus, a boy of sixteen, who ruled fairly well during the
first ten years of his reign, but who afterwards gave way to
indolence and drink.

It was in the time of Wenceslaus that the Swiss succeeded in freeing their Confederation from all external control except that of the Empire. When the Hapsburg family, taking advantage of the anarchy of the interregnum, sought to win for itself the territory of the disrupted duchy of Swabia the villages of Uri, Schwyz, and Unterwalden made a vigorous resistance. The courageous little communities would probably have been crushed had not the Hapsburg energy been deflected to the conquest of Austria. In 1291 they drew up their first articles of alliance of which we have record. In the struggles of the Hapsburg family to maintain itself in the imperial position the young confederacy found its opportunity for expansion. When, in the person of Henry VII, a Luxemburg emperor was elected, the freedom of the mountain league from all control except that of the Empire was confirmed. The effort of Austria in 1315 to check the growing power of the Confederation met with disaster in the battle of Morgarten, and three years later the Hapsburgs acknowledged the independence of the forest cantons from all but the imperial authority. Thus assured of its position the Confederacy was joined by several of its neighbors, by Lucern in 1330, by Zürich in 1351, and by Glarus in 1352. In this last year it was that the Confederacy by the conquest of Zug made the first forcible addition to its territory. The following year witnessed the accession of Bern, the last of the eight old cantons. There was as yet no central government, and the union of the eight, which had various relations with each other, was by no means uniform. It was the external pressure of the Austrian menace that held the loosely-knit confederacy together. When at last hostilities broke out again the Swiss in the battle of Sempach, 1386, won an even more decisive victory than that of Morgarten and two years later they inflicted another defeat upon the Austrians at Näfels. By the treaty of 1389 the Hapsburgs renounced their feudal claims over Lucern, Glarus, and Zug and thus left the little Confederation as a component part of the Empire subject only to imperial control.

The apathy and incompetence of Wenceslaus led the three ecclesiastical electors and the Count Palatine to depose him in 1400 and to elect one of their number, Rupert, the Prince Palatine, in his stead. Wenceslaus declined to acquiesce in the proceedings and so for ten years there was an imperial schism. Rupert ruled in the West, and Wenceslaus retained the obedience of the East. In the year of Rupert's death, 1410, the electors raised to the imperial position Sigismund (1410–37), a half-brother of the unworthy Wenceslaus who thereafter for the rest

CHAP. II
1387-1410

Progress of the Swiss Confederation

The Emperor Sigismund

of his life, restricted to the affairs of Bohemia, remained in a state of " innocuous desuetude." To Sigismund, a valiant warrior who had exerted every effort to check the invading Turk, was chiefly due the effort to solve the grave problems of the time by summoning the Council of Constance. The failure of the council to effect the desired reforms rendered impossible the fulfilment of Sigismund's cherished plan of building up a strong monarchy in Germany. Everywhere the prevailing discontent deepened. The Hussite wars broke out in Bohemia, and all the disintegrating forces in the Empire gathered headway. When Sigismund died in 1437 the male line of the house of Luxemburg became extinct. His daughter had been married to the man who succeeded him, Albert of Austria, and so a union of the two houses of Hapsburg and Luxemburg had been effected.

Unfortunately Albert II, a man of justice and energy in whom all those who desired law and order reposed the greatest confidence, survived his election only a year. He left no son, and so a Hapsburg of the younger line, Frederick III (1440–93), was elected his successor. The fifty-three years' reign of Frederick, a man altogether lacking in the qualities required by the critical condition of his country, was a disastrous period for the imperial interests. On the West the national feeling in England, France, and Spain had resulted in each of those countries in a compact national union. France acquired Dauphiny, Provence, and Burgundy, and thus extended her territorial possessions to the border line of Germany. In the East the Turks were steadily advancing; Poland, which had declared her independence in the interregnum, secured additional German territories for herself; and Bohemia acquired Silesia and Moravia and became practically independent. Internally the imperial losses were even more serious. Never had the imperial power sunk so low. All the centrifugal forces were unchained. " The Empire is attacked by a mortal sickness," said Cardinal Nicholas of Cusa, " and it will certainly perish if a cure be not found immediately." Let us then pause to glance at the rival forces that were making for the dismemberment of the Empire.

First there were the rising houses. When the custom of dividing the lands of a ruling prince among his children, a great hindrance to the growth of powerful houses, had been done away with by the introduction of primogeniture, houses that aspired for national supremacy began rapidly to develop. These new rivals appeared especially along the frontier for there it was easier to acquire additional territory. In 1423 the house of Wettin, which for long had held the mark of Meissen, became one of the most important of the princely houses by the acquisition of the electorate and duchy of Saxony. The power of the house was greatly lessened, however, by the division of Saxony in 1484 into the Ernestine and the Albertine branches. The house of Hohenzollern at first held some scattered territories in Swabia, then others in Franconia. Then it acquired the mark of Brandenburg and afterwards it grew by various means, conquest and inheritance, until at the end of the fifteenth century it was a great Germanic power. To the west of the empire there lay the loosely connected territories of the Burgundian Capetians, substantially increased in the reign of Duke Philip the Good (1419–67). Philip hoped to weld his motley aggregation of possessions into an organic whole, to fuse them with a national life, and to transform his duchy into a kingdom, but the dream was vain. His son, Charles the Bold (1467–77), inherited his father's ambitions. He thought to win for himself a spacious kingdom between Germany and France, and gradually his dreams grew greater and before his eyes there floated the alluring phantom of the imperial crown. Within the Empire there were lesser dynasties rising into power. When in 1268 the last Duke of Swabia died a considerable part of the duchy fell into the hands of the count of Würtemberg. Then the possessions of the house of Würtemberg, which was the first to make imperative the indivisibility of territory, adopting the principle of primogeniture in 1482, grew steadily until in 1495 they were made a duchy. Two other rising principalities were the margraviate of Hesse, which was substantially enlarged by Henry of Brabant who secured possession when in 1247 the line of the former rulers, the landgraves of Thuringia, became extinct, and the margraviate of Baden, whose scattered territories had once been part of the now extinct duchy of Swabia. Owing to the frequent subdivisions of its territories the once powerful house of Welf was a waning force and was destined not to become prominent again until the eighteenth century when a prince of its house became King of England.

The second force that made against national unity in Germany was the increasing power of the electoral princes. The right of voting in the imperial elections had, as we have seen, been confined by the *Golden Bull* to seven princes of the realm. None of the good results that might be expected to flow from the new plan of electing the emperor came to pass. It was seldom the sole concern of the electors to choose the best man, but rather did they choose men whose power they did not fear, or those who had offered the most tempting bribes. Then when the Hapsburgs grasped the scepter they never let it slip from their hands, with a single unimportant exception in the eighteenth century, until the title was abolished. Candidates were obliged to purchase their elections with relinquishments of imperial power that left the emperor ever more and more a mere shadow. And just as the imperial power was diminished that of the electoral princes increased.

A third disrupting force was that of the city leagues, the Hansa associations in the North and West and the Swabian League in the South. In the fifteenth century the Hanseatic League reached the height of its power, carrying on its commercial operations not only in Germany, but also in Lithuania, Poland, Russia, Denmark, Norway, Scotland, England, France, Spain, and Portugal. Charles IV had realized the dangerous disintegrating tendencies of the municipal confederations and in the *Golden Bull* he sought to cripple them by requiring all such associations to obtain the sanction of the territorial lord and forbidding the towns to bestow their citizenship upon people outside their walls and to give shelter to fugitive serfs. In spite of all restrictions, however, the towns continued to develop. Never were the city leagues so numerous as during the decades immediately following the promulgation of the *Golden Bull*. The Hanseatic League was never so powerful as at the end of the third quarter of the fourteenth century. The Swabian League was able to compel Charles to grant them the right of union that had been denied to them, and under the feeble Wenceslaus its gains were so marked that it boasted a membership of seventy-two towns and the command of ten thousand men-at-arms.

The City
Leagues

A fourth element making for decentralization consisted of the imperial knights, belated remnants of feudalism, living from hand to mouth, hostile to all the other forces, the princes, the burghers, and the bishops, that were slowly crushing them out of existence, and preying upon them whenever opportunity offered.

The
Imperial
Knights

Finally, among the forces hindering the development of an effective central government, were the Vehmic courts, survivals probably of the courts of Charles the Great. Appearing first in Westphalia, where they flourished best and acquired an immense power, and thence spreading throughout the empire, these secret tribunals played an important part in the life of Germany from the end of the twelfth century to the middle of the sixteenth. They were of two kinds, open and secret. The open courts took cognizance of civil suits and ordinary crimes. The secret courts, to whose meetings only the members of the Holy Fehm were admitted, took charge of crimes of a serious nature, especially heresy and witchcraft. Their rise was due to the failure of the

The
Vehmic
Courts

imperial power to enforce law and order, and at first they were
a beneficial institution; but gradually their secrecy and the arbitrary character of their rules changed them into the ready tools of the lawless and selfish forces they were designed to resist.

Such were the concrete causes that made for the impotence of Germany as a national power. To these must be added a cause **Effects** more impalpable but none the less potent in its disastrous effects **of the** — the theory that held the Empire to be an international power **Imperial** **Theory** and thus led to the dissipation of its energy. Instead of regarding themselves solely as the kings of Germany and making themselves the leaders of the national sentiment, the emperors allowed themselves to be lured by the will-o'-the-wisp of the imperial title and tradition into the quagmire of international diplomacy and warfare. Thus all through the Renaissance era was Germany an aggregation of principalities and powers and not a robust monarchy.

Leaving the conglomeration of conflicting elements of which the Germanic Empire was comprised, we have now to deal with a people who became imbued with a powerful sense of nationality and who achieved an effective national union. When Henry II **Causes of** of Anjou became King of England in 1154 he retained his great **the Hun-** **dred** French possessions, Normandy, Maine, and Anjou. Later on he **Years'** secured the overlordship of Brittany, and when he married **War** Eleanor of Aquitaine he obtained Poitou, Aquitaine, and Gascony. He was succeeded first by his son Richard Lion-Heart, who left no direct heirs, and then by his third son John, who, by a forfeiture that the French kings regarded as absolute, lost all the French possessions except Aquitaine and Gascony. In 1259 there was concluded the Treaty of Paris by which Henry III definitely renounced all the revived claims of England to Normandy, Anjou, Maine, Touraine, and Poitou, and by which he agreed to hold Gascony as a fief of the French king. On his part, Louis IX acknowledged Henry as the Duke of Aquitaine (which had become known as Guienne) and ceded to him several minor territories. The treaty was disliked by the French because of the surrender of territory and by the English because of the abandonment of their wide-sweeping claims. The chief thing to note is that the agreement confirmed England in possession of territory that hindered the development of the French monarchy and thus left a cloud upon the horizon. The predominant characteristic of Edward I (1272–1307), one of the greatest of the medieval kings of England, was his conscious devotion to the cause of his country. Equally devoted to the welfare of France was Philip IV (1285–1314), who included among his projects the ending of the independence of Flanders under its counts and the conquest of Guienne, in both of which plans, however, he failed. The brief reigns of Philip's three sons, Louis X (1314–16), Philip V (1316–22), and Charles IV (1322–28), were all insignificant, save that in the time of Charles, with whose death the main line of the house of Capet came to an end, the French encroached upon Gascony. Uneventful, too, and dismal was the reign of Edward II (1307–27) of England. It was left to the successors of these kings to witness the opening of the long impending war.

Philip VI (1328–50), Count of Valois, the first of the Valois kings, nephew of Philip IV, inherited his uncle's ambition to wrest Aquitaine (as the two provinces of Guienne and Gascony came to be called) from the English. Opposed to him was Edward III (1327–77), one of the most energetic of the English kings, who exhausted his country in his efforts to ruin France. In their reigns it was that there broke out the long and terrible struggle called the Hundred Years' War. What were the causes of the conflict? On the one hand it was always with reluctance that the English kings did homage to the French kings for their territories over the water; while, on the other hand, the French kings, actuated as they were by the natural desire to win for their country all the territory from the Pyrénées to the English Channel and from the Atlantic to the Alps and the Rhine, seized every opportunity to loosen the hold of the English kings upon the French possessions that still remained to them. This was the fundamental cause of the war. There were several more immediate causes. First, the bitter rivalry of the French and English sailors and fishermen resulted in constant quarrels in the Channel. Second, the French frequently gave assistance to the Scots in their wars with the English, and the latter were becoming convinced that it would be possible to conquer Scotland only after France had been crushed. Third, the English were determined to resist the encroachments of France upon Flanders. The independence of Flanders was of prime importance to England. English wool, the chief product of the island, was woven into cloth in Flemish looms and from that cloth much of the clothes of Northern Europe was made. The export-tax on wool was the largest single source of revenue that the English crown possessed down to the sixteenth century. Fourth, Edward III, through his mother, laid claim to the French crown. If a woman could inherit the crown, Edward certainly had a right prior to that of Philip. The French, of course, balked at the idea of an English king in Paris; and so it was declared that a woman, un-

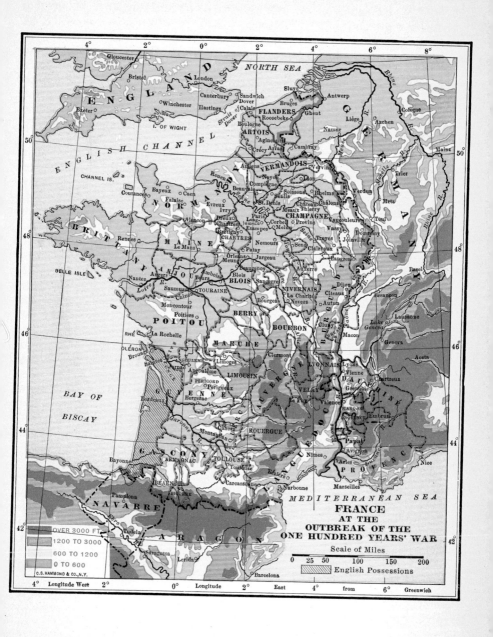

FRANCE
AT THE
OUTBREAK OF THE
ONE HUNDRED YEARS' WAR

Scale of Miles

| 0 | 25 | 50 | 100 | 150 | 200 |

English Possessions

OVER 3000 FT.
1200 TO 3000
600 TO 1200
0 TO 600

C.S.HAMMOND & CO., N.Y.

Longitude West — Longitude — East — from — Greenwich

NORTH SEA

ENGLAND

ENGLISH CHANNEL

CHANNEL IS.

GERMANY

BAY OF
BISCAY

MEDITERRANEAN SEA

Gloucester
Bristol
London
Canterbury
Winchester
Exeter
Hastings
Sandwich
Dover
Strait of Dover
Calais
Boulogne
I. OF WIGHT

Sluy
Bruges
Antwerp
FLANDERS
Roosebeke
Ghent
Liège
Namur
Aachen
Cologne

ARTOIS
Agincourt
Crécy
Arras
Cambray

Coutances
Bayeux
Caen
NORMANDY
Rouen
AMIENS
VERMANDOIS
Noyon
Laon
Vervins
Trier
Metz
Verdun
Toul
Mainz

Evreux
Ivry
Dreux
Chartres
Alençon
MAINE
Le Mans
Patay
Beauvais
Compiègne
Senlis
St. Denis
Paris
Lagny
Corbeil
Melun
Étampes
Nemours
Sens
Soissons
Reims
Meaux
Château Thierry
Châlons
CHAMPAGNE
Provins
Vassy
Joinville
Vaucouleurs
Domrémy

BRITTANY
Rennes
Nantes
BELLE ISLE

ANJOU
Angers
Saumur
Chinon
TOURAINE
Tours
Amboise
Blois
BLOIS
Orléans
Meung
Jargeau
Beaugency
Bretigny
Moncontour
Poitiers
POITOU
La Rochelle
RHÉ
OLÉRON
Broussac
Saintes
Angoulême
ANGOUMOIS
Cognac
Périgord
Périgueux
Bergerac
Bordeaux
GUIENNE
Montauban
Cahors
Agen
GASCONY
ARMAGNAC
TOULOUSE
Toulouse
Carcassonne
Béziers
Narbonne
Bayonne
BÉARN
BIGORRE

Sancerre
Auxerre
NIVERNAIS
La Charité
Nevers
BERRY
Bourges
BOURBON
MARCHE
Limoges
LIMOUSIN
Clermont
AUVERGNE
Cluny
Mâcon
Autun
Citeaux
Dijon
BURGUNDY
Langres
Besançon
Basel
Lausanne
Lake of Geneva
Geneva

LYONNAIS
Lyons
Vienne
VELAY
Le Puy
Valence
LANGUEDOC
Nîmes
Arles
Marseilles
PROVENCE
Avignon
Papal
Nice
DAUPHINÉ
Grenoble
Chartreux
Aosta
Embrun
MARGON
Provence

Pamplona
NAVARRE
Tudela
ARAGON
Saragossa
Lérida
Barcelona

able herself to inherit the crown, cannot even transmit the crown. As a result, the personal relations of the two kings were embittered; and the animosity of Philip increased when Edward gave refuge to his mortal enemy Robert of Artois, and that of Edward deepened when once more the French gave assistance to the struggling Scots. The horizon had long been darkening. At last the storm broke.

Men and money were gathered in England for the imminent war; and alliances, which, however, proved of little worth, were made with the Netherlandish princes and the Emperor Louis the Bavarian. The English won a great naval victory at Sluys in 1340, and at Crecy in 1346 they were even more overwhelmingly successful on the land. For nine years, with the exception of the capture of Calais, the war was practically at a standstill. Hostilities continued to smolder; but both countries were exhausted, and throughout Western Europe there swept the terrible scourge of the Black Death, the most fatal of all the visitations of the plague, leaving untold desolation in its wake. In 1349, by treaty and purchase, France secured the important province of Dauphiny; and in the following year Philip was succeeded by his son John II (1350–64), who, burning with desire to avenge the disaster of Crecy, attacked Edward's eldest son, the Black Prince, at Poitiers in 1356 with greatly superior numbers, only to meet with a defeat equally as decisive as that sustained by his father. John the Good was himself taken captive and was sent to England where he " went a-hunting and a-hawking in Windsor forest at his pleasure." Under the dauphin the degeneration of France, that had been going on since the outbreak of the war, increased. The peasants, who had suffered terrible hardships, rose in revolt and were put down with extreme brutality. At last, in 1360, the first period of the long and devastating war came to a close with the Peace of Bretigny in which Edward renounced his claim to the kingship of France and to all territory north of the Loire in return for full ownership without homage of Calais, Guienne, Gascony, and Poitou. England also agreed to end the alliance with Flanders, and France that with Scotland; and for the release of John the sum of about $2,500,000 was to be paid.

The fundamental cause of the war remained. Indeed, the very considerable increase of the English possessions in France secured by the Treaty of Bretigny served to make that cause still more potent. So, before long, the struggle was renewed. John was succeeded by his son Charles V (1364–80), who since his father's capture at Poitiers had been the practical ruler of France.

The First Period of the War

The Second Period of the War

By temperament the new king was a man of peace. Even had he been so minded, his arm was too weak to wield a weapon. But he fully merited the epithet of "Wise," for he was patient, tactful, and diplomatic. His policy of peace and of the rehabilitation of France, of the dressing of its bleeding wounds, of the strengthening of its defenses and the reparation of its material loss and its moral ruin, was exactly the policy calculated to result eventually in the expulsion of the invaders. He subdued unruly nobles, cleared his land to some extent of the vulture hordes of mercenaries, punished the infraction of law, and prepared for the inevitable renewal of the conflict with the hitherto invincible English. In the second period of the war the wisdom of the cautious tactics of Charles and his commanders was fully demonstrated. The French avoided pitched battles, kept themselves shut up in the fortified towns, and left the English to be wasted by want and disease and to be harassed by guerrilla attacks. The Black Prince, stricken with fever, returned to England, where his death was soon followed by that of his father and by the accession of his only child, Richard II (1377–99), a forlorn little boy of ten. For five years the English had lost command of the sea, and further defeats made even the voyage from Dover to Calais a perilous one; while on the land the English possessions melted away one after the other. But heavy losses befell the French, for the death of Bertrand du Guesclin, the ablest of their generals, was followed in a few weeks by that of Charles, the wisest of their kings. With the passing of all these great figures the second period of the war came to a conclusion.

The Third
Period of
the War

Charles VI (1380–1421) was also a child when he came to the throne. Like Richard of England he was a handsome and lovable boy; but like Richard, too, he was unfitted to rule in so tempestuous a time. About the lad there clustered his uncles, the Dukes of Anjou, Berry, Burgundy, and Bourbon, each greedy to advance his own personal interests, each oblivious to the welfare of the country, who plunged him so deeply into voluptuousness and sensuality that they led him on to madness. All through the remainder of his life he was lucid only at intervals and was always subject to the dictation of whomsoever happened to have control of his person. So oppressive were the financial burdens of this third period of the war that everywhere from the Alps to the Bay of Biscay and from the Pyrénées to the Cheviot Hills the people, with an essential identity of cause, rose in rebellion. Under Wat Tyler the peasants from the Southeastern counties of England demanded the abolition of serfdom. At Rouen the coppersmiths opened the prisons and destroyed the charters; the

Parisians seized twelve thousand mallets and for three days were masters of the city; in Flanders the burghers rallied around Philip von Artevelde only to be cut to pieces by the French at Roosebeke; and in Auvergne, Languedoc, and the old Swabian duchy the uprisings of the peasants and the townspeople, goaded to desperation by the misery of war and taxation, were suppressed with unspeakable cruelty. The quarrels between the relatives of Charles gradually resolved themselves into one between his younger brother, Louis, Duke of Orleans, and his youngest uncle, Philip, Duke of Burgundy. The Burgundians were clever enough to enlist the support of the tax-ridden people, being especially diplomatic in winning the support of the Parisians; while their opponents, the Orleanists, who from their leader received the name of Armagnacs, represented the forces of feudalism. All France became involved in the war of the factions, the whole country was ravaged, and for two years Paris was in the hands of the turbulent proletariat.

In the early years of this war of Burgundian and Armagnac neither Richard II nor his successor, Henry IV (1399–1413), was in a position to make an effort to regain England's lost possessions; but with the accession of Henry V (1413–22), a wild prince suddenly transformed into a sober monarch of iron will, conditions changed and a fourth period of the war began. Once more English fleets swept the narrow Channel; and, in 1415, the field of Agincourt was reddened with the blood of the flower of French chivalry. The rivalry of the French factions continued to paralyze the national activity, the king was mad and the queen was licentious, and so when two years later Henry began the conquest of the country in earnest he found but a feeble opposition. The murder of the leader of the Burgundians by an Armagnac retainer drove the former party into the arms of the English. By the Treaty of Troyes, signed between the English and the Burgundians, Henry was married to the daughter of the crazy king and declared to be the Regent of France and the heir of his father-in-law. The dauphin Charles, who was associated with the Armagnacs, did not approve of the iniquitous agreement; but the opposition was powerless to stay the advance of the English and Burgundian armies, when suddenly, in 1422, Henry died, and a month later he was followed to the grave by that sad symbol of his country's decadence, the mad king Charles. Henry VI (1422–61) was a babe of nine months when he became King of England and, so far as the treaty with the Burgundians could make him, King of France, while his rival, Charles VII (1422–61), was a youth of nineteen. Son of a mad father and a dissolute mother, it is little wonder that Charles, who spent most of his years safe inside the walls of strong castles, proved weak both in body and mind. He held his court at Bourges, while the Duke of Bedford, uncle of the infant Henry and Regent in France, made his capital at Paris. This, then, was the condition at the close of the fourth period of the war. Roughly speaking, all the territory North of the Loire and East of that river as far south as Lyons refused allegiance to Charles, while in the South much of the country that surrounded Bordeaux was loyally English. The remainder of the Southwest was held by self-seeking nobles not actually committed to either side; and in the Southeast Provence was practically independent. Only the center of France, a mere remnant, acknowledged Charles. Armagnacs, Burgundians, and English, hordes of armed brigands who cared little for the cause for which they fought, ravaged the wretched country, laid desolate the fields, sent up the villages in smoke, tortured and killed the starving peasants, and found the only effective resistance to their plundering forays in the walls of the cities whose inhabitants, forewarned by experience, denied admittance to them one and all. Such was the mournful situation when, while the siege of Orleans, the gate-way to the central provinces, was under way, there appeared upon the scene the last and fragrant flower of medieval civilization, Jeanne d'Arc, the savior of France.

We do not know a great deal about Jeanne before she was drawn into the whirlpool of war. She lived at Domremy, a little village in the green and narrow valley of the Meuse, on the highway from Dijon to Flanders. But whether Domremy belonged to France or to the Empire, to Champagne or to Lorraine, we are altogether uncertain, so complex were the feudal relations of that border region. Even her name is uncertain. The name " Darc " came to her from Arc, the place from whence her father came. But in those days a girl usually had no surname. She was known only by her first name, or if she had another it was from her mother that she got it and not from her father. The habit of taking the father's name was only just coming into vogue. Jeanne of Domremy was called Jeanne la Pucelle; and when she was ennobled she took the name Jeanne du Lis, doubtless from her banner. Her own village was devoted to the Armagnac-French cause, while the neighboring village of Maxey was attached to the Burgundian-English side. Between the two villages there were frequent disputes upon the burning question of the time; up and down the highway there traveled the news of the weary struggle, and on the northern horizon

Jeanne more than once saw the columns of smoke that marked
the trails of the bands of soldiers that harried the countryside.
So all through her childhood and youth she must have been
familiar with the sore plight of France. Slowly there dawned
upon the peasants the consciousness of the fact that the first step
to end the horrors to which they were subjected was to expel
the English; their French oppressors could be dealt with after-
ward. And that belief was implanted in the heart of the child.

One summer noon when Jeanne was in her father's garden she
had a vision of the archangel Michael, and to the frightened little
girl the angelic visitor returned again and again in succeeding
days. Gradually her fear passed away. Other heavenly visi-
tants appeared, and St. Catherine and St. Margaret bade her
to go to the help of the unhappy King. For several years she
kept the apparitions a secret. In the house and in the fields
she worked, a true peasant's daughter. She nursed the sick, and
loved to hear the angelus sounding sweetly the twilight benedic-
tion. For some years the " voices," as she chose to call them,
repeated, though indefinitely, their injunctions to save France.
In 1428 the village of Domremy was raided and set on fire,
after which the commands of the voices became more definite.
Orleans was to be delivered from the English investment, Charles
was to be consecrated and crowned at Rheims, and then there
were vague words about driving the English from France. In
her own day men did not deny that voices spoke to Jeanne, but
wondered only whether they were divine or devilish. In our
day men wonder whether she was mentally deranged or an impostor. Both of these modern impressions are wrong. All of
us have visions unless we have been educated out of them. It is
the hardest thing in the world to discriminate between what we
know and what we imagine. It must ever be remembered that
Jeanne was a peasant girl, that the only education she ever received was the religious teaching given in the parish church, that
it was a natural thing for her to hear voices, that many in that
time saw visions and dreamed dreams, that the woods that surrounded her village were full of spirits and fairies, baleful and
beneficent, who had lived there since the days of Merlin, aye,
and beyond that in those far-off days of which we have not even
a legendary record. The sincerity and the sanity of Jeanne are
certain. Whatever one may think of her visions and her voices,
be sure they were to that sound and sweet and noble girl the
gravest of realities.

At last, in the middle of February 1429, after meeting with
many humiliating refusals of aid, clad in male attire and accom-

CHAP. II

1429-53

Jeanne
Career
and
Death.

panied by six armed men, Jeanne set out from the nearby castle
of Vaucouleurs for Chinon where Charles was keeping his court.
Through the heart of France they rode, often avoiding the inns
for fear of detection and sleeping in the winter fields. After
protracted examinations at Chinon and Poitiers she was sent
at the end of April with a little army of about three thousand
men and several of the ablest of the French captains to put an
end to the weary siege that Orleans had suffered for seven
months. In this manner did the fifth and the last period of the
war open. She infused new courage into the hearts of the
demoralized French soldiers and with undaunted energy drove
the English from the outlying and strongly fortified tower of
the Tourelles, which they had captured, and compelled them to
abandon the siege. The effect of this victory upon the morale
of the French may well be said to have been miraculous. The
downcast, downtrodden, and despairing country was thrilled with
a fierce confidence in its new leader, the boastful assurance of
the English began to disappear, and the whole course of the war
was changed. There were, however, two parties at the court.
At the head of one was La Trémoille, a selfish and unscrupulous
nobleman who had secured control of the weakling king, and who
saw his own defeat in the establishment of an orderly government
that would follow a final triumph of the French arms. So a
month was lost in indecision before the campaign to drive the
English from the valley of the Loire began. Jeanne wished
Charles to be crowned at Rheims without delay, but she was
overborne in the matter. When military operations were resumed the French captured Jargeau, Meung, and Beaugency;
and at Patay the English, greatly outnumbered, after a feeble
resistance left 2,500 dead upon the field. With such evidence
as this the ecstatic faith of Jeanne in her mission became more
contagious than ever and despite the fact that the road, lined
with fortified towns, ran for one hundred and fifty miles through
the hostile country of Champagne, the cowardly king at last
yielded to the urgent pleadings of Jeanne that he go to Rheims.
The danger was not nearly as great as it appeared, for the English garrisons of the towns were small and the French inhabitants
not difficult to win over. The march was accomplished in safety;
the king was crowned; and Jeanne, then at the culmination of
her career, was eager to press forward in the work of driving
the English from France. Troyes had already submitted, and
now in quick succession Beauvais, Senlis, Laon, Soissons, Châ-
teau-Thierry, Provins, Compiègne, and other towns acknowledged Charles as their king. If quick, aggressive action had

been taken the hated foe could unquestionably have been expelled. But the old indecision and delay caused valuable time to be spent in aimless wanderings. The intrigues of La Trémoille made the further success of the French army practically impossible; and so when in September Jeanne led the troops in an attack upon Paris that was repulsed, she met with her first bitter disappointment. She never wavered in her belief that she was divinely inspired, but the unbounded confidence she once instilled in the hearts of men was gradually dissipated. Thereafter most of her efforts resulted in failure, and at the end of May in the following year she was captured in the siege of Compiègne. The story of her trial need not detain us long. For three months, with an interval of sickness, the unlettered peasant girl of nineteen years, enfeebled and harassed by the brutal treatment of her jailors, confronted the learned theologians and legists. " I see many counselors," she might well have said, as did Mary Stuart at Fotheringay, "but not one for me." Yet she had not much need of a legal counselor, for her fate would have been the same, and her simplicity, sincerity, and native shrewdness enabled her to evade the most ingenious attempts to make her convict herself of wrong-doing. On May 30, 1431, the fagots were lighted in the old market-place at Rouen and the last word that Jeanne uttered with her blistering lips was the name of Jesus. So perished the peasant girl of Domremy, while in all the long months of her imprisonment and trial there had come from those whom she had delivered from the depths of despair never a letter offering ransom, never a message threatening retaliation upon the captive English leaders, and never a lance to attempt her rescue. Yet the life of Jeanne d'Arc was not in vain. About her name there gathered the memories of the sorrows inflicted upon France by the foreign foe. In her the spirit of nationality found an inspiring leader. Because of her devotion and her deeds the fierce hatreds of Burgundian and Armagnac began to cool. Out of her life, " stainless amid all the corruptions of the camp and compassionate amid all the horrors of war," a new patriotism was born in France. For her country she brought together its shattered elements, made it hale and whole, and into it she breathed the spirit of her sweet and tender heart, her noble and unconquerable soul.

The English gained very little by the capture and judicial murder of Jeanne. Not all the criminal self-seeking of La Trémoille and the other perverse counselors of the miserable puppet of a king could turn back the growing tide of French patriotism. All that it could do was to delay the final ex-

pulsion of the English for a score of years. In 1433 the traitorous favorite was surprised in his bed by the opposing faction
and thrown into prison. Gradually the French auxiliaries deserted the English ranks. Bedford, the leader of the English
forces, died in 1435; and in the same year Philip of Burgundy
broke his alliance with the invaders. The Norman peasants,
made desperate by the license of the English soldiers, rose to the
aid of the bands of mercenaries in the hire of France. Paris
was regained in 1436. Still the dreary war dragged on. The
French soldiers were nothing less than brigands; *écorcheurs,*
skinners or flayers, their captains were called; and they were
dreaded alike by those whom they came to deliver and those
whom they came to despoil. In order to rid France of the invader it was necessary to reorganize the military forces. So
the indiscriminate forming of free companies and the carrying
on of private war were forbidden, and all the troops were paid
out of the royal treasury and placed directly under royal authority. In order to procure the necessary revenue to do this
the taille was taken out of the hands of the nobles and made
exclusively a national tax. The men to whom these reforms were
chiefly due were Richemont, constable of France and long an
enemy of the worthless La Trémoille, Dunois, a captain who had
fought with Jeanne d'Arc, and Jacques Cœur, a wealthy merchant
of Bourges. Thus was the monarchy sent once more along the
road to absolutism. A formidable revolt of the nobles, the
Praguerie, against these measures was suppressed, and with the
reorganized army the English were at last expelled from France,
retaining of all their great possessions only the town of Calais.
The warfare of a century had laid desolate the land of France.
Everywhere the condition of the peasantry was wretched, and
the prosperity of many of the towns had long been halted. But
out of all the misery there was born a deepened national feeling.

**Turk and
Mongol in
Europe**

Before we proceed to consider the break-up of Italy and the
building of Spain we must stop to note the coming of the Turk
and the Mongol into Europe, and to glance at the dying empire
of the East. The Mongols originally came from the valleys of
the upper tributaries of the Amur in Northern China. Their
greatest leader was Jenghiz Khan (1162–1227) whose victorious
armies swept from the plains in central Asia westward as far
as the Dnieper. Long before this great invasion the Seljukian
Turks, who were also from Northeastern Asia, had established
themselves in Asia Minor. After the Mongolian invasion another division of the Turks, the Ottomans, moved westward to
the Mediterranean, and, in Asia Minor, mingled with the kindred

race and confronted the decaying Byzantine empire. The Ottoman Turks were a young nation and to the freshness and vigor of their life was added the fanaticism of the conquering religion of Mohammed. Under Orkan (1360-89) the Turkish possessions were made to include all of Asia Minor and were consolidated with consummate skill, while the dwindling Greek dominion remained, as it had always been, a collection of heterogeneous nationalities. Then under Murad I (1360-89) European conquests to the west of Constantinople were made, and Bayazid I (1389-1402) pushed those conquests to the Danube. No sooner had this been done than still another kindred race under the dreaded Timur (1338-1405), or Tamerlane as we call him, which had been sweeping westward, captured Bagdad, Aleppo, and Damascus. Thus for a time the attention of the Turks was diverted from their westward advance to their Eastern frontier. Indeed, with the defeat and capture of Bayazid by Tamerlane the Turkish power seemed to have crumbled to dust, and the existence of the Byzantine empire indefinitely prolonged.

At the opening of the thirteenth century the fourth crusade had been deflected from its destination to Constantinople, that capital had been captured, and a Latin empire, with Count Baldwin of Flanders at its head, had taken the place of the effete Byzantine empire. The Byzantine rule was restored in 1261, but only a miserable remnant of its once extensive territory remained. So it was but a feeble resistance that could be offered to the Turks, who after the death of Tamerlane regained their vigor and continued their western conquests. The appeals of the Byzantines to the Christians of the West to help them to stay the infidel tide fell upon heedless ears, and so the Turks were able to continue the systematic and gradual extension of their possessions. Constantinople, left like an isle in the midst of the Mohammedan sea, was surrounded by their conquests. But on their Western frontier it was Latin Christendom the Turks now confronted, and they found it able to offer a more stubborn resistance than Greek Christendom had shown. Under the adventurous knight and able general John Hunyady, the Hungarian forces drove the Turks back across the Balkans; but they failed to press on to Adrianople, the Turkish capital, and finally met with defeat. In 1453 the Turks captured Constantinople. At last the day of Byzantium had come to its end and the night had fallen. For more than a hundred years the Turkish invasion of the Christian continent had been in progress and the fall of Constantinople could not have been difficult to predict.

Yet it came as a great shock to the Christians of the West. They were ashamed to think they had lifted not a hand to avert the capture of the last citadel of the ancient Greek civilization. They were afraid of the further advance of the Mohammedan tide, now that every vestige of the intervening barrier had disappeared. Their apathy had allowed the Turks to secure possession of one of the most famous capitals of their continent, to cement the hitherto divided territory in Asia and Europe, and to become a European power. But when the first sorrow died away, the old indifference was resumed. Europe was separating into distinct nations, each with its own problems, and the ideals of the age of the Crusades lived on only here and there, in the heart of a Prince Henry the Navigator or of a Christopher Columbus.

**Italy after the Hohenstaufen**

While France, England, and Spain were rising into vigorous national life, Italy was sinking into political insignificance. It was a mere congeries of principalities. Let us then glance at the seven Italian States that were the chief divisions of the peninsula in 1305 at the beginning of the Avignonese captivity. In the South the kingdom of Naples and Sicily belonged to the house of Anjou, summoned, in the person of Charles I (1266–85), a younger brother of King Louis IX of France, by the Papacy across the Alps to Italy to assist in driving the imperial power from Italian soil. In 1282, fifteen years after the coming of Charles, the Sicilians revolted against his harsh rule, compelled the withdrawal of his forces from the island and persuaded Peter III of Aragon to accept the crown. Thereafter the Angevin possessions were confined to the kingdom of Naples. Charles II (1285–1309) was succeeded by his second son, Robert (1309–43), who, having outlived his own son, Charles of Calabria, left his grand-daughter Giovanna I (1343–82) his only direct heir. An attempt to make the rule of a female more secure by a marriage with her cousin, Andrew of Hungary, resulted in arousing the jealousy of some of the Neapolitan nobles and in creating opposition to the Hungarian influence. The story of Naples and its rulers we shall continue later on. We are here concerned only with the beginnings of the principal Italian States.

Venice was founded by men who, fleeing in terror from the ferocious Huns, left the rich and pleasant plains of Padua for the shallow salt-marshes and low sandy islands of the Adriatic While the mainland of Italy, overrun by the pitiless robber bands, was falling into ruins, these peaceful islanders went their way building slowly, with tireless energy, their unique city of the

ITALY
AT THE CLOSE
OF THE
FIFTEENTH CENTURY

Scale of Miles

0 10 20  40  60  80  100 120 140 160

sea. Independence was the first and constant thought of the Venetians, and it was maintained with the utmost tenacity and courage. Their political life, dominated by a powerful aristocracy, enjoyed a stability unknown to the principalities and communes of the mainland; and when the riches of the Orient were in part disclosed to Western Europe their city became the gateway to those shining lands and grew to be a commonwealth unsurpassed in commercial prosperity.

It was in the confusion resulting from the Lombard invasion that Genoa began to gain her independence. Additional immunities were obtained from time to time by contending nobles until at last it became a self-governing commune. Its prosperity was greatly enhanced by the expansion of commerce consequent upon the Crusades, and Genoese traders established themselves in the Levant, on the shores of the Black Sea, and on the banks of the Euphrates. For two centuries a fierce rivalry raged between Genoa and Pisa, but after the victory of the former in the battle off the island of Meloria, in 1284, the latter lost most of its maritime power and Genoa was left to contend for commercial supremacy with Venice.

Milan, one of the most important of the Roman cities, at the conflux of great commercial highways, had been the capital of the decaying Empire. Seated in the middle of a great and fertile plain it never lost its importance and became a great center for the manufacture of wool, silk, armor, and jewelry; and a center, also, of a great agglomeration of republics and lordships.

Florence, unlike Milan, was one of the least important of the Italian cities in the days of the Empire, and she developed later than did the cities of the Lombard plain and still later than the maritime republics. But gradually the little town began to grow and to enter upon a career of conquest until at last it became the capital of the most important republic in Tuscany.

Last of the important provinces in Italy at the opening of the Renaissance era was the Papal State, acquired by real or pretended gifts of emperors and other rulers, and occupying the center of the peninsula. It must be remembered that these seven States that we have noticed, Sicily, Naples, Venice, Genoa, Milan, Florence, and the Papal State, were only the principal divisions of Italy at the opening of the fourteenth century. The many minor communities in the Northern part of the discordant peninsula we shall not stop here to notice.

Such was the disrupted condition of Italy when the popes took up their residence in Avignon. The inhabitants of the peninsula did not speak of themselves as Italians, but as members of the

State to which they belonged, as Florentines, Milanese, or Nea-politans. The aim of every one of the numerous political divisions of the peninsula was merely to secure free-play for personal interests or party intrigues by making still weaker the central authority, by keeping alive the antagonism of pope and emperor. The significance of Guelf and Ghibelline had long evaporated, but the innumerable factions still conjured with the names and sought their petty local and personal interests in the deepening anarchy to the sacrifice of the common welfare. Yet there were men who dreamed of a united Italy. Dante longed for some leader who could rise above the paltry politics of his own State and undertake the task of healing the dissensions of his country, of welding it into a nation. Petrarch, too, never considered himself as merely a Florentine but as an Italian. When he saw the Italian communities either oppressed by the yoke of sanguinary tyrants or torn by internal dissensions and ruined by fratricidal wars among themselves he uttered in his *Italia Mia* a passionate plea for national union that was pathetically premature. All these dreams were doomed to defeat for yet five hundred years. The tragic drama of Italian politics moved rapidly to scenes of still greater degradation. Italy failed utterly to understand the profound change that was being consummated by the creation of a deep national sentiment in other countries. She had few statesmen who perceived the signs of the times and none who could command effective support. Let us note, briefly, some of the more important of the political events that took place in Italy at this time.

Italy During the Absence of the Papacy

The Holy Roman emperors had not yet either explicitly or implicitly abandoned their claim to suzerainty over Italy, but for sixty years they had failed to make any practical assertion of it. In 1311 Henry VII entered the peninsula. Never had there been an emperor so well-fitted for the task of replacing anarchy with unity. Far above the petty intrigues of German princes and Italian despots Henry moved serene with his heart set upon justice. He was the chivalrous ideal of all Italians who longed to see an ending made of their deplorable political divisions. Dante wrote an impassioned address to the rulers and people of the peninsula hailing the new Emperor as the deliverer of Italy. But Henry failed. In spite of his desire to keep aloof from either faction, the situation forced him to ally himself with the Ghibelline party, and then in 1313 he died suddenly of fever.

The Scala family at Verona may be chosen as the type of the despotic rulers of the period. When the cruel Ezzelino da

Romano, whose thirst for blood was never satisfied or equaled, died in 1259, Mastino della Scala was chosen by the citizens as their chief magistrate, and the tyranny that he established became dynastic and continued in power for more than a century. The most illustrious of the family was Cangrande della Scalla (1308–29), an able and ambitious soldier, a bold and clever statesman, one of the greatest of the Ghibelline chiefs of Northern Italy. He made considerable additions to the already extensive territory of his family; and, with no mere selfish end in view, dreamed of the political unity of the whole peninsula; but he died suddenly when he was only thirty-eight years of age.

Summoned by the Ghibelline leaders in a time of need, another emperor, Louis IV, called by the old chroniclers in scorn and hatred "the Bavarian," entered the peninsula in 1327, had himself crowned in Rome, deposed as a heretic Pope John XXII of Avignon who had excommunicated him, set up an anti-pope, and then hurried back to Germany to look after his interests there without having given any effective aid to his Italian allies.

The next invader of Italy was King John of Bohemia, who entered the peninsula in 1330. Son of Henry VII, he could rightfully expect the support of the Ghibellines. Friend of Pope John XXII, he had a good claim upon the allegiance of the Guelfs. And so many communities hastened to place themselves under his control that it seemed for a time as if the dream of Italian unity would come true. But the legacies of hate were still too deeply cherished to be dispelled by the first effort. The affairs of Bohemia demanded John's hasty return, and when he went back to Italy he found the task to be a hopeless one. So he turned his back upon the warring factions and made his way over the Alps.

The invasions of Henry of Luxemburg, Louis the Bavarian, and John of Bohemia had left behind them bands of mercenary soldiers who lived by brigandage or were taken into the employ of the despots in the work of putting an end to the independence of the republics and aggrandizing the despotisms. Knowing little about the cause for which they were fighting and caring less, concerned only with their pay, their plunder, and the gratification of their lust, these pitiless robbers and murderers left desolation and death in their wake. "*Un écorcheur ne peut pas aller en enfer,*" boasted such a bird of prey, "*parce qu'il troublerait la repos du diable.*" The republics were not slow to follow the example of the despots in hiring these mercenary troops. The *condottieri,* as the leaders of these soldiers-of-fortune were called, found numerous opportunities for self-advancement. They became commanders of independent armies, lending their aid to those who offered the highest pay. They became wealthy. Some won for themselves ephemeral territorial possessions, while others conquered important States, and founded famous dynasties. At first these mercenaries were foreigners, but in the latter part of the fourteenth century they were gradually replaced by Italians. Among the more famous of the *condottieri* were " Duke " Werner, Moriale, Lando, Barbiano, Attendolo, Braccio, Francesco Sforza, John Hawkwood, Colleoni, Gattamelata, and Carmagnola.

In this period it was that the death of Robert of Naples plunged that kingdom into indescribable anarchy. His heir, as we have seen, was his granddaughter Giovanna I (1343–82), a girl of sixteen, who in her childhood had been married to her cousin, Andrew of Hungary. Giovanna grew to be a wilful and dissolute woman and her husband proved to be a worthless rake. Giovanna wished to be the actual ruler and to regard Andrew as being merely her husband; but Andrew, being the nearest male heir, claimed the right to rule as king. In 1345 Andrew was murdered, and rumor accused his wife of being an accomplice if not the instigator. Two years later Andrew's brother, Louis of Hungary, came to avenge the crime and assert his own claim to the throne. Many Neapolitan nobles flocked to his banner, and a desultory warfare lasted until 1351 when the affairs of his kingdom compelled Louis to return to Hungary. Giovanna, who had no children, retained the throne for thirty years more. When the schism in the Papacy began in 1378 her nearest male heir, Charles of Durazzo, who as a claimant of the Neapolitan throne assumed the title of Charles III (1382–86), supported Urban VI, while she upheld Clement VII. So Giovanna sent to France to invite Louis of Anjou to become her heir. The offer was accepted. This creation of the claim of the second house of Anjou to Naples, while it failed to effect the disinheritance of Charles of Durazzo, resulted in a century of intermittent warfare and furnished to Charles VIII of France an excuse for his invasion of Italy.

It was in the midst of this anarchy that there came the apparition of Rienzi, whose story, briefly touched upon in the preceding chapter, is one of the most romantic in an age of romance. Rienzi, born in the most squalid of all the quarters of Rome, was the son of a tavern-keeper and a washer-woman. His mother died when he was still an infant, and he was sent to a relative at Anagni where he acquired a fluent command of Latin, read widely in literature, and perhaps became imbued with his special hatred of the house of Colonna. At the age of twenty he returned to Rome, then, in truth, a city of desolation. The Colonna family had surrounded with a palisade the section of the city they claimed as their own; the Orsini had fortified another quarter in the same manner; the Savelli were entrenched in a third position; and the Frangipani held the Colosseum. The Roman populace, some thirty thousand in number, led the most precarious existence in the ruined capital. Rienzi brooded over the desolation of Rome and dreamed of raising her from her abject prostration and of reviving her freedom and her glory. His fluent and impassioned eloquence won the support of the people; and on May 20, 1347, he was able to effect a bloodless revolution. He promulgated the laws of " the Good Estate," a brief and excellent code, the administration of which brought peace to the tumultuous city. Although invested with absolute power he took for himself the title of " Tribune " which in the olden days had been associated with the cause of popular freedom. His plans were not confined to the papal State. They included the pacification and unity of all Italy; and for a time in that crowded and dream-like summer it seemed as though that dearest dream was soon to be fulfilled. But the summer drew to its close, and the autumn opened in strife and bloodshed. The swift ascent of the Liberator turned his brain; his pretensions, despite his sincerity and his disinterestedness, became not only vain but impious; and the nobles recovered from their consternation. On November 20 a fierce conflict took place in which a dozen of the leading Roman nobles, including several of the house of Colonna, were slain. Rienzi permitted the bodies to be grossly insulted, inaugurated a season of riotous feasting, and failed to follow up the victory with vigorous measures. From that time his influence declined. " Of the two alternatives," said old Stefano Colonna, the venerable head of the house, " it is assuredly better to die than to submit any longer to the tyranny of this peasant "; and he placed himself at the head of the baronial faction. A few weeks later, seven months after his accession to power, Rienzi fled to Naples.

Suddenly, as if man had not done enough to devastate Italy, the crowding calamities of the country were increased in the spring of 1348 by a visitation of the plague, conveyed to the peninsula by a Genoese ship returning from the East. In Siena eighty thousand people, three-quarters of the population, died; in Pisa, where five hundred people a day were buried, seventenths of the population perished; and the pestilence was equally virulent and fatal at Venice, Florence, Rome, Naples, and other parts of the peninsula. "We go out of doors," said Petrarch, "walk through street after street and find them full of dead and dying; and when we get home again we find no live thing within the house, all having perished in the brief interval of our absence." The *morbo nero* carried off one-third of the entire Italian population and added to the anarchy of the time.

The wanderings of Rienzi during the years of his exile may be quickly passed over. In 1354 he was sent by Innocent VI from Avignon to Rome to aid Cardinal Albornoz to restore order in the papal State. After some months he decided to act independently of the warlike legate, and on the first day of August he reëntered the imperial city in triumph. But Rienzi was now broken in body and unbalanced in mind. In October he perished in a tumult of the populace, and confusion reigned again. There are two reasons for the sudden fall of Rienzi. The degraded Roman populace were quite unfitted for democracy, and Rienzi lacked every one of the stern qualities demanded by a time so disordered.

It was a double and a difficult task that had been given to Cardinal Albornoz. He had to resist the inroads of secular rulers upon papal territory and to restore to order and obedience the unruly population of the State. But so successful was the indefatigable Spaniard, alike in war and in diplomacy, that he succeeded in depriving the princes of most of their usurped possessions, of recovering practically complete the temporalities of the Church — though he failed to subdue Perugia — and in restoring something like order within the papal State. The warrior-cardinal, however, died in 1367, and the old lawlessness soon returned.

The third stage in the melancholy story of the break-up of Italy is the recounting of the most important events that occurred during the papal schism and the time of the councils. The history of the schism, and of the councils that attempted to end it, has already been given. So we are free to turn our attention to the first of the important events, the struggle between Venice and Genoa for maritime supremacy, that transpired in Italy while they were in progress. There were at first three Italian competitors for the trade of the East — Venice, Pisa, and Genoa. But the maritime power of the Pisans received a blow in the battle of Meloria from which it never recovered. Then began a long and sanguinary struggle between the victor and Venice, in which the strength of the two great maritime republics was wasted, while the constant encroachments of the Turks became a peril ever more urgent to the West, and which ended in 1380 with the irreparable defeat of the Genoese at Chioggia. Thus Venice, left comparatively free from her rivals in commerce, became mistress of the Mediterranean sea.

We have seen something of the rise of Milan into industrial and political importance. It lost its independence in 1295 and came under the dominion of the Visconti family, the greatest of whom was Gian Galeazzo, in whose subtle mind there was born again the dream of a kingdom that should embrace all Italy.

No sooner had Venice made herself mistress of the great inland sea than she aspired to conquest on the mainland. Great States were springing up all about her, and she deemed her dominion of the lagoons to be no longer secure. So she entered upon a new stage of her history, acquired a territory that extended, roughly speaking, from the Alps to the Po and from Triest to the lake of Como, became involved in the intrigues of Italian politics and by her success excited the jealousy and the fear of rivals who later on were to combine and cripple her.

Florence, as we have seen, rose from comparative obscurity to be the most important republic in Italy. It found prosperity in the pursuit of the wool and silk trade. But, like every other commune, it became divided by the rancorous strife of its various factions. A plutocratic aristocracy of merchants, bankers, and manufacturers gradually arose, of which, amid tumult and conspiracies, banishments and proscriptions, first one party gained the upper hand and then another. The wars of conquest in which the republic engaged and which made her the greatest power in Tuscany, necessitated heavy taxation; and when, in 1427, the people clamored for a more equitable system of raising the sums needed to meet the expenses of the State, Giovanni de' Medici, the richest banker in Italy, openly sided with them. Giovanni had long lurked behind the people and did not fail to seize the opportunity to put himself at their head. Thus the Medici rose above the level of their fellow-citizens and began their remarkable history. No other family has so influenced the destinies of humanity. Slowly they absorbed the governmental power by their cunning and traditional policy of identifying themselves with the popular interest. Giovanni died in 1429. Cosimo (1389–1464), his son, more daring and less cautious than his father, engaged in an open effort to secure ascendancy. But his rival, Rinaldo degli Albizzi, was too powerful to be overthrown at once, and the attempt resulted in Cosimo's exile.

Hardly a year passed, however, when at an election in Florence the tide turned, Rinaldo was banished and Cosimo reëntered the city triumphant, to be thereafter its virtual ruler. Consummate financier that he was, he was also an extraordinarily clever diplomat and politician. The outward show of a republican form of government he kept, but little by little he gathered more power to himself until he became as truly a despot as was to be found in Italy. The Medici continued their regular pursuits of trade after acquiring the attributes of sovereignty; and in finance, the patronage of art, domestic government, war, and diplomacy, they displayed an insight, a grasp, a varied capacity, and an enterprising spirit that was unexcelled. Piero (1419–69) succeeded his father in 1464, but, weak in health, he was not able to keep so firm a grasp upon the city. Lorenzo (1449–92) became the ruling spirit even before Piero died and with inflexible will he continued in the path that led to an absolute personal despotism. "*Maravigliosamente*" is the word chosen by Machiavelli to describe Lorenzo, and the characterization is most apt. The chains with which he bound Florence were golden chains. Nowhere else was there to be seen such splendid pageantry, such frequent festivities; and the licentious abandonment of the carnival time was complete. So were the Florentines beguiled; and so was the sober spirit of their earlier days transformed into the most pronounced paganism. But relentless and cruel as was Lorenzo's determination to make himself supreme, he was yet a genuine as well as a generous patron of art; and about himself he gathered the greatest painters and poets and philosophers of the age.

The dynastic struggle still dragged out its weary length in Naples. When Giovanna I, because of their difference regarding the papal schism, passed over Charles III of Durazzo and made Louis I of the second house of Anjou her successor, war broke out again. But Charles III, his son Ladislas, and his daughter Giovanna II, who belonged to the first house of Anjou, succeeded, each in their turn, in keeping the throne until the death of Giovanna in 1435. This second Giovanna, like the first one, was also childless. She chose as her successor Alfonso of Aragon and Sicily, until whose death in 1458 Naples and Sicily were reunited. But the second house of Anjou did not abandon its claims. The Neapolitan nobles were divided in their allegiance to the Aragon and Angevin houses and so a prolonged war distracted the unhappy country, until in 1442 Réné le Bon of Anjou abandoned the struggle. Alfonso who was King of Sardinia as well as of Aragon, Sicily, and Naples, was

styled by the humanists " The Magnanimous." His court was
filled with scholars, and there men who were persecuted in
other places for their opinions found an asylum.

During all this time that Italy was torn with conflict the
Turks were approaching ever nearer. In 1457 they gained
Athens, and five years later the Morea was in their possession.
Thus had they come into distinct contact with Venice, who had
expended so much of her strength in crushing Genoa and securing for herself a dominion on the mainland. Here we pause
for a time in the unhappy narrative of the disruption of the
peninsula. Italy, it has been well said, was not a nation but
merely a geographical expression.

The career of the most westerly of the Mediterranean peninsulas, the chronicle of the up-building of Spain, is altogether a
different story. When, in 1266, the Moors were driven beyond
the mountains and shut up in Granada the long warfare of Christian against Moslem paused for nearly two hundred and fifty
years. The effect of the united and protracted struggle to expel
the infidel, which had been carried on at intervals for seven hundred years, had been to weaken the provincial jealousies, which
in the Italian peninsula had been growing ever more intense,
and to infuse into the Spanish peoples something of the sentiment of nationality. With such a foundation it did not take
long to weld the Spanish States into a strong modern power.
At the opening of the Renaissance era there were four of these
States — Navarre, Aragon, Castile, and Portugal. Navarre was
made up of territory on both sides of the Pyrénées. Aragon had
been formed by the union of the three provinces of Aragon,
Catalonia, and Valencia; and later it gained Sicily, the Balearic
Isles, and Sardinia, and, for a time, Naples. Castile, when it
was united with Leon, became the largest of the Spanish States.
Portugal was at first a comparatively unimportant State. In
1139 its count, Alfonso I, assumed the title of king; and Denis
the Laborer (1279–1325) succeeded in consolidating the kingdom. The work of uniting Aragon, Castile, and the Spanish
part of Navarre into one country, Spain, was accomplished by
the house of Trastamara. Alfonso XI of Castile (1312–50)
was succeeded by his son Peter the Cruel (1350–69). But Alfonso left a number of illegitimate children, the eldest of whom,
Henry II of Trastamara (1369–79), killed Peter and placed himself upon the throne of Castile. He was succeeded in turn by
four male descendants and then by the famous Isabella (1474–
1504). The succession to the throne of Aragon came into dispute. The Cortes offered the crown to Ferdinand I (1412–16),

a prince of the reigning house of Castile, who accepted. So the family of Trastamara, despite its illegitimate origin, became the royal family of both Aragon and Castile. In due time Ferdinand was succeeded by two of his sons, and then by his grandson, Ferdinand II (1479–1516) the Catholic. In 1469 Isabella and Ferdinand were married, and thus the two branches of the house of Trastamara were united. The two kingdoms, however, although directed by the same policy, remained distinct until after the death of Isabella. In 1513 Ferdinand conquered all of Navarre south of the Pyrénées and added it to the kingdom of Spain.

Having made an attempt to study the history of the Papacy throughout the period that intervened between the end of the Middle Ages and the opening of the era of the Protestant Revolution — more definitely from the accession of Boniface VIII in 1294 to the close of the Council of Basel in 1449 — and having glanced at the political conditions of Germany, France, Italy, and Spain during the same period, we are now ready to turn our attention to that effort to recover the intellectual and artistic inheritance of Greece and Rome, to develop that inheritance and to utilize it in all the channels and aspects of life, that constitutes the Renaissance. It seems advisable to insist, at the outset, upon the fact that the development of the classical inheritance was of much greater importance in ushering in the modern world than was the recovery of the actual inheritance itself. It would be fatal to think that the Renaissance consisted exclusively of the attempt to recover the classical literature and the classical art; or, indeed, to deem that attempt to be its most important constituent. The effort to resuscitate the remains of the antique thought and art was indispensable, it is true. At least the modern era would have been greatly delayed without its aid. The spirit of the Middle Ages was one of intellectual constraint, while that of Hellenism had been one of intellectual freedom. The passage from the one to the other was like the passage from a prison to fields that stretched unbounded to the blue sky. But the inheritance of the past was merely a point of departure. Far from being no more than a renewal of antiquity, the Renaissance was a new life, indigenous, autocthonous, such as the world had never before witnessed. The mere revival of Greek and Latin letters soon developed into a pedantic classicism that, with its back turned to the future, looked only to the past. It would be wrong to think that these philologians, who disdained the work of helping to create the national languages and literatures, preferring instead slavishly to copy the forms of tongues that were dead, were the most potent figures of the period. It was not they who made the Renaissance; but rather was it those Italians, and, later, those men of other countries, who, in spite of their ardent admiration of the ancients, gave expression to their own personalities, voiced the national sentiment of their own countries, found utterance for the spirit of their own time, who looked keenly and lovingly into the world about them and scanned with eager eyes the far horizon of the future. It is the various " revivals," each of which was more of an inauguration than a revival, which these men imbued with the deepening spirit of modernity effected that constitute the true Renaissance. One other word of warning may be permitted. Politics and wars had even less than the revival of letters to do with the Renaissance. That is why they have been relegated to the background.

# CHAPTER III

## THE REVIVAL OF THE NATION

1. Nationality.
2. How it had been lost.
3. How it came back.
4. Where it came back.
5. Where it lagged and why.
6. The Value of Nationality.

IN dealing with the revival of the nation it is necessary, first of all, to arrive at the meaning of the terms " nation " and " nationality." In doing this it is perhaps well to come to an understanding of the meaning of some words that are not synonymous with them, but which are sometimes considered to be so. First, there is the word " State," which means the entire political community, all its ordinary citizens. It should not be confused with the term " nation." Austria-Hungary is a single State; but its multifarious peoples with their diverse interests and mutual antagonisms by no means constitute a single nation. Magyars and Slavs and Germans remain as distinct

**Nationality**

under the crown of St. Stephen as they were eight hundred years ago. The term " government " is likewise not equivalent to that of " nation." It is used to designate the person or the persons in whose hands rests the function of political control; and it also includes the body of electors. Beneath a single government there are oftentimes distinct elements that, like oil and water, refuse to unite. The term " society " is applied to all human communities no matter how loose their organization may be, and regardless of whether nationality has been achieved. A nation is none of these things. It is a body of people united by common ideals and a common purpose. It is the " unity of a people."

What is it, then, that gives a people unity, that makes of them a nation? Is it race? Race is oftentimes an important factor in forming a nation, but by itself it cannot create a nation. If racial unity were the essential factor there would be no nations to-day, for there is not a single pure race in Europe. Every modern nation has mixed blood. The Spanish are one of the most homogeneous of peoples, and yet they are the product of mixed blood. It is true that race is the most popular of the rule-of-thumb solutions for the question of nationality, but so vigorous a nation as the English includes prehistoric Briton, Celtic Briton, Roman, Saxon, Angle, Dane, Norman, Fleming, and Huguenot.

Does language make a nation? It, too, can help to make one; but it, too, by itself is powerless to create one. It would seem to be the most obvious mark of nationality, and at times it has been held to be an indispensable condition. The difficulty of uniting populations speaking different languages has appeared to be insuperable. But the Irish despite the fact that they speak the same language are not united to the English by national feeling. And Switzerland's three languages have not prevented her from becoming one of the most unified of nations with a popular and parliamentary government carried on by oral and printed discussion. Similarity of language invites the unity of a people, but does not compel it.

Nor does religion determine nationality. It is true that religion had much to do with the formation of the Spanish nation. The Perpetual Crusade against the infidel in the Spanish peninsula did much to weld the Christians into a nation. But that was an exceptional case. There is not a single nation to-day that has religious unity. For some time religion has been in the process of becoming a personal matter, a matter of the individual conscience. It no longer has any influence in the determination of political boundaries. If a common religion were an indispensable condition the leading nations of the world to-day would not exist.

Geographical unity may help to make a nation, but it is by no means the controlling factor. It has been well said that the limits of a nation are not written on a map. It is violence at times and at other times the wisdom of concession, and not nationality, that have as a rule determined political boundaries. Switzerland is altogether lacking in geographical unity, and yet for centuries she has had pronounced nationality; while on the other hand Italy with her striking and unusual geographical unity was able to achieve national unity only in the nineteenth century and then only because of other things. Political boundaries are shifting and comparatively unimportant. What is the width of the sea, the height of the mountains, or the breadth of a river, that amounts to political severance?

Similarity of physical environment cannot in itself make a nation. It is written that "we are what sun and wind and waters make us." Of course even inert environment counts. It has its effect upon man. It helps to condition his life. But man is not under the complete control of his environment. He is able to modify and to change it. One must take into consideration the seed as well as the soil. It is the seed that tells, more than the soil. The innate potency of men is responsible for national feeling far more than their physical surroundings. Similarity of environment may contribute toward nationality, but it cannot of itself produce it.

Nationality, the unity of a people, is not produced exclusively by race, or language, or religion, or geographical unity, or similarity of environment; nor does it come as the result of any number of these things, nor of all of them combined. Two things produce a nation — a rich inheritance of memories and the desire to preserve those memories. A nation is a spiritual unity that has been brought into existence by complex historical conditions, by similar traditions and a similar imagination. A nation, like an individual, is the product of experience, of achievement and of failures. Common triumphs to rejoice in; common sacrifices to remember. Common sorrows are especially the basis of nationality. Grief and sacrifices are a more potent element in the creation of nationality than are the common joys. When a people begins to look back upon a loved hero or heroine, upon those who have been brave and true, upon a Cid, a Richard Lionheart, a St. Louis, a St. Francis, or a Jeanne d'Arc, or when it begins to look back upon a common foe, upon the Northmen, the Mohammedans, upon England, the Empire, or the Papacy, then it begins to be conscious of a unity that not all the other contributory forces could have produced. Men are not bound together or kept apart by external and incidental things. They are not united or disunited by racial, or linguistic, or religious, or geographical conditions. Ireland has been united to England for centuries by linguistic ties. She has largely lost her own language. Yet she cherishes memories that keep alive the sense of Irish nationality. For a long time Poland has been dismembered; Russia has taken one part, Austria a second, and Germany a third. Yet the Poles keep in their hearts the memories of the past, and so the Polish nation lives to-day, though one shall look in vain upon the map for the country of Poland. It is the influence of common experience, penetrated by poetry and by passion, that is fundamental in the creation of a nation. The national bond is not necessarily dependent upon similarity of race, or soil, or religion, or language. It is wanting between the Spaniards and the Portuguese who are so nearly allied in all these respects. It is present among the Swiss where nearly all these things are absent. Like an individual, a nation is the result of a long past of triumph and of sacrifice, of devotion and of defeat. Service and sacrifice in the cause of a beloved ideal seal the soul to the object of its devotion. To toil and to suffer for the common welfare and for the fruition of the common hopes, to win life eternally through losing it, is the sure road to that high unity of a people that we call nationality. And there is in all the world no confirmation of a faith like that of abuse, contumely, and defeat endured in its service.

Nationality had been lost among the Romans. Originally there was a single state unified by the common experiences and aspirations of its people. By the process of absorption and conquest this was gradually changed. In the place of Roman nationality there came the conception of a world-wide State. And this State was conceived merely as a jural society, bound together only by its common laws and the power to enforce them. Such a conception is obviously too narrow and imperfect. Such a bond is based neither upon reverence for the past nor upon hope for the future. It is powerless to spread the contagion of sacrifice for the sake of the future. And yet this is the chief thing that conserves the life of nations. When Roman life came to be conceived of as consisting only of relations established and defined by the Roman Law, all that was vital, and noble, and inspiring, disappeared. When this was the only bond that united Romans, the Empire itself was doomed.

Nationality was dormant throughout the Middle Ages. Before the Teutonic peoples invaded the Roman Empire they lived under a crude form of tribal unity. They were united to each other by personal allegiance to their leaders. The various tribes combined with each other and fusion with the Roman population was gradually effected. Homogeneous peoples with common traditions and common aims, like the Franks, began to appear. But the Church gave to Charles the Great the title of " Emperor," and thus the national feeling of the various Teutonic peoples was side-tracked. It is true that the Empire after Charles was only a shadowy institution, but " the idea of the world-State continued to fascinate men's minds long after it had lost material existence." One looks in vain for any vital manifestation of nationality in medieval institutions. Civil law and canon law alike were international, and feudal law and custom were local. In the Middle Ages the wars were not an outcome of national feeling. It was not for national purposes that the crusades were fought. The long-continued struggle between the Empire and the Papacy was one for world-wide supremacy. The innumerable petty strifes of feudalism were the very denial

of nationality. It is not until the Hundred Years' War that
national feeling is visibly present. Even religion was arrayed
against nationality for it was universal and inter-national. In
the Middle Ages the European countries were nothing but vast
feudal nebulæ.

Only very gradually was the sense of nationality restored.
It was a silent transition due to many influences slowly interfused. One thing that caused the universalism of the Papacy
and the Empire to dissolve and the merely local feeling of feudalism to give way to nationality was the fusion of the races. Men
of Wessex and men of Northumbria disappeared. The Englishman came in their stead. Norman and Gascon were merged
into the Frenchman, and Catalonians and Castilians were replaced by Spaniards.

The growth of the royal power was another factor in the revival of nationality. As the power and authority of the king
grew, the imperial idea became fainter and fainter, the secular
claims of the Papacy were successfully disputed, and the disintegrating forces of feudalism were crushed. The king was a
symbol of national unity, and in him were centered the national
aspirations. The increase of kingly power was a concrete and
effective force in the gradual consolidation of the heterogeneous
feudal nebulæ into compact and homogeneous countries.

Another force that made for the resuscitation of nationality
was the rise of the vernacular literatures. In the Middle Ages
all Latin Christendom was bound together by the Latin language.
It was the language of the Church, of the secular as well as the
ecclesiastical law courts, and of all educated men. A district
in a city in which a university was situated was called the Latin
Quarter because there Latin was not only written but spoken.
The vernacular tongues were spoken, but they were regarded as
dialects are to-day. They were not organized. They had no
grammars and no literatures. But gradually, and almost simultaneously, in France, in Italy, in Spain, and in England, the
vernacular tongues acquired a greater dignity, and national literatures arose. These vernacular literatures displaced the idiom
of the Church and became both an expression and a guarantee
of national feeling.

The advent of the Third Estate was still another force in
the revival of the nation. The peasants did not gain representation and a voice in the national councils. That still lay far in
the future. But the townspeople, the bourgeoisie, succeeded in
gaining recognition in the national assemblies. The middle
classes were far more national in their feeling than were the

feudal nobility, and more so, too, than the clergy. Retrospection did not lead them to regret a time of feudal independence. It was only with the growing power of the nation that they had won their emancipation from the thraldom of feudalism. Only as the nation grew in power could they hope to compete in social matters with the feudal aristocracy; only as the nation grew in strength could feudal warfare be made to give way to the king's peace, and peace was necessary for the commerce and industry of the towns. Nationality affected the interests, touched the hearts, and fired the imagination of the townsfolk. More important in the history of the Middle Ages than the struggle between the empire and the Papacy, was the struggle between the secular and the spiritual power. And this in its last analysis was nothing less than a struggle between the natural instinct of nationality and the universal authority of the Church. With the growth of the towns and the consequent increase of secular culture, the sense of nationality received a great impetus. In general it may be said that at the end of the thirteenth century the medieval ideal of universality began to give way before the rising tide of national spirit.

Nationality came back in France. In the days of Hugh Capet, France had been the name of only a single duchy. It was merely one of a number of feudal lordships, and it was by no means the most powerful of them. But step by step the Capetian kings had subdued the feudal nobles and built up a compact nation. They encouraged the towns and made them valuable supports of the kingly power and they assumed direct lordship over the peasants. And so, as we have seen, in the struggle with Boniface VIII the French kings could appeal successfully to a sense of nationality. Papal excommunication was pronounced in vain. But more than all else it was the Hundred Years' War that kindled French nationality. Jeanne d'Arc is the godmother of the French nation. Around her name there clustered the memories of the misery and the humiliation of the long and cruel war which the French people had suffered in common. Their common memories of the past gave them a common aspiration in the present. The peasant maid of Domremy became the patron saint of their patriotism. Where Nationality Came Back

England also witnessed a revival of nationality. The geographical conditions were particularly favorable. Feudalism had never been so rampant as on the continent, and England had never been affected greatly by the idea of the medieval empire. But the popes had disposed of English benefices in the most arbitrary way; and its kings had been men of foreign blood who had introduced alien elements into the land. Edward I, whose long reign began in 1272, was unmistakably English. He gave preference to Englishmen and to English customs. Parliament was made more widely representative by the introduction of the middle classes, and the laws were developed and codified. The papal pretensions were resisted by Edward III, whose parliament gave him its support; and Edward IV and the Tudors continued the work. The English custom of sending the younger sons of the nobility into the ranks of the commons helped to consolidate the people; and the opposition of the people to Poitevins and Gascons served to develop in them a strong sense of national unity.

In Scotland the sense of nationality was developed by the struggle under Wallace and Bruce for independence. And the Bohemians, who, despite the fact that their kings received investiture from the German emperor, and were included among the seven electors, kept aloof from the general politics of the Empire, were drawn together by the brilliant conquests of Ottokar II and the struggles of the Hussite movement. The feeling of nationality was greatly strengthened by its association with the religious reform movement which was directed to the establishment of a national Bohemian church. In the Spanish peninsula the long warfare against the infidel drew the people together. Provincial jealousies were weakened, they were relegated to the background by the greater interests of the common enterprise. So the Spanish peoples were welded by the Perpetual Crusade into a nation. And when the elements of a strong national life had thus been gained, Ferdinand of Aragon married Isabella of Castile and thus hastened the definite political union of the Spanish kingdom. So strong did the sense of nationality become in Spain that ecclesiastical affairs were in a large degree withdrawn from the dominion of the Curia and made subject to the Crown.

From this movement towards nationality Italy and Germany stood aloof. In Italy the Papacy, which thought that its own position would be weakened by the union of the numerous Italian States, effectively opposed political consolidation. Ever since the days of the Lombards it had been the traditional policy of the Papacy to thwart any attempt of a secular leader to secure national sovereignty in the peninsula, and the papal restoration had made it strong enough to carry out this policy effectively. Then, too, Italy at this time seemed to be more concerned with intellectual emancipation than with political consolidation. It is true there were dreamers who had visions of a united Italy,—

**Where Nationality Lagged**

Dante and Henry of Luxemburg among others. But Italy had become relaxed by prosperity and still further disintegrated by the rapid mental enfranchisement of the Renaissance movement. For a long time the Italians had been accustomed to the shifting combinations of the many States into which their peninsula was divided. The changes in these combinations were "a game of ceaseless check and counter-check." Oftentimes the moves in this game were directed with extraordinary astuteness, but the great principle of nationality was lost to view. More important to Italians than the unification of Italy seemed to be the preservation of the distinctive marks and the privileges of a Florentine, a Venetian, a Neapolitan, or a Roman. And so, "the swelling tide of nationality passed them by to wash other shores." It was not until the days of Garibaldi and Mazzini that the sense of nationality was developed in Italy, and it is still only opening its wings.

The medieval idea of the universal lordship of the Holy Roman Emperor, although it had grown more shadowy with each succeeding century, had much to do with retarding national consolidation in Germany. The emperor was bound to assert his suzerainty over Italy. Although many attempts were made, this proved to be an impossible task. But it engaged the energy that might otherwise have been directed against the disintegrating forces that distracted Germany, and so Italy became the sepulcher of German national unity. Germany was dissolved into a confederacy of States and cities and classes each bent upon the furtherance of its own special interests. Towards the end of the Middle Ages there were some forty secular princes and seventy ecclesiastical princes, besides an uncounted host of greater and smaller imperial cities and inconsequential nobles. The emperor became nothing more than the titular head of this loose confederacy. Yet the medieval ideal of empire was not the sole cause of the disintegration of Germany. Other historical conditions, such as the opposition of the agricultural and urban interests, and geographical differences were by no means unimportant factors.

The revival of the nation had its roots deep in human nature. It is by the maintenance of wholesome relations with one's fellow-men that the individual can best secure his own development. The ties that bind men together are not so much the accidental and incidental things of race, language, theological creed, or geography, but rather the common memories of a people and the will to perpetuate those memories. A nation, therefore, is not an artificial expedient devised to attain certain special and tem-

The Worth of Nationality

porary ends. Its elements, distinctive character, treasured his·
tory, deep and passionate desire, are to be found in human nature itself, in the indwelling necessity for the association of men.
Yet there should be no narrow conception of nationality. A too
limited idea of nationality inevitably results in spiritual disaster.
It makes of patriotism only a magnified selfishness. It is only
with a generous and an expanding ideal of nationality that the
solidarity of human interests, the essential brotherhood of all
men, can be concretely realized. It is only with such an ideal
that individuality can find its finest development.

# CHAPTER IV

## THE REVIVAL OF THE INDIVIDUAL

1. Individuality.
2. How it had been lost.
3. How it came back.
4. When and where it came back.
5. The significance of Individuality.

THE word "individuality" means the quality of not being capable of further division. Society is an organization of men. It is not an organism. It is dependent upon the organisms which it includes. It derives its life from the individuals who compose it. Society cannot be resolved into anything more fundamentally simple than the individual. The individual man is the atom of human society. He is a real concrete entity, incapable of division and incapable of fusion. He remains forever separate. Individuality, the force of separate self-hood, is the most important fact in human life. Only as a man stands squarely and solidly upon his own feet can he deal in the most effective way with the world of nature and the world of men. It is only through the channel of individuality that new thought and new art can come into the world; and thought and art, immaterial though they be, are the matrix that shapes the issues of life. Personality is the central fact and force of human nature. The reverse of the old saying that there is nothing new under the sun is true. There is nothing under the sun that is not new. No two leaves upon the same tree are identical. No two animals, even of the same parentage, are exactly alike. Every life is a new combination of old forces. Every personality is original and unparalleled. The difference between men is so great as to become, in the case of genius, incalculable and illimitable. The difference of our faces and our voices is merely symbolical of mental and emotional differences vastly more important. "No other man's fingerprint," said a recent English poet, "has the same pressure as mine, and I shall see that it appears on everything I handle, everything I adopt, everything I own. The gloves of party, of culture, of creed, wherewith men hide their fingerprints lest they should be caught in the act of being themselves, I decline to wear." The process of multiplication is powerless to produce an admirable society when the units multiplied are themselves contemptible. "If I see nothing to admire in a unit," said Emerson, "shall I admire a million units?" It is through individuality that the force of creation flows on continually in the world. *"Je n'en sais rien,"* said Napoleon when asked the origin of his new tactics, *"je suis fait comme ça."* So every powerful individuality is a channel through which new truth comes among men. The certain reality of the self is the starting-point of modern philosophy. The one key to the great enigmas of life is personality.

The Greeks to a certain extent had realized the importance of individuality. It is to this that their supreme achievements in art were largely due. Yet despite the fact that Greek art tells us of a high development of individuality, the political thinkers of Greece gave the State the first claim. And Rome endeavored to substitute for the diminished individuality of that time her comprehensive and formulated law. Individuality sank from sight still further in the Middle Ages. The Church taught that individuality was rebellion and sin. Conscience, which is the individual judgment of what is right and wrong, might exist between man and man, but not between man and God. Man must not be content to live his own life. Instead, it should be his aim to live over again, as far as possible, the life of the saints, the life of Christ. He must divest himself of selfhood. Instead of seeking to create he should endeavor only to imitate. All utterance of the carnal self was fraught with danger or with sin. Self-abnegation, self-annihilation, was the goal of the medieval Christian life. It was a sort of Buddhism, save that the Nirvana of the Christian was God and not mere oblivion. The spirit of implicit faith, of unquestioning obedience, inculcated by the age of faith, was destructive of individuality; for mere right-doing in obedience to external commands leaves the power of individual thought and judgment in abeyance. It empties action of all rational significance. The ideal of life of the Middle Ages was one closed about with the circumscribing walls of a cloister. Yet its vision, though narrow, was lofty. It ignored as much as possible the world of nature and the world of men, but it opened upon the infinite like "the chink which serves for the astronomer's outlook upon the abysses of heaven." Individuality was also restricted in other affairs of life in the Middle Ages. It was so in political matters. When the cities threw off the yoke of feudalism it was a collective, communal, liberty they enjoyed, not individual freedom. They were free as societies,

but as individuals they were still unemancipated. It was so in
industrial matters. The peasantry on the manorial estates were
chained to the wheel of labor. And in the cities the life of the
craftsman was directed in all essential respects by the trade at
which he worked, the corporation to which he belonged, the
parish in which he worshiped, and the quarter of the city in
which he dwelt. His station in life was determined as im-
mutably as that of the villein. There were few things in which
his individual taste or opinion was a deciding factor. It was a
time of aggregate and not individual strength. Feudalism and
the ideals of universal empire and universal church had bound
together the various peoples of Europe " in a rigorous hierarchy
which imposed order on the confusion of barbarism. On all
the stages of the immense pyramid, united one to another by an
invisible force, there reigned the fundamental law of the new
society. The individual was only part of the whole. Isolation,
had it been possible, would have been fatal to him; for he had
no value except as a member of the group to which he belonged,
and his group was held together only by its subordination to
masters who in their turn were subordinate to a still higher
group. Thus the unity of the feudal and Catholic edifice was
maintained from stage to stage; kingdoms, duchies, counties,
baronies, bishoprics, chapters, religious orders, universities, corporations, the obscure multitude of serfs. At each stratum
the human being was fettered and protected by the duty of
fidelity, by perfect obedience, and by community of interests and
of sacrifice. The individual who tried to burst his bonds, the
baron who revolted, the tribune who agitated for liberty, the
unbelieving doctor, the heretical monk, the Jacques or the Fraticelli, were crushed." All through the Middle Ages man knew
himself only as a member of a family, a race, a party, a guild,
or a church. He was for the most part unconscious of himself
as an individual. The central figure of Joinville's *Histoire de
Saint Louis,* says Gebhart, is the one clearly individual character
which the Middle Ages have left us. The story of the Renaissance is the story of the revival of the individual — in science,
invention, in discovery, in art, in literature, and in religion.
The deep, underlying cause of the Renaissance was the revival
of the individual. And it was in Italy that the individual first
began to emerge from the guild, the corporation, the commune,
the religious order, and the hierarchy.

This emergence of the individual was not a sudden apparition;
nor did it occur only when the hour of the Renaissance was
about to strike. It was a gradual evolution; and its workings

may be observed long before the appearance of Petrarch who has been called the first modern man. It was at the close of the thirteenth century, while the peoples of other countries were still cognizant of themselves only as members of their respective races and associations, that individuality began to assert itself in Italy. Italians acquired the desire and the courage to be themselves. No longer were they afraid of being singular. Even in the matter of dress, expression was given to personal idiosyncrasy and taste. In Florence there came to be no longer any prevailing fashion of dress for men. It was in the matter of taste, the thing that differentiates us from our fellow-men in what we like to eat, or smell, or hear, or see, that the re-birth of selfhood first became apparent. Nowhere is the significance of individuality so evident as in literature and art. Indeed, art depends upon individuality for its very existence. Upon all poetry that has left its impression upon humanity there can be seen the seal of personality — the " keen translunar music " of Milton, the " cloudless, boundless human view " of Shakespeare, Shelley's " flush of rose on peaks divine," and the " wizard twilight " that Coleridge knew. Before Dante there were poets in Italy who were able to stamp their work with the unmistakable impress of their personality, but it was he who for the first time poured " in all his writings a stream of personal force by which the reader, apart from the interest of the subject, feels himself carried away." Others following in his wake expressed themselves in lyric, epic, novel, and drama. Petrarch was explicitly aware of the fact that the highest conditions of culture can be attained only by the free evolution and interaction of self-developed intellects. By the recognition and expression of their individuality were the Italians enabled to emerge from the bondage of the Middle Ages and become the apostles of humanism to the modern world. Men became animated by an overpowering desire to make the best of themselves. All around them were the priceless riches inherited from the past, the architecture, sculpture, literature, and philosophy of the bygone days of a golden age which the inundating wave of barbarism had hidden and Christianity caused to be neglected for many centuries. They became filled with a deep belief in the desirability and possibility of man's perfection. They were reinstated in their human dignity as one by one the trammels of authority were discarded and they began to feel, to think, and to act as their own thought and instinct directed. And as a powerful stimulus there came about a rehabilitation of the pagan idea of fame. The desire for immortality upon earth was coupled with the hope for immortality in a world to come, and, indeed, in many instances, replaced it altogether.

The story of the development of Italian art, like that of Italian literature, is also the story of the gradual revival and unfolding of individuality. Little by little the spell of the Church which had held art in thrall, and allowed it to be nothing more than its handmaiden, was broken. Gradually the architects, the sculptors, and the painters dared to be themselves. Instead of mere conformity to long-established traditions, instead of blind obedience to canonical conventions, the artists learned to look within themselves, to look out into the world of nature and of men, and then to record their visions. Some of the arts require greater independence in the artist than do others. Architecture is one of the least exacting. More than any of the other arts it is dominated by the national genius and by the prevailing force of the age. The cathedrals of the Middle Ages are the expression not of the genius of individual architects but of the spirit of the Age of Faith. They do not bear the stamp of individual thought and feeling so much as that of popular instinct. Their beauty and their spirit belong to the age that gave them birth. In the architecture of the early Renaissance one can witness the exercise of individual taste. It was this exercise of individuality that gradually revived the Greek and Roman styles of architecture, changed them first in one respect and then in another, and finally combined them into a new style that received its name from the age. Sculpture and painting demand a more complete exercise of individual taste. The statue or the picture is far less a common product of a people or of an age than is the temple or the cathedral. Every picture and every statue that has attained to the rank of art is unmistakably the product of an individual. So the individuality of the Italians found fitting mediums of expression in these arts. Although the expression of personality by the sculptors and painters was very feeble at first, one has but to recall their names, Cimabue, Duccio, Giotto, Orcagna, Ghiberti, Donatello, to realize distinctly how differentiated they became. It is of course only by the expression of their contrasting personalities that this differentiation was produced. Each recorded his own vision. Despite the fact that Donatello was the first sculptor of the Renaissance to make a free-standing nude figure he refused to follow the conventions of classic scuplture, of which there were doubtless many memorials about him, and trusted to his own fine power of observation. Very feeble is the expression of personality in the pictures of Cimabue, one of the first painters

of the Renaissance, but it is unmistakable in Giotto, charming in
Perugino, opulent in Raphael, and overwhelming in Michelangelo.

In curiosity, as well as in taste, individuality found a channel
for expression and development.  Not the ignoble curiosity of
"my landlady's neighbor, she who lives behind us to the left,
whose window commands our garden," but the curiosity that
inspired Roger Bacon, Newton, and Darwin.  In the Age of
Faith curiosity was a cardinal sin.  The idea that it is a duty
or that it is the part of wisdom to find out the reality of things
was quite foreign to the time.  It was dangerous to trust to the
guidance of one's depraved self.  Revelation was the sole source
of truth.  But when Peter the Hermit preached the first Crusade
he unconsciously helped to set in motion forces that resulted in
the Renaissance.  Travel incited the curiosity of men and
brought them into contact with the wonderful civilizations of
Byzantium and the Saracens.  Men became filled with curiosity
not only to know the civilization of other countries, but to learn
something of men who had lived in distant ages and who had
been actuated by different ideals of life.  This curiosity came to
be a powerful and important force.  It extended the narrow
horizon of the Middle Ages.  It produced a revival of learning
and of research, it resulted in invention and in discovery, and
so it was the starting point of modern civilization.  It " whis-
pered to Columbus, plucked Galileo by the sleeve, and shook the
apple off Newton's apple-tree."  It initiated the experimental
method.  It implanted in the hearts of men the desire to study
and to know the world for themselves, unencumbered by the
bonds of authority.  It spurred them to the most daring voyages
and the most patient and careful investigations.  It was perhaps
in the field of learning that the stirring of curiosity first became
evident.  And when knowledge of the classic tongues was increased and men became able to see the world from the Greek
and the Roman points of view, the aroused interest of man, his
developed intelligence and his critical curiosity led him into other
fields of activity.  Thus it was that the Renaissance of science
and literature and art came about; with the awakening of curiosity there had come into existence " that which at once produced
and was produced by all these — thorough perception of what
exists, thorough consciousness of our own freedom and powers
— self-cognizance.  In Italy there was intellectual light, enabling
men to see and judge all around them, enabling them to act wit-
tingly and deliberately.  In this lies the immense greatness of the
Renaissance: to this are due all its achievements in literature

and science, and, above all, in art,— that, for the first time since the dissolution of antique civilization, men were free agents, both in thought and in deed."

Individuality also made itself felt in the field of religion. In the Age of Faith men had but to hearken and obey. The postulate of an infallible church that was the sole custodian of truth rendered unnecessary the exercise of the reasoning faculty of man. To trust one's unaided instinct or reason was to run the risk of being deceived. But with the revival of individuality men began to trust something within themselves — the consensus of their faculties, which we have narrowed into the word "conscience." Against the authority of the Church men asserted the reliability of the reasoning faculty, even its sovereign power, and the dignity of the individual conscience. The only test of truth, said Abelard, is its reasonableness; and the wandering scholars who had flocked in tens of thousands to hear him sowed the seed of his method everywhere. In Provence, in northern Italy, and elsewhere, there were found people who thought they could live a religious life unassisted by the priesthood and directed only by conscience. They dispensed with sacraments and with clergy. The Cathari and the Patarini in Lombardy, the Albigenses in Provence, the Lollards in England, the Hussites in Bohemia, and the Waldenses in the Alpine valleys were the principal groups of heretics. But not all those who were borne along on this wave of intellectual emancipation became heretics. There were those who stayed within the pale of Mother Church, who denied none of her doctrines, but strove to effect a reform in the morals of clergy and laity. Francis of Assisi, Dominic, Bernard of Clairvaux, Bernardino of Siena, Savonarola, numbers of the trans-Alpine humanists, and many another reformer, were filled with a passionate desire to regenerate society. The movement of emancipation, the casting aside of the accepted rules and criteria of the medieval period, led to moral recklessness, to that practice and tolerance of vice which constitutes the worst feature of the Renaissance; but the age was by no means given over wholly to immorality. It is often-times the striking feature, the abnormal condition, that arrests attention.

The Crusades, as we have already seen, had much to do with the revival of individuality. They opened hitherto unknown distances to the European mind. They awakened a passion for travel and adventure; and travel is perhaps the best method of setting men free from prejudice. Gradually this passion became coupled with a thirst for knowledge. The two became allied in Italy. So to study the beginning of the revival of individualism, the interest in the individual that overleaps all the claims and bonds of race, nation, and church, one must go back to the Crusades. The Crusades were the realization of the Age of Faith, the triumph of the Church. But the results were far from those expected by the Church. New groupings were made, new associations formed. Englishmen, Neapolitans, Spaniards, Germans, Frenchmen, and Italians, were brought into most intimate companionship with each other. There were new crystallizations. Everywhere, in camp, during truces, in hospitals, on the way, and in pilgrimages, men were taken out of their old environments, out of the hearing of their village church-bells that constantly recalled them to the piety of their childhood, and confronted with new things. They mingled with the Mohammedan infidels and found them to be human, kindly, intelligent, and prosperous, and sincerely devoted to the worship of what they believed to be the true God. The Crusaders got a new standard of life from the comforts and luxuries of the Saracens. They got intellectual stimulus. They lost their provinciality. No longer were they content with the common and uniform nourishment of Mother Church, but each began to crave for himself individual stimulus to beauty and religion. It was the common broadening effect of travel raised to a higher power. It did all that travel can do to emancipate men in a brief space of time. It set them to discovering that the present world is interesting and beautiful, real and God-given. It helped to make their vision less vertical and more horizontal.

The last part of the twelfth century and the first part of the thirteenth was the time of the Goliardi, the wandering scholars, who lived the life of the open road, the free song, and the flowing bowl. Theirs was a care-free, jovial life. They turned their backs on convention and gave full vent to impulse. Their vagrant life along the roads and in the villages and towns of Europe was filled with youthful exhilaration, irrepressible fun, and madcap pranks. Everywhere they were received with pleasure. Their songs, "the spontaneous expression of careless, wanton, and unreflective youth," were listened to with eagerness. Perhaps it was the new thought which these songs contained that made them so appealing, thought that helped men to peer beyond the bounds of feudalism and ecclesiasticism. They were charged with the new message of humanity. They made men pause and wonder whether after all there might not be something worthy and necessary in the impulse of nature. They breathed the freedom of man. It is true that these songs of the Goliardi were in Latin, but it was significant that a particular class of society should be making its own songs. The transition from this to lyrics in the vernacular was not long or difficult.

In Provence individuality found a fruitful soil and a congenial climate. Most beloved of all the possessions of Rome, it was known in imperial times as "the Province." And not only the name of this province *par excellence* bore memories of Rome, but its roads, its bridges, its towns, and many a less prehensible inheritance. Immigration had brought to it not only Romans, but Phœnicians, Ionian Greeks, and Saracens. Its civilization was stamped with the genius of the East as well as with that of the West. Its town life had not been obliterated by the wave of barbarism. Always some traces of the old ideals and the old culture remained. Commerce flourished and brought with it from distant places not only necessities but also luxuries. Its burghers early won for themselves a large measure of freedom, and its nobles were less exclusively concerned with warfare and the chase than were those of the more feudal North. In the twelfth century the lyric poets of this country, the troubadours, struck the note of modernity. Men of the proletariat as well as the men of the palace became poets; and the songs of all of them appealed to the whole populace and had for their burden the passions and the dreams of men. Things that are not the exclusive privilege of birth, a generous and a brave heart, a fearless mind, courtesy, and, above all, love that has forgotten itself and that is the birthright of every youthful soul, furnished the themes of the troubadour. Individuality found a wide field in which to roam. Their verse-forms, too, were diversified. They had the stately *chanson,* the dramatic *sirvente,* the elegiac *complainte,* the pliant *tenson,* for the morning love-song at the shy hour of dawn the *aubade,* for the twilight the *serenade,* and for the poem of idyllic mood the *pastourelle.* It was a vibrant lyrical poetry, this of the troubadours. It gave expression to the life of the whole people. The bonds of feudalism and ecclesiasticism had been burst asunder. The individual emerged from the medieval shell. Freedom of thought in secular matters led to independence in religion. Criticism of the clergy increased. Heresy took root and flourished. But at length a crusade was preached against the Albigenses. The French king, in part because of political considerations, gave his aid to the pope, and Provence, devastated by fire and everywhere stained with blood, lost its liberty and its civilization; and so its awakening individualism was extinguished.

This yearning for youth and love, this responsiveness to nature, quenched in Provence, found a home in Sicily. It is there that one finds the first well-rounded type of manhood in that intellectual adventurer and oriental dreamer, Frederic II, wit, statesman, philosopher, poet, skeptic, and theologian, who evoked a premature Renaissance at his southern court. This descendant of Barbarossa, who was born in Italy, and who spoke Italian, French, Greek and Arabic from his childhood, was far removed in spirit from the Middle Ages though he lived eighty years before Dante. The civilization that he encouraged was essentially rational and generously liberal. Its prime concern and dominant element was intellectual culture. The Italians, who before many years had gone by were " to be charmed by personal energy more than by virtue, and who in the following century permitted their masters to do anything provided only that they accomplished great things, . . . admired this Emperor who tried to wrest the world from the grip of the Church and who, while amusing himself among his poets, astrologers, musicians, and singers, was reconciling Christian Europe with Mohammedan Asia." In his conflict with the Church, Frederic, who was excommunicated, dispossessed, betrayed by his chancellor, and compelled to defend his possessions in all parts of the peninsula, died as defeat was coming upon him. But his work left a lasting impression upon the course of civilization. The stimulus he gave to the development of individuality by example and by patronage was by no means ephemeral.

In the city-republics of the Italian peninsula individuality found opportunity to unfold. The cities themselves had thrown off the dominion of the Empire, and this emancipation, no doubt, was an example to the individual. The Latin intelligence and fine imagination of the Italians was sharpened by the quick life of the towns. The change of rule from one party to another induced the successful leaders to exercise an ever-increasing degree of watchfulness, thought, and power. The exigencies of the situation compelled the leaders to develop every ability they possessed. So more and more did these political leaders become marked by their distinguishing characteristics. The hope of securing their lost positions was likewise a stimulant to the defeated leaders to greater and more thoughtfully-directed energy. The lack of such hope led them to turn their attention to other lines of activity, to literature, or to the other intellectual and artistic pursuits that were beginning to attract the attention of men. It would be a mistake to think that the incessant civil discords and political convulsions always hindered the progress of the communes and the development of individuality. It was in the midst of such struggles that personality was formed. It was only for the purpose of defending or aggrandizing their own interests that the free citizens of the commune took up arms,— the interests of their city against a neighboring commune, the interests of their party against a rival party, and their own personal interests against those of their opponents. Even exile played a part in this revival of individuality. Banishment " either wears an exile out or develops what is greatest in him." The emigrants gave to their new cities a cosmopolitan air, and cosmopolitanism is attained only through the widening of the horizon by means of an increased individualism. All of them had learned to resist authority that they deemed to be arbitrary, and when independence has been asserted in one sphere of life it is less difficult to assert it in the others. But these city-republics gradually lost all the essential features of a republic; they eventually became self-governing communities in name only. They passed into the control of the despots, of the men who by the force of their individuality had made themselves the masters of their fellow-men.

The age of the despots " fostered in the highest degree the individuality not only of the tyrant or *condottiere* himself, but also of the men whom he protected or used as his tools — the secretary, minister, poet, and companion. These people were forced to know all the inward resources of their own nature, passing or permanent; and their enjoyment of life was enhanced and concentrated by the desire to obtain the greatest satisfaction from a possibly very brief period of power and influence." Up to this time the Italians had been arrayed against each other only in solid masses, town against town. But the age of the despots produced a condition even more favorable to the development of individuality, for " the qualities, virtues, passions, and even the vices, which the Italians had up to that time employed for the collective good of their town were henceforth diverted to their own private advantage with an energy all the greater because their effort was egotistical and solitary. It no longer sufficed to act in self-defense to avoid destruction. One must attack and conquer in order to secure to-morrow's peace and to content one's pride. In this struggle of man against man it was, of course, the one equipped with the better arms that triumphed. Wealth, knavery, and boldness proved excellent arms; but the most certain of all was intellect." The conditions of the time called into play the varied potentialities of each individual. So there came into existence those versatile men of the Renaissance who are the wonder of to-day. In order to win control of a state it was not necessary to be of noble birth. Any one might make the attempt, a soldier, a priest, or a tradesman, an adventurer, or even a criminal. The ability of the individual was not circumscribed by convention. Provided only that he had sufficient daring and the talent of success the way was open to any one, even though of the most obscure or illegitimate birth. Ability enabled one to climb from the lowest rung of the social ladder. Gismondo Malatesta, who is in many respects a typical despot, proceeded upon the assumption that to the individual all things are possible. He trusted his own powers implicitly and in them he placed his sole reliance. He gave free rein to his desires. He realized that only his own capacity could protect him against the increasing power of the pope and the growing hostility of his powerful neighbors. He displayed the indifference to humanity, the relentless cruelty, of the Middle Ages, the political sagacity for which every early Italian statesman became famous, and the intellectual independence of the age in which he lived. Italy was a seething mass of struggling despotisms in which personal power, intellect and skill, were essential to success. And when political success had been attained every ruler proceeded to satisfy his personal desires in his own way. The will of the despot was supreme. But even the subjects over whom the despot ruled, as well as the poets, artists, scholars, and philosophers whom he patronized, felt the impulse of individuality. The large majority of these acquiesced in the despotism, especially when it was unmistakably benevolent in character. They were, of course, without political power; but that did not prevent them from engaging to the fullest extent of their capacity in any others of the varied activities of the social life of the time. Aside from the lack of participation in the control of the State, the conditions of life in the Italian despotism seem unquestionably to have fostered the development of individual thought and power. " The private man, indifferent to politics, and busied partly with serious pursuits, partly with the interests of a dilettante, seems first to have been fully formed in these despotisms of the fourteenth century." The democracies and despotisms of Italy were the seed plots of individuality. It was there that man first emerged from the bondage of the age of feudalism and the Age of Faith.

The insistence upon individuality was the greatest of the many factors that gave rise to the Renaissance. It caused men to question the authority of external control, and inspired them to develop their latent powers beyond the restricting confines of authority. It made them ready to question the conventional standards of conduct. It filled them with a vivid apprehension of life and a zeal for activity of all kinds. Endowed with confidence in their own powers they faced without fear every problem that confronted them. They " dared to be themselves for good or evil without too much regard for what their neighbors thought of them." The energy which their intense individuality created found a wide range of expression, from superlative intellectual activity and artistic creation to the depths of pagan sensuality. The standards of internal moral control had not yet been developed, and those of external control had been discarded. It is this that produced such violent contrasts of emotion and conduct and that " makes the psychology of the Renaissance at once so fascinating and so difficult to analyze." It was the seemingly illimitable vitality of the individual force of princes and popes, of statesmen and scholars, of poets and of painters, that made the Renaissance one of the most remarkable eras in the history of the world. " A man's mind," said the wise author of *Ecclesiasticus,* " is sometime wont to tell him more than seven watchmen, that sit above in an high tower." The desire to study and to know the world, to put aside the fetters of arbitrary authority and discoloring prejudice, and see things as they really are, gave birth to new thought, to literature, science, and art, and it revived the experimental method of investigation without which it is impossible to extend the horizon of man's knowledge. It produced the Renaissance and the modern world in which we live. The consciousness of the individual is the only creative faculty in life. In the last resort it is the only center of good and evil, the sole home of values.

> " For what avail the plow or sail,
>     Or land or life, if freedom fail? "

Without the freedom and development of the individual the modern world would have been impossible. And, one may add, without the devotion of the emancipated individual to social service the salvation of the modern world shall be sought in vain.

The wise man recognizes the truth in the principle of individualism and in that of association, and preserves a balance between these two opposing forces. It was Descartes who, in a later century, first clearly suggested the reconciliation between the fullest individual development and the pursuit of a social end.

# CHAPTER V

## THE REVIEW OF LITERATURE

CHAP. V
1275-1300

Why the Renaissance did not Begin in France

IN the twelfth and thirteenth centuries it was France that held the intellectual supremacy of western Europe. But, as we have seen, the premature Renaissance of Provence was extinguished with fire and sword. This was not the sole cause, however, of the decline of southern France. The civilization of that country contained intrinsic defects. It was essentially lyrical, emotional, and egotistical. It was incapable of that calm, dispassionate, objective view of life which is indispensable to intellectual progress. Then, too, after its rapid emancipation from feudalism it had received certain streams of thought which threatened to detach it from the civilization of Christendom. It listened eagerly to the iconoclastic whisperings of Manicheism, it gave welcome to the austere rationalism of the Vaudois, neither of which was calculated to encourage the development of art or of science, and it furnished votaries of Averroism, which set its face against the revival of Greek culture. It was because of these things that southern France failed to become the seat of the Renaissance. Northern France had produced the most spiritual architecture that the world has ever seen. The sculpture that adorned her Gothic churches, delicate product of a refined religious sentiment, was, in its way, well-nigh perfect. Of the seemingly lost art of stained glass that made her cathedrals glow with the splendor of the sunset she was the chief mistress. She possessed the epic spirit and the deep earnestness that were lacking in the south. Her language was known and used all over the civilized world. Civil liberty had made great progress in her towns. And Abelard, in his lectures at the great University of Paris, had shown the way to intellectual freedom. Why, then, did northern France fail to carry forward the lighted torch of civilization? Scholasticism blighted its thought. Observation of the world of nature and of men, investigation, was not practised. Men were engrossed with the method of reasoning. They held logic, and not investigation, to be the sole key to knowledge. They made the syllogism the very end of science instead of recognizing it as being merely one of the instruments of science. Given over to the discipline of the syllogism, they failed to base their premises upon the data of experience, and they failed to verify their conclusions. Instead of going out into the world to gather data upon which to base their generalizations they were completely absorbed in the processes of logic. So their ingenious and interminable disputations, that remind one of a squirrel going round and round its cage with exceeding skill and arriving nowhere, were barren of results. The intellect of northern France was benumbed by its system of education. Logic is too thin and bloodless a thing to direct and govern life. It is possible to reason forever and yet to learn nothing. A second reason is to be found in the decline of the independence of the towns. The social conditions that had come to exist in the municipal democracies favored the development of thought and the progress of civilization. But in the process of the centralization of power in the hands of the king, the towns lost their independence. As a political force the middle class grew more and more insignificant. Thus northern France lost the two conditions that are indispensable to the development of civilization — freedom of thought and political liberty. The springs of her intellectual life ran low. So that the Renaissance which might have been cradled in France found a birthplace in Italy.

In Italy all the conditions necessary for the success of such a movement as the Renaissance were present. She possessed freedom of thought. Scholasticism had never been accepted as the sole and infallible method of thought. The Italian genius, unlike the French, did not lend itself to the study of logic for its own sake. It was concerned with the concrete realities of the world rather than with mental abstractions. This was illustrated in the principal university of each country. At Paris dialectics, which was nothing more than mental gymnastics, reigned supreme. At Bologna it was law, which has to do with the actual deeds and interests of men, that flourished. The Italians made law the basis of their liberal education. They were not afflicted with the intellectual disease of an excess of dialectics that rendered the French mind incapable of innovation. Unwarped by the narrowing discipline of scholasticism the Italians developed the critical sense and assigned to reason the domain which of right belongs to it. They were able to distinguish clearly between feeling and fact; they combined a capacity for deep emotion with scientific procedure. All their autobiographical and historical writings reveal them to have been consciously aiming to produce at one and the same time a scientific document and a piece of literature. French memoirs, on the other hand, always so artistic and agreeable, are literary creations rather than scientific documents. Social conditions also favored the development of the Renaissance in Italy. The rise of the communes, each one of which was essentially though not absolutely an autonomous republic, relieved her from the oppression of feudalism. The struggle between the Empire and the Papacy, resulting as it did in the enfeeblement of the contestants, enabled Italy to lighten the burdens they had imposed upon her. Thus she relieved the pressure of a triple yoke — feudalism, the Empire, and the Church. And in the process of this emancipation, and as one of its results, there came about, as we have seen, a revival of individuality. The age of the commune passed into the age of the despots. This in its turn resulted in an intensification of personality. And the despots, perhaps without a single exception, gave encouragement to literature and to art. A third cause that made Italian soil fertile for the Renaissance was the preservation of the classic tradition. In Italy the civilization of the ancient world had never so completely disappeared beneath the wave of the barbarian invasions as it had done elsewhere. It was always believed that the grandeur of Rome had suffered only a transient eclipse, that her destiny was divine and her power eternal. They found no hero, as did the French and the Germans, in the ranks of the feudal aristocracy. The only national traditions which they had were those of Rome. So the Renaissance, in one sense, was but a continuation of a tradition which the accidents of history had never abolished. This admiration and love for the Latin civilization in medieval Italy was by no means confined to a few cultured minds. It was " a popular sentiment, a living passion. It was left in men's minds by paganism, and Rome devastated, its temples overgrown with brambles, its statues of the gods mutilated, its Forum and Coliseum haunted by wild beasts, still spoke with a mysterious voice to the heart of the people." The writings of Vergil, the Latin tongue, the Roman law, each in its way contributed to the preservation of the classic tradition. Nor was the inheritance of Greece wholly lost. Greek traders and the descendants of Greek colonists used the Greek language; and the negotiations between the Greek and Latin churches compelled attention to it.

In every one of the medieval centuries there were Italians who were students of Greek. The classic tradition, then, was for Italy "a long continuity of memories." A fourth reason that enabled Italy to become the first seat of the Renaissance was the fact that she had gradually become possessed of a language capable of giving complete expression to the spirit of the people. This fact was demonstrated by Dante when he wrote his immortal epic in which "there is no sense of damnation, no sigh of love, no outburst of anger which does not find its form, its colour, or its precise note." And in his hands Italian prose also proved its capacity to express with exactitude the most subtle shades of thought and feeling. It was at the right moment that the Italian language, "so delicate and so sonorous, emerged from its Latin chrysalis and became a perfect form for Italian literature."

Such were the fundamental and permanent causes of Italy's primacy in the Renaissance. There were in addition certain subsidiary and temporary causes. In the Middle Ages the Italian peninsula was the meeting place of many civilizations. In the mosaics of her churches may still be seen something of the widespread and long-continued influence of Byzantium. Even more general was the influence of the Arabs. Indeed, "all Europe felt the prestige of this elegant race, of whose strange and refined customs some glimpse had been gained during the Crusades." In science, in art, and in poetry they were for a long time supreme. The Normans superseded the Arabs in the political control of Sicily. But the two races lived peaceably side by side, and the political capacity of the Normans was interfused with the Arabic civilization. This composite civilization was carried over to the mainland by Frederic II, whose reign, as we have seen, was a prelude of the Renaissance. Something of the genius of Provence was interwoven with that of Italy when the court of Frederic gave asylum to the troubadours and their lyrical poetry. More lasting in its effect was the influence of the epic and romantic literature of northern France. Many an Italian, long before the time of Dante, Petrarch, and Boccaccio, found his way to the University of Paris. And other French schools, Tours, Orleans, Toulouse, and Montpellier, were not without their students from across the Alps. Still another cause was the fact that when the Renaissance began to dawn Italian writers and artists found ready and generous patrons in the popes of Avignon.

The special aptitude of the Italians, their penetrating sense of reality, their freedom from prevenient judgment, their lack of prejudice with which to clothe the naked truth, their dearth of cherished illusions that had to be saved at any cost, their æsthetical sensitiveness as opposed to ethical sensitiveness, led them into many lines of activity, into commerce, industry, finance, war, politics, philosophy, literature, art, and religion. And with their sense of reality, their clear understanding of men and of things, their ability to see things unblinkingly in the white light of fact, there went to complete the Italian character of the Renaissance period a deep-seated passion that found its vent in love, pride, and ambition, and an indomitable will that brooked no obstacle to its sovereign sway. These qualities, this *virtù*, this perfection of the personality, that which makes a man, the power to will (the word is untranslatable), resulted in lives that were compounded of wisdom and folly, brutality and kindness, of unspeakable immorality and religious ecstasy, of unscrupulous selfishness and the most liberal generosity. The virtuoso acknowledged no limit to his desires and set no bound to his deeds. It was his aptitudes that produced Italian civilization with all the amazing variety of its manifestations, a civilization that for the three centuries of the Renaissance period remained essentially the same.

The first field of art in which this genius of the Italians found expression was that of literature. There had long been a popular poetry in Italy, as elsewhere, giving expression to the joys and sorrows of the common people, and little known to us to-day because it was intended to be sung and not read. The first written poetry of any importance was that of the troubadours. Driven by the horrors of the crusade against the Albigenses many of the troubadours left their native country and wandered from one end of the Italian peninsula to the other. Admiration of these wandering minstrels engendered imitation, and so before long Italian troubadours, scarcely to be distinguished from those of Provence began to sing, in the language of Provence, of love and war, the basic elements of chivalry. Individuality is but faintly indicated in their songs, and there is little regard for nature. Later on, in Sicily, at first under the patronage of Frederic II, there were poets who wrote in Italian. They were dominated by the Provençal influence, but they were not without an originality of their own. They were innovators in that they were the first to raise one of the Italian dialects to the dignity of a poetic idiom, to make of it something more than a mere dialect. They invented several verse-forms, among them the *canzona*, which Dante chose, the sonnet, which Petrarch carried to perfection, and the *strambotto,* which in after years suggested

Italian
Literature
Before
Dante

the fluent and noble stanza of *The Fairy Queen*. Dante tells us that the influence exerted by the Sicilians was most potent. It was by this Sicilian school that the seed of Italian literature was sown. Just when the movement began to spread northward, and what route it took, cannot now be determined, but the seed sprang up with marvelous rapidity. St. Francis of Assisi and his followers did much to elevate the vernacular into the rank of a literary language. The rhythmic prose of the *Poverello* constitutes the earliest example of religious literature in an Italian dialect. In the latter half of the thirteenth century there were a few poets who had something of personal inspiration, in whose poems something of individuality may be found. Among them were Guittone di Arezzo, the first conspicuous name of the indigenous Italian school, and Guido Guinicelli, of Bologna, which seems to have been one of the first cities to respond to the Sicilian influence. Before long the practice of writing verses in the vernacular prevailed at Arezzo, Pisa, Pistoia, Florence, Lucca, Padua, Pavia, Ferrara, Faenza, and other towns, each of which was bent upon developing to the utmost its local dialect. It was the Florentine dialect that finally prevailed in the formation of the Italian language. The central situation of Florence, her commercial prosperity, her political importance and the striking degree to which individuality had been developed among her citizens all contributed to this result. But of greater importance than these causes was the fact that of all the Italian dialects that of Florence was best fitted to become the fundamental element in the formation of the Italian language. More than any other it had succeeded in combining the regularity, the precision and the gravity of the Latin with the vital characteristics of a living tongue. So, evoked from the chaos of dialects and the darkness of the dead Latin, there came into being a language whose liquid and melodious vocables invite like limpid waters, a tongue of delicate grace and of tragic accent. With the work of Lapo Gianni, Guido Cavalcanti, Cino da Pistoia, and others, the Italian language was ripe for a literary Renaissance, and with unparalleled swiftness the literature of Italy reached, in the great epic of Dante, the greatest height it ever attained.

There are but few events in the life of Dante degli Alighieri (1265–1321) of which we have certain knowledge. We know that he was born in Florence, that his youth was devoted to study, to poetry, and to the affairs of public life, that he married **Dante** Gemma Donati by whom he had several children, that because of his participation in political matters he was exiled in 1302 from his native city, that for twenty years he was a wanderer in Italy and France, knowing the salt taste of patrons' bread, alternately trembling with hope and disheartened by cruel disillusions, and that he died at Ravenna, where often he had mused in the pine forest by the sea and where his remains still rest far removed from the city of his birth, which he loved with such passionate intensity. Dante came at the end of an era, but he was not merely the last great writer, the last great personage, of an age. The deep currents of life that were silently producing a profound change in human affairs affected his thoughts, his dreams, and his deeds. It is true that with matchless power he summed up the Age of Faith in his great epic; but to summarize an era is to end it. The world cannot stand still. Life is dynamic. It flows on ceaselessly, forever changing in its aspects and its vision. When it seems to stand still it is but the end of an oscillation of the pendulum. Deep as was the sympathy of Dante with the Middle Ages, he was nevertheless a child of the new birth. In his poetry individuality is supreme. One of the most striking characteristics of the Divine Comedy is its autobiographical element. His concern with the secular problems of his day is not that of a medievalist. And in religion he held that virtue and inner peace are to be attained by ethical rather than by supernatural means. He wished to bring the world back to a way of thinking that was far older than the Middle Ages. He wished it to think of God as the creator and guide of human life, and of heaven as the ultimate goal of man. He saw the new paths that were opening for the feet of men. He, too, was possessed with a zeal for knowledge. He was the most profound scholar of his time. He saw, though it may be but dimly, the new realms of knowledge that were looming vaguely along the horizon. It matters not that he saw the new world but indistinctly. It is the direction of a man's gaze that is of chief importance.

Something of the morning freshness of the time, the thrill of awakening life, is to be discerned in the earliest and most directly autobiographical of Dante's writings, *The New Life*. What is this new life of which the poet writes with such tenderness and frank simplicity, whose charm it is impossible not to feel? Is it simply the story of his early life? Or is it the story of the new life revealed to him by the poignant experience of love? The latter seems to be the true interpretation. *La Vita Nuova* is the story of Dante's life sublimated by the thaumaturgic presence of Beatrice. It does not recall the facts of the poet's life in their due order, but it rearranges them freely and always in the light of a glowing imagination and always for the purpose of revealing a spiritual thought. And under this story of love, with its note of spiritual ecstasy, there seems to be the story of a soul torn with a conflict between faith and science, the two things that disputed the allegiance of every thoughtful man in the thirteenth century. Such, it would seem, is the inner meaning of this book with the enigmatic title. Turning from the subject-matter to the form, one can say that *The New Life* is the first great example of Italian prose, and that its poems mark a great advance in Italian poetry.

The Divine Comedy is one of the great epics of the world. Embracing as it does not merely a single aspect of life but the whole of life it is one of the greatest conceptions that ever issued from the mind of man. It is the drama of the soul. Eternity is involved within its lines. Written in the last years of Dante's life, after joy and sorrow had in turn come to him, after he had labored and thought, it may be said that the great poem is the story of his own soul's pilgrimage written in characters so universal as to possess vitality for all succeeding ages. His actual mind may doubtless be seen filled with bitterness in the gloom of the *Inferno,* calmed by reflection in the *Purgatorio,* and lifted above the world and its disappointments in the *Paradiso.* Endowed with the keen sense of his race for reality, Dante wove his tremendous epic about himself and filled it with the details of his own life and the personages of his own time. Beatrice sent Vergil to guide him through the dread scenes of Hell and the purifying realms of Purgatory to Paradise. The story of the awful journey is given with great minuteness of detail. For each of the lost souls in Hell the principal motive that actuated him upon earth has become his inexorable fate. Against that fate the character of the individual still struggles. In the midst of hopeless death in this kingdom of everlasting pain each is still undefeated. Instead of repenting, the damned persist in their sins. All blaspheme the God who inflicted punishment upon them. The terrible tragedy of the poem lies in the fact that this struggle is in vain. Something, too, of earth's passion still survives. The dwellers in the black wastes of Hell retain the loves and the hatreds of their earthly lives. This place of damnation is, then, a world of fatal passions. In the Purgatory each soul remembers his earthly life dimly as a dream. But each is concerned with his former life only because of its consequences. The hostilities of the bygone days are forgotten. Each soul is animated with the single passion of repentance. This place of penance is a world of contrite sorrow. Yet this place of expiation is illuminated by the assurance of ultimate salvation, and so it has a brooding peace. The souls are joyful in the midst of the flames, for they can sin no more, and are sure of obtaining in due time eternal felicity. The Paradise, with its radiant and celestial imagery, is a world of rarefied air, too thin for mortals to breathe. In it there is no force of individual character. Each soul, steeped in the beatitude of the Divine Presence, is simply a reflection of the divine love, a single note in the divine harmony. This place of beatitude is a world of perfect accordance with the will of God. The Divine Comedy may also be regarded not as a description of the future world, but as one of the existing spiritual world with its three states of sin, trial, and beatitude. The poem is called a " comedy " from the fact that the pilgrimage is not a tragedy ending in death, but a story " issuing in triumphant life," and from certain external and less important characteristics, such as the fact of its being written in the vernacular. The epithet of " divine " was given to the poem by its admirers among whom was Boccaccio. There are large tracts of the great epic which are not poetry at all, but merely sections of scholastic philosophy, such as the explanation of the Thomist doctrine of love, or medieval science, such as the explanation of the spots on the moon, forced into rime; sections of matter that the poet failed to melt and fuse with his emotion and to subordinate with the power of his imagination. These intrusions of tedious and prosaic passages are now no more than records of a vanished civilization. It is impossible adequately to indicate here the wonderful beauty of The Divine Comedy, the remarkable vividness of its personages, the canorous melody of its majestic lines, the lurid glare that illuminates some of the scenes, the soft pervasive glow in which others are steeped, the touching conception of human love, the delicacy of heart, the pity, the tenderness, the exquisite sadness, its beautiful descriptions of nature that are so often touched with tears. Dante's mission was to show " how the soul of man, lost in the mazes of life and defeated by the fierceness of its own passions, can learn its peril, escape from the stain and power of sin, and enter into perfect blessedness," that the foes of man are not the adverse accidents of his history but his own tumultuous passions, and that it is possible for every one to change his life from the darkest tragedy to the most glorious comedy. This message he uttered in a clear and penetrating voice. It is the message of a lonely spirit, whose vision was as vast as time itself.

The reader who turns from Dante to Petrarch is like a man who comes suddenly into a drawing-room lighted by wax candles after a walk through a great autumnal forest which the setting sun had filled with red-litten spaces and mysterious shadow. The wild and somber beauty is left behind, but the chamber is exquisitely furnished and admirably proportioned. Up to Petrarch (1304–74), the world was essentially medieval. It is with him that the modern world begins. Some of his predecessors were fore-runners of the Renaissance; but he may be said to be its founder. Some of the scholars who had preceded him had looked at the world from the modern point of view, but it was their own exclusive possession and private practice. They did not communicate it to society at large. Not one of them had been able to make it a power in the world by kindling the zeal and quickening the souls of his contemporaries. But Petrarch inspired others not merely to read ancient literature, but to think as the Greeks had thought, to think as modern men think, to go to nature in the spirit of free inquiry for the data of one's premises, to attempt to appraise the things of life at their just value by means of the critical faculty which had been ignored all through the Middle Ages, to see something of the beauty and the nobility of the world, to regard the present life as worthy of investigation and improvement. It is not altogether an exaggeration to say that he was the first modern man, that he was the founder of humanism. Some quality of his spirit enabled him to spread among men the contagion of the new attitude towards life and to make it a living force. It is in this rather than in his poetry, exquisite as are so many of his sonnets, that his historical importance lies. It is with him and in his time that the Renaissance takes definite shape, with its many-colored lights and its sinister shadows, with its vital and versatile spirit, its squalor and its nobleness, its cruelty and its refinement, with its richness and its splendor, at times so gorgeous and at times so baleful.

Yet it is as the author of a series of beautiful lyric poems that Petrarch is best known. His love for Laura, her of the golden hair and beautiful eyes, whom history has failed to reveal, seems to have been the most critical of his personal experiences. It seems to have touched his nature to a larger and a fuller life. It is, however, merely with the poems themselves that we are here concerned, with their masterly technique, their interpenetration of sense and of sound that approaches the condition of music, their delicacy of expression, their moving melody, and the wide range of feeling they portray. But the art of these sonnets is greater than their thought. One looks in vain for the impress of distinguished mental quality. The discipline of hopeless love brought to the poet neither wisdom nor consolation. At the end one finds him as lachrymose and as sentimental as at the beginning. Such a finished and musical expression of love will always claim attention. The sonnets will remain a landmark in Italian literature because of their intrinsic merits and because of their contribution to the development of the Italian language. But it is as the chief " initiator of the Renaissance" that Petrarch's fame grows with our increasing knowledge of the potent influences which he exerted at one of the most critical periods of the world's history.

Into his great epic Dante brought the macrocosm of the universe. For the subject of his sonnets Petrarch chose the microcosm of man's inner life. Boccaccio wrote of the outward and the common life of his day. The first of this triumvirate sang of heaven and hell, the second of the recesses of the heart and the sanctuary of the soul, the third of the city streets and the gardens of country villas. Several things contribute to the **Boccaccio** importance of Boccaccio (1313–75). He made adventures in different directions and was something of an innovator. His *Filocopo* indicates the transition from the medieval metrical romance to the prose novel of modern times. His *Ameto* is the first definite pastoral romance this side of the Middle Ages. It opened one of the most delightful veins of literature. His *Fiammetta,* an introspective and subjective story, burning with passion, perhaps the most striking picture of the passions of love which the Renaissance knew, pointed out a field, that of the psychological novel, destined to remain practically uncultivated for a long time. But the popularity of Boccaccio rests upon the *Decameron,* a book such as one might expect from its author. Boccaccio was far less imbued with the classic spirit than was Petrarch. His mind lacked the elevation and his character the reserve and the dignity of the older scholar. He was much more of an Italian of his day. He delighted in the movement, the gaiety and the license of the polished and vivacious court of Naples, where his youth was spent, and where he divided his time not altogether impartially between literature and the ladies. If the tragic accent of life fell upon his ears its echo soon died away. It was the romantic aspect of life that arrested and held his attention. He was an artist who delighted in the shifting panorama of life, from which, and from old romances, he gathered material for his stories. Invention is to be found in the *Decameron* in the variety of incident and the skilfulness of some of the plots; and the narrative is often witty. But one looks in vain through all the hundred stories for a single touch of poetry. Imagination and eloquence one shall find, but not poetry. Most of the characters are mere masks. They are mere marionettes, though it is true they are moved by the hand of a master. It is but a few of them, such as Ser Ciappelletto and the Ferate Cipolla, that appeal to us as living personages. There are no heights and there are no depths. Love is the most frequent theme, but it is not love in any high and noble sense. And it is not merely the failure to regard love in anything but its lowest phase that one misses, but the lack of all the things that vitally concern human society. Only very seldom does one find stories touched with tragedy, or heroism, or generosity, or courtesy, such as those of the fourth and the tenth days. The greatest defect of the book, however, is its licentiousness. It is customary to excuse this by pointing to the social standards of the time. Dante, of course, stood far above his world in ethical purity, but Petrarch could write of love with delicacy and refinement, and in a far less civilized land, in a society more barren of resources, Chaucer, although of the earth earthy, could touch the many stops of emotion and passion without constantly reveling in obscene buffoonery. The *Decameron* has a beautiful framework, a lovely *mise en scène,* in which the art of the author almost wholly resides. It bubbles with merriment, and its style is one of exceptional beauty. But its lack of nobility of thought prevents it from being a great book.

Petrarch became the initiator of the Renaissance by inspiring others with the spirit of the classical world, by inculcating an ideal of life that fostered the emancipation of the individual. This he did chiefly through the medium of Latin, and so he had for his followers the scholars of the various countries of Europe. Boccaccio diffused the humanistic spirit among the middle class of Italy by giving it expression in the Italian language. It was a similar service that Chaucer (1335?–1400) did for England. No other poet of his age in any land was so well-fitted for popularity as Chaucer. Though he is at times too garrulous and long-winded for modern readers he is brevity itself compared with medieval romancers. His stories are told with a singular directness, his limited power of imagery does not find vesture in allusive and difficult metaphor but is confined to explicit similes. He is a master both of broad humor and sly, subdued pleasantry; and his pathos, far less frequent than his laughter, is always true and tender. He is concerned with deeds and not with meditation. He is lucid, shrewd, cheerful, content with life as he found it, and filled with its zest. He is full of an unfailing freshness. He has a confiding felicity, and he reveals here and there a quality rarely found in the literature of his time — intimacy. Unexcelled until Shakespeare's day in the variety of his characters and the skill exhibited in their portrayal he was the best story-teller of the whole Renaissance period, and is still unsurpassed as a writer of humorous narrative verse. Chaucer created a literary style in England where before none had existed. He extended the range of the literary interest. He portrayed aspects of life which the poets of chivalry had ignored. He did not reveal the labor and the sorrows of the lower classes, the down-trodden peasantry. One has to go to the *Vision of Piers the Plowman* for their distressful tale. But of the weavers, the dyers, the millers, the carpenters, the sheriffs, the friars, and their like, he wrote many a realistic and not unsympathetic story. In this and in many another thing he was essentially modern. The course of the Renaissance in England, which he did much to inaugurate, was, however, interrupted by social and political events, by the ravages of the Black Death, by the dynastic civil war that ended with the murder of Richard II, and by the still more disastrous Wars of the Roses. Even without these obstacles its growth would have been slow, for the soil of England was far less prepared for such a seed than was that of Italy.

The Italian language had been used by Dante, Petrarch, and Boccaccio. Its scope and its diversity had been demonstrated. It had proved capable of expressing the widest range of feeling from the most exalted emotion to the most profane ribaldry. It had given expression not only to the primary impulses of man, but also to the most delicate shades of his feeling. It could lay claim to be the fitting and adequate vehicle of a great national literature. But the attention and interest of scholars was then turned to a revival of classical letters, and so far as literature in Italian is concerned a sort of literary interregnum ensued. All through the Middle Ages the Latin language had existed though in a degenerate form. It was the language of the western church, and it was the language of men of culture in all parts of western Christendom. Instruction in the schools and lawsuits in both the civil and canonical courts were conducted in it and commerce transacted. The libraries of such great monasteries as those of Monte Cassino and Bobbio were rich in classic authors. The Italians cherished a love for Vergil throughout the medieval centuries. And Greek was not unknown. Something of Aristotle and of other Hellenic writers the Middle Ages always possessed. Each succeeding medieval century, moreover, regained something more than its predecessors possessed of the lost inheritance of the classic past. But the names from the litera-

tures of Greece and Rome that lingered throughout the Middle
Ages were only imperfect memories, echoes of echoes, distorted
conceptions, " phantoms whereof the positive historic truth was
lost." Men did not read the ancient authors in order to obtain
knowledge of the civilization of antiquity, nor with the desire
of improving the conditions of their own time by means of the
culture of the past. They read them only for the purpose of
medieval thought. They heard but the murmur of classical culture reverberating ever fainter and fainter in the cloisters of
their medieval monasteries. They did not dream that within
the yellow pages of those old manuscripts was to be found a
talisman tnat could exercise a potent power in the creation of a
new world. So, although Greek and Latin writings were by no
means unknown in the Middle Ages, although as time went on
more and more of them were recovered, they had little effect
upon the life of that time. The capacity for understanding
them was in abeyance. And for the most part they were to be
found only in the hands of men who were antagonistic to their
spirit.

Dante wrote in Latin. But his writings in that language have
always the air of a literary exercise. They lack the stamp of
personality. As we have seen, Petrarch did much to spread
knowledge of the classic authors. He recaptured their spirit, he
instilled it into others, and he did much towards making it one
of the most powerful forces of the time. " Vergil, Horace,
Livy, and Cicero. These," he said in writing to Boccaccio, " I
have read and re-read, not once, but a thousand times, not
cursorily, but studiously and intently, bringing to them the best
powers of my mind. I tasted in the morning and digested at
night. I quaffed as a boy, to ruminate as an old man. These
works have become so familiar to me that they cling not to my
memory merely, but to the very marrow of my bones. They
have become so identified with my own genius that, even were
I never to read them again, they would still be there rooted in
the deepest recesses of my soul." Petrarch had a fine sense of
literary style. In speaking of his study of Cicero when a boy,
he said : " At that time I could not understand what I read, but
the sweetness of the language and the majesty of the cadences
enchanted me so that whatever else I read or heard sounded
harsh in my ears and quite discordant." He was the first
humanist who assiduously collected Latin manuscripts, inscriptions and coins. " Whenever I took a journey," he writes, " I
would turn aside to any old monasteries that I chanced to see

in the distance, saying that possibly some scraps of the writings I courted might lie hidden there." After the middle of his life he was seldom without a copyist or two in his house, and at times he had as many as four, making copies of the manuscripts that he had discovered or borrowed, and he did not a little of this work himself. His life-long devotion to Cicero and his burning zeal in the collection of classical manuscripts were rewarded by the singularly happy accident of his discovery of Cicero's private correspondence with Atticus in a dusty library at Verona. His own attempts at literature in Latin, successful as they were, need not detain us here. It was not merely classical manuscripts and a better mastery of Latin style that Petrarch restored to the modern world. His chief service was the revival of the lost faculty of intelligence, the lost power of sympathetic appreciation of those writings, the lost attitude towards life of the pagan world. At his touch the spirit of that bygone time arose from the grave and together with what was retained of the Age of Faith furnished a new ideal for men to follow. One of the most ardent of Petrarch's followers in devotion to the Latin classics, and one of his most diligent assistants as a collector, was Boccaccio. He wrote a good deal in Latin, though his work in that line has little value. He acquired a wide acquaintance of the Latin poets, but he was not so deeply interested in the spirit of Latin literature as was Petrarch, being concerned chiefly with minor matters of style.

The revival of Latin letters was carried on by wandering teachers who went from city to city communicating their zeal to different groups of students. First among these was Giovanni da Ravenna (1346?–1406) who succeeded in arousing in his pupils a passion for Latin literature, especially for the writings of Cicero. Among his pupils were the foremost teachers of the succeeding generation. Gasparino da Barzizza (1370?–1431) after teaching in Pavia, Venice, Padua, and Ferrara, settled in Milan. He was especially successful in developing a new style of epistolary Latin imparting to it something of the careless grace of refined conversation. He was the first apostle of that Ciceronianism of which we shall see more later on. The man who may be regarded as the founder of a new system of education based upon the ideals of humanism is Vittorino da Feltre (1378–1446). Under the patronage of Gian Francesco Gonzaga, Marquis of Mantua, he established a school in which he carried on a broad system of education. He aimed to develop all the faculties of his pupils, intellectual, moral, and physical, and to make them good and influential members of society. Noble youths from all the courts of Italy came to his school, but all of his sixty or seventy scholars were placed under exactly the same discipline. The Latin classics were made the basis of the intellectual training. They were taught in a large and liberal spirit that stimulated the interest of the students. The long list of the pupils who attended this school shows how great was its influence upon the times.

Meanwhile the quest for classical manuscripts, inaugurated by Petrarch, who had discovered two speeches of Cicero at Liège and his letters at Verona, went on unabated. Boccaccio discovered writings by Ovid, Martial, Ausonius, and other Latin authors. Salutato recovered writings by Cato, Maximianus, Germanicus, Pompeius, and the *Familiar Letters* of Cicero. When the Council of Constance was convened agents of the papal curia carried on a most industrious search for manuscripts in the libraries of central and northern Europe. Poggio and his assistants found more writings by Cicero, a complete copy of Quintilian's *Institutions,* some of the works of Valerius Flaccus, Asconius, Priscian, Vitruvius, Vegetius, Pompeius Festus, Lucretius, Manilius, Silius Italicus, Ammianus Marcellinus, Columella, Petronius, and the grammarians Caper, Eutyches, and Probus. In an old chest the bishop of Lodi discovered still more writings by Cicero. The *History* and the *Annals* of Tacitus were recovered, and writings by Celsus, Gellius, Curtius, Plautus, Frontinus, Cornelius Nepos, Donatus, Suetonius, Pliny, Porphyrio and other Latin authors. The most obscure monasteries and church libraries were ransacked in the hope that some forgotten document containing the dearly prized lore of classic times might be found.

It must not be imagined that humanism, this new learning, or rather this new attitude towards life, was accepted immediately, universally, and without question by scholars who had been trained in other lines of thought. The aim of humanism was to interest men in all things pertaining to human life, to destroy the shackles which medieval authority had imposed upon the mind of man. It lacked the piercing spiritual vision of the Age of Faith; but, in its purest form, it was by no means devoid of the element of religion. It sought to unite the feeling for beauty with the spirit of religious exaltation, not in moods of rapture and ecstasy, but in a manner more expressive of the daily and normal life of man. It was a revolutionary movement having for its purpose the liberation of thought. It emphasized the ideal of the self-development and individual responsibility of man as opposed to the ideal of self-surrender and vicarious redemption. It sought to break the bonds of medieval religion, to break the fetters of medieval philosophy, and it therefore met with opposition from the representatives of that religion and that philosophy. Medieval religion had depreciated human nature, while humanism sought to rehabilitate it. Scholasticism, as we have seen, was concerned with the processes of logic, while humanism was concerned with the concrete realities of life. At first the jurists, doctors, grammarians and theologians of the universities were mostly hostile to humanism. It is only in our own time that schools have endeavored to give new thought to the world. At the dawn of the Renaissance the universities were merely the custodians of the truth that was already known, and their sole function was to pass the accumulated lore on to the succeeding generations. They were not the cradle of the new intellectual activity that was effecting such momentous changes. Nor was humanism brought in by a sweeping movement of the popular mind. In the beginning it depended upon powerful and wealthy patrons who gave aid to the humanists and enabled them to secure audiences in the various Italian cities. It made its way slowly at first. It had to pass through a militant period. Petrarch made war upon the scholastics whose learning filled him with sovereign contempt. All his life long he protested against them and boldly assailed the medieval tradition. In its beginning humanism was more of a religion than a science. It derived its moral force from the emotions rather than from the intellect. The humanists were filled with a yearning love for the wisdom of the past. They were imbued with sympathy for the attitude towards life of antiquity. They saw once again, as did the Greeks of old, the divine rendered visible in the human; and they believed that self-control rather than self-sacrifice is the way of life. But they were not as yet animated solely by the sober curiosity of the scientist. The medieval and humanistic ideals are irreconcilable and mutually exclusive. One or the other of them had to give way. In the struggle that ensued it was the former that succumbed. It is true that scholasticism, which for four centuries had dominated the thought of Europe, did not receive its death-blow until the *Epistolæ Obscurorum Virorum* were published (1515–17), but it began to yield with the first attacks of the humanists.

Somewhat later there came a revival of Greek letters. It was a revival that had the greatest importance. But the value of the revival of Latin letters should not be underestimated. Latin literature is not merely imitative of that of Greece. The Roman poets adapted as well as adopted the forms of their Greek models. Their age was something more than a mere echo of the golden days of Hellas. The Odes of Horace, for instance, are far more in spirit and even more in form than mere copies from the Greek. Rome, quite as much as Greece, was the foundress of modern civilization. Greece was affected very largely by Oriental influences, and in some things she had remained very largely Oriental. Then, too, because of its lofty idealism and indifference to biographical details, Greek literature has an impersonal character; it is lacking in individual traits. Latin literature, on the other hand, does not rise to so sublime a height, and is informed with a greater interest in the daily life of man. The Renaissance, therefore, obtained from the Greeks literary models and philosophical ideas; while from the Romans it learned much regarding the living man himself. It was instinct at first rather than knowledge that led scholars to divine the importance of Hellenic thought. Petrarch had a vague knowledge of Plato through Augustine, and of Homer through Vergil, and he ardently desired to read them in their original language. So he studied Greek, first with Barlaamo and later on in Venice. But he never succeeded in acquiring a reading knowledge of it. Yet despite his own failure to acquire the key to the literature of Hellas, he urged others to undertake the study of Greek. It was upon his advice that Boccaccio took up the study. The author of the *Decameron* chose Pilato for a master and secured his installation in the University of Florence in the first chair of Greek in Italy. It was an exceedingly difficult matter to study Greek at this time. There were no Greek grammars or dictionaries written in Latin or in any of the Romance or Teutonic languages. The only way in which a western European could acquire something of Greek grammar and vocabulary was through a Greek-speaking teacher. Greek sailors and traders were to be found in the seaports of the Mediterranean, but they spoke a patois, and they were without scholarly knowledge of ancient Greek. Even in Constantinople men with such knowledge were rare. Yet it was these men from the vanishing Byzantine Empire who revived in the occident the forgotten knowledge of the Hellenic past. First of them was Barlaamo, a Calabrian monk who had long resided in Constantinople and who returned to Italy on one of those fruitless missions to obtain help for the Eastern Empire against the Turks. Pilato, who was also a native of Calabria who had gone to live in Constantinople, knew little more than the Greek that was then current in the Byzantine capital. Yet so great was the dearth of adequate teachers that, as we have just noted, he was made the first professor of Greek in a western university. The first effective teacher of Greek in Italy was Manuel Chrysoloras (1350?–1415), another of those agents of the Byzantine Empire who had come to implore aid against the conquering infidels. He was a man of wide learning, a gentle-hearted visionary given to meditation, who proved to be a sympathetic and inspiring teacher. He was induced to teach at Florence and began his work there in 1397. An extraordinary crowd of students thronged to hear his lectures. He also taught at Pavia, Milan, Venice, and Rome. Italians were given for the first time a scholarly and sympathetic presentation of Greek culture. Above all else in importance Chrysoloras brought with him the intellectual contagion which is characteristic of the Greek spirit. The charm of Hellas began to work again. Men received new inspiration in their quest for a new manner of living, a new ideal of life. Trapezuntios (1395–1484), another of the Greek schoolmasters, came to Italy about 1420. He taught at Florence and Rome, among other places, and he worked at the papal court as a translator of Aristotle and Plato. Gradually a new world opened to the Italians, one in which, even more than in the days of the Roman civilization, men lived in happy communion with nature, whose pleasures they enjoyed without question, and whose secrets they explored without fear.

The advance of the Turks sent a stream of Greek exiles into the west. Not all of them were of much use in the revival of Greek letters. Some of them were not men of letters, and many of those who were scholars were ignorant of Latin and had only a smattering of Italian. But their presence was a lively stimulus to the study of Greek. They increased the passion that had been created for the philosophy of Plato. In Gemistos Plethon (1356?–1450), who came to Florence in 1438, the Florentines found a man able to give them something of the Greek idealism for which they craved. There was much more in the teachings of Gemistos that came from Alexandria, where the philosophy of Plato had become tinctured with that of later writers, than that which came from Athens. Yet something of the thought of Plato he was able to give, and all that the eloquent old man had to say was accepted as pure gold. Theodoros Gaza (1400?–75) came to Italy about 1430, and after teaching in various places settled in Rome where he found employment in the palace of Cardinal Bessarion as a translator. Greatest of the Byzantine Platonists was Bessarion (1395 or 1403–1472), who very early in life had risen to a high station in the Greek church. As the Archbishop of Nicæa he attended the Council of Florence in 1438–9, and there, after the attempt to bring together the eastern and the western churches failed, he went over to the Latin church. He was made a cardinal, and his palace in Rome, which contained a considerable library of Greek and Latin authors, became a haven of refuge for the exiled Greeks. In the bitter controversy that arose among the Greeks as to the respective merits of Plato and Aristotle he displayed a serenity and tolerance in striking contrast to others who joined in the fray, professing respect for Aristotle as well as admiration for Plato. Joannes Argyropulos (1416–86) taught Greek in Italy as early as 1441. He lectured at Padua, Florence, and Rome. Struck by the excellent translation and pronunciation of Reuchlin, one of his German pupils, he exclaimed: "Lo! through our exile, Greece has flown across the Alps." Another Greek who taught in Italy before the fall of Constantinople was Chalcondyles (1424–1511) of Athens. The most prominent of those who settled in the peninsula after the fall were Apostolius, Callistus, Constantine Lascaris, Janus Lascaris, Musurus, and Callierges.

As we have seen, the work which had been begun by Petrarch in Florence soon spread to other cities. But Florence had long shown itself to be the brain of Italy. Nowhere else had the traditions of the Roman civilization been so faithfully preserved. Nowhere else had individuality been developed to so great an extent. All classes of society had experienced, at least for a brief time, the intoxication and the difficulties of governing. Wearied somewhat, perhaps, with perpetual revolution it had settled down to enjoy a period of stability and a government apparently democratic. The dissembling Medicean autocracy was of course far from being democratic. But it was the government which the Florentines had accepted, and it flattered their passions and pleased their pride. From the beginning of the fourteenth century Florence had enjoyed an increasing commercial prosperity which reached its maximum in the middle of the fifteenth century. The oil of commerce filled the lamp of culture. The wealth of the city made possible a high standard of comfort and produced a luxury and a sense of refinement that called into activity the energies of artisans and of artists. And all the people of the city profited by the wealth of its merchants. They shared in the pomp and the splendor of the civic and religious festivals which were paid for by the rich merchants and bankers. They enjoyed the artistic buildings that were erected. They saw the pictures, read the poems, and witnessed the dramatic performances that were made possible by the wealth of the patrons. Christianity still maintained a

The Spirit of Florence

hold upon the people. It determined not a little of the social activity of the public palace, the corporation, the family, and the individual. Even the most ardent of the humanists, the men most enraptured with the rediscovered and the resurgent pagan attitude towards life, were, as a rule, respectful Christians. But it was no longer the Christianity that held complete renunciation of the world to be the highest virtue and self-maceration to be a principal secret of peace. Indeed, Christianity was losing ground. It was coming to be more and more merely a veneer. It was the architecture, the decoration, and the ritual, that attracted the most cultured of them to church; the perfection of the lines of pillar and dome, the perfume of the incense and the sweetness of the songs, things that aroused sensuous emotion. Florence had come to be a city of epicureans. In its intelligent, sober, and industrious citizens human nature manifested itself in all its multifarious aspects. They had a passion for their city, a deep-rooted sense of their citizenship. They had a love for what was beautiful, and a keen critical sense that enabled them to insist upon a high plane of achievement. Such was the city to which we have now to turn our attention.

Florence had become a hive of learned men, congenial coteries of whom gathered in palaces, in convents, and in villas. The first of these groups was the one that met in the convent of Santo Spirito under the leadership of Luigi Marsigli (?–1394), a teacher of mediocre ability who nevertheless exerted a widespread influence. There came to be a passion in Italy for these societies. In many of the towns there existed a literary group that organized itself into an academy. Another Florentine humanist of this period was Coluccio Salutato (1330–1406), who became chancellor of the city, and who did much by the exquisite Latin prose of his official papers to make a correct and graceful Latin style an indispensable accomplishment of any one who sought to occupy a position as secretary in any of the republics or courts of Italy. Thus an important field was thrown open to the humanists. The revival of letters and of art found generous supporters in several members of the Strozzi family. It was the noble and generous Palla Strozzi who was chiefly instrumental in the renovation of the University of Florence and in bringing Chrysoloras to it as one of its teachers, thus making it the center of Italian Hellenism. Had he not been banished from the city he might have excelled his rival, Cosimo de' Medici, as a patron of learning.

A second period in the literary and artistic history of Florence began with the patronage of Cosimo de' Medici (1389–1464) who became the autocrat of the city in 1434 and held the position for thirty years, with the exception of a brief period of exile. Cosimo was in many ways a consummate ruler. He maintained a perfect harmony between his own aims, ideas and aspirations and those of the Florentine people. Very early he realized that the Renaissance movement was one of profound importance. He perceived that it was something greater than a national movement. "You might as well try to control the stars in their courses," he wrote to one of his friends, "or the sea in its tides as to bind the Renaissance to Italy. It is a European, perhaps a world-wide influence." And he determined to make himself its foster-father. He identified himself with every aspect of it. Eminent as he was in finance and politics he was nevertheless remarkable as a man of notable and varied culture. He gathered about him the most prominent classical scholars, architects, sculptors, and painters. By his discriminating judgment and sympathy, as well as by his financial support, he did much to evoke the latent genius of many of these men. He employed agents to collect coins, inscriptions and manuscripts. He not only accumulated libraries but made provision for housing them and making them accessible to the public. It was he who founded the Platonic Academy at Florence. Among the members of his circle were Niccoli, Bruni, Marsuppini, Manetti, Poggio, Traversari, Guarino, and Filelfo. Each was actively engaged in furthering the revival of letters, and each was specially interested in the study of Plato. Niccoli (1363–1437) was an excellent Latinist, an indefatigable collector and copyist, an able critic and a man of wide learning. Leonardo Bruni (1369–1444), who had been one of the pupils of Chrysoloras, became chancellor of Florence and one of its historians. He is chiefly famous in the revival of letters as a translator from the Greek. He possessed a critical mind, and he gave a great impulse to textual criticism and philosophy. Carlo Marsuppini (1399?–1453) succeeded Bruni as chancellor of Florence. He placed little value upon the Christian faith, and upon his deathbed he refused the rites of the Church. His work was chiefly that of a teacher and lecturer. Manetti (1396–1459) studied Hebrew as well as Latin and Greek. He was an ardent collector of manuscripts, copies of which he circulated among the poorer scholars. The pagan learning that led other scholars to moral laxity served in his case for the elevation of his character. Poggio (1380–1459) was the most diligent and fortunate of all the searchers for classical manuscripts. He was the first scholar to prove himself an original writer. His Latin is full of Italianisms, but it has the spontaneity and the vivacity of a living language. Despite the fact that he held papal offices under eight successive popes he was surpassed by few in his contempt for Christianity. His facile pen was ready not only to copy classical manuscripts, but to lend itself to the licentiousness that marked the later years of the revival of letters. Traversari (1386–1439) another of the pupils of Chrysoloras, became general of the Camaldolese Order. He made his convent in Florence a meeting place for scholars, and he wrote to other scholars all over Europe. He had the happy faculty of uniting the Christian virtues with the pagan culture. Guarino da Verona (1374–1460) was still another pupil of Chrysoloras, having studied in the house of the master at Constantinople. With Vittorino da Feltre he was one of the great schoolmasters of the early Renaissance. He taught in many places, Venice, Verona, Trent, Padua, Bologna, Florence, and Ferrara. He was perhaps a better Greek scholar than any other Italian of the time, and unlike many of the humanists his moral character was above reproach. Filelfo (1398–1481) had also studied in Constantinople under Chrysoloras. Two years after his return to Italy he began to teach in Florence. He was conceited and arrogant, and he quarreled with most of the humanists and with Cosimo, their patron. His genuine enthusiasm for letters and his undoubted mastery of much of the literature of Greece are overshadowed by his venomous and obscene vituperation.

Italian Paganism

In speaking of the revival of letters we have been compelled to notice the increasing paganism of the Italians. It would be incorrect to think that it was the study of Greek and Roman life that gave to the Italians their pagan attitude towards life. Nothing could be further from the truth. It was the innate sense of reality of the Italians that led them to govern their lives so largely by their senses, a sense that had been emancipated by the revival of individuality, that gave to them the pagan conception of life. When they read the classic authors they were at first surprised and then delighted to find men who like themselves were bent upon enjoying to the full the pleasures of the present life. The resuscitation of the paganism of antiquity was merely a confirmation of their own. The paganism of the Italians, then, was in large part a matter of temperament; but it was also something of an intellectual epidemic, a youthful exuberance, a reaction against the trammels from which they had but recently become emancipated. Eventually they discovered that " a system which sacrificed what was inward " could not satisfy them; and, profound as was the indebtedness of the

Renaissance to the new paganism, much of the finest work of the era was accomplished when " the glow of medieval faith " inspired it. Michelangelo's greatness, for instance, was due to the fact that his genius was " spiritualized by the reverie of the Middle Age, penetrated by its spirit of inwardness and introspection," that he lived " not a mere outward life like the Greek, but a life full of inward experiences, sorrows, and consolations." So, in the later Renaissance, did the Hellenistic and medieval ideals tend to mix and mingle, to become concurrent and concomitant forces.

A third period in the development of letters and a new period in the development of literature and art began with the patronage of Lorenzo de' Medici (1449–92), who after the brief interval of five years in which his father, Piero de' Medici, held sway, succeeded, in 1469, to the position formerly occupied by his grandfather, Cosimo. Lorenzo was only twenty-one years of age when he came into power, but he had already displayed the qualities that made him successful. We have here to regard him as a patron and a poet, rather than as a ruler. As a patron of literary men and artists he surpassed even his grandfather. In an extraordinarily complete way he represented the varied aspirations of his day, and he spared no effort to make Florence the mistress of literature and art. Under his patronage Greek scholars were brought to the Tuscan capital. " Athens, root and branch," said a contemporary Florentine, " has been transplanted hither, here to make her abode. Not Athens in ruins and in the hands of barbarians, but Athens as she was, with her breathing spirit and her very soil." To assist in the classical studies of his circle he made costly and valuable collections of books, coins, medals, inscriptions, and other antiquities. His patronage was marked not only by lavish expenditure and generosity but also by tact and a most judicious discrimination. He was able not only to recognize men of genius and to honor them, but also to inspire them to the highest achievements of which they were capable. With the most diverse forms of the many-sided life of the Renaissance he could sympathize. In an unusual degree he possessed the artistic temperament, a keen sensitiveness to the thought and feeling of those amongst whom he lived. Philosophers deemed him a sage. Scholars were aware of his exquisite appreciation of literary style. In him architects, sculptors, and painters found a patron of faultless taste. To libertines he was a boon companion, who wrote carnival songs that are often highly licentious, who danced and masqueraded with the most abandoned, and who plunged into all the orgies of the carnival festivities. The pious knew and honored him as the author of mystery plays and of hymns steeped in genuine religious emotion. Unless one realizes the rich and variegated life of the Renaissance, Lorenzo, who was at once sensual and spiritual, spontaneous of emotion and subtle of mind, as well as many another man, will seem a paradoxical being.

We have already seen that there was a tendency among the men of culture to form themselves into groups for the purpose of discussing their intellectual and artistic interests. These coteries usually came to be known as academies. It was not long before academies sprang up all over Italy. There was a need for them. They afforded the humanists definite organizations, gave them a corporate existence, and added greatly to their influence. They provided opportunity for the intercourse of sympathetic spirits, and they made possible the free play of the lately aroused critical faculty. The Platonic Academy at Florence, a circle of friends much more informal than the academies that were organized in other places, was conceived by Gemistos Plethon, founded by Cosimo de' Medici, and carried to its acme by Lorenzo de' Medici. It is not difficult to understand the ardent devotion of the men of the Renaissance to Plato. Aristotle was coupled with scholasticism, with the submission of the human intellect to external and arbitrary authority. Plato appeared to them as the prophet of freedom, as the philosopher to whom, more than to any one else, was due their emancipation from the fetters of the Aristotelian scholasticism. He spoke to them of the mystery of life, he corresponded to the new instincts that stirred within them, to the new vision that floated before their eyes, to the imaginative yearnings that filled their hearts. The way in which Plato fused the material and the immaterial world had for them an unfailing fascination. Moreover, their temperaments were naturally Platonic. So they turned to Plato with a passionate devotion. Out of this devotion grew an attempt to find the Christian doctrines contained implicitly in the body of his teachings, to reconcile him to Christ. But their Platonism was very largely their own. The teachings of the Athenian philosopher had come to them in a roundabout way and in an adulterated form. They possessed only that system of philosophical and religious doctrines and principles, compounded of Platonism and oriental beliefs and then colored by Christianity, which had originated at Alexandria. Their Platonism was not Greek. It was Christian, medieval, and chivalrous. Yet their Platonic feeling was genuine. It was the same passionate pursuit for something permanent in the midst of a world of change as that in which the disciple of Socrates was so active a participant. It was in its essence the same eternal Platonism to which the material is but the symbol of the ideal, the phenomenal of the noumenal, the visible of the unseen. It made their intellects emotional and their passions cold. It was much more than a mere imitation of Plato. It was a veritable reincarnation of his spirit divested of the environment of his far-off pagan world. And if the Florentines have been surpassed in their knowledge of Plato by more recent scholars, no others have loved him better. They believed that no other philosopher had expressed the eternal verities in speech of such consummate beauty. They built a shrine to him, and before it they kept a lamp continually burning. They crowned his bust with laurels. They made the day of his birth a festal day; and on the anniversary of his death they pronounced stately and solemn panegyrics. This Platonic cult exercised an immense influence upon the literature, the art, and the culture of the age. The conception of God as the supreme unity of all the diverse parts and forces of the physical and moral universe penetrated the literature of the latter half of the fifteenth century and permeated its art. It made men of culture opponents of ecclesiastical dogma and apostles of a general reconciliation.

Among the members of the Platonic Academy in the time of Lorenzo was Marsilio Ficino (1433–99), who in his childhood had been set apart by Cosimo de' Medici for the purpose of becoming an interpreter of Plato's philosophy. All his energy was fervently devoted to the reconciliation of Christianity and Platonism. He regarded Plotinus, the chief Neo-Platonist of Alexandria, as the greatest exponent of the teachings of the Greek philosopher because he found more features of resemblance between Christianity and Platonism in the writings of the disciple than he did in those of the master. His enthusiastic ardor in the study of Greek literature and in promulgating the doctrine that all religions are really one had an enormous influence not only in Italy but beyond the Alps. The Academy met, according to the season or the circumstance, in the Medici palace in Florence, in the pleasant gardens of the Badia at Fiesole, in Lorenzo's villa at Careggi, and in the forest that surrounds the convent of Camaldoli. In his *Camaldolese Discussions* Christoforo Landino (1424–1504) has left a vivid and charming picture of the life of the scholars of Lorenzo's circle. In the revival of letters he is notable as an annotator of Horace and Vergil and a translator of the elder Pliny. And with his commentary on Dante he did not a little to assist in the revival of literature in the vernacular. He was one of the leaders of Florentine scholarship. Poliziano (1454–94) was probably the first Italian whose mastery of Greek was equal to that of the contemporary Greek scholars. He was an able interpreter both of Greek and Latin literature. Students from all parts of Europe came to hear him lecture. He wrote poems in Greek at the early age of seventeen, and his Latin poetry possesses a singular grace and beauty. As a humanist he stands easily first among the Italians. He was able to divest his scholarship of pedantry and to infuse into it vitality. Pico della Mirandola (1463–94) did much to further that unity and belief that was the aim of Florentine neo-Platonism, that was directed against the prevalent materialism of the Aristotelian school of philosophy and the ignorance and corruption of the clergy. The soul, he said, comes from God. It yearns to become more deeply conscious of its relation to God. It desires reunion with Him. Every religious creed has this desire for its basis. He was, therefore, intellectually tolerant of all creeds. Pico, who died at the early age of thirty-one, was a young man of noble birth and singular beauty. He was eminent as a scholar, and he became the idol of Florentine society. Between the dim figures of the half-forgotten gods of Greece and the pallid, blood-stained Christ of Calvary, between the old faiths and the new, he craved with a wistful passion to effect a reconciliation that should bring to the world the peace of which he dreamed.

Italian confined to the Common People

When, after the death of Boccaccio, the men of culture practically ignored Italian, it descended below the surface and continued its career in subterranean channels. The common life of the people with its joys and sorrows, its victories and defeats, its aspirations and its dreams, demanded expression. So a popular literature of ballads, tales, romances, letters, chronicles, and hymns, sometimes the gradual result of composite authorship, and sometimes the product of men whose names were speedily forgotten, gave voice to the daily life of town and country-side.

Value of the Study of Classical Letters

It has been the fashion to decry the renunciation of Italian in favor of the literature of Greece and Rome. But the situation seems to justify such action, if not to have made it imperative. Dante's great poem, despite the fact that he himself foresaw something of the coming change, summed up an era that was ended. He did not point out new paths to literature. And because of the fact that the culture and technical accomplishment of Petrarch and Boccaccio were greatly superior to that of other writers of their time and the generations immediately succeeding them, those writers founded no school. General culture and the mastery of technique had to be acquired, and this was done by the study of classical letters and literature. The work of the humanists was not a mere harvest of barren blossom without fragrance and without fruit. Nor did it warp the Italian genius. Though they may have been for the most part unconscious of the result, the work of the humanists, which was not always that of mere imitation, served to educate and develop the Italian genius. As the years went on they began to create an original literature in Latin. This literature, whatever its defects may be, contains in germ some of the characteristics of the renewed Italian literature that was about to appear. It contains history, oratory, and the depiction of contemporary manners in prose. It came to be penetrated with Italian life. The work of the revival of classic letters was then concluded. The revival of Italian literature was at hand.

Leo Battista Alberti (1404–72), poet, philosopher, mathematician, inventor, athlete, architect, painter, sculptor, and musician, one of the many-sided men of the Renaissance, realized the need of a national language to express the national life, and so in a treatise he championed the cause of the Italian tongue, and by his example did much to bring about a second flower time of Italian literature. The study of Greek and Latin letters was fast becoming merely the work of pedants given over to imitation and stylistic affectation. Alberti took up the development of Italian prose where the interruption of the revival of classical letters had left it. His prose is somewhat artificial in its imitation of Latin, but his verses have a notable freshness and spontaneity.

*Renewed Revival of Italian Literature*

Lorenzo de' Medici was essentially a poet, elegant if not powerful, vivacious and always spontaneous. His sonnets have precision of technique and grace of diction and in their passages of graphic description they give ample evidence of a loving observation of nature, though they fail to reveal a temperament that was finely sensitive to her varying moods. His idylls, in which he displays an easy mastery of various verse forms, are the most elaborate of his poems. They contain portraits of rustic folk drawn from life, and their diction is admirably suited to their pastoral character. His carnival songs conformed to the popular taste of the time, and so they are sometimes exceedingly licentious, and they always disguise immorality under the mask of gallantry. His songs and ballads are sometimes delicate, sometimes coarse, and always lyrical. They are spontaneous, rising out of the life of their time, but they are monotonous in theme. His sacred poems express a side of his nature

*Lorenzo as a Poet*

that was as genuine as the one disclosed in his lascivious carnival songs. They are often eloquent, the emotion is often deeply moving, and at times the thought rises to the purest sphere of tragedy and religion. The dominant note of all his poetry is that of love touched with the wistfulness of a thoughtful man. As a poet he was accomplished rather than great. And as a writer in prose and verse he did much by example to lift the Italian language into its rightful place as the medium for the expression of Italian life.

The use of Italian, which had been renewed by Alberti and Lorenzo de' Medici, was continued by Luigi Pulci and Poliziano. The first force of the revival of letters was now spent. The passion for antiquity had begun to cool. Its effects were far-reaching and it had by no means been brought to a conclusion. But the exclusive devotion to classical letters which had made **Pulci** the century between Boccaccio and Alberti almost a blank in the history of Italian literature came to an end. Men were no longer content to devote all their energies to mere letters, a mere concern with the technique of literature, and to be dependent upon the literature of the past. They began to exercise their own creative power. They passed from letters to learning and to literature. They broadened and deepened. Their audience consisted no longer of little scholarly groups scattered here and there. It became the living world of men. For his *Morgante Maggiore*, Luigi Pulci (1431-2—1487-90) took the legends of chivalry that were suited to his purpose and wove them into a romantic burlesque. It was written part by part to be recited before the brilliant and cultured society of the great Florentine palace of the Medici. Mere amusement was its aim. It had no serious and sustained object. It is at once romantic, heroic, and ironical. It is a series of gay and reckless narratives, written with spontaneity and vigor, convincing in its delineation of character, shining with touches of a rich fancy, and full of the bold and pungent irony that is a characteristic of the Italian genius.

The greatest man in Lorenzo's circle was Poliziano. As we have seen, he was the foremost scholar among the men of letters. **Poliziano** He was also the greatest poet of the revival of Italian literature in the fifteenth century. He freed the Italian chrysalis completely from its Latin shell and reinstated it as the literary language of the Italian people. His poetry does not soar to great heights. It lacks the elevation of Dante and the rich imagination of Ariosto, but it is limpid, pliant, and melodious, and it possesses an incomparable freshness. *La Giostra* which he composed chiefly for the pleasure of Giuliano, the brother of Lorenzo de' Medici, lacks any noble or even central thought, but it is extraordinarily varied in its movement and its melody. He wrote his play *Favola d' Orfeo,* the first non-religious play in Italian, in two days, when he was only eighteen years of age. It contains passages of golden melody, but the dialogue never attains true dramatic quality. Without the music for which it was meant it seems only the shell of a play; it lingers in the memory as a thing of lyrical beauty rather than of dramatic power. His minor lyrics have the exquisite refinement, the limpid grace, and the enchanting melody that are their author's chief characteristics. It is not passion, however, that pulsates in these poems, but only the tender and delicate feeling of a nature keenly sensitive to the beauty of the world in which it lived. Poliziano's poetry and Botticelli's painting are expressive of Florentine Platonism. The inspiration of each is love turned into an enchanting and passionless ideal.

Florence was the central school of Italy, but the revival of letters, of literature, and of art flourished in all parts of the peninsula. And in some respects Florence was equaled if not eclipsed by her rivals. In the first half of the fourteenth century Siena, within whose rose-colored walls there was such an apparently paradoxical union of commercial astuteness, military spirit, and contemplative passion, was the teacher of architecture, sculpture and painting to half Italy. In Siena more than in any other Italian city did the Renaissance assume a spiritual aspect. To this aspect of life she gave eloquent expression in painting, but she contributed nothing of importance to Italian literature. Most of the Greek scholars who came to Italy passed through Venice and carried on their work in other places. The city of the lagoons never produced any literature of distinction. In the early stages of the Renaissance she seemed completely engrossed in politics and commerce. Later on the rich merchants as well as the wealthy nobles patronized men of letters and filled their palaces with works of art. It was not until the printing press had been invented that Venice became a literary center. Individuality had been developed to a far less extent in Venice than in Florence. In the republic of the Adriatic the state and not the individual was held to be of paramount importance. Even in her glorious period of painting in the sixteenth century it was aliens from the mainland rather than Venetians who made Venice famous. When Petrarch as a boy sailed from Genoa on his way to Avignon that Italian town seemed to him " a city of kings, the very temple of prosperity, and the threshold of gladness." But Genoa produced nothing of importance in literature or in art.

Beyond the walls of Florence it was at the courts of princes rather than the capitals of republics that letters and literature flourished. Moral corruption abounded in these courts; and guile, hypocrisy, cruelty, and deceit were seldom absent. Yet these princes, who with their courtiers were often guilty of the **Humanism** grossest immorality, were also possessed of extraordinary merits **at the** and ability. They were generous to their friends and filled with **Italian** a keen zest of life. They were discriminating lovers of litera**Sourts** ture and intelligent and lavish patrons of art. They vied with each other to secure and retain men of talent. They made their courts brilliant with all the men of genius they could allure. A purely literary or artistic career was scarcely possible without their aid. At Naples, as we have seen, Frederic II succeeded in producing a premature Renaissance. But the culture of his court did not become deeply rooted among the people. Culture flourished at intervals at Naples after the death of Frederic, but it was always dependent upon the patronage of the ruling prince. Almost a century after the death of Frederic, Robert the Wise became a friend to Petrarch and a patron to Boccaccio. Another century later Alfonso the Magnanimous proved himself to be a munificent promoter of learning. It was in his reign that the Academy of Naples was founded. Antonio Beccadelli (1394–1471), one of the humanists of the court of Alfonso, prostituted his ability by producing a book that invested with voluptuous grace all the vices that accompanied the recrudescence of paganism. Lorenzo Valla (1406?–57) possessed one of the keenest intellects of the early Renaissance. His critical mind was trained in the methods of scientific investigation. Three years after Alfonso made him his private secretary he gave to the public his famous treatise on the *Donation of Constantine*. He exposed as a forgery this medieval document that testified to the transference by Constantine of the sovereignty of Italy and the west to Pope Sylvester. And he called into question the tradition that the Apostles' Creed was the joint composition of the twelve apostles. So great a storm did he arouse that he was compelled to take refuge in Barcellona. Later on, humanism, in the person of Nicholas V, crept to the papal throne and then Valla was given a place in the papal curia. Thus was typified the passing of humanism from its militant to its triumphant period. Pontano (1426–1503) was a distinguished Latin scholar and his Italian lyrics reveal much of the many-colored life of the Renaissance. Cangrande della Scala, whom Petrarch calls " the consolor of the houseless and the afflicted," was a patron at Verona. It was in his time that Dante lived there. But Dante had a noble pride, and he found the patron's salt to be bitter, and his stairs hard to climb. At Padua the University founded by Frederic II in 1238 had been growing steadily in importance. Jacopo II da Carrara, who had secured his lordship by forgery and murder, was untiring in his zeal to promote the interests of literature and art. After repeated entreaties he induced Petrarch to reside at his capital for a time. His son Francesco was also a man of cultured intellect who did much to further the cause of humanism. But Padua failed to become a noted literary center in the early Renaissance period. At a later day it became famous as a place of intellectual freedom. For many centuries Milan had been the second city of importance in the peninsula. It was one of the first among the cities of northern Italy to secure municipal independence. The commune did much to improve the city, and the work was continued when the Visconti and the Sforza were the despots of the principality. It is to Lodovico Sforza that the Milanese school of painting owes its origin. But Milan did not distinguish herself in letters or in literature. As we have seen, Gian Francesco Gonzaga, Marquis of Mantua, chose Vittorino da Feltre to teach his children and thus ensured for his capital high rank among the centers of humanism. Lodovico Gonzaga, who succeeded his father in 1444, was also a liberal and intelligent patron of art and letters. In the sixteenth century the court of Mantua was made splendid by the residence of Bembo, Bandello, Ariosto, and Tasso. Ferrara played an important part in the development of Italian literature. The revival of Italian in the fifteenth century took place almost simultaneously at Florence, Naples, and Ferrara. The golden age of culture at Ferrara began in 1402 when its university was reopened. It had no part in the great literary movement of the thirteenth and fourteenth centuries, but in the fifteenth century, under its Este lords, it became celebrated for its literary and artistic splendor. Under Frederic, the most ideal Italian prince of his age, Urbino gained a literary as well as a political importance. The little duchy was scarcely more than forty miles square and the larger part of it was unsuitable for cultivation. But Frederic, who had been a pupil in Vittorino da Feltre's school at Mantua, was a man of culture, and the finest general of his day. So noble youths flocked to his court, the model court of Italy, to learn manners and the art of war. Frederic was a liberal patron of arts and letters; and his son Guidobaldo followed in his footsteps. Gismondo

Malatesta, one of the most brutal and licentious despots in an age when such men were numerous, was a patron who succeeded in making Rimini a center of humanism. But with his death the literary glory of his capital came to an end. Thus we have seen that although Florence was the birth-place of humanism its influence spread far and wide. At every Italian court there were to be found scholars, poets, sculptors, and painters, all intensely interested in the surging life of the time and bent upon giving expression to their thought and their vision in some form of art or of literature.

It was impossible for the Papacy to remain unaffected by the progress of humanism. We have seen that after the Captivity and the Schism the Papacy was restored to something like its old power and prestige. But it was very far from having become the vigorous power that it was in the years of its medieval supremacy. Captivity, schism, and conciliar struggles had seriously crippled it. So had it been disposed to stem the flowing tide of humanism it would probably have found itself unequal to the task. The Avignonese popes were in sympathy with the new art and the new literature, and this attitude of the Papacy was maintained, in general, until the Council of Trent. In the first years of the fifteenth century Innocent VII attached Bruni and Poggio to the papal curia as secretaries; and humanists gathered about Eugene IV, despite the fact that that pontiff cannot be considered as being favorably disposed towards the new movement. With the election of Nicholas V (1447-55) the Renaissance definitely ascended the papal throne. Extremely poor, he had nevertheless managed to secure a university education at Bologna. Step by step the little, ugly, bright-eyed, active scholar, once a bell-ringer, crept up the ladder until at last he found himself seated in the Chair of St. Peter. From his time Rome became the literary and artistic capital of Europe, and with brief intervals the Papacy gave its chief attention during the Renaissance period to art and literature to the neglect of religion. Not until half Christendom had withdrawn itself from the pale of the church did the Papacy abandon its interest in the revival of literature and art and turn its energies to ecclesiastical matters and the recovery of its lost possessions. Nicholas was completely penetrated with the spirit of humanism. He collected the books that were in the various papal buildings and became the real founder of the great Vatican library. His agents were to be found in all likely places seeking for manuscripts, and he employed the most skilful copyists. He was not only generous but tolerant, or at least indifferent, to those who did not subscribe to all the doctrines of the church. Among the large number of humanists employed in his service was Lorenzo Valla. Calixtus III, the successor of Nicholas, whose pontificate lasted three years, was chiefly interested in prosecuting the war against the Turks. Pius II (1458–64) was also devoted to the success of the crusade. But he was not such a fanatic as his predecessor. Before his election he had been a man of the world and a man of letters, who did much to carry humanism across the Alps. The humanists expected a great deal from him as a patron. They were disappointed. It was only a mild encouragement that he lent them. Yet humanism had succeeded in establishing itself in the capital of Christendom. It proved a subtle enemy of the Papacy that gave it patronage, for it encouraged men to think for themselves and to rely upon their own reasoning powers. It did not in an outright way contradict any of the essential dogmas of the Church, but it cultivated an attitude of mind that was inimical to many of them. And from the standpoint of the Papacy, had the latter been aware of the fact, or had it not been indifferent to it, this mental attitude was far more dangerous than an unequivocal heresy. An unmistakable heresy could be condemned and persecuted. But a mental attitude was a less prehensible thing. It could scarcely be defined, let alone condemned. So humanism went its way, quietly inculcating disbelief in things that were fundamental to the Age of Faith.

It was in the city republics, at the courts of princes, and in the papal retinue, that humanism found its most congenial quarters. It had by no means taken full possession of the universities as yet. Petrarch tells us that when he went to the University of Bologna the educational methods of the day seemed to him to be radically wrong. " Philosophy is so prostituted to the fancies of the vulgar," he said, " that it aims only at hair-splitting on subtle distinctions and quibbles of words. . . . Truth is utterly lost sight of, sound practice is neglected, and the reality of things is despised. . . . People concentrate their whole attention upon empty words." And more than a century after the death of the father of humanism most of the universities were still dedicated to medievalism. Theology interwoven with the scholastic philosophy, medicine, and the civil and canon law were the principal subjects of study. And the method of instruction was fixed by tradition and prejudice that rendered every subject comparatively lifeless. The bitter hostility and the arrogant scorn which the humanists displayed against the medieval instructors was reciprocated in kind. Medievalism defended its position in the universities with all the tenacity of a vested in-

terest. It fought with vigor against the forces of the new movement which it did not understand. But despite all the skill and
vigor displayed in its defense the great medieval educational
system was doomed. It gradually fell into decay, and the universities became slowly permeated with the spirit of the new
learning.

When humanism was a century old in Italy it crossed the Alps
and began to infect the whole of western Europe. With magnetic touch it roused the slumbering nations of the north to

vigorous intellectual life. It took on varied qualities and aspects
in accordance with the ethnic traditions, the racial temper, the
national characteristics, of the various peoples by whom it was
taken up. Yet in spite of all the mutations of expression the
fundamental principle of the new movement remained the same
in every country it entered. In Germany it did not consist as
largely as it did in Italy of a revival of the spirit of classical
antiquity, of a return to the rational and pagan spirit of Greek
and Roman civilization. It was rather a return to primitive
Christianity, or at least to what was understood to be primitive
Christianity. The German mind is deeply earnest and more
given to introspection than is the Italian. It lacks all instinctive
sympathy with the pagan spirit. So when the Renaissance penetrated into Germany it assumed a character that differed very
greatly from the one it had displayed in Italy. The French mind,
although it adopted humanism with great readiness, did not surrender itself as fully to the spirit of pagan antiquity as did the
Italian. It retained more completely its own essential qualities.
With a serene detachment it appropriated those qualities of classical antiquity that appealed to it and combined them with those of
its own which it retained. The effect of this combination of Gallic
and classic qualities is to be seen in all French art and literature.
Two things combined to make England receive the Renaissance
with less instinctive sympathy than did France. The English
national temperament is conservative and tenacious of whatever
custom has made familiar, it has a deep-seated aversion to
change; and, unlike France, the race is of Teutonic and not
Latin origin. It is characteristic of the English temperament
that the first use of humanism in England was to spread learning and not to produce art. Humanism was less fruitful in Spain
than in Germany or France or England. The Spaniards are not
a great artistic race like the French or the Italians, nor are they
a race of abstract thinkers and philosophers like the Germans.
Yet the achievements of the Spaniards are remarkable because
of their variety and their audacity. In discovery the Iberian

peninsula can point to the achievements of Columbus, its adopted

son, Cortes and Vasco de Gama; in religion to St. Teresa, St. John of the Cross, Loyola, and Xavier; in literature to Cervantes; and in painting to Velasquez. The essential characteristic of the Spanish genius seems to be that its exponents have worked by themselves; that, with the exception of mysticism, the life of the nation has been unmarked by any great movements such as those which have appeared in other countries. Spain, as a whole, then, was little affected by humanism. Only little isolated groups of humanists sheltered by powerful patronage were able to bid defiance to the hostility of the church.

The humanistic movement was a broad one. It included the revival of Greek and Latin letters. Much of this was mere pedantry, and became more and more so as the years went on. It was concerned primarily with form to the neglect of thought. Yet that was a necessary stage. Grammars had to be constructed, dictionaries had to be compiled, texts had to be determined by the comparison of manuscripts, and commentaries had to be written. And pedants are sometimes good schoolmasters. They lay the foundation for the work of men of nobler mind. Humanism also included criticism. With this it furnished a key to new thought and prepared the birth of modern science. It led to Machiavelli and the study of man as a social being, to Erasmus and the study of man as an ethical being, to Vesalius and the study of man as a physical being, and to Bruno and the study of man as a part of the sidereal system. It did all of this because it produced a new attitude towards life.

# CHAPTER VI

## THE REVIVAL OF ART

1. The Relation of Art to Life.
2. The Revival of Architecture.
3. The Revival of Sculpture.
4. The Revival of Painting.

**CHAP. VI**
**1275-1400**

**The Forces that determine Art**

ART is a language. It gives expression to the spirit of the age, the nation, and the individual that produced it. These three creating forces of the age, the nation, and the individual may be discerned in every work of art. They make of art the most eloquent expression of life. In the novels of Dickens, Thackeray, and George Eliot, for instance, it is easy to see the spirit of the nineteenth century. No one who is at all acquainted with the history of civilization would think of assigning them to any other time should the dates of their composition by some mischance become lost. And equally easy would it be to assign them to the British nation. They are strikingly differentiated from the products of other nations by the English genius that informs them. Nor would it be difficult to come to the conclusion that they were the product of three writers, quite distinct each from the others, should the names of their authors become forgotten. Usually, in a work of art, it is the force of the individual that is paramount. The painting of Corot and the music of Mozart were influenced by the gentleness of their lives. But architecture is more impersonal than any other art. It is informed chiefly with the spirit of the age that gave it birth. It is always a particularly true exponent of the quality of the civilization that created it. Each epoch of the world develops its own proper form of expression. Greek architecture is the embodiment of supreme serenity, of self-restraint, and the sense of inevitable fate. It is the expression of an ideal of life that never sought to leave the earth, the ideal of a sound mind in a sound body. Its impulse is purely pagan. Roman architecture, with its bridges and aqueducts, its triumphal arches, its domes and its auditoriums, speaks of the majesty of the Roman government, of the imperial scope of its power and its law. When paganism had fallen and Christianity had built a new civilization upon the wreck of the old, Gothic architecture gave expression to the new spirit, to the new ideal of life, to the new vision that soared aloft until it was lost in the blue sky. Pure beauty was the sole object of Hellenic art, but Gothic architecture strove to voice the aspirations of the human soul. The predominant lines of classic architecture are horizontal lines, which are restful and belong to the earth, while those of Gothic architecture are vertical. In a Gothic cathedral, slender window, towering pillar, pointed arch, lofty vault, delicate pinnacle, and soaring spire, irresistibly carry the eye upward. Classic architecture was rooted in the rational faculty; Gothic was born of the spiritual. The rational faculty looks about it with understanding. The spiritual faculty aspires with rapture to God. But it is not form alone that creates the impression produced by a Gothic cathedral. The windows, made up of separate fragments of glass, ruby, or sapphire blue, or emerald green, let in mellow light and permit mysterious shadow. The lofty interior is steeped in the brooding richness and solemn splendor of a strange twilight. The effect is profoundly emotional. It is the language of the soul become articulate. "When the house of God," wrote the abbot of St. Denis in the middle of the twelfth century, "many-colored as the radiance of precious stones, called me from the cares of this world, then holy meditation led my mind to thoughts of piety, exalting my soul from the material to the immaterial, and I seemed to find myself, as it were, in some strange part of the universe, which was neither wholly of the baseness of the earth nor wholly of the serenity of heaven, but by the grace of God I seemed lifted in a mystic manner from this lower toward that upper sphere."

The Renaissance was in part a harking back to classic ideals. The neo-classicism of the time demanded an architecture that could give it expression. Gothic architecture could not express the lucidity and the sanity of Greek thought, nor the grandiose nature of the Roman civilization. Nor could it express the combination of classicism and modernity that formed the spirit of the Renaissance. A new style of architecture was required. The pure Gothic of northern and central France had never found a congenial soil in Italy. Only a modified form of Gothic, in which the horizontal principle held an important part, had flourished there. Breadth rather than height was its characteristic attribute. The spire was almost unknown, its place being taken by the dome. In retaining something of the character of classic architecture Italian Gothic expressed the genius of the Italian people, a genius with a classic inheritance, as contrasted with the genius of the French people, a genius with a marked Celtic strain. In the creation of an architecture that should give expression to the semi-classic spirit of the Renaissance, a less radical change was required of the Italians than of the northern nations. The spirit of the Renaissance appealed to the Italian mind promptly and decisively. A new style of architecture, that rapidly reached maturity, gave expression to that spirit.

The architecture of the Renaissance began in Florence under Brunelleschi (1377-1446). To find him as the original inspiring mind of Renaissance ecclesiastical architecture one should not go to the enormous dome of the Duomo in Florence, for, despite the unique beauty of its wonderful curve, it is chiefly remark-

able as a great engineering feat and not as a high artistic achievement. Rather one should go to the smaller churches of San Lorenzo and Santo Spirito in Florence. Here one finds the towering Gothic pillars of the Age of Faith replaced by classic colonnades, and the high vaulted roof by lower and broader ceilings of the Roman type. There are in these churches the strong, exact proportions of classic architecture, its level lines, its ample spaciousness, and its chaste and simple decoration. Yet despite Brunelleschi's free use of classical details the effect of his work is quite unlike that of antiquity. The classic inspiration was one thing to the man of antiquity; it was quite another to the man of the early Renaissance. To the former it was genuine, sincere, and irresistible; to the latter it was less vital because it was not born of the time but was merely retrospective. The intervening centuries had changed the complexion of life. The architecture of Brunelleschi and his followers express the spirit that resulted from the intermingling of pagan and Christian ideals. It is less single-hearted and more eclectic than either the Greek, or the Roman, or the Gothic architecture. A still closer approach to the spirit of antiquity was achieved by Alberti (1404-72), that many-sided man of the Renaissance whose writings we have already noticed. Much of his gracious and elegant work still exists. It was not only in central Italy that the new architecture, deriving its inspiration from both pagan and Christian sources, arose. While the Florentines were faithfully following the course Brunelleschi had laid down, Bramante (1444-1514) was doing similar work at Milan. In 1499 he went to Rome and there after he had steeped himself in the neo-classic spirit of the time he became the greatest architect of his age. It is true that, broadly speaking, Brunelleschi and his associates had anticipated almost all that was best in the architecture of the

succeeding century. But some things Bramante added. He had
a large conception of his art, sound judgment, and refined taste.
His buildings have simplicity of form and unity of effect. To
this structural symmetry all the details of decoration were carefully subordinated. He achieved proportion and grace and elegance. Something, too, of the vigor of the north he interfused
with the majesty of the south. With him the first stage in the
revival of architecture was concluded and the second begun. All
during his life architecture went on its way with a due regard
for proportion and a fine feeling for a restrained richness of
decoration.

The Greeks serenely enjoyed the external world. They drew
the inspiration for their sculpture from the men and women they
saw about them. They were not much disturbed by the moral
struggles and the ceaseless and often-times painful questionings
regarding the destiny of the individual soul that Christianity
emphasized. As we have seen, this change in the attitude
towards life, coming by imperceptible degrees, brought with it a
change in the ideals of art. The Greek temple gave place to the
Gothic cathedral. And when men began to recover something
of the pagan attitude towards life the architecture of the early
Renaissance gave expression to that spirit. A similar change
took place in all the arts, in sculpture and in painting. In sculpture the Italian sense of reality had never been completely extinguished. The carving of leaves and flowers and fruit in the
medieval churches of the peninsula give testimony to a certain
power of observation. Yet the Italian sculptors were in no
small measure bound by the subjection of their art to the exclusive service of the Church. The men of the medieval centuries
were exceedingly skilful carvers of stone. Indeed, the medieval
sculptors made the thirteenth century one of the great periods of
their art. But the spell of the Church under which sculpture
worked is seen in the almost exclusive devotion to ecclesiastical
subjects, in the thin and gaunt figures, the emaciated faces, the
angular gestures, and above all in the spirit that informs it. It
was Nicholas of Pisa (1207?–80), not a Pisan but an Apulian,
who, disregarding the limiting traditions of the past, first instilled
something of the new life into the forms of medieval sculpture.
In the panels of the pulpits at Pisa and Siena and those of the
tomb of St. Dominic at Bologna one can see something of the
detachment, the purity of feeling, and the sense of the dignity
of the human form, that were possessed by the Greeks. The
aim and the ideal of the sculptor are evident, despite the halting
technique. It was not alone the example of antiquity that in-

spired Nicholas. He was not a mere imitator. He went direct to nature. And from him onwards not one of the Italian sculptors copied classical statuary in a slavish manner. So into the sculpture of the Renaissance, as into its literature, its architecture and its painting, there flowed from the beginning two streams of inspiration, that of classic art and that of nature itself. John of Pisa (1240–1320), the son of Nicholas, was much more concerned with nature than with antiquity. It was his aim to see nature as it is. He carried no cloak of convention ready to throw over its truth. And coupled with his naturalism was a genuine religious feeling. The sculpture of Nicholas of Pisa was semi-classic. The sculpture of his son John was picturesque, intellectual, daring in innovation and full of movement. Above all it indicated to Italian sculpture its true path, the study of nature. Andrew of Pisa (1270–1348?) had for his aim the portrayal of beauty rather than that of the naked reality. Nowhere is this more evident than in the large doors he made for the Baptistery in Florence. His panels tell the old biblical stories not with strict lines whose sole purpose is intelligibility, but with lines instinct with grace, with refined and swaying figures, whose one aim is beauty. Even the soldiers who have just beheaded St. John the Baptist stand in attitudes of gentle grace. The great painter Giotto was teaching the Florentines that art could make things real. Andrew of Pisa taught them that it could make them beautiful. Orcagna (1328?–68), another of the many-sided men of the Renaissance, goldsmith, painter, poet, architect, and sculptor, extended the range of sculpture. In his hands the art which the Greeks had used to express impassible serenity became a medium for the portrayal of tender and even spiritual emotion. Orcagna was a great artist. The refined and lovely figures of the tabernacle of Or San Michele indicate what he might have achieved in sculpture had he confined his attention to that art. But he was more of a painter, in which art he was the greatest of the followers of Giotto, and more of a goldsmith than a sculptor.

Such were the pioneers of Italian sculpture. They had broken the bonds of medieval tradition. Their work was imbued with certain classic qualities as they understood them, with grace and suavity. But in them was kindled a passion for the beauty of the living world about them, and this was the greatest force that determined the progress of their art. We have now to turn to the masters of that art. Jacopo della Quercia (1371–1438) was an artist of pronounced individuality, of bold vision, of noble sense of form, and of vigorous thought. His power to express movement was so great and so rare that it had to wait three-quarters of a century to find in Michelangelo its equal. And in his sepulchral effigy of the Lady Ilaria del Carretto, one of the most beautiful figures in all sepulchral art, there is a perfect expression of the quality of repose.

Two pairs of gates for the Baptistery of Florence represent the artistic product of the life of Ghiberti (1378–1455), for he devoted the greater part of his life to them, and although he executed other works in the same years they have either disappeared or are much less successful. The first set of gates were for the north portal. They are a pendant to the gates made by Andrew of Pisa. Despite the graceful lines of the Pisan the panels of his gates tell the biblical stories with a direct and some-times incisive clearness. It was with a greater and a more refined grace that Ghiberti told the stories that he chose from the same stately pageant of dramatic narrative. He was far more concerned than Andrew with the manner than with the matter. Always when one looks at the panels of the Pisan it is the story that dwells in the mind; but when one looks at the panels of the Florentine it is the graceful attitudes and the harmonious composition that appeal most strongly. So pleased were the Florentines with Ghiberti's gates that they removed those made by Andrew from the east portal, the main entrance, to the south portal where they now stand, and commissioned Ghiberti to execute a set of gates in their place. With ceaseless care and infinite love the master wrought upon the new gates for twenty-seven years. Seldom, indeed, has a life been so single-hearted. The result was a thing of beauty of which art had never dreamed before. Each one of the ten scenes is beautifully staged. Each has an elaborate background of landscape or architecture. In each the figures are arranged with masterly skill. The figures, the trees, and the temples recede. Usually in bas-relief there was only one plane, but Ghiberti's figures are arranged in three and even four distances. Thus he achieved the illusion of perspective which is an element of painting rather than of sculpture. This skilful use of many planes, this illusion of depth, has earned for the panels the name of " pictures in bronze." The pictorial character of the gates is a defect in that it oversteps the limits of noble sculpture. And another defect is that each one of the numerous figures in all the panels, the youthful David and the giant Goliath, the honest Esau and the cunning Jacob, the lowly shepherd and the Queen of Sheba, moves to the same melody. It is not Hebrew strength but Latin grace that informs these gates. But the consummate skill and exquisite feeling of the figures grouped before spacious porticos, or under spreading trees, fading into the dim distance, moving in dreamy grace to an unheard melody, are incomparable. In his youth Ghiberti practised the art of the goldsmith, and these gates are goldsmith's work rather than sculpture. Yet they are the incarnation of rhythmic grace and exquisite beauty, and they won from Michelangelo the name of the Gates of Paradise.

Fortunately the Italian sculptors of the Renaissance were turned from the wrong path into which the fascinating pictorial art of Ghiberti had threatened to lead them by the strong realism and abounding imagination of Donatello (1386?–1466). His statue of St. George illustrates one period, or aspect, of his genius. Without notable grace or elevation it has a quiet dignity and the vigor of youth. It is a connecting link between Gothic and

**Donatello** modern sculpture. Under the armor one feels the presence of the supporting muscles. But more important than the realism of the statue is its imagination, the expression of the soul of the manly and militant saint, ready to battle against the prince of darkness. His bas-relief of the Annunciation shows the influence of classic art. It is a more elaborate piece of work than the St. George, but it has the same simplicity and honesty of thought, the same freshness of vision, the same vital realism, and the same power of imagination. With simple candor the story is told, with dignity and with grace. The statue of David reveals his mastery of the classic principles and his power to use them without servile imitation. It is the first nude bronze statue of the Renaissance, but it is no mere imitation. The idealism of Greek art is tempered with the realism of the Florentine. This David might have been a goatherd of the Campagna. This happy combination of idealism and realism is also seen in Donatello's famous singing gallery where the single impression is that of children exultantly dancing to a joyous melody. More mature work may be seen in the masterly statue of the *condottiere* Gattamelata which still stands in the Piazza at Padua, the first equestrian statue since the one of the Emperor Marcus Aurelius. In this noble work the splendid creative power of Donatello came to a climax. All his freshness of vision, his vivid realism, is there. The anatomy of the horse shows careful observation, and the movement is only slightly defective. The rider is a man of Donatello's own time, a convincing representation of a figure from a Renaissance pageant. The fine imagination and the inexhaustible creative power are there. The rider and his horse are correctly related to each other and in the man there dwells the power to lead his fellow men. The insight of the sculptor, his splendid and untrammeled genius, has revealed to us the essential character of the *condottiere*. Donatello not only exerted a desirable influence upon sculpture by offsetting the pictorial example set by Ghiberti, but his studies of the nude and of drapery were of great service to the painters who were also turning their attention to the things of the present world.

Luca della Robbia (1400–82) was more Greek in spirit and more sculpturesque in his aims than either Ghiberti or Donatello. Ghiberti mingled the plastic and the pictorial. Donatello merged the plastic with the dramatic, and his thought and feeling were essentially Italian. But Luca della Robbia had the Greek spirit. He kept strictly within the classic limits of sculpture. His subjects are ecclesiastical, angels and saints, Christ and the Madonna. But in all of his work there is the same theme of a happy unity of physical and emotional well-being. It is the Greek serenity uttering itself in a modern tongue. And it is a theme that can easily be expressed within the comparatively narrow limits of sculpture. Luca della Robbia was the inventor of a new art. He worked with a new material, glazed terra-cotta. His bas-reliefs were modeled in clay, and then over the surface he put a coat of enamel in which color, pure white and pale blue, was sparingly used. Thus he made his figures clear and bright and rendered them more durable. It was a wise innovation, for the ductile clay lent itself admirably to the delicate feeling of the artist. Luca della Robbia's figures are full of a tender humanity. Each has its own individuality, but each gives voice to the same melody, each is imbued with the same spirit of youth and serene happiness. His tender pathos is not so deep as that of Ghiberti and his range and dramatic power are narrower and feebler than those of Donatello, but in classical beauty and stately repose he was far nearer to the Greeks than were they, while at the same time his lyric Christian sentiment and appealing humanity made him, quite as much as they, an artist of his own age.

There were, of course, many minor sculptors in the early Renaissance period. Andrea della Robbia (1437–1528?), Luca's nephew, produced work equal to that of his uncle in its exquisite feeling, but in general inferior in power. Desiderio da Settignano (1428–64) had creative power and charm of sentiment. Verrocchio (1435–88) was the creator, in part at least, of the world's greatest equestrian statue, that of the *condottiere* Colleoni. But none of them added any essential feature to the art which had been so enriched by the bold spirit of Jacopo della Quercia, the golden melody of Ghiberti, the fresh vitality of Donatello, and the tender grace of Luca della Robbia.

In the Middle Ages painting was merely the handmaid of the Church. Its function was not to reveal to man the beauty of the present world, but to help him to win the salvation of his soul in the next. In the later medieval centuries the only school of painting was the Byzantine school. It is true that the Greek church had been separated from the Latin church for centuries, but the painting of the former dominated that of the latter. Byzantine painting was completely under the spell of the Church. The subjects of the pictures were taken from the Scriptures, from the legends of the Church, or from the lives of the saints. An arid symbolism, void of all initiative, dominated art. If the infant Child upon His mother's knee held up two fingers, it meant one thing; if his hands were clasped, it meant another. Peter was known by his keys, and Paul by his sword. Even the colors were prescribed. Blue became the canonical color for the outer robe of the Virgin. The style of treatment, the attitudes, the composition, and the colors, were all determined by traditional rules. This was done in order to make the didactic story told by the picture as quickly recognized and as easily intelligible as possible. So one painter simply copied the work of another who had faithfully obeyed the rules. There was no direct reference to nature. All that painting had to do was to assist the Church in its teaching. It had no separate and independent existence. But softly and unnoticed a new era dawned upon the world. In the thirteenth century life began to animate painting once more as it had done in the days of Greece and Rome, and as it was already doing in Italy in literature and sculpture. Men once again became sensitive to the beauty of nature and the significance of humanity. Among the painters who first made their art more expressive of life were Guido of Siena, Giunta of Pisa, and more important, Cimabue (1240?-1302) of Florence. Some of Cimabue's frescoes, sadly faded, may still be seen in the Upper Church of San Francesco at Assisi. He was the most advanced master of his time. A painting that has been called the first picture of the Renaissance is the famous Madonna, that still is to be seen in the church of Santa Maria Novella at Florence. The author of this altar-piece is unknown. He was long thought to be Cimabue, but now we know that he was a Sienese, and perhaps he was Duccio. Whoever he was he did not accomplish a sudden advance in art. He followed the traditional injunctions of Byzantine conventionalism. But, in a slight degree, he tempered the chill atmosphere, and put into his picture a touch of the tenderness and the pathos of the modern world which was unexpressed by the Greeks and maybe unknown to

them. Perhaps this timid infusion of humanity was inspired by
the spirit of St. Francis of Assisi which " fertilized the religious
ideal with the simplest and sweetest instincts of mankind."
Duccio (1260?–1320?) painted an altar-piece for the cathedral
of Siena, which even more than the picture we have just noticed
shows the influence of the new and refreshing stream of humanity. It has more of tenderness, more of refinement, and a greater
degree of grace.

The beginning of the revival of sculpture preceded that of
painting by almost half a century; but the genius of one great
man, Giotto (1276–1336), raised painting to so high a pitch that
it overtook and overshadowed the development of sculpture.
The traditions which Cimabue and other painters who preceded
him and who were contemporaneous with him timidly attempted
to modify, Giotto resolutely abandoned. With masculine vigor,
and a quick, unfailing invention, he effected the regeneration of
painting. He studied under Cimabue, but soon the tradition of
the master and the budding invention of the disciple parted ways.
With a vivid dramatic feeling Giotto painted scenes that have
the air of actuality — the Raising of Lazarus, St. Francis receiv-
ing the Stigmata, St. Francis before the Soldan, the Death of St.
Francis, and many another similar scene. He had a keen realization of the place in which each scene was enacted, and an extraordinary faculty of design. He arranged each one of his characters in a picture so that all should contribute to the general
impression. The backgrounds of his pictures are varied. Landscape is utilized, though it is but crudely mastered; and the
buildings of the time appear, though distorted by an imperfect
command of perspective. Gesture is abundant and varied. It
explains, directs, and commands. It expresses the most varied
emotion. His figures are lifelike, and in their faces is seen an
astonishing variety of feeling. They are faces that resemble
those of the men and women about him. He even attempted
portraiture, painting among others the portraits of Boniface VIII,
the youthful Charles of Valois, and Dante, with whom he was
intimately acquainted. The results show methodical and experienced observation. He painted at Florence, Assisi, Rome,
Naples, Gaeta, Rimini, Bologna, Ferrara, Ravenna, and, so we
are told, at Arezzo, Lucca, and Avignon. Thus he traveled up
and down the peninsula, scattering with tireless energy the seeds
of the new art, infusing a vitality into painting that has not yet
been exhausted. He stands apart, a towering figure, the Dante
of painting. There was no immediate successor to take his place.
His followers were a feeble folk, lacking his embracing human

sentiment, his dramatic force, and his penetrating insight. They were unable to follow the path that he opened toward the study of nature. Something more of technique they learned, but their art was only an echo of his.

Almost a hundred years passed away before a shy and silent youth took up the art of painting where Giotto had left it, and in his brief, lonely, and poverty-stricken life gave it a new impulse and left it assured of its future greatness. Although Giotto infused life into painting he had left it with only a secondary function to perform. The chief service of his pictures is to assist in the inculcation of ecclesiastical doctrines or to perpetuate the legends of the Church. But Masaccio (1402–29?) lived at a time when the strong new wine of naturalism was being infused into thought and into art; and he realized that the highest function of art is to express life. So he went to the world about him for his material and his inspiration, and thus he gave to painting a new aim, a new vision. Perhaps something of this new point of view he owed to Masolino, his master, who in his turn had been a pupil of Ghiberti, but more than all else it was his own creative power that enabled him to open to painting the vast prospect of freedom in the portrayal of life. With him ecclesiasticism and painting began to part company.

There was one artist who did not accept the new point of view. The art of Fra Angelico (1387–1455), a painter seemingly born out of his due time, was completely devoted to the service of the Church. But he was the last of the painters whose work is exclusively religious. He was a dreamer who throughout his cloistral life was absorbed in heavenly visions. Into the lamp of art he poured a stream of religious enthusiasm and spiritual imagination that caused it to burn with a pure and heavenly radiance. In his frescoes the gold of earth is always glistening in a celestial blue. But though he raised his eyes to the sky and strove to leave the earth with its hindering limitations he did not wholly escape the strong current of naturalism that was flowing into the art of the time. Despite the fact that seemingly he shunned the world of men, he was exquisitely sensitive to the beauty of the world of nature. And he was not so deficient in technique as might be thought. He could draw features with skill, and he had a flower-like grace of line and color. The sources of his feelings were medieval, but his power of expression is unmistakably modern. A considerable part of his life was passed in the convent of San Marco in Florence where many of his frescoes may still be seen on the walls. Painting in fresco requires spontaneity. The colors are mixed with water and the

painting is done while the plaster is still damp. The work has
to be done somewhat rapidly, and there is neither the leisure nor
the chance of correction that is afforded in oil-painting. Fresco
painting requires for success not only spontaneity but also a
lyrical spirit. It is a process admirably suited to the art of Fra
Angelico. More spontaneous and more exquisite wall pictures
than those of the corridors and cells of San Marco it is difficult to
conceive. One of the most beautiful of them all is that of the
Annunciation where, in the quiet twilight, the angel Gabriel conveys to Mary the message that she is to be the mother of God.
It is so exquisite in the beauty of its accessories, the gray walls
of the cloister, the pale rose of the angel's robe, the tender green
of the leaves and the grass, the delicate grace of the distant
flowers, and it is so single in its thought, so child-like in its simplicity, and so imbued with the spirit of devotion, that its beauty
penetrates the beholder. In the field of painting the work of
Fra Angelico was the final and supreme flower of the Age of
Faith.

Despite the devotion of Fra Angelico, the old lamps were sold
for new. Painting became more and more concerned with the
present world, its freshness and its wonder, and the spirit of the
time found its way even into the convents. Fra Lippo Lippi **Fra Lipp**
(1406–69) followed the road opened by Masaccio and departed **Lippi**
still further from the traditions of the past. He was completely
engrossed in the world about him, finding it to be, poet that he
was, a pageant of unfailing interest. Only the lingering spell
of the Church induced him to paint religious subjects. The patronage of art was shifting from the Church to the rich burghers
and the princes, but her influence was still potent, and even
the new patrons did not always prefer secular subjects. Left to
himself Fra Lippo Lippi would probably never have chosen
ecclesiastical themes. A human quality pervades his work.
Keen observation of his fellow-men, clear characterization of their
varying individualities, and a lively sympathy with their interests,
are fully displayed in his pictures. For the saints that he painted
he found models in the men and women of Florence. He could
portray different moods by means of facial expression. He was
one of the first, if not actually the first, of the artists of the Renaissance to make the face the window of the soul. This is the
most important thing that he contributed to the development of
painting. His realism is never crude, but is often-times tender
and poetic. And though his work is never distinguished by
elevation of spirit or depth of emotion it is always refined, lovely,
and harmonious. The shore of romance had now been reached

The veil had been lifted. Before the eyes of men there loomed the world with all its wonderful beauty and its inexhaustible interest.

When we dealt with the revival of literature we saw that many of the Italian courts were centers of literary production. Among these courts was that of the Gonzaga family at Mantua. There it was that Vittorino da Feltre established his famous school. And it was to this court that Mantegna (1430–1506) was sum- **Mantegna** moned; and there, with the exception of two years spent at Rome, he remained until the end of his life. He was a painter who had been nourished upon antique sculpture and he had for companions scholars who were busy with the revival of Greek and Latin letters. So because of these external facts and still more because of the predilections of his temperament he became the most Roman of all the Italian painters. They were Roman qualities that entered into his work, sobriety, dignity, self-restraint, discipline, and masterfulness. His genius was essentially masculine. It would be vain to seek in his paintings for the facile grace and the soft charm of Lippo Lippi. Mantegna was cold and austere, though not altogether lacking in tenderness. But he was a master of characterization. Every figure in his pictures has its own unique individuality. He was a skilful portrayer of personality. And he was a great technician. On the vaulted ceiling of one of the rooms in the palace at Mantua he painted a circular opening, surrounded by a marble balustrade, through which the spectator seems to be looking at the blue sky with its white clouds. In boldness of conception and skill of execution this study in perspective excelled anything that had thus far been accomplished in Italy.

Of all the artists of the fifteenth century none was so gifted with imagination as Botticelli (1447–1510), and there are few who so well represent that stage of the Renaissance in which the medieval and pagan currents of inspiration were intermingled. Many of his themes are the oft-repeated ones of ecclesiastical history, but they are painted with a romantic imagination, and they are made vital by intensity of feeling, highly wrought emotion, bold invention, a vivid sense of life, expressed with unusual power. It was not only religious subjects, however, that he painted. The poetic legends of the pagan world appealed to his imagination quite as strongly as did the saintly legends. But his Madonnas are not the simple saintly souls of Fra Angelico; nor are his goddesses the serene women of an untroubled world **Botticelli** of beauty. Botticelli was a poet and a dreamer, and he was steeped in the Neo-Platonism of his time. Like Pico della

Mirandola and others, he dreamed of the reconciliation of paganism and Christianity, and he gave to this intellectual fantasy and spiritual yearning its highest pictorial expression. It is the dreamy poetry of this thought that inspires so much of his work. In the faces of his Madonnas one always finds a pensive sadness, in their eyes a melancholy reverie. And the same wistful pathos he gave to his goddesses. Both have that Vergilian sense that makes the work of Ghiberti so melodious. In both he gave expression to the same sentiment of infinite but ineffectual desire. In spite of his vivid sense of reality, that gave to him his tender and flower-like delicacy of color, and led him to paint with such delight the loveliness of youth, floating draperies, filmy veils, fluttering roses, the deep forest and the blue sky, the green fields and the undulating sea, he was not interested primarily in the external world. It was a beauty more remote for which he yearned. He did not strive to lend glory to the common things of life, but to reveal a world of more recondite beauty that would become intelligible to the beholder when he learned to share the emotions that were shadowed forth in the picture. He was the most sensitive spirit of the early Renaissance, and to the most subtle thought of that age he sought to give expression.

Luca Signorelli (1441–1523) was a great artist of stern ideals who declined to follow Fra Angelico, Fra Lippo Lippi, and Botticelli in the valley of peace, in the path of tender sentiment and romantic imagination. He traveled a more virile and robust road, the road of vigor and dramatic action. It was an austere power that he possessed, and with it he became a potent delineator of physical life and strength and action. Taking men and women whom he selected for their special fitness for his subjects as models he advanced the study of the human form for its own sake much further than any of his predecessors. In this respect he was the precursor of Michelangelo; but the masculine force of Signorelli was never tempered like that of Michelangelo with a pathos of spiritual import. With great technical accomplishment, in a broad and swift manner, he painted noble and masterful men and women of grandeur, refinement, and grace. His work was always seriously and even solemnly conceived, and this with his sonorous color, his stately architectural backgrounds, and his dignified composition, lends to it an air of majesty. Fra Angelico had abjured antiquity and Mantegna had discarded the inheritance of the Middle Ages. But up to this time most of the artists of the Renaissance had striven to unite the pagan and the Christian elements. It was only very gradually that the classical and the modern were amalgamated. We shall have to wait for

Michelangelo and Raphael to witness the perfect fusion, but the works of Signorelli made a near approach to that unity which later artists, who learned much from him, were destined to achieve.

Ghirlandajo (1449–94) was a skilful but plebeian artist who, lacking poetic vision, saw only those things that are perceived by every one, the superficial phenomena of life, and so did nothing to extend the vision of his fellow-men, but merely repeated it in all its narrowness and imperfection. Yet just because he saw exactly as did the rest of the world he enjoyed a wide popularity, for the world delights to have its own vision and its own thought confirmed. He was a careful and successful craftsman, a facile and prolific worker in fresco, who painted the wealthy bourgeoisie of Florence, their customs and their costumes, the splendor of their social functions, and who received in return their patronage and applause and remained their favorite for more than a quarter of a century. As a technician he possessed the accomplishments of all his predecessors. He was able to render external things with great exactness. He had an unusual command of stately and sumptuous composition. But his pictures of biblical and legendary subjects have no spiritual feeling, and into them he introduced groups and processions of wealthy Florentines dressed in the rich robes and jeweled ornaments that were worn so lavishly in his day. It was the practice of many of the Renaissance painters to place their patrons in the most august company, but none had yet done it so boldly and so baldly as did Ghirlandajo. His pictures may be taken in at a glance. There is no wistful mysticism to set one dreaming as in those of Botticelli and no enigmatic smile to arrest one's attention and to disturb one's thoughts as in those of Leonardo. All lies upon the surface. As a portraitist he was more successful than as a frescante, but his chief importance lies in his expression of the average taste of his time.

From an artist who was so completely objective we turn to one who was just as completely subjective. Perugino (1446–1524), the painter of contemplative ecstasy, of serene rapture, was an artist of inward vision, who had for his single theme a mood of the soul. There is one picture, the beautiful triptych that he painted for an altar-piece at Pavia, that may well be considered his masterpiece, and that sums up his genius. So we may come to know the painter through a study of this picture. In the central panel the Virgin adores the infant Jesus. On the left is the archangel Michael clad in armor. And on the right there is the archangel Raphael with the youthful Tobias. All

the figures are completely detached from their surroundings.
Steeped in quiet spiritual ecstasy, they are unconscious of the
presence of the physical world. Perugino was the painter of a
gentle mysticism, of rapt communion with God. Especially in
the figure of Michael is the painter successful in rendering the
lyrical and tender feeling of the soul, the beatitude of contemplation, that formed his single melody. One must note, too, the
lovely landscape that unfolds itself so softly in the background,
for it is an essential part of the picture. Landscape had been used
for backgrounds since the days of Giotto, but never had it been
made so organic a part of the composition, never had it so insidi-
ously infused the whole and reinforced its special beauty. A
serene charm of brooding peace has descended from the blue sky
and suffused the quiet valley with its winding river, the distant
hills and the slender trees. All is steeped in a soft and golden
light, in an ineffable beauty, and the beholder, like the figures in
the picture, seems to be listening to some silent song. It is in
this spiritual note, transmitted to the men who came after him,
and finding its place in the eclective ideal of art, that the work
of Perugino has its chief importance.

So at last we come to the summer noon of the Renaissance in
literature and art. The widely divergent accomplishments and
ideals of individual writers and artists and the changing life of
the time had gradually extended the gamut of technic and the
scope of art. The dawn of the Renaissance had found art with
a restricted language. Its noon did not find it with a universal
language, it has not yet acquired that, but with one that could
express a wide range of the emotions of humanity. During these
three centuries three streams had been flowing into art, medieval
life, classical life, and contemporary life. The first one early
began to diminish; the decline of the second began at a later time;
while the third, the love of all that is earthly, an interest in all
that is human, flowed on with ever increasing force. All three
fertilized the soil for the wonderful harvest of the high Renaissance.

# CHAPTER VII

## THE REVIVAL OF SCIENCE

1. Science in the Middle Ages.
2. Thirteenth-Century Scientists.
3. The Relation of the Revival of Science to the Revival of Letters.
4. The Revival of Research.
5. The Revival of Invention.
6. Results of the Revival of Science.

CHAP.
VII

1150-1315

Medieval
Science

THE intellectual strength of the Middle Ages did not lie in scientific knowledge and achievement, but in a vivid quickening of the spiritual imagination. The scientific learning of the time. far from being a well-ordered system of knowledge, was merely a compilation of detached and ill-comprehended fragments. The medieval man had little ability to look things squarely in the face; he had no clear-eyed perception of the visible world. It was not his practice to deal in an objective way with the facts of the actual world about him. All things were veiled with a mist of subjectivity. The things that he saw were treated as symbols, and the things that he heard were understood as allegories. " Supra-sensible things," said Chrysostom, " are ministered to man by sensible things." The speculative life was held to be vastly more important than the practical life. The world was but a house of probation; wherein, then, lay the wisdom of earthly knowledge? So the medieval man devoted himself to the study of philosophy. But his philosophy was defective and misleading. It suffered from the dictation of the Church. It was not a free inquiry into the constitution of the world of nature and the world of men. It was not an unhindered attempt to conceive of the universe as a rational entity. Instead it was merely an effort to put the theology of the time into a logical form, to prove that the teaching of the Church was identical with the universal and self-consistent truths of philosophy. To reinforce the unassailable authority of the medieval Church the scholars of the time invoked the infallible authority of medieval philosophy So medieval philosophy was no more and no less than an endeavor to give a scientific statement of medieval theology. Another thing that acted as an obstacle to the progress of science in the Middle Ages and deprived men still further of the use of their own eyes was a slavish devotion to Aristotle. Not all of Aristotle's works have come down to us, and some of those that we possess have been recovered from the cataclysm of the barbarian invasions only in an imperfect form. They may be divided into four groups, according as they deal with logic, metaphysics and natural science, ethics, and art. Up to the thirteenth century Aristotle was known to Christendom only through some of his logical writings, a part of the *Organon* and the *Categories*. But the Greek philosopher's works can be understood only when studied in their entirety, and the fragments which the medieval scholars possessed are precisely the ones that have most need of the others in order rightly to be apprehended. Two other things added to the misrepresentation of Aristotle. The few books of the philosopher possessed by the medieval scholars had come to western Europe by way of Alexandria where they had been colored with the Neo-Platonic thought, and a number of books not written by Aristotle were ascribed to him. The real Aristotle was almost completely obscured until the thirteenth century. Medieval man knew him only as a logician, and even in that respect they knew him only imperfectly. Thus deceived by the infallible Doctor they wandered still further from the path of scientific thought than they had been sent by their perverted idea of the aim and the scope of philosophy. Logic was the key delivered into their hands by Aristotle, and with it all the doors of knowledge should be opened. By the aid of logic alone should all truth be revealed. It is easy to see how this belief retarded scientific progress. With this magic key in one's hand, what need could there be to interrogate nature? What need of careful and extensive observation? What need of induction? Alas! it was long before the futility of logic apart from observation dawned upon the consciousness of men.

By the middle of the thirteenth century much of the missing work of Aristotle had been restored. The additional thought of the Greek philosopher came into western Europe, in a circuitous way, from the Mohammedan schools in Spain. The acquaintance of the Mohammedans with Greek philosophy dates as far back as the eighth century when they penetrated into Persia. Some of their translations of Aristotle into Arabic, made for the most part in the ninth century by Persians who had embraced the Nestorian form of Christianity, were from the Syriac versions and others from the original Greek. It was an impure form of the Aristotelian philosophy which they obtained, and it was further adulterated by its passage through the schools of Alexandria, that great melting and mixing pot of oriental and occidental thought. Still, with all this, the Mohammedans in Spain had much of Aristotle's philosophy to give that Latin Christendom had not hitherto possessed. It was gladly accepted as pure gold, and the scholar with whom the gift is chiefly associated is Averroes (1126–98) who became acknowledged as the Aristotelian inter- preter *par excellence* and was known as the " Great Commen- tator." With this new guide the Europeans could proceed to something like a systematic and positive study of the world in which they lived. Later on, when the menace of the Turkish invasion grew more threatening, scholars from the Byzantine Empire brought the writings of Aristotle to Italy in the original Greek texts. Then the syllogism was dethroned and investiga- tion set up in its place. This substitution of experiment and observation, however imperfectly it was applied, for the *a priori* methods of scholasticism constituted one of the most potent of all the revivals of the Renaissance. In every stage of culture the physical and the psychical faculties of man are subtly co-ordinated. Bodily activity affects thought, and thought determines action. So the mere dealing with external realities assisted in the mental task of understanding and interpreting them. The days of the solitary thinker, immured within his cell, dealing with signs and symbols, were numbered. Confidence in the value of experience steadily increased, and confidence increased in man's ability to interpret that experience. This confidence in the mind of man was at once the seed and the fruit of the Renaissance. Without it all the vast change in the life of man that is the distinguishing characteristic of that era would have been impossible.

**The Thir- teenth- century Fore-Run- ners of the Revival of Science**

Among the thirteenth-century fore-runners of the revival of science three names stand out above all the others. The first is that of Albertus Magnus (1193–1280), a Dominican friar, who became convinced by the study of Aristotle and by his own inves- tigations that a science of nature was possible. " The visible world," he said, " was made for man's sake in order that man might arrive at the knowledge of God through observation of it." So despite the hindrances of the time he began to search like any modern scientist with the instruments of analysis and synthesis into the secrets of nature. He catalogued the trees and plants known in his time, and he noted the influence of the physical environment upon human, animal and vegetable life. " All that is here set down," he wrote in regard to his work, " is the result of my own experience, or has been borrowed from authors whom we know to have written what their personal experience has con- firmed; for in these matters experience alone can be of certainty."

The second of these intellectual pioneers was Roger Bacon (1214–94), a far-sighted genius, one of the most powerful minds recorded in history, who made many important discoveries, and to whose credit must be placed a number of brilliant anticipatory guesses of modern science. Greater, however, than any of his discoveries, and more important than all of them combined, was the scientific method that he employed. He devoted his life to the reformation of the existing methods of scientific thought. The science of the Middle Ages descended from the highest concept, that of pure being, down to individual things. It set its seal of disapproval upon the method of proceeding from the particular units of a class upwards. In other words it declared the inductive method to be reprobate. For its own part it dealt only with a universe evolved from its own inner consciousness. If it dealt at all with the causal relation of earthly things it did so only in so far as that relation lent itself to the support of the *a priori* theories of the time. " Secular science intoxicates, but not with charity," said Bernard of Clairvaux: " it obstructs, but does not fortify." Quite opposite was the opinion of Bacon. He warned his fellowmen against servile subscription to the tradition of authority, declaring that it confined thought in an ever identical circle. " We must not give our adhesion to everything we hear and all we read," he said; " on the contrary, it is our duty to examine with the most careful scrutiny the opinions of our predecessors in order to add to them what is lacking in them and to correct what is false and erroneous, though with all modesty and discretion. For the truth is ever growing by God's grace. It is true that a man never reaches perfection or an absolute certitude, but he is ever perfecting himself; that is why it is necessary not to follow the ancients blindly, for if they could come to life again they would themselves correct what they have said and would change their mind on many things. In like manner the learned men of to-day are ignorant of things the veriest schoolboy will know some day." To the writer of these words more than to any other one man is the modern world indebted for the perfection of the experimental method which has been so powerful a means of extending its mental horizon. The third of these forerunners of modern science was Raymond Lull (1235–1315), a philosopher half-Mohammedan and half-Christian, theologian and naturalist, missionary and troubadour, the acutest intellect of the Spanish countries in the Middle Ages, whose aim it was to devise a system, an *ars magna,* for the purpose of ascertaining all truth by means of logical analysis. His teachings gradually inter-

**Relation
of the Re-
vival of
Science to
the Revi-
val of Let-
ters**

ested his followers in the observation of reality and in convincing
them of the importance of a systematic study of the world of
nature.

This preliminary revival of science was at once the cause and
the effect of the revival of letters. It received a great impetus,
as we have seen, from the restoration of the writings of Aristotle.
It quickened men's perception of facts, and it helped to renew
the connection between words and things which scholasticism had
done away with. It interested men in observation rather than in
concepts. It taught them to proceed from individual things to
abstraction, from example to application. Naturally they became curious to know more of that ancient world from which
the intervening centuries separated them. So they looked about
them with eagerness for further writings of those far-off Greeks,
and the more they read the more were they impelled to their work
of research and invention. By his reading of Latin authors
Petrarch was helped to obtain a firm grasp upon the fundamental
principles of science. Such was the inter-relation of the revival
of science and the revival of letters. Men read the ancient
authors, learned to see with their eyes and to imitate their observations and experiments. Then by their own work in observation,
testing and correcting they arrived at independent and additional scientific achievements. Thus did they take up the threads
of scientific investigation where long ago they had fallen from
the hands of the ancients. In medicine they went back to Hippocrates and Galen, in botany to Theophrastus, Dioscorides and
Pliny, in zoölogy to Aristotle, in mathematics to Euclid, Era-
tosthenes and Hipparchus, in physics to Archimedes, Vitruvius
and Heron, in astronomy to the Pythagoreans, in jurisprudence
to the *Corpus Juris,* and in politics to Plato as well as to Aristotle. All the great scientific investigators of the eras of the
Renaissance and the Protestant Revolution lit their torches on
the altar of the ancients. Each of the various revivals of the
time contributed to the success of the others, for each, in addition to its own definite contributions to knowledge, aided in the
production of an atmosphere that was favorable to the new
thought. So was the narrow horizon of men pushed back; so
was self-confidence restored to the reason of humanity.

**The Revi-
val of Re-
search in
Philosophy
and His-
tory**

The revival of research was witnessed in many lines of human
activity. In philosophy the thought of Plato, Aristotle, Socrates
and other Greek philosophers and the works of Latin philosophers were recovered. As a result the ancient systems were extended and a new philosophy, of which we are to see something
in our last chapter, was born. In the field of history we begin

distinctly to discern the spirit of scientific criticism in the writings of Petrarch, and it is found as the controlling force in the work of Lorenzo Valla. Indeed, Valla, who was one of the greatest historians of the entire era, has been described by some writers as the founder of historical criticism. He proved the *Donation of Constantine* to be a forgery. With keen insight he made a critical examination of the writings of Livy, Aristotle, and the Areopagite; he described Moses and the authors of the four gospels as being simply historians; he denied that the apostles were the authors of the so-called Apostles' Creed; in his *Notes on the New Testament* he pointed out the corrupt state of the Vulgate in comparison with the earlier Greek texts; and he began an examination of the scriptural writings for the purpose of formulating the standards of textual criticism. It is difficult to realize how much elementary work had to be done by the critical writers of the early Renaissance. For one thing, the correct spelling of Latin had to be determined again, and the use of the diphthongs, a troublesome question, decided. Many scholars were engaged in such work. It was their endeavor to settle disputed points by appealing to the evidence of old manuscripts, coins, and inscriptions, by scientific investigation and comparison. But in Valla, to whom the modern world is so greatly indebted, we see, more clearly than in any one else, that the writers of the time were by no means given over to a mere blind admiration of the ancients but that on the contrary the principles of criticism which they suggested were soon turned against the classical writers themselves.

The medieval universities recognized mathematics as a standard study, but the subject appears to have been kept in a very subordinate position by the favorite studies of logic, philosophy, and theology. The knowledge of the Arabic notation had become general throughout Europe, but it was not the custom to reckon numbers with pen or pencil. Instead, counters, with which comparatively complex calculations could be made, were employed. The only books on arithmetic that had been left by the ancients were those of Euclid, and they were neglected in the Middle Ages. So arithmetic was regarded merely as an aid in carrying on the affairs of daily life and not at all as a deductive science. Only such rare geniuses as Leonardo of Pisa, Jordanus of Saxony, and Roger Bacon, in the beginning of the thirteenth century, rose to a higher level; but, because they were too far in advance of their time they did not exercise a widespread influence upon their contemporaries. Still from this time onward a slow evolution of arithmetic may be perceived. Geometry was in much the same condition. All through the medieval centuries only the propositions of Euclid were given; the proofs, by a singular error, being suppressed. Theoretical geometry, then, had in reality no existence. Practical geometry, however, was used with great skill by the architects of the time, and it was also employed by the surveyors. Before the opening of the thirteenth century Mohammedan mathematics had begun to penetrate into western Europe. Part of the mathematical knowledge of the Moslems was derived from the Greeks and part from Hindoo sources. With this aid they had acquired an excellent command of arithmetic, algebra, geometry and trigonometry, though it cannot be said that they extended the bounds of mathematical science. It was principally from Spain that their mathematics, like their philosophy, filtered into western Europe. But Greek mathematics, like Greek philosophy, was brought direct to Italy later on when Byzantine scholars began to flock to the peninsula to escape the on-coming Turk; and by the middle of the fifteenth century the principal results of the ancient Greek studies were accessible to western students. Then the discovery of printing made the dissemination of the gathered and combined knowledge a comparatively easy matter. The next century and a half witnessed notable developments in syncopated algebra and trigonometry and symbolic algebra, and it saw the beginning of the science of dynamics. Among the most important mathematicians of these years were Cardinal Nicholas of Cusa (1401–64), who opened up new paths in mathematics and physics, and who in astronomy prepared the way for the great discoveries; Regiomontanus (1436–76), the greatest mathematician of his time; Leonardo da Vinci (1452–1519), whose suggestions in mathematics were of greater value than his accomplishments; Niccolo Tartaglia (1500–57), who contributed more than any other scholar of his generation to the development of algebra; Girolamo Cardan (1501–76), a gambler and perhaps a murderer, whose genius was allied to madness, but who, in his *Ars Magna*, gave to the world the best text-book on algebra that had thus far been published; and Franciscus Vieta (1540–1603), who wrote the first book on symbolical algebra.

With the development of mathematics that had taken place during the fourteenth and fifteenth centuries it was possible to

proceed to new discoveries in astronomy. And astronomy was helped by the pursuit of astrology. It was necessary for the astrologers to determine the position of the heavenly bodies as they were at the hour of the birth of the person whose career was to be foretold. In order to do this correctly it was necessary to employ the same scientific calculation that is required in astronomy. The practice of astrology was carried on in both Greek and Latin Christendom all through the Middle Ages and it resulted in an increase of astronomical knowledge and a development of astronomical processes. To this were added the achievements of the Mohammedans. Then, about the middle of the thirteenth century, an Englishman, John of Holywood, better known as Sacrobosco, summed up his *Treatise on the Sphere* all the geometrical knowledge necessary for the study of astronomy. Yet despite the fact that the western Europeans were now equipped with far better apparatus for the development of astronomy than any previous people had been a pause of fully a century occurred in the progress of the science. Then two Germans, George of Peuerbach (1423-61), and Regiomontanus, owing not a little to the inspiration of Nicholas of Cusa, inaugurated another period of development. The prevailing astronomical theory, laid down fourteen hundred years before by Ptolemy, averred that the earth is stationary and that the apparent movements of the planets and the sun and the stars around it are actual movements. Six centuries before the opening of the Christian era Pythagoras had dimly suggested that the earth and the planets might rotate about a central sun; and three hundred years later Aristarchus had advanced the same theory with greater precision. In the fifth century of our own era it made a furtive appearance in the writings of Martianus Capella. Then it remained concealed for a thousand years until, inaccurate and incomplete, it came to light again in the writings of Nicholas of Cusa. Almost a century later Nicholas Copernicus (1473-1543), the first great founder of modern astronomy, a simple scholar who lived in Poland far out on the frontier of civilization, gave to the world a distinct statement of the theory that the earth turns upon its own axis and also, together with the planets, revolves around the sun. Each of the previous statements of the theory had been a simple hypothesis given with more or less plausibility. The claim of Copernicus to be the real discoverer of the theory that bears his name rests upon the fact that he was not content to advance it as a mere statement but that he supported it with a strict train of reasoning. The new theory displaced the earth from its central position in the universe, and contradicted many statements in the scriptural writings. The patient scholar well knew that the result of his long and lonely researches would arouse a storm of opposition, so he delayed the publication of his discoveries until he was an old man. When he lay paralyzed upon his death-bed he intrusted the publication of his great work, *De revolutionibus orbium coelestium,* to Rheticus, one of his pupils. Rheticus rashly intrusted the final care of the printing to Andreas Osiander, a Protestant theologian of Nuremberg, who slipped in an anonymous preface in which he stated that it was not the intention of Copernicus to state the theory as a fact but merely to suggest it as a hypothesis. The deception succeeded. Only seventy years later, when the theory was boldly announced as a fact by Galileo and supported by the revelations of his telescope, did the papal authorities proceed against it. Galileo (1564–1642) was an Italian scientist whose chief work was that of a pioneer in mechanics and especially in dynamics. He was also an astronomer, and in 1609, virtually inventing the instrument, he constructed a telescope that had the power of magnifying thirty-two times. With the discoveries he made, which included the satellites of Jupiter, he confirmed the theory of Copernicus. Alarmed for the credit of the Bible, whose statements relating to matters of science were universally accepted, the Inquisition declared the system he upheld to be false and threatened the scientist with the rack; and the Congregation of the Index forbade the reading of any book that advocated it. The " starry Galileo " may be regarded as one of the chief workers in the revival of science because he did much to remove the obstacle of medieval Aristotelianism from the path of progress. In his own day Aristotle was a fearless investigator who strove to inform himself of the facts of the subjects which he studied and to base all his conclusions and principles upon the ascertained facts. In the field of politics there was an abundant supply of facts at his disposal, his procedure was scientific, and so his conclusions are of great value even to-day. But in the field of natural science the supply of facts was far from being ample, and observation, as we practise it, was unknown to him. He was unable to distinguish between fact and fable. When, therefore, his writings that deal with natural science were regarded as a bible by the men of the Middle Ages, when it was believed that all information regarding the world of nature was to be found in them, they became a bar to progress. It was Galileo's great work to point men away from this cast-iron Aristotelianism to the world of nature itself. This revolt against the authority of the past paved the way for the expanding science of the future.

One cannot say that anything like a science of physics existed in the Middle Ages. Some facts were retained from the days of Greece and Rome and others were restored by the Mohammedans. But, at the best, the laws and the facts of nature that were known to the ancients were comparatively few. Simple instruments for the measurement of time, such as water-clocks and sun-dials, the Greeks had. They knew the law of the reflection of light, the law of the lever, and certain of the laws of sound and hydrostatics. The Romans seem not to have made any advance upon the knowledge of the Greeks in physics; and the interest of the Mohammedans was confined very largely to optics. Medieval Christianity had checked the development of the physical sciences for more than fifteen hundred years. It had produced a soil in which it was impossible for the seeds of science to grow. Instead of questioning nature for her facts in order to discover the laws which those facts reveal it was the practice to summon nature solely for the purpose of supporting theology. And instead of going directly to nature men went to Aristotle. Science, then, if such it may be called, was studied in the library and not in the laboratory. The principal physical problem discussed in the Middle Ages was that of matter, of the constitution of natural bodies. The discussion was carried down into the Renaissance period by such thinkers as Albertus Magnus, Roger Bacon and Nicholas of Cusa, but for the most part it was purely academic. The real contributions to physics consisted of work like that of Galileo, to whom we are practically indebted for the establishment of the science of dynamics. By observing the oscillations of a swinging lamp in the cathedral of Pisa he discovered the isochronism of the pendulum; and, in opposition to the teaching of Aristotle, he demonstrated that the rate of descent of falling bodies is not proportional to their weight. He also made discoveries in the laws of projectiles, and did much to anticipate the laws of motion as eventually demonstrated by Newton.

Chemistry was born of alchemy, the pseudo-science that sought to transform base metals into gold and silver and to prolong human life indefinitely. It was but a scanty knowledge of chemistry that the Middle Ages inherited from antiquity. And because of the fact that throughout the period chemistry, like every other branch of science, was dominated by traditional belief, very little was added to the store until the time of Roger Bacon. That alert and indefatigable investigator discovered many chemicals and, what was still more important, many chemical laws. But, while doubting whether transmutation had ever been achieved, he believed in its possibility. Gradually, however, men began to neglect the formulas couched in meaningless gibberish and the magician's wand of the " black art," and then alchemy began to change into iatro-chemistry. The first great scholar who taught that the aim of chemistry is not the production of the philosopher's stone was Paracelsus (1493–1541), a Swiss savant of rare originality, who definitely connected chemistry with pharmacy. The mutual inter-action of chemistry and medicine, resulting in the enrichment of each of them, is the principal characteristic of the science throughout the period in its development that ended with the middle of the seventeenth century.

The same fundamental defect that had hindered the progress of the exact and the physical sciences in the Middle Ages, the dependence upon the traditions of antiquity and the consequent failure to observe phenomena carefully and systematically, operated to prevent the development of the natural sciences. But gradually the fabulous lore of the medieval "Bestiaries" was supplanted by the knowledge that the stimulated curiosity of men had brought to light. With the dawn of the Renaissance men awoke to a realization of the beauty of the world in which they lived. This drew people to nature. They began to study not only her physical laws but also her forms and her works in plant and animal life. The zoölogical works of Aristotle were restored and his method of observation was noted. Physicians especially devoted themselves to these new studies. Chief of them was Conrad Gesner (1516–65), a distinguished scholar who issued editions of Greek authors and wrote an important *History of Animals*. Interest in animals became widespread. Menageries were kept by nobles and rich burghers, and the breeding of horses for the perpetuation and increase of desired characteristics was undertaken in a systematic manner. Hand in hand with the new interest in animals went a new interest in plants. Botanical gardens as well as menageries were kept by rulers and wealthy men, one being founded at Padua in 1525 and another at Pisa in 1544. The works of Albertus Magnus contain remarks on the organic structure and physiology of plants that could have been obtained only by a careful examination. Gesner did considerable work in botany. He was the first to devise a methodical system of classification based on the fructifying organs. Among other botanists of the sixteenth century were Jerome Bock (1498–1554), whose *Neu Kraeuterbuch* was so popular that it ran through ten successive editions; Lionel Fuchs (1501–66), who with keen observation described some four hundred plants; and Valerius Cordus (1515–44), whose botanical explorations were carried on in many parts of Europe. These old herbalists were interested in plants chiefly for their medicinal virtues, but their discoveries led to a more purely scientific interest. A beginning was also made in the science of mineralogy. Chemistry deals with the constitutents of a body and with its properties. There was needed a science to deal with the external characteristics of things. It was this office that was undertaken by mineralogy. The father of the new science was George Agricola (1494?–1555), who in 1530 issued the treatise *De re metallica*.

The ancients had possessed only a slight knowledge of anatomy. They held the dead body as being especially sacred, and so the cadaver was examined but rarely. The Greeks made some progress in the science of anatomy; and at the Alexandrian school dissection was publicly practised for the first time. Then the darkness of the medieval centuries intervened and it was not until Mohammedan knowledge and skill penetrated into western Europe, through Spain but principally through the school at Salerno, that there came a revival of the science. At the medical school of Montpellier the cadavers of criminals were regularly dissected; in 1308 the senate of Venice provided that each year a human body should be examined; early in the same century Mundinus, at the University of Bologna, publicly dissected several bodies; and dissection was practised at Prague from the very foundation of the University in 1348. But nowhere was there made a careful and systematic study of the structure of the body. All that was done was to open the great cavities and then examine the viscera in a superficial manner. Great reliance was placed upon the Greek authorities, Galen and Hippocrates, and upon the Mohammedan commentators. First of modern men to insist that the structure of man should be learned from a systematic examination of the human body instead of by depending upon authority was Andreas Vesalius (1514–64), of Brussels. In 1543, in his *De humani corporis fabrica*, he gave to the world the first careful description of the body based upon actual observation. Many errors of the old authorities were corrected, and students were continually urged to test every statement by going to the ultimate source of information, the body itself. By thus substituting the method of interrogating nature for the medieval dependence upon authority he founded, in a time when the path of scientific progress was beset with every form of superstition and hampered with crass credulity, the modern science of anatomy. He proved the fallacy of the belief in the one "incorruptible, incombustible bone, the necessary nucleus of the resurrection of the body." With this work and that of his students and followers there gradually disappeared the old superstitions about the body; and dissection came to be regarded as a necessary and desirable means of obtaining knowledge of the structure of the body and its functions. Other investigators who contributed to the development of anatomy were Michael Servetus (1509–1555), who discovered the lesser circulation of the blood between the heart and the lungs; Eustachio (1520?–74), a papal physician, who described the Eustachian tube and the Eustachian valve, who is the first histologist of whom we have any record, and who shares with Vesalius the honor of founding the science of anatomy; Fallopio (1523?–62), who taught anatomy at Ferrara, Pisa, and Padua, and whose name was given to the tube he discovered; Fabrizio (1537–1619), who discovered and described the valvular folds in all the veins of the extremities; and William Harvey (1578–1657), who demonstrated the general circulation of the blood.

The knowledge of the medical practice of the Greeks had become lost to a large extent in the period of the barbarian invasions. All through the Middle Ages medicine was nearly as dogmatic as theology. What need of chemical preparations when relics were at hand? Here and there, however, in defiance of the edicts of the Church and in the face of the superstition of the time, was to be found a layman or an ecclesiastic who based his practice upon study rather than upon tradition. Then the Mohammedan physicians, whose knowledge had come down to them from the Greeks, and who were held in high repute, exerted a great influence. From Spain and from Salerno they introduced new preparations into the European *materia medica* and made known the first elements of pharmaceutical chemistry. So at the end of the Middle Ages some of the European physicians made valuable observations, studied cases and wrote histories of them, and taught at the bed-side. Among the things they accomplished were the segregation of erysipelas and the prevention of its spread, and the partial control of the spread of leprosy. The revival of learning enabled them to study medicine from Hippocrates and Galen. Thus gradually, along with the increase in knowledge of the organs of the body and their functions, there was developed the science of medicine. The diseases of the different organs were studied and remedies based upon experiments, and to which chemistry contributed, were prescribed. Surgery, which is differentiated from medicine by its treatment of disease conditions with mechanical methods rather than by the administration of medicines, underwent a like development. Operations were performed on various parts of the body, wine was used as an antiseptic, and two or three forms of anæsthetic were employed.

So did there come about a gradual revival of research. Very early the Middle Ages disprized the method of observation and induction. "It is not ignorance that makes us think lightly of science in general," said Eusebius, the most learned man of the day, about the opening of the fourth century, "but contempt for useless labor, while we turn our souls to better things." What need was there to keep trimmed and replenished the lantern of science when in the heavens there shone the sun of theology? The revival of research was one of the most important phases of the Renaissance and one of the greatest services ever conferred upon mankind. In all its different fields it was essentially the same. Of course it varied somewhat in its superficial aspects of the differing conditions necessitated by the differing subject-matter of the several fields; but in every line of investigation the fundamental process of observation, experimentation, and induction, and the guiding spirit, were essentially the same. Like any other revival of the era, and like all progress that we witness to-day, the revival of research was a normal sequence of the revival of individuality.

Side by side with the revival of research went a renewal of invention, the first notable instance of which contributed to the development of navigation, to the ability of men to direct the course of vessels and to ascertain their positions. First in point of importance was the invention of the compass. Instances have been cited of the use in China of a needle rubbed with a lodestone to give it the power of polar direction as far back as the second century of the Christian era; but the first mention of it in Europe has been traced to Alexander of Neckham, about 1190, and to Guyot de Provins, about 1200. It seems to have been in general use in Europe at that time, for both of these writers speak of the "ugly black stone" not as the guarded secret of a few scholars, but as a common possession of seamen. So it was probably employed by the Genoese explorers when, in the last quarter of the thirteenth century, they made their first explorations in the Atlantic. The magnetic needle was made more useful by connecting it with a compass-card. Thus mariners were provided with an efficient portable guide, and, as far as simple steering was concerned, they were rendered independent of the heavenly bodies and emancipated from the coasts. This made possible a momentous revolution in geographical knowledge. As early as the eleventh century the astrolabe, an instrument invented by the Greeks and used chiefly to ascertain the time of day, was borrowed from the Mohammedans. It enabled seamen approximately to determine positions. Regiomontanus improved it, but since then it has been superseded by more perfect instruments. The quadrant, an ancient instrument for measuring alti-.

tudes, indispensable in astronomy, surveying and gunnery, was improved; and a similar instrument, the sextant, useful to navigators because it enables them to measure angles between distant objects, was invented. Then with the aid of these and other instruments the science of navigation was gradually developed and a great impetus was given to exploration and commerce. By the end of the thirteenth century the use of the compass, the beginning of scientific surveying, and the ascertaining of positions by astronomical calculation had produced a marked advance in the mapping of coast lines. Reliable maps were an indispensable aid to seafarers, and so the improvement in cartography is an important feature in the prosecution of exploration and the expansion of commerce as well as in the perfecting of the science of navigation. The scientific charting of coasts may be said to begin with the " handy-maps," the *portolani,* of the Mediterranean, the earliest specimen of which that has come down to us is the *Carte Pisane* that dates back to the opening of the fourteenth century. As a result of these inventions mariners came to have a working knowledge of oceanic conditions and the science of navigation witnessed a continued development.

Invention produced an equally great revolution in the art of war. Gunpowder may have been known to Bartholdus Schwartz, for it was mentioned in 1220 in his writings. Forty-seven years later Roger Bacon, who perhaps had learned of its use in Spain, described it after a careful examination of several forms. He was certain that men would eventually learn to control it and that then many things could be accomplished that previously had been impossible. The means of controlling explosions was provided by the invention of cannon. At first mortars and cannon were made of brass and threw stone projectiles. After a while they were put on wheels and iron projectiles were employed. By the end of the fourteenth century they were used extensively over Europe. In 1375 the gun that is fired by powder began to displace the crossbow and the longbow, which for several centuries had been the chief weapons of infantry. The first guns were very cumbersome, but gradually they were made somewhat lighter. The method of igniting the powder remained very crude for a long time, and as a consequence the bow and arrow still figured in war in Cromwell's time. As a sequence of these inventions both tactics, the handling of military forces, and strategy, the directing of the larger movements of a war, were changed and developed. They came to be something of a science as well as an art; systematic observations of the clash of armies were made and books were written upon military manœuvers.

Invention also came to the aid of book-making. Before the opening of the tenth century the use of papyrus, the writing material made from the reed of that name grown in the delta of the Nile, was generally abandoned, and, although instances of its later use may be found, parchment came to be the material commonly employed. But the cost of parchment was a serious problem which even the use of palimpsests failed to solve. So when a new, cheap, and suitable writing material made its appearance it was seized upon with avidity. Paper was invented at a remote time in eastern Asia. Its manufacture became known to the Mohammedan world after the capture of Samarkand in 704, where the conquerors became familiar with its merits. By the middle of the thirteenth century it was used to a considerable extent in the Byzantine empire; and it was first manufactured in western Europe by the Mohammedans in Spain and in Sicily. Cotton was the raw material used in the Mediterranean countries, but when the industry crept northward woolen rags were employed and then, in the first years of the fourteenth century, linen. The making of books in the *scriptoria* of the medieval monasteries was a slow and laborious process. Every volume had to be transcribed anew. The cost, therefore, was very high; and there were many more opportunities for mistakes to occur than there are in the making of a book to-day. These disadvantages were not overcome when the universities became great book-making establishments. Books were still so costly, being five times as expensive as they were after the invention of printing, that in public places they were secured with chains. Between the writing of books and the printing of them with movable type there was an intervening process. Books were printed from engraved blocks. An entire page was engraved on a single block. Most of these blocks were devoted to pictures with a few explanatory words; but here and there an entire page of text was engraved on a block. At first all the blocks were of hard wood, but later on copper ones were used. These block-books, that were printed only on one side of the page, seem to have had their origin in the Netherlands; and perhaps Laurence Koster (1370?-1440) of Haarlem, who has been credited by some writers with the invention of movable type, was an engraver of these printing blocks. The invention of printing with movable type was a gradual process. It resulted from a long series of experiments carried on by various craftsmen in different places. The principal merits of Johannes

Gutenberg (1400?–68?) of Mainz, who in 1450 produced a practical printing-press, seem to have been his ability to produce a complete book with the new process, to teach others to do so, and to improve the mechanism of the press so as to make possible the printing of larger sheets. Gutenberg, then, was not the first printer, for books were printed from engraved blocks before his time. Nor was he the first printer of books from movable type, for the Chinese employed separate type four centuries before his printing press was set up in Mainz. But he was the first European to make practical the process of printing with adjustable type. The first book that was issued from his new press was a Latin version of the Bible that was printed somewhere between 1454 and 1456, a copy of which in the year 1911 was sold for fifty thousand dollars, by far the highest price ever commanded by a single book. The city of Mainz in which the modern art of printing was inaugurated was not a university town, but was the most important commercial center of the middle Rhine district; and from the beginning the new art was in the hands not of scholars but of craftsmen. So in Germany the choice of the books to be printed was determined very largely by the interests of the reading public. The reverse was true in France where the first printers were connected with the University of Paris. The new art quickly spread to other places. In 1462 Mainz was captured and plundered by the soldiers of Archbishop Adolph of Nassau, and the printers fled to other towns. Strasburg, Cologne, Zürich, Augsburg, Ulm, Nuremberg, Leipzig, Frankfort, and especially Basel, where the larger works of Erasmus were printed by Froben, all became centers of the new industry. In 1464 German printers set up the first Italian printing-press in the Benedictine monastery of Subiaco; and six years later German craftsmen began the work of printing in Paris. The introduction of printing into England was due more than to any one else to William Caxton whose long residence in Bruges had made him acquainted with the production of books on the continent, and who from his press at Westminster issued ninety-eight works, principally romances translated by himself from the French. Nearly all the great publishers, such as Aldus of Venice, Froben of Basel, Estienne of Paris, and Caxton of London, as well as many of the less important ones, carried on their work not merely with a view to pecuniary gain but from a real love of truth and learning. All of them made sacrifices for the perfecting of their art and the production and distribution of the books they loved.

The application of research resulted in inventions in still

other fields — in optics and in the measurement of time. Mirrors of polished bronze were in common use among the Egyptians, Greeks and Romans. The Greeks had also mirrors of polished silver, and the Romans of polished obsidian. Mirrors of artificial glass, marking a great improvement upon their predecessors, were first made in Venice about the opening of the fourteenth century, and in the next century their manufacture became a regular industry. Roger Bacon discovered many of the properties of concave and convex lenses. At first they were made of gum or crystalline stones, but in the early seventeenth century they were made of artificial glass. Their power to magnify minute and distant objects was of incalculable aid in the revival of science. Roger Bacon has also been credited with the invention of spectacles, with having evolved the idea of using concave glasses for far-sighted eyes and convex for near-sighted ones; but some writers attribute the invention to Alessandro di Spina, a Florentine monk. Bacon invented the telescope, but it did not come into practical use until the opening of the seventeenth century when it was used by Galileo. After that it was employed in many lines, in navigation, surveying and astronomy. Roger Bacon and others used simple microscopes; but the first to construct a compound microscope, which allows a far closer and more careful focus, was Zacharias Janssen, a spectacle-maker of Middleburg, in Holland. Among the precursors of the modern clock were the sun-dial, the water-clock, and the hour-glass. The invention of the true clock is an uncertain matter. Perhaps the first of which we have record is the one sent by the Sultan of Egypt to Frederick II in 1232. A great clock was made in 1326 for St. Albans, a town near London. In 1379 a clock was set up for Charles V of France. The law of the pendulum, which was discovered by Galileo, was probably applied to clocks about the middle of the seventeenth century. The invention early in the sixteenth century of a spiral spring to take the place of a weight to drive the wheel-train produced a portable time-piece; and although these first watches were heavy, large, and cumbersome in comparison with those of to-day they were useful for ascertaining the difference of longitude between two places and for many other purposes.

The revival of the spirit and the process of research and the application of the knowledge thus obtained and the method of experimentation to the daily affairs of life had the most momentous results to society. It was at once the result and the cause of that irrepressible curiosity that forever inquires into the constitution of the universe, seeking to learn its laws and

The So-
cial Re-
sults of
the Re-
vival of
Science

to acquire control of its forces. The scientific method is a stiff and formal process; and it is fitted to deal only with number and with measurement, which implies number. It is powerless to demonstrate any proposition in which the emotions are directly concerned. We are coming to see that all that science can do is to afford us an orderly way of looking at things, a convenient way of arranging phenomena, and that it is incapable of giving us knowledge or truth in the philosophical signification of the words. Too long have we set up scientific truth as the type of all truth. Too long have we ignored the imagination as a means of ascertaining truth. In our concern to be rid of a dictatorial theological orthodoxy we have allowed an almost equally dictatorial and intolerant scientific orthodoxy to take its place. But nevertheless the recovery and development of the scientific method has been one of the most potent of all the forces making for the emancipation of man. And just as the spirit and method of research are greater than any of their concrete results, so, too, the spirit of invention and machinery that was restored to man and developed in the era of the Renaissance is of greater value than any of the actual inventions. The sense of machinery, like the exclusive claims of science, has its danger. It has caused us to lose something of the sense of personality. In our age of machinery we are all too prone to regard a man exclusively engaged in, say, making pin-points as a machine and not as a human being. But most undoubtedly the sense of machinery, the inclination to invention, has performed a service past all calculation in helping mankind along the road of progress. And the immediate results of the concrete inventions can by no means be neglected. They made possible an age of exploration and a vast expansion and change of commerce. They leveled the walls of castles and rendered of little avail the baronial keeps that hitherto had been impregnable. They put power into the hands of the middle classes by providing them with artillery and thus abolished feudalism; and they gave to civilized peoples a greater power over savage and barbaric races. By making literature cheaper and more accessible they scattered everywhere the seeds of the new thought. "I do not think I am far out," said Lorenzo de' Medici, "when I say that a century hence the peasant will be able to purchase the volumes that are now within the resources only of the prince. As waters cover the sea, so I believe will literature cover Europe from end to end." They created public opinion and thus introduced a new and potent factor into all the affairs of life. So it was that the revival of science revealed

the invalidity of the old method of thought and provided one in
its place which, though far from being sufficient in itself to give
to men knowledge of the truth of things, was yet an incalculable
advance upon the one it displaced.

# CHAPTER VIII

## THE REVIVAL OF CONSCIENCE

1. Conscience in the Middle Ages.
2. The Critics.
3. The Ecclesiastical Reformers.
4. The Biblical Reformers.
5. The Mystical Reformers.

**CHAP.
VIII**

**33-63**

THE revival of conscience was the last of all the revivals to
bloom. Conscience and religion, with which it is inseparably associated, are always the last things to be changed in an
age of new birth, for only as new generations, nourished upon
new thought, come into power can they be altered. They take
hold of what is most sacred and permanent in human life. They
are the most vital of all the concerns of man. The questions of
conscience and religion are practically one and the same. They
determine the conduct of life, and so they are of permanent and
fundamental importance to history.

**Definition
of "Con-
science"**

The word " conscience," derived from the Latin *con-scientia,*
means a combined knowledge, a knowledge of some matter obtained by the consensus of one's faculties. In popular usage it
means the power, or the faculty, with which one, when confronted by two alternatives, decides between right and wrong.

**Why the
Individual
Conscience
Was Re-
placed by
Implicit
Faith**

In the first generation that followed the death of its founder,
Christianity had for its basis the simple and fundamental ethical
precepts of the Sermon on the Mount. It was possible for every
one, under that condition, even for the unlettered Syrian peasants who formed the first Christian community, to decide for
himself all questions of right and wrong and thus to direct himself in the new way of life. And that, a new and a better daily
life, was all that Christianity was in those early years. But
as the years went on, as Christianity gradually won its way into
the sophisticated and subtle civilization of the Greeks, the emphasis of the new teaching was changed from conduct to creed.
It was the Greek world with its great cities, not the simple countryside of Galilee, that gave to the dominant Christianity of the
subsequent centuries the body of doctrine upon which it has
placed its chief emphasis. That doctrine, which by gradual

accretion grew to be of great proportion, soon came to be beyond the knowledge of the laity, and in many points it became so subtle that it proved to be beyond their understanding. An authoritative external custodianship and interpretation were, therefore, felt to be necessary. Thereafter the individual was no longer free to determine for himself what things are necessary for salvation, nor was he free to interpret according to his own reason the creeds that were declared by the Church to be essential. So, from the age of Constantine, when the first great council of the Church performed its task of deciding what creeds were to be deemed essential and how they were to be formulated, and when for the first time the arm of the State enforced the decisions of the Church, to the age of Abelard, when a great effort was made to enfranchise the human mind, the individual conscience suffered a strange eclipse. In those intervening centuries even the very word " conscience," in the sense now current, virtually disappeared from the life of men. The individual conscience was replaced by implicit faith in the external authority of the Church. The notion that within one's self is to be found a trustworthy criterion of truth, of right, of goodness, was discredited and forgotten. It came to be held that the highest duty of man is to accept blindly the guidance of the Church; that, as the heavens are above the earth, so the thoughts of God are higher than those of men and need not, indeed, seem reasonable to man in order to be authoritative and true.

The doctrine of implicit faith is as old, at least, as Gregory of Nazianzus (325?–90?), who admonished those desiring baptism to accept implicitly the orthodox Christian dogmas of that time and to trust to him for their defense. An imperial edict of 380, which made it a civic duty upon the part of all the inhabitants of the Empire to acknowledge the orthodox doctrine of the Trinity, whether or no they could understand it, lent the sanction of the State to this doctrine of implicit faith. The doctrine grew apace. Augustine (354–430) boldly declared that he believed in many articles only upon the authority of the Church, that, indeed, it was only upon the authority of the Church that he believed the Gospel itself. Thus the Church acquired an immense importance. She was present in every act of faith. Faith sank from the level of reason to that of mere obedience. Every difficult dogma was relegated to the background as far as the individual conscience was concerned. Inner conviction gave way to external authority. It is true that Augustine's doctrine of faith is among the most obscure of his dicta, but in his *De Utilitate Credendi*, one of the most carefully written of all this ardent writer's works, the statement *Quod intelligimus igitur, debemus rationi, quod credimus auctoritati, quod opinamur errori* distinctly excludes any individual experience of faith. Strong support for the doctrine of implicit faith was given by the utterances of Pseudo-Dionysius the Areopagite, who probably flourished in either the fourth or the fifth century and whose writings exercised an enormous influence upon medieval thought. Gregory the Great (540?-604) lent the pontifical sanction to the doctrine. Anselm (1033-1109), one of the great teachers of the Church, declared the dogmas of the Church to be identical with divine revelation. His maxim *credo, ut intelligam, non quæro intelligere, ut credam* signifies the complete subordination of the reason, of the individual conscience, to external authority. It requires faith, and nothing but faith, whether rational grounds can be adduced for that faith or not.

The first notable opposition to the doctrine of implicit faith was made by the eminently critical mind of Peter Abelard (1079-1142), who, in his *Introductio ad Theologiam,* contended that the Christian should be ready to give an account of the hope and the faith that are in him. He required that not only should the mere wording of the articles of faith be grasped, but that there should also be a certain knowledge, even though it be only of an approximate character, of the grounds of the dogmas to be believed. Faith may be above the reason, he admitted, but it should never be contrary to reason. Only so is it possible to accept faith, for that which is contrary to reason cannot proceed from God. He did not discard authority. Reason and authority, in his thought, mutually supplement each other. But realizing that implicit faith, unintelligent and mechanical faith, that makes no effort to understand and then to test its accepted dogmas, imperils the freedom of inquiry and the pursuit of knowledge, he was its sworn foe. Abelard, in the first half of the twelfth century, stood alone in his advocacy of the desirability and the necessity of the exercise of the individual conscience. For a long time his voice was that of one crying in the wilderness. Yet it was not possible that his thought regarding the function and the reliability of the conscience, of the legitimacy of the exercise of the reason, in matters of daily conduct and religious belief should fail to affect his contemporaries. The sharp discussions, so deeply colored with bitterness, even with malice, that were provoked by his teachings and writings were followed by modified forms of the doctrine of implicit faith.

Hugo of St. Victor (1096-1141) said that faith may proceed from knowledge or from *affectus,* a desire to believe. The latter kind he declared to be the more praiseworthy. But he admitted that a certain amount of knowledge must always be bound up with faith, otherwise faith would lack any directive power. Even Bernard of Clairvaux (1091-1153), the greatest exponent of the ideal of medieval monasticism in the period of its highest development and chief of the many foes of Abelard and his rationalism, admitted the desirability of an infusion of knowledge into faith. By the time of William of Auxerre (?-1215) distinct progress had been made in the revival of the individual conscience. It is sufficient for the simple laymen, William contended, if they believe certain articles explicitly, upon the basis of reason, and others implicitly, upon the word of their pastors; but the pastors themselves are obliged to believe all articles explicitly, for they are bound to give an account of the faith that is in them.

But the advocates of implicit faith abated nothing of their claims; indeed, Innocent III (1161-1216) greatly extended its scope and exalted its value. According to him, should man implicitly believe an erroneous doctrine he is not guilty of heresy, but, on the contrary, wins and retains merit merely because he believes that the Church believes as he does. William of Auvergne (?-1249), bishop of Paris, insisted that there are certain articles of faith which all men must believe. The learned must, by special acts of faith, believe each single article by itself to be true; whereas the simple layman must believe them collectively for the sole reason that the learned hold them to be true. Innocent IV (1243-54) held that the only articles necessary for the unlettered laity, if not for all the laity, to believe explicitly are the existence of God and the rewarding of men according to their works. All other articles of faith, he declared, may be believed implicitly. The lower clergy, he added, because of their lack of opportunity for study, need believe no more articles explicitly than it is necessary for the simple laity so to believe. The scholastic theologians of the thirteenth century lent their ingenious logic to the discussion of the doctrine of implicit faith. Albertus Magnus (1193-1280) insisted upon its necessity, for otherwise, he declared, men would not be bound to believe what they can in no wise understand. If I am uncertain whether a new doctrine of the faith that is laid before me is true, he said, I go to the man who knows, the priest, and I believe or do not believe in accordance with his judgment. Finally Thomas Aquinas (1228?-74), the Universal Doctor, the very incarnation of Scholasticism, whose influence upon the theology of the Church has been rivaled only by that of Augustine, gave the

Resistance
of the
Advo-
cates of
Implicit
Faith

support of his great name to the doctrine of implicit faith. He divided science into two sections. The first section consists of all the mundane sciences; the second is made up of the revealed Christian science. Man arrives at the truth contained in the former by means of his understanding; but the truth of the latter is beyond the grasp of the understanding and is made known to man only by divine revelation. The revelation contained in the Scriptures is often difficult to discern; long study and much practice are required to disentangle it from its context. Many have neither the time nor the ability to do this. Implicit faith upon the part of many, therefore, is necessary.

Abelard was condemned by two councils of the Church; but truth crushed to earth shall rise again. His refusal to regard things as being merely symbols or emblems of something else, his insistence upon the right and the ability, aye, even more, the duty, of the individual to look all things in the face, *facie ad faciem omnia intuetur,* is a method that could not be hidden from the world. It was pursued by antique thought; it is the method used by the thought of the modern world. Abelard was not the first one to apply reason to theology and to religion, but he gave movement and life to the method. Thus he became a most important precursor of the modern spirit, and a powerful factor in the revival of conscience. " Along the streets and in the squares of Paris," writes Bernard of Clairvaux, " people dispute about the faith, about Mary's motherhood of the Child, about the sacrament of the altar, and about the incomparable mystery of the Trinity." Few teachers have ever held such sway as did Abelard. Thousands of students flocked from all countries to hear him. They learned his method, they adopted it as their own, and then they scattered it in every part of Europe; and, by a strange and matchless instance of the irony of fate, his method was subsequently adopted by the Church herself.

It was not only Abelard's teachings that pollenized Europe with the new thought. Far in the south, at the court of Frederic II, there was evoked, as we have seen, a premature Renaissance. That lonely figure among the sovereigns of the age, who still remains something of an enigma, desired to secularize faith, as well as knowledge, by giving to it reason as its sole and certain guide. Still another source of fructification was the thought of Averroes, the philosopher *par excellence* for that period of the Middle Ages, who proved by the Koran itself that God requires inquiry into the truth by means of the reason and that only upon the basis of rationalism can religion be securely founded. The wise man, he declared, is he who exercises his own conscience.

The teachings of Averroes were read with avidity by thousands who were groping their way towards intellectual and religious enfranchisement and they were a factor of decided importance in the attainment of that end. But it was not only the work of these three men, Abelard, Frederic II, and Averroes, that helped men to win their intellectual and spiritual independence. All those forces that were potent in the revival of the individual, to which we have already paid attention, and the revived individuality itself, conduced to the same end. Thus gradually did men reach the belief that the individual conscience, the consensus of one's own faculties, is in itself a sure and certain guide in the conduct of daily life, and that the reason, directing and controlling the emotions, can be safely trusted to answer the eternal questions as fully as they can be answered in the present finite life.

It would be altogether unfair to the Middle Ages to suppose them to have been a series of centuries profoundly satisfied with their moral condition and altogether ignorant of their weaknesses and their shortcomings. Such was far from being the case. Though the individual conscience was in abeyance, the Scriptures and the teachings of the Church, both of which were accepted by the implicit faith of Christendom, gave literal directions for the moral conduct of daily life. Discontent with the practical workings of the Church was by no means confined to the years that intervened between Abelard and the outbreak of the Protestant Revolution. The life of the Middle Ages was one incessant struggle for reform. The ethical injunctions of the New Testament and the ascetic lives of numerous eminent churchmen were the inspiration of many efforts to recall the Church from her political and economic activity, from the things that she had inherited from Cæsar, from curialism and imperialism, to the things she had inherited from Christ, to the work of inculcating faith, hope, and charity. But the Middle Ages had run their course. They had given place to a new order of things, to a new attitude towards life, that we call the Renaissance. The principles out of which their greatness and their vitality had come had passed, or were passing, into the limbo of outworn conceptions. Their social framework was falling to pieces. The Renaissance had brought with it a new basis for morality, aye, even a new foundation for religion. The individual conscience was to be the guide to morality; the reason, directing the aspirations of the heart, was to supplant implicit faith.

No gain in the history of humanity, however, is an unmixed gain. To a considerable extent the Renaissance was also a rebirth of pagan sensuality. Some of its devotees drew from their study of the classic authors excuse for a careless life of selfish ease untrammeled and untroubled by any thought of a future world. The unbridled passions of others moved in strange orbits and gave to the life of the time a deadly iridescence. Yet the revival of the individual conscience had produced a greater sensitiveness in distinguishing between right and wrong. It was this revival of conscience that in a large measure directed progress and impelled humanity upon its way. The paganism of the Renaissance was only an ephemeral thing. Complete indifference to the destiny of the soul and serene content with the present and the external was possible only in the childhood of humanity. So conscience asserted itself. Its influence was felt in obscure and subterranean ways at first, but eventually it found a voice.

At first the revival of conscience found expression in negative criticism, a thing that is far easier than the furnishing of positive schemes for reform. It was merely a symptom of the time. Yet it was not without its value, for it kept men in a ferment and led to constructive thought. From the beginning of the thirteenth century to the end of the fifteenth there were frequent public criticisms of the Church, bantering scorn and vehement invective, directed against the decline in morality of the monastic life, the accumulation of riches by secular and regular clergy, the deplorable scandals resulting from the requirement of clerical celibacy, the corruptions of the papal curia and its financial exactions. These criticisms were no longer inspired by the evident falling away from the standard of life enjoined in the New Testament, in the teachings of the Church, and exemplified by the lives of many ecclesiastics. They were, instead, due rather to the promptings of the individual conscience, to the failure to maintain a standard of life that the reason declared to be desirable and necessary. Among the first of the critics were the Goliards, the wandering students, many of whom, in the earlier years, had listened with eagerness to Abelard, who sang their songs from one end of Europe to the other. The best of these songs were probably written in the seventy-five years between 1150 and 1225. The greed and lewdness of the monks and friars and the ignorance of the secular clergy furnish the subject-matter of many of these light-hearted songs that have so little in common with medievalism, that are so essentially humanistic and modern in their spirit, and that must have mingled so strangely with the warning of the vesper-bell. Dante, the first of the individual critics whom we shall notice, had an exalted conception of the autonomy of the human reason. The reason, he said, is the chief nobility of man; from it he derives his essential qualification; by it he is differentiated from the animals who live merely by the senses. To live without using the reason is to be dead. It is sovereign for all the actions of the will, " such as the good or evil we do to others, courage in battle or flight, chastity or debauchery." So it is the rule of manners, the living law to which all the works of life are subject. Dante lived with the evidences of the Franciscan reform round about him, but, aside from any external suggestion, his own conscience was a most sensitive one and it induced him to dream of a regeneration of the Church from within. With passionate invective he scourged popes and priests, but he never attacked Papacy and priesthood. His voice was always that of a friend. Despite the fact that its rhetorical exaggeration is palpably evident no fiercer satire of the papal court exists than is to be found in Petrarch's *Epistolæ sine titulo*. And in other of his writings the father of humanism laid bare the corruption and degeneracy that existed at Avignon. But like Dante he was a loyal son of the Church bent upon serving her by effecting her reform. Boccaccio's *Decameron* is full of contemptuous scorn of monks and nuns. His criticism, published in a popular form, was far more widely read than that of Dante. But the vices of the Church that roused Dante to austere rage and moved Petrarch to resentful melancholy merely incited the author of the *novelle* to comic raillery. Chaucer depicted the shortcomings of the clergy. In the *Pardoner* he has described a priest who preaches merely for money and who has no concern with the cure of souls. Passionate denunciation and mocking sarcasm were the weapons of the critics of the Church up to the day of Lorenzo Valla who used one that had a far deadlier effect. His fearless and scientific criticism swept away the basis of the temporal power of the Papacy, exposed inaccuracies in the Vulgate and aroused doubts as to the authenticity of the Apostles' Creed. It was the beginning of modern biblical criticism. He had to work very largely by himself, for dialectics held, as still they do to-day, more men than research. After his time there was little left that could not be submitted to the test of criticism. Each critic of the Church gave to his charges the color of his own personality. Passionate invective, regretful reproach, sorrowful supplication, or mocking levity, forms the spirit of their complaints. All combined to agitate the minds of men and to arouse a realization of the need of reform.

Most of the medieval attempts at reform assumed a monastic

direction.  Monasticism was the highest ideal of life in the Middle Ages.  It meant the complete denial of the present world as far as that was possible, the absolute submission of the body to the soul.  The devil, the world, and the flesh were all temptations to betray the soul of man to its perdition.  Each was to be shunned and avoided.  The single object of life was the salvation of the soul, and anything that detracted from this aim was to be put aside.  It is a lofty as well as a narrow ideal of

life, and it is so far beyond the possibility of attainment by the large majority of mankind that attempts to reach it must needs involve many failures.  Many who flocked into the cloisters brought with them the world and its cares.  So the places dedicated to the spirit became noisy with ambition, and monasticism became enfeebled and then corrupt by lack of zeal.  The story of every monastic order is the same.  First there is a period of unremitting and unsparing effort to attain the lofty ideal of the life contemplative.  Then there is a period of gradual decline in which formality and convention replace the spontaneous and sincere strivings of the spirit, ending at last in corruption.  Finally there is a period of revival, a return born of contrition and repentance to the ideal of the founder of the order.  In 1540 Cardinal Guiddiccioni acknowledged this to be the story of the monastic orders when he said: "In the beginning all orders are full of fervor, but they relax in time, and when they grow old the harm they do to the Church is greater than the good they did her in the beginning."

The Benedictine Order, the mother and exemplar of all the other monastic orders, fell into decay repeatedly.  And just as periodically reformers appeared within its ranks to lead it back to its original purity.  But such periodical reforms did not satisfy the most ardent of those who embraced the monastic ideal.  For them the wise and moderate rule of St. Benedict was too mild.  So austere orders were established.  The Carthusians, founded in 1084, practised severe mortification of the body.  They were imitated by the Cistercians (1098) and excelled by the Trappists (1140).  Among the other austere orders were the Carmelites (1208), the Celestins (1271), the Olivetans (1313), and the Jesuates (1355).

There were also reforms among the secular as well as the regular clergy.  Many of the secular clergy lived under rules for the regulation of their daily lives.  They were therefore known as canons.  Augustine is said to have been the first to put secular priests under such canonical regulations.  No definite rule can be ascribed to him, but an order of canons grew up that bore his name. Canons were generally to be found in the cities at large churches and cathedrals where a number of priests were required to perform the services of the church for the laity. Among the orders of canons were the Canons Regular of Prémontré (1120), Canons of the Holy Cross (1214), Canons of St. Mark (1241), and Canons of St. Savior (1408).

The two great orders of the mendicant friars had their rise in efforts to bring about reform within the Church. It was a new ideal that St. Francis held, one that was humanitarian in its essence. The monks had withdrawn themselves from the world and sought only the safety of their own souls. His begging friars should go forth into the world and have for their work the care of the souls of the laity. Without reserve they gave themselves in love to their fellow-men. What the monks had amassed for themselves the friars diffused among the laity. Into the groveling and distressful slums of the time they went carrying their message of the brotherhood of man, helping in every way they could the poor and the leprous. Their marvelous success was due to the fact that they answered the deepest aspirations of the people of the time. They made religion a function of life instead of keeping it, like monasticism, constantly at variance with life. Not since Christ has any one else inflamed the human heart and fired the imagination to so great a degree as St. Francis. And yet within a century after the founding of the Franciscan order it became a disgrace. The mendicant friars no longer wandered through the world heedless of the morrow and seeking to do whatever good presented itself. The enchanting idyll ended in the old sad failure. Like the Benedictines and others before them the Franciscans became idle and corrupt. Then came efforts at reform. The Spiritual Franciscans attempted to return to the simplicity of the Poverello, but they were unsuccessful. Dominic gave a wise and very moderate rule to his followers, full of a sympathetic understanding of humanity. It was his idea to help the cause of reform by persuading the heretics of the time that they were wrong. But this second order of mendicant friars also became enriched and fell away from the ideals of its founder. The Dominicans became the chief supporters of scholasticism in the universities and, later on, the managers of the Inquisition.

Neither of these orders of mendicant friars had their origin in the Church, which was engrossed almost completely in its worldly activities. They were a result of the new democratic culture and piety that had come into existence with the growth of the towns. But the Church prudently made use of them. She used them to satisfy the constantly increasing religious needs of the towns which both the secular and monastic clergy found themselves unable to meet. And the friars succeeded for a time in satisfying the longing of the towns for spiritual nourishment. The extraordinary privileges conferred upon them marks the last important attempt of the papacy previous to the Protestant Revolution to recover something of the moral and religious authority which it had lost in acquiring by worldly means its tremendous juristic and political power.

Among the most important of the individual monastic reformers in the fourteenth century, a time of luxurious corruption, hideous crime, and moral laxity, were Vincent Ferrer (1357–**Monastic Revivalists** 1419), Bernardino of Siena (1380–1444), John of Capistrano (1386–1456) and Savonarola (1452–98). Vincent Ferrer was a Spanish Dominican who for more than twenty years devoted himself to the reformation of morals within the Church and to the conversion of the Waldenses. Bernardino of Siena was a Franciscan who in his youth became keenly aware of the lax morality of the Italian towns. Walking barefoot throughout Italy and preaching to the crowds that everywhere flocked to hear him, he boldly denounced the corruption of the time and strove to bring back the Franciscan order to its former purity. By fervent enthusiasm and the magic of his eloquence, which in all parts of the peninsula kindled among the masses a transient flame of reform, he became the chief promoter of the religious revival of the fourteenth century and the acknowledged exemplar of all friars who engaged in preaching. Most important among the many followers of Bernardino was John of Capistrano, who was commissioned by the pope to preach in Germany, where enormous crowds thronged to listen to his exhortations. Savonarola was a Dominican friar who, from the day that he fled to the convent to the day that his body was given to the flames, was consumed with a single conviction. He was filled with a burning zeal for moral reform. He desired no change of doctrine. All his life he clung to the teachings of the Church with the most unwavering conviction. The reform of morals was his sole mission. His temperament was not suited to the ways of patient conversion; but he made himself a force in the general awakening of cities and principalities by his terrible power of denunciation, his fiery apocalyptic warnings, his passionate appeals, and his pathetic entreaties. Eventually, as we shall see in a chapter soon to follow, he was drawn into ecclesiastical and political reforms and killed by the intricate and insignificant politics of the Italian principalities. The reforms instituted by all of these revivalists had the same inherent defect. They appealed only to the emotions. They gave rise to no stream of new thought. They were vehement and spasmodic outbursts, not dispassionate and sustained movements that had their origin in intellectual conviction. When the potent personality of the revivalist was no longer present his influence gradually diminished until it vanished altogether. And so these revivals were only transient in their results.

All through the Middle Ages monasticism, as we have seen, provided the chief means for reformation within the Church, but all the monastic reforms were unsatisfying, save as they taught men forever how mightier than policy is purpose. We have seen that every monastic order goes through the same round of fervent zeal, gradual relaxation, corruption, and another outburst of reform. Such is the inevitable consequence of the attempt to attain so unworldly and difficult an ideal of perfection. The bow too tightly strung inevitably snaps asunder. Then, too, a monastic order, like any other institution, grows out of the needs of the life of the time. And as life is dynamic, as its needs change with the changing centuries, the institution is outgrown. It no longer corresponds to the need of the time. it no longer is the result of spontaneous action. It has become fixed and formal. The developing forces of life no longer supply it with vitality, but instead are engaged in its dissolution.

Several of the popes endeavored to institute reforms. The Avignonese captivity and the protracted schism had lessened the power and the prestige of the Papacy, and since then the activity of the curia had become more than ever juristic, financial and political, and less moral and religious, so that at the end of the fifteenth century the character of the Papacy was predominantly that of a worldly institution. Something of this was perhaps dimly perceived by Martin V (1417–31), Eugene IV (1431–47), Nicholas V (1447–55), Calixtus III (1455–58), Pius II (1458–64), and Paul II (1464–71). The reaction against the paganism of the humanists began with Calixtus and was continued by Pius and Paul. These reforming efforts of the Papacy were purely personal. They were ineffective because they were not directed to the root of the evil. The pontiffs were too largely dependent upon the members of the curia. The Papacy had become essentially a worldly institution, and until the spirit of the time imperatively demanded its reform it was impossible for any pontiff who was not also a great statesman to effect any substantial reform. The circumstances of the time would have made reform difficult even for another Hildebrand; so the efforts of these papal reformers of far less power ended in failure. They availed nothing to make new the heart of Christendom. The spiritual significance of the Papacy steadily declined. Its fiscal oppressions increased. Nepotism was practised in the most unblushing way. And in the person of Leo X paganism seemed to have installed itself upon the papal throne.

The attempts of members of the Church to bring about a reformation of the institution in root and branch assumed another form toward the end of the fourteenth century when the age of the reforming councils began. The theory of the conciliar reformers is well expressed in the famous decree of the Council of Constance: "A general council has its power immediately from Christ, and every one of every rank, even the pope himself, is bound to obey it in matters pertaining to the articles of faith, to the extirpation of heresy, and to the reformation of the Church in head and members." The conciliar movement had its birth in France, and found in Pierre d'Ailly and Jean Gerson, two eminent French ecclesiastics, its most able advocates. But the theory that a general council is above the pope found vigorous opposition from the Papacy of multifarious activity and worldly power that the Middle Ages had produced. So a struggle ensued.

Something of the activity of the councils of the fifteenth century we have already seen. We have here to regard them from a somewhat different point of view. The first of the reform councils was convened at Pisa in 1409. It was summoned by the College of Cardinals and met under the protection of Charles V of France. It was widely representative, and it had for its chief purpose the ending of the schism. It deposed the rival popes and in their place elected Alexander V. As neither of the deposed pontiffs acknowledged the action of the council a triple papacy resulted. The work of the council in effecting a reform of morals was insignificant. A second council was held at Constance (1414–18). The ending of the triple papacy was the chief task that confronted it; but it also debated questions of morals and questions of faith. Its efforts in the first direction resulted in the unity of the papacy. The reformation of morals was largely lost sight of by the conflicting elements of which the council was composed. The revival of synods, the summoning of general councils at stated intervals, the reorganization of the College of Cardinals, the reform of papal taxation, the reform of ecclesiastical law courts, the control of papal grants, dispensations and indulgences, and the morality and zeal of the ⁀lergy, all failed to receive settlement at the hands of the council. A few inconsequential decrees were the only result of the efforts of the council to effect reform within the Church. This failure was due in part to the opposition to the conciliar theory, in part to the conflicting interests of the members of the council, and in part to the organization of the members who were arranged in nations and who thus felt the full force of political antagonism. The attempt of the council to secure unity of faith resulted in the burning of John Hus and Jerome of Prague. Twelve years later practically the same tasks, with the exception of the elimination of superfluous popes, confronted the Council of Basel (1431–49). Again divergent national interests prevented unity of action. Again the Papacy successfully opposed itself to the council. The council came to an end without having accomplished the expected reforms. The tide of the conciliar movement was fast ebbing. In vain it had spent its force against the rock of the Papacy. The last council of the Renaissance period was the Fifth Lateran Council (1512–17), which received its name from the church of St. John Lateran in Rome. It was made up exclusively of Italian prelates; and in that time of national spirit, commercial expansion, and secular thought, it commanded little attention. There were earnest men in the Church, and many members of the council had a deep sense of the necessity of reform; but the council bears witness to the hopelessness of the conciliar cause. The Pragmatic Sanction of France, which was a recognition of the claims of the conciliar reformers, was revoked at the dictation of the triumphant Papacy. Thus the last vestige of the conciliar movement for reform disappeared.

The conciliar movement which had begun with so confident a hope of success failed in the course of fifty years. Its slight victories were nullified with apparent ease. The general discouragement was well expressed by the abbot Jacob of Junterburg: "I can scarcely believe that an improvement of the Church can be brought about; for first the papal curia must be reformed; and how difficult that is the present course of events shows. There is no nation which so vehemently opposes the reform of the Church as the Italian." The earnest supporters of the conciliar idea were too few in number. They were members of the upper classes only, and the people were not behind them. The relative power of pope and council was for the masses a purely academic question. The one concrete thing that appealed to the people and increased their wrath and contempt was the shameless worldly conduct of the Church, the avarice and the immorality of the clergy. The vested interests of the

Papacy at which the movement was aimed were too powerfully entrenched. So the movement failed. The worldly interests and entanglements of the curia increased. The moral laxity of the clergy became ever more grievous, and the spiritual needs of the common people ever more neglected.

The ecclesiastical reformers — monks, friars, popes, and conciliar theorists — had all failed to effect any permanent reform within the Church. We come now to another group of men, the biblical reformers. The doctrines of the Church had grown by accretion through many centuries. So vast a body of thought exceeded the capacity of some of the members of the Church. It appeared to them to be superfluous, and burdensome. It disturbed them with an incomplete sense of belief or with a distinct sense of disbelief. And the contrast between the material Church, with all its vast possessions and its worldly activity, and the simplicity of Christianity in apostolic times, the simple internal religion of Christ, was so striking that reactions against medieval Catholicism were inevitable. So here and there a group of men limited the body of religious doctrine, lessened the range of religious interest, sought to intensify truth within that range, and opposed themselves to the accumulation of worldly wealth. They endeavored to state the fundamental truth of religion in its simplest form. This phenomenon was not confined to the eve of the Protestant Revolution. Scarcely had society begun to settle down after the barbarian invasion when such sects sprang up on all sides. And although they suffered persecution such reactions characterized every one of the medieval centuries, for they were natural reactions arising out of a need that otherwise would have remained unsatisfied. As a rule these groups of simple believers flourished in those parts of Europe where centrifugal forces were most potent. They were not only dissatisfied with the doctrines of the Church because of their bulk and difficulty, and with the greed, selfishness, and immorality of the clergy, but they were also filled with social discontent. They indulged in dreams of social as well as religious reconstruction. So they were deemed to be perilous by the state as well as by the Church. All of them attempted to restore the simple brotherhood of apostolic times and to live according to the social doctrine of the Galilean.

*The Biblical Reformers*

One of the most important of these groups of reformers were the Waldenses, a sect which originated, somewhere about 1170, in the two streams of the peasants of the valleys of the western Alps and the Poor Men of Lyons who were the followers of Peter Waldo. They translated the Bible into their daily tongue

*The Waldenses*

and, discarding all allegorical interpretation, accepted only its literal meaning. They dispensed with the priesthood as unnecessary. Every believer in Christ they held to be as much a priest as any other. The apostles were laymen, they said, and so were the first disciples of Christ. Then why should not every good layman in subsequent times be a priest? So all of them were admitted to preach, without distinction of age, or rank, or sex. The only sacraments they retained were baptism and communion, and these could be administered by any one. They rejected also all other external and extraneous aids such as indulgences and the adoration of saints. But despite the fact that the Waldenses increased with great rapidity and spread from Aragon to Bohemia they did not succeed in making any great and permanent impression upon the religious life of the time. Europe was not yet ready for their ideas. And they were poor and lowly men, unable to influence leaders in Church or State.

Essentially similar to the principles of the Waldenses were those held by John Wiclif (1320–84), a master of Balliol College at Oxford, a royal ambassador, and later a popular preacher. He, too, insisted upon the priesthood of every Christian, and thus put himself into direct opposition to the claims of the clergy; and he, too, with bold logic held the seven sacraments to be unnecessary. In short he attacked the entire system of the Church and insisted upon the sufficiency of divine grace and individual faith as did the reformers of the sixteenth century. Everywhere along the roads of England, in churchyards and market-places, could be seen the "pore preestis" of Wiclif preaching to crowds of the common people. And, with the aid of two friends, Wiclif translated the Bible into English and placed it in the hands of the common people. It could be understood, he said, by any one who led a religious life and sought for truth in a humble spirit. But hostile forces rallied to the defeat of the new movement. The rising of the peasants under Wat Tyler and Jack Straw had filled the barons and the burghers with fear. Wiclif's movement was regarded as dangerous, and so it was put down.

The teaching of Wicliff failed to produce a lasting impression in England; but in the person of John Hus (1369–1413) it had a potent influence in the distant country of Bohemia. Richard II of England had married Anne of Bohemia and the Bohemian students, among whom was Jerome of Prague, who followed her to England, were instrumental in bringing Wiclif's writings to the attention of Hus. But important as was the influence of Wiclif upon Hus it would be a mistake to regard the Bohemian reformer

as no more than a copyist of the English preacher. Their doctrines were similar, but they had used the same sources and were
inspired by the same writers. And, moreover, Hus was the heir
of a long series of Bohemian reformers. Matthew of Janow had
already asserted that only by a revolution could the Church be
brought back to the primitive simplicity and purity of the first
years of Christianity. In Bohemia the clergy were as corrupt
as elsewhere; and there, too, a brigand baronage oppressed the
people. The deep religious feeling that was roused to active life
by the passionate preaching of Hus had long been stirring. The
torch that lit the funeral pyre of Hus at Constance was the signal
for a long and terrible war in Bohemia. But, at last, war and
weariness broke the spirit of the reformers and crushed their
reformation.

In addition to these two great biblical reformers there were
several minor ones of whose writings the great reformers of the
sixteenth century knew very little, although they contained implicitly and explicitly the doctrines of the Protestant Revolution.
**Minor Biblical Reformers** John of Goch (1400–75) asserted that the Bible is the only necessary guide of life, and that the Church in her teaching is sub-
ject to error. "Only the Bible," he said, "has an irrefragable
authority. The writings of the fathers of the Church are of
value merely in so far as they are in conformity with the sacred
books." He held that the New Testament is a law of internal
sentiment. It secures the salvation of man by uniting him to
God with the bond of love. He was a recluse by temperament,
so his doctrines did not gain a wide audience in his lifetime, and
they were not published until the sixteenth century. John of
Wesel (1410?–81), who after teaching in the University of Erfurt became a popular preacher at Mainz and at Worms, boldly
discarded the authority of the Church. Incited by the abuses of
the time to denounce indulgences he eventually declared the Bible
to be the only true religious guide. "We must believe nothing,"
he said, "except that which is in the Bible. Christ commanded
his disciples to preach the gospel. He did not tell them to introduce new laws." And in his attack upon indulgences he was
more radical than Luther in his celebrated theses, for he not only
denounced their abuses but denied their principle. "The grace
of God," he said, "raises the sinner from his fall. There is,
therefore, no reason for the mediation of the Church. Everything passes between man and God." Only two of his books
have come down to us. One was published in the sixteenth century and the other in the eighteenth. Wessel Gansvoort (1420?–
89), a wandering humanist, also rejected the tradition of the

Church and recurred to the Bible as the sole basis of authority. He held that faith in Christ, finding its vent in devotion to the cause of one's fellow-men, is sufficient to ensure salvation. The true unity of Christendom, he held, is not to be found in the external authority of the Church, but in the uniting of all Christians to Christ by " one faith, one hope, and one charity. It matters little who are the chiefs under whom they live, whether they be one or many. The unity of the Church under the pope is a mere accident. It is not the pope who is the bond of union, but the Holy Spirit." He was the boldest of all the forerunners of the Revolution. He denied the real presence of the body and blood of Christ in the wafer and the wine of the Eucharist, admitting only a sacramental presence. In this respect his position was exactly that of Zwingli, the leader of the Swiss revolt from Rome. It was not until more than a generation after his death that the first of his books to be printed came from the printing press.

All of the biblical reformers ostensibly remained within the Church. Yet their fundamental thesis of the sole authority of the Bible is essentially antagonistic to the claims of the Church. None of them secured a wide following; and it is not known that Luther derived any of his ideas from their teachings. So they cannot be regarded as direct contributors to the revolutionary movement. They must rather be considered as intimations of the profound unrest that was stirring Germany in the fifteenth century.

Still another group of men who attempted to effect reform within the pale of the Church were the mystics. Mysticism is a term not easy to define. It is not an articulate system of doctrine or philosophy. It is an attitude towards life, a mode of thought, an atmosphere. It is the result of temperament rather **Mysticism** than of intellect. It cannot be demonstrated by logic; neither is there any logic that can disprove it. The basic conviction of mysticism is that under all the diversity of outward things there is unity at the center. All things that surround and confront us are merely manifestations of the divine life that constitutes the center of existence. Visible and prehensible things are but ephemeral phenomena. The divine life that is present in them alone possesses immortality. Dwelling in the heart of man is a spark of the divine life, and only through this part of his nature can man know God. The aim of the mystic is to attain to union with the One, the divine. So he ignores the fleeting phenomena of life as such and concentrates all his faculties upon the spark of the divine that glows within him and upon God with whom he desires union. Only like can comprehend like. For the contemplation of spiritual things there is required a faculty that is itself essentially spiritual. Such a faculty the individual possesses in his soul. The soul is his spiritual eye by which he may gradually come to see God. The soul is to be trusted for the discernment of spiritual truth just as implicitly as the organs of sensation are trusted to perceive material fact. This spiritual insight is an emotional state of being. It is not a mental process. The consciousness of physical existence must gradually be lessened, and then by degrees the consciousness of spiritual existence will take its place. So eventually shall the mystic be carried into a complete fusion with the divine life that lies at the heart of the universe, so shall he soar to those transcendental heights where all distinction between creator and created is abolished. But absorption in the Eternal Word is not the sole aim of the mystic of the western world. His mysticism is not incompatible with the practical life. His outlook upon the facts of earthly life is not less clear because he sees beyond them. The green earth on which he lives and his human nature are not devoid of meaning and are not without their uses. The world is not to be neglected. It is a road upon which one walks to God. The duties of daily life are purgative and they teach the principles of measure and discipline which are divine characteristics. The mystic is never to be idle. His time is to be spent in prayer, or meditation, or in work for the common good.

" Not alone, not alone would I go to my rest in the heart of my
        love:
    Were I tranced in the innermost beauty, the flame of its tender-
        est breath,
I would still hear the cry of the fallen recalling me back from
        above,
    To go down to the side of the people who weep in the shadow
        of death."

It is only in the hours of silent contemplation that the mystic becomes lost in lonely ecstasy, in the seemingly actual presence of divinity. Mysticism, like so many other types and phases of religion, had its cradle in the Orient. But in the East mysticism led to inactivity, to quietism, to Nirvana. It was seldom revolutionary. It indulged its bold speculations under the cloak of convention. In the West mysticism has generally been associated with reform and sometimes even with revolt. All of the great mystics of the West have been men of energy and influence.

Mysticism is not confined to any particular creed. It finds its followers among Catholics and Protestants and among men of every race. It breaks down all social barriers. It lives in a region far above the clash of creeds and the diversities of racial characteristics. It is because of this that the books of the mystics have always made so wide an appeal, that they have brought to members of every sect comfort and consolation. But mysticism, being born of temperament, needs a special condition for its propagation. It is a seed that will not grow in alien soil. The words of a mystic fall meaningless upon the ears of a man who is not fitted by temperament to apprehend them. The proportion of men thus fitted has never been very large. So it is impossible for mysticism to produce a great religious movement. Its voice is resonant only in the chambers of its own dwelling. Yet in the fourteenth century it was a powerful though intangible force.

Mysticism did not flourish in France, the country that contributed most to the development of scholasticism, as it did in Germany and in the Low Countries. The French genius is not given to mysticism. It requires concrete doctrines, lucidly and logically defined and systematically articulated. Yet France, like every other country, has produced mystics. Foremost among the French mystics was Bernard of Clairvaux (1091–1153), who was believed to have accomplished the mystical " flight of the alone to the Alone," to have seen God in mystic ecstasy face to face. His activities were by no means confined to the cloister. He realized keenly the corruption of the Church and did all that he could for its correction. He boldly pointed out to Eugene III the abuses of the papal curia, and he was a constant and powerful advocate of a better daily life. Hugo of St. Victor (1097–1141) was a Saxon who went to Paris and there developed a new theory of spiritual reality that was a distinct addition to the thought of mysticism. A life of faith, he said, in the living world is the indispensable precursor of an eternity of contemplation. No individual may reach perfection without having done his part in making the world better. Richard of St. Victor (?–1173), a Scotchman who was attracted to France, also contributed to mystic thought and was active in promoting the practical, ethical side of life. " Let him who thirsts to see God," he said, " make his own spirit bright." Jean Gerson (1363–1429) was the last of a group of French thinkers who tried to combine scholasticism and mysticism. By his participation in the Council of Constance he became one of the most notable figures in Europe. Yet he was essentially a mystic rather than an ecclesiastical politician. Realizing the relation of the life contemplative to the life active he wrote and preached in his mother tongue, emphasizing the simple facts of primitive Christianity, and in later years he devoted himself to the education of children. But after all his scholasticism made his mysticism an arid and a formal thing.

Joachim of Flora (1132?–1202) may be regarded as the first important personage in Italian mysticism. He was born in Calabria, a province in which there were numerous Greek monasteries of the Order of St. Basil, which formed a sort of connecting link between the Greek and the Latin Churches, inasmuch as they acknowledged obedience to the Roman pontiff while at the same time they used in their services the Greek language and liturgy. Courtier, crusader, Cistercian, and hermit in turn, he founded a new monastic order, whose strict rules were perhaps derived from those of the Basilian monks, and he became the principal initiator of the stream of mystic and communistic thought in which dissatisfaction with the practical workings of the Church expressed itself in the twelfth and thirteenth centuries. Yet Joachim was not a thinker of the highest type. His importance is somewhat fortuitous. His writings were caught on the crest of the great Franciscan wave, and then, carried far and wide, they were probably changed (the revolutionary doctrines which they suggested being given more explicit statement) and they certainly gave rise to a movement of greater scope than any that he anticipated.

Three of Joachim of Flora's books were put together and to them was added an introduction usually ascribed to Gerard of Borgo San Donnino. Then somewhere about 1254 the book, under the title of *The Everlasting Gospel,* made a great sensation by its presentation to the public in Paris. It was radical in its teachings, and it was cherished by the Spiritual Franciscans as being scarcely less important than the Bible. It held that there were three ages of the world. The age of the Father, a wintry time of fear and trial in which men were slaves, a time of nettles, a time represented by the Old Testament, illuminated by the stars, had passed away. The age of the Son, the springtime of wisdom and action, in which men were freemen, a time of roses, a time represented by the New Testament, illuminated by the moon, was rapidly coming to an end. In six years the age of the Holy Ghost, the full summer, a time of love and contemplation, in which men were to be friends, a time of lilies, a time represented by *The Everlasting Gospel,* illuminated by the sun, was to begin. Monastic clergy, rather than the

hierarchy, devoted to the welfare of the people, were to be the
chief religious guides of the new age. Poverty and love were
to replace wealth and arrogance in the Church. Men were to
be so trustful of each other that all property was to be held in
common. The laity received the book with great applause and
eagerly devoured it, for its indictment of the corruption of the
Church coincided with the popular conviction. Soon the name
of *The Everlasting Gospel* broadened from that of a book
into that of a doctrine. It was too revolutionary to remain long
without the disapprobation of the Church. In 1255 the book,
or at any rate the introduction, was formally condemned because
of heresies it was alleged to contain.

No other group of men so immediately and so eagerly welcomed *The Everlasting Gospel* as did the Spiritual Franciscans. Very soon after its institution the Franciscan Order began
to acquire property and to show signs of moral laxity. Grad- *The Spirit-
ually two parties were formed within the Order — the Spiritual- ual Fran-
ists and the Conventuals. The former wished the rule of St. ciscans*
Francis to be observed literally; the latter by ingenious interpretations evaded the prohibition to acquire property. Bitter
enmity existed between the two parties. The Conventuals were
quick to seize the opportunity offered by the connection of the
Spirituals with the revolutionary teachings of *The Everlasting
Gospel*. They succeeded in securing the removal of John of
Parma, a member of the Spiritual party, from the generalate of
the order. A schism in the order was prevented only by the
wisdom and the commanding personality of Bonaventura, the
succeeding general, who was committed to neither party. But
dissension continued; the Spirituals still denounced the engrossment of the Church in worldly affairs and continued to insist
upon the literal acceptance of the Franciscan rule. Some of them
went to great extremes and the Church persecuted them.

Still another sect arose within the Franciscan order, the Fraticelli, the little brothers of the life of poverty. They were moderate Spirituals who, nevertheless, held that the popes who had *The Frati-
favored the Conventuals and sanctioned their possession of prop- celli*
erty had condemned the life of Christ and were unlawful popes.
Poverty, they said, was the law of Christ, and therefore when the
Church acquired property it became the synagogue of the devil.
The assertion that neither Christ nor the apostles had held property was made a test for heresy by the Papacy, and many of the
Fraticelli who persisted in the assertion were burned at the stake.
In turn the "little brothers" pointed to the idleness and the
immorality of the clergy, and declared the whole Church to be

heretic. They carried their proselytizing activity into various lands, but at last they succumbed to persecutions and the sect became extinct.

According to *The Everlasting Gospel* the year 1260 was to witness the beginning of the age of the Holy Ghost. Emotional excitement increased as the appointed time drew near. Processions of flagellants scourging their naked bodies filled the highways of Italy. Among those touched with the contagion of penitence and reform was Gerard Sagarelli ( ?–1300), an uneducated youth of Parma, of lowly birth. He imitated the dress of apostolic times as represented in the mosaics and frescoes of the churches, and he gathered about him a body of rustics who professed to practise the simple life of the apostles. Later on their ranks were augmented by members of other classes. Eventually the new Order of the Apostolic Brethren was proscribed and Sagarelli was burned by the Inquisition. The widespread religious unrest of the time, the profound discontent with the moral condition of the world, increased the membership of the Apostolic Order, despite the persecution that it suffered. A new leader was found in Dolcino ( ?–1307), a man of intellect and some learning, who with 1,400 followers fled to the Alps and there for several years with great skill and bravery, succeeded in escaping the clutches of the Inquisition.

Italy was at this time the " hostelry of sorrow." The popes were absent in Avignon. The peninsula was in a state of anarchy. The immorality of all classes was constantly increasing. The spirit of worldliness had taken complete possession of the Church. Not the least among the mystic revivalists who attempted to reform this state of affairs, and among the most practical of them, were two women. The first, St. Bridget (1304–73), was a Swedish princess who founded in Italy a new order of nuns that had for its ideal the combining of the life contemplative, as exemplified in the life of Mary, with the life active, as represented by the life of Martha. She protested against the deplorable state of the clergy and endeavored to secure the return of the papacy to Rome. The second, St. Catharine of Siena (1347–80), daughter of a dyer, is a luminous figure in the somber picture of the time. She led a remarkable life of contemplation, filled with an intense and passionate desire for personal communion with Christ, and at the same time in her extraordinary public activity she displayed unusual worldly wisdom and sagacity. In impassioned utterance she urged the abandonment of Avignon, strove to heal the wounds of Italy, and to unite the European nations against the Turk.

In penetrating accents she pleaded for the redress of the moral evils of the time, that were so gross, so open, and so avowed. She made herself the leading statesman of Italy in the fourteenth century, but she was happiest in her narrow cell that for her was often " filled with the fragrance of the lilies of Paradise and sweet with its ineffable melodies."

Mysticism found in Germany a soil well fitted to receive its seed. It became the most important feature of the spiritual life of that country in the fourteenth century. In the German genius there is a strange intermingling of materialism and sentiment, of crude and violent desires and tender and intimate religion, that often-times assumes the form of mysticism. Because of his philosophical genius Meister Eckhart ( ?–1328), the greatest of all speculative mystics, may be considered as the founder of German mysticism, though before his time Mechtild of Magdeburg, who also worked for the reformation of the Church, made an exposition of mysticism and pointed out its relation to the social problems of the time. Not much is known of his life. He became a Dominican friar and taught with distinction in the University of Paris. Then he became an official of his order in Saxony and in Bohemia and a teacher of theology at Cologne. He died in the midst of the proceedings of the Inquisition against him for heresy. Despite the fact that his philosophy logically leads to withdrawal from the world, the modern spirit induced him to take an active part in the life of the time. When he preached to the German people in their own tongue he often dwelt upon the operation of the spirit of God through a life devoted to the common welfare. His writings contain frequent expressions of dissatisfaction with the immorality of the time; and he rejected external ceremonies and observances as unnecessary and emphasized the virtues of humility and love.

All the mystics who followed Eckhart were primarily concerned with an active, helpful life. Not one of them added anything of importance to mysticism as a speculative system. Their mysticism was known, as every religion is best known, by its fruits. The vivid *Life* of Heinrich von Berg (1295?–1365), better known as Suso, written with a keen sense of reality, reveals a mystic who, though much occupied with the phantasmagoria superinduced by mental concentration and bodily anguish, was not concerned with the spiritual image of eternity to the complete exclusion of the daily life of earth. This autobiography, full of poetic fervor, shows that its author greatly desired a reformation of the world about him. He accepted the monastic

Meister
Eckhart

Suso and
Tauler

life as the highest life, though many years of his career were devoted to active usefulness. The real successor of Eckhart was
John Tauler (1300?–61), a mystic less neurotic than Suso, a
preacher of robust eloquence, a thinker as well as a preacher,
who devoted his life to active work, and who deemed everything
and every person to be a medium through which God could be
heard and seen. No priest is necessary, he said, to bring the
individual soul into relationship with God. The sacraments are
not essential to salvation. He insisted upon the necessity of a
practical religious life. " No one," he said, " may leave off
doing good works."

German mysticism effected several important practical manifestations of itself. The first of these was the formation of a
secret organization of men and women, initiated probably by the
mysterious person known as the Friend of God in the Oberland,
who has been held by some writers, though seemingly incorrectly
so, to have been Nicholas of Basel. The members of this secret
fellowship were not very numerous, for only individuals having
affinity for its mysticism were chosen, but though their chief
scene of action was the region of the upper Rhine, they were to
be found scattered as far to the east and south as Hungary and
Genoa. It was the purpose of the association to develop the
spiritual life of its members. They endeavored to avoid the attention of the Inquisition and in consequence of their secrecy an
air of mystery still surrounds them. A second practical outcome
of German mysticism was the association of the Brethren of the
Free Spirit, whose members first appeared in the Rhine country
and were afterwards found in other parts of Germany and in
France and Switzerland. Little is known of their creed, aside
from the reports of their trials as heretics, but they were probably steeped in pantheism, and many of their weaker members
became addicted to gross forms of immorality. One result of
their teaching was to render the individual independent of the
priesthood. They carried on a propaganda by publishing books
and pamphlets in the vernacular. Still another practical result
of German mysticism is the *Büchlein von deutscher Theologie,* written at Frankfurt in the fourteenth century by a priest
whose name has been forgotten. The unknown author was
probably a solitary thinker who cared little for fame, but his
book is one that will live. Luther discovered it and in 1516
published it for the first time. He tells us that next to the Bible
and the writings of Augustine no other book wielded so
great an influence upon him. It is a book through which flow
the deep currents of humanity and one that speaks with the lan-

guage of the heart. It inculcates a semi-mystical doctrine that
has very little to do with the Church, with its authority, its creeds,
or its discipline. It aims to make a practical application of the
mystic speculations, to make them a living force for good in the
daily life of the world.

Mysticism flourished in England. No race has shown a richer
vein of mysticism and a more profound sense of the mystery of
life than the English. Amid all the materialism of the nineteenth
century no other race produced such a wonderful group of
idealistic poets. But the English mystics as a rule have dealt
little with the theoretical side of mysticism. Instead they have
led essentially practical lives. They have instructed youth as
teachers in the schools, and as parish priests they have ministered
to the daily needs of the common people. Richard Rolle (1290?–
1349) disapproved of the hair-splitting of the scholastics and
many of the conventional views of religion of his time. He extolled the contemplative life, but he endeavored by practical
means to instil into the mass of the people an active religious
spirit. He wrote a number of treatises, all of them devoted to
right-living, and most of them intended for the common people.
Walter Hilton ( ?–1396), a follower of Rolle, was " a ful devoute
man," who like his master wrote freely in English for the religious edification of his countrymen.

Mysticism found a fruitful soil in the Low Countries. It was
there that the semi-religious bodies of the Beghards and the
Beguines arose, associations of men and women who desired to
lead a religious and communal life without being irrevocably
removed from the world by the vows of monasticism. There
were many motives that impelled men and especially women to
such a life at that time — political disturbances, economic want,
and the prevalent immorality of the time. The loss of vast
numbers of the male population by the Crusades left many
women without protectors. This was an immediate incentive to
the formation of the Beguine associations. Similar organizations of men, the Beghards, were formed at a later time. They
lived by the labor of their hands, and in their spare time they
devoted themselves to deeds of charity. They increased with
great rapidity because they answered the needs of the time and
were supported by influential and powerful patrons. Eventually
they fell away from their ideals and became idle and corrupt.
John of Ruysbrook (1293–1381) was a Flemish mystic who
founded an abbey in the forest of Soignies and lived there during the remainder of his days. He divided life into the active
life, which every man must live well in order to be saved, and

the inner life of contemplative love, to which men may attain only by the practice of the virtues and the grace of God. He realized the value of good works, but he also insisted upon the danger of exaggerating their importance. " To place chief emphasis upon good works," he said, " is to take the surface for the essence. It is neglecting the truth for the form. Man must be brought back to the internal life in order to be brought nearer to God." In his denunciation of the immorality of the time he spared neither pope, nor prelates, nor monks, nor laity. Gerard Groote (1340–84) was a man of wealth and intellect who after studying in the University of Paris led a life of cultured ease as a church lawyer until a friend who had become a Carthusian monk summoned him to a religious life. Then the seed of mysticism within him germinated. He renounced his many offices, took holy orders, became an itinerant preacher, and entered upon a new way of life. He met with great success as a reformer of the clergy, an educator of the young, and the founder of a semi-monastic society. Attracted by the personality of Groote there gathered about the eloquent preacher a group of friends, and eventually this group, under the direction of Groote and his friend Florentius Radewyn, was permanently organized into a society, under the Augustinian rule that conduced to physical health and intellectual activity, with the name of the Brothers and Sisters of the Common Life. The members of the two branches of the new order did not immure themselves in the seclusion of the cloister. They lived under a common roof, observed the rules of poverty, chastity, and obedience, but they were not bound by the irrevocable vows. They could, therefore, return to the ordinary life of the world whenever they desired. Unlike the monks they did not depend for support upon endowments and unlike the friars they did not depend upon alms. Instead they lived by their own work. They believed that purity of life and the education of youth are the prime requisites for the salvation of society. So they devoted themselves to good works and in particular to the cause of popular education. Their teaching was as practical, as liberal, and as enlightened, as the educational knowledge of the time permitted, and their lives were characterized by a sincere and simple piety that is still vocal in the pages of *The Imitation of Christ.*

Thomas à
Kempis

The new order grew so rapidly that within thirty years it had thirty-seven convents for men and eight for women. Among its convents was that of St. Agnes near Zwolle. There it was that Thomas à Kempis (1380–1471), who had already acquired the two accomplishments of singing and writing, that gave him so much pleasure, in a school having an intimate relation with the convent of the brotherhood at Deventer, went to live when he was a boy of nineteen, and there it was that he passed almost the whole of his long and quiet life. Thomas was an exquisite penman. All his heart and soul he put into his work, for he believed that the hands of the transcriber of books, the fountains of eternal life, are indeed blessed. He was glad to relinquish the various offices that he held and to get back to the quiet and peaceful round of copying books, writing his brief treatises, instructing the novices, and solitary meditation in the little cell that was so dear to him. Political disorder, spiritual unrest, and the visitations of the plague all failed to move him either to indignation or to despair. Beyond the clamor of the busy world, undisturbed by the thoughts and the deeds of awakening Europe, the serene days of his cloistral life flowed on year after year like a placid stream. There in the convent by the green hill he walked through life with the air of a pilgrim to whom the world is but a road. And there it was that he wrote *The Imitation of Christ,* a book that has been translated into every civilized tongue and more than three thousand editions of which are known to exist, a book that continues as a living force to-day. Men of the most diverse personalities have loved it — Luther and Lamartine, Doctor Johnson and Baron Leibnitz. What is the cause of such long-continued and widespread favor? It is the purity, the peace, and the simplicity of the life for which it pleads, the incomparable beauty and the unstudied dignity of its utterance, and the depth and the sincerity of its spiritual emotion. It has its limitations. Its horizon is bounded by the convent walls. It regards the actual world as the " land of the shadow of death." It is a defense of the recluse and his ideal of life. It holds that man can reach the infinite by mere negation of the finite. It ignores the virtues of family and social life in the outer and the common world of men. It is indifferent to the interests of the mass of humanity. It accepts a life of solitude and resignation as though it were the whole of spirituality instead of bearing as it does something of the same relation to the entire life of the outer world that sculptured marble bears to breathing flesh. Rightly understood Christianity is a religion of self-regard in the highest and noblest sense, not self-annihilation nor even self-abnegation. Yet all men are not alike. Life is various. There is need in the sum total of society for every kind of excellence, and the life of contemplation lends something to the ideals of humanity. Not long after the death of Thomas à Kempis a bitter dispute as to the authorship of the *Imitation* broke out. Jean Gerson, chancellor of the University of Paris, is the principal claimant put forward by those who have denied the claims of the recluse of the convent of St. Agnes. But the general consensus of scholarship confirms Thomas as the author.

The papal curia and the great prelates of the hierarchy had long been preoccupied with temporal affairs. The visible Church was busy with its vast political, juristic, economic, and financial activities to the neglect of its spiritual functions. To do away with corruption in the lives of the clergy and laity, and to bring the Church to a recognition of the paramount importance of her spiritual mission was the work of all the reformers who remained within her fold. The monks turned their backs upon the world. The friars called men to repentance. A few popes endeavored in a feeble way to improve the papal administration. The conciliar reformers strove to secure the recognition of their theory which was to be the basis of further procedure. The biblical reformers, who endeavored to recall the simplicity of apostolic times, were much more radical than the great sects of the Protestant Revolution. They passed far beyond the timid reforms of Luther and the other leaders of his time. That is why they failed. They were too advanced, too revolutionary. In order to succeed a revolution must accept the present while effecting its gradual transformation. Christianity, which was itself a revolution, had accepted the past. Only thus can progress be effected. And, again, the Biblical reformers failed because the only program they had to offer was an absolute return to the past. In their single desire to recall primitive Christianity they took no account of the progress of civilization, of the interests and the needs of modern times. They looked backwards, not forwards. A revolution in order to be successful must not only connect the past with the present, but it must be essentially a forward movement. The mystics taught the superfluity of external works save only as they are directed by a spiritual sense. And they emphasized the independence of the individual in securing his own salvation. Although their point of view, embracing as it did the liberty of the individual, did not accord with the iron unity which the Church sought to impose upon Christendom, all the mystics remained within the bosom of the Church. Yet their consideration of religion as an internal sentiment unites them in a fundamental way to the leaders of the Protestant Revolution. Mysticism is a powerful solvent of all external authority. That is why the mystics were brushed aside so rudely in the Protestant Revolution. The leaders of revolt who were bent upon

substituting a new authority for the one they displaced were distrustful of them. " I despise such men," said Luther, " they care
for nothing but spirit." Yet mysticism was a potent factor in
making possible the success of the religious revolution; and in the
time of the Catholic Reformation it enjoyed a restoration and a
new growth.

None of these movements was able to effect a general reformation; nor did all combined succeed. Yet not one of them was in
vain. They were all mingled in the great stream that was slowly
gathering force and would soon burst into a flood. Each must
be counted as a definite and permanent factor in bringing to pass
the Protestant Revolution. They went to form the general conscience, the universal recognition of the need of reform. If the
Revolution had found no echo, no response, in the general conscience of the time it would have been unsuccessful. The great
movement of reform met with success precisely because men's
minds were prepared for it and were expecting it. Every accusation that Luther made and every reform that he suggested
had resounded through Christendom long before the opening of
the sixteenth century. The successful leaders of revolt were
not a handful of men who, solely by their personal power, induced the people to follow them along a new way. Long before
their time the soil was prepared for the seed. Long ago the
conscience of men, rehabilitated by the development of individuality, had become dissatisfied with the external activity of the
papal curia, and had come to regard an interior religion as of
paramount importance. Only thus can the rapid progress of the
Protestant Revolution in all classes of society be explained. The
time was ripe for revolt, and if the Saxon friar had not precipitated it some one else would undoubtedly have taken his place.

There was still another class of reformers — the humanistic
reformers. Of them we shall see more in a later chapter.
Everywhere the intellectual revival was breathing new life into
the channels of European thought. The new attitude towards
life had made its way over the Alps. The winds of freedom
were blowing. The prosperous life of the towns was prepared
and eager to receive the new ideal. The burghers had found
places for themselves in the professions. They were able to
read and to write and to think for themselves. Commerce, industry, and material enterprise of every kind were in their hands.
The printing press was distributing innumerable pamphlets and
books. Humanism north of the Alps was unlike that of Italy.
It was content with no unfruitful skepticism. It was, as we
shall see later on, destined to help the people to effect a reforma-

Relation
of the Re-
vival of
to.the
Protestant
Revolution

tion for themselves, to turn the tremendous force of secular culture into the channel of religious reconstruction.

In the time of the Protestant Revolution several spiritual reformers, not the well-known leaders but obscure prophets, whom we are to deal with in a later chapter, drew together all the tentative, inquiring and struggling movements for reform, put an end to the dualism which the Church had established between the claims of the present world and those of the future life, and made religion an inner possession, the product of personality, and the inspiration of the finest powers of the individual.

# CHAPTER IX

## THE AGE OF DISCOVERY

1. Discovery and its Motives.
2. Its Medieval Hindrances.
3. The Influence of the Crusades.
4. The Italian, Portuguese, and Spanish Discoverers.
5. Results of the Discoveries.

D ISCOVERY was the one activity of the various revivals of the time most open to the common man. But not even discovery is universal. It has had its periods of disprizal when explorers failed to get a hearing and were left to eat their hearts out in poverty and neglect. It has had its great ages when discoverers were endowed and when learning and invention contributed to their success. Such an age was the Renaissance.

Discovery has many motives. Curiosity, not so scientific and disinterested as the spirit that animates our men of science to-day, impelled the men of the Renaissance to explore the rich and splendid East. Europeans went forth over unknown lands and perilous seas and came back with wonderful knowledge and still more wonderful fables. With stimulating imagination they told their stories of the magnificent and highly civilized Orient, of its infinite store of gold, and pearls, and spices. Geographical inquisitiveness grew upon that which fed it, and vast dreams of wealth seemed certain of fulfilment. Commerce followed hard upon the heels of curiosity and became one of the most powerful of all the motives of discovery. For the new luxuries, many of which by this time were passing over into necessities, Europe was dependent upon Asia. Still later imperial ideas as well as dreams of gain were a stimulus to exploration. And then, potent from first to last, incentive of daring and romantic deeds, resulting in astonishing triumphs and pathetic failures, was the religious motive, the crusading passion whose fires, long burning low, flamed as high as ever in the heart of Columbus.

When the destroying Turk blocked the inter-continental land routes men began to seek new ways to the East. The only new routes were water-ways. But in the Middle Ages there were many hindrances to maritime discovery. Caravans that crept

175

along the known and noted tracks, river navigation, and coast sailing, were the only means of travel at that time. The Atlantic as it appeared to medieval sailors was a Sea of Darkness, a terrifying place on which to adventure. In mist and fog, with neither sun nor stars to guide, how could they keep their way? And then they were likely to meet not only with tempests and other common perils but with the Kraken, or the Sirens, or the dreaded Bishop of the Seas with his glowing miter. The revival of science and invention removed many of these hindrances. New shapes of keel and prow were invented that made wind and wave contributory to navigation. The compass and the rudder were made serviceable. Then came the quadrant and the astrolabe that made possible something like systematic ocean navigation.

The Crusades, themselves an expression of a spirit of expansion, exercised a most powerful influence upon discovery. They failed to accomplish their immediate objects, and ended in military disaster. But they pointed out paths of future conquest to the new-born nations of the West, they suggested lines of practical religious missionary efforts, and they greatly enlarged the sphere of commercial enterprise. They stimulated pilgrimage, trade, travel, and missionary activity. Pilgrim travel was the first manifestation of medieval expansion, and for a long time it was the most vital and typical outlet of the expansive activity of Christendom. But gradually with the pilgrims went other wayfarers, travelers, merchants, and missionaries. The spirit of mercantile enterprise became ever stronger. During the Crusades the commerce between the Orient and the Occident grew to vast proportions. The merchants did not stop at the Syrian sites that were the destination of the pilgrims, but they crept on from the Mediterranean to the Yellow Sea. Back from the East in heavily laden caravels and caravans they brought silk, ivory, perfume, spices, and gems. The imagination of Europe was inflamed with stories of the riches and the wonders of the far-off East, which to every adventurous spirit became a veritable El Dorado. To the merchant was added the missionary. Envoys from Rome made their way over the plains of central Asia to the court of the Great Khan in the effort to win to Christianity the wild Mongols whose conquests were bringing them ever nearer to Europe. Their arduous journeys failed of their purpose, but over their lives there rests the halo of romance, and in their footsteps followed others who found new ways across the continent. One of the most alluring of the travelers' tales was that of "Prester John." The Nestorians, an heretical Christian sect of the fifth century, found a footing in Persia

*Influence of the Crusades*

and afterwards succeeded in establishing themselves among the
Tartars. They had converted a powerful Khan, so the medieval story ran, who had become a priest. Soon the fame of this
priest and potentate spread all over Europe under the name of
Presbyter or " Prester " John. It was said that he had broken
the power of Islam in central Asia and that his Empire extended
into Africa. In the twelfth century the papacy made several
attempts to communicate with the mythical Prester John which
resulted only in the further extension of geographical knowledge.
The Mongol tide that was rolling towards Europe in the thirteenth century and threatening to sweep Islam out of its way
attracted the attention of all Christendom. A council held at
Lyons in 1245 sent two papal emissaries to the Mongol Khan.
One took the northern route through Poland and Russia, while
the other went through Asia Minor and Armenia. The diplomat
who took the northern way was John de Plano Carpini, a Franciscan friar, who delivered his letters to the Khan and, in 1247,
returned to Lyons after a journey of sixteen months in the
heart of Asia. It is with his journey that formal intercourse
between the Mongol power and western Christendom began.
Another Franciscan friar who went on a diplomatic mission to
Mongolia was William de Rubruquis. He went with Louis IX
to the Holy Land and was sent by his master with letters to the
Khan. His journey was one of the most important ever accomplished by a west-European previous to the era of the great
discoveries. Like all the other embassies that had for their purpose the winning of western Asia by means of a Mongol alliance,
the mission of Rubruquis failed to achieve its object. But the
narratives of Carpini and Rubruquis added immensely to the
geographical knowledge of the Europeans.

From the Italian Carpini and the Fleming Rubruquis the
western world learned something of the far richer countries that
lay beyond the land actually explored by these travelers, the **The Polos**
plains of central Asia. They learned of China and the Indies,
and of far Cathay. To these distant lands, the Ultima Thule,
there penetrated three Venetian merchants, Nicolo, Maffeo and
Marco Polo. Nicolo and Maffeo were brothers. Marco was
the son of Nicolo. The two brothers made a journey to the Far
East in 1260–69; and all three of them went to China on the
second and more important journey. Leaving home in 1271 they
traversed the whole length of Asia by land, skirted most of its
southern coasts by sea, and re-appeared at Venice in 1295.
Marco was the historian of the travels, and it is to his book that
Europe owes its first real survey of the Asiatic continent as a

whole. The contributions of the Polos to geographical knowledge completely eclipsed those of all other previous travelers.
They included the first extensive and reliable account of the
riches and the splendors of Indo-China, the Indian archipelago,
and China; and they included, too, the first actual information
about Japan. So picturesque was the account, so attractive the
story, so marvelous were the facts disclosed, that thousands read
it with unabated interest for generations afterwards. Columbus
tells us that he found it an absorbing narrative. It aroused in
many a breast the desire to follow in the steps of the men whose
journeyings it recounted.

With the death of Tamerlane, the Tartar conqueror, in 1405,
there vanished all hope of the establishment of a government in
central Asia sufficiently powerful and enlightened to maintain
**Results of the Over-land Jour-neys** order and encourage commerce; and all hope of a European-
Mongolian alliance that should drive back the forces of Islam.
All the attempts of Europe to continue and extend commercial
relations with the Far East by the overland routes ended in defeat. But the journeys of her missionaries, diplomats and
traders were by no means fruitless. They had given her a
more definite knowledge of the lands to which she would win
her way, a fuller realization of the enormous value of free and
easy access to the wealth that in part now lay revealed, and a
more accurate understanding of the encircling ocean that washed
the shores of every continent, of the possibilities of a maritime
route from the west to the east. They had also added to the
legends of the fabled Christian principalities that continued to
exist beyond the Islamic barrier in Asia and in Africa, and thus,
in the subsequent attempts that were made by the western Christians to find their isolated religious allies in the east and south
and to unite with them in the attempt to restore to Christendom
the holy places of their religion, they furnished another incentive
to discovery. These various motives, separately and in combination, sent the men of Latin Christendom exploring the water-
ways that at last brought them to the land of their hearts' desire.

We see, then, that the door which the Crusades had opened
**Beginning of the Search for a Water Route to the East** to western enterprise was closed almost at once. On the long
lines of communication between Italy and India there was en-
camped in the plains of central Asia a horde of armed nomads
and between these nomadic tribes and the Mediterranean were
the hostile forces of Islam, and from neither of them could be
expected encouragement or even permission of inter-continental
commerce carried on by Europeans. The Mediterranean Sea
had therefore become a *cul de sac*. Yet the teeming millions of

Europe seemed never more restless. That fabulous world of the Orient they must needs reach. It was more than another century before they actually did reach the Far East, but meanwhile they dreamed of it, filled it with all manner of charms and riches, and built there now an El Dorado and now an Utopia. Careers opened out to every adventurous soul. To men at the bottom of society there was swung wide a door of hope sealed heretofore save to the wealthy and the fortunate. The Genoese were the first of the modern seamen to try their fortunes as discoverers in the Atlantic. It was they who invented the carrack, the first vessel capable of making a long voyage of several months far out at sea. In these new vessels they explored the western coast of Africa. We do not know a great deal of the discoveries of these Genoese seamen. It seems reasonably probable that as early as 1275 one of their fleets rediscovered the Canaries, which, slightly known by the Phœnicians, Greeks and Romans, had almost if not completely disappeared from the knowledge of the medieval world. If this first voyage actually took place its purpose has been forgotten. Another expedition in 1291 that reached the Canaries had for its definite aim the endeavor to open up commercial relations with India by a maritime way. It was the first distinct attempt to solve the great problem that was to perplex Europe for the next two hundred years. It seems quite likely that it was Italian seamen who before 1351 added the Madeira Islands and the eastern members of the Azorean group to the knowledge of Europeans. About 1345 the remainder of the Azores, with the exception of the Formigas, were discovered. Thus European exploration had got halfway to America.

Portugal continued the work of discovery. Under John I (1385–1433) a policy of expansion beyond the sea was adopted. The occupation of Ceuta in 1415, the first of the over-sea conquests, greatly aided the Portuguese in gaining a command of the Atlantic. The greatest name in the early period of African exploration is that of Prince Henry, a younger son of John. Under his direction Portuguese fleets sailed ever farther to the south searching for the end of the continent where it would be possible to turn the flank of the Mohammedan power. He took up the work in a time of depression when western Europe was inactive because of failure and exhaustion. He had convictions of his own and the courage of them. He consecrated a long and noble life to the work of circumnavigating Africa. It is with him that the new nations began to take part in that over-sea activity, those commercial, colonial and missionary enterprises,

The Early Portuguese Sailors

which hitherto had been carried on only by volunteer adventurers or the city republics of Venice and Genoa. Under his impulse the flag of Portugal was carried ever farther and farther southwards until in 1445 the coast of Guinea was reached. His last years were devoted to the discovery of the remaining members of the Azorean archipelago and to the colonization of its principal islands. He carried on his work in the reigns of his father, John I, his elder brother Edward, and his nephew, Alfonso V, the son of Edward. Negro slaves were purchased in Africa and sold in all parts of Portugal, and gold and ivory were brought home; but Prince Henry was essentially a crusader. He died in 1460. Under Alfonso V, named the " African," exploration was continued. In 1482, after the entire coast of Guinea had been surveyed, the mouth of the Congo was discovered. Gradually a vast continent extending far below the equator was revealed. Finally in 1486 Bartolomeo Diaz (1445?–1500) rounded the Cape of Good Hope and reached Algoa Bay. The long voyage was the most remarkable one, unless we accept as true that of Leif Ericson, that had yet been made. The announcement that at last Africa had been rounded arrested the attention of Europe and was an incentive to further exploration. The maritime route to India was at last demonstrated.

It was Vasco da Gama (1469?–1524), perhaps the greatest sailor the world has known, who succeeded in throwing wide open the sea-gates to the East. He was a true type of the age of maritime adventurer, a man of iron will, inexorable temper, patient, dauntless, and unswerving in his aim. In 1497 he sailed round the Cape, crossed the Indian Ocean, and, in the following year, ten months and twelve days after leaving Lisbon, reached Calicut on the west coast of India. The town was a great center of Oriental trade. To it each year there came from the various Chinese ports a large trading fleet, while other ships brought to it the products of Indo-China and the spice islands. From it Mohammedan merchants carried their wares up the Red Sea and on to Alexandria, and up the Persian Gulf and overland to Europe. There were tolls and tariffs to pay on these routes that increased the cost of the merchandise to Europe four-fold. So an enormous profit was waiting for the merchants who could avoid these exactions by carrying the products of the East all the way by water to Europe. Vasco da Gama was something of a crusader. On his first voyage he had sunk Mohammedan dhows with gusto. But there were many of them left, and their masters disliked to see so profitable a trade as that between the East and Europe slip out of their hands. The Moslem sailors were therefore hostile to the Christian seamen. So in 1500 when Pedro Alvarez Cabral sailed in charge of another expedition to India his ships were equipped with artillery. On his way he lost sight of one of his vessels and while looking for it accidentally discovered the Brazilian coast. Portuguese fleets followed each other in quick succession and the founding of an empire over the seas was begun. Goa was chosen as the capital of the new dominion. The town was captured in 1510 by Alfonso de Albuquerque (1453?–1515), who then continued the work of conquest. He captured the seaport of Malacca, the most westerly emporium of the Far-Eastern trade, cleared the Indian Ocean almost completely of Mohammedan vessels, seized the port of Ormuz near the entrance to the Persian Gulf, and was making preparations for an attack upon Aden when news came from Portugal of his removal, instigated by personal enemies at the court, from the position he held as commander of the Portuguese forces. Shortly afterwards he died. Albuquerque was equally great as a naval commander and as an administrator of empire. He dreamed of far-reaching conquest, and his dreams were always based upon a mastery of detail. Each one of his naval attacks was directed to a definite and essential strategical advantage. In the six crowded years that he spent in the East he acquired for Portugal possessions of extraordinary value and laid down wise rules for commercial development. He had a rare power of dealing sympathetically with the strange peoples and the strange faiths he met in India. In him the Portuguese character rose to its greatest height and when he died the power of his country began gradually to decline.

While the Portuguese were making their way down the western coast of Africa it occurred to other seamen that there was probably a shorter and a less dangerous way across the seas to India. This was the thought of Christopher Columbus (1446?–1506), who succeeded in discovering the West Indies. Columbus was probably born in Genoa. He had been in the service of Prince Henry. He knew the Mediterranean by heart, had been to the Gold Coast, and had gone to England and perhaps to Iceland. It is said to have been a letter from Paolo Toscanelli, an old astronomer and mapmaker of Florence, that, about 1474, confirmed him in his belief that the shortest way to the Indies lay over the Atlantic. For eighteen years he endeavored in vain to persuade first one monarch and then another, the magistrates of Genoa and the signoria of Venice, to equip him with the ships and men necessary for the discovery of the western way to the Orient. But the years of delay were full of experience, for it

The Spanish Sailor

was in the interval of waiting that he went as far south as the
Gold Coast and at least as far north as England. At last, on
August 3, 1492, a little fleet of three caravels, the *Santa Maria,*
the *Pinta,* and the *Nina,* set sail from Palos for Japan. It was
manned by a motley and ill-favored crew made up largely of the
scum of the Mediterranean ports. In spite of the murmurs, the
curses and the groans of these men, whose hearts were filled with
fear of the Green Sea of Gloom, Columbus continued his way.
At last at two o'clock on the morning of October 12, a sailor
on board the *Pinta* sighted land about six miles away, a coral
strand glittering white in the moonlight. It was one of the
Bahama Islands, probably San Salvador. Across the wintry
ocean the *Nina,* a little half-decked boat, crept back through a
violent storm to take the news to Spain. But the first tidings
that Columbus took back with him apparently created little excitement in the Spanish peninsula and still less throughout Europe. The men who took part in the next voyages that were
made across the Atlantic in the next decade were all personal ac-
quaintances of Columbus. The momentous journey did not immediately inspire a wide circle of followers. In 1493 Columbus
made a second voyage in which he discovered Jamaica, a third
in 1498 in which he went to the mouths of the Orinoco, and a
final one in 1502 in which he penetrated into the Caribbean Sea.
His journeyings were now ended. No dreams had come true
of cargoes of gold and silver and pearls with which armies were
to be raised to drive the Turk from Europe and set free the Holy
Sepulcher. Aged by hardships and broken by cruel neglect and
poignant disappointment the daring sailor died in 1506 at Valladolid. Two decades after the death of Columbus the barrier
of the new continent was rounded and the world was circum-
navigated for the first time. The voyage of Ferdinand Magellan
(1480?–1521) whose expedition left Spain in 1519 and returned
to that country in 1522 is one of the greatest ever recorded. In
comparison with his long journey of fourteen thousand leagues
the voyage of Columbus, despite its far greater popular fame,
seems to dwindle almost to a brief pleasure trip. Magellan did
not live to complete the great journey himself, but was killed in
the Philippine Islands. Columbus discovered a new earth; half
a century later Copernicus was to reveal a new heaven. Truly
the horizons of men were expanding. But to the day of his
death the Italian sailor was unaware that he had planted the Castilian banner on a new continent and thought that he had reached
the shores of the mythical and opulent empire of far Cathay.

The great discoveries had important commercial results. The

caravan gave place to the caravel. The center of commercial
gravity was shifted from the Mediterranean to the Atlantic.
Venice and Genoa lost most of their remaining trade and new
ports on the shores of the Atlantic, Lisbon and Antwerp, that
formerly were mere outposts of trade became the great places
of commercial activity. The English Channel, the North Sea
and the Baltic Sea wrested from the Mediterranean its former
proud position. Intercourse with the Orient and with the new
continent of America became comparatively easy and cheap. So
commerce not only changed its direction and passed from the
hands of the Latins into those of the Teutons but also vastly
increased in quantity. This increase of commerce resulted in the
formation of great commercial companies whose purposes were
to reduce the cost of buying and transportation and then to control the selling of their goods and wares. These combinations
became monopolies. Then prices increased and in some cases
doubled. But it was not only the formation of monopolies that
had brought about the rise of prices. Wars and the increase of
the precious metals from the German and Hungarian mines and,
later on, from those of America, had much to do with it. Yet
the economic changes wrought by the geographical discoveries
were developed only imperfectly in the fifteenth century and by
no means to the full in the century of religious revolution.

The social results of the discoveries were, eventually, even
more important. They did much to make men look forward
to new ages as well as into new lands and displaced the engrossing devotion to antiquity. Sir Thomas More was inspired by the
discovery of America to write his *Utopia*. It is scarcely possible
for us to-day to realize the powerful effect upon the imagination
of the men of the sixteenth century which the sudden discovery
of a new continent must have had. Imagination always out-
strips man's knowledge and understanding; his emotions always
carry him far beyond the narrow reach of his intelligence. What
things were not possible in that new-won world? Did not one
adventurer go there to seek even for the fountain of perpetual
youth? The finding of America did much to widen the intellectual as well as the physical horizon. It gave breadth of interest and far-reaching vision to Montaigne, and from him these
things passed to his spiritual heirs among whom was Shakespeare.
The discoveries, as we have seen, did much to accelerate the rise
of capitalism, to interest man in commerce and industry far more
than he had been in the Middle Ages when agriculture was almost
his sole concern, and it did much to cause the development of
city life. The rise of capitalism and of city life caused a vast

social dislocation.  Men engaged in new lines of activity, new forms of political organization found favor, and new social as well as economic values came to the surface.

The discoveries were fraught with important political results. Portugal acquired one empire in the East and Spain another in the West.  The medieval empire became more obsolete than ever. It was the new nations that inherited the distant lands that had

**Political Results of the Discoveries**

recently swum into the ken of men.  From the countries she conquered, Spain took more than five thousand million dollars' worth of gold and silver.  But she did not use this enormous treasure wisely.  A great part of it was employed in the effort to extinguish heresy and to repress thought.  Most of it filtered through Spain like a sieve, leaving that country worse than it had been before, and changing the purchasing power of money throughout Europe.  The piratical expeditions of Spain to America followed closely upon the conclusion of the long wars against the Moors.  Most of the men engaged in these prolonged military enterprises came to have nothing but contempt for the ordinary occupations of life.  When the wars were over they lived as parasites upon society.  Their long continued military activity eventually exhausted Spain and Portugal.  Holland and France and England became the great colonial powers and reaped the advantages of discovery.  Eventually out of geographical expansion there arose democracy, or at least a greater approximation to democracy.

Finally the geographical discoveries helped to inaugurate great religious changes.  All through the Middle Ages, upon the sure

**Religious Results of the Discoveries**

basis of the Bible, the only *terra firma,* the only habitable part of the earth, was the top side of the globe with Jerusalem as its center; so, virtually, the earth was a disk floating in the atmosphere, surrounded by circling sun, moon, and stars.  Suddenly the whole medieval conception of the cosmos was shattered by the discovery of new lands on the other, the under, side of the world that were the homes of strange peoples.  Man came at last to know by actual experience the earth beneath his feet, something of the habitable lands on the other side of the globe, something of the dimensions of our planet, and something of its relative position in our solar system and in the universe.  The earth was no longer habitable only on one side, it was no longer stationary, it was no longer the center of things; and man, the most important of its inhabitants, was therefore no longer the cynosure of all the myriad eyes of the heavens.  Instead, it dwindled to the " least of little stars."  It was merely a sphere revolving in its appointed orbit about our sun as do the other planets of the same solar system. The disillusionment was a salutary one. Slowly, very slowly, for all such changes are exceedingly gradual, the old narrow conception of the universe together with beliefs for which it served as a basis began to lose their grip and to give way to faiths with a wider scale that permit more freely the development of man's spiritual nature in many different ways. In a less direct way, too, the discoveries had an important religious result. The increase of urban population and the development of city life gave rise to a secular culture which although it did not displace the once absolute dominion of the ecclesiastical culture at least disputed it and loosened it at many points.

# THE PROTESTANT REVOLUTION

# THE PROTESTANT REVOLUTION

## CHAPTER X

### POLITICAL AFFAIRS AT THE OPENING OF THE PROTESTANT REVOLUTION

I N our study of the political affairs of Europe during the era of the Renaissance we left France with all her territory recovered except Calais. The task that now confronted her was that of consolidating the kingdom, and of centralizing power in the hands of the king, a task skilfully pursued by the crafty Louis XI (1461–83), who found himself greatly aided by the establishment of a permanent royal army and a permanent special tax for its support that had been effected in 1439 by his predecessor. The "League of the Public Good," an effort, under a misleading name, on the part of the great feudal nobles and the princes of the blood to check the policy of centralization, failed to accomplish its purpose. The intrigues of Louis against his powerful neighbor Burgundy eventually resulted in the extinction of that country. Burgundy was a complex collection of principalities united only by virtue of the fact that they were ruled by the same prince. Parts of it were held by its duke as fiefs of France and the other parts were held as fiefs of the Empire. Under Duke Philip the Good (1419–67) these loosely related territories had been greatly increased and the dukedom had become more than ever a thorn in the side of France. To his son Charles the Bold (1467–77) there was left the ambition of changing the duchy into a kingdom; but in a war with the Swiss he met an untimely death. The only child left by Charles was his daughter Mary. Louis quickly seized a considerable part of the Burgundian territories, and was prevented

Consolidation and Centralization in France

189

from seizing more only by the marriage of Mary to Maximilian, son of the Emperor Frederick III. Louis made other territorial gains including Anjou, Maine, Bar, and Provence. In the work of centralization, which he pushed forward vigorously, he received his greatest aid from the legists whose study of the Roman law had accustomed them to a supreme central authority. From this body of lawyers, the *noblesse de la robe,* the king chose his most intimate councilors; and from it, at a later time, were to come the king's chief ministers. It was this body also that furnished the Parlement of Paris with its effective membership. The Parlement was becoming increasingly powerful. The States-General, after its meeting in 1506, did not assemble again for half a century, and the provincial parlements had the right to deal only with provincial affairs. So the Parlement of Paris became the one standing body, resembling a national institution, that shared power with the king. It was primarily a judicial body, but it acquired something of a legislative character from the fact that it obtained the right of requiring the royal decrees to be entered upon its register in order for them to become valid. It is true that this right did not amount to an absolute veto, because the king could hold a *lit de justice,* that is, he could be present in person and compel the registration of an obnoxious decree. But the refusal to register a decree required the king to notice the wishes of the parlement, and was at least a suspensory veto. In the lower courts, too, by replacing feudal judges, the legists made themselves felt in the life of France. The royal army, the royal taxation, and the royal courts made the king by far the most powerful prince in the country, in whom the people saw their natural defender, "a visible image of God upon earth," and coupled with the sentiment of nationality they made of France one of the most powerful of the new nations.

In strong contrast to the process of consolidation and centralization in France was the tendency to disintegration in the empire. But when Maximilian I (1493–1519) came to the imperial throne the men who loved Germany hoped for better things. He was a gifted prince, this "last of the knights," whose gracious personality and versatile powers aroused in the hearts of his subjects expectation of the fulfilment of the dreams of reform. Few were the events and movements of his time upon which he did not leave, more or less distinctly, the impress of his individuality, but he lacked perseverance and foresight; and, by devoting most of his energy to the extension of the boundaries of the empire, and those of the house of Hapsburg, rather than to the work of consolidating the territories it already possessed and of remedying their grievances, he disappointed those who had placed their trust in him. Throughout his reign, despite his bungling attempts at constitutional reform, and his somewhat more successful effort to lift the Empire out of its military helplessness, all the particularistic forces continued to seek their own advancement to the detriment of the common union.

The building up of Spain, it will be remembered, had been hastened by the marriage of Isabella and Ferdinand. Much had to be done at first to put their respective countries in order. Castile, ravaged by frequent wars between its nobles who were practically independent, was a lawless kingdom. Aragon was far less anarchic. But in both countries there was much to do before an effective central government could be said to exist. The self-reliant character of Isabella, her courage and decision, enabled her to cope successfully with the difficulties that confronted her. To the same qualities of courage and steadfast determination as those which gave a masculine element to the character of his wife, Ferdinand united foresight, caution, and a cunning in diplomacy that enabled him to circumvent his rivals. To him probably more than to Isabella is due the restoration of order in Castile, the reorganization of its institutions and the centralization of its administration; and to his incessant activity in every line of government must be attributed the foundation of that absolute monarchy to which his descendants succeeded. A vigorous renewal of the crusade against the Moors resulted in 1492 in the capture of Granada, whose capitulation was received by Gonsalvo de Cordova, " *El príncipe de los caballeros, il Gran Capitano.*" Thus was the long and desperate warfare against the infidel ended and the crescent banished from the west. And when in 1515, eleven years after the death of Isabella, that part of Navarre lying south of the Pyrenees was incorporated with the crown of Castile the whole of the peninsula with the exception of Portugal, was united under one ruler. The Spanish conquests beyond the sea, too, went on at an amazing rate. It was only the beginning of this vast trans-oceanic empire that came in Ferdinand's time; but he it was who, in the face of great difficulties, raised Spain from feudal obscurity to the foremost place among the new nations. The most effective force in the work of centralization was the Santa Hermandad, a general association which, for the purpose of ensuring the public peace and protecting private rights, maintained a mounted military police in every part of the kingdom and made the royal authority supreme throughout the land. Italy we left a land of warring communes and despotisms.

The Papacy as an Italian Power

We return to witness it made the battle-ground on which were fought out the rival claims and ambitions of France and Germany. But to what may be regarded as a new political power in the peninsula we must first pay attention. More engrossed in political affairs than ever before, its high office and its lofty aims shamelessly relegated to the background, the papacy under Sixtus IV (1471–84) sank to the level of the contending principalities that surrounded it by becoming one of them. Yet it was only after some years of experience and a careful survey of the situation that Sixtus embarked upon his secular policy. All about him were the rival divisions of the peninsula, seething with intrigue and struggling for ascendancy. The Church had but a slight hold upon the affections of men. To rely upon popular support seemed unsafe. Each of the European powers was bent upon its own aggrandizement. To depend upon any one of them was evidently to court disaster. Was it not necessary, then, Sixtus asked himself, directly to strengthen the position of the papacy in a worldly way? In carrying out the program which he adopted of vigorous secular activity Sixtus needed first of all assistants in whom he could place the utmost confidence; so, making of nepotism a political principle, he placed his relatives in the most responsible positions. But his energy was spent in vain. The wars against Florence and Ferrara failed to carry him any nearer to his goal, while the aggrandizement of his family, his complicity in a scheme for the assassination of Lorenzo and Giuliano de' Medici, his unmistakably worldly character, his actuation by the meanest motives, and his failure to pay any attention to the omnipresent corruption of the age, debased the Papacy still further in the eyes of Europe. The pontificate of Innocent VIII (1484–92) was but an interval of indolent and aimless drifting in which the general immorality of the time became more pronounced than ever. The policy of political activity inaugurated by Sixtus was continued by Alexander VI (1492–1503), a handsome and sensual man, who while still a cardinal had made his Catalonian kinsmen all-powerful in Rome. The Papacy had certainly suffered a great change since the days of Gregory VII. The dramatic downfall of Boniface VIII, the Avignonese captivity, the schism, and now the engrossment of the papacy in its secular rôle of an Italian principality, were the chief stages in its descent. The defeat of the conciliar attempt at control left the Papacy more absolute than ever before in ecclesiastical matters; but it was not with religion that it was now chiefly concerned. Its world-wide financial system gave it the appearance of being a great financial institution, and activity in diplomacy and warfare stamped it as a political power. Its absorption in these worldly activities prepared the way for the religious revolution. Yet it was in this gloomiest moment in the history of the Papacy since the evil days of the tenth and eleventh centuries, in this time of knavery, simony, treason, and every other kind of corruption, that a final attempt was made to reform the Church from within. A prophet arose in the person of Savonarola. But first we must notice the French invasion of Italy.

When Louis XI died he was succeeded by his son, Charles VIII (1483-98), a lad of fourteen whose mind was filled with the legends of chivalry. For the first half of his reign his older sister, Anne of Beaujeu, was the regent of France. The marriage of the young king to Anne of Brittany resulted eventually in the annexation to the crown of that last of the great feudatory States of France. The country became more prosperous than ever before; and Charles, after becoming free from the restraint of his sister Anne, began to look to the fulfilment of his dreams of conquest. Spain was extending its boundaries and consolidating its power; Maximilian was evidently determined to convert the theory of the Empire into fact. Why should France lag behind? Through the house of Anjou, whose rights had descended to him, Charles had a claim upon Naples; and his cousin and brother-in-law, Louis Duke of Orleans, had a claim upon Milan. So in 1494, after making substantial concessions to England, Germany, and Spain in order to have a free hand, Charles crossed the Alps with the purpose of conquering Naples. The invasion was like the pageant of a summer day. On through Asti and Piacenza the ill-equipped and motley array went, to Florence, Siena, Rome, and Naples. But the European powers were not pleased with this easy victory. They felt the suddenly acquired preponderance of France to be a menace to their safety. They became champions of the idea of the " balance of power." At Venice, therefore, on March 31, 1495, there was formed a league between Germany, Spain, Milan, the Papacy, and Venice, whose real purpose was to expel the French from Naples. Charles retreated northward, got the better of a clash with Milanese and Venetian troops at Fornovo, in spite of being greatly out-numbered, and evacuated Italy. All his Italian conquests melted away like mist in the summer sun, and so his invasion failed to effect its purpose. But it had another and a momentous result. It took its ruffianly soldiers into the peninsula, displayed to them the glory of the Italian cities, steeped them for a year in the joys of the Renaissance, and then sent them to tell the story of the new civilization in their own countries. It revealed to the peoples of the north the richness and the weakness of Italy. It pointed the way to future invasions and made the peninsula the arena for the rivalries of the new-born nations.

Girolamo Savonarola (1452-98) was born at Ferrara where his grandfather was an eminent court physician and his father a spendthrift courtier. He was a silent and sorrowful youth made so by musing upon the immorality of the age. When he

was twenty-three years of age, after writing a farewell letter to his father telling him that "the misery of the world and the iniquities of men" had driven him to take the step, he left the luxurious corruption of Ferrara and fled across the marshy fields to Bologna where he entered the Dominican convent. There he spent the next seven years of his life. Then he went to the convent of San Marco in Florence. But he failed to impress the Florentines with his sermons, so he became a wandering preacher. His power increased and he was recalled to Florence. This time his impetuous eloquence drew great crowds to hear him. His sermons were always practical. With all the consuming ardor that filled his soul he denounced the sins of the world, called men to repentance, and in solemn and prophetic strain he spoke of an impending visitation of the wrath of God. The vast Duomo was too small to hold the crowds that flocked to hear him. In the cold and darkness of the winter nights people got up and waited in the street until the cathedral doors were opened, and then inside they waited three or four hours more until they saw above them in the pulpit the gaunt and imperious yet benign and wistful face of the man whose pure enthusiasm and impassioned eloquence held their hearts in thrall.

In 1492 Lorenzo de' Medici died and was succeeded in the control of the city by his oldest son Piero (1492-1503). Two years later, as we have seen, the French invaded Italy. "Be-

hold the sword has descended," cried Savonarola to the vast and panic-stricken crowd that hung upon his words, "the scourge has fallen, the prophecies are being fulfilled; behold, it is the Lord who is leading on these armies." Piero surrendered the Florentine fortresses and made a complete submission to the invader. The indignant citizens compelled him and his two brothers to seek safety in flight; and thus, after sixty years, Florence had regained her liberty. Savonarola then became an important political factor and disclosed an unguessed statesmanship. A plan of government, to a large extent his own creation, that resembled somewhat the Venetian oligarchy, and that won the

warm admiration of the historian Guicciardini, was adopted.
But in its actual workings the new régime was a theocracy.
For a time Florence forsook her gay dances and all her pagan
pageantry. The streets that once had echoed to the ribald songs
of Lorenzo and his dissolute companions were strangely silent
or were filled with religious processions. But the passage of
Savonarola from preaching to politics was a perilous step. It
was not for long that the Florentines were willing to submit to
such strict regulations. Puritanism found an uncongenial soil
in a city where for so long paganism had prevailed. The innate
character of the people could not be so readily and radically
changed. The alien character of the régime, the blunders of
Savonarola, the old jealousies of Dominicans and Franciscans,
and the ineradicable hatreds of the factions, brought about an
inevitable recoil. Alexander VI could not brook the opposition
of the friar to the league against France, so in 1497 he excommunicated him. And when it was discovered that Savonarola
was endeavoring to bring about the summoning of a general
council to inquire into the conduct of the pope his death was
determined. Alexander threatened to place Florence under an
interdict, and the Florentines feared the consequent loss of trade.
Over the details of Savonarola's downfall we may pass briefly —
the miserable fiasco of the ordeal by fire which was none of his
seeking, and which his supporters were ready to meet; the awful
scenes in the torture chamber where for a moment his strong soul
quailed and he was compelled to utter an agonized denial of his
divine mission; his last mass in the chapel of the Priors; and
the last scene of all in which his body perished in the flames.
Savonarola was a precursor not of the Protestant Revolution but
of the Catholic Reformation. Those kind blue eyes of his looked
not so much into the future as into the past. It was his dream
to take the world back to an earlier age in which the ideals of
asceticism had prevailed.

When Louis XII (1498–1515) of Orleans succeeded to the
French throne there were united in his person the French claims
upon Naples and Milan. Immediately he began preparations for *The Sec-*
a second invasion of Italy. The league formed at Venice *ond*
against France had little force. Its Italian members were suspi- *French*
cious of each other, and little reliance could be placed upon *Invasion*
Maximilian. The pope desired a powerful ally; and Venice, be- *of Italy*
cause of her plans of territorial expansion, wished for the downfall of Milan. So the Venetian league dissolved; the foreigner
again poured his armies through the northern passes; and Milan
was conquered. Then Louis turned his attention to the south.

In 1500 a secret treaty was concluded at Granada for a combined conquest of Naples by France and Aragon and a division of the territory. This agreement was confirmed by the pope. All the interests of Alexander VI, who occupied the papal chair, were selfish and secular. " The whole thought of the pope," said a Venetian ambassador of the time, " is to make his children great. He cares about nothing else." With every means at his command he endeavored to advance the interests of his family. He was led to put his children into important places by his passionate devotion to them, by the fact that he could trust no one else, and also because they were extremely useful as pawns in the political game he was playing. He raised his nephew Juan Borgia to the cardinalate. He married one of his daughters, the radiantly beautiful Lucrezia, in turn to three important princes. His third son, the handsome and iron-willed Cesare, whom he chose for an ecclesiastical career, was made bishop, archbishop, and cardinal, and given an enormous number of benefices, before he was nineteen years old. But Cesare was interested in secular affairs, and, using every means that came to his hand, conquest, treachery, simony, and extortion, he made his father the first pontiff who actually ruled the unruly papal State. Alexander died in 1503, probably from having contracted the fever of the Campagna. The full responsibility for having invited the second French invasion cannot be laid upon him, but with him must rest a large share of the blame. He did not inaugurate the secularization of the Papacy, but he did much to degrade it still further to the level of the surrounding and self-seeking Italian principalities. The conquest of Naples was accomplished without serious difficulty. But the provisions of the treaty of Granada were by no means precise, and a war broke out over the spoils in which the Spanish troops were victorious. The matter ended by the agreement of Louis to give his Neapolitan claim as a dowry to his sister's daughter, Germaine of Foix, whom Ferdinand, in 1506, Isabella having died two years previously, took for his second wife. Thus did Naples fall into the possession of Spain.

No such nuptial agreement, however, was destined to ensure peace to the unhappy peninsula. It put an end to the war in the south only to permit another to break out in the north. Venice had reached the height of its power and splendor. It is true that the Turks had robbed her of some of her possessions in the east and that the discovery of the route to India by the Cape of Good Hope twenty-two years before had shifted westward the center of commerce and left her to pursue a career

of continuous decline that lasted for three hundred years. But
this loss of economic importance was not yet apparent. She
ranked as one of the great powers of Europe. Her foes looked
with greedy eyes upon her possessions and coveted them for
themselves. Chief of those who plotted for the division of the
maritime republic was the martial Julius II (1503–13), who,
after the brief pontificate of Pius III that lasted less than a
month, succeeded the infamous Alexander, and who was determined to make the papal State the strongest political power in
Italy. The others were Maximilian of Germany, Ferdinand of
Spain, Louis of France, the republic of Florence, the Duke of
Ferrara, and the marquis of Mantua. A league was signed between some of the conspirators in 1508 in the little Flemish town
of Cambray, and by the others later, for the partition of the
Most Serene Republic. Venice was defeated. All the possessions she had acquired in the fifteenth century were lost.
And perhaps she would have fared even worse had not her foes
fallen to quarreling among themselves.

The warlike Julius now desired to expel the French from
Italy. Possessed of Milan, they were too powerful and too dangerous a force in the peninsula. So in 1511 he induced Spain
and Venice to sign the Holy League with him to effect that end.
A month later the compact received the adherence of Henry
VIII of England who had plans of his own for the division of
France. In less than a year the French were driven back across
the Alps. And Ferdinand proceeded to the conquest for himself of that part of Navarre that lay south of the Pyrénées.
The confederates then restored the Medici to Florence, which
had favored the French, and the Sforza to Milan. On the
death of the *pontefice terribile,* Leo X (1513–21), second son
of Lorenzo de' Medici, began his splendid but scandalous pontificate in which he proved a most magnificent patron of the
Renaissance and a most unworthy Vicar of Christ. He continued his predecessor's policy of hostility to France, and with
Henry of England, Maximilian I of Germany, and Ferdinand of
Spain, he signed the treaty of Mechlin, 1513, for the partition of
that country. An attempt of France to retake Milan with the
aid of the Venetians met with disaster in the battle of Novara;
and in the " Battle of the Spurs " at Guinegate the French suffered defeat at the hands of the English. But the idea of the
balance of power made some of the confederates hesitate at
the further disablement of France. Dissensions, therefore,
broke out among them. Then a new king, Francis I (1515–47),
came to the French throne, a youth of twenty who was filled

with the desire to retrieve the military disasters of his country. His victory at Marignano, 1515, regained Milan. In the following year the death of Ferdinand of Spain brought still another new figure upon the scene in the person of Charles, whose mother was Joanna, daughter of Ferdinand and Isabella, and whose father was Philip, son of Maximilian. Philip had died in 1506, and since then Charles had been Arch-duke of Austria. When his grandfather Ferdinand died he became, at the age of sixteen, the ruler of Spain, the Netherlands, Naples, Sicily, and the rapidly expanding Spanish possessions across the sea. For some years he had lived in the Netherlands as the governor of those unruly provinces, and there, frequently reminded that France had taken some of the fairest possessions of the House of Burgundy, whose heir he was, he had come to regard his western neighbor as his hereditary foe. But as yet he was in no position to carry on war with France. He was too insecurely established in his vast and scattered possessions and he lacked money. So at Noyon, in 1516, he concluded a peace with Francis. Three years later his other grandfather, the Emperor Maximilian I, that knight-errant of a bygone time, died; and then he became ruler of the Austrian hereditary lands. A new emperor had to be elected. Three candidates offered themselves — Henry VIII of England, who was not an aggressive contestant, Francis I of France, and Charles I of Spain. The last was chosen and became Emperor Charles V.

Charles was only twenty years of age when he was elected to the imperial position. He lacked a strong physique. The traces of the unhappy inheritance from his mad mother, whose tainted blood wrought so marked a change in the Hapsburg stock, could be plainly seen. But he had an iron will, and not a little of the unbending pride and stiff precision that proclaimed him to be more of a Spaniard than a German. In intellect he was, perhaps, inferior to either of the two men who had contested with him for the imperial crown; but he possessed qualities that both of them lacked, freedom from their flagrant immorality, and a stern and inflexible sense of duty. Nor was he as selfish as they. The hope that he cherished in his heart was that of a restoration of the medieval empire and the medieval church, not so much for personal aggrandizement as for the reason that they were in his opinion the secular and the spiritual agencies of God, the ultimate organization of humanity, the final and effectual instruments for the extinction of evil. For the fulfilment of this ideal he employed all the means at his command, every art and every weapon with which he was familiar. But this

silent, serious, and lonely man, the last heroic figure among the
emperors, was doomed to spend his years in vain endeavor and
to know at the end the bitterness of a double defeat.

Having now sketched very briefly the political situation at the
opening of the sixteenth century we are to turn our attention to
other aspects of the great revolutionary wave that was sweeping through the thought and the life of the time and transforming the medieval into the modern world.   The Renaissance was
one aspect of that movement, and the Protestant Revolution another.   The political, industrial, social, and religious conditions
of the Middle Ages were all giving way and becoming transformed into conditions that more nearly resemble those of our
own time.   Ecclesiastical change, then, was not an isolated
phenomenon.   It was but one aspect of a general change.   All
the various aspects, or lines, of this general change were inextricably interwoven with each other.   So it would be both difficult and inadvisable to attempt to separate them, to study one
without any reference to the others.   This is particularly true of
the Protestant Revolution.   That movement, in addition to being merely one aspect of a general change, was by no means exclusively an ecclesiastical revolution.   The Church itself at
which the revolution was aimed was concerned with many things
in addition to religious matters.   It was a potent economic factor
in the life of the time, it exercised a profound influence upon
social conditions, and it dominated the intellectual activity of men.
In each one of these phases of its activity it met with opposition.
Some men were particularly displeased with its intellectual constraint, and others with its dogmatic requirements.   Luther was
especially concerned with the practices and the teachings of the
Church; but, nevertheless, he realized that the financial motive
was exceedingly powerful, for he invoked it in his first appeal
to the German nation.   The Protestant Revolution, then, is an
elastic term.   It comprehends many motives.   It was a river
fed by many springs.   Yet, after all, though it was by no means
an exclusively religious movement, religion was its essential concern, the main current of the stream.   It was not an isolated
movement.   Other phases of that great change, of which it was
itself but a single phase, those phases for instance that we call
the Renaissance, continued their course with it side by side.
The revival of literature, art, and science, the development of invention, and the progress of geographical discovery were all going on simultaneously with the several ecclesiastical revolts.
Nor was it a sudden movement.   All through the Middle Ages,
as we have seen in our study of the revival of conscience, there

The Multi
farious
Revolu-
tionary
Move-
ments of
the Time

were men who protested against the immorality of the clergy and the neglect of their spiritual duties, and others who rejected the creeds of the Church. Something we have seen of these several classes of critics and reformers. We have delayed until now the consideration of still another class — the humanistic reformers.

# CHAPTER XI

## HUMANISM AND HERESY

ITALIAN humanism devoted itself to the study of classical records and imitated classical modes of thought for the purposes of recapturing and developing the scientific method of observation and experiment, of obtaining a more complete and accurate knowledge of the world of nature and of men, of perfecting literary style, and of increasing the appreciation of beauty. All of these things were to aid in the development and enrichment of the individual life. They were to help the individual to think, to act, and to will for himself, in opposition, if need be, to any external tradition, authority, or precedent. They were to help him to love the world as his home; to regard it no longer as a place of exile to be despised in anticipation of a life to come, but daily to win it anew by means of the recently aroused personal faculties. They were not intended to produce a general social or religious regeneration. Culture, it was believed, would relieve the individual from the pressure of external authority, would result in intellectual emancipation, and would thus give free rein to the pursuit of individual inclinations and desires. The Italian humanists were the standard-bearers of a new ideal, an ideal of the untrammeled esthetic personality whose highest quality was that of *virtù*, the power to will. Their engrossment with the achievement of this ideal of esthetic personality, complete within itself, allowed them to relegate religion to the dim realm of dreams. Only incidentally and very slightly was Italian humanism concerned with ethics and with religion. It was inclined to resign itself to the idea of a permanent division of human society into two classes, the educated and the uneducated. For the former there was to be freedom of thought; for the latter the existing traditions and conventions would suffice.

The Aims
of Cisal-
pine Hu-
manism

On the other hand, the humanism of the graver nations of the north was occupied from the first with social regeneration. It was religious in its essence, not merely esthetic. It desired the development of individuality, of course, but chiefly as a means toward social improvement in the broadest sense of the term. The trans-Alpine humanists were interested in the welfare of society at large. It was for the enlightenment of their fellow-men that they studied, translated, and wrote, and not solely for the perfection of the individual.

The Effect
of Transal-
pine Hu-
manism
upon Re-
ligion

It is not difficult to see why the humanism of the north, differing in its aims as widely as it did from that of Italy, exerted so profound an influence upon religion, while the humanism of Italy was non-religious in its temper. The Italian humanists were animated with the ardor of research, they were observant, and they were critically-minded. They had won mental emancipation for themselves, they were absorbed in the attainment of a highly developed esthetic personality, and they were satisfied. From the beginning of the pontificate of Nicholas V to the end of that of Leo X the Papacy was a foster-mother of the new humanism. Popes and cardinals were humanists themselves. The mere outward conformity to the requirements of the Church, that was the sole demand made upon the humanists, was readily granted. Within himself, and within the various groups of humanists, the man of letters found a safe harbor of thought. So outward affairs were allowed to go as they would. The Italian humanists were occupied with their studies. They were but little concerned with ecclesiastical abuses and theological dogmas. They smiled at the former, and if the latter momentarily arrested their attention a shrug of the shoulders was the only response. Italian humanism did not incite to social action. It ended with the mental emancipation and the esthetic development of the individual. The humanism of the northern nations was concerned from the beginning with the betterment of the life of the time. It was in travail with the deep desires of the soul. It was rooted in religion. It labored first of all to eradicate the prevalent ecclesiastical abuses; and then, later on, it turned its attention to the dogmas of the Church and sought to reconstruct what it deemed to be a degenerate Christianity. It therefore led to heresy, to ecclesiastical revolution. The Transalpine humanists, especially the Germans, were not content to regard culture as an individual possession. More and more they became social reformers who sought to effect a change in moral and ecclesiastical affairs.

There was, of course, no general unanimity of thought among

the humanists in the north upon the subject of religious reform.
There was no concerted movement among the nations.  In each
country the movement was *sui generis*.  And neither was there
any general and definite agreement among the individual humanists in any one country.  As time went on some of them became identified with sects that separated from the Mother
Church; others, refusing to accept the new doctrines, clung to
the faith of their childhood; while still others became skeptics
and held aloof from either camp.  But all of them, in one way
or another, were devoted to the cause of reform.  As citizens
they welcomed a reform of morals; and as scholars they welcomed an increased freedom of thought, an extension of the
principle of free inquiry.  When, later on, it was seen that within
the various new ecclesiastical folds there was no more, or even
less, freedom for individual thought than there had been in the
fold of Catholicism many of the humanists turned their backs
upon the reformers.  Erasmus, for instance, regarded Luther as
an enemy of intellectual progress, and Rabelais held Calvin to be
a bigot.  Nevertheless the spread of humanism made for the
success of the reformers, for the triumph of heresy.

One should not be surprised at the seeming boldness of many
of the early humanists.  There was no such sharp distinction in
their time between the Church and the heresies as later on there
came to be between Catholicism and Protestantism.  Within the
Church there was no general agreement upon its teachings until
the Council of Trent.  Men of widely divergent views remained
within the pale.  There was not at that time an impelling necessity to take sides with one division of Christianity or another.
This explains much of the apparent audacity in the publishing of
heretical views.  Many of the early humanists would have repudiated the charge of heresy.  They were averse to violent
partizanship.  They desired to be neither revolutionists nor innovators, but wished simply to help in the restoration of the
primitive Christianity of apostolic times.

The comparative history of humanism affords striking evidence of the powerful consciousness which the spirit of nationality had attained, for in every country the movement acquired distinguishing characteristics.  English humanism very early developed a practical tendency.  It became interested in the work
of public education, and was applied with intelligence to the work
of religious reform.  Among the earliest of the English humanists was William Grocyn (1446?–1519) who studied under Poliziano and Chalcondylas in Florence and taught Greek
at Oxford.  The physician Thomas Linacre (1460?–1524),

highly regarded as a classical scholar by his contemporaries, was another of the Oxford group who having gone to Italy, the fountain-head of humanism, returned to their native land to spread the new learning. A third member of the little band of Hellenists was John Colet (1467?–1519), the founder of St. Paul's School in London. It is in him that English humanism definitely assumed its essential character. He was much more of an innovator than most of his contemporaries. He substituted for the medieval and allegorical method of interpreting the Scriptures that of endeavoring by critical study to obtain the literal meaning of the text. Erasmus ascribes to him the leadership of the little group of Oxford scholars at the opening of the sixteenth century, "intent on high designs, a thoughtful band." Out of his own fortune he expended some $200,000 of the money of our time for the establishment and maintenance of the new school in London. He did much to call attention to the need of church reform, speaking with passionate sincerity of the purity of primitive Christianity; and he exerted a notable influence upon the work of education.

The radiant figure of Sir Thomas More (1478?–1535), him whose genius was said to be "excellent above all his nation," is the last of this group of English humanists that we shall stop

to notice. Subtly compounded of wit and gravity, of strength and tenderness, of cheerfulness and religious fervor, the character of the high-souled chancellor is one that makes an unfailing appeal to men of every place and time. He had a wide and thorough knowledge of Greek and Latin literature; and, like Colet, he was filled with an ardent desire for a reformation of the Church from within. In the long line of pictures of an ideal state of society that begins with Plato's *Republic,* and is augmented from time to time by the vision of some dreamer of dreams, his *Utopia* holds an honorable place. Through the thin veil of humor one may read an indictment of the social conditions of the time, of poverty that is undeserved, of riches that are idle and unmerited, of persecution because of religious faith, of the infliction of the severest penalty of the law for minor crimes, of the many deplorable evils that are the inevitable accompaniment and aftermath of war, and of many another glaring evil that filled the soul of More with "divine discontent." And there, too, one may read the suggestions, some of them paradoxical, others merely ingenious, others obviously tentative, but many of them set forth in all sincerity, that were to serve as lamps to guide the feet of men toward a better and a juster organization of society. The marked differences between rural

and urban life were to be lessened as much as possible, towns
were to be made sanitary and inviting, the naked places of the
country were to be made green and shady with trees; monasticism was to be abolished; no one was to be idle, six hours each
day was to be the maximum time devoted to manual labor so
that all might have leisure for intellectual progress; religious
toleration, save that all were to believe in the existence of God
and the immortality of the soul, was to be practised.  The book
was originally written in Latin and addressed to the educated
class of Europe; but it was translated into English and other
modern languages, and it became influential in the struggle for
social reform in Germany.  Even to-day it is still a counsel of
progress.

This brief treatment of English humanism would be incom-
plete should we fail to note the influence of Erasmus, with whom *The Influ-*
we shall deal at some length later on.  So great was the power *ence of*
exerted by this chief protagonist of the new humanism upon the *Erasmus*
*in England*
scholars of his time, and indeed upon the time itself, that only the
influence of Voltaire upon the eighteenth century can be compared to it, an influence far more circumscribed than that exerted by the little Dutch scholar.  Erasmus went to England in
1499 when he was thirty-three years of age.  " England pleases
me as no other land has yet pleased me," he wrote to one of his
friends; " the climate I find most agreeable and healthful, and I
have come upon so much accurate and elegant scholarship, both
Greek and Latin, that I hardly care now to go to Italy, except for
the sake of seeing the country."  Endowed with " the capacity
for friendship which is a mark of the true humanist" he made
friends wherever he went, in Oxford, in Cambridge, and in London; and his witty and satirical attacks upon obscurantism, his
method of scientific research, and his advocacy of ecclesiastical
reform, won adherents to the cause and incited imitation.

From the beginning French humanism allied itself with heresy,
due perhaps to the fact that combined with the passionate devotion of the French scholars to ideals was a logical impatience *Early*
of compromise.  Among the Parisian humanists of the early *French*
*Humanists*
sixteenth century was Jacques Lefèvre (1455?-1536) of Étaples.
In his *Commentary on the Epistles of St. Paul,* published in 1512,
Lefèvre distinctly enunciated the doctrine of justification by
faith alone, which, as we shall see, was the fundamental tenet
of Lutheranism.  Guillaume Budé (1467-1540), the leading
French humanist of his time, though not the leading French
writer, was concerned primarily with secular studies.  It
was he who wrested from Italy for France the claim to the

first place in the world of scholarship. In Greek scholarship and in technical knowledge of Latin he equaled if he did not surpass Erasmus, but he was by no means so great an intellectual force. Guillaume Briçonnet (1470–1533), who in 1516 became Bishop of Meaux, was a humanist and a patron of scholars. He withdrew from uneducated ecclesiastics the privilege of preaching in his diocese and replaced them with pupils of Lefèvre. Nicolas Bérauld (1473–1550) was an ardent student of the classical literatures, ranking high as a Greek scholar. His teaching interested many men, especially Admiral Coligny and his two brothers, the cardinal and the general, in the cause of ecclesiastical reform. Étienne Dolet (1509?–46), who was more directly indebted to the Italian Renaissance for his scholarship and literary predilections than any other French humanist of the time, was believed by most of his contemporaries to be a materialist, if not actually an atheist, but his writings seem to warrant the conclusion that he was a sincere believer in the existence of a divine creator and in the immortality of the soul. Yet it was a vague and shifting idea of immortality that he had. The faith that recommended itself to him was one of " duty in relation to this world only," a faith troubled very little, if at all, with the future, holding that to be " a matter of which nothing can be certainly known, and concerning which it is useless to speculate or to reason." His heretical views together with some regrettable infringements of the law caused him to be put to death. Despite his faults of head and of heart he was a man of many fine qualities, of no inconsiderable ability, of a genuine love of knowledge, and possessed of a keen desire to impart it to his fellowmen. Jean Bonaventure Despériers (1510?–44) was another writer of the time whose books were colored with heretical thought. He seems to have abandoned Protestantism because of his dislike of the Calvinistic doctrines and to have become an avowed skeptic.

Rabelais
The fame of all these French writers has been overshadowed by that of Rabelais (1495?–1555?) in whom the humanistic spirit of the time found its veritable incarnation. He, too, has been charged with atheism, but it is impossible to doubt that he believed in the existence of a beneficent deity. He was a critic of contemporary society rather than a reformer in that he seems to have had no definite program to offer. He lacked the zeal of the reformer, the narrowness of vision, the concentration of interest, the fanaticism, if you will, that characterizes such a moral leader as Savonarola. Yet in a general way he indicated the road upon which he thought it would be well for men to travel

One of the greatest satirists of all time, he delighted in pointing out the follies of his fellow-men to whose welfare he was sincerely devoted. He was impatient of tradition and of many of the accepted canons of conduct. His novels of *Pantagruel* and *Gargantua* are among the most vigorous onslaughts ever made upon pedantic and ostentatious scholarship. He believed in the inherent goodness of human nature as contrasted with the inherent tendency towards evil preached by so many of the reformers. He believed in freedom of thought, and in the reliability of the reasoning mind of man as a guide in faith and conduct. His views brought upon him the charge of heresy, and it seems not improbable that the charge contributed to the vagabond character of his life. He believed in the solidarity of human interests, and in the brotherhood and equality of men. In the activity of the awakening world in which he lived he was keenly interested, being concerned chiefly with science, which he made the principal pursuit of his life. Only secondarily was he a man of letters.

It was not only at Paris that humanism flourished in France. It found itself well received in quite a number of the more important provincial towns — at Bordeaux, Nismes, Bourges, Orleans, Toulouse, Montpellier, and especially at Lyons, whose literary activity exceeded that of the capital. Humanism in these places did not suffer so early from the blighting influence of the Sorbonne, the relic of a bygone age, a citadel of orthodoxy. Upon the French men of letters Erasmus exerted a pronounced influence. *Pater mi humanissime* is the title bestowed by Rabelais in a letter avowing his indebtedness to the writings of the great humanist. The idea of a reform of the Church by means of education and by the eradication of the moral abuses of the time, which was urged by Erasmus, was widely prevalent among the French humanists. But already before the time of Rabelais's literary activity humanism in France was a waning force. It was either running to seed in the pedantries of its devotees or its activity in religious matters was being checked by reactionary forces. The religious renaissance in France had come from above not from below, from the cultured few and not from the masses. It had " flowers everywhere and roots nowhere." The sympathy of the prelates and the protection of the king, the two supports upon which it relied, gave way when, under the inspiration of Caraffa, the Church in every country ceased to parley with the rebel leaders of reform, when, at the dictation of logic, she closed the *via media* realizing it to be the avenue through which so many of her sons were escaping, and when the disaster of Pavia fell upon Francis and threw him back for support upon the enemies of religious revolt.

In the long reign of John II of Castile, which extended from 1406 to 1454, humanism received a certain encouragement in that country; but the civil tumults which increased upon the death of that monarch did much to obliterate its traces. Later on Isabella proved to be an effective patron of learning. So the humanistic movement once more got under way in the heart of the peninsula. Chief of those who lent their fostering care to the new learning was the great Cardinal Ximenes (1436?–1517). It was he who established the University of Alcalá which opened its doors in 1508, which was destined to surpass its ancient rival the University of Salamanca and to become the *alma mater* of many leaders of Spanish learning. Before long large numbers of students flocked to the new school, that became famous principally for its philological studies. In 1514 it gave to the world the first Greek text of the New Testament ever printed. Six years later this was followed by the renowned Polyglot Bible, which was also the first of its kind. The work on this famous Bible was intrusted by Ximenes to a number of scholars, converted Jews, a Greek, and Spaniards, who pursued their labors under his direction. Six volumes, published at the personal expense of the cardinal at a total cost of almost $125,-000 of our money, were required to contain the text and notes. In the prolegomena Ximenes gave his reasons for the expenditure of so much time and money. " No translation," he said, " can fully and exactly represent the sense of the original . . . It is necessary, therefore . . . that we should go back to the origin of the sacred writings." For a century and a half this Bible exerted a great influence upon the texts of the New Testament. The editors did not have access to the best and earliest manuscripts, perhaps none older than the ninth century. Their work was surpassed by subsequent recensions of the biblical texts; but they will always retain the honor of having produced the first polyglot bible, and for Catholicism their conservative attitude set the standard of criticism.

Foremost of the Spanish humanists was Elío Antonio de Nebrija (1442?–1522), who after spending twenty years in Italy, returned to become the father of classical learning in the Spanish peninsula. He had a wide range of literary interests; and he lectured at various places, at Seville, Salamanca, and in the new University of Alcalá. Because of his criticism of textual errors in the Vulgate he was prosecuted by the Inquisition, but, thanks to the powerful protection of Ximenes, he was permitted to con-

*marginal notes:*

Cardinal Ximenes

Other Spanish Humanists

tinue his labors. Among the first masters of Castilian prose was
Juan Valdés (1500?–41), one of the earliest of Spanish critics,
judicial in temperament and gifted with keen insight, whose
earliest work *The Dialogue of Mercury and Charon* holds up
to ridicule abuses in both church and state. In his writings the
Lutheran doctrine of justification by faith alone was mingled
with Spanish mysticism. His heresy went so far as to hold that
the personal enlightenment which is said to come as the result of
mystic contemplation is of far greater importance than the
Bible which is a mere primer of the Christian faith. Juan de
Vergara (1492–1557), one of the most noted of the Castilians
for learning and culture, was a writer of elegant Latin verse, and
one of the forerunners of historical criticism. He was in the
midst of preparing a complete edition of the works of Aristotle
when the death of his patron, Ximenes, put a stop to the undertaking. Last of the Spanish humanists whom we shall note was
Luis Vives (1492–1540) a native of Valencia, the most influential schoolmaster of his time, who passed a considerable part
of his active life in England and in the Spanish Netherlands.
According to Erasmus, who was his teacher, no man was better
fitted than the *Doctor Mellifluus*, as the Oxford students loved to
call him, " to overwhelm the battalions of the dialecticians."

Upon Spanish humanism, as upon that of other lands, Erasmus
exercised a great influence. He was admired by the Emperor The Influ-
Charles V, and he came to be the model of all who aspired to ence of Erasmus
culture. But when Charles left Spain in 1529 the friars and in Spain
the scholastics, who very early had detected the germs of heresy
in the freedom of speech encouraged by the circulation of the
writings of Erasmus, were to exert an effective opposition.

Gradually Spanish humanism sank into silence. Born under
an ardent sun, endowed with passion that could find its vent only The Col-
in attachment to a real object, the Spanish people were unat- lapse of Spanish
tracted by the pale abstractions of Florentine Platonism. They Humanism
had, too, a deeper sense of sin than the voluptuous Italians, who,
often incredulous, became scoffers only too readily. Less intoxicated with beauty for its own sake, they gave more thought to
morality, and their scholarship was always closely coupled with
theological thought. Yet despite these facts a humanism, modified to suit the Spanish temperament and predilections, would
doubtless have developed and exerted a great influence in the
life of the nation had it not been for the stern repression of
the Inquisition. Spanish humanism was seemingly stretching
its wings for a bolder flight when it was sharply checked and
brought to a pathetic collapse by the Inquisition, the institution

whose object it was to suppress all pregnant thought; and not until the nineteenth century was Spain destined to witness a resuscitation of the passion for knowledge.

The first of the German humanists with whom we shall deal are those scholars, knights-errant of humanism and also of heresy, who wandered restlessly from place to place, arousing interest in the new learning, sowing seeds of new thought, teaching youth in the universities, disputing with the scholastics, and in their pagan self-indulgence stamping themselves as cousins to the Italian humanists. Peter Luder (1415?–74?) was one of the earliest of these itinerant scholars. After studying in Italy he became a lecturer at Heidelberg, where he incurred the enmity of the orthodox members of the faculty; and from there he went, among other places, to Ulm, Erfurt, Leipzig, and Basel. Conrad Celtes (1459–1508), after studying at several universities, became a wandering scholar. Out of his meager earnings he contrived to save enough to support himself for six months in Italy. There he studied at Ferrara, Padua, and Rome. Returning to his native land he became a veritable apostle of the new thought. Everywhere he strove to inculcate the spirit of the new learning. His wanderings extended as far as Poland and Hungary where he founded humanistic societies like the Italian academies. His poems are tinged with paganism, and his teaching made for independence of thought. Last of these roving scholars that we shall notice is Hermann von dem Busch (1468–1534), who after spending five years in Italy lectured in many of the universities and towns of northern and central Germany, speaking not only of the Latin classics but also of the neglect of the intelligent study of the Bible.

In the first years of the fifteenth century Germany had seven universities — Prague 1348, Vienna 1365, Heidelberg 1386, Cologne 1388, Erfurt 1392, Leipzig 1409, and Rostock 1409. And far away at Cracow in Poland a university was established in 1420. Most of these institutions were centers of the old scholasticism, which though waning in power and unable to boast of any leader of marked ability was still arrogant in temper and militant in mood. Theology still kept its place as the study of chief importance, and to it all other studies were regarded as preparatory or subordinate. In the outer world the study of arts and of letters was fast assuming a threatening importance; but ready to come to the support of the theologians was the Church, and in particular the powerful mendicant orders. A quarter of a century passed in which humanism made pronounced headway, and then, largely due to its impulse, new universities were estab-

THE UNIVERSITIES OF GERMANY
AND THE IMPERIAL CITIES
AT THE MIDDLE OF
THE SIXTEENTH CENTURY
Scale of Miles
0 10 20 40 60 80 100

DENMARK

BALTIC SEA

Greifswald (1456)

Ritzebüttel

Rostock (1409)

Hamburg

Lübeck

Bremen

Frankfort-on-the-Oder (1506)

Wittenberg (1506)

POLAND

Dortmund

Goslar

Nordhausen

Mühlhausen

Leipzig (1409)

Cologne (1388)

Aachen

Marburg (1527)

Wetzlar

Erfurt (1392)

Cracow (1420)

Trier (1472)

Fried-berg

Frankfort-on-the-Main

Schweinfurt

Königsberg

Prague (1348)

Mainz (1477)

Worms

Heidelberg

Windsheim

Verdun

Landau

Spires

Nuremberg

Metz

Heil-bronn

Rothenburg-on-the-Tauber

Weissenburg

Tübingen

Dinkelsbühl

Ratisbon

Strasburg

Reut-lingen

Döpfingen

Giengen

Nördlingen

Ingolstadt (1472)

Schlettstadt

Gengenbach

Ulm

Augsburg

Freiburg (1460)

Buchau

Biberach

Pfullendorf

Ravensburg

Memmingen

Kaufbeuren

Überlingen

Vienna (1365)

Basel (1460)

Leutkirch

Kempten

Isney

SWISS

CONFEDERATION

HUNGARY

SAVOY

MILAN

VENETIAN REPUBLIC

C.S.HAMMOND & CO.,N.Y.

○ University Cities. Figures
show date of establishment
of University
◉ Imperial Cities and territory
which each controlled

Longitude    10°    East    from    14°    Greenwich

lished — Griefswalde 1456, Freiburg 1460, Basel 1460, Ingolstadt 1472, Trier 1472, Tübingen 1477, Mainz 1477, Wittenberg 1502, Frankfort-on-the-Oder 1506, and Marburg 1527. Most of the German universities, like those in other lands, witnessed frequent struggles between the advocates of the new learning and the defenders of the old. The preëminence of theology and the educational methods of scholasticism were seriously menaced. The conservatives with their backs to the wall were fighting for the supremacy which for so long a time they had enjoyed.

One of the most important cradles of humanism north of the Alps was the Rhine country. A vigorous intellectual activity was rife in those provinces. Schools imbued with the new ideal of education were to be found in many places; and so important did the Rhineland become as an educational center that students flocked to it from Scotland, Scandinavia, and the Slavic lands. Rudolf Agricola (1443–85), a student first in one of the schools of the Brethren of the Common Life and then for ten years in Italy, may be regarded as the chief restorer of Greek in Germany. After he went to teach in the University of Heidelberg that institution became a center of humanism. In the purity of his life, in the religious inclination of his temperament, and in the serious purpose of his work he is typical of the social humanists of the north as distinguished from the individualists of Italy. Only his early death prevented him from exercising a far-reaching influence in the literary and religious revivals that were going on hand in hand in Germany. In many places new schools were being founded, printing presses established, classical writings translated, new books written in Latin and in German, and libraries collected. One of the most important of these schools was that founded at Deventer, in what is now Holland, in 1481 by Alexander Hegius (1433–98), the greatest German teacher of his time. Unfortunately after his death there was no one to take his place and so its glory declined. Still more important was the school at Schlettstadt, which under the direction of Ludwig Dringenberg (?–1490), became the point from which the new ideas radiated in the country of the Upper Rhine. Johann von Dalberg (1445–55?–1504), after studying in Italy, was made Chancellor of the University of Heidelberg and Bishop of Worms in the same year. He strove to make both towns nurseries of the new culture. Jacob Wimpheling (1450–1528) put into definite literary form the ideas carried out in practise by Hegius. "The better education of the young," he wrote, "is the foundation of all true reform, ecclesiastical, rational, and domestic." So great was the demand for his writings that up to 1520 almost twenty thousand copies of them were sold. To the end this " Schoolmaster of Germany " hoped for a reformation of the Church from within. Still another humanist who dreamed of a reformation of the Church by itself was Sebastian Brant (1457–1521). In Basel, where he lived for many years, humanism was fostered by the new university, and classical and other texts were issued by three printing presses. He is famous chiefly for his pungent satire *The Ship of Fools,* a story of a ship directed by fools and sent to sail the troubled seas of life. More than a hundred fools embark, among them the book-fool, the miser-fool, the fashion-fool, and the fool of useless studies. They sail past the land of idlers until they come to the land of fools. The immorality and ignorance of the clergy are dealt with in unmistakable terms. It became the most famous German poem of the time, appealing as it did to the widespread discontent with the condition of affairs, and it found more than one imitator. One of the most important of the humanistic reformers who remained within the pale of the Church was Geiler von Kaiserberg (1445–1510), who boldly denounced the prevalent vices and exerted every effort to effect a reform in discipline. He was an eloquent preacher and was highly esteemed throughout Germany. Favorably known for the wide range of his knowledge was John Trithemius (1462–1516), abbot of the Benedictine monastery of Spanheim. But he kept close within his convent walls and so failed to exert a popular influence.

German Cities as Nurseries of New Thought

The more important of the German cities, planted along the highways of the world and subject to the cosmopolitan influences that are afforded by frequent intercommunication, had long been strongholds of civil liberty. They now became nurseries of intellectual freedom and religious independence. When men found others sharing their thoughts they became emboldened to speak and to write. They felt the impulse to dare and to do. It is in the towns, the humming hives of humanity, rather than in the placid country-side, that new thought is given birth. The culture from which the new ideals of life were given birth was essentially urban in character. It grew up in the towns that were very largely outside feudalism. It had an industrial and a commercial basis, in contradistinction to the purely agrarian basis of the culture of the Middle Ages, and it was at first but little concerned with religious affairs. But the great widening of the physical horizon and the unprecedented expansion of trade was followed by a time of intellectual elevation. Gradually the medieval consciousness was dissolved and a new

atmosphere of emotion and intellectual tendencies was created
which left the old culture and its principles far behind. The
strength of the old culture had lain in the ascetic ideal. It had
borne the stamp of the Church. The strength of the new culture lay in the development of earthly life. It bore the stamp of
the laity. In this process of emancipation from the ideals of the
Age of Faith the Italian cities led the way. In time the movement spread to other places. The German cities attained their
greatest height of self-reliance from the twelfth to the fourteenth centuries. In the fifteenth century, owing to the activity of the territorial princes, their political power was a waning force. But they continued to play a most active part in the
history of civilization. Within their walls it was that individuality was revived, that man found himself free to think and
free to act in a much larger measure than had been possible for
many centuries. In the truest sense of the phrase the towns were
the nurseries of modern life.

Commercial prosperity had brought to Augsburg riches and
power. It was the center of German finance, for it was the
home-city of the great family of the Fuggers, the most important of all the new capitalistic associations. Its citizens were
intelligent, and devoted to their fatherland. They were con- Conrad
scious of the fact that the interests of the papal curia did not Peutinger
coincide with those of Germany. They were aware of the shortcomings of the clergy. With the educational aims and methods
of the scholastics they were dissatisfied. Even the Fuggers were
no mere worshipers of Mammon. They had a deep realization
of the cultural and social mission of wealth. There was in the
city, as elsewhere, an air of impending change. Chief of the
Augsburg humanists was Conrad Peutinger (1465–1547), a
learned patrician, friend and literary coadjutor of the Emperor
Maximilian, who became the secretary of the city. He had
studied with Poliziano in Italy and when he returned home he
became active as a writer, as a collector, and as a patron of
scholars.

Nuremberg, situated in the center of the Germanic lands, the
German world in miniature, was another of these civic centers
of humanism, the most important of them all. It was esteemed Pirk-
as "the brightest jewel of the empire." The ramifications of its heimer
trade extended throughout the known world; and so many and and Dürer
so important were the craftsmen, the artists, and the men of
letters who lived there that it easily held its position as the
Florence of Germany. Most important of its devotees of humanism was Willibald Pirkheimer (1470–1530), patrician and

patron, friend and counselor of untold numbers of scholars, who sought to sum up in himself the combined culture of the age. He had spent a number of years in Italy in happy friendship with distinguished men of letters. Despite the fact that there was a distinct touch of paganism in his character he was sincerely interested in the cause of religious reform. But the extremes of revolution and obscurantism were alike distasteful to him. In the many-sided activity of Albrecht Dürer (1471–1528), Germany's greatest artist and one of the world's great painters, may be found a full expression of the new life that was surging in his native land. In him in several ways, in his somewhat gross and materialistic pleasures and in his concern with social and religious matters, the German Renaissance was incarnate. In the record of his journey to the Netherlands he denounced "the unchristian Papacy which strives against the freedom of Christ," which puts upon the laity such " heavy burdens of human laws for which we are robbed of the price of our blood and sweat that it may be expended shamefully by idle, lascivious people, while thirsty and sick men perish of hunger.' He denounced, too, the " blind teaching which the men, whom they call the Fathers, have invented and set down whereby the precious Word is in many places falsely explained, or not set forth at all." Yet anxious as he was to see a reformation of the evil living of the clergy, the curtailment of the power of the papal curia, and a return to a more primitive state of Christianity, he clung to the creeds and the conventions of the old Church. At least he did not break with them publicly. In this respect he was like many another humanist, anxious for reform, but not rebellion.

The Erfurt Humanists

Very early in the German Renaissance the University of Erfurt became distinguished for its work in the classical languages and literatures, and later on under the leadership of Maternus Pistoris (1465?–1534) it added to its reputation. Round this teacher there gathered a notable group of scholars who took an important part in the struggle between humanism and medievalism. More remarkable as a thinker was Mutianus Rufus (1471–1526), better known as Mutian, one of the most attractive of all the German humanists, whose learning, wide and ready sympathy, and power of suggestion, made him the center of a group of scholars strongly tinctured with heresy. Among his followers were Spalatin (1484–1545), Eoban Hess (1488–1540), Ulrich von Hutten, with whom we are soon to deal, and Crotus Rubianus (1480?–1540). All of them were filled with an ardent devotion to the new learning and were ac-

tively arrayed against the lingering scholasticism that was still
intrenched in many places and that could rely for support upon
all the power of the papal curia.   The active mind of Mutian was
interested in all the grave problems of the time.   Yet he did not
give his thoughts to the public through the press; he committed
them to writing only in letters to his friends.   With the theological creeds about which so many battles of words were raging
he, together with so many others of the humanists, was little
concerned.   Quietly he lived his life, collecting books, reading
and discussing them, a gentle scholar " who loved and sought the
truth."

In our story of humanism and its relation to heresy in England, France, Spain, and Germany only a few of the more celebrated scholars have been mentioned.   It would be a mistake
to think that these names exhaust the list of humanists in those
countries.   In order to gain an adequate idea of the literary
activity of those countries one should realize that the list can be
extended very greatly.   Especially is this true of France and
Germany.   Ardent and active resident scholars could have been
found in every important town in those countries.   " No German town," said Irenicus, " is so far removed from all literature that it cannot point to its learned Greek scholars, to say
nothing of the rest.   Who could count them?"   Everywhere
darkness was being dispersed and the stagnation of scholasticism
disturbed.   It must be noted also that as time had gone on the
humanists had become more and more radical.   The older German humanists were grave scholars deeply desirous of helping
in the general intellectual and religious development of their
country.   But while they earnestly desired a reform of the current abuses they did not favor ecclesiastical rebellion.   The
younger humanists were more eager for conflict.   Like their
captain, Ulrich von Hutten, they were Hotspurs of reform if
not of revolution.

The first important battle between the humanists and the
scholastics took place upon a question that had little to do with
the things over which the two camps were in dispute.   Johann
Reuchlin (1455–1522), one of the most notable personages in    Reuchlin
the history of German humanism, was deeply interested in religious matters.   He became a student of Hebrew and wrote the
first important grammar of that language.   His pioneer work
in scientific philology was inevitably bound to conflict with the
unscientific method of the old medievalists, to demolish it, and
to sweep away the theological ideas that were based upon it.
He bravely pointed to errors in the Vulgate, the Latin transla-

tion of the Bible that had been accepted all through the Middle Ages; he suggested corrections, and he dwelt upon the necessity of going back to the ultimate sources of information. He cast aside all traditional commentaries and endeavored to ascertain the literal meaning of the various books of the Bible in their original language. As a scholar he won for himself a European reputation. But his principal occupations were those of a lawyer and a statesman, and not those of a man of letters. As old age approached, he relinquished diplomacy for study and retired into the country, there to spend his remaining years quietly. It was then that the storm burst about him.

**The Obscurantists *Versus* the Humanists**

The scholastics were well aware of the impending struggle. Instinctively they felt that the scientific method of the humanists and the increasing freedom of thought were fatal to their position. To us it seems a hopeless struggle; medievalism on one side and modernism on the other,— darkness and light. But to its defenders obscurantism by no means appeared a forlorn cause. It was a daring thing to deal with Hebrew in those days. The Jews were the people who had crucified Christ. Were not they and their tongue things to be shunned by every faithful Christian? Was there not good reason to suspect of heresy any one who devoted himself to the study of the Jewish language? In accordance with an imperial order Reuchlin was required by the Archbishop of Mainz to give his opinion on the question whether all Hebrew books with the exception of the Old Testament ought to be taken from the Jews and committed to the flames. In his reply Reuchlin arranged the Jewish books in seven divisions, only one of which, he said, and that with no certainty, deserved the fate of being burned. As a result a bitter controversy developed, first between Reuchlin and Pfefferkorn, a converted Jew, and then, when the latter was seen to be no match for the scholar, between Reuchlin and Jacob Hoogstraten, dean of the Dominicans at Cologne and chief inquisitor in that part of Germany. The course of the controversy was followed with breathless interest for ten years by all educated Germany. Despite the fact that the question in dispute was only slightly related to the things upon which the two hostile forces were divided the humanists rightly regarded the trial of Reuchlin for heresy as an attack upon themselves and their principles. On the one side were the mendicant orders, especially the Dominicans of Cologne, supported by the Inquisition, and on the other were the younger scholars and poets, apostles of scientific research and freedom of thought. Two trials in Germany did not suffice to settle the case. An appeal was taken to Rome.

Then judgment was given in favor of Reuchlin. But Leo X, instead of confirming the sentence of the commission that heard the appeal, imposed silence upon both sides, with the practical effect of prolonging the struggle indefinitely. The failure to secure the condemnation of the humanist served only to increase the enmity of the Dominicans.

The hostility between the two camps gained in bitterness. The publications born of the fight were not only adorned with learning and enlivened with wit, but were also disfigured with licentiousness. Yet despite the depths to which the controversy sometimes descended there was revealed more and more clearly the essential differences between the humanists and the medievalists. Chief of these literary missiles was a collection of letters called *Letters of Obscure Men,* the first series of which, containing forty-one letters, appeared in 1515. The writers of these epistles are supposed to be members of the clerical party who desire to receive or to give information regarding the Reuchlin controversy or who appeal to Gratius, a professor at Cologne, to settle points that were in dispute. The letters were written purposely in " the choicest bad Latin," and were signed with fictitious names, some of which are absurd. In an apparently unconscious manner they disclosed the most astonishing ignorance and asked the most ridiculous of questions. Piety and pruriency, pedantry and profound ignorance, go hand in hand in them; gluttony is portrayed in the broadest farce, and immorality with boisterous mirth. Yet so true was this satire upon the obscurantists that the *Letters* were at first accepted as genuine and serious. A second series, containing seventy letters, was published in 1517. The *Letters* appeared without the names of the real writers and their authorship has always been a matter of dispute. It is now thought that Crotus Rubianus and Ulrich von Hutten were the principal writers; but it is possible that many humanists, by direct contribution or by suggestion, aided in the work of compilation. Everywhere the letters were received with shouts of laughter; but while their appearance is a dramatic event in the struggle between humanism and scholasticism their importance must not be over-rated. At that time actual rebellion against the Church was already too near at hand to be greatly accelerated or retarded by such a pasquinade.

Chief of the militant humanists was Ulrich von Hutten, (1488–1523), a man of noble birth, a lover of literature, a rake, a patriot, and, later in life, the most fiery of reformers. He realized keenly the injury that Germany had suffered from the financial exactions of the Papacy. He saw his country divided and distracted with internal conflict; and the chief cause of this political abasement he attributed to the Roman curia. Despite the fact that he spent the greater part of his short life in poverty and in disease he was unremitting in his attacks upon the oppressors of his fatherland. He had been to Rome and the things that he saw there furnished material for his pungent epigrams. With unsparing banter and savage satire he leaped into the fray and remained a foremost combatant until he died, alone and in poverty, still young in years but worn with the arduous fight. More than any other man he gave voice to the vague but deep-seated resentment of Germany against the Papacy for its long-continued oppression. " We are fighting for a common freedom," he wrote to Luther, " to liberate an oppressed Fatherland." In him it was that the humanistic culture for the first time lent itself definitely to the aid of the Protestant Revolution. It was his mission to declare open war on the part of the new culture against the old.

Encouraged by the reaction against the financial exactions of the papal curia and the growing sentiment of German patriotism the humanists lent themselves more and more to the cause of revolt. But there was one, the greatest of them all, Erasmus, (1466?–1536), who refused to lend his name to one camp or to the other, who instead addressed himself exclusively to the emancipation of the individual. " I seek truth," he said, " and find it at times in Catholic propositions, and at times in those of the Protestants." From the enlightenment of the individual he expected that religious as well as social reform would eventually issue. Without violence, through the working of mind upon mind, the new culture would gradually and silently change the Church. Under its benign influence superstition would disappear, the external things of religious practice, such as fasts, pilgrimages and ascetic penances, would be relegated to the forgotten past, creeds that are impossible of reconciliation with reason would vanish, simplicity would be restored to public worship, and religion, thus born anew, would become essentially moral and practical. The whole evil of the time he thought was due to ignorance. To this prince of letters men in all parts of Europe turned for guidance in the journey from the cloisters of the Middle Ages to the light of an ampler world. His work of education took the form of writing. In all his books, even in his prefaces and his notes to the books of others which he edited, one finds, mingled with genial wit and with penetrating satire upon conspicuous follies, the same appeal for truth, temperate procedure, and for tolerance. His writings, therefore,

possess a deep and undying human significance far above any
connection they may have had with the controversies of their
day.

Among the more remarkable of his works the *Adages* is first
in point of time, though the first edition of the book, which was
published in 1500, was only the germ of what the work afterwards came to be. In its final form it is a collection of 4,251
Greek and Latin proverbs that are explained and enforced with
discursive commentary. Ancient literature seems to have been
ransacked for the adages themselves and also for matter for
their elucidation. When they were first given to the public
they were devoured with great avidity.

In 1501 there appeared the *Enchiridion Militis Christiani*, the
*Dagger of the Christian Knight*, in which Erasmus first gave to
the world his general ideas of Christianity. "I wrote the *Enchiridion*," he said, "to remedy the error which makes religion
depend upon ceremonies and an observance of bodily acts, while
neglecting true piety." The Church, he said, needed greatly
to be purged of formalism. Behind her ceremonies there is a
truth, but it is a truth only too easily and frequently lost to
view. "The best way in which to adore the saints," he said,
"is to imitate their virtues. The saint cares more for this kind
of reverence than for a hundred candles that may be burned before his shrine." It is a little book of practical piety, simply
and deeply ethical, intended to be a devotional manual.

A book that added very greatly to the author's reputation is
*The Praise of Folly*, published in 1511, and based upon his experiences in Italy. In that country, as elsewhere, he had seen
not a little of the degenerate condition of the monastic orders;
but more particularly in Italy he had come into contact with the
new paganism; he had met scholars who outwardly conformed
to the practices of the Church and profited by its endowments
while in their hearts they disbelieved its fundamental doctrines.
Everywhere among the cultured clergy he found at the most only
an eviscerated Christianity; and the flatteries of those accomplished Ciceronians failed to overthrow his dissatisfaction and
his disgust; for Erasmus was a Christian as well as a humanist;
he was not content to study the classics for their own sake; he
desired to devote the new learning to the cause of religious reform. The book was illustrated by Holbein; and so great was
the demand for it that it went through twenty-seven large editions in the lifetime of the author. In polished and easy-flow-
ing phrases, with sparkling wit and graceful yet caustic satire,
Folly claims with ostentatious pride the degenerate monks, the

narrow theologians, the effete scholastics, bishops, cardinals, and popes, as her offspring, and boasts of their wonderful deeds. The things that were amiss in the State were not spared. Scorn was heaped upon princes as well as upon prelates whose deeds were detrimental to the public welfare. All these darling children of Folly are sketched with an unusual power of humorous observation. Europe laughed at these pictures so true to life, sketched with such an airy grace, and bitten in with such a mordant satire.

**The Biblical Studies**

In 1516 Erasmus gave to the world his edition of the Vulgate, the translation of the Bible into Latin by St. Jerome, which had been the only authorized version of the Scriptures all through the Middle Ages, and also his edition of the Greek Testament. In those days there were not so many early manuscripts of the books of the Bible available to the scholar as now, and the general knowledge of the value of such manuscripts and the ability to use them were not so great as at present. But Erasmus examined all the manuscripts he could find and gave the results of his study to the world. His edition of the Greek Testament was accompanied by a new translation into Latin which differed in important details from the Vulgate; and there were notes in which misinterpretations and misconceptions that had gathered about certain passages in the Vulgate were exposed. It was his aim to ascertain as exactly as possible what the writers of the New Testament had actually written. This edition of the Greek Testament is one of the most important services rendered by the classical revival to the cause of religious reform.

**The Colloquies**

Last of the books of Erasmus that we shall notice is the *Colloquies* that appeared in 1521. In it are exposed once more the ecclesiastical abuses of the time, the idleness and immorality of the monks, and the prevalent superstitions. Youth is warned against rash vows of celibacy; and the wickedness of war is dwelt upon. The author's power of witty and satirical expression is again evident, the brilliant raillery, and the keen and unsparing criticism. The book is written in Latin with all the author's graceful and fluent command of that language; and like the other productions of his pen it was read far and wide.

**Erasmus's Solution for the Problems of the Age**

We have seen something of the widespread influence of Erasmus. He was recognized throughout Europe as the chief man of letters of his time. Latin was then the universal language of educated men, and so the writings of the great humanist were read wherever European civilization had found a footing. One should not leave unnoticed the intense earnestness of the great writer, the courageous persistency with which he maintained his position outside the two great camps, and the devotion to learning that led him to decline many offers that would have afforded him a life of greater ease but of less opportunity for literary work. But what of Erasmus's fundamental idea that the abuses of Church and State could safely be left to melt away before the slow approach of the new culture, as an iceberg detached from some continent of the north melts away in the kindlier currents of a warmer sea? It seems a delusion. A delusion to which a scholar, one whose intellectual activity and the realization of whose ideals required both inner and outward peace, might be expected to become subject. The appalling conditions of the time demanded more immediate, more direct, and more drastic action. Too long had reform been delayed. The dam was breaking. Already were the floods let loose. Old bounds and old landmarks were being swept away. A life of quiet contemplation was impossible in the keen air of that time. Collisions that resulted in bloodshed were already occurring. It was no time for the harmonious perfecting of the individual. The moods of men, even of scholars, were too greatly affected by the daily vicissitudes of life. Such a program of silent erosion, of the gradual leavening of the inert mass of society, as that desired by Erasmus was impossible. The humanistic ideals of individual culture vanished in a time of inevitable warfare. Indeed, the younger generation of humanists, of whom Ulrich von Hutten is the most conspicuous example, were themselves given over to the policy of aggression. The first two decades of the sixteenth century clearly revealed the irreconcilable opposition of the old and the new ways of looking at the world. Compromise between humanism and scholasticism was impossible. It was rejected with contempt. Revolution was at hand.

Humanism furthered the religious revolution; but it would be a superficial view to think that it was the sole cause. Humanism and heresy were alike the result of the Renaissance. They mutually aided each other, it is true; but they were separate and independent. Each was born of that momentous change in human affairs that we speak of as the rebirth of man and of which the essence was the revival of the individual. Each, in its own way, so its devotees thought, was what Machiavelli called a "*ritorno al segno*," a return to the original source. Humanism was a return to the classical attitude towards life, to a concern with the present world, to an ideal of the development of the individual who is free to think and free to act. The religious reformers desired a return to the conditions of apostolic times for the cleansing and rejuvenescence of

Relation of the Humanists to the Reformers

religion. They built upon the foundation of belief in the Bible and in that alone. Reason was the guide of the humanists; belief that of the reformers. The most essential condition for the fulfilment of the ideal of humanism, the perfection of the individual, was that of free will. But free will was denied by the reformers. They declared, as we shall see, that salvation depended entirely upon the gratuitous grace of God. Sooner or later, therefore, there was bound to come a parting of the ways. But before the separation the humanists lent substantial aid to the heretics. And still to-day humanism is unceasingly preparing the way for " the golden heresy of truth."

# CHAPTER XII

## THE GERMAN REVOLT FROM ROME

I F ever there was an accidental reformer, ever a man who had no intention of turning the world upside down, it was Martin Luther. A peasant's son, born at Eisleben, on November 10, 1483, a little village far removed from the current of new thought that made so varied the activity of Augsburg and Nuremberg, he had no share in the belief common to many of the mystics and humanists of the time that the blame for the deplorable conditions of the age lay with the leading classes in wealth and authority and that from the common folk only could reform be expected to come. His father was a hard-headed, practical burgher who cherished the ambition that his son, a promising lad, should begin where he himself had been obliged to stop. So when Luther was fourteen years of age he was sent to school at Magdeburg, a prosperous Hansa town, where he remained for a year. Then he went to Eisenach, where he had the good fortune, while singing in the streets to earn his way, to win the favor of Frau Cotta, a lady of gentle birth, who took him to live in her house. In his eighteenth year he was sent to the University of Erfurt. Here, too, as at Magdeburg and Eisenach, his father insisted that, in part at least, he should earn his way. By this time Luther was a sturdy lad, fond of books, though not so fond of them, perhaps, that he would have gone forward without his father's push. He was fond of society, too, of music, and of the students' festivities, and withal soundly moral and pious. Erfurt, it is true, was a center of humanism, but with its brilliant circle of scholars Luther seems to have come into contact only very slightly.

Against the wishes of his father, who desired him to become a lawyer, Luther, in 1505, entered the Augustinian convent at Erfurt. What induced him to take this step? Several ex-

Why
Luther
Became a
Friar

ternal reasons have been given, but it seems certain that whether it was the immediate outcome of a thunder-storm or the death of a friend, or neither, there came, as a result of a profound impression of his own sinfulness, a resolution to set himself right with God. There was nothing unusual in this. It is a perfectly normal phenomenon of healthful youth, now made a matter of common knowledge by the study of the psychology of religious awakening. Very often in the age of adolescence a profound change comes over the entire personality. The life of emotion and of will seeks its expression in activity. Latent ideas, of which hitherto the consciousness has had but a dim apprehension, assume more definite significance and become a controlling factor in the life and character of the individual. It is at this time, when the organism is strained by the physiological readjustments that are taking place, that the majority of the instantaneous "conversions" occur. There was only one way at that time in which one could hope to make oneself altogether acceptable in the eyes of God and to secure the boon of inward peace, and that was by adopting the life contemplative. A boy left to himself and beset with the sense of sin, especially if the monastery door was left open, as it was sure to be to a boy of promise, would be very likely to seek the shelter of the cloister. So Luther took the vow to lead an ascetic life. He remembered only that His are those who love naught else, not even the joy of student life, or power, or the ambition of parents, so well as His will. It was not theology that led him to take the irrevocable step. Theology in itself had no attraction for him. It was religion. So Luther entered the convent of the Augustinian friars, a preaching order, and there he was given the humblest duty, that of begging. He had no theory for reforming the world. He had simply decided to try the accepted means of reforming himself.

In 1508 Luther went to teach at the University of Wittenberg, which had opened its doors only six years previously. About three years later he set out for Rome. When for the first time he saw beneath him the great dome of the city and the many towers he fell on his knees exclaiming, " Hail, holy Rome! Thrice holy place where the blood of the martyrs was shed!" There had been much to win his admiration on his way through Italy. The fertile soil, the genial climate, the well-paved streets, the spacious architecture, the clean and orderly hospitals and foundling asylums, and the splendor of the civic life. But soon in his walks from the Augustinian convent of Santa Maria del Popolo to the various shrines of the papal city

The Visit
to Rome

he saw many things that filled his heart with dismay. About the pope, Julius II, there fluttered a throng of gay and thoughtless courtiers. Everywhere he saw the extravagant expenditure in worldly things of the princes of the Church, and noted the general laxity of life. He returned to Wittenberg as devoted as ever to the Mother Church; but as time gave him opportunity for reflection upon the things he had heard and witnessed at the capital of Christendom, as the city of saints gradually vanished, there stood before him Rome the center of corruption. Some months after he returned to Wittenberg he was graduated in theology and became a somewhat noted teacher, and a far more famous preacher. In common with other earnest men of the time he called attention to the prevalent ecclesiastical evils, one of the principal ones of which was the abuse of the sale of indulgences.

What is an indulgence? Every sin, so the Catholic Church holds, entails two consequences — guilt and punishment. Guilt is the stain upon the soul. It can be removed only by genuine contrition, the act of confession, and a sincere purpose to amend his ways in the future, on the part of the sinner, and by the absolution given by the priest in the sacrament of confession. After the guilt has thus been removed the punishment still remains. Punishment may be undergone by the penitent either in this world or in purgatory. Only when every stain, all guilt, is washed away from the soul, and all the punishment that has been incurred has been fulfilled, is it possible to enter the kingdom of heaven. When Christ underwent the sacrifice of the cross more merit resulted than was necessary to save those who had lived upon earth up to that time. This superabundant merit was increased by that which resulted from the life of Mary, the mother of Christ, and it is still further and constantly augmented by those saints whose lives have been such as to enable them to earn merit more than sufficient for their own salvation. This store of supererogatory merit is in the keeping of the Church. It can be dispensed, by means of indulgences, at the discretion of Christ's vicar upon earth, the Pope. There are two kinds of indulgences, partial and plenary. A partial indulgence is a remission of a part of the penance incurred up to that time by the penitent sinner; and a plenary indulgence is a remission of all the punishment that has thus far been incurred by the contrite offender. Indulgences were granted for prayers, pilgrimages, and other good works, and, later on, for money. Such is the theory of indulgences, a theory which as yet has not been authoritatively defined by the Church.

CHAP.
XII

1508-17

The Sale
of Indul-
gences
Like many another theory this doctrine of indulgences is capable of abuse in practice. And that it was grossly abused in Luther's time there is no doubt. So many frauds of all kinds were connected with the sale of indulgences that an outbreak against them was inevitable. Great numbers of the sellers of pardons were like the one described for us so vividly by Chaucer, intent upon personal gain rather than upon the cure of souls. Leo X needed money for the completion of the great church of St. Peter at Rome, which was begun in 1506. So he issued a plenary indulgence, the price of which was to vary from twenty-five golden gulden for the well-to-do to the saying of prayers and the keeping of fasts for the wretchedly poor. For the purpose of the sale Germany was divided into three districts, at the head of one of which was the Archbishop of Mainz, primate of Germany and arch-chancellor of the Empire, a youth of some twenty-six years. The profits of the sale were to be equally divided between the pope and the archbishop. So it is quite natural that the latter prelate should look about for an effective seller of pardons. He chose John Tetzel, a Dominican friar, a man of commanding appearance, with a sonorous voice and a ready tongue, who, like those ministers and laymen to-day who go about from church to church raising debts, had gained a reputation as a preacher of indulgences.

It was the consciousness of sin that had driven Luther into the convent. There he sought, by the time-honored ascetic means, by the zealous performance of penances and good works, to obtain the inward peace for which he longed with all his soul. But the sense of peace which he craved so ardently seemed ever to retreat in the distance before him, like a mirage in the desert, till at last he came upon the doctrine of justification by faith alone. What is this doctrine, and how did he come upon it? Under the guidance of the good and wise Johann von Staupitz, vicar of the Augustinian order in Germany, Luther read not only *The Imitation of Christ* but also the writings of St. Augustine, among the Fathers of the Church, and those of St. Paul in the New Testament. It was in these writings, particularly in those of St. Augustine, that he became aware of the doctrine that was to be the starting point of Protestantism. The authority of St. Augustine was all-powerful during the Middle Ages. Yet it was in his name that Luther rose against the medieval Church. This contradictory influence of the greatest of the Fathers of the Church is to be explained by the fact that in his writings there are two points of view. The practical aim of his teaching is humility, the entire subordination of the will of the individual to God. In the Middle Ages the Church and God were inextricably associated in the minds of men. The unquestioning humility inculcated by St. Augustine ended, therefore, in giving to the Church an unlimited sway over the minds of men. But among his theoretical writings is to be found the Pauline theory that salvation comes to the individual as a gratuitous gift of God, that whatever man may do he can never himself earn eternal life, that all that is necessary in order to gain admission into the kingdom of heaven is to have faith in Christ and his power to save men. All through the Middle Ages, however, the Church recommended certain acts such as fasting, pilgrimages, the giving of alms, and the obtaining of indulgences, as being in a high degree meritorious, as being very largely efficacious in helping to effect the salvation of the soul. The two doctrines are irreconcilable. The doctrine of justification by faith alone leads, in the end, to the annihilation of man before God. " Free will," said Luther, " is a fiction, a word that has no reality corresponding to it." The doctrine of salvation by faith and works, on the other hand, leads, eventually, to the recognition of the liberty of man and the efficacy of his own deeds. But it did not lead to liberty in the Middle Ages because the Church claimed the right to determine what works were necessary to salvation and also the right to control them. The Church quickly recognized that with the acceptance of the doctrine of justification by faith alone, which, for the most part, had remained dormant, an esoteric dogma, throughout the medieval period, her entire sacramental system would be rendered unnecessary. It was incompatible with her claim to loose and to bind. It would make men independent of her aid and her direction. It left them slaves before God, it is true; but it made them free before men. So she opposed it in the most uncompromising manner. Thus arose the great question of salvation that preoccupied the minds of thinking men in the sixteenth century. How shall a man be saved? The Catholics answered: by faith and works. The Protestants replied: by faith alone. In any judgment that may be passed upon either or upon both of these two positions it must be remembered that all through the Middle Ages the performance of meritorious works, prescribed exclusively by the Church, had usurped so dominant a place as very largely to exclude the element of personal faith; and that in the period of the great Revolution the opposing doctrine proved a most effective weapon with which to combat that usurpation.

Luther, as we have seen, sought in vain through the performance of ascetic works to gain the inward peace, the sense of being acceptable in the eyes of God, that he desired so ardently. The sense of alienation was still strong upon him. The consciousness of communion, that other of the two poles between which religion oscillates, was as yet far from his possession. But the very sense of want that he felt, the feeling of dissatisfaction, lies near to the heart of religion. It is a recognition of one's weakness or unfitness and the desire to harmonize one's life with the unchanging laws of the universe. Perhaps he came to the belief that the one thing needful was to have faith in the atoning sacrifice of Christ as a result of his own spiritual struggles and mental anguish, and was merely confirmed in it by the writings of St. Augustine and by the Commentary of Lefèvre, the French humanist, on the Pauline Epistles. But, by whatever road he had traveled, that was the goal at which he had arrived. Before him stood the appealing figure of Christ with the promise of reconciliation with the Father upon the one condition of absolute faith. His faith reached out for the promise and all was consummated. There was no more to be done; salvation was assured. Such was Luther's discovery or resuscitation of the Augustinian doctrine of justification by faith alone. He did not carry it to its logical conclusion, for his was not essentially a logical mind. He did not sweep away in its entirety the sacramental system which it renders unnecessary. Instead, later on, he effected a compromise, as all such natures do, and reduced the sacraments from seven to three. He found peace in the new conception. The ceaseless introspection, the pursuing sense of sin, came to an end. He had found the way of salvation. And like the boy that he still was he set himself with all his heart to tell others of it. He did not realize as yet that his teaching would be contradictory to the position of the Church. He did not dream of dividing the seamless robe of Christ. He was not by nature a theologian, and he never made a thorough study of the theology of the time. The one thing of which he was definitely convinced was that things had been made too complex, and that he had found a way to simplify them.

Suddenly there appeared upon the horizon the figure of John Tetzel, the preacher of indulgences. Stories of his unscrupulous methods had preceded him, and doubtless they had not grown pale with travel. The Elector of Saxony declined to admit him to his territory, and the bishop did not approve of him. Out of loyalty to his superiors, and to his own general line of thought, Luther decided to protest against the abuses connected with indulgences. He had not as yet arrived at his final position of the

complete dispensability of works, and so he did not deny the
usefulness of indulgences when properly conducted. There
would be a great gathering on the feast of All Saints at Wittenberg, when the thousands of relics accumulated by the elector
would be solemnly exposed in the castle church. Why not
seize the opportunity of a public discussion of the matter? So
on the preceding day, October 31, 1517, after the fashion of his
time, he nailed to the door of the church a crude and evidently
not well-digested set of theses, which seem to have been already
printed, set forth in Latin, and sent a copy of them to the Archbishop of Mainz, who forwarded them to the pope. It does not
appear that any one accepted the challenge to discuss the theses;
but, translated into German and circulated in printed form, they
aroused a surprising amount of popular interest. Scores of men,
in a far more effective way, throughout many years had protested against the abuses of indulgences. Why, then, did Luther's theses create such a stir? The reason why popular excitement was so quickly generated was that the fuel was ready for
the flame. The leader for whom Germany had long been waiting had appeared upon the scene.

Indulgences were an accepted item of papal revenue. Leo X
was a member of the Medicean family of bankers. He was not
disposed to curtail the income of the curia by restricting the
sale of indulgences. In 1518 he summoned Luther to Rome.
But the Saxon preacher desired to be allowed to defend himself
in Germany, and, with the aid of his protector, Frederick the **The Pa-**
Wise of Saxony, such an arrangement was made. A meeting **pal Con-**
took place at Augsburg between Luther and the papal legate, **demnation**
Cardinal Cajetan, a Dominican friar. Cajetan demanded unconditional recantation. Luther asked for a properly conducted
trial. When it was evident that no agreement was possible
Luther left the town secretly, at night-time, and returned to
Wittenberg. The next event of importance was the disputation
at Leipsig, which took place in the following year, and in which
Eck, Carlstadt, and Luther were engaged. Eck, the learned
vice-chancellor of Ingolstadt, was a born disputant, greatly skilled
in all the niceties of the scholastics. Andrew Bodenstein,
usually called Carlstadt, was a teacher in the University of Wittenberg. The debate was not confined to the subject of indulgences, but included many other points. The religious views
with which Luther's brain was seething were by no means clearly
defined and well formulated at this time. They had yet to be
"beaten out on the anvil of disputation." In the course of the
discussion Eck succeeded in extracting from Luther the asser-

tion that general councils of the Church are subject to error and that they have fallen into error in the past. With this declaration the breach, as Eck at once perceived, became irreparable. The Church holds herself to be ever one and the same guardian of divine truth; that at every time she possesses the faith in all its fullness; and that its principles are only "defined," that is, fixed intelligibly, as often as necessity arises. The net results of the disputation were that Luther obtained a clearer understanding of his own views which up to this time had been slowly fermenting, that the belief that his own views accorded with the position of the Church was revealed as a delusion, and that two distinct parties began to form themselves in Germany. "The die is cast," said Luther, "I despise the fury and favor of Rome; I will never be reconciled to them nor commune with them." On June 15, 1520, the bull *Exsurge Domine* was issued. It condemned forty-one articles taken from the works of Luther, ordered all his books to be burned, forbade him to preach, and commanded him, under pain of excommunication, to recant within sixty days.

Before the appearance of the bull in Germany, Luther knew that proceedings were being instituted against him at Rome, and probably he expected that adverse action would be taken. But he must have been encouraged to face the issue by the knowledge that the great bulk of public opinion favored religious reform, and that the determination of the Germans to resist the exactions of the papal curia was constantly increasing. Before he learned of the issue of the bull against him he put forth the first of his great publications, *To the Christian Nobility of the German Nation*. The book is an arraignment of the entire hierarchical structure, and a stirring appeal to his countrymen to put an end to the wrongs from which Germany had suffered so long. Luther denied the distinction between the clergy and the laity. Every Christian man, he said, is a priest. He denied the claim of the Church to the exclusive right to interpret the Bible. Interpretation, he said, is the right of every individual who has accepted the Christian faith. He denied the claim of the pope to the sole right to convoke a general council. Such a right, he said, rests with the Church at large. Here, in brief, were the main lines of the religious system that he afterwards advocated. And in simple and fervid words, with directness and with earnestness, he pointed out the abuses and the oppression under which Germany had suffered so long, and indicated a definite line of reform. He spoke as a prophet, with all the burden of his country stirring his heart to passionate indignation, and as a practical guide who saw a way to better things. It was the trumpet blast of the Ecclesiastical Revolution.

Soon after Luther knew the contents of the bull against him he issued a second pamphlet, *On the Babylonish Captivity of the Church,* intended primarily for theologians and scholars. He had been greatly encouraged by the popular support he had received in all quarters. The hour for revolt had come at last, and Luther, made so by his intensity and simplicity, was the man for the hour. He was a born party leader, seeing only one side of the question, seeing it simply and strongly, and possessing the ability to present his ideas in a way that all who heard could understand. In this second blow that he struck at the papal system he accepted some of the logical consequences of his doctrine of justification by faith alone. All things that stand in the way of the direct relation of man to Christ should be discarded. So he abolished the sacraments with the exception of three — baptism, penance, and communion. And the Church, he again insisted, does not consist of the clergy superimposed upon the laity, but is made up of all believing Christians.

The last of the three great books that Luther issued in 1520 is the little tractate *On the Freedom of a Christian Man.* In a direct and simple way it deals with the daily life of the Christian man. It develops still further the individualism which is the outcome of his basic doctrine of justification; and it rounded out the publication of his views. In the first of these three books he spoke as a statesman, in the second as a theologian, and in the third as a man. The books are stamped with all the characteristics of his future utterances. They have the same fiery language and unrestrained passion, the same ardent and impetuous spirit, and the same striking contrasts between the gross and the sublime. In these three books the Lutheran revolt was unmistakably declared; for in them he disowned the " character indelebilis " of the priest and discarded the medieval doctrine of the sacraments and thus created a schism beyond repair. Calvin, with all his subtlety, merely completed the separation.

For some time bonfires had been made of Luther's books, in accordance with the papal command, but there had been frequent and unmistakable expressions of hostility on the part of the people to the papal authority. Encouraged by such evidences of popular support Luther decided to retaliate in a similar manner. So on the morning of December 10, 1520, in the presence of a concourse of students and townsfolk, he committed to the flames the recent bull, and a collection of the canon law. It was a bold and dramatic event, and it won the applause not only of the assembled students but of the greater part of Germany. When Luther lit the fire that burned the pope's decrees he lit another fire, the fire of revolution, for which the materials were already at hand.

The first diet of the reign of Charles V was held at Worms, January to May, 1521. There were many difficult questions to be settled, the most important of them being (1) the succession to the hereditary dominions of the House of Hapsburg in Germany, (2) the settlement of the form of government of the Empire, (3) the war with France, and (4) the course of action to be taken with regard to Luther. This last problem was by no means the most important in the eyes of the authorities; it was regarded by them merely as a troublesome incident; yet it was destined to prove the gravest and most difficult of all. Charles solved the first problem by retaining the Netherlands and Franche-Comté and relinquishing to his brother Ferdinand all the hereditary Austrian lands and the claims upon Hungary and Bohemia. The question of the imperial government was met by the restoration of the Reichsregiment, the Council of Regency, an institution which had been in existence for the two years of 1500–02, which had the initiative in arranging foreign alliances and adjudicating feudal questions, which had administrative power in the absence of the Emperor and which, at other times, acted as his adviser. Among the conditions of the election of Charles had been a pledge for the establishment of a central government. The Council of Regency was a compromise between the demands of the nobles and those of the Emperor. The Reichskammergericht, the Supreme Law Court, was remodeled. Three members were nominated by the Emperor, two more were to represent the Hapsburg dominions, and the others were to be elected by the seven electors and the six circles. The members were to be paid by the Empire so as to guard against their dependence upon the Emperor. The war with France had already broken out and Charles was most anxious to prosecute it vigorously, but the Diet provided for only 4,000 cavalry and 20,000 infantry.

The Diet summoned Luther to appear before it; and so unmistakable were the signs of approval showered upon him by the people that his journey from Wittenberg to Worms was a triumphal procession and his entrance into the city was like that of a conqueror. On April 16 the Emperor, a youth of twenty-one years, utterly unfitted to deal with the momentous problem before him, and the heretic friar confronted each other, at the end of an April afternoon, in the great hall where the Diet met. In the presence of Charles, the great princes of the realm, and the representatives of the free cities, Luther acknowledged the authorship of his books; but in answer to the question of his withdrawal of them he asked time for consideration. He was granted twenty-four hours. In the interval much encouragement was given him, and on the following day, in a highly dramatic scene, he bravely refused to recant any of his teachings. Then in the midst of tumult he made his way from the hall. A few days later, at the command of the Emperor, he quitted Worms before he knew what the action of the Diet would be. Upon the day following Luther's refusal to recant, Charles expressed his determination to stake all his dominions, his friends, his life, and his soul, upon the extinction of the Lutheran heresy. On May 26 an edict was issued against Luther, proscribing him as a heretic, forbidding men to give him food or shelter, commanding them to deliver him to the imperial officers, and ordering his books to be burned. Thus Luther was placed under the ban of the imperial authority as well as that of the Church. But no decree issued against the person of the Saxon friar could bring the religious question to a conclusion, neither was it to be ended by the burning of his books. In him all the burdens and aspirations of Germany received expression. But they would have found another voice had the fate of a martyr befallen him. The Revolution had gone too far to be ended with the death of a single man. It had gone so far, indeed, as to render the execution of the Edict of Worms impossible. But Charles left Germany deeming himself to have met with success. He believed he had checked the encroachment of oligarchy, engaged the support of Germany against his foreign foe, and scotched the snake of heresy. He was destined not to return to the fatherland for nine years. In the meantime the religious revolution was to continue with ever increasing momentum.

On his way home, while riding through a wood, Luther was seized by some men and carried by devious ways to the castle of the Wartburg, one of the residences of the Elector of Saxony, whose emissaries the abductors were. There "Junker Georg" began his great work of translating the Bible for the German people. A number of translations of the Bible and parts of the Bible into German were made before the Protestant Revolution, but they were based upon the Vulgate and thus perpetuated opinions which the reformers declined to accept. Luther endeavored to base his translation upon the most recent results of Greek and Hebrew scholarship. But the great success of his translation was due to its literary form rather than to its scholarship. He grieved because of his lack of classical scholarship, yet it may be said that, with his power of direct appeal to the imagination and passions of men, he created the German language. Of course the great development of German is not due entirely to him. Other men have contributed to the work. But his was the river that determined the route to the sea. It is no detraction that it was swelled by tributary streams along the way. The first edition of his translation of the New Testament was issued in September, 1522; and his translation of the entire Bible was finished in 1534. Meanwhile, here and there, in a few places, Luther's books were burned; but his supporters did not decrease in numbers, nor was any rigorous prosecution of them attempted. The Edict of Worms was a dead letter.

While Luther was hidden in the Wartburg the social and religious ferment at Wittenberg did not cease. Scholars, animated by varying motives, continued to flock there; and the University and the town declined to acknowledge either the papal bull or the imperial edict. Chief among the teachers there were Philip Melanchthon (1497–1560) and Carlstadt (1480?–1541). More than any one else it was Melanchthon who infused the humanistic element into the revolutionary movement in Germany. Previous to his contact with Luther he was interested chiefly in the restoration of classical science and the recovery in its unadulterated form of the ancient philosophy. Later on he gave himself to the service of religious reform. He was not one of the militant figures of the movement, and he never ceased to regret the quiet and peaceful life of the student. He had come to Wittenberg as a teacher of Greek, and it was due in part to his reading of the New Testament and in part to the dominating personality of Luther that he lent himself to the cause of revolt. Carlstadt was ambitious to be regarded as the leader of the new movement during the absence of Luther. He was a man of considerable learning, a mystic, and a radical. His mysticism led him to place but slight value upon all external observances and rites. He accepted the Zwinglian doctrine that in the sacrament of communion the elements of bread and wine are merely emblems, he desired the abolition of the worship of the Host in the mass, he advocated the compulsory marriage of secular priests, and he denounced the institution of monasticism. These teachings resulted in a riot against the mass at Wittenberg. The radical movement was accelerated by the coming to the University town of a number of so-called "prophets" from Zwickau, a town in southern Saxony, near Bohemia, among whom were Nicholaus Storch, Thomas Münzer,

and Marcus Stübner. They relied exclusively upon the direct
inspiration of the Holy Spirit. To them the Bible and the
Church were alike unnecessary. Historians have sought to iden-
tify them with the Anabaptists, but more recent scholarship
seems to reject any such connection. At Wittenberg they allied
themselves with Carlstadt and his group and increased the radical nature of his propaganda. They advocated the distribution
of the property of ecclesiastical corporations among the poor;
and declared, because of the direct guidance of God, all institutions of learning to be unnecessary.

In January 1522, a new Pope, Adrian VI, a man already sixty-
three years of age, ascended the chair of St. Peter. He was a
native of Utrecht and had been the tutor of Charles V. He was
a cold, austere, and simple man, sincerely devoted to the cause of
moral reform and to the disengaging of the Papacy from the
secular aims to which it had been committed for so long. He had
no conception of the Renaissance movement, and no sympathy
for the art and learning of which his immediate predecessor was
so willing a patron. Unfortunately the circumstances of the
time did not permit him to undertake separately the work of reforming the Church. It was not an easy matter to get rid of
the political entanglements of the Papacy. Questions that could
not be brushed aside required his attention. Despite his un-
willingness he was drawn into the quarrel between France and
Germany. So his brief pontificate of twenty months came to a
pathetic close with little progress made in the reform that he
cherished as his chief aim.

In his retreat Luther had learned of the proceedings of the
radicals at Wittenberg and was greatly displeased. So, regardless of the ban of the Empire and the instructions of the Elector,
he left the Wartburg and arrived in Wittenberg on March 6,
1522. For eight successive days he preached to the people and
succeeded in winning them from the support of the radical
leaders. Soon Carlstadt, Münzer, and Stübner left to carry on
their work in other places, and Luther continued to live in the
Augustinian convent. No action was taken against him by the
imperial authorities.

When Charles, at the close of the Diet of Worms, believing
that he had put things in order, had gone off to the Netherlands,
he had really left Germany in a dangerous condition. For one
thing, there were many classes that had no voice in the affairs of
government and their dissatisfaction rapidly increased and began to take definite form. The peasantry, as we shall see in our
next chapter, were seething with discontent. The burghers were

ill at ease. And the Ritterschaft, the knights, were on the verge of insurrection. These parasitic military adventurers had been called into existence by the innumerable feudal wars that had continued for so long a period in the absence of any effective central government. When those wars gradually grew less frequent the knights were left to prey upon their peasants and upon society at large. Whatever reason for their existence there may have been in the past had vanished with the approach of modern life. They lacked "the blessing of a great task." They looked back upon a proud past. They had once embodied the warlike strength of the nation, and they had been its chief class, politically, socially, and in literature. Their period of brilliance had gone by. Yet they were puffed up with a boundless pride; they clung to their old ideals, endeavored to preserve the old conditions, claimed a position of precedence in politics and society; and struggled passionately against the new economic conditions and the modernized conceptions of state and law that were gradually making their way in western Europe. Few of them adapted themselves to the changed environment; and others, sunk in poverty, resorted to robbery upon the highway. Some of these knights became mercenary soldiers, finding in the national wars of the time a restoration, in an altered form, of their former occupation. But from the fall of the Hohenstaufen dynasty to the reign of Maximilian the Empire had hardly waged a single war worthy of the name. Consequently those knights who had depended upon the Empire had lacked the opportunity for a legitimate exercise of their military calling. And in the wars of Maximilian so little glory was to be won under his banners that it is not improbable that many knights disdained the imperial service. Thus there was developed in them all the evil qualities of the unemployed soldier. The warlike force that fermented in them discharged itself in guerilla warfare with each other, or with the secular and ecclesiastical princes, or in the wild life of the bandit. Most conspicuous of this class was Franz von Sickingen, one of the most prominent of Luther's supporters, who soon after Charles had left Germany made a raid upon the Archbishop of Trier. The attack resulted in the defeat and death of Sickingen and in the disappearance of the knights as an independent and effective force in the political affairs of Germany.

In the absence of the Emperor the Council of Regency attempted to control the affairs of the country. But it had neither men nor money, and it proved altogether ineffectual. It failed to check the aggressive movement of Von Sickingen and it failed to check the retaliatory measures of the princes who had combined for the relief of Trier and the ending of the power of the knights. The towns were hostile to its economic policy, the princes opposed it because it interfered with their individual independence, and Ferdinand, who was its president, believed that its enfeeblement would enhance his own power. The majority of its members viewed with displeasure the swelling tide of Lutheran opinion, but they were too precariously situated to undertake repressive measures. So when Pope Adrian urged the enforcement of the Edict of Worms they referred the matter to the Diet.

The Diet met at Nuremberg, from November, 1522 to March, 1523. A locality more favorable to the Lutheran cause could scarcely have been chosen. The town was enthusiastic and unabashed in its support of the heretical friar. The majority of the members of the Diet belonged to the orthodox party, but with a few exceptions they were not inclined to a policy of active suppression. To the Diet the lay estates submitted one hundred Gravamina, recounting the more important of the papal abuses from which Germany had suffered. The outcome of the meeting was that word was sent to Adrian that any attempt to enforce the edict would result in civil war, that the existence of evils in the Church had been admitted by the Pope himself, and that the best remedy for the situation was the summoning of a council in which laymen as well as ecclesiastics should be permitted to discuss the grievances. It cannot be said that either the list of grievances presented by the lay estates or the communication of the Diet to the Pope can be taken as an expression of support of the Lutheran cause; but the delay that ensued contributed in no small degree to the success of the movement. It is clear that the religious revolt had now acquired a political aspect, that it had secured recognition as a national problem whose solution could be found only in the reform of the conditions that had called it into existence.

*The Diet of Nuremberg*

For the time being, then, the revolt was allowed to spread. Luther himself was the feeblest of organizers, but the Lutheran revolt answered to the needs of the time. It had already found a fruitful soil in the cities. The city age in the development of German civilization was at hand. It was making culture more democratic, and it was creating new needs, new tendencies and new aims. The culture of the Middle Ages, represented by the clergy and to a lesser extent by the nobility, was passing away. The development of city life was causing the upheaval of social strata that hitherto had been intellectually dormant. Far-reach-

*Spread of the Revolt*

ing dislocations were taking place. The age of feudalism had permitted the Papacy to build up, by violent means when necessary, its vast juristic and political power. The age of capitalism and the new democratic culture was to witness the retaliation. And together with the proletariat of the towns, in the sharing of the new social ideals, there must be associated the peasants. Political thought had brought to the surface the doctrine of the sovereignty of the people; and from the bosom of the Church had come the gospel of the equality and brotherhood of all men. These two ideas were intoxicating the minds of the masses. We shall soon see how they led to the social revolt of the peasants. At present we are concerned only with their influence upon the religious revolt. At first this quickening of life in the cities assumed the form of a crusade against the exasperating religious abuses of the time, a stirring of the spirit of nationality, and an intellectual awakening, rather than a desire to supplant the creeds of the Church with new doctrines. Still it was true that the theological views of Luther and Zwingli were gaining ground.

Lutheranism also spread among the princes, the most powerful political force in Germany. The defeat of the knights under Von Sickingen, who had espoused Luther's cause, seemed for the time to be a great blow to the Lutheran revolt. But in much the same manner as the revolt increased the national opposition to the papal curia did it connect itself with the oligarchical opposition to the monarchy. Then, too, the princes as well as the lesser nobility, the burghers and the peasants, had suffered from ecclesiastical pretensions and exemptions. Frederick the Wise, Elector of Saxony, to whom the German revolt owed its preservation from the grave perils of its earliest years, was won over to the Lutheran cause much more definitely and much earlier than has commonly been supposed. His brother John who succeeded him at his death in 1525 was less circumspect, and favored the new doctrines more openly. Among the other princes who early lent themselves to the Lutheran cause was the youthful and talented Philip of Hesse, who was won over by Melanchthon in 1524. He was an important acquisition to the movement. His state was one of the first rank, and he himself was able and ambitious. In the same year the Margrave Casimir of Brandenburg, acting in conjunction with his Estates, adopted the Lutheran profession; and Duke Ernest of Lüneburg, a nephew of the Elector Frederick of Saxony, inaugurated reformatory measures at Celle. In the following year Albert of Hohenzollern, Grandmaster of the Teutonic Order, renounced his religious vows and changed his ecclesiastical office into an hereditary duchy under the protection of Poland.  George of Culmbach also became a convert to Lutheranism; and the banished and brutal Ulrich of Würtemberg, who doubtless hoped the success of the revolt would enable him to recover his duchy, proclaimed his adherence to the new religion.  Lutheranism found a Danish patron in Christian II, a brother-in-law of Charles V, who urged Luther and Carlstadt to carry on a propaganda in his kingdom, and when that brutal and lustful ruler was deprived of his throne it found a much more desirable promoter in his successor, Frederick I.

The strength of Luther's mission was that it kindled the hearts of those who were so rooted in the old ideals that they could not be touched by the radicals, by the teachings of those scholars who hastened on to the emancipation of the individual in which both mysticism and rationalism resulted.  His earliest teaching appealed to the masses who wished to keep in touch with the assured past.  The successful founder of a new religion has always been a devotee of the old, a more ardent disciple and a deeper lover of the ancient ways than others.  The power to make the hearts of his followers burn within them is the power to reveal to them still further the beauty and the consolation of the book they already hold sacred.  He comes never to destroy, but always to fulfil.  His message purports to be a better interpretation of the ancient faith.  There is nothing new about Luther, said Erasmus, not without a touch of disdain, except his grand phrases.  The corruption of the clergy and the unbelief and skepticism engendered by the new learning had brought about a visible decline in religion that extended even to the ranks of the peasantry.  It was Luther's object to restore religion. It was necessary, so it seemed, to carry on a simultaneous warfare against the ecclesiastical abuses and the increasing rationalism of the time.  He did not fight under the banner of humanism. On the contrary, he distinctly repudiated reason as a religious guide.  In the beginning he did not realize how far his religious views would carry him.  No one would have repudiated more passionately than he the things which eventually became the essential characteristics of Protestantism.  It was the tide of events, the great upheaval of the time, of which, paradoxical as it may seem, he stands out as the leader, that carried him forward.  But he always faced backward.  His greatness, like that of other leaders, consisted not in unlikeness to his fellow-men, but in ability to see things from their point of view.  The great leader is always comprehensive, never unique.  He sees the things that should be done with such a singleness and intensity of vision and he strives for their fulfilment with so definite and passionate a conviction as often to bring upon himself the charge of narrowness, and sometimes that of fanaticism. But it is precisely these qualities that make him a leader. Luther had the elements of a great man in that he shared the point of view of his contemporaries; he caught the trend of the new movement with extraordinary reality and intensity; the simplicity and directness of his nature gave to him the power of vivid and appealing speech; and his vital imagination gave him a power, seldom equaled, to move the hearts of men. New religions are wont to start in the backwoods. One started in an unimportant province of the great Roman Empire nineteen hundred years ago, and grew in power from its humble beginnings in Nazareth until to-day it nominally embraces the Christian world. So, too, in Saxony, a frontier province of the German Empire, crude and undeveloped, touched but slightly as yet with the transforming humanism of the time, a new religion was born.

# CHAPTER XIII

## THE SOCIAL REVOLUTION

1. Its Medieval Forerunners.
2. The Peasant Outbreaks of 1513-17.
3. The Social Effects of the Lutheran Schism.
4. The Second Diet of Nuremberg.
5. The Social Revolution.
6. Why as yet the Revolution Failed.

CHRISTIANITY in its first years became connected with socialistic views. It insisted upon the equality of all classes of men in the sight of God and it gave a high value to voluntary poverty. In the Middle Ages it went still further. It held up, as the condition of life in the apostolic age, as a condition of life to be regained, the ideal of community of property. Private property, it taught, had come into existence only as a result of the fall of man. This communistic ideal never prevailed in actual life. From time to time first one ascetic order and then another attempted to attain it, but sooner or later each fell by the wayside. Yet their efforts were by no means wholly in vain. The radiant ideal of St. Francis of Assisi, so expressive of the tender personality of the most poetic of all the saints, appealed to the laity with a heart-compelling force and exercised upon them an incalculable effect long after it had become forgotten by his professional followers. So at intervals there appeared heretical sects who included community of property as an essential part of their program. Such a sect were the Waldenses. To this part of their creed the Church could not consistently object; and so in 1206 one division of the Waldenses, known as the "Catholic poor," received the papal sanction. This amalgamation of religious and social questions was destined to have momentous results. Two churches existed side by side, or rather one existed within the other; first, the outward and visible Church, the rich and powerful hierarchy with its worldly interests and activity, the empirical Church; and, second, the invisible church, the community of saints, held together by no organization, united only by the common devotion to a religious ideal of life. The political, economic, and social changes that took place in Germany in the fourteenth, fifteenth, and sixteenth

CHAP.
XIII

1200-1381

Medieval
Forerun-
ners

centuries put the masses into a state of ferment.  This discontent was accentuated by the dissatisfaction of the invisible church with the wealth and the worldly activity of the visible Church. Ominous threats against the captains of industry, the princes, and the prelates, who were held responsible respectively for the economic, political, and ecclesiastical evils of the time, grew ever more frequent.  The people must fall upon them all, was the burden of the popular German poetry of the end of the fourteenth century, upon priestly, princely, and capitalistic vampires alike, for " they are full day and night, while our bellies are empty."  Already, as one of the intellectual products of the Renaissance, there was spreading abroad the theory of the political sovereignty of the people ; and from the bosom of the Church there came the doctrine of the equality and brotherhood of all men.  The two thoughts united to increase the social discontent of the time.  They pointed towards a golden age and intoxicated the minds of the masses.  The only outlet for this discontent that was consequent upon the break-up of ecclesiastical and secular feudalism was revolution.  So the storm broke and all the deplorable disasters of the social revolt came to pass.

The first outbreaks of importance occurred in England.  In that country the conditions of the peasants had been improved; but it was precisely because the peasants had caught a vision of better things that they became determined to secure a greater degree of amelioration.  The uncertain personal services that had formerly been demanded of them had to a considerable extent been commuted for definite rents, and the devastations of the Black Death, which in a few months had swept away one-third of the population of England, had depleted the supply of labor and caused an increase of wages.  The landlords, by means of the Statute of Laborers, tried to put back the hands of the clock, to compel a return to the conditions of feudalism.  The irritation caused by this attempt was increased by the communistic teaching of the Lollards.  The demand for a reformation of morals had become coupled with a belief in the equality of men, and a desire for the redistribution of property, at least of ecclesiastical property.  In the beginning all men were equal, said John Ball, a wandering priest ; the subjection of one man to another that has come about is against the will of God.  The primitive freedom and equality which is the birthright of every man can be regained only by war upon the oppressors of the common man.  At last in 1381, when the grievance of an obnoxious poll tax irritated the malcontents, friction developed into violence.  The rebellion, which lasted only three days, found a leader in Wat Tyler, a quick-witted adventurer of uncertain antecedents. The Kentish mob streamed along the highways from Canterbury to London where Tyler confronted the youthful king. Richard promised a redress of grievances. At a second conference Tyler was killed in the course of an altercation with one of the king's attendants. Instantly realizing the gravity of the situation Richard rode forward exclaiming to the rebels: " Take me for your leader; from me shall you have all that you seek." He led them beyond the walls into the fields where they were induced to disperse. When some days later he was asked to fulfil his promise he made the harsh reply, " Villeins ye are still, and villeins ye shall remain." Then the royal forces fell upon the insurgents and defeated them. There were minor outbreaks in various parts of England, but all of them quickly subsided. The immediate results of the rebellion were in many cases distinctly unfavorable to the peasants. The old bonds were tightened anew. But the forces of economic change were working silently, and gradually they brought about the desired transformation from villeinage to free tenure that revolution had failed to accomplish. The misery of the peasants and their dreams of amelioration found expression in the poems grouped under the title of *The Vision of William concerning Piers the Plowman*. They have usually been ascribed to a single author, William Langland, but there is much evidence to support the conclusion that they are the work of several writers, each with his own eyes to see the corruption and the injustice of the time, each with his own heart deeply sympathetic with the sad plight of his fellow-men, and each with his own peculiar voice giving utterance to his indignation in passionate protest.

The ideas that produced discontent in England also found their cognate social application in Bohemia. In the reign of Charles IV (1347–78) that country reached the height of its prosperity. In 1348 Charles founded at Prague the first university on German soil. The national spirit of the Czechs was stimulated and in 1409 the German element was expelled from the University. The most influential spokesman of this revival of national feeling was John Hus, a teacher and a priest. From Wiclif and from a long series of Bohemian thinkers he inherited heretical views. On July 6, 1415, he was burned at the stake at Constance, where he had been induced under a guarantee of safety to attend the general council. The treacherous death of the popular leader kindled a terrible war. The Bohemian revolt was distinctly national in character. All classes of society participated in it. The insurgents, inspired by the fanaticism and

Revolt in
Bohemia

aided by the strategic skill of John Ziska, burning churches and
monasteries, swept over Bohemia, and made devastating expeditions into various other parts of the empire. Everywhere the
Christian socialist views had produced the most inflammable material and only the spark of the shameful betrayal of Hus had
been necessary for the conflagration. The Hussite extremists,
who were known as the Taborites from their custom of giving
scriptural names to the hills where they held their meetings,
demanded along with ecclesiastical reforms the secularization of
church property, and they desired to institute a socialistic theocracy based upon their conception of the primitive Christian
life. In the Bohemian revolt there were interwoven an insurrection against the authority of the Church, an outbreak of the
national spirit, and an attempt to settle the fundamental problems
that confront secular society. Unfortunately it came to include
a disprizal of culture and a belief that the golden age was to be
reached not by a gradually increasing development but by a sudden and stupendous catastrophe. In Bohemia the revolutionary
movement succumbed to the persistency of the warfare against
it and to its own excesses; but its ideas spread throughout the
German lands increasing everywhere the fermenting and foreboding discontent.

We have arrived at the beginnings of the social revolution in
Germany. But first we must stop to note the example of the
Swiss. The struggle for freedom made by the people of the
three forest cantons in the first years of the fourteenth
century, was the first great successful peasant rebellion. The
rebels were greatly aided by the mountains which they knew
thoroughly and loved well. In the battle of Morgarten 1,300 of
them were able to defeat 10,000 Austrians. Between 1424 and
1471 the peasants of the Rhætian Alps were successful in a
similar rebellion. So two little republics were formed in the
heart of the mountains, and eventually a new nation was born
in Europe.

Somewhere about the year 1437 there was written a remarkable little book, called *The Reformation of Emperor Sigismund,*
that boldly sketched the program of the social revolution that
was impending in Germany. It is not certain who wrote it; and
equally uncertain is the reason for naming it as the work of
Sigismund. The authorship has been attributed, among others,
to a secular priest of Augsburg and to the town notary of an
imperial city. Its title may be due to the current belief that
some day a great reformer, in the person of an emperor, would
come to end all the sorrows and burdens of the people, or to the

hope that the emperor would accept its program of reform as his own. This earliest of the German revolutionary pamphlets appeared in print for the first time in 1476, and so it was not until long after it was written that it became widely known and exercised a wide-spread influence. Indeed, it was not until the second decade of the sixteenth century that it reached the apogee of its power. Then it became "the trumpet of the Peasants' War." It demanded the abolition of serfdom as a sin against the word of God. All opponents of the emancipation of the peasants it declared to be deserving of death. The peasantry was essential to the existence of every other class of society; in truth, it was the oldest and most respectable of all classes. It should be freed from all its oppressions, from tithes and tolls and rents, and from secular and ecclesiastical punishment; and it should have free access to the waters, woods, and meadows. In the towns there was need of a similar emancipation for the workmen. The guilds and the great capitalistic corporations, the most unanimously and bitterly hated of all the new phenomena of the economic life of the time, of which the chief was the remarkable family of the Fuggers, were to be abolished; and wages and the price of food were to be regulated by representatives of the handicrafts. In addition to such definite demands the book contains much vague suggestion that is equally characteristic of the contemporary state of feeling. Verily the humble should be exalted and the mighty be put down from their seats. The last age of the world was dawning. All evil was to be rooted out and happiness was to become the common lot. The book is expressive, too, of the exceedingly varied elements of the discontent that everywhere was rife, and of the idealization of the peasantry and the proletariat and the religious ennoblement of agriculture and the handicrafts that characterize the literature of the fifteenth century.

Before we begin the story of the social revolution it would be well to attempt an analysis of this wide-spread discontent. It was not due entirely to economic need. Long ago the legal condition of the peasant had altered in his favor. Here and there could be found peasants who were free, upon whose persons and property no lord had any claim. And most of the former serfs had become partially free. They were free tenants who combined with complete personal freedom a limited right of usufruct in their farms. In general they paid to the lord of the manor a fixed rent; they and their heirs, therefore, were able to enjoy the fruits of their industry; and they were able to profit by the increased demand for agricultural products

caused by the growth of urban population and the rising standard of life in the towns. It is true that this improved economic
condition of the peasants was not uniform. Some there were
who " had neither hay nor straw." Most of these unfortunates
were to be found in Swabia and the bordering provinces. Yet
even these poorer peasants were not landless thralls. Here and
there poverty and subjection were to be found; but nowhere was
there general poverty; and nowhere was there slavery without
legal rights. It would be a mistake, therefore, to attribute the
uprising solely to economic need. " New inventions and designs," new burdens that had been imposed upon them within the
memory of living men, the raising of their dues to the lords of
the manors, the changing of occasional and voluntary services into
regular and required duties, the shifting of the demands of the
State from the shoulders of the landlords to those of the tenants,
and the levying of heavier taxes directly upon them, figure everywhere in the peasants' programs of reform. The abolition of
these intolerable innovations became the watchword of the dis-
contented peasants. Then, too, the peasants whose economic condition had, in general, been improving, had caught a glimpse of
better things. They were no longer content to render even the
old services as a matter of course. They began to demand legal
title and counter-service. All things not in harmony with divine
and human law were to be rejected even though they were sanctioned and sanctified by immemorial tradition. To return to the
conditions of primitive Christianity, to establish a new order
based upon social justice and fashioned after the will of God —
that was the central demand of the peasants. It informs, as we
shall see, the Twelve Articles, their principal program of reform. In addition to these grievances against the lords of the
manors the peasants bitterly disliked the great associations of
capital, the Fuggers, Welsers, Höchstetters, and others, which
had formed monopolies in so many lines of industry, and which
had, so it was believed, arbitrarily and wantonly raised prices.
The guilds of the towns also came within the scope of their disapproval, for did not they, too, control industry and raise prices?
And even the clergy had become more grasping than ever.
Thus the peasants believed themselves to be surrounded by a
world of enemies, given up without hope of rescue to the greed
and caprice of the higher classes. Every man sought to enrich
himself at their expense; whoever outraged a peasant was guilty
of no wrong. In the phrase " the poor man," as applied to the
peasant of that time, there lies a deep meaning. And against
these hardships no aid could be expected from the State. Only

in certain of the Germanic lands did the imperial power come into direct contact with the peasants; elsewhere it was too far off. The territorial power, especially in the diminutive political districts of the southwest, was in most instances harsh and exacting. Embarrassed by the increased cost of administration, and still more by military necessities, the territorial power placed additional burdens upon the peasants. And, not content with increasing the burdens of the peasants, the State, like the lords of the manors, encroached upon their rights. It seized the common lands, the pastures and the still more valuable woods and forests; it could not even restrain the transgressions of its own agents; its officials plundered the common man, loaded him with fees and administrative expenses, and practised upon him every conceivable act of violence. The necessities of the political life and the demands of high politics were things the peasants could not understand. They saw themselves prejudiced by the State and kept under, and they found it to be no helper in time of need. The great tendencies of national life either surged past the peasants or whirled them to destruction. They had no voice in the councils of State; the aggressive activity of the capitalists ground them to dust whenever they were in its way; and neither manor nor State cared for the education of these men in whom lay fallow so rich a treasure of intellectual and moral force and who, despite all the discouraging circumstances, managed in a few mighty personalities to render great service to the national culture. Finally, the peasants were only too often compelled to receive the blessings of religion, their only spiritual refreshment, and their mainstay in the hour of trouble, from the hands of a corrupt clergy. It availed the peasants little that a few powerful personalities from their ranks won a place for themselves in the world. The generality of their class was excluded from it. Yet their eyes were opening. They were beginning to gaze down the vista of progress. For sometime, as we have seen, they had ventured to criticize the upper classes. They were becoming aware of their worth, of their rights as well as their duties. Psychical causes were at work. The revolution was at hand. It was, then, not so much economic distress that caused the peasants to revolt as the sense of social exclusion, the powerlessness, under existing conditions, to defend themselves by lawful means against injustice and exploitation, and the hopelessness of waiting for redress at the hands of the State.

The first actual outbreak that followed the Hussite wars and the revolt of the Swiss peasants took place in the spring of 1476 in the idyllic region of Würzburg. Hans Böheim, known

**The Piper
of Niklas-
hausen**

as the Piper of Niklashausen, was a son of that mixed race of
West-Franks and Swabians whose dreamy and deeply religious
temperament, combined with a deep-seated craving for freedom
and a choleric disposition, made them ever ready to receive
revolutionary suggestions; and who were, perhaps, more deeply
moved than any other of the Germanic peoples by the dynamic
social and political ideas of the time.  One day this peasant piper
lit a fire before the pilgrimage church in the little village of
Niklashausen and cast into the flames his musical instruments.
Then turning to the assembled people he began to preach.  With
eloquent words he told them of a vision of the Mother of God
who had informed him of the great changes that were at hand.
All authority, secular and ecclesiastical, was to be abolished, all
taxes were to be repealed and all property was to be held in common.  Every man was to work, even the bishops and the barons
were to earn their daily wage, for one man is as good as another.
The kingdom of God would soon come upon the earth.  Emperors and popes, princes and prelates, would all disappear and
all men would be brothers.  Quickly the news of the new prophet
was carried in all directions, and from the villages and countryside around came crowds to hear him.  His teaching was not
confined to the inculcation of socialist doctrines.  He preached
repentance for sins.  In Niklashausen, he said, which was specially dedicated to the Virgin Mary, there was more grace than
in Rome.  Whosoever confessed in that place was sure of
heaven.  Hans was soon regarded as a saint, and pilgrims poured
into the little village to hear him.  But one night the sleeping
piper was spirited away by a troop of cavalry and imprisoned at
Würzburg.  There, singing a hymn of his childhood to Mary,
he perished at the stake and his ashes were thrown into the
Main.  Sometime later the village church was demolished.  But
the memory of the piper-prophet lived on among the peasants,
who for forty years continued to meet by night on the ruins of the
little church, and his teachings spread far and wide.

The whole south and south-west of the empire now became the
center of seething discontent that rapidly developed into rebellion.  The kind of shoe usually worn by the peasants was one
tied with strings, called a *Bundschuh,* and such a shoe, the symbol of their revolts, they adopted as their emblem; while for
their motto they chose the saying " Only what is just before
God."  They demanded the abolition of all tithes, customs, and
rent, and the confiscation of all property belonging to the Church
and the nobility.  At that time nearly two-thirds of the land in
the empire was owned by ecclesiastics.  Everywhere could be

**The Bund-
schuh**

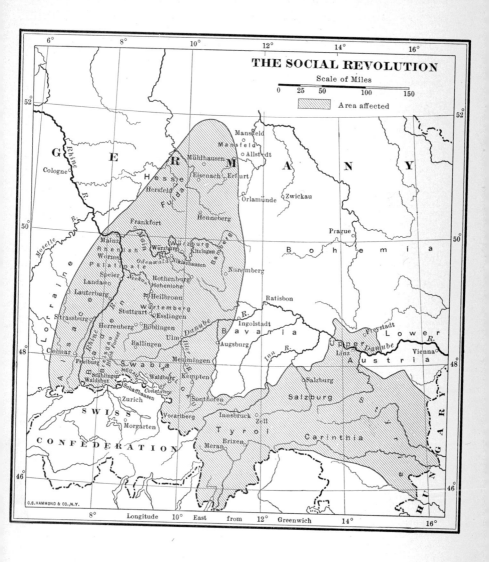

THE SOCIAL REVOLUTION

Scale of Miles

0   25   50      100      150

Area affected

GERMANY

Cologne

Rhine R.

Mansfeld
Mansfeld
Mühlhausen    Allstedt
Eisenach  Erfurt
Hessia    Orlamünde    Zwickau
Hersfeld
Fulda R.
Henneberg

Frankfort

Mainz    Main R.
Rhenish    Würzburg    Würzburg    Kitzingen
Worms    Odenwald    Niklashausen
Palatinate    Saale R.
Speier    Neckar R.    Rothenburg    Nuremberg
Landau    Hohenlohe
Lauterburg    Heilbronn

Prague    Bohemia

Wörtemberg
Stuttgart    Esslingen
Strassburg    Rhine R.    Herrenberg    Böblingen
Ulm    Danube R.    Bavaria    Ratisbon
Colmar    Ballingen    Ingolstadt
Freiburg    Swabia    Memmingen    Augsburg    Inn R.    Lower
Stühlinger    Waldburg    Kempten    Upper    Danube    Freystadt    Vienna
Waldshut    HEGAU    Salzburg    Linz    Austria
Schaffhausen    Constance    Sonthofen
Zurich    Vorarlberg    Salzburg

SWISS    Morgarten    Innsbruck    Zell
Tyrol    Carinthia    HUNGARY
CONFEDERATION    Meran    Brixen

Mosette R.

Lorraine

Alsace

O.S.HAMMOND & CO.,N.Y.

8°    Longitude    10°    East    from    12°    Greenwich    14°    16°

heard the mutterings of the deepening discontent, in the inns and the hostelries, at church festivals, in the city workshops and in the harvest fields. Ominous harbingers of the coming storm flitted through the air. Constant uprisings of the common people that were quickly quelled occurred in the third quarter of the fifteenth century. But the cruel treatment of the defeated insurgents did not stop the movement. In the years from 1490 to 1503, which were years of frequent famine, more determined rebellions took place. Class hatred became increased in bitterness. The nobles still thought they could safely afford to despise the masses. They failed completely to understand the deep religious and social needs of the people. They had not yet experienced the fearful results of their wrath. They still deemed it possible to extinguish the prevalent discontent by brute force. But the storm of the social revolution continued to lower over Germany, and lightning flashes continued to announce its coming.

It was not only the peasantry that continued to menace the peace of the land. The population of the towns, oppressed with similar wrongs, attempted in many places to throw off their burdens by means of revolution. There was no economic homogeneity in the towns. The medieval guilds obstinately held their ground and were able, in no small measure, to impede the march of the new economic forces, to keep the craftsmen in their ancient subjection, and to deny to many an aspiring workman entrance to the trade he desired to follow. The activity of the great capitalistic associations, hated and feared alike by the peasantry and the proletariat, boldly pursued its conquering way and despised the outworn prejudices that endeavored to obstruct its path. Thus both the guilds and the new capitalism increased still further the distance between the rich and the poor and enhanced the social tension. As a result of all this there came to be two distinct classes in the towns. First, there was a thin superstratum of merchants, manufacturers, and persons of private means, who, in the matter of social development, had left the proletariat far behind; whose life was comparatively easy, rich in color, and full of enjoyment. To them the expansion of commerce and industry were ever opening up new sources of wealth; and already were they greedily reaching for the title of nobility and aspiring for greater influence in the affairs of State. On the other hand there stood the increasing mass of those who possessed little or nothing; — the numerous artisans, living for the most part in modest circumstances, especially the weavers; the small trades-men, who, together with the artisans, were oppressed by the new capitalism, who were weakened by a serious crisis in their trade and threatened with a speedy reduction to the ranks of the proletariat; the small agricultural holders who lived within the walls; the day laborers, the domestic servants, the journeyman artisans; and, finally, the professional beggars and other shady characters who formed in some towns no small percentage of the population. In the disproportion between these two municipal classes lies one of the deep-rooted causes of the social revolution. It was one of the most important of the many painful rifts that were appearing in the social life of the time. All these members of the second class had been injured rather than healed by the economic and financial changes of the time. They had become more exigent in an age that increasingly valued the pleasures of life; and they were without political rights. So it was with envy and hate that they looked up to the possessors of wealth and power. Nor were they without specific injustices of which to complain. City finances were invariably kept secret and new taxes were imposed without the consent of the community. So demagogues found the proletariat easy of persuasion. " Down with the powerful and plunder the rich " became a popular watchword. Thus it was that a considerable proportion of the city population combined with the peasants in the social revolt. These continued convulsions of the body politic made thoughtful men look with anxious fear into the future.

**The Revived Bundschuh and Other Uprisings**

A lull of the storm of some ten years took place and then in 1515 the *Bundschuh* broke out again, in the country of the upper Rhine, with redoubled force. Joss Fritz, a soldier who had been implicated in former uprisings of the peasantry and who had fled to Switzerland, was the leader. Silently, with much power of persuasion and skill of organization, he had prepared for the revolt. The league included many supporters in the Breisgau, in Alsace, and in Swabia. The authority of every master except the pope and the emperor was to be abolished; feudal dues were to cease; and the woods, the fields, and the waters were to be free to all. But the plans were discovered before the day of the uprising and the revolt was crushed with pitiless cruelty. Four years later the dauntless leader was again busily engaged in preparing for revolution; but again his plans were betrayed untimely and once more rebellion was mercilessly suppressed. One of the most threatening of all the uprisings was caused by the financial exactions of the tyrannous duke of Würtemberg. It broke out in 1514 under the direction of a romantic leader named " Poor Conrad." Townsmen and peasants and members of the middle-class joined in the insurrection and the entire insurgent body became known as *Der arme Konrad*.

All these uprisings, and others that took place in Hungary and in Austria, were premature. Grievances in that era of change the "poor folk" had in abundance. But they lacked an effective leader. The powerful impetus that mining had received in Germany caused a marked depreciation in the purchasing power of money. Later on there came a rise of prices. These things made the old burdens of the poorer classes, in town and in country alike, more oppressive than ever. The contemporary belief that all this was due to the arbitrary and wicked interference of men, to the fiscal policy of the political rulers and to the manipulations of the monopolists, only added to the bitterness of feeling that rapidly increased the separation of the various classes of society. Ulrich von Hutten passionately denounced the speculations of the new capitalism and its effects. The financial exactions of the papal curia gave the first impetus to ecclesiastical revolt, and financial distress led to the attack upon civil authority. Such were the grievances that the people suffered while they waited for a hero to guide them out of the land of bondage. At last the great leader for whom they had longed so passionately, the man who could give voice to their hopes and direct their aspirations, was at hand. He did not come from a privileged social rank, but from the common people. Full of the spiritual power of the German peasantry that as yet had never revealed itself in all its fullness, sharing their deepest loves and their bitterest hates, acquainted with the most intimate emotions of their daily lives, he was, moreover, brave enough to take the foremost place in the van of the inevitable attack. Had not his great doctrine of justification by faith alone emancipated man from thraldom to the hierarchy? And by the same reasons was not man justified in his determination to secure secular freedom? How could the individual be free as a believer and a slave as a man? Surely the man for the hour was Martin Luther.

Luther did not leave the Germans to inference. In his pamphlet entitled *On secular authority and how far it should be obeyed* he spoke directly of the wrong-doings of the secular rulers. "Kings are made for their people," he said; "they ought to seek only the good of their subjects." But the princes have not fulfilled this duty. "They are of the world," said the bold friar, "and the world is the enemy of God; they live according to the world and against the law of God. . . . From the beginning of history a prudent prince has been a very rare

The Long-Awaited Leader

Luther's Social Teaching

thing, an upright and an honest prince still rarer. They are generally the greatest fools or the greatest scoundrels in the world." It was easy enough for the masses burning with their wrongs to pass over the qualifying statement that "government should not be opposed with force but with knowledge and truth." The voice of Luther was the voice of the people. "Oh, masters and lords," he adjured, "govern with moderation and justice. Your subjects will not long put up with your tyranny. This is no longer what it once was, a world where men could be hunted like wild beasts." Just a year before the great outbreak he said: "The laboring man, tried beyond all endurance, overwhelmed with intolerable burdens, will not and cannot any longer tamely submit; and he has doubtless good reasons for striking with the flail and the club as Hans Pitchfork threatens to do. I am delighted so far to see the tyrants trembling."

No wonder that the spokesman of such bold and decided words appeared to the common people as a veritable apostle of civil as well as religious liberty. Luther's preaching enormously increased and accelerated the insubordination that everywhere from Switzerland to the Baltic Sea was filling the land with tumult. The fuel of social revolution was everywhere ready for the flame and without realizing the gravity of his action he flung the torch that kindled the conflagration. When the peasants first resorted to arms he insisted upon the need of moderation. But moderation under the circumstances was out of the question. And many of his followers did not hesitate to urge the insurgents to the most extreme measures.

We have seen that while Luther lay concealed in the Wartburg radical preachers stimulated the social and religious ferment at Wittenberg, and that when he returned to restore order the extremists left the Saxon capital to carry on their work in other places. Münzer carried on his iconoclastic propaganda with great success at Allstedt, a little town in Saxony, until his expulsion was secured by Duke John and Duke George, a brother and a cousin of the Elector. When he was banished from Allstedt he went on to Mülhausen. Only two months elapsed, however, before he was expelled from there. Then he became a wandering missionary in south-western Germany sowing everywhere the seeds of revolution. Carlstadt continued his revolutionary teachings at Orlamünde. Both of these radicals preached the equality of all men, social as well as religious, and appealed to force for the destruction of all who stood in the way of their program. Other preachers in other places were equally incendiary. In the pamphlets of the time that flooded the country the peasantry were exalted into the one class capable of regenerating society. They were wiser than the lawyers and more learned than the theologians. It was Karsthans and New Karsthans, the typical peasants, who alone, in the satirical literature of the time, saw the way of social salvation, and who with their rude implements stood ready to clear the road of every obstacle. It was evident that Germany was on the verge of a tremendous social upheaval. Almanac-makers and astrologers, whose prophecies were read and pondered by all classes of society, foretold that the storm would burst in 1524, and doubtless the prediction had not a little to do with the precipitation of the catastrophe.

It will be remembered that at the Diet of Worms, held in the first months of 1521, the attempt was made to settle the question of the imperial government by restoring the Council of Regency which in the absence of the Emperor was to administer the affairs of Germany. But no sooner had Charles gone to Spain after the Diet was over than the Council began to totter. Because of the lack of funds with which to carry out its projects it was ineffective from the beginning. All the centrifugal forces in the empire, all the vested interests, the towns, the knights, and the princes, were making for its speedy dissolution. At the second Diet of Nuremberg, 1524, it made a last attempt to control the imperial government. But the task was too difficult. New problems confronted it at every turn. Germany was fast dividing into two religious parties, and toward both of them the Council, though inclined somewhat favorably toward Lutheranism, tried to act in an impartial manner. What should be the attitude of the imperial government toward the religious question that every day was becoming more acute? It was not left to the Council of Regency to decide. It was obviously impossible for that body to become an effective factor in imperial affairs without provision for financial support. This support the Diet refused to supply and thus the Estates brought about the practical extinction of the Council. It is true that the Council continued to exist until 1531. But it was a mere ghost. With the removal of this obstacle, never a formidable one, the centrifugal forces of the Empire were once more in full swing. The disorder that resulted from the pursuit of their own particular interests by the conflicting elements of the Empire afforded an unrivaled opportunity for a general insurrection of the masses. With the Council of Regency confirmed in its impotency it was the Estates that had to face the religious question. The papal legate in attendance at the Diet demanded the renewal of the

The Second Diet of Nuremberg

Edict of Worms. The Estates promised to enforce the decree "as far as it was possible to do so." The Papacy, they added, had admitted the existence of serious abuses. So a general council should be summoned to consider the ecclesiastical situation. The reply, obviously an evasion, failed to satisfy either Luther or the legate. The former at once pointed out the inconsistency of the Diet. By promising to enforce the Edict of Worms as far as it was able the Diet, he said, had condemned him; yet by demanding a general council in which he should be given an impartial hearing it had acknowledged that such a condemnation was premature. The matter was taken up again in the Congress of Ratisbon that met a few months later. In the meantime the cleavage between the two religious parties was perceptibly widening and the governmental disorder and popular discontent were constantly increasing.

Outbreak
of the
Great
Peasants'
War

It is not surprising that under such circumstances the social revolution broke out again in 1524 with greater determination and redoubled fury. All the various causes that had provoked the previous uprisings had for some time been increasingly active. The grievances of the peasants had become more galling than ever. The revolt began in the hamlet of Stühlingen, not far from Schaffhausen, where the Rhine, that pathway of missionaries and merchants, rushes on its way from Switzerland into Germany. Under the guidance of Hans Müller, a former *landsknecht,* a thousand peasants made their way down the river to Waldshut where perhaps they hoped to be joined by the proletariat. The lords were unprepared and resorted to a protracted parleying in the course of which many of the insurgents returned to their homes. But the insurrection continued to manifest itself in various places in the region of Lake Constance, and then spreading northward it broke out among the peasants in the Black Forest. A conference of representatives of the rebels met at Memmingen in which an Evangelical Brotherhood, that emphasized the religious aspect of the movement, was organized and the famous Twelve Articles were adopted.

The
Twelve
Articles

The Twelve Articles in their essential details had been foreshadowed by the lists of grievances drawn up in previous social insurrections. The peasants demanded (1) the right to choose their own pastors who should preach the unadulterated Gospel; (2) exemption from the small tithe; (3) release from serfdom; (4) the right to fish and hunt; (5) a share in the forests for their household needs; (6) a mitigation of feudal services; (7) payment for all labor in addition to the contracted requirements; (8) a reduction of rents; (9) security against illegal punishment and a return to the old law; (10) the restoration of the common lands; (11) the abolition of the death duty that permitted the seizure of the most valuable chattel of the deceased tenant; and (12) the submission of these demands to the test of Scripture, it being promised that every demand not in accordance with the biblical teaching should be withdrawn. It is uncertain to whom the drafting of the articles is due; but that is not a matter of great importance, for the main demands had long been fermenting in the minds of the lower classes and the problem at Memmingen must have been merely one of selection and phraseology. The articles are doubtless wider in scope than were the grievances of the peasants in any one particular locality and therefore they may be regarded as giving expression to the entire movement. They are remarkably restrained and dignified in tone, and temperate and reasonable in character. Every demand is written carefully and clearly, and every one carried its justification upon its face.

The Twelve Articles were circulated throughout the empire with great rapidity. But they were rejected with contempt by the lords who continued their trick of protracting negotiations so as to gain time in which to gather their forces. The insurrection spread like wild-fire, from village to village, and from province to province. From the shores of Lake Constance and the north bank of the upper Rhine the conflagration spread into the farthest parts of the old Swabian duchy. Then toward the east it spread into Salsburg, Styria, and Tyrol; and toward the north into the Rhenish Palatinate. In the early spring of 1525 nearly all Germany was in the throes of revolution. Only Bavaria and a few provinces in the far north and north-east were exempt from the upheaval. The proletariat of the towns, linked by their common grievances and hostilities, joined the peasants. The ranks of the insurgents were further swelled by the influx of criminals and other roystering recruits who sought to gain their own private ends amid the general uproar, and very soon these undesirable allies by their violence and cruelty brought the movement into disrepute. Castles and convents were pillaged and burned, towns were occupied, and here and there regrettable atrocities were committed. The insurgents met with many successes, and in the heat of their apparently successful rebellion their demands went far beyond the modest stipulations of the Twelve Articles, extending to the social equality of all men and uniformity in the possession of property. But they lacked an effective general organization and were unaccustomed to military discipline, and so when the dissensions that were inevitable in such

Rejection of the Articles and Spread of the Revolution

motley armies began to appear among them, especially the differences in policy that arose between the extremists and the moder-
ates, their situation became precarious. The insurgent armies
suffered a series of grave disasters at the hands of the princes.
Atrocious reprisals, such as the tearing out of the eyes of fifty-
nine inhabitants of Kitzingen and the prohibiting of any one to
give them assistance of any kind, filled their hearts with fear.
Then the revolution was gradually stamped out with unparalleled
cruelty. At least a hundred thousand peasants had been destroyed, and other untold thousands were homeless fugitives.
The revolt failed to effect any improvement in the hard lot of
the peasantry. Indeed, it served only to sink them deeper in
serfdom and they remained until the beginning of the nineteenth
century the most oppressed of all the countryfolk of Europe.
But it was not only the peasantry and the proletariat that suffered from such brutal repression. Germany's leadership in
the religious life of Europe passed to other lands, and her proud
scholarship and awakening art sank into ignominious silence.

It was no mere implicit sanction that Luther had lent to the
struggle of the peasantry to improve their condition. He had
spoken in unmistakable terms of the wrong-doings of the secular authorities, and he had preached the doctrine that government exists for the benefit of the governed. What, then, was
his attitude toward the revolution that had resulted from the
determination of the masses to secure an amelioration of their
condition? When in the belief that he was in sympathy with
their aspirations the peasants sent him a copy of their Twelve
Articles and asked him for his opinion of their demands he
paused to warn the rulers to put an end to their tyranny, and
then, admitting the justice and reasonableness of some of the
articles, denounced, with Bible in hand, the demand for the abolition of serfdom forbade the peasants to resort to the use of
arms and advised that the whole problem should be solved by
negotiation. Continued endurance of the old wrongs; continued submission for the sake of God to their age-long burdens!
Such was Luther's message to the peasants. Little wonder
it was received with bitter disappointment. Little wonder it was
disobeyed. The answer of the leader for whom they had waited
so long and yearned so passionately was but another sorrow.
When Luther saw that his advice was not heeded he began to
denounce the insurgents. "Peasants must bear the crack of the
whip and the whiz of the bullet," he said; "if they refuse to
obey, let the cannon balls whistle among them or they will make
things a thousand times worse." Doubtless, in addition to being

disgruntled with the refusal of the peasants to follow his advice, he feared that the social revolution would endanger the success of the ecclesiastical revolution of which he was the leader. Whatever may have been the reason, his invectives against the rebels became ever more vehement. "Dear lords," he urged, "smite, stab, destroy . . . Whoever dies fighting for authority is a martyr before God . . . I pray every one to depart from the peasants as from the devil himself." Strange words to proceed from the lips of a man who was himself the greatest rebel of his time! They were words that reacted upon the spokesman and the cause he cherished, for Luther rapidly lost the good will of the people; and, lacking the support of the masses, his own revolt was delivered into the hands of the self-seeking princes. From that time on both he and the cause he represented deteriorated. In both of them it is easy to see a marked decline in spirituality and a corresponding emphasis upon dogmatism. Disowned as a leader of thought and the aspirations of the people, a position for which he was fitted above all other men of the time, Luther became a mere theologian. And the church to whose construction his energies and his interests became confined was narrowly circumscribed by the personal dictation of the political rulers upon whom it depended.

One reason for the failure of the social revolution of the sixteenth century was that the insurgents, armed with few weapons other than farming implements, lacked efficient organization and direction and therefore they suffered an easy defeat at the hands of the trained forces, clad in mail and commanded by experienced officers, that confronted them. But there is a deeper reason. When the demands of the rebels went beyond the Twelve Articles they went beyond the possibilities of the time and became impracticable. Indeed, they went beyond the possibilities of our own time, for they went beyond democracy and arrived at socialism. Like so many other revolutionaries, the peasants broke too sharply with the past, and so they added one more pathetic failure to the long list of the attempts of men to throw off intolerable burdens with a single sudden stroke.

Why as yet the Social Revolution Failed

# CHAPTER XIV

## PROTESTANTISM AND THE BALANCE OF POWER

1. Why the Edict of Worms was not Enforced.
2. Lutheranism as a Political Power.
3. The French King and the German Protestants.
4. The Schmalkaldic War.

CHAP.
XIV

1521-26

Why
Charles V
did not
Enforce
the Edict
of Worms

THE Diet at Worms in 1521 had placed Luther under the ban of the empire. Charles V had left Germany in the belief that the edict would be enforced and thereby an end made of the religious trouble. But such was not to be the case. Three things prevented the execution of the edict; the condition of Germany, a rebellion in Spain, and war with France. Something of the condition of Germany we have seen. The particularistic interests were ready to sacrifice anything, religious or national welfare, in order to gain their own selfish ends. A complexity of causes contributed to incite the revolt in Spain, the most immediate of them being the thoughtless dismissal of Spanish office-holders, their replacement by officials from the Netherlands, and the general dislike of an arrogant foreign king. It is true that Charles was much more of a Spaniard than a German; but he was also much more of a Burgundian than a Spaniard. The revolt was suppressed in Castile before the arrival of Charles, but there was much to do in Aragon. Finally the uprisings were put down and peace restored. Then the impending war between Francis and Charles broke out. Italy was the battle-ground. The important victory of the imperialist forces in 1522 at Bicocca led to the evacuation of Milan by the French. Personal differences between Francis and his most powerful vassal the Duke of Bourbon, whose head was full of schemes for personal aggrandizement, brought about the defection of that prince to the imperial banner. Bourbon hoped for the dismemberment of his country and the creation for himself of a new kingdom in the center and south of France. But France rose to the support of its king. Bourbon, who had made an unsuccessful attack upon Marseilles, fled before the approach of Francis, and the latter crossed the Alps and retook much of the territory from which his troops had been driven. The battle of Pavia, however, fought on February 25, 1525, resulted in his defeat and capture. After a captivity of eleven months he signed the treaty of Madrid by which he renounced his claims to Milan, Genoa, and Asti, surrendered the overlordship of Flanders, Artois, and Tournai, and engaged to secure from the States-General and the Parlement of Paris the cession of that part of Burgundy which France had taken, or, failing in that, to return to prison. But no sooner had Francis set foot on French soil than he repudiated the agreement.

It was not a difficult matter for Francis to start intrigues against the growing power of Charles. So vast an empire seemed to threaten many interests. In May, 1526, the league of Cognac was formed. It consisted of France, Milan, Venice, Florence, and the Papacy. The reigning pontiff was Clement VII (1523–34), an illegitimate nephew of Lorenzo de' Medici, who for the sake of his house as well as that of the Papal State desired the success of Francis. All of the confederates were inspired by the dread of an overwhelming preponderance of power on the part of Charles. Meanwhile the Turk was creeping steadily westward. Belgrade was captured in 1521, Rhodes was taken in 1522, and with the battle of Mohacs in 1526 the greater part of Hungary was won. But such was the condition of western Europe that no concerted action could be taken to stay the Moslem advance. Not a great deal came of the new league. The members were irresolute, and so the imperial forces continued to be successful in northern Italy. On May 6, 1527, a body of German *landsknechts,* joined by the half-starved Spanish troops under Bourbon, and by straggling Italian soldiers, took Rome, and for eight days the city was given over to all the horrors of lust and loot. Thirty thousand inhabitants lost their lives, by fire, sword, famine, and plague; and thirteen thousand houses were burned. The French sent additional forces to Italy only to meet with reverses. The situation seemed hopeless to the pope, so he became reconciled to Charles; and then, on August 3, 1529, peace was signed between Francis and Charles at Cambray. Charles was not reluctant to cease hostilities with France. Spain and Germany required all the attention he could give them. Then, too, the Turks were advancing up the valley of the Danube, and they were to be stopped only by the stout walls of Vienna and the approach of reinforcements for the Christian cause.

The
Struggle
between
Charles V
and
Francis I

We must now turn our attention to the development of Lutheranism and see how it became a political power. When Charles

How
Luther-
anism Be-
came a
Political
Power

left Germany in 1522 he had left behind him two serious problems, the political and the religious. He thought he had solved the former by the establishment of the Council of Regency, and the latter by the Edict of Worms. But the council, without power to enforce its regulations, met with complete failure. Central authority was a fiction and particularism reigned supreme. And conditions were such as to make any attempt to enforce the edict foredoomed to certain defeat. So Lutheranism went on its way. It gathered to its support, as we have seen, a number of influential princes. It had been compelled to rely upon those princes to a far greater extent than would otherwise have been the case by the attitude of Luther toward the social revolution. Charles, however, was obstinate. He was determined that the edict should be carried out. He was densely ignorant regarding the character of the social revolution, deeming it to be nothing but an uprising of the Lutherans. Lutheranism, he was resolved, should be rooted out; and once his hands were free the task could be accomplished with no great difficulty. An attempt, then, to suppress the German heresy seemed to be impending. So two parties began to form. In the Imperial party were, among others, Duke George of Albertine Saxony, the electors of Brandenburg and Mainz, and Duke Henry of Wolfenbüttel. The principal members of the Lutheran league were the elector John of Ernestine Saxony, and Philip of Hesse. When the diet met at Spires in June, 1526, Charles, still detained in Spain, was represented by his brother Ferdinand of Austria. He demanded the unconditional enforcement of the Edict of Worms. Should the edict be executed, he promised, pressure would be brought to bear upon the pope to summon a general council in which the religious difficulty might be settled. The diet declined to enforce the edict and decided that indemnity should be granted for past offenses against the edict, and that until a general council should be held in a German city, each State should so conduct its religious affairs " as it hoped to answer for its conduct to God and the Emperor." It would scarcely be possible to construct a more gelatinous stipulation. It meant, practically, that for the time being each one of the innumerable political divisions of Germany was at liberty to conduct its religious affairs as it saw fit. Thus national action with regard to the Lutheran problem was suspended indefinitely; and, in the meantime, the control of ecclesiastical matters passed to the princes and the free towns.

This right of the princes to determine ecclesiastical condi-

THE PRINCIPAL GERMAN
ECCLESIASTICAL TERRITORIES
AT THE
OUTBREAK OF THE
SCHMALKALDIC WAR

Scale of Miles

0 10 20   40   60   80   100   120   140

C.S. HAMMOND & CO., N.Y.

tions in their territories was a fortunate thing for Luther whose propaganda, now that he had abandoned the peasants and the proletariat in their desperate efforts to secure social amelioration and had cast in his lot with the princes, would have perhaps fared ill with a democratic form of Church government and would certainly have suffered had the central government vigorously opposed any such assumption of authority on the part of the various political divisions of Germany. It was the beginning of the definite organization of a Lutheran church in each of the principalities that had espoused Luther's cause. Luther did not fail to see the opportunity afforded by the respite and to make the most of it. All his energy was devoted to the aid of the princes. He cut himself loose completely from all democratic ideas of ecclesiastical organization and enjoined obedience in all things to the territorial ruler. He provided for visits to the various parishes to see that the incumbents were conducting their duties in a fitting manner. Episcopal jurisdiction, of course, had been abolished. The princes had replaced the bishops. In them resided all the powers of ecclesiastical government. They it was who were the guardians of doctrine, the dispensers of ecclesiastical justice, the custodians of ecclesiastical property and revenue, the patrons of benefices, and the persecutors of dissent. There was much to do, too, in the matter of ritual and doctrine. In these things Luther did not make so wide a departure from Catholicism as did Zwingli and Calvin. He retained the mass with the exception that it was celebrated in the vernacular instead of Latin and substituted for transubstantiation, which teaches that the bread and wine are changed into the actual body and blood of Christ, the theory of consubstantiation, which maintains that the body and blood are present, without actual change, in the bread and wine, just as fire is present in red-hot iron. He wrote a number of fine hymns, among them his *Ein' feste Burg ist unser Gott,* which Heine has called the *Marseillaise* of the Protestant Revolution. He published a German catechism, and also an abridgment of it, "a right Bible," he said, "for the laity." The strength of Lutheranism as a new religion lay in its message of the spiritual liberty of man, of the sufficiency of individual faith, of freedom from dependence upon the elaborate apparatus of a mediatorial sacramental system in the exclusive keeping of a highly organized Church. There was much that was vague in Luther's teaching at first, much that was inspiring and opened limitless vistas of religious thought. But this element evaporated. It passed into mysticism or Anabaptism. Lutheranism itself, its doctrine and its discipline, became crystallized. It became dogmatic, as much so as the Church from which it had separated.

At the second diet at Spires in 1529 the clause in the ordinance of 1526 upon which the foundation of the Lutheran territorial churches was based was revoked. The Lutheran princes and the Zwinglian towns of southern Germany, the two most formidable and antagonistic of the separate elements that went to make up Germany, joined in a protest against this action, "a protest, let us remember, not for the subject's freedom to choose, but for his sovereign's to prescribe"; and it is this protest that gave to all the schismatics of the century, whether or no they deserved or desired it, the name of Protestants. It was in the very plenitude of his power and on the eve of his return to Germany that this defiant protest to the Emperor was made. It is true Charles was more powerful in appearance than in reality. The vast extent of his dominions and the problems that pressed upon him for solution from all sides made it impossible for him to give any one part of his empire the attention it required. Yet he seemed as able as he was impatient to take up the problem of the German heresy that had been so long delayed. The diet was opened at Augsburg on June 20, 1530. Charles wished to settle the differences by persuasion; should this fail, however, he was ready to proceed to the use of force. Luther, being under the ban of the empire, was not present. The mild and timid Melanchthon took his place as the adviser of the Protestant princes. It was he who drew up the Confession of Augsburg. He aimed to reduce the differences between Catholicism and Lutheranism to a minimum. The Confession gives a brief exposition of the doctrine of justification by faith alone, and then it enumerates the beliefs and practices of Catholicism to which the Lutherans cannot subscribe — compulsory celibacy of the clergy, transubstantiation, compulsory auricular confession, monastic vows, and the exercise of secular authority by ecclesiastical officials. The Confession is a faithful reflection of the conciliatory character of its author. It was signed by the elector of Saxony, his son John Frederick, margrave George of Brandenburg-Ansbach, dukes Ernest and Francis of Lüneburg, landgrave Philip of Hesse, Prince Wolfgang of Anhalt, and by the delegates of Nuremberg and Reutlingen. Zwingli, who looked with scorn upon so mild an *apologia,* drew up a statement of his own in which he boldly published his differences from Catholicism. Four towns in southern Germany, although they had accepted the Zwinglian creeds, were not willing to sanction so daring a deed. So they drew up a third Confession. The Lutheran statement was answered by a Catholic "Confutation" which displays some signs of the purifying process that Catholic beliefs were undergoing and that culminated at the Council of Trent, but which made such slight concessions that even Melanchthon, eager as he was for compromise, was not satisfied. A committee of fourteen was then appointed to reach a temporary working compromise and to leave as few disputed points as possible for settlement by the next general council. This attempt also failed, and then Charles accepted the "Confutation" as a statement of his own faith. On September 22 the Catholic majority in the diet voted to give the Lutherans six months grace in which to decide whether they would conform to the Confutation. If on April 15 of the following year they were not ready to subscribe to it they were to be coerced. So did the diet end, a failure in its purpose of compromise and conciliation, a drawn battle.

It was a traditional privilege of the imperial estates to join together in unions or leagues. Of this privilege the Protestant princes and delegates of cities availed themselves on the last day of the year when in the little town of Schmalkalden they formed the league that took its name from the place of its birth and that included nearly all northern Germany and the more important towns in the south. They made themselves ready to resist the expected attempt at repression. But the period of grace allotted to the Lutherans came to a quiet end. It was impossible for Charles to enforce the decision of the diet. Trouble was brewing on every side. The Turks were advancing upon Vienna; the pope disliked the talk of a general council, and he was not a very reliable supporter of the imperial interests in Italy; one heresy was rife in northern Germany and another in Switzerland; all was not quiet in the Netherlands; Moslem pirates were ravaging the coasts of Sicily and Spain, and the latter country was especially clamorous for its ruler's presence; the relations with Henry of England were by no means friendly; and, finally, France was irreconcilable. When the diet met at Nuremberg in July, 1532, Charles realized that he was powerless to bring force to bear upon the Lutherans and so he agreed to another extension of the period of peace for the dissenters. For a brief time the emperor was now comparatively free to turn his attention to the Turks. But the sultan Solyman and his army, having been repulsed at Guns, retreated; and Charles failed to follow them up and recover Hungary. Then he crossed the Alps into Italy to make secure his interests. Once

*Why the Summons Could not be Enforced*

more the ecclesiastical revolution had found safety in the vast extent of the emperor's possessions. The innumerable demands upon his time and energy had made it impossible for Charles to attempt the suppression of the heresies that divided Germany. They had given additional time to the revolution, and time was its chief requisite. For another decade Protestantism was allowed to develop as best it could.

Charles hoped, by binding the Italian States to him with personal ties, to shut out France and thus preserve peace in the peninsula. To this task he devoted himself for a time with **Charles in Italy and Africa** some success. Then he turned his attention to Tunis, a nest of Moslem pirates who were headed by Barbarossa, the Corsair who had become Sultan's admiral, strategically situated so as to command the narrow passage between itself and Sicily and to be a source of annoyance to southern Italy and southern Spain. He captured Tunis in 1535 and won the gratitude of all southern Europe; although Barbarossa, who shifted his port to Algiers, was soon as active as ever. In the meantime Clement VII died. In his pursuit of Medicean and papal political interests he had greatly hampered the movements of Charles, and thus he had done more than any other man to secure the success of the religious revolution. His successor was Paul III (1534–49), who seemed much more favorably inclined to the summoning of a general council. In 1535 the house of Sforza became extinct and the question as to who should control Milan once more became acute. Francis had long been intriguing with Protestant and Turk to work disaster to his rival. He immediately turned his attention to the vacant duchy. Between Milan and France there lay Savoy. Conjuring up a flimsy pretext Francis invaded the intervening kingdom. The act precipitated another war with Charles. But the latter, harassed by the Moslems and filled with apprehension by the growing power of the Lutherans, was anxious for peace and Francis was not unwilling to cease the struggle provided he could secure good terms. By the truce of Nice, 1538, which was to last for ten years, each side retained the conquests it had made. Those of France included the greater part of Savoy.

In January, 1541, Charles, after an absence of almost nine **Failure of the Policy of Reconciliation** years, once more entered Germany. In this period a change had taken place almost as great as that which transpired during his first absence of nine years between the diets of Worms and Augsburg. Protestantism had made marked progress. In 1534 Duke Ulrich of Württemberg had been restored to his duchy from which fifteen years previously he had been driven by the Swabian league and which in the meantime had been held by the emperor's brother, Ferdinand of Austria. This had been accomplished by Philip of Hesse who defeated the Austrian forces. No sooner had Ulrich been reinstated than he established Protestantism in the duchy. In 1539 the elector Joachim II of Brandenburg seceded from Catholicism and established a state church of his own much like the Church of England. In the same year Henry, who had already gone over to Lutheranism, succeeded his brother George as duke of Albertine Saxony; and he in 1541 was followed by his son Maurice. Margrave John of Brandenburg-Ansbach, who ruled in Cottbus and Peitz, had also become a Lutheran. Many other princes of lesser importance had also embraced the spreading heresy; and so, too, had many of the towns. So strong was the movement away from the Mother Church that the three ecclesiastical electors of Mainz, Cologne, and Trier meditated the abandonment of Catholicism and the changing of their territories into secular principalities of which they were to be the founders of the ruling houses. Protestantism, evidently, was no longer on the defensive. Once more Charles tried the old plan of effecting a working compromise between the two religious parties until a general council should settle to the satisfaction of all the points that remained in dispute. It was in pursuance of this policy that a religious conference was held at Ratisbon. Never did Catholicism and Protestantism so closely reapproach each other as they did at this meeting, yet like all the previous similar attempts the colloquy failed to effect its purpose. Two insurmountable obstacles prevented its success, the fundamental incompatibility of the subjective character of the Lutheran heresy with the external authority of Catholicism and the political selfishness of the German princes, Protestant and Catholic alike, who feared that a settlement of the religious trouble would lead to a dangerous accession of power to the Emperor. So the conference proved of no avail except as it revealed the fact that the heretics would not abide by the decision of any such meeting, nor, indeed, by the decision of a general council whenever one should be called; and that, therefore, if religious unity was ever to be regained force would have to be employed. This was recognized even by Contarini, the most conciliatory of the Catholics; and by Melanchthon, the most moderate of the Protestants. Defeated in his policy of reconciliation Charles fell back upon his expedient of suspension, of postponing final action and making in the meantime a temporary arrangement.

The time seemed opportune to Francis for a renewal of the

Final
Struggle
of Charles
and
Francis

struggle with his rival. Charles had recently suffered two disasters at the hands of the Turks. Solyman had inflicted a crushing defeat upon his brother Ferdinand and captured Buda-Pesth; and an attack upon Algiers, led by the Emperor in person, had been turned into a lamentable failure by violent storms. So, taking advantage of the misfortunes of his enemy, Francis in 1542 began the war again. This time it was France that witnessed the shock of battle and not Italy. Peace was signed in 1544 at Crespy; and then Charles, freer than ever before, and convinced at last of the failure of conciliation, turned to the coercion of the Protestants.

Charles Determines to Crush Protestantism and Territorialism

Not only was heresy to be crushed in Germany, but also the aggressive territorialism with which it had allied itself. The recent conversion of the Elector Palatine and the archbishop of Cologne had given to the Protestants a majority in the electoral college. It was now quite possible that the next Emperor would be both anti-Catholic and anti-Hapsburg. Clearly the situation was one of peril to the Catholic and imperial cause to which Charles had devoted his life. First of all the general council, so long delayed, must be summoned to meet in Germany. The Mother Church herself was to be reformed. That was an integral part of the program. Something of a compromise was to be offered to the Protestants; and then, if this was refused, war should begin. Paul III bowed to the inevitable and summoned the council to meet at Trent. But the pope had outwitted the Emperor. Trent, it is true, was situated in German territory, but it was in reality an Italian town. Plainly the council would be a pliant tool in the hands of the pontiff. This the Protestants were not slow to perceive. They declared the council to be neither free, nor Christian, nor general; and until it conformed to all three requirements they declined to attend. War was imminent. Charles busied himself with efforts to consolidate the Catholic party, and to disintegrate the Protestant league. The duke of Bavaria was the most important of the Catholic princes hostile to the Hapsburg power. Concessions secured his benevolent neutrality and a gift of money and artillery. The Schmalkaldian leaders, elector John Frederick of Saxony, and Philip of Hesse, had long been at variance with each other. There were also other divisions among the Protestant princes. Harmonious action between them was at least dubious. Several of them were won over and others were persuaded to remain neutral. Chief of all these successful intrigues was the winning of the neutrality of Maurice of Albertine Saxony, who was greedy for the title and the terri-

THE PRINCIPAL GERMAN
SECULAR TERRITORIES
AT THE
OUTBREAK OF THE
SCHMALKALDIC WAR

Scale of Miles

0 10 20    40    60    80    100    120    140

G.S.HAMMOND & CO.,N.Y.

tory of electoral Saxony. The division of Saxony into the Ernestine and Albertine lines had taken place in 1485; and the lands have never again been united.

On February 18, 1546, while the war clouds were thus darkening the skies of Germany, Luther died; and four days later his body was buried in the castle church at Wittenberg to the door of which almost a generation before he had nailed his famous theses. He had lived to see Lutheranism the accepted religion of a large part of Germany and to see it legally established in Denmark, Norway, and Sweden. But he had also lived to see the beginning of those doctrinal disputes between his followers that were to be quite as bitter and as barren as any of their kind; and to realize, in part at least, the unfortunate results of the dissociation of his revolt from the sympathy of the masses and its abject reliance upon the support of the princes.

Charles asserted that his object was not to repress heresy, but only to punish political insubordination. The Lutherans, however, insisted that their religion was the object of attack. The truth is that the Schmalkaldic war was both a religious and a political war. Protestantism had become so closely interwoven with the forces of decentralization that it was impossible to separate them, and war against both had become inevitable. Decisive action on the part of the league, despite the defection of Maurice of Albertine Saxony, would have insured victory to the Lutherans; but through indifference and timidity the opportunity was thrown away. The war ended without much fighting in 1547 with the imperial victory at Mühlberg. All Germany, with a few minor exceptions, seemed to lie at the Emperor's feet. When the diet met at Augsburg Charles prepared to impose upon the country a political and religious organization that should suit his purpose. But he found it impossible to carry out his original plans; and so in 1548 a compromise measure, the Augsburg Interim, was adopted. The Interim, "a master-piece of ambiguity," was intended as a temporary expedient to unite Catholics and Protestants until a final settlement should be attained; but it proved a dismal failure.

Many things now contributed to the undermining of the Emperor's popularity and power, neither of which had ever been very pronounced in Germany. The intense hostility to foreign dictation aroused by the presence of Spanish troops stationed in various German towns was increased by the desire of Charles that his son Philip should succeed to the imperial position. Maurice of Saxony, the "Judas" who had betrayed the Protestant cause and who had been rewarded in 1547 for so doing with his cousin's title and a considerable share of his territory, was exceedingly unpopular with his subjects. The Emperor was his chief support, and the prop was failing. So Maurice rejoined the cause he had deserted and conducted for the Protestant princes a conspiracy with Henry II of France against Charles. War broke out between the allies and the Emperor in 1552 which ended in the same year with the Treaty of Passau and resulted in 1555 in the Peace of Augsburg. By the terms of the Religious Peace the legal existence of Lutheranism was permanently established. The Lutheran princes were granted security in their faith. In their lands the jurisdiction of Catholic bishops was to cease; and in their lands, also, all ecclesiastical property (with the exception of that directly controlled by the empire) that had been secularized previously to the Treaty of Passau, was to remain in their possession. Each secular ruler henceforth was free to choose between Catholicism and Lutheranism, and all his subjects were to be bound by his decision. *Cujus regio ejus religio.* Should a subject find himself unable to accept the religion of his ruler, it was his privilege to go elsewhere. Should a Catholic prelate abandon his faith, his territory and title were to be forfeited. It is true that this settlement at Augsburg gave Germany internal peace that lasted with scarcely a perceptible break for two generations and so permitted a greater degree of prosperity than it had enjoyed for some time; but nevertheless, it contained the germs of discord. The "ecclesiastical reservation" was certain to cause further difficulties. Then only two creeds were recognized, Catholicism and Lutheranism. In the negotiations the Lutherans had considered only themselves. Yet the followers of Zwingli were numerous in southern Germany; and those of Calvin were beginning to increase in the south-western provinces. And from the mass of the people even this limited choice between two creeds was practically withheld. Their religion was determined for them by the prince in whose jurisdiction they happened to reside. The alternative of exile, in most cases, was but a mockery. Peace, indeed, the agreement brought; but temporary peace only. The Thirty Years' War lay in the future.

# CHAPTER XV

SWITZERLAND, as we have seen, had its origin in 1291 when Uri, Schwyz, and Unterwalden, three peasant communities grouped about the lake of Luzerne, formed themselves into a loose confederation. It was the second of these communities that later on was to give its name to the Confederation. Schwyz was the most determined of all the little forest States in its opposition to the German nobles. To this nucleus of the Swiss nation other cantons were added from time to time; Luzerne in 1332, Zürich in 1351, Glarus in 1352, Zug in 1352, and Bern in 1353. These five additional cantons were all united to the three original cantons; but they were not then necessarily connected with each other. Their relations with each other were exceedingly varied and can be explained only by the circumstances of their admissions into the Confederation. Then gradually an outer circle of five more cantons was formed. Freiburg was admitted in 1481, Solothurn in 1481, Basel in 1501, Schaffhausen in 1501, and Appenzell in 1513. These five newcomers were all allied with the eight previous cantons. But they were admitted to the Confederation upon less favorable conditions. No more cantons were admitted until the end of the eighteenth century when the old Confederation was replaced by the Helvetic Republic.

Dependent upon the Confederation were some lands, the "common bailiwicks," that had been taken by force, whose government by various combinations of the thirteen cantons was often the cause of friction between the members of the Confederation. And near by were other leagues, such as the various Rhætian leagues and that of St. Gall, with whom the Swiss union maintained relations. Each of the thirteen cantons governed its own internal affairs as it deemed best. They formed little more than an agglomeration of independent communities

269

held together principally by the enmity of Austria. These fed-
erated States differed greatly from each other in many respects.
They were not, as we have seen, all on the same footing as
members of the league, for they had been admitted at different
times upon different conditions. They differed from each other
in their separate governments. They were made up of diverse
social elements. Some of them, such as the forest cantons of
Uri, Schwyz, and Unterwalden, were rural communities with
primitive democratic governments; while others, such as Bern,
Zürich, and Basel, were aristocratic municipal communities with
oligarchic governments. The one federal governmental institution was the diet, which met alternately at stated intervals in the
larger towns. It was made up of two delegates from each canton and one from each of three associated districts, the abbey of
St. Gall, the town of St. Gall, and the town of Bienne. Its members were strictly limited by the instructions of the districts they
represented, and their decisions were not binding upon the
minority except in matters relating to the subject lands that were
held in common. The administration of the federal laws devolved upon the government of each canton. Federal enactments, however, were confined chiefly to foreign affairs. The
protection of individual life and property was in the sole charge
of each sovereign canton. Through the service of their mercenary troops in Italy, the Swiss had become particularly well
acquainted with the political character of the Papacy, its absorption in secular interests and ambitions; and for more than
a hundred years they had been gradually restricting the area
of ecclesiastical jurisdiction, so that by the end of the second
decade of the sixteenth century the clergy were very largely
subject to the secular courts. Under these conditions, then, we
shall expect to find the Confederation as a whole conscious of
the need of ecclesiastical reform and each canton determining for
itself the form of religion that shall prevail within its territory.

The history of the Swiss revolt from Rome centers about the
name of Ulrich Zwingli (1484–1531) whose activity in the
northern and German-speaking cantons of the Alpine federation was carried on simultaneously with that of Luther in Saxony. But though the work of these two reformers was parallel
in time it was entirely different in character. One was a friar,
the other a humanist; one looked to the past, the other to the
future; one was emotional, the other intellectual; one was a
conservative, the other a radical. Zwingli was born in the little
village of Wildhaus in the territory of the abbey of St. Gall.
For some time he went to school at Basel; and then, when he

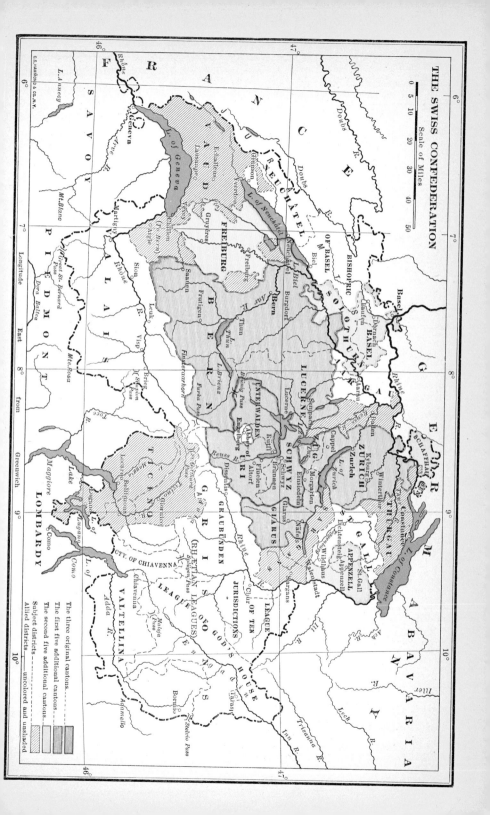

THE SWISS CONFEDERATION

Scale of Miles

0  5  10    20    30    40    50

was fourteen years of age, he was sent to Bern where he studied under Heinrich Wölflin, a poet who had traveled in Italy and Greece. There he became enamored of Greek and Latin literature and began his journey along the road of humanism that led to heresy. Then for two years he studied at the University of Vienna, where perhaps he came under the influence of Conrad Celtes. After that he returned to Basel, where he steeped himself in the Neo-Platonism of Pico della Mirandola and where he came under the influence of Erasmus. Then in 1506 he became the parish priest of Glarus, where every day he found time to dip still further into the writings of Erasmus, whose personal acquaintance he had made. Ten years later he went to occupy a similar position at Einsiedeln, the most famous shrine in southern Germany, only twenty miles from Zürich.

At the close of the year 1518 Zwingli, who had become famous as a preacher, was elected to the office of people's priest or vicar in the Great Minster at Zürich, one of the most important of the Swiss towns. His sermons showed the influence of his humanistic training and sympathy. They included suggestions for both ecclesiastical and political reform; for in his mind State and Church were intimately related to each other. They protested with ardent patriotism against the ruinous and demoralizing practice of mercenary military service; they opposed monasticism and asceticism, the belief in purgatory and the adoration of saints; and they declared tithes to be merely voluntary offerings. Naturally they gave rise to controversies. At last a series of public disputations before the great council took place. Zürich had long maintained a closer supervision of the clergy than other municipalities, and so it was but natural that the public discussion of ecclesiastical matters should be held before a civil body. For the purpose of the first debate Zwingli drew up sixty-seven theses that contained the essence of his doctrinal innovations. The Church, he said, is made up of all Christians. It is a democratic institution; and its external direction, as far as any is necessary, rests with the secular authority and not with popes and bishops. The Bible is the only rule of faith, and its interpretation does not rest exclusively with the Catholic Church. Clerical celibacy, the mass, adoration of saints, the belief in purgatory, and Lenten observances should all be abolished. The first disputation was held in January, 1523, before an audience of about six hundred people, and resulted in making it evident that the reformer and the town had irrevocably departed from the fold of the ancient Church. Thus encouraged Zwingli proceeded in his course. A second disputation was held in October of the same year in which he argued against the use of images in churches and contended that the mass is merely a representation of the sacrifice on the Cross and not a repetition of it. A private disputation was held in January, 1524, with which the Catholic party ended its formal opposition to the innovations in creed and worship. At the conclusion of these discussions the civic authorities definitely espoused the cause of religious revolution. Images were removed from the churches in every case where a majority decided against them, monasteries were suppressed, the mass was abolished, and the last sacrament was no longer administered. In place of the episcopal authority an ecclesiastical organization was effected and ecclesiastical courts were established to take care of conduct and cases relating to marriage. At the head of all civil and ecclesiastical government stood Zwingli, the guiding spirit of the revolt.

Very different from that accorded to Luther was the treatment of Zwingli by the Papacy. The Saxon rebel was regarded as an

upstart friar who was to be silenced in a summary manner. The Swiss priest was the leading citizen of Zürich, from which the Papacy hoped to secure further military aid in carrying out its military projects, and he was therefore to be won over by the most conciliatory measures. It was not the Papacy that gave Zwingli trouble at first. It was the extremists. At Zürich, as at Wittenberg, there were men more radical than the leader of revolt. Among the radicals were Conrad Grebel and Felix Manz, sons of influential citizens. Later on they were joined by Carlstadt, Hubmaier and other German radicals, who came to Zürich or its neighborhood. They separated themselves from the Zwinglians and effected an organization of their own. They opposed infant baptism and rejected all authority, secular and ecclesiastical. Rigorous measures were taken to suppress them. Manz was drowned in Lake Zürich and other leaders were banished. For a time, despite all the efforts of the magistrates to stamp it out, radicalism continued to flourish, but eventually that form of it known as Anabaptism became almost extinct in Switzerland.

Zwingli went much further than Luther in changing the form of worship. The organs were removed from the churches and

the hymns were sung without instrumental accompaniment; and then even vocal music was abandoned. At the end of the century, however, music was restored to the Zwinglian churches. The mass, as we have seen, was not merely modified but abolished. The sermon was made the center of the religious service.

In 1525 a theological seminary was established in which the Hebrew and Greek biblical texts were studied and commentaries made in German. Not only the regular students attended the school, but also the city clergy; and townspeople came to hear the lectures in the vernacular.

Religious change involved the Swiss Confederacy in new difficulties. The forest cantons were opposed to the innovations adopted by the towns. In order to solve the problem the diet arranged a disputation. The public debate was held in 1526 at Baden, twelve miles from Zürich. Zwingli realized that the conditions would be the reverse of those under which the disputations at Zürich had been held, that the majority of the audience would be Catholics. He was not present at the debate. The Catholics were represented by John Eck, the most distinguished of their German theologians. The Zwinglians had for their chief champion John Œcolampadius; but Zwingli himself exerted a great influence by means of letters and messengers. By a vote of eighty-two to twenty it was decided that Eck had established his theses. The effect of the disputation was to strengthen the Catholic party.

The religious revolt, as we shall see, broke out in other cantons. The Confederacy became divided into two hostile groups and preparations were made for war. At the close of 1527 Zürich entered into a league with Constance, which, because its terms were not accepted, had declined to become a member of the Confederacy, for mutual help. In the middle of the following year Bern was included in the compact; and then other cities and cantons were admitted, the town of St. Gall, Bienne, Mülhausen, Basel, Schaffhausen, and Strasburg. This Protestant league was answered by a Catholic union. In 1528 the five forest cantons, Uri, Schwyz, Unterwalden, Luzern, and Zug, banded themselves together to preserve the ancient faith and to effect an internal reformation of the ancient Church. In the following year they entered into an alliance with Ferdinand of Austria and with the district which at the end of the eighteenth century became the canton Valais. The theological differences between the cantons entered into the problem, already a difficult one, of the government of the subject lands, and thus the tension between them was greatly increased. At last, on June 8, 1529, Zürich, the leader of the Protestant league, declared war. But the mass of men in both armies did not wish for war; and, as it was the custom in the cantons to allow the troops to decide whether there should be war, it was not difficult to negotiate peace. Unfortunately the peace, signed at Cappel on June 24, 1529, was

**The Con-
ference
at Mar-
burg**

lacking in precision of statement and so it contained the germs of future dispute. It was merely a truce.

The ablest political leader of the German-speaking heretics was the Landgrave Philip of Hesse. He was exceedingly desirous of eliminating the differences in creed that stood in the way of their united political action. Dangers to the dissentients were thickening. He saw only disaster in their continued separation and enmity; and in their differences he recognized nothing that was fundamental and irreconcilable. In order to effect a union he was determined to bring about a conference between the chief disputants "though it should cost him six thousand gulden." So on September 30, 1529, he gathered together in his castle at Marburg the leading theologians of the Lutheran and Zwinglian communions. Luther went with reluctance and Zwingli with alacrity. Melanchthon and Œcolampadius and many other of the principal supporters of the two groups were there. But the differences proved deeper than Philip had believed. Zwingli was the most radical of all the leading Protestants, while Luther was the most conservative. Concessions were made by both sides, especially by the Zwinglians, but they failed to agree " as to whether the true body and blood of Christ are bodily present in the bread and wine." Zwingli, who deemed the mass to be without any sacramental efficacy whatsoever and who regarded the practice of communion as being merely a commemorative ceremony possessing value solely because its performance necessitates the bringing together of a group of worshipers and thus ensures a social act, declined to accept the dogma of consubstantiation. This Luther held to be sufficient to prevent the recognition of the Zwinglians as members with the Lutherans of the Christian Church. So the purpose of the Landgrave was not accomplished. His plan for the formation of a league that should include all the Protestant forces was defeated.

**The Sec-
ond Swiss
Religious
War and
After**

There were many things that tended to bring about a second outbreak of war in Switzerland. More than ever before Swiss and German politics had become entangled. And Zwinglianism had become more and more closely connected with politics. It had therefore come to be regarded by Ferdinand of Austria as being more dangerous to the empire than Lutheranism. He was determined to take measures against it. And internal troubles still disturbed the Confederation. The Catholic cantons still nursed their grievances. The conditions of the Peace of Cappel were not at all to their liking. On the other hand Zürich was determined to enforce free preaching in all the cantons. Enmity increased until the Protestant cantons stopped the sale of grain, wine, salt, iron, and steel to the Catholics in their mountain homes. The result was inevitable. The desperate forest cantons declared war. In the battle that was fought on October 11, 1531, at Cappel, ten miles south of Zürich, Zwingli was killed. On November 23 a second Peace was signed at Cappel. It provided that in each canton the government was to be determined by the majority and that each canton was to be left free to manage its own religious affairs. The common lands that had accepted the new faith were to be allowed to retain it, and those who desired to keep or to return to the old faith were to be allowed to do so. All leagues with powers outside the Confederacy were forbidden. This agreement checked the progress of the Swiss revolt from Rome; and it prepared the way for the reaction towards Catholicism that set in soon afterwards. The new religion, shorn of its political character, was directed by Henry Bullinger (1504–75) the successor of Zwingli at Zürich.

In the meantime religious revolt had occurred in other places. In Bern, politically the most important city in the Confederacy, a humanistic school had been opened by John von Stein, in which one of the teachers was Heinrich Wölflin, a scholar under whom Zwingli studied. It was the first school to adopt in a large measure the educational ideals of the Renaissance and it did not a little to prepare the way for heresy. In 1518 Sebastian Meyer, a Franciscan friar from Alsace, began to preach against the ecclesiastical abuses; and three years later Berthold Haller, a companion of Melanchthon in their student days, who was also bent upon reform and whose eloquence had made him very influential, was elected people's priest in the cathedral. Both of these priests were encouraged and assisted by Nicholas Manuel, a painter, dramatist, and statesman, who possessed great political power in the city. Early in 1527 the number of the reformers had so increased as to give them a majority in each of the two governmental councils. Then, before many months had gone by, the civic authorities decided to hold a disputation. Haller, with the assistance of Zwingli, drew up the following ten theses: (1) The sole foundation of the church is the Bible; (2) the only binding ecclesiastical laws are those in consonance with the Bible; (3) only through Christ is it possible to win salvation; (4) it cannot be proved by the Bible that the miracle of transubstantiation takes place; (5) the mass is contrary to the Bible; (6) only Christ should be invoked in prayer; (7) because there is no mention of Purgatory in the Bible, prayers for the dead are in vain; (8) the use of sacred pictures should be discontinued; (9) marriage is not forbidden by the Bible to any class of men, but unchastity is forbidden to all; and (10) unchastity on the part of the clergy is more provocative of scandal than among the laity. These propositions embody the essential doctrines of the Swiss revolt; and it was the fourth assertion that caused the greatest discussion. The disputation resulted in the decision of the government to abandon Catholicism for Zwinglianism. The ten theses were enacted into law. Sermons were substituted in place of the mass; images were removed from the churches; the cathedral organ was destroyed; and monasteries were secularized. In 1532 a synod of the canton adopted an ecclesiastical constitution (a church polity and discipline) and provided for the holding of a Synod each year. Thus Bern in the west and Zürich in the east, the two cities that dominated the plain outside the mountains, were committed to the cause of religious change.

Basel, the wealthiest city in the Confederation, was an important center of German humanism. Its position at the head

of the medieval navigation of the Rhine, where the transparent green waters of the great river bend from the west to the north, and its situation on the highway from Burgundy to Constance, made inevitable its commercial prosperity. It was the seat of a young but famous university; and even before Erasmus settled there in 1521 and became Froben's general editor and literary adviser it could boast of the most famous printing press in Europe. It was at about the same time that Erasmus made his home there that John Œcolampadius (1482–1531) returned to the city. He was a man of wide sympathies, and second only to Zwingli in importance among the Swiss reformers. He had studied Greek and Hebrew, and had made the acquaintance of Reuchlin, Melanchthon, and Erasmus. He had come back to Basel as a lecturer on the Bible in the University. His lectures and sermons excited so much comment among the townspeople that the bishop ordered their cessation. Then a series of disputations were held. The results were encouraging to the reformers. In 1525 Œcolampadius was appointed by the city council as the public preacher in St. Martin's church and empowered to make such innovations as were justified by the Scriptures. Three years later, in the midst of tumult that caused Erasmus, Clareanus, and other humanists, and most of the teachers in the University to forsake the city, the mass was abolished and the images were removed from the churches. Thus Œcolampadius's five years' struggle ended with success. The few years that remained to him were spent quietly in developing the change he

had inaugurated. From his death, in 1531, his work was carried
on by Oswald Myconius (1488–1552), who like his predecessor
was both a pastor and a professor in Basel.

Religious reformation in the thoroughly Alpine canton of
Glarus, the scene of Zwingli's first labors as a priest, centers
about the names of the Tschudis and Glareanus. The influential
family of Tschudi traced its ancestry back to the days of Charlemagne, though, it is scarcely necessary to say, it never proved
it. Three of its members were connected with the Swiss revolt
from Rome. Ægidius Tschudi (1505–72) is the most famous
of all of them. In his history of Switzerland, a work that won
high praise from Goethe, he embodied the romantic legend of
William Tell. He remained a member of the ancient Church,
but by his moderation won the respect of both parties. His
brother Peter went over to the Zwinglians. Valentine, his
cousin, succeeded Zwingli as the pastor at Glarus. At first the
new pastor adopted a middle course; saying mass for the
Catholics, and preaching sermons to the Protestants that met
with their approval. Afterwards he married and ceased to say
mass; but he continued to give sermons to both parties and by
his learning and conciliatory disposition retained the respect of
all. It is this spirit of compromise and conciliation that characterizes the reformatory movement in the canton; and even
to-day it may be seen in the joint use of the church at Glarus
in which at one hour mass is celebrated by the Catholic priest
at the altar and at another a sermon is preached by the Protestant pastor from the pulpit. Another name involved in the religious history of the canton is that of Henry Loriti (1488–
1563), better known as Glareanus, the most distinguished of the
Swiss humanists, who became strongly inclined to heresy, but
who withdrew from the Protestant movement when Erasmus
repudiated the revolution of Luther and Zwingli. From Freiburg, whither he went with Erasmus and other humanists who
left Basel in 1529, he wrote to Ægidius Tschudi and worked
with him for the retention of Catholicism. The final settlement
of the religious question in the canton was that of tolerance.
The members of the two faiths lived amicably side by side.

Into the territory that is now included in the canton of St.
Gall the new religious beliefs and practices were introduced by
two men, Vadianus and Kessler. Joachim von Watt (1484–
1551), more commonly known as Vadianus, was a humanist,
physician, and statesman, and a correspondent of Reuchlin and
Erasmus. In the town of St. Gall, where he practised as a
physician, and where he was several times elected burgomaster,

Protes-
tantism in
St. Gall
and its
Dependen-
cies

he displayed an active interest in religious matters, calling to the city several ministers and teachers of the new faith. He took part in the theological disputations in Zürich and presided at the one held in Bern. John Kessler, after studying theology at Basel and Wittenberg, preached the new doctrines in the town of St. Gall and the neighboring villages while earning his living as a saddler. The abbey and the town of St. Gall were two communities with separate interests. It was in the seventh century, so the legend runs, that St. Gall, an Irish monk, fell ill at this place and upon his recovery vowed to devote the remainder of his life to the conversion of the wild tribes in the neighboring mountains. He built his cell a thousand feet above Lake Constance, where to-day stand the abbey and town that bear his name. The abbey became famous as a place of learning, and its library is still a treasure-house of priceless manuscripts. As the years went on a town bearing the same name grew up beside the abbey. For long there had been jealousy between the towns-people and the monks. The former wished to be free from the jurisdiction of the abbot. Perhaps this accounts in part for the fact that when Zürich abandoned the old faith St. Gall was the first town to follow its example. To take part in its administration, and to protect it, the cantons of Luzern, Zürich, Schwyz, and Glarus each in turn sent a bailiff every two years to the abbey. It was Zürich's turn in 1528 to send the officer. The abbot was on his deathbed and Zwingli was determined to use the opportunity to further his revolt. So the Zürich bailiff was instructed to seize the convent as soon as the abbot should have breathed his last, secularize it, and introduce the new religion. But the impatient townsmen broke into the abbey several hours before the death of the abbot. The monks elected another abbot who fled over the green delta of the Rhine to Bregenz on the shore of Lake Constance, from whence he protested against the seizure of the abbey. This high-handed procedure did much to precipitate the war that broke out between the cantons. The second Peace of Cappel provided for the restoration of the abbey. The new doctrines also found their way into the Toggenburg valley and the canton of Appenzell, both of which had been under the jurisdiction of the abbot of St. Gall.

Into Schaffhausen, also, the only canton that lies altogether on the German side of the Rhine, the new teachings found their way. Chief of the propagandists in that territory was Sebastian Hofmeister (1476–1533), a Franciscan friar who became an ardent admirer of Zwingli. Because of the discord created by the appearance of some Anabaptists in that canton he was sent into exile and a reaction towards the old faith took place; but in 1529 Protestantism was definitely established in the canton.

The mountainous region that now forms the canton of Graubünden did not form a part of the Swiss confederation in the sixteenth century. It was included in three confederacies each of which was separately allied to certain of the Swiss cantons. Each valley and each separate group of people was isolated by the snow from the rest of the world for six months in the year. In each community, as a consequence, a natural and compulsory autonomy prevailed. There was an absence of continued episcopal discipline; and tolerance, or rather impunity, was assured to heretics. Chief of the Zwinglians in these high valleys were Comander, Gallicius, and Campell. John Comander (?–1557) drew up eighteen theses based upon the teachings of Zwingli for the disputation which, in 1526 at the order of the diet of the three confederacies, was held in Ilanz. His work and that of his assistants resulted a few months later in the decision of the diet to allow every individual to choose between Catholicism and Zwinglianism and to permit every parish to elect or dismiss its priest or pastor as it desired. Tolerance was extended to the members of the two principal faiths, but not to the minor heresies or to individual heretics. Philip Gallicius (1504–66) labored principally in the valley of the Engadine; and he took part in the disputation at Ilanz that resulted in the legalizing of the Zwinglian doctrines. Ulrich Campell (1510?–82) also worked in the Engadine. The very situation of the different valleys and communities, isolated by the mountains and the snow, made religion in Graubünden not a cantonal but a local matter. From the diet of Ilanz to our own day each congregation has remained supreme, choosing its religion and electing, maintaining, and releasing its pastor at its will. In the Engadine and neighboring valleys there is still spoken by some forty thousand people a Rhæto-Romanic language which has a literature, chiefly religious, of its own.

Zwingli, it will be seen, is the great outstanding figure in the Swiss revolt from the Mother Church, just as Luther is the dominating figure in the German revolution. In many respects the teaching of these two leaders is similar. Both of them rejected the authority of the Church for the authority of the Bible; both preached the doctrine of justification by faith alone; and both, declaring every Christian to be endowed with all the qualities of priesthood, erased the line of demarcation between the clergy and the laity. But there was a fundamental difference in the character, the outlook, and the teaching of the two men.

Luther was a conservative who looked to the past, while Zwingli was a radical who looked to the future. Luther accepted the dogma of original sin without question; but Zwingli, while admitting it in appearance, in reality destroyed it. The Swiss reformer taught that what is called "original sin" is merely an inclination toward sin and not sin itself; and that this innate inclination toward evil is not the result of any sin on the part of Adam and Eve but has its origin in nothing else than the union of the soul with the body. Man is inclined to sin, therefore, simply because he is a finite and limited being. In advancing this doctrine, Zwingli went far beyond the Christianity of his time. From it proceeded the bold statements that he made in the *Confession of Faith* that he addressed to the king of France. "We may hope to see in the realm of eternal life," he said, "all the holy, brave, faithful, and virtuous men who have lived at any time in the history of the world." Among them will be Socrates and Seneca, Aristotle and Aristides. "In fact," he continued, "there is no good man, no holy spirit, no faithful soul, that will not be seen there with God. What more beautiful, more delightful, and more glorious spectacle can be imagined than this?" It was from philosophy, from the Neo-Platonism of Pico della Mirandola, not from the Christianity of the sixteenth century, that this doctrine was obtained. Zwingli always remained deeply attached to the Greek and Latin writers, and to the humanists of a more recent age, whom he had read with delight in his youth and early manhood. Valerius Maximus he had learned by heart; Plato he deemed to have been divinely inspired; Seneca he esteemed as being with Paul an equal witness of the truth; and he loved the magic of Lucian's words and the tranquillity of his soul, finding in his books, where spring laughs eternal, "the double dowry of counsel and delight." The essence of religion, so Zwingli thought, was the confidence of the child in its father, in the confident belief that the creator will turn to the best use all the sorrow and suffering in the world. He regarded revelation as a personal and inner enlightenment that comes from God and that enables the individual to recognize God and to live in harmony with the divine will. This revelation, this spirit or inner word which in itself is sufficient to effect salvation, is not connected with any book or organization. Neither is it to be found only within the pale of Christianity. It comes immediately from God to the individual; and it has been present and can still be found where no syllable of the Scriptures has ever penetrated. In the ears of Luther such a doctrine seemed the most audacious blasphemy. "I despair of his salvation," said the Saxon friar, " for he has become a pagan by admitting impious pagans, and even an Epicurean Scipio, a Numa, the instrument of the devil in instituting idolatry among the Romans, to the ranks of the blessed souls. What is the good of baptism and the other sacraments, the Bible and Christ himself, if the impious, the idolaters, and the Epicureans, are saints in heaven? What else is this than to teach that each man can be saved by his own religion and belief?" The doctrine of original sin was regarded by both Luther and Calvin as part of the fundamental basis of Christianity; and in this respect they were at one with the Church from which they had severed. Neither was so daring nor so liberal as the cheerful-minded Swiss reformer with his wide culture and his breezy and wholesome vigor. One wonders how far he would have gone had not his work been interrupted and left incomplete by his violent death.

It seems certain, however, that Zwingli would not have gone in the direction of those Anabaptists who denied the need of political organization and of social progress and who deemed an inner enlightenment to be the sole necessity in life. Religion, in his view, found its fruition in social advancement as well as in individual salvation. His conception of the act of communion illustrates his emphasis of the social aspect of religion. He denied, as we have seen, even Luther's half-way theory of consubstantiation, regarding the rite as being devoid of all sacramental efficacy, and held the virtue of the commemorative ceremony of communion to reside solely in the fact that it was a corporate, social act in which a body of worshipers participated. Another fact would have prevented his approach to the position of the Anabaptists. He was interested almost as deeply in the political welfare of his country as in the work of religious reformation. The two things were intimately associated in his mind. The Anabaptists held that the Christian man should take no interest in worldly affairs, that he should divide his goods among the poor, that he should never take an oath, nor draw the sword, nor serve as a soldier. In answer to this Zwingli distinguished between an inner and ideal conception of the state of society, possible only among actual saints, and the external, actual, state of society that exists as the result of the weakness of man. By recognizing and controlling the right of private property a nearer approach can be made to a state of perfection than by its abolition. Then, too, the fact that the State includes non-Christian members precludes an absolute return to the conditions of the apostolic age. The political atmosphere of his native land and the ideas of the ancients combined to make Zwingli burst the bonds of primitive Christian society, abandon the ideal of the passive resistance of a peaceful community of believers to the secular authority, and substitute in its stead the duty of the faithful to coöperate in the formation and administration of the civil constitution. According to Zwingli the ideal organization of society is a republican State interpenetrated with the lofty social sentiment of the Galilean. The combination of political democracy with the social creed of the first age of Christianity forms an ideal that is still pregnant with change.

# CHAPTER XVI

## THE FRENCH REVOLT FROM ROME

OUT of the soil of France, also, there grew a movement of religious reform; one that possessed characteristics distinguishing it from the similar and simultaneous movements in Germany and Switzerland. It failed to win the support of the mass of the populace, owing in part perhaps to the skeptical temperament of the people with whom it had to deal, a people swayed by common sense rather than by enthusiasm and so more or less apathetic to the cause of religious reform, or at least dubious of its possibility. Yet it found a minority animated by a passionate idealism whose intellectual qualities made them impatient of a middle course and whose separation from the Mother Church was cleaner cut than that which occurred in any other land. Another characteristic of the French revolt was that it was more closely connected with humanism, and for a longer period, than were the reform movements in any other country. The French humanists recovered not only the secular writings of Greece and Rome but also early versions of the biblical narratives.

First of the French humanists who led the way to heresy was Lefèvre of Étaples (1450?–1536), who at the opening of the sixteenth century was a teacher in the University of Paris. In 1512 he issued a translation from the Greek to the Latin of the Epistles of St. Paul accompanied by a preface and a commentary. Prefaces at that time filled the place since then taken by newspapers, magazines, and monographs. " In them gushed forth freely the passions of the moment; in them appeared quite unexpectedly many a new opinion. Now as naïve as a book of intimate confidences, now ardent with the reverberations of yesterday's controversy, now as grave as a declaration of principles, these prefaces are the most vivid record of the ideas of the

CHAP.
XVI
———
1512-26

Characteristics of the French Revolt

Lefèvre of Étaples

283

sixteenth century." In his dedicatory preface, anticipating the action of Luther, Lefèvre stated in the most definite manner his belief in the exclusive authority of the Bible and in justification by faith alone. "Let us not speak of the merit of works," he said, "which is very small or none at all." In 1522 he published in Latin a Commentary on the Gospels, in the preface of which he pleaded for the restoration of primitive Christianity, and for the sole authority of the Scriptures. "To know only the Gospel," he affirmed, "is to know everything." Because of the gathering enmity to him at Paris he accepted the invitation of Bishop Briçonnet to take up his residence at Meaux, a little town twenty-eight miles from the national capital. There he devoted himself principally to the work of translating the Bible. In 1523 he issued his translation of the New Testament into French. It did not mark a great advance upon the existing French versions, but yet it served to increase the knowledge of the life of Christ. With that life the French people were none too familiar; and when it was placed before them, in all its penetrating simplicity, to be inspired with the spirit of Christ made up the sum of religion, "all else vanished into the background." A few years later he completed a translation of the Old Testament.

About Lefèvre, in the University of Paris, there had been grouped a little band of scholars. Quite the opposite to the gentle master was the fiery and impetuous Guillaume Farel. Others were Gerard Roussel, touched with mysticism and gifted with the power of eloquence; Michel d'Arande, who, like Roussel, remained within the Church and became a bishop; François Vatable, who revived the study of Hebrew in France; and Louis de Berquin, a noble of high position, famous alike for his unusual learning and the purity of his life. All of these humanists were tainted with heresy. So they incurred the hostility of the Sorbonne, the college that had assumed virtually all the instruction in theology given in the University of Paris, whose decisions in questions relating to the doctrines and practices of the Church had come to be regarded as conclusive. The Sorbonne was the very citadel of orthodoxy. In 1521 in a pronunciamento relating to all who held heterodox views it asserted that "their impious and shameless arrogance must be restrained by chains, by censures, nay, by fire and by flame, rather than vanquished by argument." The Parlement of Paris was equally hostile to the heretics. In 1521 it commanded all of Luther's books that had found their way into France to be given up; and two years later it seized and condemned the library of Louis de

Berquin and would have proceeded against the humanist himself had he not been saved by the interposition of the king. Clearly the path of heresy in France was beset with peril.

Guillaume Briçonnet had been appointed bishop of Meaux in 1516. Previously he had been the abbot of St. Germain-des-Prés in Paris. He attempted to introduce into his diocese reforms that he had long cherished. He invited as preachers certain of the scholars who had studied under Lefèvre, and he instructed them to read the gospel narratives to the people in French, to accompany the readings with easy explanations, and to endeavor to arouse a genuine religious feeling. These things, he thought, were sufficient to remedy the evils of the time. He did not desire a revolution. But some of his new preachers were busy inculcating heretical views. Not long after this program had been put under way Margaret of Angoulême, the sister of Francis I, and her mother, Louise of Savoy, visited Meaux. Both of them favored such an internal reformation. Margaret was two years older than her brother, and upon him she exercised considerable influence. A poet of distinct talent, she was sensitive to all the currents of the Renaissance that were then pulsing through the veins of France. She was, says a contemporary writer, "a solitary violet in the royal garden," to which were attracted all the better spirits in France, "as the wild thyme attracts the bees." In her the earlier French Renaissance found not only its epitome but also its "good fairy." For a brief time she was able to interest both her mother and her brother in the work of Briçonnet. So the reformation at Meaux went on its way until, owing to the hostility of the Sorbonne, the timid bishop withdrew his support. Not content with mere negative action the Parlement applied additional pressure in consequence of which Briçonnet forbade the circulation of Luther's books in his diocese. The war with the Empire entailed the absence of the king. So his mother, Louise, was made regent. Acting upon the advice of the Chancellor, Cardinal Duprat, and of the Sorbonne, she began to take more aggressive measures against the spreading heresy. When the king was defeated and captured at the battle of Pavia in 1525 there seemed to be an imperative necessity of acting in concert with the papal power in order to secure its support against Germany. A special commission was appointed by the Parlement to deal with the heretics. Farel, who had proved to be far more radical than Briçonnet desired, had already left Meaux; and one by one the other reformers fled before the gathering storm. Behind them were left the people who had embraced the new doctrines and who fur-

**The
Changed
Attitude
of the
King**

nished some of the earliest victims of the French revolt from
Rome.

In March, 1526, Francis I returned from his captivity in
Madrid. By the terms of the treaty of release he had promised
to coöperate in the suppression of Lutheran and other heretical
sects. He was a generous patron of arts and letters, giving
substantial encouragement to poets, philosophers, architects,
painters, and sculptors. Up to this time he had viewed the
reformation carried on at Meaux with distinct approval. His
own religious convictions, however, were not very deep, and
doubtless it did not require any very great pressure to convert
his favorable attitude toward the reformers into an unfavorable
one. The paramount consideration with him was doubtless the
expediency of securing the papal support. Then, too, the
French clergy agreed to contribute 1,300,000 livres to the expenses of the war with Charles V, which had broken out again,
provided that measures were taken for the suppression of heresy.
So, after the self-indulgent king had made up his arrears of
pleasure and had left the capital, persecution began in earnest.
One of the most prominent of the victims was Louis de Berquin.

**The
Heretics
Become
Aggres-
sive**

In 1533 an event occurred which for the time being still further connected the royal power with the cause of orthodoxy.
Henry, the second son of Francis, was married to Catherine de'
Medici, the niece of Pope Clement VII. And then, too, just as
circumstances seemingly conspired to make the secular authority
more hostile to heresy, the heretics themselves became more aggressive. On November 1, 1533, Nicholas Cop, the newly appointed rector of the University of Paris, made a public address
in which he contended that salvation is the gift of God and cannot be obtained by the performance of good works. The address
was a misjudgment of the temper of the time and the place.
It created an uproar, and the rector was compelled to seek
safety in flight. Six months later, a certain John Calvin who,
so rumor said, was the actual author of the address, was also
obliged to flee from Paris. A year later when the inhabitants
of Paris woke up on the morning of October 18, they found
copies of a placard denouncing the mass posted on the walls of
the principal streets. This gratuitous attack upon the central
ceremony of Catholicism infuriated the populace, and the anger
of the king was likewise aroused when a copy of the offensive
placard was found affixed to the door of his bedchamber. Three
months later a solemn expiatory procession, in which, immediately behind the Host held aloft in a silver cross, the king walked

with head uncovered, wended its way to the celebration of high mass in the cathedral of Notre Dame. A censorship of the press was established; and the burning of heretics was carried on more vigorously than ever. Almost four hundred were committed to the flames in less than a year.

In July, 1535, the Chancellor, Cardinal Duprat, died. His successor, Antoine du Bourg, was more favorably disposed toward the reformers. A week after his succession to office the king issued the Edict of Courcy which provided that only incorrigible heretics were to be persecuted and that those who renounced their errors within six months were to be pardoned. The Edict of Lyons, issued in the following year, was still more favorable to the dissenters. But these measures of comparative mildness did not succeed in checking heresy. In consequence the king from about the year 1538, in which the mild Du Bourg was succeeded by Guillaume Poyet, became wholly committed to the policy of active suppression. Especially given to persecution of the religious dissenters was Cardinal de Tournon who obtained a complete ascendancy over the king. From that time on heretics were burned all over France. In 1545 three thousand Waldenses, men, women, and children, who had affiliated themselves with the Lutheran creed, were massacred with exceeding brutality. The Edict of Fontainebleau, published in 1540, provided for rigid measures for the discovery and punishment of heresy. The most prominent of the victims was Étienne Dolet, of whom we have seen something in our study of humanism and its relation to heresy. Because of the unsubstantiated charge of atheism he was burned to death in 1546, in the Place Maubert in Paris, where to-day there stands an expiatory monument erected to his memory. His cruel death was applauded by Protestants as well as by Catholics. On March 31, 1547, Francis I died. Under his successor, Henry II, the persecution increased in severity, but instead of suppressing heresy it simply compelled it to seek subterranean ways and transported its center from Paris to Geneva. It is, therefore, with the work of the French reformers in Geneva that we have now to deal.

The King Committed Wholly to the Policy of Persecution

Geneva lies at the south-west end of Lake Leman, at the point where its blue waters run swiftly into the Rhone. It is near the most frequented of the Alpine passes, and so it was a center of the commerce carried on between France, Germany, and Italy. In the early part of the sixteenth century its varied population, derived from Latin and Teutonic sources, amounted only to some twelve or thirteen thousand. Early in the twelfth century it had come under the overlordship of the German em-

Geneva

perors and was in consequence technically regarded as an "imperial city." In actual practice it was under the sovereignty of the bishop of Geneva, who acknowledged the emperor as suzerain. The bishop delegated his temporal power to a *vidomme,* an office which from 1290 to 1525 was held by the dukes of Savoy. The *vidomme* exercised seignorial rights, but to the citizens there was left a considerable margin of municipal self-government. The city was thus governed by bishop, *vidomme,* and commune. The attempt of the House of Savoy to consolidate its territories seemed to Geneva to threaten the loss of her liberties. So in 1504 war broke out between the Genevese and their *vidomme.* The struggle for independence, in which Geneva received the aid of Freiburg and Bern, lasted for twenty years and resulted in the abolition of the *vidommate.* This was followed by the repudiation of the governmental power of the bishop. Freiburg, the first ally of Geneva in her effort to throw off the yoke of Savoy, was a staunch supporter of the Mother Church. The Bernese Vaud, on the other hand, the most powerful member of the Swiss Confederation, had accepted Protestantism in 1528; and that canton desired to see the same faith introduced into Geneva. Freiburg was opposed to the suggested change. When confronted with the conflicting desires of her allies, Geneva decided somewhat negatively in favor of the party of religious change. The decision was beyond doubt determined by political expediency and was not the result of a sincere religious belief, for the Genevese had as yet evinced little sympathy with the new doctrines.

To Geneva there came in October, 1532, armed with a letter from Bern, Guillaume Farel, the most aggressive of the reformers of Meaux, who since his flight from that bishopric had been actively engaged with others in the work of converting to the evangelical cause the French-speaking part of Switzerland. But the ardent and uncompromising preacher so offended the Genevese that in a few days he was compelled to flee from the city. He did not abandon the effort to win over Geneva, but persuaded Antoine Froment to carry on the work of evangelization in his absence. Froment took up the mission while engaged ostensibly in the work of a school teacher. Outbreaks continued to occur between the Catholics and Protestants. Freiburg and Bern sent representatives to further their conflicting religious interests, and with the delegates from Bern came Pierre Viret, one of Farel's assistant preachers. In December, 1533, the indomitable Farel ventured to return and resume his impassioned and eloquent preaching. The last stage of the long struggle for municipal independence was directed, as we have seen, against the bishop. It was perhaps inevitable that this should assume the color of a revolt against the Church. This feeling of opposition, reinforced by the effect produced by the ignorance and immorality of the Genevese clergy, and combined with a slight but increasing degree of Protestant conviction, lent favor to the cause of the reformers. The new-born independence prepared the way for a new-born faith. In 1535 the cessation of the mass was ordered, and thus the city was officially committed to Protestantism. On May 21 of the following year the citizens voted their determination " to live in this holy evangelical law and Word of God, as it has been announced to us, desiring to abandon all masses, images, idols, and all that which may pertain thereto." Two months later there came to the city a wayfarer, John Calvin, seeking rest for a night before resuming his journey from France to Strasburg.

Calvin was born on July 10, 1509, at Noyon, a little town in Picardy, sixty-seven miles to the north-east of Paris. His parents belonged to the lower middle class. His father was a lawyer who also held several ecclesiastical benefices; and his mother, a beautiful and pious woman, was the daughter of a retired innkeeper. Both of them realized the value of education and it was from them that their son inherited his predilection for scholarship. Calvin's father intended him for the Church, and when he was fourteen years of age sent him to the University of Paris. The University had lost its former preëminence in the world of scholarship. It clung to the scholasticism that was gradually being discredited, and only an occasional humanist was to be found within its walls. One such teacher the young boy met in Maturin Cordier, who strove to make Latin a living thing for his pupils and succeeded in helping Calvin to acquire a good command of the language. Five of the formative years of youth Calvin spent in Paris, and then in 1528, just as Ignatius Loyola entered it, he left the capital to go to Orleans. Acting upon his father's advice he had decided to abandon theology for law. He went to the University of Orleans to be able to profit by the lectures of Pierre de l'Étoile, the most famous among the French legal scholars of the day. After a year at Orleans he went still farther south to Bourges in order to study with Andrea Alciati, an Italian scholar, who was the most scientific legal teacher of the time. After the death of his father in 1531 Calvin decided to devote himself to letters. In the same year he published a commentary upon Seneca's *De Clementia.* The book is a plea addressed to a ruler for the exercise of clemency. In his preface Calvin boldly denounced the malad-ministration of justice in the public courts. It was probably a year or two after the appearance of this his first book that he definitely withdrew from the Catholic fold. It was in the latter part of 1533 that, because of his alleged authorship of Nicholas Cop's heretical address, he was obliged to seek safety in flight from Paris. It is impossible to say definitely what it was that brought about Calvin's change in religious belief. From his mother he had inherited a zeal for religion, and the swelling tide of the Protestant Revolution was therefore very likely to sweep him from his old moorings. He himself regarded his conversion as a sudden one, and as being the direct work of God; but it was probably a gradual change. After leaving Paris he wandered up and down France for a few months and then went to live in Basel, one of the most important centers of hu-manism north of the Alps, a city in which Protestantism had gained a firm footing, a place of refuge and repose, such as he needed at the time, where he could carry on his literary work un-hindered. There it was that in 1536 he completed the first edi-tion of the *Institute of the Christian Religion* which he had begun in Angoulême.

It is with the *Christianae Religionis Institutio* that the doc-trinal development of Calvinism started. The first edition is

merely an outline of what the work subsequently became, but it contains in embryo all the fundamental views of its author. The changes that were made were changes of form and emphasis and not of doctrine. Unlike the later editions it places chief stress upon ethics and the practical conduct of religious affairs rather than upon dogma. Viewed from the standpoint of doc-trin: it is an explanation of the Apostles' Creed accompanied by a commentary. In the Creed there are four fundamental as-severations of faith: (1) I believe in God the Father; (2) and in His Son, Jesus Christ; (3) and in the Holy Ghost; and (4) in the Holy Catholic Church. The *Institute* is divided into four parts each of which explains and comments upon one of these basic sentences. Viewed from the standpoint of ethics, of worship, and of ecclesiastical polity, the book has six chap-ters that deal with (1) daily conduct, (2) faith, (3) prayer, (4) the two sacraments authorized by the Scriptures, (5) the false sacraments established by the Catholic Church, and (6) the re-lation of the Church to the State. The book is very considerably indebted to thinkers who had preceded Calvin, especially to the leaders of the Protestant Revolution who came immediately be-fore him. It is more the work of codification than of creation.

It gathered up, with the art of a master builder, the scattered bits of heretical thought and made of them a symmetrical structure. Its logical precision and lucidity of statement made it incomparably the most effective exposition of Protestantism that had yet been made. Yet something it did add that was new and peculiar to Calvin — the Romanic idea of religious reform, which proved to be better adapted for international propaganda than either the Lutheran or Zwinglian forms. Prefixed to the book is an address to Francis I, implying that heresy is intolerable but repudiating for the French Protestants, whom it defends, all heresy and all sympathy with heresy.

Before the *Institute* had come from the printing press Calvin left Basel for Italy to visit Renée, duchess of Ferrara, the youngest of the two daughters of Louis XII, the late king of France. We are sure neither of the reasons nor the details of the visit. Renée was a patroness of the new learning and sympathetically disposed towards the heretical reformers. Perhaps Calvin hoped to persuade her to use her influence in France on behalf of the persecuted reformers; perhaps he hoped to make Ferrara a center of Protestantism; or maybe it was merely the fulfilment of the dream that every humanist harbored in his heart some day to visit Italy. His visit was a brief one. Alone and on foot, by the steep pass of Duranda, he returned to Basel; and from there he went to his birthplace, where his brother Charles had recently died, to arrange his family affairs. On his way from France to Strasburg he stopped for a single night at Geneva.

It would be well before taking up the story of Calvin in Geneva to sum up very briefly the condition of the city in which he was to find his principal field of work. Geneva, as we have seen, had overthrown the dominion of the duke and the bishop. Thereby she had secured political independence. But the government that had taken the place of those authorities was not a democratic one. Power was concentrated in the hands of a few men. In ecclesiastical matters the Genevese lacked both organization and creed. They were committed to Protestantism and they supported Protestant preachers. That is as much as can be said. The old religious edifice had been torn down, but a new one had not yet been erected in its place. Genevan society in the years that intervened between the achievement of political independence and the arrival of Calvin has been described as being given over to license and disorder, though this appears to be an exaggeration. There seems to be no proof indicating that the Genevese were more given to corruption and lawlessness at this time than were the inhabitants of any other European city of the same size. Finally it should be borne in mind that liberty of conscience had not been established. Laws had been passed that restricted freedom of religious opinion.

Such, in brief, was the condition of affairs in Geneva when, one day in August, 1536, there entered the gates of the city to rest for a night before resuming his journey, a frail young Frenchman, with a refined and scholarly air about him, singularly pallid of face, with lustrous eyes that retained their brightness even to his death. It was John Calvin on his way to Strasburg where he hoped to lead the quiet life of a scholar. But Farel heard that the author of the *Institute* was in the city and hastened to tell him that Geneva needed his aid. Calvin declined to stay. He pleaded his unfitness for the work that was to be done, and asked to be allowed to go upon his way. "May God curse your studies," answered Farel, "if now in her hour of necessity you refuse to lend your aid to His Church." Thus did the zealous old man morally compel Calvin to renounce the life he had contemplated and take up his work in Geneva.

**Calvin Persuaded to Stay**

It was not long before a *Confession of Faith* was drawn up, intended "to give some shape to the newly established Church," a brief creed of twenty-one articles, written probably by Farel, but indebted for its thought and arrangement to Calvin. By means of the *Confession* the inhabitants of Geneva were to be separated, the Protestants from the Catholics. There was to be no equivocation. Each was to choose one creed or the other. And all those who declined to accept the new creed were to be driven from the Genevan territory. The *Confession* was approved by the Little Council and its enforcement authorized. The Council of Two Hundred also approved it, though not without some opposition, and it was adopted by citizens assembled in the cathedral. Then, on different days, the captains of the several divisions of the city took the people to the cathedral where in groups they accepted the new creed on oath. But there were those who disapproved and stayed away.

**The Confession of Faith**

Together with the *Confession of Faith* there was submitted to the magistrates of the city a *Discipline* that sketched an ecclesiastical organization and outlined the relation of the civil to the ecclesiastical power. Discipline, the control of daily life, had been a prime concern of the early Church, and Calvin deemed it to be an equally essential concern of the Church then in the process of establishment. The ecclesiastical sentences for breach of discipline were to extend to the extremity of excommunication. "It is expedient," it was contended, "and accord⁄

**The Discipline**

ing to the ordinance of God that all open idolaters, blasphemers, murderers, thieves, adulterers, and false witnesses, all seditious and quarrelsome persons, slanderers, pugilists, drunkards, and spendthrifts, if they do not amend their lives after they have been duly admonished, shall be cut off from communion with believers until they have given satisfactory proofs of repentance." The censures of the Church, Calvin insisted, were to be enforced by the civil authority. Secular enforcement of discipline was adopted by the councils, but they declined to approve the penalty of excommunication. Later on, when Calvin returned from exile, he succeeded, after meeting with great opposition, in securing the adoption of excommunication, though not in the way he had desired.

Another thing to be done was to provide for elementary religious instruction. So Calvin wrote a *Catechism,* designed for children, but also intended to be useful to the adult citizen, which was published in 1537. It explained the Ten Commandments, the Apostles' Creed, the Lord's Prayer, and the sacraments, being a condensation of the *Institute.* Calvin intended it to be easily comprehensible, but it proved to be altogether too difficult, too theological, too minute, for children, and in 1541 it was replaced by a revised edition.

No definite office was given to Calvin at first, but two months after he entered the city he was made one of its pastors. This was the only office to which he received a regular appointment. Yet in an incredibly short time he became the virtual dictator of the city, ruling it until his death, except for the three years of his banishment, with a rod of iron. It was a gay and pleasure-loving people with whom he had to deal. Their days of labor were relieved with many festivals. They were fond of dancing, of music, and of masquerades. To the strolling mummers they gave a hearty welcome, and they delighted to see the "merry-andrews making mirth on the green." In the evening, after the day's work was done, they gossiped in the cabarets over their wine or indulged in a friendly game of cards. But especially at weddings did they dance and feast to their hearts' desire. All this was now to be abandoned and in its stead was to be substituted a "holy reign of terror." All citizens were obliged to attend two sermons on Sunday, those who played cards were exhibited publicly in the pillory; to laugh at Calvin's sermons or to speak disrespectfully of him in the street was accounted a crime. No more could a bride be adorned as of old, her hair unbraided and flowers at her breast. To wear one's hair in graceful tresses or to be decked too gaily was a violation of the moral code. No more were weddings a time of special rejoicing. To have too many guests at a feast, or too many dishes, or to dance, was a crime. An old woman who lighted a taper and mumbled a litany was whipped severely; and a child who struck its parents was beheaded. Did all this lead to an improvement in the morality of Geneva? It is at best doubtful. Most likely the stern regulations and harsh punishments simply drove immorality below the surface. "True holiness is that which men live and grow into in the strength of high principles and noble affections, not that which is bolstered up by regulations and protested by penalties."

Reaction
and the
Banish-
ment of
Calvin

Inevitably opposition arose against so harsh a régime. It consisted principally of the Eidgenossen, the patriotic citizens who had fought for independence against the duke and the bishop and who saw their hard-won liberty disappearing before the encroachments of a new tyranny; but it included also the worst element of the population; and so it received from the Calvinists the undeserved name of the "Libertines." So powerful was the reaction that at the election of the four syndics early in 1538 three of them were chosen from the ranks of the "Patriots." Closely connected with this reaction against the drastic regulations and inquisitorial procedure with which Calvin sought to effect a renovation of the Genevese character was a quarrel over theological matters with the Bernese authorities. Presuming upon the assistance rendered to Geneva in her struggle for independence the Bernese authorities demanded that their neighboring city should conform to certain ecclesiastical usages, among which was the celebration of communion with unleavened bread. This Calvin refused to do. The Patriots at once saw the opportunity. They upheld the demand of the Bernese. Calvin and Farel refused to yield. So, in the year 1538, both of them were banished. The bow had been strained until it snapped asunder. Calvin's drastic and despotic rule proceeded from the best intentions. It had a lofty aim. Perhaps he recognized in part that the great need of the time was not so much the acceptance of a new theological system as the perfection and practise of a social discipline. But three things militated against his success. In the first place he had altogether too exaggerated an idea of sin. The minute and rigid regulations — over two hundred in number they came to be — place a ban upon almost every form of amusement. In the second place his procedure was sudden and dictatorial instead of being gradual and persuasive. In the third place he placed far too slight a reliance upon the individuality of the Genevan citizen; he was not content slowly to develop an internal moral force, but sought instead to control every action immediately by external restraint.

When they left Geneva the two preachers went to Basel and afterwards parted ways. Farel, who was then almost fifty years of age, went to Neuchâtel where he labored for yet another generation. Calvin, who was not yet thirty years old, continued his work in Strasburg, the most important stronghold of the Protestant Revolution in south-western Germany. Among the men with whom he was associated there were Martin Bucer, who proved a wise councilor and a kindly companion, the conciliatory Wolfgang Capito, and Jacob Sturm, a municipal official who was an influential promoter of Protestantism and a distinguished educational reformer. Here, too, he found several hundred French refugees who elected him their pastor. Very soon he had a well-organized congregation to which he preached four times each week. His salary was very small, and oftentimes he suffered financial distress. His activity became varied. He taught theology in the public schools, took part in religious disputations, and continued his work as an author. In the field of theological criticism he wrote a *Commentary on the Epistle to the Romans,* and in the field of theology itself he issued in 1539 a revised and greatly enlarged edition of the *Institute,* which, while inferior to the final edition of 1559 in logical arrangement, reaches the culmination of the author's doctrinal system.

The Emperor Charles V greatly desired religious union, if only for the sake of making possible united action against the Empire's foes. For the advancement of their cherished particularism the Catholics and the various Protestant sects had not scrupled to further the interests of the enemies of Germany. So conferences, whose object it was to effect the desired religious unity were held at various times in various places. Early in 1539 Calvin, in an unofficial capacity, attended the meeting at Frankfort; in 1540 he went to the meeting at Hagenau; in the same year he was sent as a delegate of Strasburg to a meeting of the Diet at Worms, in which he took a prominent part, and when the Diet was adjourned to Ratisbon (Regensburg) he was again an active participator. Whatever political results these conferences may have had they all failed to effect a religious reconciliation. Calvin, indeed, seems not to have desired a reunion. Only by mutual concession could a reunion have been effected, and to compromise Calvin was constitutionally opposed.

In the meantime how had things been going in Geneva? Apparently the moral condition of the city was much the same as

CHAP.
XVI

1538-41

Geneva in
the In-
terim

when Calvin first arrived there. But the two opposing parties remained unreconciled. In the struggle the Patriots lost ground. They were successful only while protesting against the unduly rigorous ordinances. When Calvin was driven from the city their activity ceased. Seemingly they had no constructive program to offer. On the other hand Calvin's supporters were animated and unified by the idea of regenerating humanity, and their program for moral purification was a definite one. The dissensions between the citizens seemed to afford a favorable chance to win back the city to the ancient faith. So in 1539, at the suggestion of Pope Paul III, Cardinal Sadoleto, bishop of Carpentras, in Dauphiny, wrote a conciliatory letter to the municipal authorities and the citizens appealing to them to return to the Mother Church. Sadoleto was a distinguished humanist, and a man of genial disposition. Irreproachable in his own life he sincerely desired the reform of the abuses of the Church without changing any of its essential creeds. His letter was sent by the Genevan authorities to the Bernese officials who, in turn, requested Calvin to answer it. The exiled reformer wrote the most eloquent defense of the entire religious revolt that had yet been made or that was destined to appear for a long time, a dignified, gentle and moderate reply that gave expression to the feelings of Protestantism and doubtless made many friends for its author. At last the incessant agitation and strife in Geneva resulted in the victory of the Calvinists; and then, on October 22, 1540, a letter was despatched requesting Calvin to return. But he was in no hurry to comply; and when finally he consented he insisted upon certain conditions, the chief of which was the establishment of a Consistory, or tribunal of morals, to consist of pastors and elders, that should have supervision of the daily lives of the Genevese. The conditions were granted, and on September 13, 1541, the exile reëntered Geneva after an absence of three and a half years.

When Geneva abolished the dominion of its duke and its bishop it did not establish a democracy, but instead the city with its adjacent territory was ruled by an oligarchy. It is to the component parts of this government that we must now devote our attention. First of all there was the General Assembly, which consisted of all the citizens, that is, of all the heads of families. It was supposed to meet at least twice each year to conduct business that related to the entire community. It elected the four syndics, the treasurer, the secretary, and the lieutenant of justice, and it made alliances and proclaimed the laws. But as time went on the General Assembly was summoned less and less frequently, and most of the powers formerly exercised by the duke and the bishop were acquired by the Little Council and the Council of Two Hundred. The syndics were the administrative officials of the city. They had charge of the most important criminal jurisdiction, and it was their duty to see that order prevailed from sunset to sunrise. The Little Council had twenty-five members in whose election the people had scarcely any voice. The syndics and the treasurer holding office and the syndics of the previous year were always entitled to membership. The other members were chosen by the Council of Two Hundred; but this latter council was itself nominated by the Little Council. Thus only five members of the Little Council (the syndics and the treasurer who had been elected that year) could be chosen by the people in any one year. Yet this council was a most powerful factor in the Genevese government. It was the supreme court, and it was an inner legislative and administrative body. All told, it exercised a wide range of powers. There was a Council of Sixty, called into existence to decide matters too important for the Little Council. Its members were elected by the Little Council. But the oligarchic tendencies of the Genevan government soon rendered this body insignificant. It very rarely took action. Finally there was the Council of Two Hundred, established in 1527, whose members were chosen by the Little Council. It was this body that had practically arrogated to itself the functions of the otiose Council of Sixty. Such was the civil polity, the aristocratic government of Geneva, with which Calvin's ecclesiastical polity worked — " two parts of one machine."

The influence of Calvin upon the civil government of Geneva was undemocratic. It was due seemingly to his advice that the General Assembly of the citizens was summoned as infrequently as possible. And it was doubtless due in no small degree to his personal attitude of unfriendliness that the mere desire to call a special meeting of the Assembly was regarded as an indication of treason. He greatly curtailed the governing power of the people by arranging that nothing should be discussed in the General Assembly that had not previously been considered in the Council of Two Hundred, that nothing should be discussed in the Council of Two Hundred that had not already been debated in the Little Council. Thus all legislation had its origin in the Little Council. Between the Little Council and the Consistory there was a most intimate connection, and the dominating influence in the Consistory was Calvin. Thus he became " the mainspring of the Genevese republic. He set all its wheels in motion." It is impossible to define his exact political position. Nominally he held no political office; but in reality he made the laws, while the councils confirmed them and the syndics carried them out.

According to Calvin's theory the church was made up of all clergy and laity who agreed upon the fundamental articles of **Calvin's** the Calvinist theology. Church and State each was to be su-**Church** preme in its respective sphere. This idea of ecclesiastical inde-**Polity** pendence was inherited from the Catholic Church which had often fought to maintain it. Luther and Melanchthon consented to the subjugation of the church to the civil power; and in England the monarch was at the head of the Church as well as the State. Calvin modified the Catholic idea by giving to the laity a voice in the government of the church. The secular power was to enforce the laws and doctrines of the church. In practice the government of the Genevan Church was vested in the Consistory which was made up of six ministers and twelve lay elders. The lay members of this powerful court were all nominated by the ministers. Two of them were chosen from the General Assembly, and ten from the Council of Two Hundred. For their services they were paid two "sols" a day derived from the fines which they imposed. According to law one of the syndics should have presided at the meetings, which were held every Thursday, but Calvin, although it would seem that he did not actually usurp the office of president, certainly exercised the preponderating influence until the end of his life. It was the establishment of this institution that Calvin had made the chief condition of his return to Geneva. It had jurisdiction over the conduct of the morals and the belief of the citizens of the town. It summoned inhabitants of every age and rank to appear before it, and its procedure was incredibly minute. It was empowered to pronounce the extreme ecclesiastical penalty of excommunication. In many instances it handed the accused persons over to the civil authorities for punishment by fine, imprisonment, torture, or death. Between 1542 and 1546 fifty-eight persons were sentenced to death, and seventy-six to exile. "From his cradle to his grave the Genevese citizen was pursued" by the Consistory with its "inquisitorial eye." Calvin's powerful influence was exerted in behalf of an increase in the penalties and an unrelenting and pitiless execution of the laws.

Having seen something of Calvin's supervision of morals, let **Calvin's** us turn to his theology; not to the ideas that he held in common **Pivotal** with contemporary and traditional Christianity, but to those that **Dogma** are distinctly his own. According to the doctrine of justification by faith alone, man is impotent to contribute to his own salvation. God alone can save him. God is omniscient and omnipotent. Some men are saved and others are lost. It must be, then, that some are predestined to be saved and others to be lost. God must have known and ordained their fates in the beginning. But Luther did not pursue his doctrine of justification as far as this. In his eyes the church had still a part to play in saving the souls of men by producing in their hearts the indispensable faith in Christ. Predestination was always a torment to him. He shunned it. Not so with Calvin. Predestination is his pivotal dogma. He faced the issue squarely. His theology begins and ends with the supremacy of God. Before the existence of time God arbitrarily determined, without any reference whatsoever to the character of the individual, the eternal fate of every human being. Any attempt at coöperation on the part of the individual is fruitless. Man cannot contribute to his own salvation even in the slightest degree. "Everything," said Calvin, "depends upon the mere will of God; if some are damned and others saved it is because God has created some for death and others for life." But why, it might be asked, did God create those men who were eternally to be lost? Calvin was not abashed. He did not recoil. He was ready with an answer. It was for His glorification. Such is the central doctrine of Calvin's theology. How did so terrible a belief find such ready and wide-spread acceptance? Did it come as a consolation to those who had left the ancient fold? Did it convince them, this doctrine of the inefficacy of man's works, that the ritual they had abandoned was of no avail? Nothing clings to men so persistently as the things intertwined with their emotions. Long after the intellect has declined longer to subscribe to a creed the ritual and the associations of the abandoned church appeal with almost irresistible force to the emotions. Feelings are ever more conservative than intellectual convictions. The thing that is reasonable to the mind is often treasonable to the heart. The religion which the first Calvinists had left behind was one whose roots were entwined with the very fiber of their being. It possessed the most stately and solemn ritual known to history. What could be more momentous than the words of consecration pronounced by the priest over the bread and wine while the deep-toned bells announced the miracle, daily renewed in the remotest village as well as in the capital of Christendom, to the listening world? Was it possible that sometimes the fear crept into their hearts that after all salvation might depend upon the sacraments which the Church they had

renounced alone could administer? Then was it not with consolation that there came to them the teaching that salvation is
to be found only in the hollow of God's hand, that it is dispensed without reference to any human mediation, and that it
depends entirely upon the unsearchable will of the creator?
With this belief taken to their breasts no evil could befall them
No one had power over them, not even their persecutors, for all
things had been determined even before the foundation of the
world.

This doctrine of predestination, of the helplessness of man,
would seem to lead to moral paralysis, for it leaves to the elect
no need for self-restraint, and to the reprobate it offers no
incentive to reform. Yet such has not been the case. Calvinism does not appear to have decreased the moral vitality of any
nation that has accepted it. This result is difficult of explanation. Perhaps the dogma of predestination was never really accepted by the mass of Calvinists even in Calvin's time. It was
the theme of innumerable polemical discussions, but perhaps for
the mass of men it had never more than an academic interest.
Perhaps from the first the human conscience, always a better
guide than logic, revolted against the idea that man is a slave before God, and that God chooses from his slaves a few for election
and delivers the majority to the eternal torments of hell. Men
do not look to their religious leaders for a systematic theological
system. They are interested not so much in theology as in religion. Their deepest need is an inspiring interpretation of the
aspirations of the heart. The stern morality of Calvinism flowed
from Calvin's character and not from his theology. Character
is ever more potent than intellectual power. If Calvinism had
inherited from its founder only a well-articulated theological
system it would have sunk from view, sooner or later, in " the
quicksands of doctrinal dispute."

In less than two years after Calvin returned to Geneva hostility to his rigorous rule began to make itself evident. And,
as before, the opposition included varied elements. In 1546
came the first serious clash. Calvin was victorious, but for the
next two or three years his situation was precarious. Among

**Bolsec**    those who, in later years, opposed Calvin was Jérôme Bolsec, a
physician who came to Geneva in 1551, and, by his ability, learning and character, quickly succeeded in winning the respect of
the community. He soon took exception to the doctrine of predestination. Calvin evidently desired his death, for a letter
written by him and his colleagues said: " It is our wish that
our Church should be purged of this pest in such a manner that

it may not, by being driven home, become injurious to our neighbors." But in the end, owing to the councils of moderation from Bern, Bolsec was banished.

We have now to deal with the chief example of Calvin's intolerance. Michael Servetus (1511?–53) was a Spaniard, who after studying law, perhaps in Toulouse, spent some years in Germany, where he issued two heretical books on the Trinity. Fear of persecution led him to flee the country. He took up the study of medicine in Paris and won a reputation as one of the best physicians in France. Gifted with a highly analytical and keenly observant mind he discovered the pulmonary circulation of the blood three-quarters of a century before William Harvey. He went to live with the archbishop of Vienne, an old pupil of his, and to practise his profession there. There his heterodox views regarding the Trinity, objectionable to Catholics and Protestants alike, got him into trouble. His manner, too, was not likely to win him friends. He was arrogant and contemptuous of those who differed from his opinions. Sincere in his conviction that his beliefs were of the greatest importance to humanity, he continued to publish them. In the course of the discussions that ensued Calvin meanly forwarded to the Catholic Inquisition, for the purpose of delivering him to death, some letters that the accused physician had sent to him in confidence and under the seal of secrecy. Servetus was imprisoned, but made his escape. After lingering for some time in France he set out for Italy by way of Switzerland, alone and on foot, and by some irony of fate stopped at Geneva. He reached Geneva on a Sunday and in the afternoon he went to hear Calvin preach. He was at once recognized and was arrested, at the instance of Calvin, before the service began. In prison he was subjected to cruel treatment; and he was denied the benefit of counsel. Calvin appeared against him in the courtroom, displaying great eagerness to secure his conviction, and from the pulpit he incited the people against him. On October 27, 1553, on the little knoll of Champel, just outside of Geneva, the lonely heretic, who to the last persisted in his beliefs, was burned to death. Servetus was merely a visitor in Geneva, a wayfarer who had stopped for a time on his way from France to Italy. His religious views had neither been printed nor uttered in Genevan territory. The Genevan government, therefore, had not the slightest legal justification for his arrest, imprisonment, torture, and death. Many excuses have been offered for this lamentable deed. It is said that fanaticism, devotion to one idea so intense as to lead to the undervaluation

**Servetus**

or exclusion of all others, destroys the judgment. But Calvin was not a fanatic. He was a constructive statesman alike in the field of religious thought and in that of social organization. He was by no means absorbed by a single idea. Then, too, his temperament was cold, deliberate, and calculating. His emotions pulsated but feebly. It is said, again, that religious persecution was the prevailing temper of the time, that " it was not Calvin who burned Servetus but the whole sixteenth century," and that every other religious leader of the day would have committed Servetus to the flames with equal readiness. But the idea of tolerance, derived neither from skepticism nor indifference but based upon reason, no mere hazy presentiment but a systematic vindication of complete religious liberty, was contemporary with Calvin. There were many who there and then raised their voices in protest against the cruel deed.

Chief of those who spoke at this time in behalf of tolerance was Sebastian Castellio (1515–63), a scholar of deep and wide **Castellio** learning who had come to Geneva as a teacher. He wished to enter the ministry, but to the proposed change, because of differences in biblical interpretation, Calvin objected. Castellio withdrew from Geneva to Basel, and when in 1554 Calvin, with the aid of texts taken from the Bible, made a defense of the execution of Servetus in particular and argued for the suppression of heresy in general, he and several others issued, a month later, a *Treatise on Heretics,* signed with the pen name of Martinus Bellius, and addressed to the laity at large. It contained a well reasoned plea for tolerance, and it was reinforced by quotations advocating tolerance from a score of writers among whom were Augustine, Chrysostom, Jerome, Luther, Erasmus, and Calvin.

From Geneva the teachings of Calvin spread to France. By a coincidence the first edition of the *Institute* appeared in 1536 **Calvin's** the very year of the death of Lefèvre. The teaching of the **Teachings** most venerable of all the reformers of Meaux, although it had **in France** included the doctrine of justification by faith alone, had been chiefly ethical. Calvin's book gave to the Protestantism of his native land an articulated creed. In accepting this dogmatic system the French heretics abandoned the most essential characteristics of the humanism that had led them out of the beaten path of orthodoxy, for they had surrendered the right of the individual to think for himself. Thus it was that French humanism and heresy, so closely interwoven at first, parted ways. Compactness was gained, it is true, but only at the price of freedom.

In 1541 Calvin finished a French translation of the second and greatly enlarged edition of the *Institute*. In addition to this he carried on a tireless correspondence with dissentients in France, sustaining the weak, encouraging the hesitating, advising organization, and becoming definitely recognized as their spiritual leader. The knowledge of the continued spread of heresy made the French government more energetically repressive than ever. But, as we have seen, the increased severity of Francis I failed to effect its purpose, and on the death of that monarch all that had been accomplished was the driving of heresy below the surface and the transferring of its headquarters from France to Geneva.

All the circumstances that surrounded Henry II when he succeeded his father in 1547, and all the influences brought to bear upon him, made for still more rigorous efforts to stamp out the obnoxious religious views. The new king lacked the strength to maintain the monarchy at the height to which it had attained. Slowly but steadily it slipped back into impotence. Once again the great feudal families raised themselves above the sovereign and their bitter rivalry overshadowed all the land. Henry was a sickly king. He knew the battlefield only by hearsay, and he seemed to be inseparable from the elderly ladies who were his mistresses. The task of extinguishing heresy was not an easy one, for everywhere the new opinions had been conveyed up and down the rivers and highways throughout the length and breadth of the land, but it was taken in hand with grim determination. In the first year of the new reign an additional court, the notorious *Chambre Ardente,* was established in Paris for the exclusive purpose of dealing with heretics. In two years it had condemned some two hundred people to death. Suppressed in 1549, because of the jealousy of the ecclesiastical courts, it was revived in 1553 and continued its nefarious work. It must not be thought that this was the sole tribunal engaged in the work of condemning heretics and confiscating their property. Provincial parlements and ecclesiastical courts were equally active. In the face of this pitiless persecution French Protestantism did not waver, but took up the work of organizing "churches" which for almost a decade had been suspended. A "church" was made up of a body of worshipers, a preacher, and a consistory that included elders and deacons. The work then consisted in the giving of sermons and the administering of the sacraments. Before 1560 some thirty-six churches had been completely organized in France, others had been partially organized, and many pastors had come from Geneva. Among the earliest and most important of these churches was the one established in 1555 at Paris.

Henry realized that his efforts thus far had been in vain. He desired to introduce the Inquisition into France, but to this the Parlement of Paris refused to consent. So from Compiègne he issued another edict against heresy on July 24, 1557, that was registered by the parlement six months later. But torture chamber and stake alike failed to arrest the progress of religious dissent. Heresy not only continued to spread among the middle classes but began to invade the upper strata of society. Late one afternoon in May, 1558, in the public grounds of the University, known as the Pré-aux-cleres, a favorite promenade of the Parisians, a few voices began to sing one of the psalms recently translated into French by Clément Marot. It was not long be-

fore the singers were joined by large numbers of those who were taking the air in that leafy place or playing games. For several successive evenings the performance was repeated. Included among the recruits to the chorus were such important personages as Antoine de Bourbon, who next to Henry II and his children was the first prince of the blood; his wife, Jeanne d'Albret, in right of whom he was the titular king of Navarre; his youngest brother, Louis, prince of Condé; Gaspard de Coligny, admiral of France; and one of the Coligny's brothers, François d'Andelot, who because he was the most active of all the converts among the nobility to the Huguenot cause was called the fearless knight. The psalm-singing was stopped, but not before the spread of heresy among the middle and upper classes had been given a most impressive demonstration; for, so it was said, five or six thousand had taken part in the performances. To the Huguenots it seemed time that the churches established in France should be united in a national organization. So on May 26, 1559, the first Protestant synod in France was held in Paris. It was only a small gathering, and it was conducted, perforce, in the utmost secrecy, but it drew up a confession of faith, based upon Calvin's theological teaching, if, indeed, it was not actually written by him, and it formulated a plan of government. To the king the situation appeared so serious that he attended a meeting of the Parlement of Paris, a most unusual thing for the monarch to do, in which the entire religious question was considered. Several speakers, chief of whom was Anne du Bourg, expressed their disapproval of the policy of repression that was being employed against the Protestants, and this so enraged the king that he commanded the arrest of four

of them, including Du Bourg whose death at the stake he swore
to witness. Some months later Du Bourg met his terrible fate
with great dignity, and his death, so it was said, "made more
converts among the students than did all the books of Calvin."
But the king had not lived to see the spectacle.

On July 10, 1559, Henry died as the result of a wound accidentally given in a tournament. All his persecution had failed
of its purpose. It had not only left the religious dissentients
as recalcitrant as ever but had actually stimulated their ardor
and their zeal. So from Geneva, as from a watch-tower, Calvin
saw the great panorama of his revolt unfold itself in France.
His own position, after the burning of Servetus, became more
firmly established than before. Hostility to his strict and unrelenting rule broke out again, as we have seen, in less than two
years after his return from exile; but the uprising of the Libertines was crushed, and its leaders, their property confiscated,
were either expelled from the republic or beheaded.

Not a little of the success of Protestantism in France was due
to Théodore de Bèze (1519–1605), better known as Beza, the
Latin form of his name that he occasionally used, who in the
wide range of his experiences excelled any other leader of religious revolution in the sixteenth century. His gentlemanly
manners helped to give him access to a stratum of society un- Bez
known to either Luther or Calvin; and to the Catholic aristocracy
of France he was more acceptable than any other Protestant
propagandist. There is not space at our disposal to dwell upon
his life — his work as a teacher at Lausanne and Geneva, his
fearless activity on behalf of the Huguenots in France, his participation in the Colloquy of Poissy (which, as we are to see in a
later chapter, failed to effect a reconciliation between the members of the two faiths that were dividing France and proved
instead to be the parting of the ways), his literary activity, and
his administrative ability as the successor of Calvin whom he
survived by forty-one years. In him Protestantism found its
ablest representative in the most vigorous moment of the attack
of militant Catholicism.

Of Calvin's theology we have spoken, and something has been
said of the details of his supervision of personal conduct. In
the heart of every inhabitant of his city he endeavored to cultivate a stern morality similar to his own. Moral self-control and
self-direction was the deepest need of the time. All through the
medieval centuries the religious and ethical direction of the individual had been arrogated to himself by the priest, and all
political direction had been assumed by the prince. The power

of self-direction had become very largely atrophied. When the religious revolution threw off a part of this external restraint the power to direct oneself in moral matters was not suddenly restored. That would have been impossible. A long period of education was necessary in order to restore the enfeebled will. Paradoxical as it may seem, it was this education that Calvin endeavored to supply by means of the galling restrictions, the savage legislation, that he imposed. The errors of his policy have already been intimated. The time has come to speak of them explicitly. Calvin's supervision of men's lives had far too distorted an idea of sin, for it included in its disapproval actions that were by no means detrimental to the individual or to society. It was summary and dictatorial both in its spirit and its procedure. And it was altogether too timorous in its trust of the individual. In so far as appetites and passions are concerned his

policy of ruthless repression aided men to form habits of abstinence. But in helping to establish those habits it did nothing to develop the power of self-control. Such a power can be developed only in the presence of freedom of choice. Self-control is positive in its character, whereas repression is merely negative. Self-control requires resolution and voluntary effort upon the part of the individual to shun evil and accomplish good; and these two things were both ignored by the Calvinistic supervision of conduct. It has been claimed that this repression, exercised in Geneva and elsewhere, produced a sterling character in those who were subjected to it. But the repression was always incidental to the character; the character was never the result of the repression. Indeed, the reverse of this claim is true. The effect of the narrow and inquisitorial supervision of conduct inaugurated by Calvin was distinctly detrimental to character. It was in the highest degree anti-educational. It brought about the decay of self-reliance. It served not only to arrest the growth of the faculties; it starved and stunted them, doubtless in many cases irretrievably. It produced prudes and Pharisees, not men. Those who lived under it and remained men were men in spite of it. The one touchstone which through the ages has separated the moral from the immoral life is the freedom and the power to choose the good in preference to the evil. And only where "the winds of freedom are blowing" can such a power be developed.

# CHAPTER XVII

## REVOLT IN THE NORTH AND HERESY IN THE SOUTH

THE Scandinavian lands lagged far behind the other countries of western Europe in civilization; and their revolts from Rome were not occasioned by popular uprisings but by politics. It was the rulers and not the people who revolted. Yet the revolts became complete. For more than four hundred years Denmark, Norway, and Sweden had existed as separate monarchies. In 1397 they were brought together by the Union of Calmar; but the year 1523 witnessed the dissolution of the compact. Christian II (1513–23) was the last king of the three turbulent countries. He was a man of much learning, devoted to the interests of the people, but unstable in temper and untrustworthy in character. He attempted to do away with a number of ecclesiastical abuses, and he had two Lutheran preachers sent from Saxony. His plans for governmental and economic reforms were far-reaching and wisely conceived. He was determined to lessen the power of the nobles who had placed many limitations upon the kingly authority, and to increase that of the burghers and peasants. His cruel effort to repress the recalcitrant Swedes ended in their final withdrawal from the Union. Denmark and Norway remained united; but in the same year that Sweden went her own way Christian was expelled from the southern kingdom.

Before the deposition of Christian, humanism had begun slowly to penetrate into Denmark. The first name of any note connected with the movement in that country is that of Christian Pederson, a priest, who, after becoming a Lutheran, published in 1529 a much better Danish version of the New Testament than the one already in existence. Another humanist was Paul Elisen who desired a reformation of ecclesiastical life and doctrine without a separation from the Catholic Church. He trans-

Scandinavia under the Union of Calmar

The Danish Revolt from Rome

lated some of Luther's works into Danish and delighted in those of Erasmus. A number of Danish students went to Wittenberg. Among them were Hans Tausen, who became known as the Danish Luther, and Jorgen Sadolin. The prince who succeeded Christian II was the Lutheran duke of Schleswig-Holstein, Frederic I (1523–33). The position of the new king was so difficult that at his election he felt obliged to pledge himself not to permit the teaching or the preaching of heresy. Despite this oath, however, the reign of Frederic witnessed the revolt from Rome in Denmark. Lutheran preachers, including Sadolin and Tausen, were at work in many places. In 1526 Frederic took it upon himself to fill the vacant archbishopric of Lund and to take the confirmation fees that had formerly been paid to the pope. This revolutionary act was approved by the diet of Odense in the same year; and in the following year when the Catholic prelates protested to the diet against the preaching of heresy the king declined to proceed against the propagandists. Lutheranism, left unmolested, made rapid progress. After the death of Frederic there was a disorderly interregnum; but his son Christian III (1536–59) succeeded in defeating those who opposed his succession. In the first year of his reign Christian summoned a national assembly at Copenhagen. This body, in which the nobles were the most active participants, decreed the abolition of the bishoprics and the transference of all ecclesiastical property to the crown. Bugenhagen then came from Saxony to organize the Lutheran church in Denmark. Seven superintendents, who later on were styled bishops, were placed over the people and the preachers, an ordinance that became the fundamental law of the new church was drawn up, a liturgy was compiled, and the Augsburg Confession and Luther's Lesser Catechism were adopted.

Lutheranism in Norway and Iceland

There had been far less dissatisfaction with ecclesiastical affairs in Norway and Iceland than in Denmark. There was, indeed, in those countries, no popular demand for a change. Yet Lutheran preachers were sent into Norway with letters of protection from Frederic I; and ecclesiastical property was either destroyed or systematically confiscated by the crown. Under Christian III Norway lost its position as a joint kingdom with Denmark and became a mere dependency of the latter. Lutheranism, much to the social detriment of the people for some fifty years, was forced upon the country. Even more arbitrary was the imposition of the new creeds upon Iceland where it required years of repression to quell the opposition.

The establishment of Swedish independence had been prac-

tically the work of one man, Gustavus Vasa (1496–1560).
After driving out the Danes he was elected king. It was
a difficult situation that confronted him. The nobles had
been accustomed to a large degree of feudal independence;
the peasants, upon whom he chiefly relied for support, were by
no means easy to control; and from one end to the other the
country had been made desolate by war. In his sore need Gustavus turned to the clergy for financial help and a long series
of bickerings took place. During these years Lutheranism
spread apace in the country so that when the diet met at
Westeras in 1527 other things than money matters had to be
discussed. It was decreed that all ecclesiastical property not
absolutely needed by the church (and of the necessity the king
was made the judge) was to be turned over to the crown; certain church lands were to revert to their former owners, others
were to be made over to the government; and provision was
made for a future settlement of doctrine. Two years later a
synod held at Örebro provided for the preaching of Lutheranism. Outbreaks against the new ecclesiastical régime were
easily crushed, and no one met death because of adherence to
the old religion; the kingly power was greatly increased; and
the country, because of the development of its mines and manufactures, rapidly became wealthy and powerful. The Swedish
church had its own service-book, hymn-book, and mass-book;
and it had twelve bishops and one archbishop.

In the middle of the twelfth century Finland was invaded by
Swedish forces but it was a long time before the conquest was
made complete. Gradually the Swedish civilization was introduced into the country and the Finlanders were granted the
same civil rights as those enjoyed by their conquerors. Gustavus Vasa was quick to appreciate the secular advantages to be
derived from a revolt from Rome. He, therefore, put into force
in Finland a religious policy parallel to the one he had carried
out in Sweden. His designs were furthered by the fact that for
some years the country had been without a bishop duly recognized and confirmed in office. The first man to preach the
Protestant doctrines in Finland was Peter Särkilaks who had
listened to the teachings of Luther and Melanchthon at Wittenberg. Little is known about this man who, disappearing as
suddenly as he had come, left behind him a great reputation as a
preacher. His work was continued by Michael Agricola (1510?–
57) whom he had won over to the new ideas and who went to
Wittenberg to conclude his studies. The mass of the Finnish
people were still half heathen; and what appealed to them most

CHAP.
XVII

1496-1560

The
Swedish
Revolt
from
Rome

Catholi-
cism Sup-
planted in
Finland

in Christianity was probably the impressive ceremonial of Catholicism. Only a few of the better educated of the clergy were in a position to weigh the conflicting ideas. It was only gradually, therefore, that the new doctrines made their way. Gustavus, without pronouncing definitely upon the doctrinal disputes of the time, commanded the Finnish clergy in general terms to work along evangelical lines. Gradually both doctrine and ceremony were modified. The economic position of the Catholic church was attacked with greater decision. Hostile measures ruined the monasteries whose revenues were then devoted to secular purposes. During the progress of disendowment the king's appetite for ecclesiastical property developed. The inferior clergy were taxed, a portion of the property set apart for their maintenance was confiscated, and the churches were plundered of their ornaments and valuables. This led to robbery of the Church by private individuals. The suppression of the monastery schools left education in a deplorable condition. When Agricola returned from Saxony he was made rector of the school at Obo; and later on, when the single Finnish bishopric was divided, he was made one of the two bishops of his country. He was a great pioneer in religious and secular instruction. Among other works, he translated Luther's Lesser Catechism and the New Testament and portions of the Old Testament into his native tongue, in all of which he maintained a moderate position. His writings formed the nucleus of a national literature; and his name is a glorious one in the history of Finnish culture.

Protestantism in Prussia

The German knights of St. Mary, better known as the Teutonic Knights, entered Prussia in 1231, and devoted themselves to the conquest of the heathen peoples on the shores of the Baltic. Soon after the next century opened all their activities were confined to these lands. And gradually the aims of the Order became political rather than religious. For a time the knights were very successful, but when their neighbors, Poland and Lithuania, were united in 1387 their power began to decline. In their semi-ecclesiastical state the relations of Church and State were unusually close and complex; but that did not prevent the early introduction of Lutheran ideas, especially in the cities. For the purpose of strengthening itself against Poland the Order, in 1511, made Albert of Brandenburg its grand-master; but in spite of that Poland succeeded in conquering West Prussia. Albert had looked for aid from the house of Hapsburg and when this failed him he renounced his allegiance to the Church as well as to the Empire. In 1525 he became a

Lutheran, secularized the Ordersland, and changed his title of master to that of duke. When he had thus converted Prussia into an hereditary principality he held it as a fief from Poland. A Lutheran church was then established in the duchy. The recently opened University of Königsberg became a center of Lutheranism and from its printing press there issued many pamphlets for the persecuted Protestants in Poland. In 1549 Albert brought into his duchy Osiander, whose heterodox Lutheran doctrine we shall notice in the next chapter, much to the anger of his orthodox Lutheran subjects. The nobles, who were disaffected by the encroachment of the ducal power, seized the opportunity to fan the flames of discontent. Osiander died in 1552, but a still more serious outbreak occurred in 1566 against John Funck, his associate, who was publicly put to death at Königsberg. A strictly orthodox Lutheran belief was then made imperative for every office-holder, ecclesiastical or secular, in the duchy, and the nobles recovered their privileges. So bitter was the struggle among the Lutherans that when Albert died in 1568 there spread abroad the rumor that he had become reconciled to the faith of his fathers.

At the opening of the thirteenth century Christianity was being ruthlessly forced upon the heathen of Livonia by the Brothers of the Sword. At the end of the fifteenth century the master of the Order, Walter von Plettenberg, had won for himself a position of great importance, and in 1527 Charles V recognized him as a prince of the empire. Despite this action the emperor neglected the imperial interests in the Slavonic provinces of the Baltic and so eventually Livonia, after being held by Poland and then by Sweden, was incorporated into the expanding domains of Russia. The country was divided in 1550 between Russia and Poland. Eleven years later the grandmaster, Kettler, embraced Lutheranism and from that time on his domain was confined to the duchy of Courland. For some forty years before the grand-master formally adopted Protestantism the doctrines of the Saxon friar had been making headway in Livonia. The clergy were corrupt there as elsewhere; and large numbers of Livonians after attending German schools scattered the seeds of criticism in their native land. The Protestant ideas found a fruitful soil in this northern land, especially in Riga, the capital of the country, which signed the Augsburg Confession as early as 1530. But iconoclastic raids by "the sovereign rabble" marked the course of the Livonian ecclesiastical revolt; and the movement, becoming involved in the complicated political troubles of the country, lost almost all

*Protestantism in Livonia*

traces of the religious spirit with which it had once been stamped. Finally Livonia was absorbed by Russia; and Esthonia, and, later on, Courland, into both of which Lutheranism had found its way, went with it.

When Poland and Lithuania were dynastically united in 1386 they made a new power of the first rank. It was a wild land in which the burghers had few rights and the peasants none at all, and in which the nobles gradually gained so many privileges as to become a lawless and turbulent oligarchy. Ecclesiastical abuses similar to those existing elsewhere prevailed in the dual kingdom. The clergy were ignorant and corrupt, the bishops amassed enormous wealth, efforts were made to reserve the episcopal positions exclusively for nobles, and the financial exactions of the clergy and their exemption alike from governmental burdens and governmental control were most galling. Discontent helped to spread the doctrinal ideas of Hus and his followers in these Slavic lands throughout the fifteenth century. And after the Lutheran movement got under way in Saxony it

was not long before it spread to Poland and became permanently entrenched in Polish Russia. It was not only orthodox Lutheran views that invaded the two countries; more radical opinions made their appearance. Under the patronage of Queen Bona Sforza a humanist society was formed at Cracow of which Francis Lismanini was the leading spirit, and from which there radiated Anti-Trinitarian doctrines. In 1548 the ranks of the religious dissenters in Poland were considerably augmented by the coming of the Bohemian Brethren, or Moravian Brethren or, as they preferred to call themselves, the Communion of Brethren, a sect holding radical Hussite views, that had been expelled from Bohemia. They placed chief stress upon conduct rather than upon creed and made a notable effort to revive the life of primitive Christianity. It is true that they sojourned in Poland only for a time, going on into Saxony; but in their wake they left many converts. The spread of religious dissent naturally met with opposition; but owing to the decentralized government, described in a later chapter devoted to the Magyar and the Slav, little could be done. The diet of 1552 granted to the clergy the right to judge heresy but withheld from them all power to punish it with any other than an ecclesiastical penalty. Four years later the diet gave permission to every nobleman to adopt in his own house the form of worship he desired, provided it conformed to the Bible. Protestantism had now reached its apogee in Poland. The reformers were divided among themselves. The Lutherans, Calvinists and the members of the various sects, by no means dwelt in harmony with each other. It was hoped that Jan Laski, sometimes known as John à Lasco, would be able to unite the different factions into a national church. He was a Polish noble who had studied abroad, made the acquaintance of Erasmus and other humanists, left the ancestral church, and made a name for himself as the head of the congregation of foreign refugees in London. But he died without having effected the desired conciliation. The dissensions among the Protestants continued and all hope of their union died away when Fausto Socini, whose work we are to consider later on, gave to the Anti-Trinitarians a definite organization.

Protestantism gained but a slight foothold in the Mediterranean lands. The Italians have always been addicted to the preservation of institutions and customs that have long been emptied of real significance. Unlike other nations they have never attempted a sweeping removal of the vestiges of an ancient régime. But aside from this fundamental fact the Papacy was more strongly entrenched in Italy than elsewhere because it aroused no national animosity, but, on the contrary, was predominantly an Italian institution, flattering the vanity of many Italians and adding to their material prosperity. The Italian character of the Papacy was a source of weakness in all the countries that lie north and west of the Alps, but in Italy it was a source of strength. It was not without pride that the Italian realized that the presence of the Papacy in Rome made the most important city of his country the capital of Christendom, and the innumerable and tangible material advantages that resulted from the residence of the popes in Rome were also the source of no small degree of satisfaction. The general interest of his country, the Italian concluded, lay not in the destruction of the Papacy, but in its preservation. *Italy and the Papacy*

In Italy the revival of the individual had been inaugurated and carried to its greatest extreme. Now individuality naturally makes for the dissolution of dogma and ecclesiastical authority. Opposition to the Papacy was impeded in Italy by the forces and the facts we have just noticed, but the creeds of the Church evaporated in the atmosphere of the Renaissance, in the presence of the unrestricted liberty of the individual. Under the disguise of outward conformity the most heterodox opinions freely circulated among the various groups of scholars up and down the peninsula. All varieties of thought were tolerated as long as their outward expression was not too indiscreet; and this tolerance, or rather indifference, continued until the Church parted company with the Renaissance movement and *The Trend Toward Paganism* perfected its machinery of repression. Under the cloak of an easy-going participation in the ceremonies of the Church there spread throughout Italy a new paganism. This paganism, as we have seen, was due in part to the revival of Greek and Latin culture, but it was also, in a much larger degree, an indigenous growth, an exhalation of the Italian soil. The most famous exemplar of this paganism in its relation to the religious side of the life of the time is Pietro Bembo (1470–1547), secretary of Leo X, who was subsequently made a cardinal by Paul III, and who is said to have advised Sadoleto not to read the Pauline epistles because of the possibly unfavorable effect upon his style of their unclassical Greek. It was not only the literature and the art of the time that was deeply colored with paganism but also philosophy and religious thought. The paganism of the Renaissance has been decried as a thing wholly undesirable. Such, however, was not the case. By no means can the vices of the Italians be ascribed entirely to their paganism; while, on the other hand, certain merits resulted from their absorbing interest in the affairs of the world about them. For one thing the frank naturalism of the humanists acted as a solvent of the ascetic ideal of life, and eventually there was formed an eclective ideal that includes the best of both the ideals that clashed in the sixteenth century.

The Trend Toward Rationalism

Side by side with the tendency toward paganism there was a trend toward rationalism, stimulated first by the writings of Arabic thinkers, particularly those of Averroes, and later by the recovered remains of Greek and Latin thought. In the Italian universities, where theology had virtually been replaced by philosophy and science, especially in Padua, there existed a freedom of thought that elsewhere would have been sought in vain. The revival of the learning of antiquity was bound to result in bold flights and daring syntheses of the individual mind. The classical point of view was that of the rational faculty; its conceptions and its ideals were the result of the reasoning process. Reason alone guided the classical man, rendered him self-reliant and made him self-sufficient. From the time of Lorenzo Valla the batteries of criticism were leveled against medieval orthodoxy; and so bold did rationalism become that its most extreme exponents did not hesitate to call into question the immaterial nature of the human soul. The most noted of these bold thinkers who insisted upon the right and the power of the human reason to search out for itself the truths of philosophy and religion was Pietro Pomponazzi (1462–1525) who was a professor of philosophy in the University of Padua and later in that of Bologna. He was a cold and unimpassioned thinker into the fiber of whose being was interwoven an irresistible tendency to doubt. His chief merit is his noble advocacy of a pure and unselfish morality; a morality that, seeking no external rewards, is content to accept virtue as its own reward and to see in the results of vice its own punishment. The morality of a people is always closely related to its religion. In an age when men were becoming increasingly unwilling to accept the ecclesiastical sanctions upon which morality had hitherto been based this promulgation of the permanent and unchanging laws of morality was of the greatest value. In 1516 Pomponazzi published his treatise *De Immortalitate Animae* in which he denied the Christian doctrine of immortality. Such opinions were widely disseminated. Yet they were opposed with energy. To Christianity in its true sense, as embodied in the words and life of its founder, rationalism was by no means antagonistic. Only a small minority of the rationalists of the Renaissance dreamed of denying the essentials of Christianity. It was merely to superfluous dogmas that they refused to subscribe. Rationalism, whenever it pays due regard to the instincts and emotions, results not in the disintegration of the religious faculty, but in its increase and purification. Machiavelli's statement that all Italians of this time were super-eminently irreligious is incorrect. The growing disbelief in the long-established creeds did not leave the cultured Italians devoid of all religion. Their foregone faiths were replaced in many instances by an increased devotion to the one Supreme Being, a devotion that led, as we shall see, to Anti-Trinitarianism. The new thought to which the Renaissance had given rise was making itself felt not only in the fields of politics and science, but also in those of philosophy and religion. But it made itself felt among the Italian scholars in a way quite different to its manifestation amid the peoples of the cismontane countries. The Italians lack the gloomy fanaticism of the Spaniards, the predilection to dogma of the Germans, the fatal scholastic logic of the French, and the readiness to establish a public compromise that characterizes the English. The cismontane saw the Church only from afar. The thing that impressed him most forcibly was her immutable dogma for which she made the high claim of infallibility. He was not near enough to hear the human accents of the papal voice. When he left the ancestral Church he hastened to found a new one, for he was unprepared for the solitude of free thought. He was too timid to strike boldly at the supernatural and set up reason as the sovereign guide of his body and his soul. He did not dare to leave the accepted circle of Christianity. So his revolts took the form of schisms or heresies. Not so the Italian. He knew that the Papacy was in no small degree his own production, the continuous creation of the Italian genius. In the voice of the Vicar of Christ he heard the passions of humanity; and within the sacred precincts of the sanctuary he saw the stirring of earthly interests. The weaknesses as well as the virtues of his teachers had always been known to him, and he had not been found unsympathetic. All that did not approve itself to his clear brain he nevertheless accepted as being merely symbolical. Dante may be regarded as a perfect example of the conscience of the educated Italian. He was an implacable enemy of popes but not of the Papacy. He harbored no thought of heresy and entertained no dream of division. Yet he interpreted the dogmas of the Church to suit his views. He toned down their desolating severity. Nowhere did he consign to hell the Christians who had lived without the pale of the sacramental practices; while on the other hand he placed Averroes, Plato, and Saladin in a region of semi-beatitude, made Cato the guardian of purgatory, and installed the Emperor Trajan in paradise. Everywhere his great poem is pervaded with a religion that is Franciscan in its tenderness and in its hope. So for the majority of Italian thinkers the mantle of the traditional faith never became too heavy to wear; and for the small minority who could no longer wear it a far bolder separation than the various revolts in the countries north of the mountains was the one way of life.

Among the lower classes of the peninsula orthodoxy was firmly established. In the northern countries Christianity had displaced the heathenism of the barbarians; but in the southern peninsula Christianity had gradually been blended with the ancient paganism of the peasants. The old deities were never quite supplanted in Italy. There still continued to be paid to them a popular cultus. The soft and mellow religion that resulted from the interweaving of the ancient and medieval faiths permeated the life of the masses of the people. It formed the basis of secular passions and of secular art. It still speaks to us through the life of St. Francis, the poetry of Dante, and the sculpture and the sculpturesque painting of Michelangelo. Few there were among the Italians who had not a relative in the priesthood. They feared the hierarchy no whit. Their Catholicism was their own, permeated with the tenderness of the most lovable of all the saints, appealing to the heart more than to the mind, knit completely into the fiber of their national life, expressed in the splendid ceremonials so indispensable to the southern imagination. So they made no effort to rend the " seamless coat."

In the years 1512–17 the Fifth Lateran Council held its twelve sittings. It was never regarded by the cismontane countries as being an œcumenical body because it was comprised exclusively of Italian prelates. It displayed a good intention to effect reform and passed a number of measures to that end; but as far as the general Church was concerned it came to naught. Leo X continued to neglect the well-being of Christendom in his patronage of art and pursuit of the political interests of the house of Medici. The curia remained corrupt, and the widespread scandals of the clergy were undiminished. Yet upon Italian thought the council was not without effect. It roused many of the prelates in the peninsula to the need of reform and encouraged those who were already alive to that necessity. The stimulus that it gave to religious feeling found expression in the rise of the new religious confraternities and the activity of the mediating reformers with which we are soon to deal.

Effect of
the Fifth
Lateran
Council
on Italian
Thought

North of the Alps revolt was upon the verge of breaking out. The spirit of the German reformers, as we have seen, was intensely anti-Italian. The government of the Church was dominated by Italians. The curia did not include more than two or three Germans and Englishmen. Leo X and the Lateran council were alike oblivious of the impending catastrophe in the north. The German saw the promise of the future to lie in a successful attack upon the Papacy; the Italian deemed that promise to reside in the defense of the Papacy. Such a situation naturally made Italy hostile to the German ideas of reform.

Hostility
of Italy
to the
German
Ideas of
Reform

The pagan Leo, with his indescribable charm of speech, his magnanimity, his learning, and his love of art, gave place to the austere Adrian VI (1522–23) who was received with ill-concealed contempt as *un pontefice di nazione barbara*. The new pope, born in Utrecht, had been a tutor of Charles V; and from humble origin he had risen to be cardinal-bishop of Tortosa. He had been the papal legate in Spain and had done much in that country to reform monastic life. But he had never set foot in Rome until he entered it as pontiff, and there his personality was altogether unknown. His ascension to the papal office marked an abrupt transition; and as his plans for a thorough-going reform, not only of Rome but of the entire Church, were unfolded the contempt in which he was held by Leo's retainers deepened into hatred. But Adrian was not able to complete the gigantic task he had undertaken. He was, indeed, scarcely able to begin it. Confronted with the implacable hostility of the curia, he found the funds at his disposal altogether inadequate and, making the situation more difficult, the pestilence became epidemic in the Eternal City. Then, too, the increasing peril of the Turks demanded his attention. Adrian met all these obstacles with determination; and the chief cause of his failure to carry out his program was the brevity of his pontificate which lasted only twenty months. On September 14, 1523, the last of the non-Italian popes died, and he was succeeded by another Medician pope, the worldly, shifting, and procrastinating Clement VII.

But there was left in Italy a man quite as much bent as Adrian had been upon a sweeping reformation within the Church,

Caraffa
and the
Begin-
nings of
his Cath-
olic Ref-
ormation

Giovanni Pietro Caraffa (1476–1559), a member of the Neapolitan nobility. In 1504 he had been made bishop of Chieti and he had then worked strenuously to eradicate the abuses in his diocese. After that he had been employed in the papal service as legate to England and nuncio to Spain. He was a typical representative of southern Italy, eloquent and impetuous, zealous but not always wise, obstinate and ruthless, an indefatigable worker in the cause he had at heart. In Spain he had seen the work of the great reformer Cardinal Ximenes; and there, too, he had known Adrian who afterwards became pope. Black as were the stains upon the Church he saw the feasibility of purification if only the pope would adopt the proper plan. A similar reformer was Gian Matteo Giberti (1495–1543), bishop of Verona, whose work was especially effective among the lower and middle classes.

Among the earliest signs of the spirit of reform within the

Church were the awakening of the existing religious orders and the establishment of new ones. The Germans were bent upon the abolition of monasticism, but the Italians desired its retention and regeneration. Even in the times of the deepest depression, as we have seen in our study of the revival of conscience, men had arisen within the ranks of the Church with the purpose of effecting reform without revolt. Once more such men took up their task. While the Papacy was given up to politics and the prelates to paganism certain clerics and laymen united at Rome, in 1517, soon after the close of the Lateran council, to form the society known as the Oratory of the Divine Love. By their own example they endeavored to lead the way in the abolition of the prevalent abuses; and they did not confine their work to religious exercises but devoted themselves to offices of charity. Similar communities, connected with the one at Rome, were established at Verona, Vicenza, Brescia, and Venice. But from the nature of their organization and the claims of other duties they did not exercise a wide influence. The Brothers of Charity, founded in 1519, was another order devoted to reform. Its members helped the poor, visited the prisons and hospitals, and buried those who had died in poverty. More important was the Theatins, an order founded about 1524, whose chief purpose was to improve the character of the parochial clergy. The requirements for membership, which was limited to the nobility, were so strict and its vow of poverty so severe, that after nine years it could claim only a score of members. But it was a *corps d'élite,* and, becoming a seminary for bishops, won for itself in the work of reform a position of unquestioned importance. Its most noted members were the gentle and retiring Gaetano de Thiene and the impulsive and bigoted Caraffa. A fourth order was established about 1531 at Milan. Its members called themselves the Sons of St. Paul, but they became known as Barnabites because of their residence in the ancient convent of St. Barnabas. They made a far wider appeal than the Theatins, preaching in the open air to great crowds of people. For a decade northern Italy had been devastated by war, in the wake of which followed desolation and disease. In order to take care of the numerous orphans Girolamo Miani, a Venetian senator, formed a congregation of regular clergy known as the Somaschi, from their place of meeting, the village of Somasca, which lies in isolation some distance from Bergamo. Their principal work was the conduct of their orphanages, but they also aided the sick, the poor, and the ignorant. But most important of all the new orders were the Capuchins. Very early the Franciscan order had fallen into decay. The reformatory movements of the Spirituals and the Fraticelli we have already seen. Another such movement received the papal sanction when in 1526 Clement VII authorized Matteo de' Bassi to organize into a new order a body of Franciscans who desired to restore the primitive simplicity and poverty of their beloved founder. With their robe, made of the roughest material they could procure, they wore a square-pointed hood, *cappuccio,* and from the diminutive *cappuccino,* which means " little hooded fellow," a title bestowed upon them half contemptuously and half affectionately, as is the Italian way, they derived their name. Their chief work was that of revivalists. They preached repentance to the masses of the people. But they also administered the last sacrament to the dying, took care of orphans, and gave succor to the destitute. In 1534 they admitted to their ranks the most famous preachers in the peninsula, Bernardino Ochino and Bernardino of Asti,

They became a powerful instrument of reform and more than any other order thus far established did they keep within the fold of the Mother Church the mass of the people of Italy. But although all these orders in a lesser or a greater degree contributed to the regeneration of Italian Catholicism it was another and a later order, the Jesuits, to whom we have devoted a later chapter, that effectively checked the advance of Protestantism in the peninsula.

We have now to deal with a group of men whom we shall call the mediating reformers, men who hoped to effect a conciliation between Catholicism and Protestantism, men who were concerned with the spirit of creeds more than with their letter, men who valued theology less than religion, men who laid greater stress upon life than upon mechanism. Before and during the various revolts from Rome they denounced the curia and demanded the reformation of morals and discipline. But had their power developed even earlier than it did and become greater than it was it is scarcely probable that the breach could have been healed, so rapidly did Luther's opinions, in spite of their author, demonstrate themselves to be incompatible with the fundamental postulate of the Church and so quickly and deeply did they strike root in the minds and hearts of men. Among the generous minds who entertained this noble Utopian dream was that of Gasparo Contarini (1483–1543), a distinguished Venetian senator, who became a member of the Oratory of Divine Love. He suggested to Clement VII the relinquishment by the Papacy of its territorial possessions and the concentration of its activity upon the general welfare of Christendom. In 1535 Paul III made Contarini a cardinal. Six years later he was sent to the diet of Ratisbon; but he was distrusted and hampered by the curia, and so, owing to that reason and to the suspicion and disinclination of the Lutherans, that last genuine effort to conciliate the German revolutionists came to naught. The mediating reformers believed in justification by faith, as the Church had always done, but they also insisted upon the fruition of that faith in good works. Their attitude is well expressed in the communication sent by the scholarly and eloquent Cardinal Jacopo Sadoleto (1477–1547) to the Genevans in an attempt to win them back to their forsaken fold. "We obtain this blessing of complete and perpetual salvation," he wrote, "by faith alone in God and in Jesus Christ. When I say faith alone I do not mean, as those inventors of novelties do, a mere credulity and confidence in God, to the exclusion of love and other Christian virtues. This indeed is necessary, and forms our first access to God. But it is not enough. Our minds must be full of piety towards God and desirous of performing, by the power of the Holy Spirit, whatever is agreeable to Him." In no other man of the sixteenth century were the graces of humanism and the spirit of Catholicism so happily blended as in Sadoleto; and in all the letters that were exchanged between him and Calvin he displayed a far finer Christian spirit than did his powerful opponent. Cardinal Giovanni Morone (1509–80), who when he entered Modena in 1533 as its bishop set himself at once to reform the clergy of his diocese, preceded Contarini as the papal nuncio at Ratisbon. He repeatedly urged upon Paul III the necessity of a general council and a vigorous prosecution of reform as being indispensable to the recovery of Germany. Youngest of the mediating reformers was Cardinal Reginald Pole (1500–58), an Englishman whose greatest aim in life was to effect a reconciliation between his native country and Rome. When Contarini was sent to Ratisbon he conferred with Pole and both agreed upon a conciliatory policy. The diet was an event of great importance. Had the policy of the mediating party prevailed the Protestant Revolution would doubtless have assumed a greatly different aspect. But, as we have seen, all attempts at compromise failed and the revolt went on its way.

When Paul III (1534–49) became pontiff the party of the mediating reformers came into power. It was he who elevated Contarini, Sadoleto, and Pole to the Sacred College. He appointed a commission of nine members to report upon the necessary reforms. Their report, *Consilium de emendanda Ecclesia,* presented in 1537, is an out-spoken enumeration of the abuses that prevailed throughout the Church. So scathing was the indictment, so complete the exposition, that it was decided not to publish it. But it was privately printed and by some means or other a copy reached Germany where it was at once reprinted with satirical annotations calling attention to the fact that a papal commission had approved all the German demands for reformation. Little seems to have been done, however, in the way of reform. War broke out in Italy between Charles V and Francis I; and the pope, who was growing old and feeble, began to lose his interest in reform. After the death of Paul III there came the brief pontificates of Julius III (1150–55) and Marcellus II (1555); and then with the reign of the bigoted Paul IV (1555–59) the predominance of the mediating party at Rome came to an end. The Catholic world assumed an aspect of gloomy fanaticism, and all the high hopes of Contarini and his associates dwindled into dust.

There were in Italy not only men and movements whose purpose it was to effect a reform within the Church but also men
who entertained distinctly Protestant opinions, and there were
centers in which those opinions were propagated. In a number
of towns in Italy there were literary circles that gradually acquired a religious complexion. They were made up of men and
women who were deeply penetrated with the new humanism and
who at the same time felt within themselves the piercing power
of the contemporary religious impulse. A marked diversity of
opinion prevailed among these groups, and, indeed, among the
members of each single group; but a large number of those who
made up these circles entertained, with varying degrees of meaning, the belief in justification by faith alone. But this article of
faith, and other opinions analogous to Lutheranism, did not
lead, as they did in Germany, to revolution. The conviction,
still obtained that the Church is one and indivisible, and that the
pope is the Vicar of Christ upon earth; and many of the customs
and ceremonies of the Church were too closely interwoven with
the very fiber of their being to make possible any general departure from the ancient fold. "No corruption," said Isidoro
Clario, "can be so great as to justify a defection from the hal-
lowed communion of the Church." And then, he added, "Is
it not better to repair what we have than to endanger all by
dubious attempts to produce something new? Our sole endeavor should be to improve the old institution, to free it from
its defects." It must be borne in mind, therefore, that the
opinions approximating those of Luther entertained by Italian
scholars were tempered by their attachment to the Church.

One of these centers of Protestant ideas was Ferrara. In
1533 Ercole II succeeded to the ducal throne. Five years previously he had married Renée (1510–75), daughter of Louis XII of
France. She had been brought up in France with her cousin
Margaret, who afterwards became queen of Navarre, and the
two girls had become tinctured with the new religious thought
that was spreading abroad in the land. When she went to Ferrara, in 1527, she took these new opinions with her and she
gathered about herself a group of kindred spirits. Included in
her circle were the French poet, Clément Marot, a French historian, Languet, and scholars from Germany, Crete, and various
Italian cities. In Ferrara itself adherents were gained chief
of whom was Pellegrino Morato, a professor in the university,
and, later on, his daughter, the eloquent and learned Olympia.
In the midst of this little circle there appeared in the spring of
1536 the stern figure of Calvin, who had come thither one

knows not why. A not unlikely reason is that he wished to startle the world by creating a Protestant State in the very center of the Catholic peninsula. Little is known of the proceedings of the great theologian in Ferrara. Very soon he departed as he had come, silently and alone. It was not to be much longer that heretical opinions were tolerated or endured in the duchy of the Este. Fannio, a poor youth of Faenza, who had preached heterodox ideas throughout Romagna, was put to death in 1550 in accordance with a papal order. This is the second recorded death for religion at this period in Italy. The first one was that of Jamie Enzinas, a Spanish Lutheran, who three years earlier was burned at the stake in Rome. Renée sent her heretical followers to Mirandola, in whose count they found a protector. In 1554, under pressure from Rome, the duchess received the sacraments of confession and communion, though she remained at heart a Calvinist. Once she was banished by her husband for her heretical sympathies to Consandolo in the pestiferous delta of the Po; and once she was shut up in a tower as insane. In 1560, two years after her husband's death, she took up her residence in Montargis, in France, where she became openly a Calvinist, though at times she was filled with doubt and desired to return to the bosom of the Church of her childhood, and where she gave assistance to the Huguenots. Heresy was not allowed to linger in the duchy after her departure. There were continued arrests and punishments.

Modena, the other capital of Ercole, was also a center of humanism and heresy. The bishop himself, the learned Morone, whom we have noticed as one of the mediating reformers, gave no little encouragement to the Protestant views. It was at his express command that the book *On the benefits of Christ's death,* which we shall notice later on, was printed. When the ruthless Caraffa became pope, Morone was himself suspected of heresy and thrown into prison where he remained for about two years until he received the papal absolution. Everywhere in the city, according to Tassoni, a contemporary writer, the people engaged in disputes upon the faith and the law of Christ until the town became known as a " second Geneva." But soon all suspected persons were required to sign an explicit declaration of faith. Long after this, however, there were many names enrolled upon the register of the Inquisition as suspect of heresy. Punishment was inflicted throughout the duchy with a ruthless hand and at Modena, in a single year, 1568, thirteen men and one woman were burned at the stake.

Very naturally, the Lutheran views made their first appearance in upper Italy between which and the cismontane countries there was a constant stream of commerce and travel. Many students made their way to Bologna, there to study the Roman law. At a number of places in the Romagna there was an outcropping of Protestant ideas. In 1547 a papal brief was issued

for the suppression of the Lutheran heresy in Faenza; and preachers at Forli, Ravenna, and Bagnacavello, came under suspicion. Vendors of heretical books were prosecuted and "persuaded" by the Inquisition to disclose the names of their patrons. In 1550 twenty-eight members of the Servite order were compelled to do penance for their heretical opinions, three were expelled from the order, and others were debarred from performing ecclesiastical functions. Still later other members of the same organization were punished for having Lutheran literature in their possession.

Venice was one of the greatest commercial centers in Europe. Many foreigners found their way there, and they were able to make public their religious views because toleration was practised by the government. So the Protestant ideas found it a favorable place. There, too, were to be found the scattered

literati of Rome, Florence, Milan, and other cities that had been torn by factions or had suffered in one way or another by the long-continued wars. A number of these men gathered about Contarini whom they regarded as their leader. Most of the men who were engaged in spreading the Lutheran teachings were members of religious orders. In answer to a demand for repression the Council of Ten, in 1530, refused to take action. In the same year Caraffa was commissioned by the Papacy to proceed against the offenders in Venice and from this time forward the chief passion of his life was the extinction of heresy. Two years later he called the pope's attention to the wide prevalence of heresy in the Venetian territory, especially to the "apostate" monks and friars, who were everywhere busily engaged in inculcating the obnoxious views, and to the unrestricted and public sale of heretical writings, a veritable fountain-head of heresy. In 1533 Aleander was sent as nuncio to Venice, and his reports reveal the fact that heresy was beginning to make its way even among the lower classes. A branch of the perfected Inquisition was set up in Venice in 1547, and from that time heresy and heretical literature began to disappear from the dominions of the doge. The signoria of Venice was at first very unwilling to take any measures at all against the heretics. But owing either to pressure from Rome, or the turn of political affairs, or their own conclusion that the progress of heresy must be stopped, the

Venetians finally proceeded against the accused upon their own initiative. Yet the signoria always kept the control of affairs in its own hands; and for some time it restricted with firmness the demand of the Church to punish heresy with bodily maiming or death. Heresy, it was held, could be eradicated without the aid of the rack and the stake. Eventually the death penalty was inflicted. Baldo Lupetino, who had propagated Protestant ideas among his fellow-prisoners, was perhaps the first one to suffer the extreme penalty for his faith. He was drowned in the stagnant waters of the lagoon.

In Lucca, also, the tendency toward Protestantism assumed something of the aspect of a popular movement. Some of the principal citizens and nobles joined a group of scholars in the study of the Pauline epistles; but by 1551 the last of the Lucchese heretics had been compelled to seek safety in flight. Siena and Viterbo also became centers of heresy. Cardinal Pole resided at the latter place as the papal legate from 1541 to 1545; and Heresy at Lucca, Siena, Viterbo, Padua, Brescia, Como, and Milan during that time Cardinal Morone, Ochino, Vittoria Colonna and other scholars were there. The reformers met in Cardinal Pole's residence, and all of them were deeply imbued with the doctrine of justification by faith. The same doctrine was spread in Padua by Michael Geismayr, a peasant leader from Salsburg. The principal teacher of heresy in Brescia was Pallavicini, a Carmelite monk; but the new opinions never obtained a decided support there. At Como there was a little group favorably inclined to the still more radical views of Zwingli. Milan, because of its proximity to Switzerland and the Waldensian valleys, and because of the fact that, like Venice, it was a great center of commerce, was especially exposed to the infection of heresy. Among the clergy, both secular and regular, and among the laity, the Protestant ideas found acceptance. Down through the Grisons, the Valtelline and the Val di Chiavenna the new doctrines found their way with the commercial caravans; and the material interest of the Milanese demanded that the stream of traffic with their northern neighbors be not interrupted.

But the most important center of the Protestant ideas in Italy lay far to the south and had for its guide and leader not an Italian but a Spaniard. The reform movement at Naples centered round the gifted Juan de Valdés (1500?–40?) who, in or- Heresy at Naples der to avoid persecution at the hands of the Inquisition, left his native land in 1529, and after five years of wandering settled in the south Italian capital. There he attracted the finest spirits of the time. It cannot be said that he was a disciple of any one of the religious revolutionists. Rather was he a follower of

Erasmus whose ideas he carried to their logical conclusion. He remained always within the pale of the Church, but in his teachings "there is an infinite potentiality of rebellion against the whole ecclesiastical system." In his catechism may be found an enunciation of the doctrine of justification by faith; yet his Lutheran tendencies were mixed with a large infusion of mysticism, for he held that above reason is the divine inspiration that comes from the abandonment of self to the contemplation of God. The remarkable circle that Valdés gathered about him consisted of men and women who represented both the clergy and the laity. It included among others Ochino, Giulia Gonzaga, and Vittoria Colonna. Over this select group he exercised a profound influence; and his influence was by no means confined to this academic and aristocratic circle but went abroad and affected a very large number of people. Of all the noble ladies who were included among the adherents of Valdés the one who accepted most completely his teachings was Giulia Gonzaga (1499?–1566) reputed to have been the most beautiful woman in Italy. She gained a reputation as a poet, and to her Valdés dedicated one of his books. After the death of Valdés some of his immediate followers scattered themselves throughout Italy. The remainder looked up to Donna Giulia as a leader. Vittoria Colonna (1490–1547) was the most gifted and illustrious woman of her age; her father, head of the long-descended baronial house, was the grand constable of Naples, and her mother was a daughter of the duke of Urbino. Her husband, the marquis of Pescara, had died in 1525, and since then she had devoted her life in retirement at her villa near Naples to poetry and religion. Then, after spending some years in Rome and visiting the duchess Renée at Ferrara, the beautiful and high-souled woman became one of the disciples of the Spanish scholar. She realized keenly the need for reform within the Church. "I see thy ship, O Peter," she wrote, "so over-laden with mire that it is in danger of sinking at the first attack of the waves." From such passages in her writings it is clear that she ardently desired a reformation of morals in the Catholic world; but despite the community of ideas with Margaret of Navarre, as revealed in her letters, and her tolerance of dissenters, it does not appear that she stepped beyond the pale of the Church.

We have now to deal with a number of men who were not definitely connected with any particular group. First we may notice Antonio Bruccioli, a Florentine scholar, who when exiled from the Tuscan capital became a printer in Venice. In 1532, two years before Luther completed his translation, he published his Italian version of the entire Bible; and afterwards he gave to the public a voluminous commentary. He was imprisoned by the Inquisition in 1546 on the charge of heresy, and although the accusation was never substantiated he was troubled throughout the remainder of his life by that engine of repression. Giovanni Battista Folengo (1500–59), the learned Benedictine prior of Monte Cassino, was another Italian imbued to a more or less degree with the doctrine of justification by faith alone. He wrote a commentary on the psalms, that contains many indications of a leaning toward Lutheranism. He attributed justification to faith alone and protested against placing emphasis upon works, such as fasts, prayers, masses, and confessions. Yet he passed all the years of his life from the age of sixteen to sixty in the quiet life of his convent on the mountain. In one of his letters Marc Antonio Flaminio ( ?–1550), a man of true piety and unquestioned morality, a retiring student, put forward the doctrine of justification by faith alone. " The gospel," he said, " is no other than the glad tidings that the only-begotten Son of God, clothed in our flesh, has satisfied for us the justice of the Eternal Father. Whoever believes this enters the kingdom of God; he enjoys the universal forgiveness; from being a carnal creature, he becomes a child of grace and lives in a sweet peace of conscience." This announcement of the Lutheran postulate is certainly clear and explicit. Yet in his preface to his commentary on the psalms Flaminio referred to the pope as " the warder and prince of all holiness, the vice-regent of God upon earth."

The Italian version of the doctrine of justification by faith alone received its best and most popular expression in a little book called *The benefit of Christ's death*. Its authorship has been ascribed to various persons, including Juan Valdés, but the consensus of the most recent opinion is that it is the work of Benedetto of Mantua, a Benedictine monk, that he wrote it in his convent at the foot of Mount Etna, and that at his request Flaminio revised it both in subject-matter and in style. It was circulated at first in manuscript and then in printed form. " It treats in an insidious manner of justification," says a report of the Inquisition; " under-valuing works and merits, it ascribes all to faith; and as this is the very point upon which so many prelates and monks are stumbling, the book has been widely circulated." So eager and wide-spread was the demand for the book that, so it is said, more than 40,000 copies were printed in the one city of Venice; and so thoroughly and ruthlessly did the Inquisition carry on a campaign of extirpation against it that it was thought every copy had been destroyed until in 1855 one, bearing the name of Paleario, was found in the library of the University of Cambridge. It seems to be the voice of a group of like-minded associates rather than that of an individual; and it endeavors to strike a compromise between the one extreme of justification by faith alone and the other of justification by works without faith. In this respect it has justly been called the *credo* of the Italian reformers who entertained Protestant ideas.

The hope of the mediating reformers, as we have seen, was frustrated. The division of Christianity had become irreparable.

And the hope of all those spiritual-minded men who, touched with the humanistic temper, desired to see Catholicism not only purged of the immorality of its priests and recalled from its extreme engrossment in worldly affairs but also broadened and liberalized was likewise doomed to disappointment. For, instead of becoming more liberal, the Papacy put aside the indifference of the Renaissance period and became ruthless and relentless in its persecution of all that savored of heresy. At the instigation of the inhuman Caraffa, ardently seconded by Loyola, the bull *Licet ab initio,* July 21, 1542, was issued for the purpose of reorganizing the Roman Inquisition in a manner similar to that of Spain. Caraffa was its first head. It presupposed the fact that the existing local inquisitions in Italy and elsewhere were unable to cope with the situation. It was intended to have a wide jurisdiction and to be an effective instrument for the carrying out of the rapidly extending and sinister designs of the Papacy. For sometime after its reorganization it was inefficiently administered and remained unprovided with the necessary secular support. But it was not destined to remain thus comparatively impotent. Later on it gained the fearful repute of making the most frightful and terrible decisions upon earth; and so effective did it become that long before the century was ended all the contaminating seeds of heresy had been stamped out of the peninsula, and their most important expression, the widely distributed *Sui benefizii della morte di Cristo,* was thought to have been utterly destroyed.

Of the many who suffered persecution and death at the hands of the revived Inquisition we have space to mention only two. Pietro Carnesecchi (1508–68) was a Florentine of noble birth who became an influential private secretary to Clement VII. After the death of that pontiff he entered secular life. The turning point of his career was his meeting with Valdés in Naples. He accepted the Spanish scholar as his spiritual guide.

He was a broad-minded man who believed the fundamental Lutheran doctrine with the customary Italian reservation that he did not entirely discard the efficacy of good works. After trial and acquittal, subsequent imprisonment and escape, after years of wandering in France and Italy, consorting everywhere with heretics, inclining now toward Calvinism and now toward Lutheranism, he was put on trial once more, this time in Rome, and after a stubborn defense he was beheaded and burned. Aonio Paleario (1500–70), though of a complaining and somewhat quarrelsome disposition, was a great scholar, interested in doctrinal reform, who taught with success in many of the important towns in northern Italy. Oblivious or unmindful of danger he continued to publish heretical views and to correspond with cismontane reformers after his interrupted trial in Siena for heresy. In 1570, in the presence of the implacable Pius V, who himself had been an inquisitor, he was condemned as an impenitent heretic and shortly afterwards he was strangled and burned in Rome.

In addition to all those who suffered death either for the particular doctrines they cherished or for the cause of liberty of thought itself, there were other Italians who escaped the clutches of the Inquisition and spent the remainder of their years in exile. The number of these refugees was very considerable. In many places in Switzerland and in some of the German cities they formed independent congregations. Still others were to be found in France, in England, and in the Slavonic lands. The most notable in some respects of these exiles was Bernardino Ochino (1487–1565) of Siena, vicar-general of the Capuchins and Italy's most eloquent and beloved preacher. He was won over to the new ideas by his association with Valdés at Naples. Multitudes flocked to hear him in the various cities in which he preached. The churches were too small to hold the crowds. Young and old, men and women, scholars and peasants, pressed eagerly to listen to his message. Clad in the rough garment of his order, his body enfeebled by fasting and his face illumined by his ardor, he had the aspect of a saint. " He who hath made thee without thine help," he asked, " shall He not also save thee without thine aid?" For some time under suspicion, he was summoned in 1542 to appear before the Inquisition at Rome. On his way thither he stopped to visit the dying Contarini at Bologna; and, meeting with Vermigli in Florence, the two, convinced of their danger, fled to Switzerland. At Geneva and Zürich and Basel he became the pastor of congregations of Italian fugitives. But his emotional temperament and his radical views did not permit him to stay long in any one place. After preaching at Strasburg he accepted Cranmer's invitation to go to England. In London he became the pastor of the Italians who attended the Strangers' Church. He stayed in England three years and then returned to Zürich. From thence he was driven out because in a volume of religious dialogues he had permitted one of the interlocutors to question the doctrine of the Trinity and to uphold the lawfulness of polygamy. He died on reaching Moravia, almost seventy-eight years old. Peter-Martyr Vermigli (1500–62) had been prior of the great convent of the Austin canons at Naples and visitor-general of the order. He, too, had come under the influence of Valdés. In 1541 he went to Lucca where he gathered about him a congenial group of scholars. The attendance at his Sunday sermons continually increased, and upon his hearers, as we have seen, he enjoined participation in the Eucharist merely as a commemoration of the sacrifice of the cross. Within a single year no less than eighteen members of his order left Lucca and put themselves in safety beyond the Alps. After his flight to Switzerland he was invited to England by Cranmer where he exercised a great influence at Oxford and in the English episcopacy. Another notable exile was Pierpaolo Vergerio, a Venetian lawyer who became an important figure in the papal diplomatic service. After being elevated to the episcopate he continued to act as an agent of the Papacy pursuing simultaneously and aggressively plans for reform and schemes for his personal advancement. In France he met Margaret of Navarre and in Germany he came into contact with Melanchthon. At the diet of Worms he admitted the existence of grave abuses in the Church, but pleaded earnestly for union. Then he went to his diocese of Capo d' Istria, where he endeavored to eradicate the ecclesiastical evils. The reading of heretical literature filled his mind with doubt. When suspicion resulted in accusation he laid his case before the Council of Trent, but that body forbade him to return to his bishopric. At the close of 1548 he made known his determination to secede from the Church and this brought about his deposition and excommunication. He fled to the Grisons, taking with him the manuscript of Valdés's *One Hundred and Ten Divine Considerations*. This, with a prefatory commendation by Curione, he was instrumental in having printed and published at Basel. The last nine years of his life were spent at Württemberg where he created the impression of being a self-seeking and a disappointed man. Ludovico Castelvetro (1505–1571) was one of the members of the academy at Modena who were suspected of heresy. A papal brief was issued for his arrest on the ground of having translated into Italian the writings of Melanchthon. Later on he was persuaded to go to Rome to submit himself to trial, but before the trial was concluded he fled with his brother to Chiavenna, where he lived until his death. The Piedmontese scholar Celio Secondo Curione (1503–69) was one of the members of the group gathered about the duchess Renée at Ferrara. Previous to that he had been for three years a professor in the University of Padua and had lived in Venice. With the assistance of Renée he became one of the teachers whom Vermigli established in Lucca, when, as prior of the convent of San Frediano, the latter secured quasi-episcopal rights in that city. More daring than Vermigli he delayed his departure from Lucca until after the escape of his master. He waited, indeed, until the sheriff came to arrest him. Then, being of large and powerful physique, he cut his way through the police, jumped upon a horse, rode away, and reached Switzerland in safety. Another important exile was Valentino Gentile (1520–56) whose religious views with those of others of his countrymen came under the suspicion of Calvin at Geneva. He signed a Calvinistic confession of faith, but he afterwards retracted and eventually was beheaded at Bern for his relapse into his obnoxious opinions. Two other notable exiles, with whom we shall deal in the next chapter, were the Socini, Lelio (1525–62), and Fausto (1539–1604) his nephew.

The possibility was always slight that Protestant ideas could find a fruitful soil in Spain in the sixteenth century. The intensity of the Spanish character had produced religious convictions that were as unreasoning as they were profound. In the earlier centuries of the Middle Ages the Spanish peoples had been tolerant in their dealings with Jew and with infidel. In the protracted re-conquest of the peninsula religious zeal had played but a slight part. In the days of the Cid there were included in each of the contending armies both Christians and Moslems. Between the opposing armies there were frequently concluded, in open violation of the commands of the Church, alliances and treaties providing for freedom of trade and intercourse. The Spaniards of those days appear not to have been over-scrupulous in religious matters; they displayed little fanaticism. But the crusading era increased their religious ardor. Intolerance spread abroad in the land. A fierce and unrelenting persecution of all faiths other than Catholicism came to prevail. When the Spanish prelates returned from the Council of Vienne in 1312 they brought with them not only hostile

Effect of
The Perpetual
Crusade
upon the
Spanish
Character

canons against the Jews and Moors but also the persecuting spirit
that had produced them. The gradual re-conquest of Spanish
districts from the Moors had resulted in the presence of large
numbers of Jews and infidels in Christian territory. Under the
stimulation of the Church the old indifference to these masses
outside her fold gave place to a deep and implacable hatred.

**Backward Condition of Spanish Civilization**

The long struggle with the Moors had confirmed the feudal
character of the Spanish nobility, rendered it disinclined to adapt
itself to the changed commercial conditions of the time. Exalted pride discouraged participation in either commerce or manufacture. Oppressive taxation ruined industry and agriculture.
The burghers were denied all chance for progress in political,
social, commercial, and industrial matters. The peasantry were
sunk in profound ignorance. The wealth of the Indies poured
through Spain as water through a sieve. The fundamental ideas
of the Renaissance failed to take root in the peninsula, and those
of the Protestant Revolution fared even worse. The country
remained attached to the theological ideas of the Age of Faith.

**Dependency of the Church upon the State**

In Spain the Church was much more dependent upon the
State than elsewhere in the Catholic lands. Castile, in particular,
had always displayed its independence of the Papacy. It had
often refused to obey the canon law and it had persistently declined to permit the medieval Inquisition to obtain a footing in
its territory. Everywhere throughout Spain the secular power
insisted upon the right to appoint to ecclesiastical office, though
in tumultuous times the claim was not always carried out in
practice. Even such pious monarchs as Ferdinand and Isabella
upheld the claims of the secular power in these matters. Both
the cortes and the monarch legislated regarding ecclesiastical
subjects. The jurisdiction of the Church courts was curtailed in
open defiance of canon and decretal. Far less than elsewhere
were clerics immune from the operation of the secular law in
Spain; while the laity were safe-guarded from many of the
claims of the canonical courts. Even this was not all. The
secular power asserted its right to intervene in matters within
the Church itself. It interfered in such matters as the correction
of clerical immorality and the manner of celebrating the mass.
Thus was the Church in Spain subjugated to the State in an unparalleled degree.

**Ximenes and his Reform**

In Spain, as well as in Italy, there were men who desired to
effect a reformation within the Church and who devoted themselves to the accomplishment of their plans. Chief of them was
a Franciscan friar, Cardinal Francisco Ximenes de Cisneros
(1436–1517) who, as archbishop of Toledo, proceeded ener-

getically, and with the support of the monarchy, to stamp out Mohammedanism in his diocese and to fulfil the earliest traditions of his order by eradicating the immorality of the clergy. So vigorous were his measures that monks and friars fled before his approaching visitations to their convents. Appeals were made to the pope, but only with temporary success, against so hard a master. The indomitable spirit of the imperious reformer prevailed. Monasteries were deprived of their " privileges," and their members were disciplined. Parish priests who were unfit for their office were replaced by others whose character and zeal were tried and approved. So great was the reform that the morality of the Spanish monks and friars was greatly superior to that of the clergy in any other country of western Europe. But the work of Ximenes was not permanent. With his death it began to disappear.

When the government began its policy of eradicating heresy it was inevitable that the State should have control of the instruments of persecution. The Inquisition, which was established in 1480, was a national institution controlled by the State far more than by the Papacy. Ferdinand and Isabella saw to it that it was kept under governmental control as much as possible. In accordance with this policy a new office, not found in the preceding Inquisition, that of the inquisitor-general, was created. To this important position there was appointed the confessor of the two sovereigns, Thomás de Torquemada, a tireless and a pitiless man, to whose activity the extension of the institution throughout Spain and the improvement of its organization were due. Adapted to meet the requirements of its environment the Spanish Inquisition soon came to dominate the conscience of every individual. It made its own laws subject only to the infrequent interference of the Papacy and to the unexacting control of the crown. The arm of the State was ever-ready to enforce its will. Its summary procedure disregarded all recognized law, and its operations were veiled in impenetrable secrecy. Thus, equipped with its perfect organization, clothed with the dread authority of the Church, and armed with the power of the secular government, did it, for three centuries, eviscerate the material, the intellectual, and the spiritual life of Spain. Ferdinand desired the Inquisition to proceed with justice according to the standard of the time; but after his death, " in the turmoil and absences of Charles V and the secluded labors of Philip II over despatches and consultas," it became practically independent of the crown. It had exclusive jurisdiction over all things pertaining directly or indirectly to matters of faith; and in the

The Spanish Inquisition

wide field of civil and criminal affairs it could take what action it saw fit. Not the humblest of its servants was subject to local laws and regulations. It judged all, but was itself judged by none. Its spies were everywhere, and they were assured of immunity by the denial to the accused of the right to learn the name of his accuser. At the head of the organization was the inquisitor-general. Then there was a consultative body, the Suprema, which eventually became its ruling power. The country was divided into districts. Each district had its own local tribunal. In theory all these tribunals were subject to the Suprema, but the supervision of that distant body was at best imperfect. The local tribunal, practically a law unto itself, represented the Inquisition to the people. Each tribunal had its special building containing its prison. The tribunals derived their financial support from the fines and penances they imposed, from fees for dispensations, from ecclesiastical offices, obtained for their members, and, above all else, from the confiscation of the property of their victims.

One of the most important of the functions of the Inquisition was its censorship of the press. No book could safely be printed, imported, or offered for sale, without its permission. **The Censure** The censure was stringent, and it did much to stop the development of civilization in Spain. Against culture and learning there was waged an unrelenting warfare. The most heterodox of heresies and the most inconsequent of opinions were included in the disapprobation. So rigorous was the repression of native thought and so complete was the exclusion of foreign ideas that the intellectual and artistic development of the country was checked and then " stunted and starved into atrophy." Africa, ran the significant saying, began at the Pyrénées.

The original purpose of the Spanish Inquisition was the extirpation of the Jewish and Moorish faiths; but with the spread of suspicious doctrines among the Christians it began to turn its **The Spanish Mystics** energies in a new direction. About the first half of the sixteenth century mysticism and illuminism began their development in Spain. In our study of the revival of conscience we have seen that mysticism by bringing the individual into direct relation with God lessens the dependence upon the sacraments and other ministrations of the Church. Because of this fact the Inquisition became determined to root out this potential peril. At first an attempt was made to distinguish between the mysticism that might safely be tolerated and that which was seemingly hostile in spirit to the Church. But this, if not impossible, was exceedingly difficult. So it came about that the simplest forms of mysticism, as well as the advanced theories of illuminism and quietism, gradually became subject to the persecution of the Inquisition. Yet mysticism, in spite of this, grew apace and became deeply rooted in the Spanish character. The country became steeped in its atmosphere. Its exaggerations gave expression to the religious fervor of the people. In Santa Teresa (1515–82), Fray Luis de Leon (1528–91), and San Juan de la Cruz (1542–91) it attained its highest level of spirituality,— the sunset glow of medieval Catholicism. But even Santa Teresa was secluded in a convent and narrowly escaped transportation to the Indies; and her most famous follower, San Juan de la Cruz, was several times accused before the Inquisition.

The first distinct traces of heresy in Spain were probably those due to the influence of Erasmus. Charles V was an admirer of Erasmus and when the emperor returned to Spain in 1522 the influence of the great humanist was at its height. Nobles and clergy who had leanings toward culture read his works. The patronage of several popes and of numbers of princes seemed to stamp his opinions with authoritative approval. About 1526 his *Enchiridion* was translated into Spanish and it enjoyed an extensive circulation. So widely were his views diffused throughout the peninsula that Erasmus became convinced that Spain was to be the land in which a reformation without "tumult" would be accomplished. Gradually, however, there was developed a party opposed to him and his teachings. His scholarship was disparaged, his earnestness questioned, and his orthodoxy impugned. The *Erasmitas* secured a bull from Clement VII enjoining silence upon their opponents. But Charles left Spain in 1529 and took with him some of the most important of the followers of the great humanist and from that time his party began to decline and that of his rivals correspondingly to increase. Among the Spanish scholars who owned the leadership of Erasmus was Luis Vives (1492–1540) who, at his master's suggestion, edited Augustine's *De Civitate Dei*. He became a professor at Louvain. After that he lived in England for some years and from thence returned to Spain. He finally settled in the Low Countries; and at Bruges, where he died, he devoted himself to works against the scholastic philosophy and the preponderating authority of Aristotle. Alfonso Valdés (1400?–1532), the twin brother of Juan, was one of the emperor's secretaries, the one employed upon occasions when scholarly ability was specially required. He was a personal friend of Erasmus, with whom he corresponded; and when the Spanish ecclesiastics made a violent attack upon the writings of the famous scholar and endeavored to have them prohibited by the Inquisition he successfully exercised his influence to prevent such a proscription. He was more Erasmian, said his friends, than Erasmus. His career was cut short by his death from the plague at Vienna. To the teachings of Juan Valdés at Naples we have already paid some attention. Perhaps the foremost among the Erasmists who remained in Spain was Juan de Vergara (1492–1557), a man renowned for his culture and scholarly attainments, whom we have already noticed in our study of Spanish humanism. Ximenes appointed him professor of philosophy in the University of Alcalá and employed him upon the great Polyglot Bible. He helped to lay the foundations of historical criticism. When the reaction against Erasmus set in he was imprisoned for four years. His brother, Francisco de Vergara (?–1545), was also a scholar who came under the influence of Erasmus. He was the author of the first Greek-Spanish grammar, and he translated Heliodorus into his native tongue. Alonso de Virués was another Spanish humanist who suffered for his devotion to Erasmus. He was the favorite preacher of Charles V and it was envy of his position that inspired the charges made against him. Passages that smacked of heresy were picked from his sermons and quoted against him. For four years he remained in prison and then in 1537 having been required to abjure the views pronounced heretical he was secluded in a convent. But in the following year the emperor obtained from the pope a brief that set the sentence aside.

So deep and fanatical were the religious feelings and beliefs of the mass of the Spanish people in the sixteenth century that there never was any prospect that the Protestant ideas would get a firm footing in the peninsula. The spread of heresy was comparatively unimportant and it never constituted a real danger to Catholicism. Yet here and there were to be found Spaniards who accepted the fundamental doctrine of Lutheranism. The earliest action of the Inquisition to check the spread of the Protestant ideas was probably taken in 1527; but for some years the efforts of that institution to stamp out Lutheranism was limited to foreigners. Every divergence, no matter how slight, from the established usages or dogmas, and even casual speech that savored of heterodoxy, was classified by the Inquisition as "Lutheranism." Yet despite this fact very few cases of Protestantism were brought to light. This in itself is proof of the fact that Protestantism made little impression south of the Pyrénées. Only a few individuals, most of whom had lived in more northern lands, can be said to have been inoculated with the germs of heresy. The first Spaniard about whose heresy there is apparently no doubt was Francisco de San-Roman (?–1542) of Burgos. His business affairs obliged him to live in the Netherlands for some years and then they sent him to Bremen where he became a Lutheran. So ardently was he devoted to his new faith that at Ratisbon he attempted to convert the Emperor. He was sent to Spain and there, first of the Spanish Protestants so to suffer because of their faith, he was burned at the stake. Another Spaniard who accepted the doctrine of justification by faith was Juan de Diaz (?–1546) who studied for thirteen years in Paris and subsequently lived for some months in Geneva where he entered into friendly relations with Calvin. In 1546, at the instigation of his brother, he was assassinated in Austria because of his religious views. Jáime de Enzinas (1520?–1547), born at Burgos of wealthy and illustrious parents, was one of Calvin's innumerable correspondents. In 1547 he was burned at Rome. The most ardent wish of his brother, Francisco de Enzinas (1520?–50), was to sit at the feet of Melanchthon. The wish was gratified, for in 1541 he entered the University of Wittenberg and lived in Melanchthon's house. There he was engaged principally in translating the New Testament from the Greek into Spanish. In a treatise that appeared about 1547 he severely criticized the pope and the decrees of the first year of the Council of Trent.

The first place in Spain in which the Lutherans gathered together for the purposes of mutual encouragement, worship, or the planning of a propaganda, was Seville. The first important member of the little Protestant circle in that city was Doctor Egidio (?–1556), the magistral, or preaching, canon of the cathedral who was noted for his scholarship and his eloquence. His teachings and those of Rodrigo de Valero resulted in the formation of the little group. He died in 1556 before the storm burst; though four years later his bones were exhumed and burned. Constantino Ponce de la Fuente (1500–60), a noted Greek and Hebrew scholar who succeeded Egidio as preaching canon of the cathedral, became the next leader. Every inmate of the Geronimite house of San Isidro, one of the meeting places of the circle, became a Lutheran as well as some of the members of the Geronimite nunnery of Santa Paula. The group contained laymen as well as clerics. Indeed, every stratum of society, from nobles to rag-pickers was represented in the increasing circle which eventually numbered about one hundred and twenty members. After a more or less inconsequential inquiry the Inquisition began a second investigation in 1557, and then the prisons began to be populated. The relentless cruelty with which the Jewish and Moslem faiths had been persecuted was now turned against the Protestants. The greater number of the heretics were put to death privately; but at times, when a sufficient number of cases had accumulated, there was held an *auto-de-fé* (an act of faith), a spectacular ceremony, whose culmination was the burning of the condemned, which the Inquisition employed to spread terror in the hearts of the people. It was a great pageant, an impressive public ceremony, that loomed large in the imagination of men. The first of the *autos-de-fé* at Seville, in which fourteen persons were put to death, was held in September, 1559, in the presence, so it seemed, of all Andalusia; a second, in which ten persons suffered martyrdom, was held in December, 1560; and a third in April, 1562. Thus was Protestantism in Seville almost completely eradicated.

While the investigation was going on in Seville a similar group of Lutherans was brought to light in Valladolid at which place the court was then residing. It was through the efforts of Carlos de Seso, an Italian who had been won over to the Lutherean doctrine about 1550, perhaps by the writings of Juan de Valdés, that heresy began to spread abroad in the temporary capital. The most important conversion was made when Pedro Cazalla (1524–59), and his sister, Beatriz de Vivero, induced their brother Doctor Augustin Cazalla (1510–59), to accept the Protestant ideas. He was the favorite preacher of Charles V, who once had taken him to Germany, and he wielded a great influence in every stratum of society. Next to him the most important acquisition to the heretical group was probably that of Domingo de Rojas (1519–59), a Dominican friar, who enjoyed a wide reputation for his learning and his eloquence. His conversion was followed by that of his brother and also by that of his nephew who was the heir to the marquisate of Pozo. Men of all ranks, from the highest to the lowest, were included in the little band; though at the most they probably did not number more than three score. Strangely enough the propaganda was carried on for two or three years without its being detected. The first *auto-de-fé* for the punishment of heresy in Spain was held in May, 1559, in the Plaza Mayor. Fifteen persons were committed to the flames. At the second *auto* held in Valladolid, at which Philip II himself was present, thirteen persons were burnt. The discovery at Seville did not create much excitement; but this one at the court, in which a number of eminent persons were involved, seemed most foreboding. Then, too, Valdés, the inquisitor-general, made the most of it. He was about to be disgraced and so he seized the opportunity of the discovery, magnified the danger, and caused it to create a far greater impression upon the court than did the more serious situation at Seville. Isolated cases of heresy were discovered and punished from time to time, though more and more they were found to be of foreign origin.

There were a number of translations of the Bible into Spanish and the various dialects of the peninsula. One into Catalan, made by Bonifacio Ferrer, was printed in 1478 in Valencia. Then Francisco de Enzinas, as we have seen, translated the New Testament into Spanish. Juan Perez, as we shall see, made a similar translation; while Cipriano de Valera and Cassiodoro de Reina did not a little to perfect the Spanish version of the Scriptures. The use made by the heretics of the Bible in the vernacular caused it to be prohibited by the Index of 1551 which placed the ban even upon fragments and extracts, no matter how orthodox the translation. Yet despite all the precautions of the Inquisition many copies were smuggled into the country.

Among the Spanish Protestants who succeeded in escaping from their country was Juan Perez (1500?–1567) who had been the rector of the College of Doctrine in Seville, a municipal institution devoted to the education of youth. For four years he poured forth many writings from Geneva, including his translation of the New Testament from Greek into Spanish, many copies of which were smuggled into Spain. In 1558 the number of refugee Spaniards in Geneva was so large that they were given the use of the church of St. Germain, and Perez was appointed as their preacher. Another notable exile was Cipriano de Valera, one of the friars of San Isidro, who translated Calvin's *Institutes* into Spanish and edited the complete Spanish Bible.

The greatest ecclesiastic in Spain at this time was Bartolomé de Carranza (1503–76), a Dominican friar, renowned for both his learning and his exemplary character, who in 1557 had become archbishop of Toledo, and, therefore, primate of Spain. He aroused the animosity of some bishops whom he compelled to reside in their sees, he incurred the jealousy of Valdés, the inquisitor-general; and Melchor Cano, the greatest Spanish theologian of the time, a member of his own order and greatly superior to him in intellect, regarded him as his rival. So, despite the activity of Carranza against heresy, and despite his many claims to reverence, he was arrested by the Inquisition in 1559 and imprisoned. In some aspects the imprisonment and

The Spanish Bible

The Refugees

Carranza

trial of Carranza was the most important act of the Inquisition. All the eyes of Catholic Europe were turned upon it. Poor Carranza was a muddy thinker and an impulsive speaker. Many of his utterances were interpreted in a manner he had never intended. At a most unfortunate moment he issued his *Commentaries on the Catechism,* a rambling and discursive folio, in which are many statements that, taken by themselves, savor of heresy, but which later on are modified or contradicted. After he was thrown into prison the revenue from his property other than that retained by the Inquisition for the expenses of the trial, was enjoyed by Philip II. Over the trickery of the protracted trial, even were it profitable to do so, there is not time to dwell. After eight years' imprisonment he was taken to Rome at the command of Pius V. The case was not concluded when, five years later, the pope died. Under Gregory XIII the trial was once more resumed. Sixteen propositions extracted from his book were declared to be heretical. These he was required to abjure. A fortnight later, broken in health by seventeen years of imprisonment, the enfeebled prelate suddenly died.

In Portugal there were a few humanists with leanings towards heresy and a number of foreigners whose orthodoxy was doubtful, but there was never any prospect of the success of Protestant ideas. Yet an Inquisition, based upon the Spanish model, was established in that country. Several reasons account for this. The great increase of Portuguese commerce and colonial enterprise drew the peasants from the farms, and, as the merchants were largely exempt from taxation, there were few left to pay the taxes. So, although the Portuguese were the richest people in Europe, the king was daily getting poorer. John III (1526–57) knew that the confiscations in Spain were a prolific source of income and he determined to employ the same expedient. His wife, Catalina, sister of Charles V, also exercised a powerful influence in behalf of an inquisition. On December 17, 1531, the papal bull *Cum ad nihil,* which created the Inquisition of Lisbon, was issued. But the wealthy Jews were able to delay the operation of the institution. In sixteen years the king paid $1,500,000 to the curia to hasten the inquisitorial activity, while the Jews expended even a larger sum, in Lisbon as well as in Rome, to delay it. At last, in 1547, the bull *Meditatio cordis* put the Inquisition under way. Three tribunals, Lisbon, Evora, and Coimbra, were established. Up to 1580 when Philip II conquered the country these tribunals had turned over to the secular authority for death by fire about one hundred and sixty persons, and they had subjected about two thousand others to penance. Yet all this activity had very little to do with Protestantism. Most of it was directed against the Jews. The single heretic of importance with whom it dealt was Damião de Goes (1510?-73), the greatest Portuguese scholar of the century, who, after having lived six years in Antwerp, traveled in Germany, spent some months with Erasmus at Freiburg, and then lived at Padua. In 1545 he returned to Portugal. After being twice unsuccessfully denounced to the Inquisition he was arrested in 1571 upon a third charge and condemned to perpetual imprisonment. The king secured a mitigation of the sentence to seclusion in the convent of Batalha. Not long afterwards he died in his own home. By the time Philip II became master of Portugal all traces of heresy had disappeared, but the process of stunting the intellectual development of the country was continued with increased vigor and the general condition of the people became most deplorable.

There are several reasons why Protestantism gained no real foothold in these Mediterranean lands. The most fundamental one is perhaps to be found in the Latin character. The emotional religion of these Romanic races has always involved less of the ethical element than that of the northern peoples; and it is not so narrowly concerned with dogma. The temper of Italy, Spain, and Portugal differs greatly from that of the Teutonic nations. It requires the stately ritual of the Catholic church in which emotion is embodied in symbolism. The appealing pageantry of bells and music, of flowers and incense, of shimmering vestment and lighted taper, of processions with the crucifix held aloft, of the rosary and of the miracle of the mass, penetrates to the heart even of the confirmed believer in private judgment. Then, as we have seen, the pride of the Italians in the possession of the Papacy, the connection of their material interests with the curia, and the anti-Italian feeling of the German reformers all tended to prevent the favorable reception of the Protestant ideas in the peninsula. Many of the Italians who found themselves unable longer to subscribe to the dogmas of the Church declined to follow either the Lutheran or the Calvinistic movement. Their rationalism, which was, however, in many cases light, flippant, and skeptical, prevented their association with any such new orthodoxies. The majority of the Italians and Iberians were steeped in the old orthodoxy, which, in the case of the latter, sank into fanaticism. They saw in the innovations only danger to their countries. And while the Germans were goaded to desperation by the financial exactions of the Papacy the Spaniards and Portuguese were beginning to loot the treasures of the newly-discovered continent. Some of the mediating reformers of Italy and some of the humanists of Spain leaned perceptibly toward the Protestant heresy. For those who overstepped the bounds of Catholicism and for the heretical foreigners who ventured within the Mediterranean lands there were devised the terrors of the Inquisition.

# CHAPTER XVIII

## THE RESULTS OF THE PROTESTANT REVOLUTION

1. The Results to Faith and Worship (the New State Churches, the Sects, the Growth of Free Thought, the Rise of Tolerance).
2. The Results to Morals.
3. The Results to Education.
4. The Results to Government.
5. The Revolution Incomplete.

WE are to deal here only with the immediate results of the Protestant Revolution, not with its more remote consequences, with its direct results to faith and worship, to morals, to education, and to government.

First, then, as to its immediate results to faith and worship: It produced new state churches — the Lutheran Churches, the Calvinistic Churches, and the Anglican Church. The definite separation between Catholic and Protestants was not simultaneous with the first public appearance of the earliest of the leading reformers. The opinions of the new leaders did not at first take upon themselves a definite character. For a time it seemed not improbable that a compromise between the conflicting doctrines might be concluded. But with the opening of the second quarter of the sixteenth century all reasonable hope of such a reconciliation vanished. Then, in the Lutheran lands, the religion of the individual was made subject to the control of the ruler. Under the direction of the princes and free cities, into whose territory Lutheranism had found its way, territorial churches were organized. The lava stream of religious revolution began to congeal. There were to be as many Lutheran churches as there were Lutheran princes and Lutheran free cities. Princes in their provinces and magistrates in their municipalities assumed control of the outward fabric of the Church and even became directors of its internal life. They decided theological controversies and repressed dissensions with secular force. Lutheranism had to make its way into the definite structure of the social and political order. Having cut itself loose from the sympathy of the masses by its action in the Social Revolution it knew that its future depended very largely upon the success with which it conciliated the various rulers. So it set up no united

343

church.  Instead there were some two hundred separate constitutions of churches that subscribed to the Augsburg Confession.
Such was the consequence of the alienation of the people and the
particularism of the princes.  But there is one other cause to be
considered.  For a long time, as we have seen, the Lutheran
reformers attempted to maintain their allegiance to the Mother
Church.  It is true they adopted a reformed constitution; but
they always counted upon a future decision in their favor by a
general council.  They therefore regarded the organization of
their followers as but a temporary matter.  The numerous
Lutheran churches naturally had certain uniform characteristics,
and the degree of their dependence upon the State varied but
slightly from one province to another.  Their theologians and
preachers were merely advisers to their respective princes and
magistrates, in the Scandinavian countries as well as in the
German States.  This condition of affairs, so Capito declared in
1540, had been willed by Christ himself.  "The prince is the
shepherd," he said, "the father, the head of the Church on
earth."  But it was a condition that reduced spiritual freedom
to the minimum.  Under the dominion of political rulers the
democratic beginnings of Lutheranism were forgotten.  The attempt to return to the original condition of the primitive Christian community was resigned when the compromise with the
princes was concluded.  And this identification with the particularism of the time hindered the spread of the new faith in
Teutonic lands and caused the splendid promise of its birth to
degenerate into a condition that was in many respects petty and
unedifying.

There were, likewise, a number of Calvinistic churches.  In
addition to that of Geneva there was a church in France, one
in the northern provinces of the Netherlands, one in Scotland,
others in the Zwinglian cantons of Switzerland, where Calvin's
teaching was gradually superseding that of the Swiss reformer,
and still others in certain of the provinces and free cities in
central and southern Germany.  In these widely scattered
churches there was to be found a variety of discipline and even
of doctrine.  Zürich, for instance, declined to accept the austere
discipline of Geneva and modified its doctrinal system; and
Basel always regarded with disfavor the importance attached to
the doctrine of predestination.  Among the German States in
which Calvinism came to prevail were the Palatinate, Nassau,
Anhalt, Hesse-Cassel, and a number of smaller principalities.
Most of them issued separate and distinctive confessions of

faith, many of which were compromises between the Lutheran and the Calvinistic creeds.

The English revolt from Rome, in its method and its results, was unique. It was the work of a ruler and not of a reformer. It had, therefore, no well-defined system of theology, but one that resulted from the operation of a number of minds, one that while failing to give complete satisfaction to any one was found acceptable without serious difficulty by many. " A government," it has been well said, " always tries to strike an average, the Tudors did so in England; but an average is anathema to all extremes." It was the State, in England, and not the Church that was the paramount power. The State compelled the religious revolt. Only gradually was acquiescence in the change secured. The Anglican Church was frankly at the outset merely a transfer of authority from the pope to the king despite the fact that its government was carried on through ecclesiastical officials.

An irresistible tide of genuine religious change had swept across central and northern Europe; but the various Lutheran and Calvinistic organizations and that of the Anglicans were all essentially state churches. Was this due solely to political and economic causes? Did it come about solely from the fact that the various princes and magistrates with unanimity of purpose and tactful procedure took possession of ecclesiastical property and then as a result found themselves forced to assume the direction of the religious life of their subjects? Rightly or wrongly it is to such naked considerations that the erection of these state churches has been attributed.

The rise of a body of state churches was only one of the results of the Protestant Revolution to faith and worship. Another such result was the up-springing of multitudinous sects all of which were inspired and sustained by the dream of establishing a community of saints in the midst of the errors and corruption of a degraded world. On all sides the state churches were washed by the waves of more or less formless religious convictions. The leading reformers had substituted for the authority of the medieval church the authority of the Bible. In pictures of the sixteenth century may be seen men holding in their closed, strong-willed hands a copy of the Bible. The whole consciousness of primitive Protestantism is there expressed. But who was to determine with certainty the true meaning of the sacred texts? The reformers did not foresee what multitudinous interpretations of the biblical writings would arise. Yet it was inevitable that so heterogeneous a book should furnish the bases for the most divergent doctrines and serve as the authority for widely sundered systems. Every man could find there confirmation of doctrinal convictions born in his own heart. There, too, could he find the expression of his own moral ideas. It was not difficult in the Age of Faith to silence dissent. Terror was a most effective weapon in those days. Whatever real differences existed were often disguised beneath outward conformity to conventional symbols. But when men began really to think, it was inevitable that they should think differently. Intellectual freedom brought in its train " doubt and debate and sharp dissension " and unanimity became a thing of the past. Each one of the innumerable sects to which the individual interpretation of the scriptural writings gave rise deemed itself to be a return to primitive Christianity. But in reality each was a new and spontaneous theology. The illusion in each case failed to penetrate to the secret of the authentic and moving power of every new religion that leaves its impress upon the life of man — the renewed and varied embodiment of the ideals of the human heart, their explicit communication, and their expression in the life of the faithful. It was among the masses that these sects were formed. Everywhere groups of common folk followed logically the postulates of the new teaching, took literally Luther's preaching of the universal priesthood, and found inspiration and model in the Waldenses. They organized, of course, in a multiplication of forms, and were alike only in the growing belief that every man ripe enough for judgment should be free to choose his own faith. Absolute individualism was beginning to find champions. It seemed as though there were almost as many sects as cities and gospels as gossips.

Chief among these groups, these " Ultras of the Reformation," were those of the Anabaptists, who first appear about 1522–23 in Switzerland. Their name, which appeared later, was due to their foes, to a wish to bring them under the penalty of death prescribed by the old Roman law of the Empire for a heresy of that name. The postponement of baptism until the individual was able to decide for himself, or the rebaptizing of the individual when he had become able to reason, was with them but a secondary article of faith. Far more fundamental was their belief that revelation did not cease with the completion of the New Testament, but that day by day the word of God is revealed to man, that the divine revelation is vouchsafed to every individual, and that it is the only guide to be followed in the conduct of life. " I esteem Holy Scripture," said Hans Denck, the most reasonable and the kindest-hearted of all the reformers of his century, " above all human treasures, but not so highly as the Word of God which is living, powerful, eternal, free and independent of all elements of this world: for as it is God Himself, so it is spirit and not letter, and written without pen and paper, so that it can never more be blotted out." With such a principle for material the self-reliant and dreamy Teuton could weave many a curious fabric. Upon such a basis many a fanciful structure could be erected. So it is not a matter of surprise that among the Anabaptists there should be developed many heterogeneous tendencies. The contemporary Sebastian Franck tells us that he never found two of them who agreed with each other upon all points. Among these various tendencies the two principal ones may be called respectively the spiritualistic and the mystical tendency. Both of them started from the idea of continuous revelation. But the former declared the communications of God to be intermittent, to come only from time to time in visions, ecstasies, and other similar abnormal emotional states; while the latter declared the voice of God to be ever audible in the heart of man. Their fundamental postulates made them anathema to Wittenberg, Zürich, Geneva, and to Rome alike. Some of them held that direct communion with God made all learning unnecessary, and set their seal of disapproval upon recourse to law, upon the taking of oaths, upon the holding of civil office, and upon the possession of private property. Thus such Anabaptists as held these views made for social revolution. Their teachings were regarded as a deadly miasma, the master menace of the time; the name of " Anabaptist " became a common term of opprobrium, and rulers everywhere became bent upon their extinction.

The Anabaptists had many leaders. Some were men of high and scholarly attainments, and of these Balthasar Hubmaier (1480?–1528) was the foremost. Hubmaier had been a professor of theology in the University of Ingolstadt, its vice-rector, and probably its actual director. He was an eloquent preacher, and a man of exalted character, a man as well-fitted for leadership as either Luther or Zwingli. After leaving Ingolstadt he became a preacher at Ratisbon and then at Waldshut. From the latter place he made excursions across the Rhine and came into contact with some of the Swiss reformers. Gradually he changed his religious views and left the papal fold. Later on, about 1525, he became an Anabaptist. To escape the Austrians he fled to Zürich, where, with the connivance of Zwingli, he was imprisoned and tortured in order to compel him to recant his radical beliefs. When he was set free he went to Moravia, from whence, two years later, he was taken to Vienna and burned at the stake. Hans Denck (?–1527) had studied at the University of Basel and then found employment in one of the printing establishments of that city. From there he went to Nuremberg, a center of humanism and a forum of religious discussion, where he gradually became a heretic theologian. Differing on the subject of the eucharist from the chief pastor of the place he was expelled from the city. Then he led a roving life, engaging everywhere he went, with no little learning and skill, in theological disputation, and producing by his eloquence a religious revival. In the three years into which his activity as a religious leader was compressed he exerted a deep and wide-spread influence not only by his learning and his eloquence but also by his tender and sterling character. "He was a quiet, withdrawn, and pious man," said Sebastian Franck, "the leader and bishop of the Anabaptists." Worn out with his wanderings he returned to Basel to die. No other reformer of his time did so much to emancipate religion from the bonds of theology. "I ask no other result, God knows," he said, "than that as many men as possible should with one heart and voice glorify the God and Father of our Lord Jesus Christ, whether they be circumcised, or baptized, or neither; for I differ greatly from those, whoever they may be, who too much bind down the kingdom of God to ceremonies and elements of the world." Had he lived longer he might perhaps have become a constructive religious leader of the first rank and have exercised a due control over the disintegrating forces of Anabaptism. Little is known of the early history of Melchior Hofmann (1498?–1533), a Swabian furrier, who after preaching "the true gospel" in Scandinavian lands and on the southern shores of the Baltic, and sowing there the seeds of social revolution, left those lands for central and southern Germany and the northern Netherlands, inspiring millenarian hopes in the hearts of his followers. Among the most prominent of Hofmann's disciples was Jan Mathys (?–1534), a baker of Haarlem, who announced himself as the Enoch of the new régime. He chose twelve apostles to carry on a propaganda in the neighboring provinces. Chief of these was Jan of Leyden (?–1535), a wandering tailor whose travels had extended "from Lübeck to Lisbon," a licentious rogue, a cruel fanatic, audacious, skilful, and brave. After these men met their death, David Joris (1501–

56), a glass-painter of Delft, became a leader among the Anabaptists by reason of the fact that he succeeded in bringing the various divisions in the Low Countries to a working agreement, although even there they were never unified. Yet it was not long before his followers fell into two groups, one of which lived a decorous life while members of the other abandoned themselves to fanatical excesses, especially promiscuous sexual indulgence.

Under such leaders it was that the varied and often conflicting views that have been given the misleading general term of Anabaptism rapidly spread in Germany, Switzerland, and Holland, finding themselves welcome everywhere by the oppressed classes, forming isolated groups that obeyed no central direction either for defense or offense, requiring the acceptance of no general creed, permitting the greatest variety of practice, and, unhappily, sometimes mingling with their message of the value of spiritual intuition and the consecration of daily life a fanatical or an immoral strain. Their fundamental idea was one far in advance of their age, a truth that is slowly but surely winning its way in the world of men.

The Anabaptists were subjected to incredible persecution. A contemporary was able to say that such streams of Anabaptist blood were shed for the sake of religion " that if so much blood of beasts had been poured forth, men would undoubtedly have been horrified. . . . More than thirty thousand men in some thirty years have been killed for their religion by the command of one single man." Everywhere from the Baltic to the Alps, from Hungary to Holland, they were slaughtered like sheep after being subjected to the cruelest torture. " Like owls and bitterns," were those in Moravia who escaped, says a contemporary chronicle; " they dared not go abroad by day, but lived and crouched in rocks and caverns, in wild forest, in caves and pits." It was at Münster that a revolutionary program of a remnant of the Anabaptists left by the rigorous persecution received a formidable demonstration. Gaining the concession of legal security in the city, some of the surviving Anabaptists made thousands of additional converts there, and were reinforced by crowds of their fellow-believers who came pouring in from Holland and the near-by German towns. With the " saints " came many a sinner seeking to profit by the promised distribution of property. Mathys went there and later Jan of Leyden. It was very largely if not entirely under the stress of the long siege to which the city was subjected that the vagaries of some of the most reckless were perpetrated. The goods of the unbelieving were confiscated, the accessories of ritualistic worship were destroyed, simplicity of wearing apparel was enjoined, and, though not without opposition on the part of those who did not desire to see their morality thus polluted (opposition that resulted in bloodshed) polygamy was practised by some of the leaders. All of these things were intended to prepare for the impending coming of Christ. It was this idea of the approaching advent of the Nazarene, a belief common to the time, together with a reign of terror established by Jan of Leyden, that enabled the Anabaptists in Münster to endure the miseries of a siege of sixteen months. At last, by means of treachery, the desolate town was taken, many of the defenders were slaughtered, and Jan of Leyden, after being publicly tortured in the market-place, was put to death. The various divisions of the dispersed Anabaptists gradually sloughed off the undesirable elements of their beliefs, and in the succeeding centuries their teachings have given rise to many religious groups characterised by notable spiritual power.

The Revolution gave a powerful impetus to thought upon religious matters. Such thought carried men far. It was not possible to put a limit to a movement that was itself illimitable. Individuality had broken through the fetters of authority and tradition. Who could say to the individual: Thus far shalt thou go, but no further? It is not surprising, then, that we come upon tendencies that went beyond the bounds of Protestantism. Among the radical dissenters from the creeds of the established churches were the " Anti-Trinitarians," whose heresies were called Arianism until they became known as Socinianism. Theirs was a rationalistic stream of thought that flowed into central Europe from the south. Refugees from the Mediterranean lands found their way up the valley of the Rhone and over the passes of the Alps seeking a place in which their views would be tolerated, but finding it only in the remote countries that lay on the outskirts of civilization, in Poland and Transylvania. They found Geneva, as well as other centers of Protestantism, to be no harbor of refuge but merely a citadel of theology equal in its intolerance to that from which they had fled. All of them were highly educated and cultured men, physicians, lawyers and teachers. Endowed with a strong sense of individuality, caring nothing for historic continuity, they broke completely with all of the established churches, and apparently had no great desire to organize the loose band of followers that gathered about each of them into a definite church. A hymn of our own day gives voice to their faith.

Anti-Trinitarianism

" One thought I have, my ample creed,
So deep it is and broad,
And equal to my every need,—
It is the thought of God."

Being essentially individual and intellectual, their ideas did not make a wide appeal. Their speculations were by no means entirely new. Very early in the history of Christianity men with similar thoughts, Sabellians and Arians, had appeared; and a long though intermittent line of them may be traced through the Middle Ages.

Among the earliest of these bold and wandering heretics was Campanus (1500?–1578), who sought by means of the figure of marriage to make the mystery of the Trinity intelligible. There are in God, he said, but two persons, the Father and the Son, and they are united each with the other as are husband and wife in matrimony. The pathetic story of Servetus (1511?–53) has already been told. It is not with the fate of this solitary thinker that we are here concerned but with his faith, a strange commingling of rationalism and mysticism. His rationalism was that of the Latin heretic; his mysticism was derived from Neo-Platonism. His conception of God was essentially pantheistic. Jesus, he believed, was the son of God. In him the essence of the Godhead was actually and bodily present. But the existence of the Galilean began with his earthly conception and birth. Previous to that his personality existed only in the mind of God. Matteo Gribaldo ( ?–1564), a jurist from Padua who was a resident of Geneva when Servetus was put to death, incurred the wrath of Calvin by his outspoken condemnation of the judicial murder. He could conceive the divine nature, he said, only as two Gods, the one deriving his existence from the other. For this opinion he was driven into exile. Valentino Gentile (1520–66) had also, in the words of Calvin, " drunk dirty water from the Servetian puddle." He was compelled to recant, to burn his own writings, and to swear not to leave Geneva without official permission. But he escaped. After leading a wandering life he was captured in Savoy and sent to Bern where, although he was not a citizen of the place and therefore was not subject to its laws, he was condemned for heresy and contempt of law and was beheaded. The executions of Servetus and Gentile hastened the departure of the Italian heretics from the Calvinistic lands. The political decentralization of Poland made for a careless freedom of thought, and for some time rather close artistic and commercial relations had existed between that country and Italy. So it was to that far-off land that the Latin refugee heretics found their way; and there they were welcomed as scholars and men of culture.

It was two Italians, uncle and nephew, who drew together the threads of the Anti-Trinitarian heresy and gave to it the semblance of an organized church. Lelio Socini (1525–62), a

lawyer by profession and a man of stainless life, fled from Italy in 1547 and for the remainder of his years was a wanderer in central and northern Europe, scattering everywhere the germs of his heterodox views, never insisting or asserting that he was right, and making himself beloved by the charm of his personality. He died at Zürich, leaving to his nephew a mass of unpublished writings. Fausto Socini (1539–1604), who like his uncle was a lawyer and a man of irreproachable character, hastened to Zürich as soon as he heard of his uncle's death, collected the books and papers he had inherited, and then for ten years held the position of foreign secretary to the Medici of Florence. At last he abandoned his possessions, broke with his family, left his country behind, and went forth to obey the voice of his conscience. The first two or three years of his exile were passed at Basel where he devoted himself ardently to theological studies. His method of explicit affirmation or negation was quite the opposite to that of his uncle. The point at which he departed from the orthodox theology of Catholicism and Protestantism alike was that of the sacrifice of the cross. In what sense, he asked, did Jesus save mankind? Did he expiate our sins? Did he make a vicarious atonement? Did he render satisfaction for our transgressions in our place and our stead to divine justice? Or is it rather by the example of his life, by the power of his love, by the influence of his spirit, that he wrought for the salvation of man? Upon the answer depends the divinity of Christ. In Socini's teaching "the doctrine of the Trinity disappeared and its place was taken by those of the Unity of God and the simple humanity of Christ." Socini found the Anti-Trinitarians in Poland divided among themselves chiefly because very many of them were really Anabaptists. After long efforts he succeeded in separating this element and in uniting the remaining Anti-Trinitarians, who adopted the name of the Polish Brethren and whose principles were formulated in 1642 in the Racovian Catechism. The Anti-Trinitarians were impelled to organization far less than were the more conservative reformers. They were deeply affected by the revived individuality of the Renaissance and felt comparatively slightly the need of association with a community of fellow-believers. Such bold thinkers seldom yearn greatly for "the assuring sense of fellowship." They looked to the man of Galilee as the most perfect guide of personal life. Socini was concerned chiefly with the intellectual and ethical aspects of religion; for its emotional appeal he had little response. His exposition of his doctrines is always clear and cold. The government of the Socinian church that he founded was carried on by elders. It had a number of prosperous schools; and it exercised a powerful discipline over the lives of its members. The activity of the Jesuits, aided by the internal dissensions of the Socinians, drove it from the country, and some of its members made their way to Transylvania where to-day their Unitarian descendants enjoy a certain degree of success. The importance of Socinianism lies in its demand that Christianity, by means of a searching examination conducted according to the principles of the historico-critical process of humanism, should undergo a purification. Belief was to be limited to what could be assured by that process of proof. Its belief in the free will of man, which dominates all its writings, destroys the Calvinistic system of salvation. The path that led to Socinianism was entered upon, after the close of the Middle Ages, by Lorenzo Valla, a favorite author of Erasmus.

Other sects to which the Protestant Revolution gave rise had their origin in schisms that occurred in the Protestant churches. The Catholic Church recognized the Bible as a source of religious knowledge. She supplemented it with the tradition in her keeping; and, furthermore, declared herself to be the infallible interpreter of the scriptural writings. Protestantism insisted upon the sole authority of the Scripture, and, setting up no infallible guide to its interpretation, assumed it to contain an articulated and self-consistent system of doctrine that is apparent to every reader. But, as we have seen, when men began to read and interpret for themselves it was highly improbable that they would interpret alike. The principle of freedom of interpretation led the way to things of which the leading reformers had not dreamed. Principles are inexorable and uncompromising. They always exact their full penalty from individuals. Very soon the principle of freedom of interpretation began to exact its penalty. Divergent opinions appeared, asserting themselves at first timidly and hesitatingly, dealing with infinitely fine shades of doctrine, and then, becoming bolder, proceeding to assail more important ones, and so leading to the widest gulfs of separation. The authority of Luther and that of Calvin were overthrown as readily as those revolutionists had

The
Tendency
of Prot-
estantism
toward
Schism

once overthrown that of the pope. Out of the doctrines of justification by faith alone and of predestination there grew up a
scholasticism even more unprofitable than that of the last centuries of the Middle Ages. It is not always easy to separate
these groups of schismatics, for they overlap each other and
cross and recross in great variety. We shall notice only the
more important of them.

The first of the dissensions among the Lutherans was the
one stigmatized as Antinomianism. The chief name connected
with this schism is that of John Agricola (1492–1566) who maintained that the principles and motives contained in the New
Testament furnished the man who had faith in Christ with all
that was necessary to guide him in life and that therefore he was
exempt from the operation of all law, even from the law of
Moses. This difference between the orthodox Lutherans and
the Antinomians was exaggerated by the bitterness of both sets of
disputants. The latter were charged with holding that as long
as a man is in a state of grace it matters not how immoral his
life may be. The schism "tore the very heart" of the Lutheran
Church and left upon Luther "an abiding and melancholy impression." Another Lutheran schism was Osiandrism. Andrew
Osiander (1498–1551), who once had been a priest and who was
now one of the most powerful of the Lutheran preachers, declared that justification does not consist only of the redeeming
death of Christ upon the cross and the assertion of faith on the
part of the individual in the efficacy of that sacrifice but that it
includes another act, a change wrought within the heart of the
individual, by the same Redeemer, a "making righteous," from
which the doing of good deeds follows as a natural consequence.
Another schism that arose out of the doctrine of justification by
faith alone was known as Synergism. It was held that in the
act of conversion to a religious life there is a certain coöperation
of free-will with grace. This doctrine, advocated by John
Pfeffinger (1493–1573), was vehemently denounced by Matthias
Flack, known, from his Dalmatian birth, as Flacius Illyricus
(1520–75) who, however, went further than Luther's teaching
and thus created the schism known as Flacianism. He denied
any participation whatsoever of the free-will of man in the act
of conversion. He asserted that original sin is not an accident
but the veritable substance of fallen man and that justification
is an entirely gratuitous act of God. His doctrine, of course,
means the utter depravity of human nature. The Synergists
and the Flacians fought with extreme bitterness over the question
as to whether the term "accident" or the term "substance"

should be employed. Another schism arising from the distinction between faith and works was instituted by George Major
(1502–74) who in a more or less ambiguous way held that good
works are not only useful but necessary to salvation.

This Protestant scholasticism was more sterile than that of
the Middle Ages, narrower and more harmful, because unlike the
latter it did not seek to include the entire field of human knowledge, it paid no attention to scientific, philosophical, or political
thought. It confined itself strictly to theology, and so it failed to
avail itself of the vitalizing influence of the expanding science
and philosophy of the time. These new scholastics, moreover,
were far inferior in capacity and breadth of vision to those of
the Middle Ages. Among their number there was no one who
resembled Aquinas, Bernard, or Bonaventura. And the isolated
theology was that of a sect and not of a universal church. It
would be a difficult task to find a parallel to the bitterness engendered by these petty dissensions, many of which were merely
logical distinctions with scarcely a perceptible difference in
reality —" vacant chaff well meant for grain." Melanchthon was
profoundly oppressed by it. When the shadows gathered ever
deeper about the evening of his life, and the aim for which he
had worked, the improvement of the daily life of men, seemed
to be vanishing ever further into the distance, he gave as one of
his reasons for wishing to die the *rabies theologorum;* and the
final words to which he gave utterance were a prayer for peace
in the conflicting churches. It was inevitable that these disputes
over terms and deductions should be barren of profit. For it
is not in logic, but in human nature as a whole, that truth is
to be found. The wise man seeks for it not in a syllogism, but
in the hidden sources of life, in the fundamental and permanent
motives of activity.

A third result of the Revolution to faith and worship was the
growth of free thought,—the assertion of the right to think
freely and logically upon the great questions of life and the
practice of that right. Erasmus refused to join the Protestants, not because he lacked the courage, but because he was
no more Lutheran than he was Catholic. "There has never
been a more conservative revolutionary than Luther," says
Laurent; " far from shaking the beliefs upon which [orthodox]
Christianity is based, he exaggerated them to give them a new
force." To Erasmus the two parties were merely a Scylla and
Charybdis. He remained apparently in the Mother Church because, in his time, there had not been made a place for free-
thinkers. One must as yet belong to one of the churches, or at

least to one of the sects. Yet among the liberators who labored for the enfranchisement of the human mind Erasmus must be accorded a high rank. Another exponent of the right to think for one's self was Ulrich von Hutten, in whom love of liberty was inborn and who astonished the leaders of the German revolt from Rome by his ardent and infinite aspirations. He died prematurely. Had he lived longer, it seems safe to say, he would not have associated himself with either the Lutheran or the Calvinist Church but would have stood boldly as a forerunner of the wider religion of humanity. Another free-thinker was Cornelius Agrippa (1486–1535) who pointed out the fact that the simple teachings of Jesus had gradually been submerged by the accumulation of dogma, and who urged a return to the purity and the simplicity of the apostolic years. He failed to see an advantage in the substitution of new orthodoxies for the old one, and so he remained nominally a Catholic. Paracelsus (1493–1541), despite his cabalistic fantasies, his regard for astrology, and his unremitting search for the philosopher's stone, helped to reform medical practice by insisting upon arriving at a knowledge of diseases by the direct observation of nature. In the field of religion he pointed out the subordinate position of all that is external in faith and worship; and although he remained within the Catholic fold he approved Luther's attack upon the externalized ecclesiasticism of the Mother Church. Caspar Schwenkfeld (1490–1562), a well-educated Silesian nobleman, became a zealous follower of Luther. But his mystic temperament and his individual mind led him to withhold his approval of the hardening dogmas, and over-dependence upon the external word in the Lutheran Church, of the dwindling of its spiritual element. Religion, he contended, has for its basis the inner experience of the divine life. No external practice is indispensable to the flowing of the grace of God into the heart of man. The divine grace comes straight from God to man and needs neither scripture nor sacrament. Piety is not the exclusive possession of any church. But the inward presence of grace must always be verified by the strict morality of daily conduct. Such a position as this in the middle of the sixteenth century entailed upon its holder persecution by Protestant and Catholic alike. So this mystic prince, with his kindly heart, gentle speech, and courtly manners, spent the remainder of his life as a wanderer, gathering about himself a little group of adherents, seeking to unite them by no external organization but only by the bond of their common belief in the direct approach of man to God. He sought to the last to distinguish between the external and internal, the

formal and the real.  Similar to Schwenkfeld in his refusal to
worship at the shrine of the written word was Sebastian Franck
(1495?-1543?), preacher, soap-boiler, printer, and historian.  He
contended that the new churches placed an undue emphasis upon
the written word; and their formation of new sectarian requirements for religious association he deemed to be undesirable.  It
is the spirit of Christ, he said, that makes men pious; and that
spirit is a free thing, unfettered by any external machinery.
There is, therefore, but one Church upon earth, of which every
man who has directly received the grace of God is a member.
Insistence upon the written word and upon external observances
leads to spiritual death.  "I set much more store upon a quiet,
self-denied heart, wherein God may shrine and mirror Himself,"
he said; "for this is all that Christ thinks to be necessary to his
method and secret."  He was a prolific writer, devoting himself
to popular history and to mystical theology.  To his stories of
the Empire and the Church he added a chronicle of the heretics,
including among them Jesus himself, and Paul, and Augustine,
and "every great soul who had dared to strike out for the
Church herself new paths to truth."  When he was driven from
Strasburg he boiled soap for a time at Ulm and when for a
second time he was exiled from that Protestant stronghold he became a printer at Basel.  He was not a great scholar, but his appeal was to the common people and not to the learned.  His writings do not reveal the working of a critical mind, but they are
inspired by a rational spirit.  Another free-thinker was the
philosopher Pierre de la Ramée (1515–72), better known as
Ramus, whose vigorous and persistent battle against the prevailing Aristotelianism at Paris resulted in his death in the Massacre of St. Bartholomew.  He wished to vitalize the rigid dialectics of his day by subjecting them to the mellowing influence
of humanism, and as a first step he aimed to overthrow the abject respect for authority.  We ought to exercise our own reason and do our own thinking, he said, untrammeled by the dictation of others.  Montaigne (1533–92) said it was a waste of
time to make a revolution for the sake of the few dogmas that
separate Protestantism from Catholicism.

This disdain of all the dogmas of the time, implicit in some *The Limi-*
writers and explicit in others, is to be found in the utterances *tation of*
of all the free-thinkers of the century.  It implies the desire and *Rational-*
the hope of a more radical revolution, of the coming of an all- *ism*
inclusive religion founded upon reason.  Such a revolution, however, was not possible in the sixteenth century.  It is not possible to-day.  And in so far as it fails to take into consideration

the aspirations of the heart it is not desirable. Religion, in order to win humanity, can never rest solely upon the intellect. The human intellect is only finite, whereas the reach of religion is infinite. It is the heart that dreams and yearns beyond the horizon of the finite; and, because of this fact, religion must always be based very largely upon the emotions. Rationalism by itself can give us only philosophy. It is in the emotions that one must look for the source of the religious sentiment. Not all free thought, as we have seen, tended to pure rationalism, but much of it did.

**Free-Thought an Unintentional Result of the Work of the Leading Reformers**

These ideas of free thought made their way but slowly in the century of the Revolution. But from that movement they undoubtedly received an impetus which had not entered into the calculation of the leading reformers. The division of western Europe into so many hostile ecclesiastical camps led the way to a great variety of unorthodox opinion which in its turn has sent the world " spinning on a new track." Men found that there is no logical halting place between self-abnegation and self-assertion. It became increasingly clear that at whatever cost one must go in search of truth through the door of self, that one must find a theory for God and the universe that will make the true unity consist in fidelity to self. The truest verity in act, in thought, in feeling, and in aspiration, proceeds not from a common starting point, but from a common goal. Men are never so absolutely united as when each is loyal to his finest vision, and, renouncing all that is not genuine and sincere, strives at self-expression. But this rests upon an assumption absolutely antipodal to the postulate that prevailed in all the orthodox churches of the time. It rests upon the premise of the divinity of man, not upon his depravity, upon his essential virtue, not upon an inheritance of primal sin. Such was the natural outcome of the humanism of the Renaissance. Whatever it may be called, free thinking, rationalism, humanism, individualism, it had for its champions a group of men who belonged to neither of the two great camps of Christendom, who refused their sanction to the extremes of either side; a group of men who held an increasing feeling that as time goes on man will discover that in religion there are but few essentials and that society may safely welcome man to self-loyalty and self-expression.

**The Rise of Tolerance**

The last result to faith and worship that we shall notice in our study of the Protestant Revolution was the rise of tolerance. The most dolorous chapter in all history is the story of the torturing and putting to death of men and women because of their religious beliefs. The rise of tolerance, like the growth of free thought, was not a result at which the leading reformers consciously aimed.   All the chief reformers, as we shall see, were just as intolerant of religious views that differed from their own as the Mother Church was intolerant of them.   It was a result that came in spite of the reformers, one that took its rise out of the movement itself.   The principle of religious tolerance was not born in the sixteenth century.   It was clearly and cogently stated in 1327 by Marsiglio of Padua in his *Defensor Pacis.*   And the Neo-Platonists of Florence conceived the idea in its noblest sense.   They regarded all philosophies and all religions as being roads to God; and they endeavored to profit from all of them by wise eclecticism.

Erasmus upheld the theory of tolerance.   His temperament was averse to persecution and he was convinced that it did no good.   But he did not argue for tolerance in the sense of permitting different creeds to live peacefully side by side.   What he desired was the general prevalence of a mediating humanism that should subject the various antagonistic theologies to the slow erosion of the scientific spirit.   Naturally he incurred the enmity of both sides.   He did not wish to be at odds with any party, and yet he fell out with all.   And then, as the result of reservations, distinctions, and cautious tackings, his views on tolerance, as upon many other questions, dissolved into the most amorphous of nebulæ.   It was this habit of shrinking from a definite position that called forth Beza's disdainful remark that Erasmus " is so changeable that he has preferred to conceal what he believes rather than to tell it to the world." Erasmus

Sir Thomas More, in his *Utopia,* dreamed of a cult in which all religions could take part without giving up their distinctive characteristics.   Tolerance was to prevail not only for the sake of peace but because it would " make for the furtherance of religion."   Out of all vain and superstitious religions truth could be trusted eventually to issue and come to light.   But the humanist became the chancellor; and in the process he seems to have suffered a sea-change, for he held the propagation of heresy to be an evil for which no punishment is too severe.   The chronicles of Sebastian Franck contain many passages that argue for tolerance.   Heretics are usually misrepresented, said Franck. " If we knew Jesus only through the Jews and Romans we should see all his words perverted.   He would be called seditious, seductive, diabolical, a thorough heretic, the enemy of the law of Moses.   And is it not reasonable to suppose that this is just what has been done with Wessel, and Wiclif, and Hus? "   Neither Anabaptists nor papists ought to be put to death, he said.   Let Sir
Thomas
More and
Sebastian
Franck

CHAP.
XVIII

1545-1600

The Great
Apostle
of Toler-
ance

us take what is good in each sect and leave the rest to the devil.

The man who gave the finest and truest expression of the theory of tolerance in the sixteenth century was Sebastian Castellio (1515–63), whose protest against the burning of Servetus we have already heard. But that was not the earliest of his pleas. Two years before the fagots were lighted on the knoll of Champel he had written with sound judgment for tolerance in the preface to the Latin Bible that he dedicated to Edward VI of England. It is a strange contradiction, he there pointed out, that through zeal for that Christ who gave up His life in order that the lives of others might be spared we shed the blood of our fellow-men. We are eager to snatch out the tares although He has commanded that the tares be left until the harvest in order that the grain may not be pulled up. We persecute others for the sake of that Christ who commanded us to turn the left cheek when we are struck upon the right. Even the law of the pagan Romans held an accused man whose social status was in dispute to be a freeman until he was proved to belong to the servile class. How much more deliberate, then, should we be in religious affairs where it is so easy to be mistaken! Is it not an absurdity to use earthly weapons in a spiritual battle? The real enemies of Christianity are vices, and against them must be arraigned the virtues. The real work of the Christian lies there. It should not be abandoned to the executioner. There is no class of men in the world less to be feared than those who are ready to submit to torture and yield up their lives for the sake of their beliefs. There are none more obedient to princes and magistrates. Three years later, in the *Treatise on Heretics,* the preface of which was signed with the pen-name of Martinus Bellius, there appeared the following passage beneath the restraint of which can be felt the ardor of Castellio's passionate desire to convince men of the truth of his message. "True fear of God and charity are set at naught; men's regard for them has grown cold. Our life is passed in brawling and contention and every kind of sin. We dispute not as to the way by which we can go to Christ (which is the bettering of our daily life), but about Christ's state and office, to wit, where He now is, what He is doing, and how He is seated at the right hand of the Father, and how He is one with the Father. So, too, about the Trinity, predestination, free-will, God, the angels, the state of the soul after this life, and other similar things, which are not greatly necessary to be known, . . . nor even if they were known would make any man the better, for doth not Paul say, 'If I know all mysteries and have not charity I am nothing'?" This anxiety of men (wholly ill-directed) is not only vicious in itself, but will give birth to other and greater evils. It "engenders pride, cruelty, and persecution; so that no man will endure his neighbor if he disagrees in aught with him, as if there were not to-day as many opinions as there are men. . . . And if there is any man who endeavors to procure the white robe of Christ, the desire to live a holy and just life, all the others with one accord rise up against him and without hesitation pronounce him a heretic . . . they blacken his character and so disparage him in the eyes of the common people that men esteem it a deadly sin to listen to him. Thence proceeds that cruel and brutal rage for the use of torture," that certain persons become infuriated " if they see heretics strangled instead of being slowly burnt to death. And cruel as these things are a sin yet more horrible is committed in that it is pretended that they are done in the cause of Christ and are but the carrying out of His will." Then, after reverting to the life of the gentle Nazarene, he said: " I do not see how we can retain the name of Christians if we do not imitate his mercy and gentleness. . . . Each man must examine himself, sift and diligently scrutinize his conscience, and lay bare all his thoughts, words and deeds, and then he will see and clearly recognize that he is such that he cannot pull the mote out of his brother's eye until he has first cast the beam from his own. Wherefore it will be far better, seeing our sins are so many and we are all guilty of sin, that each man turn to himself and be careful to amend his own life, instead of condemning that of others." Castellio's evident desire in producing the *Treatise on Heretics* was to discuss in the hearing of the public at large all the time-honored arguments in behalf of intolerance and to bring the people to a clear understanding of the subject. His plea is not the work of a satirist nor that of a skeptic. It is not even the result of the scientific mind. Conscience alone impelled him to speak. His tolerance was the result of his religion. Tolerance, we are sometimes told, is the result of " the growth of rationalism, the rise of the sciences." But " that is not true," says George Lincoln Burr, " as far as my studies have led me. It was not the greatest scholars, the men of boldest views, who led the movement. They were often, as they are to-day, the most intolerant of men. It was the men of loving hearts and of broad acquaintance " who made the first pleas for tolerance and who in every age have been its true champions. The argument for tolerance may be found in the writings of Castellio in almost its final form. Immanuel Kant and the other thinkers who have considered the subject in the intervening centuries have been able to add but little. For this signal service to humanity the name of Castellio deserves to be rescued from that comparative obscurity in which it has so long remained.

Cœlius Secundus Curio, the brilliant and eloquent Piedmontese humanist, was also an advocate of tolerance. After fleeing from Italy he had taught for a time in the college of Lausanne. If he did not actually take part in the writing of the *Treatise on Heretics* he at least belonged to the group from which it came; and the most complete and boldest defense of Servetus and condemnation of his judges, if not written by him, certainly received his careful aid in the process of revision for the press. Another Italian refugee who advocated tolerance was Bernardino Ochino. A third was Giacomo Aconzio, who during his stay in Basel doubtless became connected with Castellio's group. His little book *Stratagemata Satanæ* may perhaps owe something to the suggestions of Castellio, Curio, and others. It is a manifesto in favor of liberty of conscience in the State and tolerance in the Church, and its animating spirit is the same as that which inspired Castellio. Mino Celso (?-1577), who also advocated tolerance, is the last of these fugitive Italians whom we shall here notice. Not until after his death, which occurred in Basel, did his work appear. It is made up of borrowings from various writings and it forms "a kind of little apologetic library of tolerance." It is quite a complete exposition of the subject, a veritable "arsenal of facts, texts, and arguments," ready for any one who desired to combat intolerance. It is by no means a masterpiece, but it is nevertheless an exceedingly useful manual for the aid of the defenders of liberty of conscience.

Italian
Refugees
as Advo-
cates of
Tolerance

Dirck V. Coornhert (1522-90), secretary of the Estates of Holland and writer of the first manifestoes for William of Orange, strove to effect not only the liberty of his country but, a far more difficult task, to bring about liberty of conscience. Despite the fact that he was profoundly anti-papal in his policy, and that he was the only person who had been excluded from an amnesty signed by the Catholic commander Requesens, he advocated tolerance for Catholics as soon as they should lay down their arms. A Calvinist himself, he declined to follow Calvin blindly. He made vehement attacks in public, before ecclesiastical and secular officials and in the press, at the peril of his life, against predestination, imputative justice, and, above all, against "hereticide." He discovered and translated the writings of Castellio, and after that he considered his chief work as a religious man to be the persuading of men to hate no one. He had a deep and abiding faith in the moral worth of man, a faith

Coornhert

that shed its peaceful and kindly light over his character and his
writings. It was largely owing to the influence of Coornhert
that the Netherlands became the home of freedom of the press
and freedom of conscience. " Did we but understand one another
aright," he said, " we should find that we are not so far apart as
we think."

Yet in spite of the existence in the sixteenth century of such
views of tolerance all of the men who led the various revolts
from Rome believed in the purging of heresy by fire and sword.
In the new evangelical creeds there was contained no element of
tolerance. They paid homage to the principle in the time of their
development, when they had everything to hope if only they were
secured against external opposition. But when they were safely
entrenched they would have nothing to do with it. Luther was
the first to assert not only the right but the duty of the civil
authorities to permit the preaching only of what was recognized
by them to be the true word of God. The reformers came to
look upon intolerance as a law of self-preservation. Luther
anathematized every one whose belief differed from his own.
" He who does not believe my doctrine," he once said, " is sure
to be damned." And his hatred of the Jews was quite as bitter and unrelenting as that of the Middle Ages or of the Russia
of our own time. Indeed, he was far more intolerant of them
than were his Catholic contemporaries. His theory of private
judgment involves the right of the individual to decide for himself in religion. What else but this can be meant by his democratic theory of universal priesthood? But his practice was in-
consistent with his profession. The claims of the Anabaptists
to direct intercourse with God he stigmatized as an impious
fraud. It was he who procured the expulsion of Carlstadt from
Wittenberg. Protestantism, even before the protest at Spires,
cut itself off from the doctrine of the right of private judgment.
Lutherans burned Zwinglians at the stake in Germany. When
pressed for an opinion on heresy Luther took the eighty-second
psalm as a text and distinguished between sedition and blas-
phemous heresy. The one was treason against the State. The
other was treason against the Church. Blasphemy includes the
holding of wrong opinion. If one questions the divinity of
Christ, for example, he should be put to death without a hearing.
Zwingli was ready some years before Luther to punish heresy
with death; and, as we have seen, it was with his concurrence
that Hubmaier was tortured. Calvin was thoroughly out of sympathy with the idea that individual interpretation or the trusting
of human nature is permissible. Intolerance of the most cruel

The In-
tolerance
of the
Leading
Reform-
ers

kind, naked and unabashed, is revealed again and again in his correspondence. Simply for rejecting his doctrine of absolute predestination he drove Castellio into exile. Without the least vestige of jurisdiction he committed Servetus to the flames. And he condemned all who asserted that the earth is not the center of the universe. His system and theory of the State expressly excludes tolerance. Quite as much as the medieval Church he had in mind an absolute and perfect unity of unchanging dogma.

The Intolerance of the Lesser Reformers

Among the lesser reformers connected with the great revolts tolerance is far to seek. Even Melanchthon, the most timid of the reformers, congratulated Calvin upon the burning of Servetus. "The Church, both now and in all generations," he wrote, "owes, and will owe, you a debt of gratitude. I entirely assent to your judgment. And I say that your magistrates did right, in that, after solemn trial, they put the blasphemer to death." Beza said that "blasphemers and heretics ought to be suppressed and punished by the magistrates," whom he urged to extirpate heresy even by death. "To claim that heretics ought not to be punished," he said, "is the same as saying that those who murder father or mother ought not to be punished, seeing that heretics are infinitely worse than they." Bucer and Capito both accepted the principle that the secular authority ought to interfere in the outward concerns of religion.

The Practitioners of Tolerance

It is not to the evangelical reformers that one must look for either the theory or the practice of tolerance. For the theory it is, as we have seen, to the more or less heterodox believers that one must go. Yet the heterodox believers, the isolated individuals and the members of the lesser sects, who were subjected to persecution or who feared it, were not the only ones who favored tolerance. The apostles of liberty of conscience were to be found, here and there, in the orthodox camps, though they were never leaders of their theological brethren. For the practice of tolerance it is to certain of the secular rulers of the time that one must look, to those statesmen who, standing on the verge of civil war, wished to dispel the danger by separating religious strife from politics, by leaving their subjects free to form a patriotic unity against their external foes. They begin with the Chancellor L'Hôpital, whose edict of toleration we are to notice later on. Although he was a sincere Catholic and believed in the intimate union of the Church and State he may be described as a genuinely tolerant statesman. Duke William of Cleves was another such ruler. Yet there were not many such statesmen and rulers of the time to whom could be ascribed the letter written by William of Orange to the magistrates of Mid-delburg. " We declare to you," he said, " that you have no right to trouble yourselves with any man's conscience so long as noth-ing is done to cause private harm or public scandal."

The Protestant Revolution, then, cannot be credited with either an immediate or a conscious furtherance of tolerance. Yet ultimately and unconsciously, because of the diversity of opinions to which it gave rise and the historical study of Chris-tianity which it necessitated, it made for its increase.

The theory of religious tolerance received a definitive state-ment in the eighteenth century at the hands of Immanuel Kant. Side by side with the world of intelligence, he said, is the world of the will. The laws of the latter are not those of the former. One is moved by blind forces, the other by a free force. One is governed by the laws of nature, the other by the moral law. The one is the law of the starry sky above our heads; the other is the law of duty deep down in our souls. In the one is rigorous certainty. In the other is moral certainty, the work of the will and the emotions, translating itself into a personal conviction as imperative as it is undemonstrable. In the one field the con-trolling laws are absolute; in the other, in which religion re-sides, the determining factor is the individual. Of what avail is compulsion in the latter field? Wherein lies its justification?

The Defin-itive
Statement
of the
Theory of
Religious
Tolerance

In the midst of the sixteenth century, with all its poignant interest, men looked for the first time down the vista of spiritual freedom. We have not yet arrived at the end of the road. True it is that we no longer burn men. But we still hate, al-most unconsciously, opinions that we do not share. We can put up with another's belief. But do we respect it and regard it as we should simply because it is the belief of a fellow being? Yet this is the final test of tolerance.

So much for the results of the Protestant Revolution to faith and worship. Let us turn to its results to morals. Did it make the world better than it found it? There is an enormous mass of testimony that would seem to show that its immediate effect was a relaxation of the restraints of religion and an increase of immorality. And the witnesses who testify to this effect are not all men who were opposed to the movement. The reformers themselves made many frank confessions of disappointment and discouragement regarding the moral outcome of their work. " Germany is as it were drowned in gluttony, drunkenness, avarice and luxury," said Amsdorf, the Lutheran superintendent; " and the Lutherans have really no respect for the gospel; they despise it as much as any one in the world; they insult and

The Re-sults of
the Prot-estant
Revolution
to Morals

dishonor it." In opposition to the Catholic salvation by good works the Revolution had emphasized justification by faith alone. Some of the extreme Lutherans even asserted that good works were prejudicial to salvation. In doing this they emptied faith of its essence and left it little else than a mere acceptance of the dogmas of their Church. Jacob Andreae, canon and chancellor of Tübingen, said that "as the doctrine of justification by faith alone was preached the ancient virtues vanished and a crowd of new vices appeared in the world." Bucer, who helped to establish Protestantism in Strasburg admitted that "corruption makes further strides every day in the evangelical church." Melanchthon averred that "not all the waters of the Elbe would be sufficient for me to weep over the evils of the Reformation." And, finally, Luther himself said that "there is not one of our evangelicals who is not seven times worse than before he belonged to us." Is it true, then, that the Revolution wrought only a dissolution of morality? By no means. Evidence adduced by the opponents of the movement requires to be subjected to a critical examination. And the admissions of disappointment on the part of the reformers may well be the confessions of men who were disheartened because the movement did not immediately effect a sweeping and incontrovertible reform. Oftentimes it is the friends of a movement, or an institution, who are its most exacting critics. They expect of it far more than the actual accomplishment. Then, too, the sixteenth century was a time in which we naturally expect an increase of immorality. For many generations the power of the feudal and ecclesiastical bonds had been gradually diminishing. The individual was in the process of emancipation. Men were looking forward eagerly into a boundless future. Human affairs were agitated by a tempestuous stream of new forces, that as yet had not found the channels in which to-day they flow with comparative tranquillity. Unchecked individuality manifested itself everywhere in all the activities of man. It was highly contagious. And oftentimes it made for license as well as for liberty. Immorality is inseparable in individual cases from every spiritual upheaval. In the sixteenth century it was enhanced by Luther's doctrine of justification because very naturally the pendulum swung to the other extreme from the great emphasis which the Middle Ages had laid upon good works. Calvinism, coming at a later time, was able to profit by the experience of Lutheranism. From its very beginning it endeavored sternly to repress immorality. And a practical morality, homely rather than ascetic, was eventually evolved by Lutheranism in opposition to the old medieval morality. The Revolution succeeded to the sins of the Middle Ages and to the excesses of the unwonted freedom of the Renaissance. It took place in an age of immorality. And so perhaps the severest indictment that can be brought against it on this score is that it left the world but little better than it found it.

What were the results of the Revolution to intellectual activity, to education? At first, as we have seen, there had been a rather close connection between the humanists and the heretics. They had united in the renunciation of medieval asceticism and in the application of the principles and method of historical criticism to the earliest procurable texts of the Bible. But soon their ways began to diverge. The new theological interests that were created began to thrust the work of secular scholarship into the background. "The triumph of the Lutherans," said Erasmus, "is the death of good learning." And the immediate influence of the Revolution in Germany was such as to justify the worst fears of the prince of humanists. The cause of culture was lost in the bitterness of polemics. The spirit of free inquiry engendered in the age of the Renaissance degenerated into dogmatical disputation. Luther damned the intellect as the bride of the devil; and Calvin declared natural science to be godless and harmful. Luther wished to humiliate reason, even to annihilate it, in order to make man more dependent upon faith. There is not a dogma of Christianity, he said, that does not offend human reason. Each of the new state churches developed a new scholasticism that was distinctly hostile to freedom of thought. Protestantism was quite as antagonistic to the Copernican theory as was Catholicism. Each of the principal evangelical groups seemingly endeavored to outdo the other in denouncing the new astronomical theory as being contrary to the biblical writings. The facts concerning it were carefully concealed from the students at Wittenberg. Rheticus, an able astronomer, resigned his position there and left the town in order that he might be free to seek the truth and tell it to the world. "There is much reason to believe," says Andrew D. White, "that the fetters upon scientific thought were closer under the strict interpretation of Scripture by the early Protestants than they had been under the older Church." And he adds that "in the times immediately succeeding the Reformation matters went from bad to worse. Under Luther and Melanchthon there was some little freedom of speculation, but under their successors there was none." Furthermore, because of the fact that the Reformation was a revolution it brought in its train many disasters that were fatal to education. For long years France, the Netherlands, and Germany,

were rent with war.  The struggle in Germany lasted for an entire generation and put back civilization for more than a century.
Yet, indirectly and unconsciously, the great schism did something for intellectual development.  It gave rise to debates that
compelled both Catholics and Protestants to undertake investigations and speculations.  It broke the long-prevailing unity of
faith which, by eliminating competition of thought, had been
fatal in many ways to progress.  The bitterness and enmity that
followed the separation were most deplorable; but that separation, nevertheless, was indirectly of inestimable benefit in making greater progress possible.  " So long as the average man requires stimulation from without as well as from within," says
Henry Charles Lea, " so long as progress is the reward only of
earnest endeavor, we must recognize that rivalry is the condition precedent of advancement and that competition in good
works is the most beneficent sphere of human activity."

The Re-
sults of
the Prot-
estant
Revolution
to Govern-
ment

The results of the Revolution to government, like its other results, have been stated from widely different points of view.  It
has been described by some as paving the way for democracy,
and it has been denounced by others as leading directly to absolutism.  In its origin and in its essence the Revolution was the
substitution of private judgment for authority.  But, even in the
sphere of religion, it soon became merely the substitution of one
authority for another.  It had little to do with political liberty.
All of Calvin's innovations in the government of Geneva were
undemocratic.  Luther told the rebellious peasants of Germany
that when the Bible speaks of freedom it means only spiritual
freedom and that it contains no word against secular slavery.
He firmly upheld as unassailable and divine the political organization under which he lived and labored.  Even the heathen
state, whose superiority in worldly matters he more than once
extolled, was ordained of God in his eyes.  And a prince had
better be prudent and not good, he held, than good and not
prudent.  To such a magistrate he urged the people to render
patient and implicit obedience.  All the great reformers enjoined passive obedience to the State.  Recalling the statement
of St. Paul that " the powers that be are ordained of God," they
declared the existing governments to be divinely instituted and
therefore possessed of unlimited authority to enforce their will.
Yet the effect of the Revolution upon government was far from
being altogether unfavorable.  The distinction between State
and Church was emphasized and the control of the former by
the latter was denied.  The clergy were no longer placed out-

ʲide the operation of the secular law; and immunities and special privileges were no longer claimed for them.

Was the Protestant Revolution necessary? Would the Mother Church have effected an adequate reformation? In order to answer this question it is necessary to determine what would have been an adequate reformation. Among officials of the Church there was little desire to change doctrine. The correction of the flagrant immorality of the clergy constituted their sole idea of reform. This was the aim of the councils. Discussion of reformatory measures was limited almost exclusively to discipline and the excessive power of the pope. And what could be expected of the conciliar movement when at the climax of its power, and with the full approval of its most eminent exponents, D'Ailly and Gerson, it merely deprived the infamous and irreligious John XXIII of his honors while it burned the devout but heretical Hus at the stake? The means by which the councils sought to effect their limited conception of reformation was, moreover, merely a transference of power from the Papacy to the episcopacy, and the latter was quite as much in need of reform as was the former. The impossibility of carrying out a thorough reform within the Church had become a wide-spread conviction in the fifteenth century. An institution that claims infallibility for its cardinal doctrines cannot be expected to submit those tenets to the law of progress. Infallibility cannot be reformed. It can be changed only by revolution. In so far as the Revolution effected, either directly or indirectly, a desirable religious and philosophical change, it performed a service that could not have been rendered by the ancestral Church. Could such a change have been effected by the gradual progress of civilization? Our study of the connection between humanism and heresy, and of heresy in the Latin lands, shows that educated men were going over in increasing numbers to incredulity. The literary paganism, or the cold rationalism, toward which they were tending could not have satisfied the needs of the mass of men. Of such is not the bread of life for which the people hungered. The hearts of the masses yearned for religion. In the revival of religion, in the saving of Europe from incredulity, lies the indispensability of the ecclesiastical revolt. That revolt is not to be condemned by the suffering and the sorrow that followed in its wake, any more than our own Civil War is to be condemned by the disasters that accompanied it. And how shall we say, with our knowledge of the Inquisition, that the defeat of the Revolution would have lessened the suffering of men?

CHAP.
XVIII

1545-1600

Was the
Protestant
Revolution
Neces-
sary?

The Prot-
estant
Revolution
not a Com-
pleted
Movement

　　The Protestant Revolution was by no means a complete movement. The sixteenth century saw neither its beginning nor its
end. No such vital movement comes to an end at a given date,
but continues on its way, transmuted but undiminished, along
the great arteries of the world. Life is fluid. Its horizons are
always being extended. Religion is always being reformed.
Less and less do we endeavor to confine it within the shell of
some dogmatic system. Instead we seek to interweave it with
our daily lives. It is not an institution but rather a leaven, an
atmosphere, an influence, a vital and penetrating spirit. And if
the sixteenth century has any word to say to our own it is that
any attempt to harden religion into an institution inevitably results only in sorrow, in suffering, and in failure. Absolute truth
lies beyond the grasp of man. Man must be content to increase
his store of relative truth with the changing centuries. We are
abandoning the ideal of immutable truth for the ideal of progres-
sive truth. This is an unlooked-for result of the Protestant
Revolution that is slowly but surely making its way to the surface. The deepest significance of the Revolution lies not in its
negative element, nor in the facts that it gave birth to new
dogmas and organized new churches, but in its deepening of the
religious sentiment, the awakening of which we have studied in
the Revival of Conscience, in its increasing in the hearts of men
the desire to be in harmony with God. In doing this it exaggerated the dogmas of original sin, grace, and predestination, to
such a point as to reduce man to a cipher. The rectification of
this error is the task of the later stages of the movement. "If a
man has guided humanity toward the future," says Laurent, "we
account him great among the great. If a revolution has advanced
humanity towards its final destiny, we admire and glorify it. Our
conviction is that the Reformation was one of those glorious
movements of the human mind."

# CHAPTER XIX

## THE DEVELOPMENT OF LETTERS AND ART

ALL through the agitations of the Protestant Revolution the Renaissance continued its development in letters and in art. It is to Italy, of course, that, first of all, we must turn to note the progress of culture. The revival of the art and thought of antiquity and the quickened powers and developed tastes of the Italians were resulting in a harvest that grew richer as the years unrolled. More and more did the individual become free from traditional and arbitrary servitude. This freedom is strikingly illustrated by the work of Matteo Maria Boiardo (1434–94) who, at the Court of Ferrara, where the most beautiful of all the Italian poems of the fifteenth and sixteenth centuries were written, turned from a political life to devote himself to the romance of chivalry. His masterpiece is the great romance of *Orlando Inamorato,* destined to be cut short with his untimely end and that of his country's liberty. Even in its unfinished state it is one of the most notable products of Italian literature. **Boiard(**
Something of the fascination which the legends of Charlemagne's paladins and the knights of King Arthur exercised over the Italians may have been guessed from the delight of the cultured Florentines in the *Morgante Maggiore* of Luigi Pulci. At the courts of Milan, Mantua, and Ferrara the lettered aristocracy became enamored of love and courtoisie. Boiardo determined to transform the rude warriors of Charlemagne into those knights of the Round Table whom time had rendered more gentle and therefore more acceptable to the society for which his romance, written in verse, was designed. So from the cycle of the wise and mighty emperor he took his heroes, known and loved above all others by the public that was to read his poem, and the main lines of their story; while all the remainder, the amours, jealousies, rivalries, feminine ruses, and the psychology and the

magic, he appropriated from the older cycle of the Celtic king.
Boiardo was not the first to attempt such a fusion. Both cycles,
muddled and marred by many a jongleur and weaver of romance, had lost much of their true character through fusion and
obliteration before they came to his hands. But hitherto the
combination had been accidental. The fusion effected by Boiardo
was done with such art that he created a new world of the
imagination, full of charm, that is far removed from both
the sources from which it was derived. Roland in Love —
the very name suggests the revolution demanded by the feudalism
that had become courtly and elegant, the soil from which
sprang, with the slight exception of the *Morgante,* all the
chivalrous poetry of the Renaissance. Boiardo well knew that
his heroes and heroines are merely modern men and women
accoutered in the bright trappings of the departed age of
chivalry; and either his own cynicism or the Italian incapacity
to penetrate to the heart of mysticism forbade a single one of his
characters to set foot " in the city of Sarras, in the spiritual
place." But the licentious gaiety of Pulci is replaced by the
kindly smile of the man who, though he knows that his characters
are merely figures in a literary pageant, has yet an obvious affection for them. Into the fairyland of the wizard Boiardo the
Ferrarese entered with delight; and despite the fact that Lombardy seemed transformed into a permanent battle-field the story
of Orlando was destined to be continued ere long by a poet of
greater imagination and creative power.

Lodovico Ariosto (1474–1533) took up the thread of the
medieval romance at the point where Boiardo, stricken with
grief on account of the descent of Charles VIII upon his country, had let it fall unfinished from his hands. He was a more
versatile genius than was Boiardo, having a consummate command of the language he used, a music that is orchestral in its
richness. He accepted the fusion of the Carolingian and Ar-
thurian legends that had been so effectively accomplished by his
predecessor and infused into it much that was derived from
classical sources. Thus while it continues the matter of the
earlier poems the *Orlando Furioso* is by no means merely a
sequel. It differs in spirit and in treatment, too, as well as in
matter; for while the story of Orlando in love is a romance
written in verse the narrative of his madness is an epic steeped
in the atmosphere of romance. The chaos of adventures, despite
the multitude of episodes which the epic contains, is reduced to
something like order; and on every page are to be found the interpolated remarks, relating to contemporary persons and things,

quite out of keeping with the impersonal character of the true epic, that the poet permitted himself to make. But it is in the preambles with which the various cantos are prefixed, informed with his salient common sense, enlivened with his wit, and touched with his irresponsible irony, that Ariosto, moralizing about the characters of his story and the men and the things of his own day that had arrested his attention, discourses at greatest length. So the *Orlando Furioso* goes its way, making men laugh, it is true, but above all charming them with its beauty, welding together the three streams of classical life, medieval life, and contemporary life that went to form the civilization of the Renaissance. The chief defect is the absence of noble thought. Yet its golden splendor, its soaring fantasy, which enables it to run gaily through a thousand scenes, its passionate and sometimes poignant beauty, the charm with which it depicts the deeds and dreams and loves of men, make it one of the finest expressions of the disenchantment of the Italians of the high Renaissance with all sublime faith and their absorption in the beauty of the world about them.

From his youth Nicolo Machiavelli (1469–1527), the first of the writers in prose whom we shall consider, was engaged, at home and abroad, in the practise of public affairs; and thus he gained an insight into the important questions of domestic and foreign policy. He became convinced of the inadvisability of entrusting the defense of the free institutions of Florence, his native city, to mercenaries, and wished to see it placed in the hands of the armed citizens. This was the dominating thought of his life. But his interests were not confined to a single city. He was oppressed with grief at the evils from which the whole of Italy suffered. Yet hope dwelt within his breast, for he had a boundless confidence in the remedial power of politics. When the successful conspiracy of 1512 put Florence once more into the hands of the Medici and compelled him to retire to San Cascino his life of incessant activity was suddenly changed to one of comparative leisure. To his political experience he added a study of the Roman world. The combination of experience, study, and reflection ripened his genius and he became a great intellectual power. He revealed a new aspect of mankind. In the midst of the interminable quarrels of the numerous petty States of the peninsula, of a society given over very largely to pleasure, and of unlimited ambition for self-aggrandizement on the part of unscrupulous individuals, there floated before his eyes the Roman idea of government. The State was to dominate life. And religion and morals were to be included in this control as well as politics. He was an outspoken opponent of Christianity. "This religion," he said in his *Discourses,* "makes us prize less highly the honor of the world and therefore makes us gentler and meeker. But the ancients looked upon that honor as the highest good, and were therefore bolder in their deeds. Their religion declared only those men blessed who were splendid in the eyes of the world as leaders of armies or rulers of States. Christianity, on the other hand, distinguishes the humble and lowly more than men of action. It considers the highest good to be humility, meekness, and contempt of the things of the world. The old religion looked upon greatness of soul, bodily strength, and all else that makes men brave, as the chief things to be desired. Our religion requires strength more as a means of bearing suffering than as a means of accomplishing doughty deeds. Thus the world has become a prey to wicked men who, undisturbed, dispose of it as they will." It is not difficult from this estimate of Christianity to arrive at Machiavelli's fundamental idea of all religion. Religion is undesirable unless it produces moral character, loyalty to the State and effective citizenship. And such a religion, he thought, is nothing but the invention of man. Morality might come either directly or indirectly through the medium of such a religion, but in the final analysis it was due to education by the State. Thus did he regard all human affairs from the single point of view of politics. The reports of the Venetian ambassadors of the time show us that he did not originate this simplified and objective way of looking at life; but he it was who brought it to perfection and made it the root principle of political science. In him the powerful will of the Roman system which regarded the control of all phases of human activity and thought as the sole object of life was born anew. Such a dominating will could be brought into existence only by the creation of a monarchy that should include the entire peninsula.

Machiavelli's fundamental principle is the uniformity of human nature. Men cannot alter themselves; they are bound to follow where nature leads. In order, therefore, to reach the future we must study the past. Men have always the same passions, and therefore the same cause must always produce the same effect. Upon this fundamental assumption did he base the possibility of a science of politics. Thus could the future be predicted; thus could history be utilized. His conception of society is static. The idea of progress is entirely foreign to him. And in this uniform nature of man he could find no moral autonomy. He had no idea of an independent morality proceeding from the conscience of the individual. The only morality of which he was aware is that which is inculcated by the State. Men have an irresistible inclination to fall into evil practices, he thought, if there is nothing to counteract their desire to do so. It is this inclination towards evil that in the past corrupted the primitive monarchy. The aristocratic organization that ensued passed, in its turn, by the same law of human nature, into the oligarchy with its evils, into democracy, and then into anarchy. After that, the wheel having turned full circle, the monarchy was restored. Such is the cycle run by the nature of man. The most important task of statesmanship is therefore clear. It must check the undesirable tendency of mankind. And should it have fallen from power it must not hesitate to employ any means that will effect its restoration.

The resuscitation of the Roman idea of government, the establishment of a national monarchy, Machiavelli desired to forward by his writings. He was the first among the Romanic peoples to assert the imperial and regimental idea of the Roman world under the changed conditions of modern times. The idea of dominion in all its primitive force burned within his breast. In society as he saw it there was only one really creative power — the masterful will. Religion for its own sake and the individual artistic genius in which his own age was so rich were alike ignored. The success of the dominating will, he believed, depends upon the coöperation of men with fate. "Fate decides one half of our enterprises," he said, "while she leaves the other half to ourselves." Napoleon would have been the veritable incarnation of his imperial idea; but he had to content himself with such patterns as the time afforded, with the Medicis and the Borgias.

Machiavelli's fundamental idea of human society is contained in his *Discourses upon Titus Livius;* and his idea of a dominating will found eloquent expression in *The Prince,* a book that had a great influence throughout Europe. The *Discourses* deals with the regeneration of a corrupt political life by a prince. The aim of *The Prince* was the setting up in Italy of a national monarchy. It is a minute analysis of the conditions under which the creation of a national monarchy in Italy appeared possible at that time. The prince was not to prefer unworthy methods, but he was to be hampered by no scruples. Violence and treason, if need be, he was to use. He must excel all rivals in the employment of craft and cruelty. The end would justify the means. This it is that has received the name of "machiavellism," and that has given to the author a sinister reputation. But Machiavelli did not make of these things a permanent method to be employed under the ordinary conditions of life. The separate publication of the two books prevented the recognition of the fact that in *The Prince* a physician was prescribing desperate remedies to a sick man whose case was well nigh hopeless, and that by no means did he purpose to resort to such perilous practices with every patient that came under his care. The European public failed to get the context that limited the application of the unscrupulous system it described and advocated.

Defects
of Machia-
velli's
Social
View

Too many things were left out of Machiavelli's view of society. Of economic development he took no account; of a sensitive and active conscience that determines the deeds of men he did not dream; of social progress he had no thought; of the fact that a nation cannot be made by the arbitrary will of a single man but that its growth is just as organic in its own way as is that of a plant he had no suspicion; and in an aspiring religion that transforms and sublimates the ideals of men he did not believe.

The writings of Machiavelli deal with history as well as with the theory of society and its government. To him was entrusted by cardinal Giulio de' Medici the task of writing the story of Florence. Emphasis is laid in the work upon the achievements of the patron's house. The old method of explaining events by

Machia-
velli as
Historian

the intervention of the deity is discarded and an attempt is made to interpret the laws that govern the life of peoples. The work partakes of the character of a philosophy of politics; and in it one sees the endeavor of the author to verify the theories that he professed. No interest in facts for their own sake is discernible. It is a lively narrative, richly colored, and not untouched with a certain majesty. Gradually he reëntered the service of his native city. But because of his association with the Medici he was discarded as a suspect when, in 1527, for a second time, that family was exiled from Florence. He died in the year of his disgrace, leaving to another the task of going on with his narrative from the point where he had left it.

The man who continued the history of Florence, Francesco Guicciardini (1482–1540), was one of the keenest observers of society that has ever recorded the things he witnessed. Like his predecessor he gained experience in the field of practical politics and he had a varied opportunity for direct observation. Circumstances eventually compelled him to retire into private life, and there it was that he began his remarkable *History of Italy*. It was his idea that the supreme aim of all human action is private interest. The part of wisdom, under all circumstances, is to escape with a whole skin. The social demoralization suggested by Machiavelli becomes in Guicciardini open and avowed. Machiavelli threw morality to the winds, but he did so in the faith that thereby a sacred cause would be subserved. Guicciardini believed that only a fool would prefer a public cause to personal welfare. He was more interested in the facts of history than was his predecessor and in their accurate interpretation. He was distrustful of general ideas. The critical sense was alert within him. With his eminently practical mind he pointed out the fact that the conditions of Roman regimental government could not be applied with success to the entirely different conditions of contemporary Italy. His profound experience of political affairs is set forth in his *Recordi*. With a cynicism that is perhaps unconscious he tells us how he invariably pursued his personal welfare. " My private interest," he declares, " has obliged me to attach myself to the power of the Church; otherwise I should have loved Martin Luther as much as myself." But it is his *History of Italy* that is for us his most important work. In it he narrates in chronological order the story of each of the different States of the peninsula, and at the same time he indicates their inter-relations. The history is unusually trustworthy, and through it there flows a stream of supple and vivacious thought. But its style and minuteness of detail make it laborious reading; and the total absence of the elements of morality and religion is a repellent characteristic. The explanation of this lack lies not, it would seem, so much in the character of the man as in the decadent character of the age.

Pius II was the last pope that we noticed as a patron of literature and art. From him we leap to Leo X (1513–21), that accomplished and urbane prince of the Medicean house who made Rome a protean metropolis. The character of Leo is to be found less in his official acts than in the spirit that he fostered in the Church and at his court. He was a Ciceronian, devoted to the manner of literature rather than to its matter. Spiritual things engaged his attention but slightly, while the things of art held for him an absorbing interest. He reëstablished the Sapienza, a college that had been founded by Eugene IV for the study of classical letters, and thus conferred a great benefit upon the youth of Rome. Everywhere his envoys searched for manuscripts of classical writings not yet recovered from their dusty hiding-places, and their search was not unrewarded. The energy of this literary pontiff, with his many-sided interests, was devoted to the development of letters and of art; but by the time his pontificate drew to a close the flower of humanism was fast going to seed. Humanism was becoming engrossed in the letter of literature rather than in its spirit; it was spending its energy upon form rather than upon subject-matter. The care for beauty, grace, and harmony, came to be the foundation of all moral conception of life.

Two men of letters, both of them papal secretaries, stand out above the others at the court of Leo. The first, Pietro Bembo (1470–1547), a Venetian educated in Florence, the dictator of Italian literature, was the leading exponent of Ciceronianism.

**Bembo and Sadoleto**

Perhaps the most important of his works are a brief treatise on Italian prose and a dialogue, entitled *Gli Asolani* from Asolo where the scene is laid, in which Platonic affection is explained and recommended. His mind was open, flexible, and inquiring. Lacking all creative power he endeavored to clothe in the most Ciceronian of Latin, or the most Petrarchian of Italian, the ideas he borrowed from others. His delicate sense of style and his impeccable workmanship scarcely conceal the absence of thought and feeling; but so distinguished and charming was his conversation and so tactful his intercourse with his fellow-men that he enjoyed a personal authority seldom exercised by men of letters. With the other papal secretary, Jacopo Sadoleto (1477–1547), we have already had to do as one of the Italian reformers who sought to mediate between Catholic and Protestant. His poem on the Laocoon and his treatises on various subjects display a command of Latin second only to that of Bembo in elegance of style. He was never in sympathy with the papal court; and he preferred to exercise as a peacemaker his remarkable administrative ability.

**Castiglione and his Book**

At Rome there also lived for many years Baldassare Castiglione (1478–1529) envoy of the duke of Urbino to the papal court. One of the most attractive figures of the Renaissance at its height, this distinguished diplomatist and man of letters entered in succession the service of the dukes of Milan, Mantua, and Urbino. He wrote some elegant verses in Latin and Italian, and some graceful letters that are full of delicate feeling; but the most important of his writings is the famous treatise in four books, written in 1514–18, printed by the Aldine press at Venice in 1528, and called *The Courtier*. The book purports to recount the discussions that took place at four consecutive meetings of the brilliant society in the palace of Urbino. The question debated was, What are the qualities whose union makes the perfect type of the courtier? It is a true and charming picture of the most attractive court of the time. The perfect courtier, it was decided, is one who is accomplished, noble, athletic, skilled in war, which is his natural profession, able to write and to speak

well, musical, a lover of painting, devoid of affectation, and willing and loyal in the service of his prince.   Among those who most
completely realized this ideal was the author of this " book of
gold."

In the prose narrative, also, did the development of literature *Develop-*
go on apace.   And, because it was more independent of antique *ment of*
influence and more in conformity with the realistic traditions of *Narrative*
the popular literature, the novel was the most original type of
Italian prose.   Many types of the novel abounded in Italy in
the latter half of the fifteenth century and the first half of the
sixteenth.   The earliest successors of Boccaccio were Sacchetti
(1335–1410) and his contemporary Fiorentino.   But all through
the fifteenth century there were imitations of the *Decamerone.*
Important in its influence upon the rise of the novel was the
work of the Neapolitan poet Jacopo Sannazaro (1454–1530),
whose pastoral poem *Arcadia* was derived from Boccaccio's
*Ameto* and served in its turn as the model for Sir Philip Sidney's classic romance.   Over the stories of most of the *novellieri*
we may pass quickly and pause to note *The Pleasing Nights* of
Straparola (1495?–1557?) who was the first writer to use popular folk-lore as the bases of his stories and whose fiction, despite
its shortcomings in the matter of style, possesses unusual charm,
is not untouched of passion, and has the advantage of a *mise-en-
scene* at once lovely and appropriate.   Matteo Bandello (1480?–
1561) was a story-teller who had seen many lands and who had
lived in cloisters and at courts.   He was a realist, and in his
stories there live again many of the interesting characters he met;
and there, too, are preserved the ideas and the sentiments of the
varied society in which he mingled.   His stories were evidently
freely composed, for they read like improvisations, like the spontaneous narratives of a gifted speaker, rather than like the
cleverly constructed novels of a writer capable of subtle analysis
and compact organization.

In still another line, the drama, did Italian literature find de- *Develop-*
velopment.   We have already noticed Poliziano's *Orfeo,* which *ment of*
although only the shell of a play was the first Italian drama to *the Drama*
possess a literary quality.   Plays continued to be written in both
Latin and Italian.   Among the authors who contributed to this
literary form were Boiardo, Ariosto, and Machiavelli.   The
*Mandragora* of the last author was composed in his enforced
retirement at San Casciano.   It is a bold revelation of the immorality of the age and a keen satire upon the state of contemporary society.   The action, which conforms to the classical
requirements, is rapid, the dialogue sparkles with wit, and the

characters, taken from the Florentine life of the time, are exceptionally well-drawn. The fact that this comedy of immorality threw Leo X and his cardinals into fits of laughter is singularly indicative of the temper of the time. The five comedies of Pietro Aretino (1492–1556), that literary blackguard and social parasite who besmirched the very name of his birthplace, who made profitable the practice of revealing or concealing the most salacious of private scandals, realistically depicted many of the most deplorable customs of the age. Amid all his highly-colored, witty, and vivacious scenes, there is not a single situation dealt with in a broad and satisfying manner; nor amid all his figures is there one whose characterization is complete. Yet he helped to send the drama along the right path, that of the direct observation of life, which the mere imitators of antiquity shunned.

Turning to architecture we find that the secularization of the art which we have already noticed was continued in Italy while north of the Alps the ecclesiastical revolution was swelling to flood tide. The overwhelming genius of Michelangelo (1475–1564) displayed itself in architecture as well as in sculpture and painting. His hand it was that "rounded Peter's dome." Through all the succeeding years that dome has been the eloquent symbol of the association of the Church with the classical revival, of its absorption in mundane affairs. But Michelangelo's influence upon the development of architecture was not altogether desirable. He turned the attention of builders from the expanding style of the early Renaissance, before its goal had been reached, to a close study of the Greek orders. The poetic use of leaves and flowers and vines in adorning pillar and panel, architrave and apophyge, a genuine blossoming of the Italian spirit, was abandoned, and in its stead the Doric, Ionic, and Corinthian orders supplied the material for decoration in addition to suggesting the actual construction. The genius of Michelangelo enabled him to take the three orders and employ them with surprising boldness. In the hands of his followers, however, they became a stumbling-block. To him, then, may be traced the insincerity and the bizarrerie that were to characterize much of the architecture of the succeeding age.

We have seen that sculpture was enriched by the daring spirit of Jacopo della Quercia, the golden melody of Ghiberti, the indigenous virility of Donatello that summoned into existence the very self of soldier and of saint, and the tender grace of Luca della Robbia. After their time the development of sculpture went on apace. Execution became more graceful and beautiful than ever before. And the seed sown by Donatello, the gradual

*Michelangelo's Influence upon Architecture*

*Development of Sculpture*

development of the national type that he inaugurated, brought forth many a lovely flower. This development of the Italian genius in sculpture was changed by the increased influence of the antique when Lorenzo de' Medici opened to the public his collection of classic art. No longer did the sculptors depend so greatly upon the direct study of nature as did Donatello. Instead they mingled with their observation of nature the things relating to proportion and method which they learned from the recovered statues of Greece and Rome. They became enraptured with the classical qualities of order, balance, and harmony. Regularity and restraint replaced individuality and innovation.

The great and disturbing genius of Michelangelo was not so much given over to the faithful and loving observation of nature, nor to the admiring reproduction of the spirit of classic art, as to the expression of itself. Of course Michelangelo neglected neither nature nor antiquity; but what he was always concerned with was the expression in art of the dreams and visions of his own soul. His early work in sculpture shows clearly the influence of the statues of the other masters that he preferred rather than the passions that were to surge so tumultuously within his breast; or else it is the reproduction of the living bodies that had aroused his interest, rather than the portrayal of some potent experience of his own. Two works, the David and the Pietà, stand out preëminently as the products of this first period of his career as a sculptor. The statue of David is a virile figure of a youth upon the threshold of manhood, that, unlike the wistful shepherd boy of Donatello, or Verrocchio's radiant lad, speaks unmistakably of power and purpose. The Pietà was completed a few years before the David, when the sculptor was about twenty-four years of age. Only the year before had Savonarola met his fiery death. The words of the hapless prophet must have sunk deep into the soul of the youthful sculptor, and together with the books he loved to read, the Bible and Dante, they opened the eyes of his understanding to the terrible realities of life and death. The subject of the statue, Mary and the body of her dead son at the foot of the Cross, is a traditional one; but never before or since has it been treated with such profound feeling. The sorrows and the shadows of life had already quickened the sense of tragedy in the soul of the young sculptor. He had known very little of the happiness of youth in his life. When boys of his own age were still engrossed with their games he had become interested in the serious things that engaged the attention of the more thoughtful of his elders. So to the execution of this well-worn theme he brought not only an adequate training but also a sympathetic temperament. In grief that seeks no utterance because none can be found, the mother of sorrows, majestic with the strength of calm endurance, bends her head over her Son who lies in death upon her lap where once he slumbered as a little child. Here in this statue one finds confessed something of the secret of the sculptor's soul.

After the completion of the David sixteen years went by before Michelangelo found it possible to work once more without interruption at sculpture. They were years of frustrated hopes, of disillusion, of embittered thought, perhaps of despair. Italy was distracted by war. Florence was torn by factions. Injustice had been heaped upon him. And at the command of the terrible Julius II sculpture was laid aside in order that the ceiling of the Sistine chapel might be covered with its immortal figures. It is to Florence that we must go, to the tombs of the Medici in the church of San Lorenzo, to see the statues that are typical of the second period of his career as a sculptor, that are the culmination of his genius in this art. The sculptor designed a sacristy in which he intended to place four tombs. But the tombs of Giuliano, son of Lorenzo the Magnificent, and that of Lorenzo, grandson of the Magnifico, were the only ones to be completed. Each tomb has three figures. The first, in addition to the statue of Giuliano, has figures of Night and Day; and the second, in addition to that of Lorenzo, has figures of Dawn and Twilight. There is no attempt at portraiture in the figures of the Medicean princes. The figure of Giuliano is difficult of explanation. It would seem to be that of a ruler who holds the scepter but feebly, who is content to let the world and its wrongs go as it will without effort to set it right, who is interested, as his gaze denotes, in the objective things of life. In striking contrast is the figure of Lorenzo, who leans forward upon his hand plunged in profound and melancholy meditation. Perhaps one figure was to typify hope and the other despair, the light and the shadow of life, or day and night. Underneath the Giuliano are the figures of Night and Day; and under that of Lorenzo are those of Dawn and Twilight. These are also difficult to explain. All of them are contorted and, in the absence of all physical cause of grief, give the impression of spiritual struggle, of travail of the soul. Although it is not known what Michelangelo meant to embody in these statues certain it is that some large allegory of the drama of life was intended. The names mean nothing to us; but the emotions aroused by the statues are unmistakable; the sense of the pain and the unfathomable mystery of life surges up within us.

And so in the sacristy of San Lorenzo one may see the soul of
the great sculptor laid bare.

We have seen that painting, the most important of the arts
of the Renaissance, no longer the mere handmaid of the
Church, acquired a language capable of expressing a wide range
of the emotions of humanity. That language was to be made
still more inclusive, its nuances to be made more subtle, its
vocabulary more varied and more splendid. First of those in
the noon of the Renaissance to extend still further the gamut
of painting was Leonardo da Vinci (1452–1519), one of the
most versatile and brilliant men of the entire period. He was
beyond his age intellectually, as Michelangelo was beyond it
morally. His restless and curious mind was ever inquiring, his
love of beauty in the abstract was ever unsatisfied. These two
things, intellectual curiosity and a detached desire of beauty,
though conflicting with each other at times, combined to produce
the pictures that are the expression of his subtle personality.
He was always seeking to solve the mystery of life; he yearned
for a sublimated beauty that should be identical with truth.
His pictures, therefore, are not realistic. It was the soul of
things that he sought to portray. In his paintings the objects
are veiled in a thin mist. He was the first of the great masters
of chiaroscuro, the first to understand how to combine the effects of light and shade, by the means of which he sought to
render the subtlest and most delicate gradations of form. His
pictures differ from those of his predecessors in that the light
instead of being evenly distributed in them is broken up and
confined very largely to one part while the other part is touched
with shadow or steeped in impenetrable darkness. Leonardo
realized the esthetic value of chiaroscuro. He knew that even
the faintest objects could by its means be made still more beautiful and romantic. It enabled him to reveal to others his penetrating impressionism that could catch the evanescent and
volatile sentiment of visible things. It permitted him to show
that the literal physiognomy of objects is often less significant,
or at least less suggestive, than their expression and atmosphere. With its aid he introduced into his pictures the element
of mystery that made so irresistible an appeal to his mind and
that constantly challenged his imagination. The mysterious
effect of his Virgin of the Rocks is very largely due to the
striking contrast between the light that illuminates the faces, the
luminous shadows of the distant landscape, and the deep obscurity of the curious cavern. Thus did he seek to suggest the
fugitive and elusive and unprehensible things whose existence

he suspected beneath the surface of the physical world. His *Monna Lisa,* " set as in some faint light under sea," is one of the most difficult pictures in the world to understand. What does the expression of La Joconda indicate? It is a subtle smile, perhaps intriguing; often pronounced inscrutable; certainly not for an obvious purpose; and just as certainly not the expression of a passing mood but of the very essence of the soul. Behind that quiet, intellectual face lies an animated spirit and a most alert brain. About the famous Last Supper, as Walter Pater tells us, a whole literature has gathered of which " Goethe's pensive sketch of its sad fortunes is by far the best." In all of Leonardo's pictures there is a subtle, indefinite sense of something held back, half-hidden behind an ethereal film of color, and also the sense of an unsuccessful pursuit. The painter, it would seem, declined to tell us all he knew; and failed to learn all that he himself would know. He was not a mere cataloguer of picturesque items, but an alchemist who, though denied the supreme power that he craved, could yet raise the spectrum of a dead rose, of a vanished hour, or summon a soul to an intimate interview.

The peace, the grace, the tender sentiment, and the religious aspiration of Umbria, expressed so well by Perugino, were

Raphael        united by Raphael (1483–1520) with the scientific attainments of Florence. These two elements, both of them, especially the latter, expanded with wonderful skill, inform an art that in its way has never been surpassed, an art far more popular than that of Leonardo, an art essentially simple and exterior, full of a slumberous peace, radiant with golden color, undisturbed by the enigma of life, content with the loveliness of the surrounding world, charmed with the beauty of the present day. Never were the Christian and the pagan feelings elsewhere so evenly combined in painting. And in a technical respect, also, did Raphael reveal himself as a master. He was the first great master of composition. What is pictorial composition? First the artist must select from nature the details that he deems significant. Nature itself is not art; it is only the world from which the artist selects his items. " Art is hidden in nature," said Dürer, " it is for the artist to drag her forth." Then the selected items are to be artistically arranged. Two principles, then, selection and arrangement, enter into composition. Items may be arranged according to nature as in a landscape, although even in this case the principle of selection has eliminated some things and perhaps interpolated others; or they may be arranged according to certain artificial conventions. It is in composition according to conventions that Raphael excelled. The basis of such composition is geometric — the several forms of the quadrilateral, for instance, or more often the triangle or pyramid. For some reason or other we like form and color for their own sake. The psychic elements of a picture appeal to us first, but any picture that is lacking in either form or color sooner or later appears defective. Our sense of form and color is primal. One of the most satisfying of all forms, perhaps because of its stability, is that of the pyramid. See how Raphael has employed it in the most famous of his easel pictures, the Sistine Madonna. The triangular grouping of the composition is boldly confessed. Not the slightest appearance of fortuitousness is to be found. In his great mural paintings in the Vatican the composition is less bare-faced. It is masterly. So finely composed is the Miracle of Bolsena that one scarcely realizes how awkward, with the intruding door, was the space it had to fill; and the superb composition of the School of Athens, perhaps Raphael's greatest single achievement, has never been surpassed. But let us turn to the psychic factors of his art. Raphael was a youth under thirty when he arrived in Rome, and there in the ten brief years that elapsed before his early death he gave to the world an astonishing number of paintings which though occasionally feeble are often full of beauty and sometimes touched with majesty. What enabled him to do so much and to do it so well? In the power to assimilate the ideas and the spirit of other artists, in the pliant character of his genius, he was unsurpassed. From all sides he received impressions and these he put together with extraordinary facility. Like the bee he gathered honey from many flowers. The various elements that he appropriated he fused in the alembic of his own personality. So sensitive was he that he responded to the vibrations of many notes. Every great motive that hitherto had inspired painting in Italy found a place in the harmony of his work. He did not reproduce every note that he heard. Instinctively he rejected all that was hard and harsh. When he sounded the same notes that had given him pleasure they were more golden than before, as the mocking-bird sings more gloriously the notes it has learned from other songsters. His own note was one of a golden beauty; and when he gave his music to the world there was much in it that was his own. The luminous serenity that informs all his work had its origin only in him.

No great artist can entirely escape the force of his age or that of his nation, yet the vital energy of Michelangelo (1475–

1564) was so great as to enable him to transcend his age and to make him in a large measure timeless and universal. His genius was that of a sculptor. But the powerful Julius II, the greatest of all the pontifical patrons of art, in whom he must have recognized some of the colossal qualities that characterized himself,

**Michel-
angelo as
Painter**

commanded him to work as an architect and as a painter. He was reluctant to accept the commission to cover the ceiling of the Sistine Chapel with fresco. The pope, however, insisted; and so the work began. This task that he had entered upon so unwillingly is the only one of his great designs destined to be completed. The painting, which contains about four hundred figures, is an allegory of the life of man, of the struggle in it between good and evil. All the facts of the allegory, moral as well as physical, are expressed through the medium of the human form which had become to Michelangelo the most eloquent expression of every aspect of life. For the first time the nude was made spiritual. Art, as we have seen, was enslaved when it was nothing more than the handmaid of the Church. But art has for its function the expression of life; and religion, which must not be confounded with theology or ecclesiasticism, is the highest part of human life. Art, therefore, can never afford to dissociate itself completely from religion, nor even to neglect it. Michelangelo was greatest when he gave expression to the spiritual side of human life. On the ceiling of the Sistine Chapel the majesty of God and the dignity and pathos of the life of man are here portrayed with that deep religious feeling that dwelt in the heart of Michelangelo.

No other artist of the time was as modern in spirit as Andrea del Sarto (1486–1531), who was called "the faultless painter," and who has had few equals in grace and skill. Like Leonardo he learned to merge the lights into the shadows; but his grada-

**Andrea
del Sarto**

tions are even more subtle, so delicate, indeed, as to make the point of fusion imperceptible. There is one picture that, perhaps, above all others serves to reveal the characteristics of Andrea as a painter, if not as a man. It is the portrait in the National Gallery in London, one of the most exquisite pictures in that great collection, long thought to be a presentation of himself. Touched with authentic magic, it is full of quietude and distinction; with its tranquil and silvery tone, the subtle exhalations of its shadows, exhalations like those of some fragrant flower, the melting softness of its lights, the final word, it would seem, in delicate grace. We do not know who this handsome and melancholy man may have been. Perhaps, to judge from the block that he holds, he was a sculptor. But it is a face that recalls the story of Andrea himself, the man with temperament and with skill who lacked a great soul.

The sense of tragedy is omnipresent in the work of Michelangelo. In that of Correggio (1495–1534) it is wholly absent. His entire freedom from the idea of evil, his faun-like oblivion of moral consciousness, makes him, in some respects, the most remarkable exponent of the pagan element of the Renaissance. He was a realist, but he shut his eyes to age and to sorrow and painted only youth and gladness. The happiness and the innocence of childhood was his favorite theme. Despite their occasional sentimentality, his pictures of childhood and of youth, of figures that are not so much spirits as sprites, are full of a wonderful beauty. There we find golden and melting color, rhythmic line and softest shadow, innocent gaiety, tender sentiment, the charm and beauty of earthly life.

Having followed the development of painting upon the mainland of Italy to its culmination we must now retrace our steps a little way and with Giovanni Bellini (1428–1516) begin the story of the most complete expression in art of the spirit of the Italian Renaissance,— the Venetian school of painting. The great commercial activity of Venice was carried on in an unsurpassed glamour of color. In the dawn the pearly domes of the city were reflected in the silvery stretches of the lagoons or the green waters of the canals. At noon the bellying sails of the fishing boats were orange, or red, or blue. Beneath the sunset the changing waters shimmered in their opalescent hues, the golden domes of Santa Maria della Salute sent back the crimson rays of the setting sun, the many towers glittered as though they were adorned with rubies and emeralds. And then, when the night had come, the stars of heaven were mirrored in a silver plain. Little wonder that in these enchanted isles men forgot their souls. In the early work of Bellini traces of the Byzantine origin of Venetian art may be seen. But into his figures he gradually breathed the breath of life; and, though he never succeeded in banishing altogether from his madonnas that open-eyed sleep, that solemn slumber, of the Byzantine spell, he made them sweet and tender. He felt a genuine delight in nature and joy in life. In his backgrounds there is a fresh observation of nature for its own sake. With him art, at least the art of Venice, began to dwell out of doors. Landscape, hitherto a mere accessory, became an essential. The development of Bellini's art and the entire art of painting, received a great aid from the replacing of the stiffness and dryness of the old method of painting in tempera by the Flemish method of painting in oil.

The new medium, richer and more pellucid, changed the entire complexion of pictorial art. Somewhere about the opening of the last quarter of the fifteenth century this new method of painting found its way into Venice where Bellini was one of the first to adopt it. His masterly portrait of the Doge Loredano, one of the greatest portraits in the world, shows how fine a worker in the new medium he became. It is full of the clear and golden tone that we see in so many of his pictures. The dominant notes of his religious paintings are those of stately calm and spiritual repose. He was a genuine lover of nature and of humanity, a skilful technician, a master of color, who worked along essentially traditional lines.

Venetian painting, we have said, was the fullest expression of the love of beauty and the joy of living that constituted the spirit of the age. And in the painting of Giorgione (1477?–
**Giorgione**  1511) this expression of delight in the beauty of the world received its most refined form. This mysterious artist, whose real name is unknown to us and who seems to some critics to be scarcely more than a myth, was profoundly modern in spirit. He was at once one of the most poetical and revolutionary of painters. Walter Pater has accurately and beautifully expressed his contribution to the development of painting. " All art," he says, " constantly aspires towards the conditions of music." In every other art " it is possible to distinguish the matter from the form." But " it is the constant effort of art to obliterate " that distinction. In poetry, for instance, it is usually " easy enough for the understanding to distinguish between the matter and the form. . . . But the ideal types of poetry are those in which this distinction is reduced to its minimum." Music is the art in which is found the most " perfect identification of form and matter." More than any other painter that had yet been born did Giorgione succeed in producing this interpenetration of form and matter. With him for the first time color became truly eloquent. Every touch of his brush expressed in a subtle and spontaneous way the mood that possessed him. In his altarpiece at Castelfranco, one of the loveliest pictures in the world, something beyond our analysis, the total expression of form and matter, as in a strain of music, makes the picture, despite the separation of the figures, expressive of a single thought, eloquent of a single mood.

Giorgione died at thirty-four before all he had to say to the world had been uttered. But contemporary with him lived Titian (1477?–1576), who survived him sixty-five years, and who, though he did not perpetuate the poetry of Giorgione,

learned fully the lesson of the possibilities of color.  The personality of Titian was too powerful to be dominated by another.
The genius of Giorgione was essentially lyrical, says Morelli,
while that of Titian was essentially dramatic.  And if the genius
of Titian was less refined than that of Giorgione it was more
robust.  The Venetians were less intellectual and more sensuous
than the Florentines.  They were, therefore, concerned more
with color than with form.  Form addresses itself to the intellect; color appeals to the emotions.  As masters of color the
Venetians have never been surpassed.  Not only did they freely
use the most opulent of colors and the most delicate of tints,
but they suffused everything in a flood of golden light such as
is seldom seen upon land or sea.  They did not aim merely to
copy the color of nature but to express their own sensuous natures.  In the use of color Titian was one of the greatest of the
Venetians.  And the range of his subjects was unusually wide.
It included portraiture, landscape, and secular and ecclesiastical
themes.  But above all he was a painter of portraits.  His great
canvases lack the essential decorative feeling.  When he had a
limited space and a living subject, however, he was unsurpassed.
It was always not the mere person of his sitter that he painted
but the personality.  He was a bold innovator.  His madonnas,
stately and masterful women, are entirely unconventional; and
in the composition of the groups in which they figure he cast
tradition to the winds.  His Assumption is in many respects the
greatest picture in the world.

We are now to leave the warm south and to make our way
over the Alps to the Low Countries.  There we shall find quite
another school of painting for the loving appreciation of which
the study of the Italian masters has not been the most suitable
preparation.  No emotional student of Italian art whose eyes
have been filled with its color and its glory is in quite the proper
state to appreciate the minute skill and the realistic spirit of
Flemish art.  The Flemish are a people rather warm of impulse
and free in habits who combine some German sentiment with
French liveliness and gaiety.  For long they had struggled
against adverse circumstances; and the security of their country was not accomplished until after 1385 when the dukes of
Burgundy began to extend their power over the Low Countries.
Then they became strong enough to defy either Germany or
France; and wealthy enough, through their wide-extended commerce, to encourage art.  In Flanders painting starts abruptly
with the fifteenth century.  It grew out of the work of the
miniaturists, into whose art there had poured a stream of French

influence, who decorated the medieval books with many a real-istic picture of Flemish scenery and Flemish life. When these illuminations expanded into panel pictures, oil-painting came into vogue, and the pictorial art of Flanders surpassed that of the war-ridden country to the west. The size of the miniatures was increased; but the minute method of painting remained the same. It was an indigenous art. There were no classical in-fluences, no excavated statues to copy, and no Byzantine tradi-tions left to follow. And for some time it remained uninfluenced by the art of Italy. The sudden development of Flemish art that took place at the opening of the fifteenth century was due in large part to the genius of Hubert van Eyck (1366?–1426), the elder of two brothers, who, although they did not invent the process of painting in oil, made technical improvements in the use of that medium. The technical improvement that Hubert helped to effect was, however, only one element in his contribu-tion to Flemish art. Far more important was the poetic spirit he breathed into painting. Jan van Eyck (1386?–1440), also a skilful craftsman, was a realist who sought to reproduce faith-fully the things of the outward world. The influence of the two brothers, who worked chiefly at Bruges, extended through-out the Low Countries. Roger van der Weyden (1400?–64) founded a school of his own at Brussels, and when Jan van Eyck died he became the most important and the most popular painter in the Netherlands. He was a good technician, who sometimes lost control of his emotion, but who had genuine dramatic power. The art of Hans Memling (1430?–94), who also painted at Bruges, is noted for its sincerity, and tenderness, for the pure delight with which it pictures the externals of the contemporary world, and for its touches of poetry. The Flem-ish artists painted under conditions altogether different from those that helped to determine the character of Italian art. They were not required to cover great wall spaces with the fluent work of fresco. Their patrons, the rich merchants of Bruges and Ghent and Brussels, were not without some traces of cul-ture, but they were more materialistic and less imaginative than the patrons of art in Italy. Their vision, like that of their painters, was limited by the walls of their towns or the horizons of their flat and fertile fields. The "small experiences of every day, concerns of the particular hearth and home," were the things in which they were chiefly interested. Consequently it was the details of daily life that they demanded in their pic-tures. This taste their painters loved to gratify.

Though the people did not differ very greatly from each

other, Holland produced a somewhat different quality of art
from that of Flanders. The Dutch were perhaps less versatile
and less volatile than the Flemish; less like the French and more
like the Germans. They were fond of homely joys and the
quiet peace of town and domestic life. They were matter-of-
fact in all things, sufficient unto themselves, coarse at times,
but sturdy and honest. Realism was the element in art that
most appealed to them. The details of their own lives in street,
town-hall, tavern, and kitchen were the things they loved to see
in their pictures. In the fourteenth century the illuminations
of their missals boasted a virile and indigenous style; but it was
only when Jan van Eyck came to The Hague to paint for the
Count of Holland that a notable school of panel painting began
its development. But for the most part the work of the early
Dutch painters has perished through time and iconoclastic fury.
In the seventeenth century Dutch art became original and
famous. It continued to picture native life with skill and sympathy, with keenness of insight and fine pictorial view. But it
was always limited. It never soared like Italian art. It never
became universal or world-embracing. It was essentially individual and national. Its revelation stopped short with Holland
and the personalities of the Holland painters. Heaven is unimportant in Dutch art. What is important is Holland and the
Dutch.

Next to Italy it was France that was the chief contributor to
the Renaissance. But the change from Gothic to pseudo-classic
ideals that began to overtake architecture in the fifteenth century in that country cannot correctly be called a revival because
there had never been a time in French history when architecture
had been classic in its spirit. All through the Middle Ages, as
we have seen, the classical traditions persisted in the architecture
of the southern peninsula. When the Renaissance came it was
not difficult for Italy to throw off the Gothic details that had
been superimposed upon her architecture. But in France Gothic
architecture, born of the national spirit, had found its most
logical and artistic development; and therefore its modification
and replacement were not accomplished without a struggle.
Some things there were that helped to make the change less
difficult. The ecclesiastical and feudal encouragements of
Gothic architecture were failing. The architectural needs of the
time were becoming secular and civic. Men were no longer
building castles and cathedrals but châteaus and hôtels. Ecclesiastical and secular embassies, travelers of all sorts but especially the soldiers of the several French invasions of Italy,

brought to their native land the new architectural ideas. French artists went to learn in Italy, and Italian artists came to teach in France. It was not classic architecture that found its way into France but rather the varying Italian interpretations of that architecture. The fusion of the flamboyant Gothic with the florid Italian styles resulted at first in a transitional style that was the autumnal splendor of the medieval manner; but about the middle of the sixteenth century a decided break with the Gothic past took place. The story of the second stage of the rise of the architectural style of the Renaissance in France is to be told in the last chapter that we are to devote to art.

Early
French
Painters
and Sculp-
tors

French painting, like that of Flanders, took its rise from the miniatures in the medieval missals. It is not surprising, therefore, to find that the work of the earliest of the French painters was principally decorative, and that it was characterized chiefly by its technical excellence and not by its sentiment. The first name of importance in French painting is that of Jean Foucquet (1415?–80?), an illuminator and portrait painter of some original power whose work is detailed and exact in its realism. In sculpture the first notable worker was Michel Colombe (1440?–1512) whose native and naturalistic style was gradually modified by the Italian influence. But it was not until the period of the last division of our book that either sculpture or painting in France became animated by the modern spirit. ✓

In our study of humanism and heresy we have seen something of the character of German culture. At Nuremberg, one of the most important centers of that culture, lived Albrecht Dürer (1471–1528) the greatest of all German painters. How long a time it took the Renaissance to make its way into Germany

Albrecht
Dürer and
Hans
Holbein

may be gathered from the fact that this first great worker in German pictorial art, who was always largely medieval in spirit, outlived Raphael eight years. When at last painting began to flourish in Germany it was vastly different from the same art in Italy. There was always something of the wild north in it tempered by the tenderness of homely ties and interests. It was touched with sadness and informed with sincerity. Something of gloom, too, it had, and a good deal of religious sentiment. Although Dürer is ranked as one of the world's greatest painters he was not essentially a painter in temperament. His brush did not reveal eloquently and spontaneously the spirit of the real painter. He had but a dim perception of the sensuous beauty of the world. But his appetite for fact was keen and insatiable. He was a better engraver than a painter; yet even with that art it was principally its utilitarian value that appealed to him.

Beauty of line and beauty of color in themselves, and as expressions of emotion, did not enrapture him. The minute and accurate recording of facts with which his pictures and plates are filled is the work of a scientific mind rather than of an artistic temperament. Hans Holbein (1497?–1543), whose father and grandfather were also painters with the same name, was probably born in Augsburg. When about eighteen years of age he went to Basel to find employment as an illustrator of books. There he drew the illustrations that had so much to do with the success of the *The Praise of Folly;* and there, too, he painted upon walls and panels. The increasing tumult of the ecclesiastical revolution was detrimental to the cause of art. So, taking with him letters of introduction from Erasmus to Sir Thomas More, the young painter went to England. His subsequent work belongs to the history of that country.

Thus we have seen that all during the century that extended from 1450 to 1555 the Renaissance went upon its way in Italy, neither checked nor complicated by the ecclesiastical revolutions that raged on the other side of the Alps. The Catholicism of the Italians has always rested much more upon sentiment than upon dogma. And at that time the gulf between the priesthood and the laity, so pronounced in other countries, was bridged over in Italy by the friars of St. Francis of Assisi, that most beloved of all the saints for whom the Italians cherished the most intimate affection. To the extent that Catholicism has appealed more to the hearts of the Italians than to their reason it has left their minds free to engage in whatever enterprise of the intellect attracted their interest. Far from being hostile to the Renaissance the Italian popes and prelates actually aided it and at times even assumed its direction. Under such conditions art in Italy sought to include every phase of life in its range of expression, and scientific and philosophical thought became ever bolder and more daring. In the transalpine countries, where religion was more involved with dogma and where the mass of the people were not so intimately associated with the Church by the Franciscan friars, the Renaissance coincided with the Protestant Revolution. Many of the humanists became involved in heresy; and even painters here and there, such as Albrecht Dürer, were reformers and revolutionists. For a time, then, the Church lent her patronage to the development of art that refrained from no expression of passion and to the evolution of thought that acknowledged no limit to its scope. And for a time she was indifferent to the revolution that was gathering headway in the north, indifferent to the anguish of all Teutonic Christendom.

The
Changed
Attitude
of the
Church

But all this was destined to be changed. Opposition to un-limited thought and to ecclesiastical revolution coupled with the desire to rid herself of the immorality that stained her name and the determination to give more definite shape to those of her dogmas that were the occasions of disputes arose within the Church. The Church set herself to crush those things to which hitherto she had been comparatively indifferent. Within her pale, as we have seen in our study of the revival of conscience, there were always forces making for reform. Those forces now became extraordinarily aggressive. The Church lost the stamp of the fluent and delicate genius of Italy and became im-pregnated with the ardent spirit of Spain. The culture of the Renaissance was made subservient to her interests; and Protest-antism was assailed with startling vigor. This revival of the reforming forces and militant character of the Church has been called the Counter-Reformation and also the Catholic Reaction. Both names fail to describe the movement accurately and to indi-cate its origin; and while the one that we have chosen is not as illuminating as might be desired it seems to indicate the char-acter of the movement with greater correctness than do the ones we have discarded.

THE CATHOLIC REFORMATION

# THE CATHOLIC REFORMATION

## CHAPTER XX

### THE TURK, THE COMET, AND THE DEVIL

1. The Sources of Religious Panic in Sixteenth-Century Christendom.
2. The Turk.
3. The Comet.
4. The Devil.

WE have now come to the period of history that by some writers is called the Counter-Reformation and by others the Catholic Reaction, but which we have preferred to designate as the Catholic Reformation. The truth seems to be that it requires all three of these titles properly to characterize the movement. The movement was in the first place a continuation of the efforts to reform the ancestral Church from within that we have noticed in our study of the revival of conscience and also in the chapter that deals with the Protestant ideas in Italy. These efforts were stimulated by the successes of the Protestant Revolution; and their own successes were due in a considerable degree to a reaction in favor of the historical religious establishment. This revulsion of feeling was due in part to a panic which became increasingly manifest in the transalpine countries as the first half of the sixteenth century drew to a close. This panic had three sources, the continued advance of the Turks, the appearance of comets in the skies, and the delusion of witchcraft. It is with these three causes of the panic, terrestrial, celestial and infernal, that this chapter attempts to deal.

The capture of Constantinople by no means satisfied the appetite of the Turks for conquest. The menace of the Crescent to the Cross grew apace. It was not long before the conquest of the Byzantine empire was completed. The shattered remains of that empire, Athens, the Morea, the islands of the Ægean Sea, Sinope and Trebizond on the Black Sea, all fell into the hands of the invaders. Then Servia, Bosnia, and Herzegovina, were subdued; so that when Mohammed II (1451–81) died the

397

Turkish realm had the Danube for its northern border from the Black Sea to Belgrade; and from Belgrade it extended in a direct line almost to the Adriatic. Mohammed left two sons behind him. The elder, Bayazid II (1481–1512), was satisfied with the territorial conquests of his father. Djem, the younger, laid claim to the throne; and being defeated in battle sought refuge with the Knights Hospitallers at Rhodes. But the knights betrayed the trust reposed in them by the fugitive prince. They entered into a contract with his brother, the sultan, to keep him under surveillance in return for 45,000 ducats a year. In 1489 Pope Innocent VIII became the custodian of Djem. Six years later, having been taken in charge by Charles VIII when the French King invaded Italy, the unhappy prince died at Naples under suspicious circumstances. After another outbreak of war with Venice peace was signed in 1503 between the maritime republic and the Porte and also between the latter power and Hungary. Then the sultan was able to turn his attention to the east, where Persia, under Ismail, the founder of a new dynasty and the first ruler to assume the title of Shah, had risen into new power, and to the south, where the sultan of Egypt was showing unmistakable signs of insubordination. When Selim the Inflexible (1512–20) came to the throne, the policy of aggression in Europe, after defeat had been inflicted upon Persia and Egypt and the Turkish ruler had been proclaimed the spiritual head of the whole Islamic world, was resumed. But before that policy could be put under way Selim died of the plague. Under Solyman I (1520–66) the Turkish empire reached its zenith; and among the great rulers of the time, Francis I, Charles V, Henry VIII, and Elizabeth, none was greater, either as a soldier or a statesman, than the sultan surnamed the Magnificent. Every one of the Christian sovereigns was absorbed in his own interests; and Hungary, which now lay directly in the way of the northern extension of the Turkish power was plunged into anarchy by the fact that its new king, Louis II, was still a minor. The sultan perceived his opportunity. Belgrade was captured in 1521; and, by strengthening its fortifications, it was made a Turkish outpost. Turning to the south he succeeded in making secure the line of communication between Alexandria and Constantinople and becoming master of the eastern Mediterranean by the capture of Rhodes. Left free to pursue the northern campaign, the " Shadow of God on the Earth " then led his forces into Hungary and after an overwhelming victory at Mohacs in 1526 met, before the walls of Vienna, with his first signal repulse. He failed to annex Austria, but Hungary,

Transylvania, Moldavia, and Jedisan, were added to the Turkish dominions. The mutual jealousy of France and the Empire now brought the Turks into the circle of European alliances. Charles V, apparently not content with the possession of Germany, the Netherlands, Spain, and the greater part of Italy, seemed to be meditating a further aggrandizement of the Hapsburg power. In order to offset such aggression a formal alliance was concluded in 1536 between France and Turkey. Diversity of creed was no longer a bar to political association. Political interests rather than theology had become the motive of international relations. The conflict between the Crescent and the Cross was now carried on principally in the Mediterranean. Andrea Doria, a brave Genoese captain in the employ of Charles V, had been able to inflict damage upon the Turks in the eastern Mediterranean; but when Barbarossa, the great Barbary corsair, was made commander-in-chief of all the Turkish naval forces the coasts of Italy and Spain were continually harried by the sultan's ships. One incident of this naval warfare, the expedition of Charles V against Tunis, we have already briefly noticed. One other event in the midst of the interminable fighting and looting, the siege of Malta, we have here to mention. When the Hospitallers, after a protracted and gallant defense, surrendered Rhodes they wandered for some years about the Mediterranean. At last in 1530 Charles V bestowed upon them the barren rock of Malta. Before long they had transformed it into a garden-fortress, and then they resumed the warfare against their old enemy. Finally Solyman, now an old man, determined to destroy those most persistent of all his foes. But in 1565, after a whole summer of slaughter, the last great struggle of the flower of Christian chivalry against the stubborn courage and vast resources of the Infidel, in which it is said 25,000 Turks and 5,000 Christians perished, the Turkish forces were obliged to confess defeat. In the following year the great sultan, who was then seventy-two years old, and who ruled from Budapest to the Persian Gulf, died; and although for yet another century the Turkish empire, which had made itself a central European power, remained externally unbroken, it is from his death that the gradual decline of that power may be dated.

It would be unjust to describe the invasion of Europe by the Turks as a barbarian inundation, for it did not overwhelm a peaceful and orderly civilization. Long before the fall of Constantinople the history of southeastern Europe had been an unbroken record of warfare and pillage. The crimes commonly attributed to the Turks, treachery and cruelty, were more characteristic of the conquered than of the conquerors. The Turks were at least the equals in morality and civilization of the motley inhabitants of the Balkan region who had now become their subjects, and in the virtues of courage, energy, obedience, discipline, and temperance they surpassed them. Many Christians of the time were aware of this and so the Turks were not altogether unwelcomed in Macedonia, Servia, and Bosnia. But from this it does not necessarily follow that the Christians were better off under their Turkish rulers than they would have been under rulers of their own faith and nationalities. In two respects the Turkish government rapidly began to show signs of degeneration. In the first place the sultan became changed from a comparatively tolerant military chieftain into an absolute, voluptuous, and indolent despot, who neglected the affairs of state; and, in the second place, the Turkish government gradually came under the control of unscrupulous adventurers. In another respect the Turks failed to use their opportunity to the best advantage; they failed to assimilate the conquered peoples and so they remained a mere army of occupation.

The Turk, the comet, and the devil, it was believed, were all inflicted upon man for his misdeeds; and each one of them had been foretold in far-off times. Some idea of the terror which the Turk inspired in the hearts of the Christians of the time may be gathered from the little *Libellus de ritu et moribus Turcorum* written by a European who from 1438 to 1458 was a captive in Adrianople. "Almost all the accidents and occurrences of the present age assure us," so the author informed his contemporaries, "that we have cause to be anxious, and warn us to fear the end of the world, especially as we are convinced that the end of the ages will come upon us who now live in the world. Moreover, the Holy Scriptures in both Testaments, and especially the Apocalypse, assure us of this very thing, and those terrible and awful figures in Daniel and Ezekiel, which have been written not so much for our knowledge and understanding, as to make us fear the perils of the latter days. Terrible as the descriptions are we must believe that the actual events will be more terrible still. The disposition, too, of this world plainly proves to us its age and approaching end, the tendency to evil in all classes of society, the aversion from good, the lust of domination, the reluctance to obey, and even the curiosity of the arts, the needless sumptuousness of buildings, our imagined discoveries in science, and finally in all things the adding of new vanities to the old. But among all these things that cruel beast (I mean the sect of the Turks) should cause us much anxiety, for its continuous increase, the length of time it has existed, its assiduity in fighting and persecuting threaten nothing less than great peril and scandal, tribulation and utter misery." And later on in his narrative he told his readers that when the Turks should extend their tyranny still further " the stars will waver from fear, the foundations of the sea and ocean be shaken, and all creation be dismayed." So great were the tribulations about to descend upon Christendom, he asseverated, that " when they shall appear you will think those things you have seen thus far to be solace in comparison with them. You have heard perchance and learned by experience of the great battles and victories of the Turks and wondered thereat, but know that they are but the beginning of evils. For wait but a little and you shall see in this sect such tyranny and future magnitude of victories that neither the conquests of Alexander the Great, nor those of the Romans, who subdued the whole earth, can be compared with them. For not only will there be killing of the body, as in the wars of those tyrants, but eternal destruction of body and soul alike, universal and throughout the four quarters of the world." And Richard Knolles, writing in the last years of the sixteenth century, speaks of the Turks as " the present terror of the world," appointed by the Almighty as a " scourge wherewith to punish the world."

Augier-Ghislain Busbecq, a Netherlander, who, as the ambassador of Ferdinand of Austria, made several journeys to Constantinople in the middle of the sixteenth century revealed to his contemporaries one of the fundamental reasons for the success of the Turks. " Among the Turks," he says, " honors, high posts, and judgeships, are the rewards of great ability and good service. If a man be dishonest, or lazy, or careless, he remains at the bottom of the ladder, an object of contempt; for such qualities there are no honors in Turkey. This is the reason why they are successful in their undertakings, why they are able to lord it over others, and why they are daily extending the bounds of their empire. These are not our ideas; with us there is no opening left for merit; the prestige of birth is the sole key to advancement in our public service." But the Christians who, having the power to see things clearly, had also the opportunity to observe these and other causes of the success of the Turks were comparatively few in number; the vast majority looked upon the Turk as a scourge sent to punish them for their sins.

Speculation and rumor were rife as to the wealth of the Turk. " It is commonly thought that his revenue exceedeth not eight millions of gold," said Knolles, who furnishes us with one of the contemporary estimates; "and albeit that it might seem that he might of so large an empire receive a far greater revenue yet doth he not, for that both he and his men of war (in whose power all things are) have their greatest and almost only care upon arms, fitter by nature to waste and destroy countries than to preserve and enrich them." Yet, he adds, "are his extraordinary escheats to be greatly accounted of, especially his confiscations, fines, amercements (which are right many), his tributes, tithes and tenths of all preys taken by sea or land, with divers other such like far exceeding his standing and certain revenue; his pashas and other great officers like ravening harpies as it were sucking out the blood of his poor subjects and heaping up inestimable treasures, which for the most part fall again into the grand Signior his coffers."

The Turkish soldiers filled many of the Christians who met them with admiration. "I had never seen such a sight before," declared Busbecq, speaking of those whom he saw at Constantinople, "and I was delighted with the gay colors of their shields and spears, their jeweled scimitars, their many-colored plumes, their turbans of purest white, their robes of purple and dark green, their gallant steeds and superb accouterments." And describing those who were participating in war he told his fellow Christians that "it is the patience, self-denial, and thrift of the Turkish soldier that enabled him to face the most trying circumstances and come safely out of the dangers that surround him. What a contrast to our men! Christian soldiers on a campaign refuse to put up with their ordinary food." And again he said that everywhere in the Turkish camps "order prevailed, there was perfect silence, no disturbances, no quarrels, no bullying; a state of things that must seem well-nigh incredible to those whose experience is limited to Christian camps." Yet, as we have said, it was not to such things as these that the vast majority of the Christians attributed the success of the Turks, but rather to the will of God who made use of them as an instrument of His wrath.

The most remarkable feature of the Turkish military power was the corps of Janizaries, a system of slave soldiers established and perfected in the fourteenth century. Every four years the agents of the sultan took from the Christian villages under Turkish rule one-fifth of all the boys between the ages of six and nine. They chose, of course, only the strongest and most intelligent. Severed from all their family ties and early associations they were educated as Mohammedans at Constantinople. Some of them were placed in civil service, but most of them were placed

*Turkish
Soldiers*

*The
Janizaries*

in one or another of the one hundred and sixty-five companies of Janizaries. Celibacy was enjoined upon them; and, exempt from the operation of the law, the only discipline to which they were subjected was that of their officers. They adopted the tenets of one of the most popular of the Mohammedan sects and thus they became a religious-military order somewhat similar to those that grew up among the Crusaders. Under these conditions they became a most formidable weapon in the hands of every sultan who could control them. They were the most feared of all the Turkish forces; Knolles, like the majority of the Christians, believed them to be "the greatest strength of the Turkish empire." And the author of the *Libellus* asserted that the archers among them had bows of such strength that their arrows could penetrate any shield or breastplate. About the middle of the sixteenth century the corps began to degenerate. Its members were allowed to marry; then they were allowed to introduce their children into the service; and still later the children of other Mohammedans were permitted to be enrolled. Thus the characteristics that distinguished the Janizaries from other Turkish troops were gradually obliterated.

The "heavy bondage of the Turks" was a constant dread to the Christians, especially to those who lived near the borders of the soldan's country. "Just as I left Constantinople," wrote Busbecq, "I met some wagons of boys and girls who were being carried from Hungary to the slave-market at Constantinople; this is the commonest kind of Turkish merchandise . . . unhappy Christians of all ranks, ages and sexes who were being carried off to a horrible slavery." And further on he wrote that "Slave-hunting is the chief source of profit to the Turkish soldier." And in the *Libellus* we read that "In order that their captives may more easily and conveniently be preserved" the Turks "deputed merchants to reside in all their towns for the buying and selling of men," and that "in all towns there is a special market-place for the buying and selling of men and places specifically set apart for that purpose." But from the same little book we learn that there were some mitigations of Turkish slavery; that, for one thing, "the Turks compel no man to deny his faith, nor are they very anxious to persuade any one to do so, nor do they hold perverts in great estimation."

*Slavery Among the Turks*

The corsairs, who infested the Barbary coast and who seized Christian ships and their crews and made piratical raids upon Christian countries, were a great pest. There had been pirates in the great inland sea ever since the days of Jason and the Golden Fleece; and there had been Moslem pirates before the

*The Corsairs*

fall of Granada, but that event greatly increased their numbers; thousands of Moors who had immigrated from Spain to Africa were eager to revenge themselves upon the Spaniards who had forced them into exile. It was not only Spain that suffered at the hands of the corsairs. Italy, France, and other Christian ships and shores experienced the depredations of these maritime robbers. The captive Christians were held as slaves in Africa or compelled to work the oars in the ships that harried the southern shores of Christendom. The fall of Rhodes in 1522 left the Mohammedan fleet supreme in the eastern Mediterranean; while the capture by the brothers Barbarossa of the town of Algiers a few years earlier than this and, a few years later, of the little rocky island that forms the harbor resulted in a similar supremacy in the West. The elder of the two brothers was killed by the Spaniards in 1517. The younger, known as Khair-ed-Din, was made beylerbey, or governor-general, of Algiers by the sultan Selim I and from this event dates the establishment of Turkish rule in northwest Africa. The age of the great corsairs may be said to have terminated with the battle of Lepanto which pointed to the decline of the naval supremacy of the Turks. Their maritime prestige was shattered; and the Barbary corsairs, no longer supported by that prestige, declined into petty pirates who confined themselves to plundering raids and avoided contests with Christian ships of war.

It was the belief of Christendom that in ferocity and lust the Turks were unequaled. Knolles asserted that when in 1432 Thessalonica was taken by Murad II "the Venetian soldiers fled to their galleys lying at anchor in the haven, and so got to sea; but the infinite miseries which the poor Christians endured in the fury of that barbarous nation, no tongue is able to express, or pen describe; death was less pain than the ignominious outrages and unspeakable villainies which many good Christians there suffered." And speaking of the Turks in general he declared that their cruelty, "their torments and strange tortures," and the many "strange kinds of death" were "such as would abhor any Christian ear to hear." But the author of the *Libellus* does not support the contemporary opinion as to the unexampled lust of the Turk. "Each man among them," he said, "is allowed by law to have twelve lawful wives, and as many concubines as he pleases without number or computation." Yet, he continued, "I marvel greatly when I consider the modesty among Turkish women and the indecent clothing and reprobate conduct of women among the Christians." And still further on he adds that even in their own homes it was impossible to detect among the Turks "the least sign of lasciviousness or immodesty between husband and wife, either in act, movement, or conversation."

It was not the enlightened opinion of the Turks held by men open to conviction who had dwelt in the Turkish cities and visited the Turkish camps that prevailed among the masses of Christendom, but the belief that the Turks were monsters of lust and cruelty. And gradually the conviction grew that the Turk was a scourge sent by God to punish Christians for their sins, and that God had determined within what limits "this so dreadful an empire" should be contained. So in order to foretell the advent of the Turk or to learn of his fall, many an appeal was made to the stars. It was an age of astrology. This leads us to the second source of the terror of the time — the celestial source.

From remote times there had come down a varied mass of beliefs concerning comets, meteors, eclipses, and other astronomical phenomena. Signs were displayed in the heavens, it was thought, for the purpose of warning mankind. Stars were held to foreshow felicity. A wonderful star had announced the birth of Buddha, another had accompanied that of Abraham, still another had appeared when Moses was born, "and of all the legends that have grown about the birth of Jesus of Nazareth none is more beautiful than that of the star which is said to have conducted the wise men to the manger of the peasant child." Eclipses, it was thought, gave expression to the distress of nature at the woes of humanity. The earth was shrouded in darkness, so we are told, at the death of Julius Cæsar; and at the crucifixion on Calvary "darkness overspread earth from the sixth to the ninth hour."

The Celestial Source of Panic

It was not only the uneducated who entertained belief in astrology. Every embryo science of the time was clouded by the lingering superstitions of long ago. Even Pico della Mirandola had faith in the old wives' tales that the Middle Ages had left for a legacy. "Omens, prophecies, and supernatural coincidences" accompanied him "all through life." There were "oracles in every tree and mountain-top" for him, and "a significance in every accidental combination of the events of life." The atmosphere of the time was surcharged with occultism. Belief in the mysteries of astrology was well-nigh universal. Many of the popes placed great reliance upon astrology. Nicholas V directed that litanies should be recited in order to avert the misfortune threatened by an eclipse of the sun. Paul II believed that the events of his life had been predicted by the astrologers. Leo X permitted astrological prophecies to be dedi-

Belief of the Clergy in Astrology

cated to him.   In 1524 the arms of Clement VII were impressed on the printed prophecies of an astrologer.   Paul III was the patron and the dupe of astrologers.   And Pius IV does not seem to have been free from the same delusion.   Many of the rest of the clergy were infected with the belief in astrology. Cardinals, bishops and abbots accepted dedications of published prognostications.   Cardinal Peter d'Ailly even gained great distinction as an astrologer himself.

**Belief of the Princes in Astrology**

The laity were no less dominated by the false science of the stars than were the clergy.   The belief in astrology penetrated society from the highest to the lowest stratum.   The emperor Frederick III, at whose court the " far-famed " astrologer Joseph Lichtenberger worked, was a believer in hidden forces that determine the course of events.   Maximilian I included the " influence of the planets " in his maxims of government, studied the art of star-gazing, and had an astrologer for his private secretary. Charles V, as we shall see, was powerfully impressed by the supposed significance of the comets that came in the middle of the sixteenth century ; and his brother Ferdinand was equally convinced of the truths of astrology.   It was from the prognostications of an astrologer that Maximilian II borrowed the maxims that guided his conduct and Rudolf II was himself a famous astrologer.   The astrologers of the time exercised a vast influence.   Many intrigues and moves on the chess-board of politics must be put down to their account, for almost every prince had one of them for his counselor.   " In the sixteenth century," says Friedrich in his *Astrologie und Reformation,* " the most important political events in German history were bound up with astrological predictions and (one may venture to say) brought about by them."

**Belief of the Scholars in Astrology**

Even scholars, as we have seen in the case of Pico della Mirandola, did homage to astrological delusions.   There were always professors at the various universities who busied themselves with the interpretation of astrological authors.   The most famous scholar of the time, Erasmus, questioned the astrologers as to the origin of the wrangling and strife that had broken out everywhere.   Little wonder, then, that minds of less caliber followed the universal custom.

**Belief of Protestant Leaders in Astrology**

Protestants as well as Catholics believed in signs and wonders.   The leading reformers were thoroughly imbued with the current astrological superstitions.   To the astrological delusion, which played a most important part in his life, Melanchthon was extremely addicted.   And in commenting upon a passage in Luke that deals with celestial signs Luther said: " The courses of the heavens have been so ordered from all eternity as to afford such signs of the last day. The heathen assert that the comet's appearance is a natural one, but God creates no comet that does not portend a certain misfortune." And again he asserted that " God sets His signs in heaven when a misfortune is to overtake the world and lets comets arise, or the sun and moon lose their light, or some other unwonted phenomenon appears."

Especial importance was attributed to comets as tokens of the divine displeasure. Almost every decade of the medieval centuries had seen Europe filled with alarm by the appearance of a comet in the sky which was thought to be " a ball of fire flung from the right hand of an angry God to warn the dwellers on earth." At the close of the first decade of the twentieth century superstition regarding the influence of Halley's comet was by no means infrequently encountered. May it not then be assumed *a priori* that the men of the sixteenth century connected all kinds of incidents with the appearance in 1531 of the same celestial visitant? But assumption is unnecessary when facts are at hand. For a month at the end of the summer the comet was observed throughout all Germany and Switzerland. It caused great excitement. Every evening, as long as it was visible, Zwingli was asked about it on the cathedral square at Zürich; and this boldest of all the more important reformers declared that it betokened calamity. The extensive literature that sprang up relating to the comet and the one of the following year pictures in lively colors the various disasters that were expected to result from these portents of evil. Famine, war, floods, drought, pestilence among men and beasts, and other dire calamities were to befall the earth and its inhabitants; indeed, the universe itself was to be dissolved into primeval chaos. From such a plenitude of possibilities men chose the ones that seemed to correspond with their theological views. Luther declared a comet, which seems to have been that of 1531, to be a portent of evil to Charles and his brother Ferdinand because " its tail was turned to the north and then to the south as if it pointed to both brothers." Melanchthon hoped that the comet signified catastrophe to his theological enemies. Agricola came to the conclusion that it threatened not only the Emperor but also all priests and monks and that it foretold the prevalence of drought pestilence, and bloodshed in the Hapsburg lands where the militant spirit of Catholicism was already displaying activity. To the influence of the comet of 1556 Charles V often ascribed the death of his great-grandfather, Charles of Burgundy; and the same apparition, and an earlier comet, the fiery one of 1554, were factors in his determination to abdicate and seek refuge from the tumultuous world in the convent of Yuste. Pingré, in his *Cométographie,* says that the comet of 1556 frightened Charles and caused him to exclaim " In this sign I see my approaching end." Lubienitzki, the Polish historian, writing in the middle of the seventeenth century, quotes Chytræus, who was a contemporary of Charles, as authority for the same exclamation of the emperor. And Friedrich says that, if credence can be given to Pingré and the historians upon whom that writer relied, this fear of the comet contributed in no small degree to the emperor's plan of yielding the imperial crown to his brother Ferdinand. " It is not by any means unlikely," he asserts, " that this comet at least contributed to Charles's design, which was certainly of an older date, being carried out more quickly." There was, as we have seen, a previous comet in 1554. These two comets, then, while they were not the cause of the Emperor's decision to abdicate, seem undoubtedly to have been a warning and a reminder. In 1558 there was still another comet, and Lubienitzki quotes Strada, another contemporary of Charles, as making the emperor's last illness begin with its appearance and as making his death occur at the precise hour of its disappearance.

We have said that even the lowest stratum of society, the peasantry, was permeated with the belief in astrology. It is not difficult to demonstrate that fact. Medicine was closely interwoven with astrology. The physician who knew nothing of astrology was regarded as an impostor. No treatment was adopted without a knowledge of the patient's horoscope. Astrology, in fact, dominated every circumstance of life. The common people came into frequent contact with physicians and surgeons. So it was but natural that they, too, even had they thus far escaped it, should become infected with the belief in astrology. The truth would seem to be that their own long-descended faith in the power of the celestial bodies to influence the affairs of human life received confirmation at this time. The peasants were also interested in astrology because of its prognostications of the weather. The new art of printing scattered these prophecies far and wide; and many of the pamphlets were illustrated with woodcuts that enabled those who could not read to gather the gist of the announcement. It was at this time especially the comets, mysterious visitors from the boundless realms of space, that filled every stratum of society with fear. A flood of popular calendars and other pamphlets of prognostication scattered abroad tidings and interpretations of these messengers of evil. Astrologers were consulted, as we have seen, by the powerful and well-to-do classes upon all questions of public and private life. The succession of apparitions of blazing stars that took place in the middle of the sixteenth century rendered the popular mind, already greatly disturbed by the many changes of the generation that was drawing to a close, still more distraught.

The infernal source of the religious panic of the time involved the belief in living and active powers of darkness. Down from the prehistoric past had come the conception of a living embodiment of the malignant forces of nature and the sinful inclinations of mankind. This living embodiment of evil was in time merged into the personality of Lucifer, that bright but rebellious archangel, who, with his followers, one-tenth of the angelic hosts, had been cast forth from heaven. Owing to the inscrutable ways of God the devil and his hosts were allowed to continue to exist and to endeavor with cunning arts to tempt man to destruction. Man was constantly assailed by devils and defended by angels and saints. A mighty struggle for his soul began with his birth and ended only with his death. Slowly, as the theology of the medieval Church grew by accretion, this belief in satanic aggression and saintly aid became defined with precision. The anthropomorphic devil was a familiar personage in the thoughts of men. To effect the destruction of the soul of man there was nothing at which he would hesitate, no situation in which he would not place himself. Luther's belief in the devil was exceedingly robust. Few there were who doubted his existence. The very atmosphere of the time, so full of doctrinal strife and charged with implacable hatred, increased the anxious feeling of the devil's nearness. The demonism of the dying throes of antiquity, of the dark days when paganism was found incompetent to furnish the spiritual need of a perishing world, was resuscitated. Then the vague but deep-seated feeling of uneasiness, the fears excited by the threatenings of terrestrial and celestial forces and the fear of infernal machinations, combined with the universal lust of blood to produce the wild outbreak of the witchcraft persecutions.

What was the belief in witchcraft? The idea, so well established in apostolic times, that what we now count insanity is caused by the entrance of a devil into the body, by demoniac possession, became an accepted doctrine in the Middle Ages. Even Gregory the Great, an unusually broad-minded man for his time, solemnly relates the story of a nun who when walking in her convent garden failed to make the sign of the cross before eating a lettuce-leaf and so immediately became possessed of a devil. There can be no proper understanding of the medieval mind without a realization of its consciousness of the surrounding hosts of evil spirits who were ever on the watch to lure mankind to perdition. All the new State churches of the ecclesiastical revolution accepted the doctrine of diabolic possession without qualification. No one urged it more vigorously than Luther; and Calvin shared the same belief. But diabolic possession did not necessarily mean the irrevocable doom of the unhappy man. The devil could be exorcised. Instances of the casting out of devils are to be found in the New Testament; the practice prevailed throughout Christendom in the Middle Ages; and it was performed by Luther, Calvin, Beza and other Protestant leaders. Bodily possession, however, was not the extent of the devil's cunning. All manner of wiles were employed by him. He used many temptations to win the souls of men. Some men and women were seduced by the offer of sexual relations with demons; others by the granting of magic powers to peer into the future, " to discover hidden things, to gratify enmity, and to acquire wealth," in return for the renunciation of God. Up to the fifteenth century most of the men and women whom, it was thought, by entering into such a pact with the devil, had become sorcerers belonged to the middle and upper classes; but from the opening of the century ignorant peasants, chiefly women, came to be the most common suspects of diabolical power. It is to the possession of this power by great numbers of the common people that the name of witchcraft was given. But the witch was more than a sorcerer. She had not only sold her own soul to the devil but had signed a compact to assist him in the work of betraying her fellow beings to their spiritual death. Some souls there were whom the devil could not win without the aid of a human agent. In these cases the witch was indispensable to him. It was inevitable that such a being as a witch should be held in universal abomination and that death should be the most fitting penalty for the criminal and the surest safeguard for the public. The purpose, or the theory, of the witch persecution, that most fearful product of the later medieval spirit, was to rid the world of these agents of the devil.

The epidemic of persecution was slow in getting under way. The differentiation of witchcraft from sorcery probably began in the second half of the fourteenth century. Gradually the belief in witches and their evil powers spread beneath the surface in every part of Europe; and persecution but served to scatter its seeds ever wider than before. The minds of the common people became filled with the idea that witches were the cause of almost every misfortune that befell them. Even men of intellect did not escape the delusion that they were surrounded by these malignant beings. Jean Bodin, one of the most eminent jurists and statesmen of the sixteenth century and one of its " most rational and tolerant thinkers," wrote upon the duty of punishing with death this most detestable of all crimes. So gradually the fear developed into an epidemic. Italy and Spain, where the burning of heretics left no room for the burning of witches, remained fairly free from the contagion. In England it broke out only occasionally; and France was afflicted with it only in a minor degree. The chief arena of its ravages was Germany. The delusion was greatly stimulated by the papal bull of 1484, *Summis desiderantes,* and by subsequent bulls which more than any other single agency served to encourage the persecution of witches and therefore to propagate the belief in their existence. In the " blind and senseless orgies of destruction " that lasted until the middle of the seventeenth century members of the old and the new churches rivaled each other in their ferocious and hideous delirium of fear. Indeed, the ecclesiastical revolution eventually deepened the superstition. The worst cases of witch burning occurred at times of great depression or restless excitement. No other period of European history is so filled with horror as that in which the witch-madness raged at its height. No reliable figures as to the total number of lives sacrificed to the fearful delusion are available, but it is estimated that in Germany alone in the seventeenth century one hundred thousand were put to death. No counsel was allowed to the accused; and, in order to obtain confessions that would implicate others as well as the persons under arrest, trickery and torture were employed. The witchcraft craze was " essentially a disease of the imagination "; and its results to morals and to religion were in the highest degree deplorable.

The fear of the Turk, the comet, and the devil spread throughout Europe and filled the years with terror. Panic hunted the people and reached forth for them with her clutching hands. Only here and there did reason, blown upon by these gusts of terror, shine with an untroubled light. This widespread terror helped to produce that revulsion of feeling which is called the Catholic Reaction. When one has dwelt long in the atmosphere of terror the suspicion that calamity is the punishment of innovation, of the forsaking of the ways of the fathers, grows into conviction. The prevailing mental state made for the success of the newly aroused militant spirit of Catholicism.

Panic an Important Factor in the Reaction Toward Catholicism

The Catholic Reformation was not a backward movement. It was a reforming movement within the ancestral pale con-

The Static
Character
of the
Catholic
Reforma-
tion

siderably more moderate in character than the several Protestant movements which in addition to being reformatory were
also revolutionary. It wished to eradicate the immorality of
the time and then to keep things as they were. On the other
hand the Lutheran, Zwinglian, and Calvinistic revolts, as we
have seen, distinctly faced backwards, in intention at least, to
primitive Christianity. But it is impossible to recall either a
period or an institution that has been outlived. So primitive
Christianity was not restored. There came a time when Luther
and his friends felt a revulsion of feeling against the logical
outcome of their own teachings " lest the world should go further into ruin." The fever of reform began to relax and to
give way to the timorous lassitude of repose. Passion always
flags and is followed by a revulsion in proportion to the heat.
It was found that after the authority of a Church had been discarded for the authority of a Book men did not suddenly become
generous and good; and so, as always, three out of four of the
crowd were ready to turn back. In this natural revulsion, and
in the terror that overspread the continent, militant Catholicism
found its opportunity.

# CHAPTER XXI

## THE RISE OF THE JESUITS

1. Ignatius Loyola.
2. The Society of Jesus.
3. The Generalship of Loyola.

CHAP.
XXI

1491-1520

The Youth
of Loyola
and his
Changed
Ideal

IGNATIUS LOYOLA (1491?–95?–1556) was born in the castle of Loyola, in Guipúzcoa, one of the three Basque provinces of Spain, whose inhabitants had been independent from time immemorial, some fifteen miles from the port of San Sebastian. He was taken to be educated by the high treasurer of Ferdinand and Isabella, first at a feudal castle and then at the court. There he became imbued with the predilections and aspirations of his nation and his class. He was devoted to love and to war. The glitter of arms, the fame of valiant deeds, and the adventures of gallantry were full of alluring charm to him. Thus far his life had not been very edifying. Yet despite this fact the intensity of his Spanish character, satisfied with no half-measures, had also been displayed in a fervent religious enthusiasm. Graceful and elegant courtier that he was, he had written not only love sonnets to the lady of his amorous devotion, but also verses to Peter, the first of the Apostles. In 1521 war broke out between Francis I and Charles V. Loyola had risen to the rank of captain and it fell to him to defend the stronghold of Pampeluna. In the siege his leg was broken. Admiring the courage he had displayed, his French captors sent him to the castle, not far away, in which he was born. Owing to unskilful surgical treatment he was confined to his bed for an unusually long time and his recovery was never complete. All through his subsequent life he walked with a slight lameness. In order to relieve the tedium of his convalescence he spent much of his time in reading. He had known and loved the medieval romances of knight-errantry, especially the *Amadis of Gaul*. He wished to read them again, but instead there were given to him the lives of some of the saints and also a life of Christ written by a Carthusian monk and deeply influenced by

*The Imitation of Christ.* In these books, teeming with apocryphal miracles, he read of deeds of prowess even more marvelous than the fabulous ones of Roland and Amadis, done in the service of a far greater king than Charlemagne. His passionate nature and imaginative mind, all the more sensitive to impressions because of his sufferings, were excited and inflamed by these stories of another and a greater chivalry. His shattered leg had rendered impossible the continuance of his career as a soldier of the king. Why not begin another as a soldier of Christ? Chivalry had always been closely interwoven with religion in Spain. They had been associated in the life of the young soldier. They were now to become merged in the life of the saint. Under normal conditions the transition would have by no means been abrupt. It was made less so by the morbid condition of the wounded warrior. Excluded from his former career he looked forward eagerly to becoming a knight-errant of the Church, the Spouse of Christ. Visions confirmed him in his resolution. Enthusiasm, that was alternately invigorating and depressing, produced mental phantasmagoria that seemed to him real presences.

One of Loyola's ideas, after he was able to be about, was to enter a Carthusian convent. But he wished to make a pilgrimage to Jerusalem before adopting the monastic life. On his way he stopped at Montserrat, a place of pilgrimage about thirty miles northwest of Barcelona, where in the church, after hanging his baldric, dagger, and sword before the miraculous image of the Virgin, he kept his spiritual vigil-in-arms, somewhat different in form from the vigil of chivalry but definitely suggested by the story of Amadis. From there he went to Manresa, a few

miles away, where he stayed for ten months. He inflicted upon himself the severest penances. Thrice each day he scourged himself; at midnight he rose to prayer; each day he spent seven consecutive hours on his knees; and oftentimes he fasted to the verge of starvation. Alternately he passed from passionate transports of piety to the terrible depths of despair. Visions came to his disordered brain. Luminous in the midst of light, with her child clasped to her bosom, there appeared to him Mary, the Mother of God. The apparition brought consolation. His excessive austerities did not cease at once, but gradually they were abandoned. A deep peace descended upon him. Then he realized that if he hoped to influence the lives of men it would be necessary for him to acquire learning. So he took up the study of grammar; and he began the first compilation of his *Spiritual Exercises.* The dreams and hallucinations born of a delirious mind passed away and became only dearly cherished memories. He mingled with his fellow-men again and displayed the dignified bearing, the sagacious mind, the penetrating insight and the indomitable will that were to be among his most essential characteristics during the remainder of his life. He conceived the plan of founding an organization, a company of traveling missionaries, something like the military orders that had originated in Palestine, but one that was to use the subtler arms of disputation, of which Jerusalem was to be the headquarters and the Mohammedan countries the field of operation. The plan was only partially detailed in his mind, a bright but "shapeless vision," when after innumerable hardships he arrived at Jerusalem. To the officer in charge of the Franciscans the worn but unwearied pilgrim unfolded his vague scheme. The friar was well aware of the inexpediency of the proposed propaganda. He knew that it would involve in danger all the Christians in the Holy Land. So he commanded him to depart. After another difficult and perilous journey Loyola arrived in Spain. He was still undetermined as to what should be his next work in life. One thing, however, was now certain. The foreign missionary work of the new organization that he contemplated could form only a part of its activities. So gradually there grew up side by side with the idea of converting the infidels the plan of missionary work in Europe for the conversion of the heretics. Loyola was now about thirty years of age. Spanish was the only language that he knew, strategy and tactics constituted the only science he had studied, and the fabulous narratives of knight-errantry and the equally mythical legends of the medieval saints made up the only literature with which he was familiar. Clearly it was necessary for the self-appointed captain of the Catholic Reformation to fit himself by further study for the great work he had planned. It was a difficult matter, however, for him to acquire a knowledge of Latin. His scholastic preparation was exceedingly meager, and his habit of communing with himself was distracting. But he began his studies in earnest. At Barcelona he found in Ardebalo a teacher who gave him free instruction. Then he went to study at the University of Alcalá. Several times he was suspected of heresy and imprisoned and at last he was ordered to desist from speaking in public in the diocese of Avila until he should have completed his four years of theology and philosophy. He left the bishopric and went to the University of Salamanca where he hoped to be less distracted from his studies. But similar troubles and obstacles awaited him there. Again he was forbidden to speak on religious subjects until his four years of study were actually finished. Because of this, and because his studies in the two Spanish universities had been altogether unsatisfactory, he decided to go to the University of Paris.

Before we follow Ignatius to the French capital we must stop to learn something of his remarkable little book, *The Spiritual Exercises.* During his period of convalescence in the castle of Loyola contradictory dreams of temporal glory and religious duty alternately supplanted each other in his mind. He was often left in doubt as to which course he should pursue. Then he noted how each idea arose and how it ended. He noted that the idea of a religious life fortified his faith, consoled him and left him happy. He noted, on the other hand, that the idea of a secular career, pleasant during the time he entertained it, left him dissatisfied and disconsolate. So by the effect which they produced he deemed himself able to determine what came to him from a good source and what came from a bad source. Although Loyola arrived at this distinction himself the theory was not new. It is clearly enunciated in the writings of St. Catherine of Siena, and it was well known to the Spanish mystics. Spanish mysticism, which was derived very largely from the East, demanded a complete abnegation of the will that was to be obtained by a regular mental discipline. It had as a special feature the " drill sergeant " who, following certain prescribed rules, was the director of the conscience. Those who sought peace among the distractions of a worldly life were to resign themselves unreservedly into his hands. Their inclinations and affections were to be revealed to him. He distinguished for them between the desirable and the undesirable and directed them in the art of the mortification of the individual will. Juan Valdés was one of the most important of these expert guides of souls. This work of the mystic " drill sergeant " was carried on, with a more penetrating insight, a subtler psychological calculation, and a different aim, by Loyola. His military training as well as his personal qualifications enabled him to do this. The theory of the discernment of spirits, of observing whether a given idea is persistently followed by spiritual peace or by spiritual restlessness and of then using the affective states of the soul as a guide, and the process of controlling the individual will, were embodied in a book. The plan of the book was sketched at Manresa, but for a quarter of a century, probably without modifying the general outlines to any appreciable extent, the author continually retouched it until in 1548 it was published with the papal approbation. The *Exer-*

*cises* are a strict method that are to enable the individual by means of the theory of discernment to ascertain the will of God and then by means of special exercises to fit himself to carry out that will. This is the description the author himself gives of them: "As walking, marching, and running are bodily exercises, so spiritual exercises consist of the different ways of preparing the soul to rid it of all unruly affections and when it is quit of them to seek and find the will of God, to notice what arouses a spirit of devotion and what chills it, in the ordering of one's life with a view to salvation." In following the course laid down by the *Exercises* four periods of time that vary according to the character and needs of the individual are observed. The first period is one of preparation, of the examination of conscience, of confession and penance. The second and third periods are devoted to meditation upon the life and death of Christ. The fourth is given over to restful and loving contemplation. Loyola was instinctively a soldier. In his book, in which even the postures and the attitudes that are to be maintained during prayer are prescribed, one sees everywhere the spirit of the Spanish captain; in the technique for the exact regulation, the systematic schooling, of the individual; in the punctual noting of every emotion; and in the absolute submission to the drill sergeant. Through these exercises the individual is enabled to renounce his particular inclinations and made ready to carry out with passionless energy that implicit obedience that is required of all members of the society.

In Spain and in Italy Loyola had been far removed from the principal scenes of religious revolt. In Paris, where he arrived in February, 1528, having walked all the way from Salamanca, he was much nearer to them. In the seven years that he spent there many heretics, including the noble Louis de Berquin, were burned at the stake in the capital and the provinces of France. The spread of heresy and the need of well-considered efforts to prevent it made a deeper impression upon him than ever. There were some twelve or fifteen thousand students at Paris, and many of them were devoted to license quite as much as to literature. They were grouped into several "nations"; and with the "nation of France," which included, along with French students, those who came from Spain, Savoy, and Italy, Loyola was associated. For a year and a half he studied Latin; and then for almost four years he devoted himself to philosophy; after that the remainder of his stay was given up to theology. He was then free to turn his attention to his long-cherished design. In the "nation" to which he belonged he had found several companions whose spiritual leader he had come to be. In Spain he had had a number of followers, and he had soon acquired others in Paris. Of those who afterwards became members of his society there were at first six — Peter Faber (1506-45), a Savoyard shepherd who had become a priest and who lived in the closest intimacy with Loyola; Francis Xavier (1498-1552), a talented, proud and handsome Navarrese from Pampeluna, a Basque by descent, won over to the new company only with difficulty; James Lainez (1512-65), a Castilian of Jewish descent who had come from Alcalá to Paris on purpose to meet the new leader; Alfonso Salmeron (1515-85), a mere boy who had accompanied Lainez from Spain; Simon Rodriguez (?-1579), a Portuguese of noble birth, interested in philosophy and inclined to the life of a recluse, who was a pensioner of his king at the French university; and Nicholas Bobadilla (1511-90), another Spaniard. All of them, with the exception of Xavier, had made the spiritual exercises. Almost every day they met in the room of one or the other. and frequently they took their meals together. They were united by a common devotion to the ideas and the plans of their leader, more or less indefinite as yet, but in which the conversion of the Saracens still figured. On August 15, 1534, the feast of the Assumption of the Blessed Virgin, the little group, enamored of the legends of the place, proceeded to the chapel of St. Denis in the church of St. Mary (destroyed in 1790) half way up Montmartre, then about a mile away from the city, there, in the dim and quiet crypt, to consecrate themselves to the service of the Church. Peter Faber said mass, and while he held aloft the Host all pronounced their vows. Perhaps not one of them realized how far-reaching were to be the results of those solemn words. The little band was afterwards joined by Claude le Jay (1500?-52), another Savoyard; John Codure (1508-41), a Provençal; and Paschase Brouet (1500?-63), from Picardy. In the two following years the devotees, augmented by these new recruits, renewed their consecration. With the last renewal of their vows the time had come to leave Paris and all its memories of their student days. First to depart, sometime in advance of his followers, was Loyola who went to Spain there to seek rest for a time. He was to meet the others in Venice, the gateway of the East.

Loyola arrived at the Adriatic seaport almost a year before his companions. There he made the acquaintance of Cardinal Caraffa, afterwards pope Paul IV, and his Theatines. At last, on January 6, 1537, he was joined by his companions. The little company waited at Venice until Lent before going to Rome

CHAP.
XXI

1535-43

The
Founding
of the
New
Order

to obtain the papal permission to proceed to Jerusalem. The intervening months were spent in ministering to the sick and needy. Then they made their way to Rome, but without their leader, who stayed at Venice because of the fear that personal enemies at Rome, among them Caraffa, might prejudice the Pope against his companions. After some inquiries Paul III received them kindly, consented to their going to Jerusalem, gave them money, and granted permission to those of them who were not priests to be ordained. After their return to Venice, Loyola and the others who had not already received Holy Orders entered the priesthood. War hindered their going to Jerusalem, so in the interval of waiting they engaged in charitable activity and in preaching in the Venetian territory. Then, by separate roads, they again made their way to Rome where, in the spring of 1538, they were all gathered together. They began to turn their thoughts away from Jerusalem. There was much work to be done in Europe. They began to think of a permanent organization. In the evenings they met together and exchanged and discussed their ideas of their future work. It was decided in 1539 to establish a new organization, the Society of Jesus, of which one of their number was to be chosen as the head. They had already taken the vows of poverty and chastity. They now took the third vow of obedience. The title " Societas " was chosen as being the nearest approach to the Spanish word " Campañia," the military term for a body of fighting men under the direct command of a captain; the best name for a company of men who were to be soldiers, ever armed and ever ready, of Jesus Christ. The society was to be a flying corps that was to be ready at all times and in all places to support the main army of the Church. In September, 1540, the Pope issued the bull *Regimini Militantis ecclesiæ* which gave sanction to the new order, but which, with certain other restrictions, limited its members, provisionally, to sixty. Finally in 1543 the restrictions were removed by the bull *Injunctum nobis,* and the Society of Jesus was then absolutely and unconditionally authorized to exist under its own constitutions. The new order became known as the " Jesuits," but it should be observed that the name, coined by Calvin, who certainly was no friend of the society, was originally applied in contempt. In April, 1541, Loyola was chosen to be the first general of the Jesuits. Temporary regulations governed the society for a time. The drawing up of the constitutions was a gradual process that occupied Loyola until his death. Not until two years after that event were they finally adopted by the first congregation of the So-

Selection
and
Training
of the
Members

ciety. Since then they have never been altered. What are the main provisions of the constitutions?

In order to be eligible for membership a candidate must have been born in wedlock, and, preferably, must not be an only son. He must not have worn the habit of another order even for a day, nor have held any heretical doctrine. He must be unmarried and free from any sort of obligation. He must not be deformed, or be weak in body or mind, and must be without deficiency of temper or character. Finally he must not be less than fourteen nor more than fifty years of age. Young men of the governing class were especially desired by Loyola, for he realized that those who had been successful in the affairs of secular authority would very likely be successful in the work of winning back to the cause of the Church the temporal rulers and powers whose conversion was a prime object of the society. He desired candidates who were " less marked by pure goodness than by firmness of character and ability in the conduct of affairs." The candidates for membership must all pass through a state of probation, a novitiate, in which it is to be determined whether the applicant shall be admitted to the society and, if so, to what grade in the society he shall be assigned. The novitiate opens with a month's retirement from the world, in which the novice goes through the spiritual exercises, and continues for two years, in each of which he repeats the exercises. If at that time the candidate is approved it is then determined, if a decision has not already been reached, in which of the two lines of service he is to be placed, the secular or the spiritual. The members of the society who are engaged in the secular service are called lay coadjutors. They take the simple vows of chastity, poverty, and obedience. To them is entrusted the administration of the property of the society, the superintendency of buildings, the distribution of alms, and such menial duties as cooking and washing and gardening. If it is into this branch of the service the candidate is to be placed he is now ready for assignment. But if it is decided that he is to become a spiritual coadjutor he is classified as a " scholastic " and required to enter upon a further stage of probation, which lasts as a rule from two to fifteen years. He studies languages, science, philosophy, and theology. Then he is occupied as a teacher. After that he is ready to become a spiritual coadjutor, the rank from which the preachers, the confessors, the teachers, and the missionaries of the society are drawn. These unusually protracted periods of probation are devised with exceeding skill to make the future Jesuit a pliant and capable instrument that shall be instantaneously ready to carry out the commands of his superior.

CHAP.
XXI

1535-43

The Ranks
of the
Society

The members of the Society of Jesus are divided into an intricate series of grades or classes. For our present purpose it may be sufficient to call attention to the four principal divisions — the two probationers classes of (1) novices and (2) scholastics, (3) the professed of the three vows and (4) the professed of the four vows. With the novices we have already dealt. It is in this group that we have left the lay coadjutors, even those who have risen to posts of great importance. Only the scholastics, who are spiritual coadjutors, are included in the ranks of the professed. The professed of three vows are members of the society who have taken the three perpetual vows of poverty, chastity, and obedience. The professed of the three vows have all the dignity of the true professed, those of the four vows, without being eligible for the highest offices of the society.

The professed of the four vows, an inner and a privileged body, constitute the core of the society. The fourth vow is one of special obedience to the pope to undertake any missionary service, at home or abroad, that he may require. All four vows are taken in the " solemn " form. The true professed vows to hold himself ready to set forth at a moment's notice under any circumstances and against his own judgment, if it shall be required of him, upon any mission that he might be required to carry out. In practice the fourth vow is really a special vow of obedience to the general of the society, for only the general can despatch or recall a Jesuit missionary. When differences between the Papacy and the general of the society arose, as they did, it proved to be the case that the allegiance of the true professed was to his general rather than to the pope. The relation of the general to the pope was by no means that of a military commander to an absolute sovereign; but rather it was that of a great feudal vassal to his seigneur. From its inception the society declined to obey the wishes of the pope when in important matters the papal desires diverged from those of the general. Only those whose qualifications and attainments reach a certain standard are admitted to the rank of the true professed. Their vows are taken, in the most solemn manner, after at least thirty-one years of preparation; and they cannot be annulled even by the general himself. Should it be deemed desirable to dismiss one of the true professed from the society it can be done only with the sanction of the pope, and he must always be received back if he is willing to accept the conditions that may be imposed. It is from this group that the highest officials, the general and his assistants, and the provincials, are chosen.

The Provincials

For the purposes of government the new society established a number of provinces, which have been increased from time to time until now there are twenty-seven. At the head of each of them is a provincial. Every provincial, appointed by the general, is provided with a companion, or admonisher, and also with four consultors, and these attendants are likewise appointed by the general. Usually the provincials hold office for three years.

The General and his Assistants

Highest of all the officials is the general, chosen for life, in order to ensure the continuance of obedience, from the body of the true professed, by the convoked representatives of the society (the general congregation) and entrusted with its supreme guidance. Within the scope of the constitutions his power is unlimited, and, although he cannot change the constitutions, he can for certain grave causes suspend them. It was thought desirable that the general should be subjected to supervision in order to prevent any diversion of his wide-sweeping powers to the ends of personal ambition or to ideas not in accordance with the spirit of the society. So a system of checks and counterchecks was devised. The general is supplied by the congregation with assistants, five in number at the present time, who represent (1) Italy, (2) France, (3) Spain and other countries of Spanish origin, (4) Germany, Austria-Hungary, Poland, Belgium and Holland, and (5) the English-speaking countries. They are his constant attendants and in their appointment he has no voice. A special confessor is also given him; and he is further supplied with a monitor who conveys to him any criticism or stricture that the assistants may judge advisable to make upon the performance of his duties. Thus the general, though endowed with absolute power in all things relating to the administration of the society, is yet associated with companions, whom he did not choose, of whom he is powerless to rid himself, and who like veritable shadows are forever at his side. The general is strictly required to reside only at Rome. He may not abdicate his office without the approval of the congregation, and he is subject to suspension and deposition. Yet so careful and long has been the probation any one elected to the generalship has undergone that it is altogether unlikely he will adopt a policy contrary to the spirit of the society. So in actual practice the elaborate system of limitations leaves the general still an autocrat.

The general congregation of the society consists of the general, when alive, his assistants, the provincials, and two other members from each province, elected by the superiors and older professed members. In it is vested the chief authority of the Society. It elects the general, and, for certain important reasons, it is empowered to depose him. To it also belongs the power, never yet exercised, of adding new provisions to the constitutions and of abrogating old ones. The congregation is seldom summoned except for the purpose of electing a new general, and then it is assembled by the vicar appointed by the dying general until his successor shall have been elected.

To sketch the framework of the Society of Jesus is a much easier matter than to gain and convey a just notion of its ideal and its guiding principle. It was the dream of Loyola to organize a thoroughly disciplined and mobilized body of men that should be ever ready to move at the word of command, that should move quickly and effectively against the foes of the Church. He considered the active life to be far higher than the life contemplative. Especially did the exigencies of the age, the necessity of preventing the further encroachment of heresy and of recovering the ground that had been lost to the Church, make an active life preferable to one spent in the seclusion of the cloisters. He saw that asceticism is a bad preparation for an active life in as much as it consumes more force than it supplies and lessens the flexibility and versatility that he demanded from his followers. Every article in the constitutions that he drew up is directed with incomparable logical sequence to a life of practical activity. The members of the society, then, were to find their work not in the solitude of the convent cell but out in the world of men. They were to make themselves all things to all men. To be all things to all men in order to win them over, the principle of the Apostle Paul, was adopted by the Jesuits as the guiding principle of their organization and its activity. They were to deal cautiously with the world and circumspectly with its predilections and prejudices. " Let the entrance be what it may," said Loyola, " the exit must always be ours." Absolute and unquestioning obedience was exacted of every member of the society. " He who wishes to give himself up entirely to God," said Loyola, " must of necessity deliver up not only his will but also his intellect, in such wise that he has but one and the same mind with his superior as he has but one and the same will." His followers contend that this unquestioning obedience is required of the Jesuit only in all matters wherein no sin appears.

Like all such organizations the Society of Jesus did not spring fully formed from the brain of its founder but was the result of tentative theories and gradual growth. Ten years went by from the time of its formal establishment before the text of the constitutions was submitted to an assembly of the professed members. In its first years Loyola's associates, in weekly, or monthly, or yearly letters, according to the distance of the writers from Rome, reported to him " what God had wrought through them "; and it was through his own letters that he directed the vast organization into which the society developed. Excepted from the ascetic practices that consume so much time and energy, the Jesuits went forth into every land as preachers, confessors, teachers, and missionaries. Their self-devotion to the cause of their religion was unsurpassed; their complete absorption in the character and the policies of the corporation to which they belonged was unique. Emancipating the Catholic pulpits from the bondage of scholasticism, they became the most eloquent preachers of the age, and often-times the churches were too small to hold the multitudes that flocked to hear them. Sermons were preached and masses were performed without fees. Even the customary boxes for voluntary offerings were removed from the vestibules of the churches.

Through the confessional the Jesuits gained an enormous influence. The theory and practice of confession were fully developed before the founding of the Society of Jesus. But the members of the new organization were quick to see greater possibilities and opportunities in the institution. Very early they began systematic work as confessors, and through it they won their first striking successes. They dealt warily with the sins of the world. To some of the faithful they were the strictest of spiritual directors, while to others they were most indulgent. Much depended upon the character and the circumstances of the penitent. Circumspection, accommodation of themselves with consummate skill to the circumstances of the particular confession, was the keynote of their policy in the administering of the penitential sacrament. Thus they made themselves the most popular confessors of the time, learned the secret struggles of the souls of princes as well as paupers and gained an influence that decided many a public as well as many a private question. Loyola impressed upon the Jesuit confessors the need of leniency. Every man was to be sent away from the confessional in such a frame of mind that he would be certain to return even though absolution had been withheld from him. When this leniency became a matter of common knowledge it met with the objection of the more austere Catholics, and in the middle of the seventeenth century this objection found indignant voice in Antoine Arnauld's book *On the frequency of Holy Communion.*

With the same sagacity that led Loyola to discard the unnecessary and incumbering monastic habits and rules of the older orders the Jesuits devoted themselves to the work of education. To win over the rising generation to their cause, especially to gain the sons of the governing classes, was one of their aims most intelligently and diligently pursued. Gradually they developed a carefully considered educational system, which became effective and important after the death of Loyola. In their schools, which were divided into several classes, they employed a method of instruction that from the most rudimentary to the highest grades was essentially the same. Strict attention was paid to the moral culture of the pupils and to the inculcation of correct manners. They made no charge for their tuition, being distinctly forbidden by their rules to do so. Their text books were the best of the time and their instruction covered the whole range of secular and ecclesiastical learning. Very soon, by the strategical location of their schools, their well-organized plan of instruction, their varied curricula, their unsurpassed manuals, and above all by their indefatigable activity, their incessant watchfulness, and their unity of purpose, they made themselves, in the generation that immediately succeeded the Council of Trent, indispensable as instructors to the Catholic world. And their schools won the patronage of many Protestants. Even so profound a thinker as Francis Bacon declared them to be the best teachers that civilization had produced.

The activity of the Jesuits was not confined to Europe. They " invaded all the countries which the great maritime discoveries of the preceding age had laid open to European enterprise. They were to be found in the depths of the Peruvian mines, at the marts of African slave-caravans, on the shores of the Spice Islands, in the observatories of China. They made converts in regions which neither avarice nor curiosity had tempted any of their countrymen to enter; and preached and disputed in tongues of which no other native of the West understood a word." The greatest leader of their religious activity among the heathen was the little, worn, blue-eyed Francis Xavier, canonized not only by Catholicism, but by every sect in Christendom. Whether we consider the daring and romantic spirit of his adventures, the length of his journeys, or the reported results of his endeavors, there is no other missionary quite like him in all history.

" Philanthropy was his passion, reckless daring his delight; and faith glowing in meridian splendor the sunshine in which he walked." Like a meteor he sped across the East, passing unscathed through innumerable dangers and winning everywhere, by the compelling charm of his personality, the hearts of the poor and the outcast with whom above all others he so loved to dwell. His " conversions " rapidly reached into the tens of thousands; but before long he became convinced of the uselessness of attempting to win the Orientals over to Christianity in the mass. He recognized that the eastern point of view, the Oriental cultures, must be intimately understood and that then the intellectual and spiritual leaders must be won over and persuaded voluntarily to relinquish their old religion. The problem was conceived correctly, but it remained unsolved. The Jesuit propaganda in southern and eastern Asia touched only the externals of life in those lands. It failed to seize upon the essence of the eastern culture and transmute it with the religion of the West. Consequently their missionary activity, glorious as some of its details undoubtedly are, was eventually almost an utter failure. Very soon the story of Xavier's missionary activity became blurred with the customary legendary accretion, but high above it all there rises his sweet spirit and heroic figure; and to him and to his work his Church was able to point with pride as a striking proof of her living strength in the midst of the European apostasy.

Among the heretics, as well as among the heathen and the infidels, did the Jesuits carry on a tireless propaganda. Wherever Protestantism had found a footing, Catholic princes and sometimes prelates (for the old opposition between the secular and the regular clergy found full vent in the jealousy with which the bishops eyed the Jesuits) invoked their aid. In all the northern and western countries of Europe that had departed from Catholicism they acted both as ecclesiastical and political agents. They watched over the little groups that had remained faithful to the Mother Church and confirmed them in their loyalty; and in a busy and often daring and romantic activity they endeavored to win back the deserters of the ancient fold in one way or another as a prudent expediency seemed to dictate. In this work they employed all the qualities that had been sought for in the selection of their members and accentuated by the discipline of their order; and by so doing they aroused a special distrust and fear of themselves in the apostate lands that developed into a positive mania. They had a good many striking successes in individual cases; and it is not too much to say that after the first outbreak of the Protestant Revolution they were largely instrumental in limiting its progress.

CHAP.
XXI

1540-56

Loyola
Chosen
General

Loyola's idealism, at once mystical and energetically practical in the highest degree, had at last found expression in the establishment of the Society of Jesus; and, conforming to the desire of his colleagues and the commands of his confessor, he became in 1541 its first general. Under his direction the work of the society was carried on with a zeal and a success that must have surpassed his fondest hopes.

In Italy the new society met with extraordinary success from the beginning. Its most tried and trusted leaders were sent to those places where heretical ideas had gained a footing. Lainez was sent to the Venetian territory, Le Jay was assigned to Ferrara, Salmeron was despatched to Naples, and other fathers were sent to other places where heresy had shown itself above the surface. Soon the peninsula became studded with Jesuit schools and convents. No less immediately was the influence of the society felt in that other peninsula in which its founder had been born. Despite the fact that the Spanish government regarded them with suspicion as the special emissaries of the Papacy and that the Dominicans, who were powerfully entrenched in the kingdom, viewed them with jealousy, the Jesuits made an even greater progress in Spain than they did in Italy. Very soon they were chosen as confessors by the most important members of the nobility. In John III of Portugal they found a particularly zealous patron and so rapid progress was made in his dominions. North of the Alps and the Pyrénées the society advanced less rapidly. In France, where the episcopacy was still animated by the spirit of Gallican liberty, they were opposed by the bishops and the faculty of the Sorbonne who instinctively scented dangerous rivals in the new body that professed itself to be the special flying squadron of the Papacy. But in spite of opposition an entry into France was obtained, and the progress of the society there, though very slow for a considerable time, was nevertheless steady. To secure a firm foothold in Germany was a measure specially desired by Loyola. "It is there," he said, "that the pest of heresy has exposed men to graver dangers than elsewhere." Bobadilla began active work in Bavaria and soon won the support of the duke. Before long the University of Ingolstadt became one of the two great Jesuit centers in Germany. In Austria the confidence of King Ferdinand, who soon intrusted the new priests with the control of the University of Vienna, was quickly secured by Le Jay. From these two centers the influence of the Jesuits

spread in all directions. Colleges were established in many
parts of Austria, and a Jesuit school, designed chiefly for the
education of the young Bohemian nobles, was opened in Prague.
The University of Cologne, a most important strategical gain,
fell into their hands, and in many other places the zeal, the
fervor, and the diplomatic character of Jesuit activity secured
still further successes. In the papal curia the society came to
exercise a marked influence to which their presence in the Council of Trent, as the pope's theologians, gave signal testimony.
It was a wise stroke of policy for the Papacy to intrust its cause
in the Council so largely to the Jesuits, for, more than to anything else, it was due to their efforts that the great convention,
dreaded by every pope that had to deal with it, resulted in an
increase rather than a diminution of the papal power and prestige. At the death of Loyola in 1556 the society included about
one thousand men, but its influence was far beyond that which
one would naturally ascribe to so comparatively slender a number. Thirteen provinces had been established, seven in Spanish
and Portuguese territory, three in Italy, one in France, and
two in Germany. Other European countries, too, had been
entered; and beyond the ocean, in America, Africa, and Asia,
Jesuit missionaries were busily engaged in their self-sacrificing
labors. So effective was their work in Europe that to them
must be ascribed, more than to any other single force, the largest
share in stemming the great tidal wave of the Protestant apostasy
that threatened to sweep Catholicism south of the Alps.

The establishment of the Society of Jesus and the apparently
marvelous rapidity with which it grew in power were but the
natural result of the preceding ecclesiastical and religious evolution. The Church, as we have seen, became dominated by the
**The New
Order a
Product of
the Time**
papal curia; and the activity of the curia was very largely given
over to the things of this world, to financial and political affairs.
There were many efforts to reform the consequent moral and
religious demoralization; efforts within the Church, and at last,
beginning with Luther, efforts without the Church. The actual
schisms of the Protestant Revolution made all those reformers
who deemed it best to stay within the ancient fold more determined than ever to remove the evils that had destroyed that
unity of the Church which was to them a mark of her divine
origin. They began to see that reform must be far-reaching,
that it could not stop with the mere correction of immorality,
but must go on to an increased efficiency of the clergy by means
of a better education and preparation for their work, and that
it must include a reform of worship and a simplification and

authoritative definition of dogma. If the Papacy was to retain
its position of supreme authority it was necessary that it should
put itself at the head of this reform party within the Church
whose plans had gradually grown wider and whose mood had
become increasingly militant. It so happened that at this time
a series of men committed to this very policy occupied the papal
throne. It is not a matter of surprise, then, that the Society
of Jesus, destined at first in the mind of Loyola to confine its
activity to the Mohammedan countries, should have been caught
up on the crest of the wave of reform within the Church and
swept into the forefront of aggressive Catholicism. It was born
in the very hour of need. It answered to the intimate necessity of the Church. And so the very circumstances of the time
imposed its career upon it and, in part, guaranteed its success.
The genius of Loyola is unquestionable. He had the thoughts
of a philosopher and the emotions of a saint. He matched the
cunning of every diplomat with whom he came into contact, and
neither he nor his schemes suffered from the learning of any
lawyer. But nevertheless the Society of Jesus, which he founded,
was a product of the time quite as much as were the Council of
Trent, the revived Inquisition, and the Congregation of the Index; and more than any of these institutions it was the expression of the militant spirit of Catholicism that had been aroused
by rebellion. Two forces, discipline and liberty, conservatism
and innovation, are forever at work in human life. The excess
of one engenders uniformity and stagnation, while the excess
of the other produces disorder. In both extremes is the germ
of death. The tendencies of the Renaissance toward paganism,
scepticism, and rationalism, and the result of the reformation
movement north of the Alps in rebellion, seemed to point to
discipline and conservatism as the chief need of Catholicism.
That seeming need the new society answered most effectually.
And discipline and conservatism have ever since remained its
watchword and its shibboleth.

# CHAPTER XXII

### THE COUNCIL OF TRENT

1. The Crisis.
2. The Council.
3. The Council's Sequel.

CHAP.
XXII

1555-61

The Neces-
sity of the
Council
and its
Opportun-
ity

TO the Council of Trent, in which the Jesuits played so important a part, we must now turn our attention. First of all, however, there must be noted the crisis that made imperative its convocation. Lutheranism had recovered from the defeat it had suffered in 1547 at the battle of Mühlberg; and it had spread not only in northern Germany, where it had become paramount, but also in the Scandinavian and Slavonic lands to the north; and in 1552 its inroads in far-off Iceland caused the disappearance of the last official representatives of Catholicism. In Hungary the new creed was making its way, and in Transylvania the property of the old Church was confiscated by a formal decree of the diet. In southern Germany the Lutheran tenets had become firmly established in those districts into which they had early found their way and in addition had become more widely extended. In Rhenish and Danubian lands alike the activity of the heretics was most energetic. Everywhere, it seemed, Catholicism sustained losses in worldly possessions and spiritual influence. Into the universities, too, the new opinions had penetrated and become predominant. About the middle of the century two decades had gone by in which not a single student in the University of Vienna had been ordained a priest. Calvinism, also, was spreading in all directions from its strategic center. It had found its way into eastern Germany, Hungary, and Poland. In the Low Countries and in Scotland it had risen into independent power; in England it was in alliance with the monarchy; and in France it continued not only to maintain itself but to increase in defiance of persecution. England, having separated herself from the Papacy by act of parliament, had a State church of her own. From the arctic circle to the Pyrénées and from the Bay of Biscay almost to the Black Sea the new

430

doctrines had found their way and were threatening still further encroachments. Men of all ranks, says Macaulay, were to be found in the multitude of innovators. " Sovereigns impatient to appropriate for themselves the prerogatives of the popes, nobles desirous to share the plunder of abbeys, suitors exasperated by the extortions of the Roman camera, patriots impatient of a foreign rule, good men scandalized by the corruptions of the Church, bad men desirous of the license inseparable from great moral revolutions, wise men eager in the pursuit of truth, weak men allured by the glitter of novelty, all were found on one side. . . . Within fifty years from the day on which Luther publicly renounced communion with the Papacy, and burned the bull of Leo before the gates of Wittenberg, Protestantism attained its highest ascendency." But, as we have seen, the various State churches and sects of Protestantism were by no means friendly to each other. They were not magnanimous enough to tolerate theological differences in each other. The doctrine of the Lord's Supper, for instance, was the subject of the bitterest strife between Lutherans and Calvinists, and both these groups were hostile to the Anglicans who, in their turn, reciprocated the feeling of enmity. Protestant antagonists assailed each other with extreme bitterness and reckless violence. Thus did they fail to present a united front to their reinvigorated foe and help to bring about the loss, in a large measure, of the ascendancy they had so recently gained.

Italy, Spain, Portugal, where the symptoms of dissent had been completely suppressed, and Ireland had remained wholly Catholic; and the majority of the people in France, Poland, and Hungary still professed the ancient creed. The English nobility and many of the commons were still Catholic; and so were several of the Swiss cantons, the Walloon provinces of the Netherlands, and many parts of Germany. The passive attitude of defense with which the Church had hitherto been content in the face of the great outbreak of Protestantism now gave way to one of vigorous aggression. In our study of the revival of conscience and of the inroads of heresy into Italy and Spain we have seen something of the beginnings of the Catholic Reformation; in the chapter devoted to the fears that beset men in the middle of the sixteenth century we have seen that the psychological condition of the time induced many who had abandoned the faith of their childhood to return to the ancient fold and prevented others from leaving it; and we have just noted in the rise of the Jesuits the establishment of a powerful militia that the Church was to use most effectively in her onslaught upon the seceders. All the signs of the times pointed to a great and successful outburst of militant Catholicism. The Catholic Church was determined not to abate in the least her claim of being the one true church directly descendant from Christ; and she was resolved to attempt the recovery of all the territory that had disowned her dominion. But first of all it was necessary to define her creeds and to make the line of demarcation between Catholic and non-Catholic clear and unmistakable. Hitherto too much liberty of interpretation had been allowed within her pale; but when some of her fundamental dogmas were attacked it seemed imperative that they should be submitted to a rigid definition.

The Con-
vocation,
Earliest
Sessions,
and Or-
ganization
of the
Council

Paul III (1534–49) was now the reigning pontiff. The situation that confronted him appeared most perplexing. As the head of the Church it was plainly his duty to carry on the reformation of morals and to bring about a settlement of the doctrinal disputes. It was apparent that these things could not be accomplished by the ordinary promulgation of decrees. The clamor for a general council of the Church was widespread and incessant. But councils were dangerous to the papal power. Those of Constance and Basel had made determined attempts to lessen the papal authority. Might not the conciliar theory, were another council to be convoked, secure such a new impetus in the present state of affairs as to make irresistible its fulfilment in practice? Then, too, the Pope, in addition to being the head of the Church, was also the head of an Italian principality. And Paul, as a political potentate, conceived Charles V to be his most dangerous opponent. Charles was particularly clamant for a council. Might not the powerful Emperor, who had assumed the heavy burden of putting Christendom in order, secure control of the council and curtail the authority of the Holy See? Filled with these doubts and fears the Pope delayed the summoning of the council as long as possible. At last, after many postponements, the council met in 1542 at Trent, a town in the Austrian Tyrol. Two reasons determined the choice of the town. Being just within the Empire it technically fulfilled the desire of Charles to have the council held in Germany; and being on the Italian side of the Alps it was somewhat removed from falling out of the control of the Papacy. But so scant was the attendance because of the outbreak of the last war between the Emperor and Francis I of France, that it was prorogued; and not until the end of 1545 was its first session inaugurated. In April of the following year there were only between sixty and seventy prelates in attendance; and of these the large majority were Italian. The council was therefore, at that time, very far from being œcumenical in character. The Pope was represented by three legates, Giovanni del Monte, Marcello Cervini, and Reginald Pole, all of whom were cardinals. There was no accepted method for the organization and conduct of general councils. So this important matter had to be determined there and then. The right to vote was limited to bishops and the generals of religious orders; voting was to be by individuals and not by nations; and no absentee was to be permitted to vote by proxy. Thus was there adroitly ensured the preponderance of the Italian prelates. Some years later, when the right to initiate measures for discussion was reserved exclusively to the legates, who were constantly in communication with Rome, and when all important enactments were made subject to the pontifical confirmation, the triumph of the papal party in the council was assured.

When the machinery had been thus arranged the debates did not begin without a dispute as to whether questions of doctrine or questions of the reformation of ecclesiastical abuses should take precedence. It was finally decided to consider them simultaneously. Among the earliest decisions was the one relating to tradition. Protestantism held that the Scriptures should be the sole reliance of the Christian. Catholicism declared that the tradition in the keeping of the Church should have equal weight with the Bible. Here was a fundamental clash between the two systems. It was decided, with only six dissenting votes, that the tradition of the Church is of equal importance with the Scriptures. And so to-day this idea of the importance of Catholic tradition permeates all the faithful members of the Church, laity as well as clergy. The Holy Ghost abides perpetually within the Church; she has received the explicit promise of Christ that the gates of hell shall not prevail against her; therefore the tradition in her keeping, dealing with essential matters of faith, cannot be mistaken and is of equal importance with the Bible. Then there was the question as to the text of the Scriptures. All through the Middle Ages the translation of the Bible into Latin by St. Jerome, known as the *Vulgate,* had been the authoritative text. The humanists had found many flaws in the translation, and Luther asserted it to be full of errors. But, with the injunction that hereafter it should be printed with scrupulous care, the *Vulgate* was declared to be the authoritative version. The great question of justification was then considered. Is man saved by faith alone, or is he saved by faith and good works? Salvation by faith alone was the central

Decisions
Regarding
Matters
of Belief
and De-
crees Con
cerning
Conduct

thought of Protestantism. Around it had revolved the most
bitter animosities. Its acceptance by the council would have
rendered the entire sacramental system of the Church unnecessary. It would seem that a sincere effort was made by a considerable number of the delegates to understand the Protestant
position and to deal with it justly. Yet so diametrically opposed
are the two positions, and so divergent are the two types of
piety, and the two modes of daily life that flow from them,
that the essential part of good works in the process of salvation,
although men were warned against relying exclusively upon
them, was proclaimed. When the necessity of works had thus
been declared, the seven sacraments, the most important of all
works, were pronounced to be final, enduring and indispensable.
The sacraments, with the exception of baptism in a time of
extremity, can be administered only by a duly ordained priest.
When, therefore, the indispensability of the sacraments was
enunciated the dependence of the laity upon the priesthood was
confirmed. Concurrently with these decisions were published
decrees that looked to the reformation of ecclesiastical abuses.
Preaching and the teaching of theology were regulated, residence in their respective districts was enjoined upon the
clergy, and the plurality of incompatible benefices was forbidden.

Several men stand out above the others in the discussions of
the council. Prominent among the leading debaters was Cardinal Gasparo Contarini, whom we have already met as one of
those high-minded Catholics who wished to see a thorough-going
reformation carried on within the pale of the Church and who
desired a reconciliation between the great divisions that had
arisen in Christendom. At the council he was much more interested in the reform of morals and discipline than in the disputes over doctrine. Reginald Pole, the English cardinal, was
another of the mediating reformers who hoped to see the council result in the reunion and the reinvigoration of western Christendom. Cardinal Girolamo Seripando, general of the Augus-
tinians, in whom were combined the desirable features of humanism and Christianity, was the chief advocate of a compromise
doctrine of justification. In striking contrast to these conciliatory spokesmen was the bigoted Cardinal Caraffa, of whom we
have already seen something as a reforming bishop in Italy and
of whom we are to see still more as a reforming pope. He was
one of the most vigorous opponents of the attempt to effect a
compromise upon the doctrine of justification. By the reforming energy of Cardinal Ximenes the Spanish prelates had been

made the best bishops in Europe; but they did not arrive at Trent until the discussions we have just noted were concluded. They were inflexibly orthodox, but they had a keen realization of the corruption of the papal curia and the general immorality of the clergy, and they were prepared to use the surgeon's knife in removing the evils that afflicted the Church. Finally there should be noted the two Jesuits, Salmeron and Lainez, who acted as the Pope's theologians. Both of them were able men, and the latter was extraordinarily eloquent. They had been enjoined by Loyola to resist all innovation in doctrine, and so they combated Seripando and his associates with all the skill and energy at their command. They were permitted to preach during the council, a privilege denied to the other delegates, and soon they ingratiated themselves into the good will even of the Spanish bishops. So unusual was their knowledge of the writings of the great fathers of the Church and of the conclusions of the scholastic philosophy, and so successful were they in presenting themselves as the advocates of purity of doctrine, that they came to wield a preponderating influence in the council.

Thus far, in the council, from the papal point of view, all had gone well. No impairment of the power of the Papacy had been made and the primary errors of Protestantism had been condemned. But the hopes of the Emperor had been unfulfilled. The questions of ecclesiastical reform had not been thoroughly dealt with, and the prospect of reconciliation with the Protestants seemed more remote than ever. Charles was meeting with success in Germany, and it seemed to Paul that, when he had compelled obedience there, he might go to Trent and insist upon far-reaching reforms. The danger of such an occurrence would not be so great were the council nearer Rome. So, in 1547, the outbreak of a few cases of the plague at Trent was seized upon as a pretext and the Council was removed to Bologna. It was the interests of his Italian principality, and his personal power as the Pope, rather than the unity of Christendom with which Paul was chiefly concerned. But not all the delegates acquiesced in the removal. Fourteen prelates remained to face the plague and the consequences of the imperial dictation. Charles protested against the transference of the Council as being unnecessary and unlawful, and he announced his intention of regarding its proceedings as invalid until it resumed its sittings at Trent. The death of Paul brought upon the scene a new Pope, Julius III (1550–55), who, as the cardinal Del Monte, had been one of the three legates at the council. Quite unexpectedly he yielded to the Emperor's desire by sending the council back to Trent,

CHAP.
XXII

1547-49

The Re-
newed
Sessions
at Trent

where, in 1551, it renewed its deliberations. Nothing had been accomplished at Bologna.

The second meeting of the Council of Trent was comparatively insignificant. Henry II of France, who was about to begin war with the Emperor in Italy, objected to the choice of an imperial town as the meeting place of the council. He recalled the French prelates who were there and forbade others to go. The small attendance compelled an adjournment from May to September. The new legate, Cardinal Crescenzio, was a staunch supporter of the Papacy. So the prospect of the reunion of western Christendom seemed dimmer than ever. Yet owing to the Emperor's constant pressure a number of Protestants, laymen who were the delegates of some of the Protestant princes, appeared at the council. The dogmas that had helped to bring about their separation from Rome had already been defined, so it is not easy to see what was to be expected of their participation. The wide gulf that now separated the Protestants from the Catholics could be only more clearly revealed. Still it was always the belief of Charles that if only the leaders of the two divisions of Christendom could be brought together in a deliberative assembly the breach would be healed. Affairs in Germany, Italy, and Spain might at any moment require the Emperor's presence. Charles could not be everywhere at once. So he went to Innsbruck where he could watch over the council. Thence he could march without loss of time either into Italy or Spain, or could return quickly to Germany. But no sooner had he left Germany than Maurice of Saxony began to take advantage of his absence, and before many months had gone by the traitorous prince was advancing with an army along the broad road to Innsbruck and to Trent. The Pope and his legates had already become fearful that the appearance of the Protestant deputies, and the presence of the Emperor within an easy march of three days from Trent, might induce bolder proceedings on the part of the council against the papal authority. The advance of the Protestant prince in 1552, which compelled the Emperor to flee from Innsbruck, was therefore a welcome reason for the suspension of the council.

Although the Council was suspended for only two years an entire decade was to go by before it met again. Many things hindered its resumption. The war between the Protestant princes and the Emperor in Germany was ended in 1552, it is true, by the peace of Passau. But the war between the Emperor and the king of France still continued, and so Charles found it impossible to insist upon the summoning of the council at the expiration of

CHAP.
XXII

1552-62

Why the
Council
Waited

the two years. Julius was apparently desirous not to have the council meet again. The risk to the papal power seemed too great. When he died he was succeeded by Marcellus II (1555), whose life had been free from the shadow of reproach, who was genuinely devoted to the cause of reform, but who unfortunately reigned only twenty-two days. Under the title of Paul IV (1555–59) the relentless cardinal Caraffa now became Pope. From the ardor with which he had carried on the work of reform in his Italian diocese it was to be expected that the ecclesiastical abuses would at once find in him a vigorous assailant. But reform was delayed in order that what were deemed to be the interests of the papal principality might be advanced. Paul had long disliked the Spaniards. He regarded their power in Italy as a menace to the papal state. So he wished to see them weakened if not banished altogether from the peninsula. At his request a French army entered Italy; but in 1557 a disaster to the French arms at St. Quentin on the Flemish frontier compelled its withdrawal and the Spanish power in the peninsula was more firmly established than ever. Charles V had died. The Empire had been divided. And it seemed clear that Philip II could enter Italy through Naples far more easily and effectively than could his father from over the Alps. There seemed nothing to do, therefore, but to abandon the project of dislodging the Spaniard from Italy. So, with all his impetuous energy and implacable spirit, the disappointed pontiff turned to the work of reform. He it was who gave the decisive impulse to the Catholic Reformation in the second half of the sixteenth century. None of his predecessors had so keenly perceived as he the abuses that then prevailed in the Church. But of all the popes of the Trentine period he was the only one who failed to convoke the council. How is this to be reconciled with his undoubted desire to effect reform? Public opinion was by no means unanimous in favor of a resumption of the council. At its opening the council had excited great hopes, but thus far its practical results were still to seek. The peace of Augsburg in 1555 had guaranteed equality between the Protestant and Catholic estates. All the fundamental Protestant dogmas had been definitely rejected by the council. What hope, then, could there be for a reconciliation of the two parties by means of a renewal of the conference? Paul believed in neither the efficiency nor the opportuneness of the council, and he was not without the fear of an infringement of the papal power that had actuated his predecessors. Under the guidance of the Holy Spirit, he asserted, he could carry out the task of reformation unaided. The important thing was to remove the abuses one by one, and to see that what was ordered was put into execution. He was essentially a man of action, impatient and doubtful of protracted conciliar discussions. So, hostile alike to liberalism within the Church and heresy without, he proceeded to carry out his reforms by means of commissions of which he appointed a considerable number. And although he was not personally in favor of the council his work prepared the way for its resumption and for whatever degree of success it attained.

The last sessions of the council were held in the pontificate of Pius IV (1559–65), who was the antithesis of the austere and passionate Paul. Hitherto it was Germany that had been mainly interested in the council. But now France was involved in a grave religious crisis, with which we are to deal when we come to the religious wars in that country; and Ferdinand of Austria and Philip of Spain both desired to see the relations of the bishops to the Holy See definitely defined and regulated. But kindly and conciliatory as was the new Pope he was nevertheless determined to abate no jot of the papal prerogative; and the question of the relation of the bishops to the Pope was one in which the power of the pontiff was directly involved. The council, however, was resumed, and Pius displayed great skill in the difficult position. Genial and tenacious at the same time, he managed, while appearing to conciliate, to keep the decision of every question in his own hands. So the council began its final labors. All hope of reuniting the Protestants with the Church had long vanished. The concern of the council was therefore limited to the contracted circle of the Catholic countries. The Pope appointed five legates chief of whom was Cardinal Ercole di Gonzaga. But the work of the council did not get under way without serious disputes. Was the council now assembled a continuation of the old one, or was it a new one summoned for the first time? If it were merely a continuation the legates, of course, would have the sole right to submit matters for discussion, no important measure could be passed without the Pope's approval, and thus the papal party would be in its former impregnable position. The French and German ambassadors had been instructed by their respective governments to propose a number of measures looking to reform. They desired to have the mass said in the vernacular, to have the service books revised, to have the wine as well as the wafer given to the laity in the sacrament of communion, to abolish the compulsory celibacy of the clergy, to reform the curia, to enforce the residence of ecclesiastics in their districts, to abolish the papal prerogative of granting dispensations and exemptions from the laws of the

Predomi-
nance of
the Pa-
pal Influ-
ence in
the Final
Sessions

Church, and to limit the power of excommunication. It did not seem likely that many of these questions would be submitted to the council for discussion were the sole right to propose the subjects to be debated left once more in the hands of the legates. So lively were the debates as to whether the council was a new one or merely a resumption of the former one that the assembly was in danger of dissolution. At last it was decided that the council was a continuation of the preceding one. So under the old conditions the council went to work. Soon the papal and the episcopal parties clashed. The episcopal party, whose most important members were the Spanish prelates, asserted that the authority of the bishops is not derived from the Pope but has a direct origin from Christ. Thus they struck at the very foundation of the established hierarchical system. Their success would have changed the character of the government of the Church completely. The matter was bitterly disputed for about ten months. Vigorous, too, were the debates over the question of the chalice. Should the wine as well as the bread be given to the laity in the communion? Italy and Spain opposed the concession, while France and Germany favored it. The Pope was not averse to the innovation; and the only serious argument against it was that it might create a lack of uniformity in the ritual of the mass. The legates seldom made use of their sole right to initiate measures for discussion. Consequently other measures in the German and French projects of reform, that have been outlined in the list of topics which the ambassadors from those countries had been instructed to present, were debated. These radical changes, however, were all abhorrent to the Spaniards who, although they were eager for reform in discipline, were exceedingly orthodox in all matters that related to ceremony and dogma. So there was little hope of their adoption. More than any others it was the Jesuits who determined the decisions of the council. It is true that the order itself had no direct voice in the assembly. But the brilliant and oftentimes eloquent discussions of Lainez and Salmeron had an enormous influence and were a striking demonstration of the new force that had arisen in the world. They displayed all that skill in the conduct of public affairs for which their order became so celebrated. Powerful, too, but in a different fashion, was the Cardinal Carlo Borromeo, nephew of the Pope, of whose works as a reformer we are to see something in our next chapter. Irreproachable in his personal life, saintly in character, unremitting in the performance of his priestly duties, generous to the poor and devoted to the afflicted, he was the living embodiment of all the virtues of the Catholic Reformation. Of great importance in the practical conduct of affairs was Cardinal Giovanni Morone, who, as we have seen, was one of the mediating reformers, and who, upon the death of one of the original appointees, was made a legate at the council. His skilful diplomacy was largely responsible for the victory of the curial party. In April 1563 he journeyed to Innsbruck to propitiate the Emperor Ferdinand who had been offended by the defeat of his project of reform. So skilfully was this delicate negotiation contrived that the imperial ambassadors were instructed to keep on good terms with the legates. After that the difficulty experienced by the papal party in managing the council was greatly lessened. The accomplished cardinal displayed equal diplomatic skill in conciliating many of the individual prelates who were hostile to the particular interests of the Papacy. "To him," says Von Ranke, "more than to any other man is the Catholic Church indebted for the peaceful termination of the council."

The political difficulties being thus greatly lessened it became possible to reach conclusions upon the theological and ecclesiastical questions that were acceptable to the Papacy. Although the difference is not always apparent upon the surface the conclusions of the council may be divided into two classes; (1) the canons, which relate to dogma, and (2) the decrees, which relate to discipline. In the space at our disposal it is possible for us to give only a brief analysis of the principal Tridentine promulgations. With regard to the matter of indulgences that had started the Lutheran schism it was decided to abolish the practice of selling them for money; and, for a time, the granting of them for other considerations was restricted. The belief in purgatory was confirmed, the adoration of the saints was sanctioned, and the use of images and relics commended. The existence of the seven sacraments, baptism, penance, communion, confirmation, matrimony, holy orders, and extreme unction, was affirmed. Each sacrament it was declared, instituted by Christ, confers a special grace. Only with faith in Christ and with those sacraments that the ordinary layman receives is it possible for man to be saved. Faith alone is not sufficient. The administration of the sacraments was regulated by definite ordinances. The bitter dispute regarding the relations of the episcopate to the Papacy was at last ended by the affirmation of the supremacy of the Pope. All the bishops solemnly swore to obey the decisions of the council and to subject themselves absolutely to the papal direction; and strict performance of their duties, especially that of the supervision of the subordinate clergy in their respective dioceses, was enjoined upon them. One of the most impor- tant ordinances was that which provided for the establishment in every diocese of a seminary in which boys were to be trained for the priesthood. Thus was provision made for an improvement in the character and ability of the clergy. Decrees were issued look- ing to the elimination of abuses in the performance of marriages. In order to avoid clandestine marriages it was prescribed that the sacrament should not be ministered until the banns had thrice been published in the church and unless three witnesses, one of whom was the parish priest (or another priest whom he had authorized to represent him) of one of the two contracting parties. With regard to the clergy the council declined to abolish the requirement of celibacy. Reformatory decrees relating to a number of ecclesiastical abuses, especially to that of plurality of benefices, were issued. The distinction between the canons, that relate to dogma, and the decrees, that relate to discipline, should be kept clearly in mind. The canons immediately upon their promulgation by the Pope became binding upon every member of the church. Whosoever declined to accept any one of them be- came *ipso facto* excommunicate. But discipline is a matter that varies from time to time and from place to place. Whosoever declined to accept the decrees might be rash and even rebellious, but he did not thereby become a heretic. With this distinction in mind we shall the better understand the attitude of certain Catholic countries in declining to accept the decrees of the coun- cil. The decrees by no means dealt with all the ecclesiastical abuses of the time. No reform of the curia, for instance, with its preoccupation with political and financial affairs was attempted. And the canons, far from relating to all the dogmas of the Church, dealt only with those that had been called into question by the schismatics of the century.

On December 4, 1563, the prelates, many of them deeply af- fected by emotion, met for the last time. On that day the council was dissolved. Having eradicated many of the tares sown by her worldly ecclesiastics and defined her disputed doctrines the penitent and militant Church faced the world frankly and ex- plicitly with not a little of her old serenity and assurance. The line of demarcation between Catholicism and Protestantism had been sharply drawn. The Church had driven Protestantism from her fold with anathema. She had thrown compromise to the winds and chosen instead to meet her foes in combat. Her forces were concentrated under a single direction while those of the enemy were divided. It was not an unmixed gain, however, that the Church had reaped from the deliberations at Trent. She had

Dissolu- tion of the Council

been rendered less Catholic and more Italian in character. Her practice had become reformed but her dogma had become more rigid. Less involved in the things of secular life she was also less able, because of the dynamic character of life and the static character of her doctrine, to deal with life itself.

The bull *Benedictus Deus,* issued on January 26, 1564, confirmed the proceedings of the council and enunciated the sole right of the Pope to interpret its canons and decrees. The decisions of the council were printed in order that copies might be sent to all the bishops of the Church. And on August 2, 1564, the Pope signed a bull appointing a special congregation, to consist of eight cardinals, to direct the carrying out of the Tridentine decisions. The council had left to the Pope the execution of a number of measures which because of a lack of time, it had found itself unable to perform. Among these were the revision of the breviary (the book of prayers that every ecclesiastic in major orders is bound to read each day) and the missal (the book containing the ritual of the mass), the compilation of a catalogue of forbidden books, and the completion of the new catechism which the council had left in an unfinished state. Revised editions of the breviary and missal were published and also a new edition of the canon law. More than a century before this time measures had been taken for the suppression of heretical books; and in 1559 the first papal Index of prohibited books had been published. But this was deemed inadequate by the Tridentine assembly and so in 1564 a new one was issued. A great need had been felt of a satisfactory manual for the instruction of the laity in the essential articles of the Catholic creed. It was to fill this want that the Emperor Ferdinand requested his confessor, Peter Canisius, to prepare a Catechism. This task the Jesuit father completed. It served to help the Catholic laity to entrench themselves behind the authority of the great fathers of the Church. But the catechism of Canisius did not appear to the prelates at Trent to be completely satisfactory. So a new one was undertaken; and in 1566, after several papal commissions had worked at the task, it was published under the title of *The Roman Catechism.* It is a summary of the chief doctrines of the Church designed for the use of the clergy in their own theological education but chiefly for their aid in giving theological instruction to the laity. Still another sequel of the Council of Trent was the use and extension of the bull *In cœnâ Domini* (1364–1586) which, unlike other bulls, is not the work of a single pope. It excommunicated heretics, and was read each year on the last Thursday in Lent, the day preceding the anniversary of the sacrifice on the cross. Secular rulers had constantly complained about it, because, in explicit terms, it asserted the supremacy of the Papacy over the civil authorities; but Pius V in 1567 made it more severe than ever. Finally, however, in 1770, owing to the opposition of both Catholic and Protestant rulers, Clement XIV discontinued its publication.

The militant spirit of the Church had brought victory to her banners in the great struggles of the bygone centuries. That spirit was now revived. The onslaught upon Protestantism was about to begin. Among the instruments and forces with which the Church assailed the schismatics the most important were the Inquisition, the Jesuits, the Council of Trent, the Index, and the reforming popes. As one of these instruments the Council has sometimes been over-estimated. Although it is claimed that the assembly represented the universal church, there were present in the final sessions one hundred and eighty-seven Italian prelates, whereas only eighty-one represented all the rest of Christendom. And, among the forces at the command of the Church in the struggle for her lost possessions, the Council was essentially defensive, while the others were essentially offensive. Viewed from the standpoint of the Papacy the work of the Council was a necessary part of the general strategy. But defense in itself is seldom sufficient to win victory even in religious warfare. In conclusion it may be said that the fact that the history of the Council is the history of Europe for almost a quarter of a century has been scarcely indicated. Many of the political and religious currents that agitated its meetings have not been noticed. But having seen something of the main outlines of its proceedings we must now devote our attention to the work of the reforming popes and to the activity of the Jesuits in the second half of the century.

# CHAPTER XXIII

## THE TRIUMPH OF MILITANT CATHOLICISM

1. The Reforming Popes.
2. The Jesuit Reformation.
3. The Inquisition.
4. The Index.

THE effect of Protestant aggression was to result in an equally violent outbreak of Catholic zeal. The popes abandoned the encouragement of the fine arts and discarded their temporal policy, which in the years gone by had continually involved not only Italy but the greater part of Europe in confusion, in order to devote their energies to far sterner duties. Ancient pollutions were to be washed away, heretical lapses to be punished, and, if possible, the vast secession beyond the Alps to be met and overcome. All this was not easy of accomplishment. Even the conduct of affairs with the Catholic powers, France and Spain, presented the most delicate and difficult tasks. But the popes had one great advantage over their schismatic opponents. Each in his turn was the sole commander of all the forces at his disposal, while those of the enemy were always scattered and oftentimes antagonistic to each other.

Pius V (1565–72) was well-fitted to begin the Catholic campaign. He was an Italian of lowly birth who had entered a Dominican convent when he was but fourteen years of age. The revived Inquisition had now been at work in Italy for almost a quarter of a century. Somewhat ineffective at first it had become an exceedingly vigorous institution. And Pius, as Cardinal Michele Ghislieri, had demonstrated himself to be an effective administrator as the inquisitor-general at Rome. It was well-known, too, that his personal life was free from all reproach of insincerity and immorality. These things it was, executive ability and austerity of character, that, upon the death of Pius IV, pointed him out as the man for the hour. "I was determined to consider nothing so much as religion and purity of faith," said Cardinal Borromeo, who had much to do with the election of the new pope. "I was well acquainted with the piety, the irreproachable life, and the devout spirit of the cardinal of Alessandria. I thought no other could more fitly administer the Christian commonwealth, and so I used my best efforts in his favor." When the triple crown had been placed upon his head Pius did not abandon his ascetic practices. " Under his gorgeous vestments," says Macaulay, " he wore day and night the hair shirt of a simple friar, walked barefoot in the streets at the head of processions, found, even in the midst of his most pressing avocations, time for private prayer, often regretted that the public duties of his station were unfavorable to the growth of holiness, and edified his flock by innumerable instances of humility, charity, and forgiveness of personal injuries, while, at the same time, he upheld the authority of his see, and the unadulterated doctrines of his Church, with all the stubbornness and vehemence of Hildebrand." When borne aloft in the sedia in triumphal procession he was still the unassuming friar; and often tears were seen to stream from his eyes as, lost in silent ecstasy, he bowed his head before the Host exposed upon the lighted altar. Little wonder that in a few decades after his death he was canonized. To few popes does Catholicism owe more than to St. Pius. Ruthless in his persecution of heresy he was also relentless in his punishment of immorality. Three tasks confronted the Papacy at this time — the carrying out of the Tridentine decrees, the war against Protestantism, and the repulse of the Turks. The first two especially claimed the attention of Pius. The new pope made extensive use of the Jesuits in the execution of his plans. With great precision and punctuality they fulfilled his orders; and before long they had displaced all others as the diplomatic agents of the Papacy.

No obstacle, on the part of the Catholics, had been encountered by the canons of the Council of Trent. But the reformatory enactments came into conflict with other interests. Pius IV had requested every Catholic prince to give to the decrees the validity of secular law. Such a request was not so radical a demand as it would be if it were made to-day. Little distinction was then made between ecclesiastical and secular affairs. The principal Italian states and Poland and Portugal had acceded to the request without reservation. In Germany, though they never obtained imperial recognition, they had found acceptance at the hands of the Catholic princes. In Spain they had been published by Philip II with the reservation that they were not to impinge upon the prerogatives of the crown. Their publication in the Netherlands, as we shall see when we come to the revolt of those countries, met with such vigorous opposition that the reservation was made that they were not to impair any of the privileges enjoyed by the provinces. The decrees met with much opposition in France. The religious wars were just beginning in that country and Catherine de' Medici was reluctant to offend the loyalists, who were opposed to any diminution of the Gallican liberties, or the Huguenots, who, of course, were opposed to the decrees in general. So she promised to carry out certain of the provisions without publishing them in their entirety. Practically the decrees became effective in every Catholic country before the third quarter of the century had been reached. The reformation of the Church then began in earnest. Pius V proceeded with great zeal to eliminate the remaining abuses. All future alienation of Church property was forbidden under whatever title or with whatever pretext. Dispensations from the operation of ecclesiastical laws and regulations were reduced to the minimum. Indulgences were regarded with disfavor; at least their issuance was judged to be inexpedient for the time being, and some of those already proclaimed were partially recalled. The deposition was declared of all bishops who should fail to reside in their dioceses; and heavy penalties were announced for all priests who should fail to remain in their parishes or to see that the services of the Church were duly performed. And so strict were the rules for the regulation of monastic orders that on the part of the members loud complaint arose. Kind and gentle to all whose Catholicism was unquestioned, Pius was pitiless in his persecution of those suspected of heresy. Born under the shadow of the Inquisition, and early imbued with its principles, he greatly stimulated its activity. Cases of heresy of long standing, as well as those of the day, were hunted down and rooted out with sanguinary eagerness and inexhaustible zeal. So devoted was the Pope to the reformation of immorality, the neglect of duty, and the extirpation of dissent, that in return for assistance rendered him in these enterprises, he made Cosimo de' Medici, a great ruler but a most immoral man, grand duke of Tuscany.

The Work of Carlo Borromeo

Any account of the work of the Catholic Reformation that failed to notice the work of Carlo Borromeo (1538–84) would be incomplete. True it is that created cardinal and appointed to the important archiepiscopate of Milan, when only twenty-two years of age, by the nepotism of his uncle, the reigning pontiff, he lived in Rome until the severity of Pius V compelled him to reside in his diocese. But no one can fail to admit, from the Catholic point of view, the holiness of his character. His work in the Council of Trent we have already briefly noticed; and we have seen that he had much to do with the election that placed

Pius V upon the papal throne. When he went to live at Milan he devoted himself with incessant industry and passionate energy to the reformation of his diocese. He did not scruple to use the severest penalties to extinguish heresy. And he was equally determined to eliminate immorality from the lives of both clergy and laity in his district. He was constantly traveling up and down his diocese in every direction. Even the most remote villages in high and lonely valleys were visited by him in person. When the plague raged in Milan he directed the care of the afflicted and the burial of the dead at the utmost peril of his life. He lies buried, dressed in pontifical robes, in the crypt of the great cathedral at Milan from which he had banished all the gorgeous tombs, the banners, and the other paraphernalia of ostentatious display.

Gregory XIII (1572–85) had been a man of rather easy-going disposition; immoral, while still a layman, though not dissolute, and always lively and cheerful as a priest. Yet even a man who had no touch of austerity in his make-up was unable to resist the powerful and pitiless reforming tendency of the time. His own life became not only irreproachable but even worthy of imitation. It was in his pontificate that the Jesuits attained their greatest influence in the affairs of the Church. He was particularly interested in providing for a better system of religious education, and it is doubtful if there was a single Jesuit school in the world to the support of which he did not contribute. In the Seminary of all Nations that he helped the Jesuits to build at Rome separate rooms were provided for three hundred and sixty students and instruction was given in every leading European language. He assisted the German College that was already established in the papal capital; and, in the same city, founded one for the Greeks and another for the English. No less than twenty-two Jesuit colleges owed their origin to his interest and liberality. Gregory was most fertile in expedients for the extinction of the Protestants. He lent aid to Philip II in the Netherlands, to the Catholic League in France, which he had helped to found, and in Ireland he encouraged several insurrections against Elizabeth. And, finally, it was largely due to his exertions that the Invincible Armada set sail for England. The reform of the calendar is another instance of the assiduous care with which he looked after the interests of the Church. The Julian calendar, adopted by Julius Cæsar and subsequently amended, was in use at that time. It made each calendar year longer by eleven minutes and fourteen seconds than the true solar year. This error amounted to a day in every one hundred and twenty-eight years. By decrees of several of the councils certain of the festivals of the Church had been definitely related to particular seasons of the year. These relations had been displaced by the operation of the defective calendar. The reformation of the calendar had thus been made imperatively necessary. An Italian bishop, Luigi Lilio, proposed a method of amendment. All the important universities reported favorably upon the plan which was then submitted to a minute examination by a special commission appointed for the purpose. The most active director of the entire proceedings was the scholarly Cardinal Sirleto. Finally the new calendar was proclaimed in a bull, which Gregory issued on February 13, 1582, with great solemnity. No Protestant country adopted it at once; England and her colonies conformed to it in 1753; and Sweden did so still later. Russia and the other States of Greek Christendom are the only Christian countries that still decline to accept it. The Gregorian calendar is not perfect. It exceeds the true solar year by twenty-six seconds, an error that amounts to a day in three thousand three hundred and twenty-three years. Not the least of Gregory's services was the encouragement he gave to the work of Philip Neri (1515–95), the beloved saint of cheerful temper, playful irony, shrewd mother wit, unfailing courtesy and kindly heart, whose devotion to the sick and the poor won for him the title of Apostle of Rome.

Owing to the absence in Spain of many members of the fully professed there was an interregnum of two years in the generalship of the Jesuits when Loyola died. In this situation Lainez was made vicar-general of the order. He was, as we have seen, a man of dialectic skill and oratorical power. It was not long before he proved himself to be a politician of most unusual versatility and adaptability. In 1558 he became the second general of the order. At the Council of Trent he had successfully exerted his skill and power in behalf of the papal supremacy. His vision of the activities of the society extended far beyond that of the founder; and because of the fact that he directed its energies into additional fields he may be regarded as the actual founder of the Order as it came to be. Under him the far-reaching powers of the General were increased still further, the alliance with the Papacy became still more intimate, and the close relation of the order to the cabinets of the various Catholic countries became established. The entrance of the Jesuits into France met with opposition at first. Their Spanish origin did not count in their favor in that country. The colleges, particularly the Sorbonne, were bitterly jealous of them. But in the Colloquy of

Poissy, in 1561, in which Lainez took a leading part, they were given legal recognition. Three years later they were allowed to teach in France. They possessed a remarkable preacher in Edmond Augier, who won the admiration even of Huguenots; and in Maldonat they produced a teacher whose biblical expositions attracted multitudes of the youth of the land and held them spellbound. From Lyons and Paris, where they first made themselves secure, they spread all over the country and everywhere strengthened the spirit of opposition to the Huguenots. Into the Netherlands, also, the Jesuits penetrated, their first center being the college of Douai. By 1562 they had established themselves at Antwerp, Brussels and Lille, and they had secured control of the University of Louvain. It was in Germany that Catholicism had suffered its first great losses. In 1551 Le Jay and twelve of the Jesuits arrived in Vienna, where, before long, they secured control of the university. Five years later the Jesuits were also dominant in the universities of Cologne and Ingolstadt. From these three great centers they began to spread all over the Empire. This was the first successful counter-movement against Protestantism in Germany. In their schools and colleges the Jesuits did not neglect secular instruction, but their chief energies were devoted to theology. They held public disputations that were brilliant and dignified. In accordance with the instructions of Lainez they gave their best teachers to the youth of the land. It was the general opinion that young people learned more in six months from them than they did in two years from other teachers. So Protestants sent their children to the Jesuit schools. Special schools were established for the poor. Thus was the great Revolution outflanked in its own fastnesses and its conquests not only stopped but actually diminished. When Loyola died thirteen Jesuit provinces had been established and more than one hundred colleges and houses. In this growth Lainez had borne an important part. When he died in 1565 he left behind him eighteen provinces, one hundred and thirty colleges, and 3,500 members.

The third general of the order, Francisco de Borgia (1565-72), was a Spanish nobleman who had been made viceroy of Catalonia, and who, upon the death of his father, had become duke of Gandia. Inclined in his early years toward a monastic life his tendency in that direction was increased by the solemn funeral of the wife of Charles V, the Empress Isabella. After the death of his own wife he entered the Jesuit order. Because of his temperamental predilection to melancholy he was less of an initiator than his two predecessors in the generalate, but he carried out their plans and the suggestions of his associates with decision and vigor. He contributed much to the work of perfecting the organization of the society, and to him was due its firm establishment in Spain; but it cannot rightly be said that he shares with Loyola and Lainez the title of being one of the founders of the order. His chief interest lay, very wisely, in the work of teaching, and he was responsible in no slight degree for the foundation of that system of education that was to be " pregnant with results of almost matchless importance."

**The Jesuits under Mercurian**

Everard Mercurian (1573–80) was a Fleming whom Gregory XIII compelled the Jesuits to accept as their fourth general. He was a weak and irresolute man who resigned the direction of the society into other hands. Trouble broke out in the English college at Rome, due, it was alleged, to the fact that the Jesuit instructors induced the most promising students to become members of their society and thereby diverted them from their intended missionary activity in the British Isles. After much debate it was decided to send Robert Parsons (1546–1610) and Edmund Campion (1540–81) to England. Strictly enjoined to keep themselves aloof from political affairs they started upon their perilous undertaking and entered England by different routes and in disguise. The romantic and thrilling story of the mission must be passed over very briefly. Parsons, a former fellow of Oxford, was energetic and ingenious, a skilful intriguer, an exceptionally able writer, an unsurpassed controversialist, and he possessed a winning power of conversation. The saintly Campion had a most attractive personality and he was a disputant of extraordinary power and an eloquent preacher. Other priests took part in the English mission. Many wavering Catholics were instilled with new zeal for their old faith and even Protestants were won over. Campion with several other priests, after being cruelly tortured, was put to death at Tyburn. But Parsons escaped into Normandy. After that the mission became involved in politics. It did much to encourage the cause of Mary Queen of Scots against Elizabeth and to promote the Spanish invasion of England. At Mercurian's death the Society numbered 5,000 members.

**The Jesuits Under Acquaviva**

In the person of Claudio Acquaviva (1581–1615), son of a Neapolitan noble, it was no man of indecision who succeeded to the control of the Jesuits. Only thirty-eight years of age, he was the youngest general that had yet been elected. He was the first general, too, who was not a Spanish subject. Quiet and unostentatious, even humble in his outward aspect, he was nevertheless a man of indomitable will, unswerving purpose and undaunted courage, one of the ablest legislators and most effective administrators of his age. With a hand of steel in a velvet glove he crushed a most threatening outbreak of insubordination in the society in Spain. Acquaviva was also practically the author of the *Ratio Studiorum*, for to his initiative and supervision was due the conception and execution of this authoritative embodiment of the educational system of the Jesuits. Published in 1599 it is still the obligatory guide of the method and spirit of study, though not necessarily of the matter, in the Jesuit colleges. It provides for three college classes, the *suprema grammatica*, the *humanitas*, and the *rhetorica et philosophia*, the first two of which were each designed to be completed in a single year and the other in the same or a longer space of time. They presupposed a preparation that corresponds in a large degree to that given in a modern Latin high school. Their scope is indicated by their titles. The three classes included collateral studies that gave the historical, geographical, ethnographical, critical, and other learning requisite for the proper understanding of the classical writings prescribed by the curriculum. The various authors were selected with the view of furthering the purposes of the different classes. The twenty-five hours each week that constituted the class work of the Jesuit colleges were practically devoted exclusively to the study of works in the Greek and Latin tongues; but at that time the classical languages and literatures and the medieval theological works written in those tongues were almost the only instruments of college education. The animating spirit of the *Ratio* is well expressed by the saying of Loyola —" Let us all think in the same way, let us all if possible speak in the same manner." The exercise of individual thought was discouraged. Tradition rather than speculation was promoted. At best it was the custodianship of old truth rather than the search for new truth with which the system was concerned. The generalate of Acquaviva substantially corresponded with the floodtide of the militant movement of Catholicism that was so largely the work of the Jesuits; and it witnessed the acme of the Order. Recent and rapid as had been the rise of the society it had nevertheless become established in every Catholic country and inaugurated missions in Protestant lands and in the remotest parts of the known world. It had made itself the most formidable force in the ecclesiastical affairs of the time. In its colleges many of the leading rulers, statesmen, and military commanders of the next generation were being educated. Never before or since has the society been able to boast so large a group of notable members. It was also at this time that, despite the official decree of its general congregation, the political activity of the Jesuits began to overshadow its spiritual work and the undesirable reputation in which it came to be held began to grow apace. But these things were as yet only in their incipient stages, and they were delayed by the well considered measures of Acquaviva whose election came to be regarded as an inspiration. At his death the Society boasted 13,112 members in thirty-two provinces.

It has been the vogue to see but little virtue in the activity of the Jesuits, to attribute it to nothing nobler than self-aggrandizement. But such was not the case. Many of the early Jesuits possessed admirable qualities and rendered to civilization services that were not unimportant. And the society was actuated by something more than a vast passion for power. In thought and deed it was not untouched by a passion, as its members understood it, for the service of God. It was such a passion that prevailed in their hearts when they submitted to the ordeal of the *Spiritual Exercises*, and it was such a passion that thrilled them when, like Campion, they suffered martyrdom or, like Francis Xavier, they went to the ends of the earth to do what seemed to them the bidding of heaven. The unparalleled patience, the abject self-effacement, and the ready willingness to suffer every hardship and undergo the ultimate penalty of death are not to be found among a body of men actuated only by the spirit of intrigue and self-seeking, displaying in their daily lives no moral virtue, and cherishing in their hearts no high enthusiasm.

Something of the revived Inquisition in Italy and of the recently established Inquisition in Spain we have seen in our history of the Protestant ideas in those peninsulas. We must stop here to notice the activity of that instrument for the punishment of heresy not only in those southern lands, but also in countries north of the Alps and the Pyrénées. The Inquisition continued to operate in the various Italian principalities. In Venice it was under the control of the civil authority. In Sicily the Spanish Inquisition in spite of popular disaffection caused by the arbitrary acts of the officials in their desire of enrichment, pursued its deadly work at first chiefly in the punishment of Judaism but increasingly in persecution of Protestantism; and so obviously unjust were its proceedings that it was in frequent and serious conflict with both the civil and episcopal authorities. So great was the popular opposition in Naples that it was found impossible to introduce the Spanish Inquisition there. And it was not until the opening of the second half of the sixteenth century, and then only in a partial and surreptitious manner, that the Roman Inquisition succeeded in supplanting the medieval one. In Milan, which had become a part of the Spanish possessions in 1529, the papal Inquisition proved unsatisfactory to Philip II, but popular resistance was so pronounced that he found himself compelled to abandon the project of establishing a Spanish tribunal. Under the zealous Cardinal Borromeo the Roman tribunal became more active than it had been; and " it may be questioned," says Lea, " whether the Milanese gained much in escaping the Spanish Inquisition." In the Netherlands the Inquisition was even more completely under the control of the government than it was in Spain. Charles V was thoroughly convinced that heresy was due very largely to the immorality of the clergy; and he was determined not to put the remedy into the hands of those who were responsible for the disease; and he was, moreover, convinced that it would be impolitic to increase the power of the clergy by turning over to them the function of examination and the wealth of confiscation. The Inquisition was carried into the Spanish colonies soon after their conquest; and even a traveling tribunal of the galleys, " of fleets and armies," was established. The Portuguese planted the Inquisition in the East Indies where the tribunal at Goa had jurisdiction over all the Portuguese possessions beyond the Cape of Good Hope. In France the Inquisition had been supplanted in the prosecution of lapses from orthodoxy by the Parlement of Paris and the University of Paris.

The Index of 1564 remained the standard index, with regard both to rules of censorship and the inclusiveness of its lists, until the thorough revision which in 1897 Leo XIII caused to be made. It was modified, however, from time to time and other books were included in its proscription. The use of the printing press had opened up a channel of influence of the greatest importance. Public education was beginning to pass from ecclesiastical to secular hands and to widen very greatly in its range. Words had been given wings and the " flying leaves " carried heterodox ideas into the remotest places of every land. It was necessary, so the Church thought, to protect the faithful against the baleful flood of heresy. It was her unmistakable duty to proscribe all books tainted with heresy and wherever possible to burn them. Pius V had created a Congregation of the Index which became a permanent institution. Acting under the ten rules that had been formulated by the Council of Trent for the condemnation of books the Congregation proceeded from time to time to add other publications to the list. The Index became even more arbitrary in the distinction it made between books that were permitted and books that were banned. The aim of the censorship became most comprehensive. It undertook to pass a final opinion upon all publications. The task was beyond accomplishment. But the attempt was made and as a result the Index has many omissions, is full of curious inclusions, and is characterized by other anomalies. The Index was a powerful weapon in the arsenal of militant Catholicism; but it is far easier to suppress a book than to put an end to the vital thought that informs it. Thought is too subtle and too contagious to meet extinction by any such piece of apparatus.

Circum-
stances
that fa-
vored
Militant
Catholi-
cism

Aside from the instruments employed by the Church and her own inherent power there was much in the general conditions of the time, as we have seen, to help to make successful the militant activity of Catholicism. The failure of the uprisings of peasant and burgher had dissevered the social from the religious revolution. Luther had proved to be a more staunch upholder of the power of the secular rulers and a greater advocate of the discipline of unquestioning obedience than ever had been the ancestral Church. So in their misery multitudes of the poor and oppressed turned away from Protestantism with the bitterness of frustrated hopes in their hearts. The struggle of the peasants and townfolk for better and more equitable conditions of daily life had its effect also upon the men who bore the responsibility of secular government. Such men fell into two classes, those who had appropriated ecclesiastical property and those who had not. The former had thrown in their lot with Protestantism. The latter, who had remained Catholic, were influenced by the social outbreak to resist religious innovation and to proceed to crush it where it had gained a footing. For they regarded the social revolution not as being caused by rational reasons, to be met by the granting of reasonable requests, but as being a supernatural message, a warning, an appeal. It was a protest from heaven against the ecclesiastical revolution. The answer to this protest on the part of the Catholic princes was the lending of their aid to the militant movement of Catholicism. This was only one of the many things that, appealing to men's superstitions, made the conditions of the time favorable to that movement. The dread of the encroaching Turk, the awe of the comet, and the fear of the machinations of the devil through the medium of the witches, as we have seen, all frightened men out of a quiet, sane, and rational attitude of thought. It is widely recognized that war

reduces man to the level of the brute.  Much more is this deplorable effect true of violence that transcends human conflict.
When the supposed super-human forces of good and evil are
engaged in a seemingly visible conflict in which men are merely
pawns people fall into a panic of terror and clutch at the nearest
things to them which they believe to be stable and enduring.
This is the key of that element of reaction, outside Catholicism
even more than inside it, that made the general situation of the
time so favorable to the resurgent militancy of the Mother
Church.

# CHAPTER XXIV

### THE SPANISH SUPREMACY

1.  Spain under Charles of Hapsburg.
2.  Spain and Europe.
3.  The Regency of Philip.
4.  The Last Years of Charles.
5.  Philip II.

CHAP.
XXIV

1275-1543

ONE of the greatest factors in the success of militant Catholicism was the reputed power of Spain. The zenith of the Spanish power was attained under Charles of Hapsburg whose career as the Emperor Charles V we have already noticed. It is with the story of Spain under Charles and under his son Philip that we have here to do.

The Various Parts of Spain

Spain is the connecting link between Europe and Africa. Separated from the rest of Europe by the difficult barrier of the Pyrénées, with its scanty, high, and incommodious passes, over which no railroad has yet been built, this singular country, which has for so long hovered between civilization and barbarism, " this land of the green valley and the barren mountain, of the boundless plain and the broken sierra, these elysian gardens of the vine, the olive, the orange, and the aloe, these trackless, vast, silent, uncultivated wastes, the heritage of the wild bee," is the home of a people fundamentally more African than European in character. For despite the centuries of conflict between the Cross and the Crescent in the peninsula the Spaniards were closely related in blood to the Moors. This country of primitive passions was made up of a number of component parts. There were the Aragonese lands, consisting of Aragon, Catalonia, and Valencia, each with its separate cortes and its own distinct and characteristic institutions, united only by the personal tie of their monarch. The political institutions of these lands had attained a greater degree of development than had those of Castile, but in as much as they affected only comparatively slightly the history of Spain it is unnecessary to dwell upon them. South of the Pyrénées was Cerdagne, and across them, but separated from the rest of France by the bleaker and more effective barrier of the Corbières, was Roussillon, which also

456

belonged to Aragon.  At the other end of the Pyrénées was that part of Navarre which lay to the south of the mountains; while to the east were the Balearic Isles, Sardinia, and Sicily.  But by far the greatest of the constituent parts of Spain was Castile. The dominance of this province had the most fateful significance. For Castile is a central region, made up principally of a great plateau that had but a restricted access to the ocean.  It was almost inevitable, in those times, that the people of such a region should be unprogressive and conservative to a deplorable degree. They were largely beyond the stimulus of new ideas which is so powerful an impulse to progress.  So, because it was the most important factor in the history of Spain, it would be well for us to examine somewhat closely the province of Castile.

Having been regained piecemeal from the Moors, and containing as it did a number of peoples quite distinct from each other, the laws of Castile were local rather than national.  The cortes consisted of three estates, clergy, nobles, and commons, which sat separately to discuss affairs of state.  They had no power to enact laws, but merely to offer suggestions to the monarch who alone possessed the right of legislation.  It is true that the commons possessed the right of voting or refusing supplies, but the crown had become so powerful that it was able to limit the freedom of the cortes in essential respects and thus greatly to lessen the danger of opposition.  At the opening of the reign of Charles in 1516 the cortes, because of the foolish arrogance of the king and his Flemings, assumed a less submissive attitude towards the crown.  This insubordination, as we have seen in a previous chapter, resulted in a rebellion of the Castilian towns.  When Charles crushed the *comuneros* he ignored the striking proposals for strengthening the representative system; and, despite his frequent requests for money, he kept the cortes in the position of insignificance to which they had been reduced by his immediate predecessors.  Local government was carried on by the municipalities, whose powers were nowhere very extensive, and each of whom was controlled very largely by the *corregidor,* a supervising official appointed by the crown.

Sole maker of the laws, the king was also the sole fountain of justice.  The institutions to which his legal powers were delegated were (1) the royal council which, owing to the displacement in its membership of the feudal nobles by the modern legists, had acquired important juristic power and now acted as a supreme court of appeal; (2) the *alcaldes de corte,* of which one section held irregular assizes, while the other, in accom-

CHAP.
XXIV
——
1275-1543

Political
Institu-
tions of
Castile

Judicial
Institu-
tions of
Castile

panying the crown from place to place, superseded local tribunals; (3) the two *audiencias,* situated at Valladolid and Granada,
which were courts of appeal; (4) the *corregidors,* appointed by
the crown for long terms, each of whom, by the growth of the
royal power, had become the virtual governor of the town in
which he was stationed; and (5) the municipal judges who were
elected under the terms of the various town charters. In addition to these there were ecclesiastical courts more or less independent of the civil government. The courts and their officials
had failed to win for themselves the approbation of the people.
The belief that the administrative officials and the magistrates
of the law alike were born enemies of the weak and poor, that
they were actuated solely by the motive of self-interest, was a
widespread and deep-seated conviction in Spain long before
Cervantes published his conclusion that public functions could
be exercised only at the expense of private virtues and that when
a man entered office he left behind him of necessity all that
should have gone to make him honest and kept for him the
esteem of his fellow-men. The country was pervaded by the
spirit of resigned skepticism.

Having glanced briefly at the political and legal institutions of
Castile let us look for a moment at its social hierarchy. At the
summit was a titled nobility, ranging from the grandees who
could boast a long ancestry of noble birth to those recently en-

**The Social
Hierarchy
of Castile**

nobled by the crown. It had become a class without political
importance, distinguished from the mass of the people not by
blood, as the Norman was distinguished from the Saxon in England (for in Spain every one deemed himself to be descended
from the Goths), but by the possession of wealth. Every one
recognized as a noble was also a *richombre.* Curbed and kept
in check by Ferdinand and Isabella this upper stratum of society
regained something of its former power under Charles only to
lose still more of it under his son who filled his courts and his
councils with the legists of the universities. The money which
the grandees acquired, by fair means and foul, was squandered
in extravagant living. They were often obliged to seek the
money-lenders, and sometimes, indeed, to alienate to them financial rights over the people who lived on their lands. Every man
wanted to be a noble. This itch for nobility was the great
malady of Spain. Nobility lessened greatly one's burden of
taxation. So Castile was filled with law-suits whose object was
to establish one's nobility and thus to become exempt from a
due share of the support of the government. Below the grandees
were the *hidalgos,* who, if they lived at the court or in the towns,

found service with the greater nobles, not derogatory to their
dignity, as squires, body-guards, or *duennas;* or who, if they
remained in the country, lived frugally upon their scraps of
land, idle and boastful, sometimes in sordid misery. *Hidalguism*
became a lamentable chivalric mania, the open sore of Spanish
society whose depths were probed for us by Cervantes. Not
all the *hidalgos,* however, consented to stagnate in the pitiful
idleness of rural life or to become mere adornments of the court
or the ante-chambers of the grandees. The profession of arms,
the noble career *par excellence,* was open to them. Yet the
alluring glitter of the soldier's uniform led to a precarious life
and generally ended in bitterness and want. Towards the end
of the sixteenth century the Spanish roads became infested with
military men, on leave or discharged, who, clad in tatters, begged
or robbed as the circumstances decided. After the nobility of
the sword came that of the robe. One entered this class through
the schools of the various municipalities or, better still, through
the university of Salamanca or that of Alcalá. The student
life, only too often one of want and squalor, tatters, shifts and
knaveries, led to a number of professions, especially those of
medicine and law. To those trained in the law there were positions opened from that of a humble *escribano* to that of a
counselor of the king. Below the nobility came the mass of the
people, who, as did their fellows in other countries, bore by far
the heaviest share of the burden of taxation and who were the
only creative and productive workers in the land. And at the
very bottom was the social riff-raff, the army of poverty, of vice,
and of crime, such as one may see to-day in the vast numbers of
tramps in our own country and in the inhabitants of our fast
increasing slums.

The great meseta of central Spain did not lend itself to wide-
spread industrial activity, or even to a general engagement in
agriculture. Baked by the sun in summer and frozen in winter
the elevated plains of Castile are cultivated only with difficulty.
The sterile soil compelled the Castilians to raise cattle in the
green foothills and in the mountainous valleys. So trade in
wool rather than in grain became their chief industry. Commerce with the American colonies had been confined to Castilians. Every ship employed in that trade had to enter and
leave the port of Seville. Spanish goods were forced upon the
colonies whether or no they were wanted. This gave a sudden
impetus to Spanish manufactures. So for a time Spain became
a manufacturing country. Spanish agriculture was likewise
stimulated; for the colonists were idle and would not plant; they

*The Back-
ward Agri-
cultural
and In-
dustrial
Condition
of Spain*

were hungry and thirsty and must needs eat and drink. But the cortes enacted grave economic blunders into law. Agriculture was sacrificed for stock-rearing, and serious limitations were placed upon exports and imports. Before the accession of Charles the country was infinitely behind Italy in agriculture and during his reign it suffered a further regression. In the same period the manufacture of woolen cloth, the raw material of which was Spain's most important article of export, steadily declined in both quality and quantity. A similar retrogression took place in the manufacture of leather, metal and silk. Castile, and, indeed, all Spain, fell economically into a backward condition, so much so that when we compare her condition with that of Italy or the Netherlands it appears even pitiful.

Yet Castile was the center from which not only Spain and all the new-won colonies were to be governed but also from which the Netherlands were to be ruled and the fate of Germany to be decided. Spain, under the guidance of Castile, it was believed, was the chosen instrument of God for the defense of the ancestral religion in every European land and for its extension into the lands beyond the seas. This belief was held with a childlike simplicity and with great intensity of feeling. The Castilian was utterly indifferent to all thought and activity that lay beyond the narrow circle of his own life. He displayed but little aptitude for steady and well-directed labor; and, as was the case with his ancestors the Goths, his habitual idleness was varied only with outbursts of violent energy. "The Castilian soul," says Havelock Ellis, "was great only when it opened itself to the four winds and scattered itself across the world." Sustained and systematic labor was distasteful to the Castilian. He had the creative power, the power of initiative, in abundant measure, but he lacked the ability to carry his enterprise through to completion. The routine toil of merchant and of manual laborer he regarded with contempt. And yet hardship in itself, and, indeed, pain he was able to endure with a matchless heroism. Stoicism has always been a marked element in the philosophy of Spain and it has not left its religion altogether untouched. Together with these things went a certain capacity for tender feeling, and a pronounced love, that often rose to passion, for formalism and ritual and ceremony. The whole of Spanish life was interpenetrated by an Oriental ceremonialism. It would be a profound mistake in any estimate of the Castilian character to ignore the lasting results of the mingling of Spanish and Moorish blood and of the fusion of their civilizations.

Beyond the western ocean there lay the vast, uncharted

colonial possessions of Spain. The great archipelago that
stretches from Florida to Venezuela had been given the name
of the West Indies by Columbus, who thought he had discovered
a new route to India, and who, in the name of Spain, took possession of the larger islands. Before long there began the exploitation of the islands for the benefit of Spain. Many of their
inhabitants were sent to Europe and sold into slavery, while
others were compelled to work in the mines which the Spaniards
opened in the islands. Before the accession of Charles permanent occupation did not reach beyond the islands. But exploration had been made from Florida to the River Platte, and Spain
had claimed for herself the shores of the Pacific. With the
opening of the reign of Charles the age of discovery passed into
that of conquest and organization. The insignificant settlements
on the mainland were so rapidly expanded that at the time of
his abdication Spanish conquest and settlement had almost
reached its greatest extent. The great conquests were principally the work of adventurers, like Cortes and Pizarro, who set
forth upon their own initiative from the older settlements. The
conquest of Mexico was effected in 1520 by Hernando Cortes.
In 1527 Francisco Pizarro, after enduring terrible hardships,
reached the coast of Peru, and in a few years that country became the center of Spanish power in South America. The first
Spanish invasion of Chile occurred in 1535 when an expedition
was sent there in search of gold; but a regular conquest and settlement was not attempted until 1540, and then it required almost
a hundred years of warfare to reduce the country. At first, from
1521 to 1535, the colonies were governed by *audiencias,* or courts
of justice, but that method proved unsatisfactory. The system
of vicerois was then inaugurated. There were four great vice-
royalties, Mexico (or New Spain), New Granada, Buenos
Aires and Peru. At the abdication of Charles the established
and organized possessions of the Castilian crown were Mexico
and Central America, Venezuela and New Granada, Peru, Bo-
livia and northern Chile. Argentina and Paraguay were just
being settled; and California and Florida were still in the stage
of discovery. For so short a period this testified to an extraordinary outburst of vigor. But colonial life served only to increase
the shortcomings of the Castilians,— their aversion to sustained
labor, their indolence, their avarice, and their arrogance. With
relentless brutality they drove Indian and negro slaves to work
for them. The Spanish government took measures to protect
the native population of the colonies, but they were rendered
nugatory by the inherent characteristics of the conquerors.

More was accomplished in behalf of the natives by the Spanish missionaries who in their benevolent work often found themselves pitted against their secular countrymen. Charles took the side of the missionaries against the colonists, and when, in 1524, he reorganized the Council of the Indies, which had entire charge of the colonies, he put at its head his own confessor Loaysa who infused into it the spirit by which it was long actuated. Every ship engaged in the colonial trade must sail to and from Seville. So in that city there was established the *Casa de Contratacion,* which combined the functions of a board of trade, a court of commerce, and a clearing house for the traffic with America. It collected the royal dues, and it exercised supervision over the ships and their cargoes, the crews and the emigrants who intended to settle in the colonies. Very early the western seas began to swarm with pirates and so the ships that plied between Seville and the colonies sailed in company for mutual protection. One fleet sailed for Porto Bello to supply South America with its needs, while another left for San Domingo and Vera Cruz. When they had discharged their cargoes of food and manufactures and had received their freights of precious metals they returned together. Thus did the galleons bring the gold of the Indies across the seas in safety to Seville.

Spain occupied a commanding position in Europe. She was dreaded by many nations whose statesmen dreamed for a century of her destruction. Four years after Charles ascended the

Spain's
Prestige
through
the Posi-
tion of
Charles

Spanish throne he was elected to the imperial office. The position of her king added much to the prestige of Spain. The prospect of a universal monarchy seemed to have come within the realm of possibility, if, indeed, in the fears of many who were unduly alarmed, it had not entered that of probability. It was a vast empire, with numberless and far-flung dependencies, over which in 1520 the young king began to reign. But thenceforth Spain was entangled in a policy of more than continental scope, and her greatness, already at its apogee, began gradually to decline. She was drained of her treasure and her best blood in the pursuit of quarrels which in no sense were her own.

Spain's
Prestige
through
the Wealth
of the
Indies

Through the wealth of the Indies as well as through the position of Charles was the prestige of Spain increased. At the commencement of the reign of the new king the receipts of gold and silver from the colonies were small and irregular; at its cessation the stream of precious metals from Mexico and Peru was flowing like a swollen river. Pirates swarmed the seas to intercept the lumbering galleons and swooped down upon the ill-defended ports of Spain. But this sudden stream of wealth,

while it was the envy of other nations, was by no means an
unmitigated blessing to the country into which it poured. It
produced a considerable fall in the value of money. And, as is
always the case under such conditions, the change in prices did
not affect the whole land and all branches of commerce and
industry simultaneously. Time was needed to restore the old
balance between income and expenditure. The multitude of
people, who live practically from hand to mouth, are always slow
in adapting themselves to new conditions. So the interval of
adjustment in Spain was one of great hardship for the masses
of the people; while, on the other hand, for many members of
the economically stronger classes, especially for the great merchants, who always reckon with changing circumstances and
adapt themselves with less delay to the momentary state of
prices, the alteration of prices afforded opportunity to derive
advantage. The fall in the value of money, which would have
been a serious matter even for a flourishing country, was bound
to have fatal consequences for Spain, impoverished as she was
with other causes. Spain to begin with, was, despite her prestige,
far behind her rivals economically. Then the continued wars of
Charles made necessary the trebling of her taxation, and this,
combined with the mis-management of his government, resulted
in the financial ruin of the country. What difference did it make
that the wealth of Spain grew faster than her taxation if most
of that wealth quickly found its way to other countries and if
what remained was far from being equitably distributed? In
spite of every expedient poverty descended upon the land and
the national debt grew to enormous proportions. No lasting gain
resulted to Spain from the stream of bullion that poured into the
country from the trans-oceanic colonies, because she proved incapable of employing it for the improvement of agriculture and
manufacture. It went, instead, to enrich the very people who
were to encompass the downfall of the Spanish empire.

A third thing that added to the prestige of Spain was her mili- Spain's
tary discipline. The cardinal virtue of the Castilian was for Prestige<br>through
many centuries "the primitive virtue of valor." The infantry her Mili-
battalions of Spain were the envy of the world. Her ragged tary Dis-<br>cipline
recruits, trained in Italy and quartered in the Netherlands, were
transformed into the finest infantry in existence. Brantôme, who
more than any other French writer of the time understood Spain,
was chiefly impressed by the warlike qualities of her people.
" You would have called them princes," he said, when he saw the
Spanish soldiers marching through France to Flanders, " they
were so set up, they marched so arrogantly, with so fine a grace."

It is not easy for us to realize how profoundly Europe was impressed with the military prowess of Spain. In the last quarter of the sixteenth century that impression was deepened by the splendid glory of Lepanto. But even this source of prestige was in reality a source of weakness. "The warlike nation of to-day," says David Starr Jordan, "is the decadent nation of to-morrow." The highly regarded profession of arms doubtless alienated at once many artisans from the handicrafts. It certainly drained Spain, as did the colonies, of her more ambitious sons and adventurous spirits; and it did so at a time when there was sore need of such at home. It is never the crippled and the incompetent that war demands, but the best of her manhood that a nation has to offer; and oftentimes the best of her sons are abstracted from her life without having left descendants, and so the life of the nation becomes permanently the poorer. That was the penalty paid by Spain for her attempted dominion of the world.

The religious tranquillity that prevailed within her borders was also a factor in the prestige of Spain. The reform effected by Cardinal Ximenes had made her the pattern throughout the succeeding period for reformation and reorganization within the Mother Church. And in that fact the Spaniards took no small degree of pride. The Papacy had taken no part in the reform. It was the exclusive work of the Spaniards themselves. It rested upon a fusion of the interests of Church and State that gave to the latter the controlling power. The Spanish bishops were obedient to their king who held them far more strictly to their duty than could have been done from Rome. The religious quietude that prevailed in Spain and the subordination of the prelates to the crown were the envy of many another nation.

Spain's
Prestige
through
her Championship
of Cross
against
Crescent
Still more did Spain gain prestige through her championship of Cross against Crescent and of orthodoxy against heresy. It has been said with truth that the Spaniards were the first and the last crusaders, for long before Peter the Hermit preached the first crusade against the infidels in the East they had begun the work of driving the Moors from their own peninsula, and for more than two hundred years after St. Louis led the last expedition to the Holy Land they battled against their age-long foe. To the people of other nations warfare with the infidel was merely an occasional occupation, but to the Spaniards it was a life-long vocation in which the welfare of their nation was deeply involved. It was their perpetual crusade that bred in their very fiber the lofty conviction that their nation was the one especially chosen by God to be the champion of the Christian and the

Catholic world. For centuries a holy hatred of the infidel had been the creed of Spain. The Turk was the peril abroad; the Morisco was the plague at home. The former was to be repulsed, and the latter extirpated. The last remains of the open avowal of Mohammedanism, despite the terms of the capitulation of the city of Granada, were extinguished by the end of the first quarter of the sixteenth century. After that the Jews, the Marranos, who were converted Jews, and the Moriscos, who were converted Mohammedans, bore the brunt of Spanish intolerance. Eventually, to the lasting injury of the country, the Moriscos were expelled with the utmost cruelty. With the disappearance of their patient industry whole districts became desolate and trade as well as agriculture suffered a marked decline. The expulsion of the Moors was also a fatal error in another respect. They would have kept Spain in the channel of the new culture into which she ventured but timidly and out of which she soon drifted. The story of the extinction of Protestantism in the peninsula has already been told. Thus once more it is seen that the things that contributed to the prestige of Spain were in reality sources of weakness.

Striking evidence of the prestige enjoyed by Spain is to be found in the spread of Spanish influence and the dominance of Spanish fashions. It was not only in Italy where the Spaniards were conquerors that Spanish fashions, manners and influence, played a potent part in the life of the time. In many other parts of the continent, even in Elizabethan England, which was by no means friendly to Spain, did the ruling and the noble classes and the well-to-do townsfolk adopt Spanish fashions, cultivate Spanish manners. They even became to a certain extent impregnated with Spanish modes of feeling. Yet before the end of the reign of Charles signs of the decay of Spanish power were to be discovered by those who had eyes to see; and in the time of his successor that decay made rapid strides. Charles himself and his ministers had become ever more and more engrossed in foreign policy so that the right impulse for internal affairs was lacking. His foreign undertakings compelled him to impose an ever-increasing burden of taxation and to permit his creditors, the great German and Italian banking houses, to prey upon Spain. The fundamental evil from which the country suffered was the world-policy of the Emperor, a policy that Spain, economically and socially, was unable to support.

Having thus made a brief survey of the general condition of Spain, let us now consider the leading events in the reign of Charles and his son. In 1542 Francis I proclaimed war against

CHAP.
XXIV

1543-56

The In-
structions
of Charles
to Philip

Charles, and when the latter, in the following year departed for the scene of conflict, he left his son as his regent. Philip was just sixteen years old, but so precocious had been his interest in the affairs of State that his father felt confident of his ability to safeguard the interests of the country. Two letters written by the Emperor to his son throw a flood of light upon the actions of the latter. With Philip there was to rest the final decisions in all matters, but he was to be guided by councilors who had won the confidence of his father. Among these advisers were included the heads of opposing factions. This was a precaution to prevent the young prince from falling under the control of any one group. The advisers were described; their shortcomings, their hypocrisy and selfishness were laid bare without reserve. To each of them the prince was to lend his ear. Then he was to decide for himself. The principle of distrust became one of the chief elements of Philip's policy. Added to this were self-suppression, patience and piety.

In November, 1543, Philip married his cousin Maria, the only daughter of the King of Portugal. His evident Spanish character and interests had already won for him the love of his
subjects, and their intense devotion he enjoyed to the end of his life. One of the first questions that engaged his attention was that of the economic policy to be pursued under his administration. He was convinced that the prosperity of Spain could best be promoted by keeping in the country the great stream of bullion that was pouring into it from America. So he endeavored to prevent its exportation to other parts of Europe. But the economic conditions were such as to render the attempt practically impossible. The wealth of the Indies continued to pour through Spain as through a sieve and to develop the agricultural and manufacturing activities of the very countries that were seeking to diminish the Spanish power. Food became ever dearer. The cost of production continually increased. So even in the markets of Spain the foreigner could undersell the Spanish manufacturer. In 1548, at the desire of his father, Philip began a long journey through Italy. The fervent salutation of Andrea Doria, one of the greatest sailors of the day, as Philip embarked in the Bay of Rosas, reflected the passionate devotion of the people to their prince. Through Genoa he went, through Milan, Mantua, Tyrol, and Germany, entertained and banqueted everywhere, and at last, on April 1, 1549, he joined his father in Brussels. For two years the Emperor kept his son with him, instructed him in the innermost secrets of his policy and his principles, and discussed with him the disposition of the im-

perial possessions. In 1554, his first wife having died in 1545, Philip married Mary, queen of England. It was his desire to marry another Portuguese princess, but he bowed to the will of his father who thought he saw in the English connection a great political opportunity. Serious difficulties had to be overcome before the marriage was possible. Protestantism had to be assured, English insularity had to be disarmed, and French intrigue had to be baffled. So the marriage contract provided against the political subjection of England to Spain; but Charles believed the union would redound to his son's advantage, that he would find in it compensation for the bestowal of the imperial title and power upon his uncle Ferdinand. Philip's tactfulness allayed much of the distrust with which he was regarded in England; and, because of political reasons, he and his father did all they could to postpone and mitigate the persecution of the English Protestants. Neither of them desired the extinction of English heresy as much as they wished for English aid against the French. But Mary and her ecclesiastical advisers were zealots and they impaired the cause of Spain by the barbarous punishment which they inflicted upon the Protestants.

Fortune did not smile upon Charles in the renewed war with France. He was reluctant to admit defeat in his effort to drive the invader from German soil. Success in the attempt would in all probability have left him free to crush the Lutheran princes, to secure the succession of his son to the Empire, and to force back the Protestants into the Catholic fold. These were the dearest objects of his life. But at last circumstances compelled him to yield. The raising of the siege of Metz on New Year's day, 1553, signified the renunciation of the accomplishment of his life work. Profoundly depressed, meditating the abdication of his kingly and imperial powers, he left Germany never to return. At Brussels he waited impatiently for his son to come to him. So Philip, disappointed that Mary had not presented him with an heir, left the sad and faded little woman who was his wife and hurried to join his father. The ability that Philip had displayed as a ruler combined with other circumstances, had caused his father to cherish for him his new ambition. A larger territory should be his to govern. The union of the Italian possessions and the Empire had never been satisfactory. It would be better to join them to Spain. So upon Spain there was conferred the sovereignty of the imperial possessions in the peninsula. Ferdinand of Austria was pacified and compensated by the marriage of his son Maximilian to the Emperor's daughter Maria, and by the guarantee that Maximilian should in his turn succeed to the imperial title. The Burgundian possessions were also united to Spain. Thus was it arranged that Spain, even after the abdication and death of Charles, should not be left free to solve its own problems and develop its own civilization but should remain in the whirlpool of continental politics.

**Abdication and Death of Charles**

The last war in which Charles had been engaged was directed not only against France, but also against the Lutherans and the Turks. And in every direction it had been a failure. The Emperor was weary even unto death. Step by step he divested himself of his power. In 1555 with great and impressive ceremony he transferred the sovereignty of the Netherlands to Philip. The following year witnessed his relinquishment of Spain and the Indies; and, in the same year, irrevocably abandoning heretical Germany, he invested Ferdinand with the imperial authority. Then he sailed from Flushing to Laredo and from there made his way overland to the Jeromite convent of Yuste in the province of Estremadura where for two years he lived in a little house that adjoined the convent church. There he continued to be keenly interested in the affairs of the world until an attack of fever sent him to his deathbed. At last, on September 21, 1558, holding in his hands a consecrated candle brought from the shrine of Our Lady of Montserrat, and gazing upon the crucifix which Isabella, his beloved wife, had kissed before she died, the last heroic figure among the emperors gave up the ghost. Charles V was not endowed with the strength of genius, but his position and his earnest endeavors had placed him in the foreground at one of the most difficult periods of European history. The great tasks he had set himself to do, the extinction of Protestantism, the reformation of the Church, and the political reorganization of Germany, remained undone. A part of that vast undertaking he left to his son who was himself doomed to defeat.

**Philip's Character**

Like his father, Philip II believed himself to be divinely appointed to effect the restoration of Catholicism and to perpetuate the supremacy of Spain. But he was even less well-fitted, both physically and mentally, than Charles to succeed in the gigantic task. He was altogether lacking in the easy good humor and the rough energy that had won for the late Emperor many a friend and helped him out of many a difficulty. He was capable of affection, but it was usually concealed and always subordinated to purposes of State. A refined taste led him to admire the beautiful and to become a patron of artists. He was by no means a hypocrite, but, on the contrary, acted always according to his conscience. The talents with which this melancholy

and lonely man had been endowed were distinctly moderate, and
he was, moreover, usually irresolute and procrastinating. He
was a meticulous monarch much given to red-tape. The great
solicitude which he had for the welfare of his subjects formed
the good side of his character as a ruler. In cases where the
general welfare of the nation was concerned, despite his prone-
ness to irresolution, once he deemed himself to be accurately
informed and was convinced that he could reach the evil, he
never hesitated to apply the remedy. And when they failed
to perform their duties properly he sacrificed with indifference
the highest dignitaries of the State; while for the effective fulfilment of their petty functions the *corregidors* of the meanest
villages were held in honor. So, inadequately endowed with
ability, and insufficiently supplied with means, he set to work
upon a task only less enormous than that which had defeated his
father.

The intimate union with the Papacy and the fusion of his
widely-scattered territories, which were the first of Philip's objects, met with the opposition of the Pope. Paul IV, who had
ascended the papal chair in 1555, was a member of a Neopolitan
family that had always lent its support to the Angevin party in
southern Italy, and his long-standing hostility to Spain was increased by the authority exerted by the crown over the Spanish *Foreign
Affairs*
clergy. The infuriated pontiff formed an alliance with France;
and then Philip, the most Catholic of kings, by a strange irony
of fate, found himself at war with the Pope. The Spanish
troops under Alva were victorious. Rome itself was in imminent danger; but the doge of Venice intervened and a peace
was patched up with the "accursed Spaniards." In 1558 the
death of Mary increased the difficulty of Philip's situation. It
soon became apparent that he could no longer reasonably hope
for English aid against the French. The peace of Cateau-
Cambrésis was signed, therefore, in the following year. France
and Spain mutually ceded to each other the conquests they had
made, and a secret compact was entered into between them to
suppress all heresy in Christendom. One other precaution had
to be taken. The claim of Mary, queen of Scots, to the English throne threatened the interests of Spain. Should Mary,
who was also a French princess, ever reign over both England
and France, the Netherlands would be endangered. Some weeks
after the signing of the peace, therefore, Philip was married by
proxy with extraordinary splendor to Elizabeth of Valois who
was yet but a child.

At last Philip felt himself free to return to Spain from

Persecu-
tion of
Heresy

which he had been absent for five years. Ecclesiastical affairs in the peninsula had become disturbed and unsatisfactory. The clergy were corrupt, cynicism was spreading, and heresy had begun to appear above the surface. Charles had exhorted his son to prosecute heresy rigorously and relentlessly. Such an injunction was unnecessary. Deeply implanted in Philip's heart was an inborn determination to enforce unity of faith at any cost; and in that determination he had the practically unanimous support of the Spanish people. The story of the Inquisition and the Censure has been told elsewhere and so it need not detain us here. Among the many troubles that gathered about Philip was that of the condition and the actions of his only son Don Carlos, whom he had by his first wife, and who was now

Death of
Don
Carlos

approaching his majority. Subject to epileptic fits the young prince, who was also lame and stunted in growth, displayed increasing symptoms of insanity. He became filled with a desire to escape from Spain and defy his father; and when this became known he was confined in prison. There he was either put to death by his father's orders, or, as seems more probable, brought death upon himself in the belief that otherwise he would suffer imprisonment for life.

Soon after Philip had returned to Spain he had been petitioned to suppress the Moslem pirates who raided the shores not only of Sicily and Naples but of Spain itself, where doubtless they

Rebellion
of the
Moriscos

were abetted by the Moriscos of Granada. The attempt to rid the seas of the Turkish corsairs was a terrible failure involving the loss of many ships and thousands of men. Then attention was turned upon the Moriscos. But it was not only because they were suspected of lending aid to the Moslem marauders that the Moriscos incurred the hatred of their Spanish neighbors. The Christianity that had been forced upon them, it was well-known, was but a thin veneer; and their skill in agriculture and horticulture made them more prosperous than were the peasants of undoubted orthodoxy. For a long time the Moriscos sullenly endured the persecution to which they were subjected. Then the storm burst and vengeance was wreaked upon the Christians. But the punishment inflicted upon the Moriscos by Philip was swift and atrocious. Those who escaped death were driven in chains through the snow from Andalusia where they and their forefathers had lived for eight hundred years to the strange and inhospitable northern provinces. Thus did the monarch who was so solicitous for his country's welfare hasten the industrial decline of Spain.

From warfare at home Philip turned to warfare abroad.

Urged by the Pope to strike a decisive blow at the Crescent he placed his natural brother, Don John of Austria, a handsome and chivalrous leader, at the head of the greatest fleet that had ever sailed the inland seas and sent him to make a supreme effort to rid the Mediterranean of the Moslem scourge. The Turkish fleet was encountered on October 7, 1571, in the Bay of Lepanto and a crushing defeat was inflicted upon it. Christendom was thrilled with joy from center to circumference. Thus ended the first of Philip's great naval efforts. The story of the war that broke out in the Netherlands is to be told in the next chapter. Still another war was that which ended in the annexation of Portugal. In 1578 Sebastian, the young Portuguese king, perished in an attempt to conquer Morocco. Philip was the most formidable of the host of claimants to the Portuguese throne; and there was much to make him willing to fight for the kingdom. Great wealth was pouring into Portugal and the vast possessions in Africa seemed to promise a still greater income. With these resources the lack of money and of credit, which hitherto had been so great an impediment to the fulfilment of his plans, might be overcome. Sebastian was succeeded by his great uncle, an aged cardinal, who, as King Henry, reigned only a year and a half. Then Alva was sent into Portugal at the head of a military force and on April 1, 1581, the cortes of that country took the oath of allegiance to Philip. It was not altogether an unconditional surrender. According to the terms of the agreement Portugal was to be regarded as a separate kingdom united to Spain solely by the fact that she had the same sovereign; she was to retain possession of all her colonies; and the rights and the liberties of her subjects were to be respected. Thus did all those parts of America, Africa, and Asia that had been conquered by Europeans come under the dominion of this grave and reticent king whose troubles were gathering in great clouds about his head but who moved forward to the accomplishment of his great task confident in the conviction that he was the chosen instrument of God.

Among the lieutenants whom Philip had chosen to assist him were men of no mean ability. In conformity with the advice of Charles V no civil office was intrusted to Fernando de Toledo, Duke of Alva (1508–82), who was a grandee and who was bent on his own advancement. He was employed only in foreign affairs and in war. Ruy Gomez, the bosom friend of Philip, a Portuguese by birth, was a consistent advocate of peace and moderation. He wished to have Alva removed from the circle of the royal advisers; he protested, though in vain, against the persecution of the Moriscos; and he advocated a conciliatory policy with the Flemings. At last, when Philip grew weary of the fruitless cruelty of Alva in the Netherlands, the party of the peace-maker became for a time paramount, but soon after his policy gained the ascendancy Gomez died. Antonio Perez (1539?–1611), an able, ambitious, ingratiating and unscrupulous scoundrel, was a factotum upon whom much reliance was placed. He used an old and expired commission from the king to get rid of Escobedo, the secretary of Don John of Austria, as an excuse for venting a private grudge against that unfortunate individual. This betrayal of confidence turned the king against him and the facile favorite was thrown into prison. Perez escaped to Aragon and when that province was called upon to surrender him it declined to permit any infringement of the rights of its tribunals. The fugitive was permitted to escape across the Pyrénées. Then Philip sent a Castilian army into Aragon, inflicted severe punishment upon those who had been leaders in the defense of the Aragonese rights, and effected changes in the provincial charter that favored the royal authority. A fourth assistant was Nicholas Perrenot de Granvella (1484–1550), a capable and faithful servant, recommended to Philip by Charles for employment in all matters relating to Germany, Italy, France, and England. He always cherished a love for his native Burgundy and sought to advance the welfare of his sons among whom was the Cardinal Granvella. Cardinal Antoine Perrenot de Granvella (1517–86), prime minister to Margaret (half-sister of Philip) when that princess was regent of the Netherlands, and who, after he had been compelled to retire from the Low Countries because of the growing hostility of the people towards him, was employed by Philip in important diplomatic negotiations and made president of the council for Italian affairs with headquarters at Madrid. Quite as important as any of the principal ministers was Fray Diego de Chaves, the king's confessor, who, of course possessed not only their privilege of personal approach but also a far more private intercourse from which they were excluded.

Despite these and other assistants Philip endeavored himself to conduct the enormous work of the government. We have seen that he was genuinely solicitous for the welfare of his people. He read and annotated with his own hand all the despatches, covering reams of paper, sent by his agents from almost every part of the globe. In vain he sought the help of the queen (Philip was married to Anne, daughter of the Emperor Maximilian II, in 1570) and the infantas in this endless secre-

tarial activity that he had assumed. The more papers he despatched the more he received. Timorous and hesitating by
nature, when he was not absolutely sure of his ground, the very
routine of his procedure postponed his decisions still further
beyond the appropriate h ur that would not wait. Much that
he decreed, therefore, fr led of its purpose and vanished into
thin air. The evils in the condition of Spain were in themselves
so grave and so deep-rooted that had the activity of Philip been
devoted exclusively to their extirpation the task would have
severely taxed his strength, and when there was added to it the
prodigious work of governing the vast possessions beyond the
borders of Spain it was clearly beyond his capacity. In 1586
Philip's infirmities compelled him to abandon his practice of
dealing in detail with every paper. A kind of intimate privy
council was formed to assist him. It consisted of three members, Don Juan de Idiaquez, Don Cristobal de Moura, and the
Count of Chinchon. Because of its custom of meeting every
night in the palace the council was called the Night Junta. It
went over the documents of the day before they were submitted
to the king. The three members, each of whom was concerned
with a special department of the government, were then granted
an interview with the king on the following day in which the
affairs of the various departments arising out of the documents
of the preceding night were discussed. The general policies
were then decided and the execution of the details was left to
the various secretaries of the councils. Thus was Philip relieved of much of the arduous task of government.

But the mechanical work of government still undertaken by
Philip and the cares of office were so great that they swamped
him and left him utterly defeated. Spain to her detriment was
involved in the wars of religion that were going on in France.
The Netherlands were in revolt; and designs upon the English
throne also engaged the king's attention. At home matters were
going from bad to worse. The courts were corrupt, lawlessness
was rife, the clergy meddled in mundane affairs, poverty increased, the population declined, and ignorance descended upon
the land like a thick fog. In 1588 came the tremendous catastrophe of the Armada, followed in 1596 by the destruction by the
English of the new naval force of Spain in the harbor of Cadiz.
Two years later, still firm in the conviction, despite his many
reverses, that he had been chosen of God to lead the battle
against the forces of evil, Philip died. The ruin of his country
had very largely been his handiwork, " yet his people revered
him as a saint, and still cherish his memory as a great king, not

Spain's
Disasters

Spain's
Failure

for what he did, but for what he dreamed," and his great failure they deemed to hold the substance of eternal things.

It was a peculiarly difficult problem that confronted Spain. Under Charles V she was involved in the multitudinous affairs of the German Empire; and while with the abdication of that monarch the tie that bound her to that heterogeneous congeries of warring principalities was severed she was still united to the provinces in Italy and to the Netherlands whose problems were not her own. No European nation had yet learned how to govern and develop trans-oceanic colonies; and Spain, therefore, found herself face to face with the huge and untried work of governing vast possessions separated from her by half the circumference of the globe. So the fact that the Spanish government and the Spanish people failed to meet the situation successfully does not necessarily prove their utter incompetence. No other government and no other people in the sixteenth century were subjected to a similar test; and few other countries were similarly handicapped for the performance of a like task, had such a task confronted them, by so sparse a population, by so marked an absence of constitutional unity and common feeling between its various sections, and by so backward a condition of the development of its natural resources, as was Spain. After all due allowance for mitigating circumstances has been made, however, the facts remain that Spain failed, that her history in the sixteenth century, though she was feared in every other European country, is one of deepening gloom, and that her splendid energy, expended in many a battle against infidel and heretic and squandered in the uttermost ends of the world, died away and left her barren of those economic and social enthusiasms that have animated the soul of every other modern nation.

# CHAPTER XXV

## THE REVOLT OF THE NETHERLANDS

1. The Netherlands at the Accession of Philip II.
2. The Regency of Margaret of Parma.
3. The Regency of Alva.
4. The Uniting of the Provinces.
5. The French Alliance.
6. The English Alliance.
7. Olden-Barneveld and Maurice of Nassau.

THE political State that was made up of the seventeen provinces of the Netherlands, and which is represented to-day by the kingdoms of Belgium and Holland, was created by four dukes of Burgundy, Philip the Bold, John the Fearless, Philip the Good, and Charles the Bold; and later on it was perfected by the Emperor Charles V. It lay between the two great kingdoms of France and Germany of whose erstwhile adjoining border provinces it was comprised. It was a hybrid State in more than one respect; politically, because it was made up of fragments of France and Germany; linguistically, because the inhabitants of the northern provinces spoke a Germanic tongue while those of the south spoke a Romance tongue; and geographically, because except where its low-lying shores were washed by the ocean and where in the southeast it was protected by the hills of the Ardennes there was no distinct and natural frontier. Yet it had not come into existence merely as the result of the arbitrary will of a succession of princes and of blind chance. For many centuries political, economic, and social forces had been at work drawing the various provinces together. The people of the towns desired political union; and they were very numerous and powerful in the valleys of the three rivers that flowed through the land, the Rhine, the Meuse, and the Scheldt. Their towns were situated in the greatest overland commercial highway in Europe. Their commerce was international in its range. They desired political union as a means of defense. So a multiplicity of agreements was signed between the various principalities. When the Burgundian dukes began to make a State out of these territories they did not find the task to be particularly difficult. In 1543 Charles V added the last two of the seventeen provinces to the union and thus fulfilled a plan that had been outlined in the reign of Charles the Bold.

Each one of the seventeen principalities had preserved its own constitution and its own institutions and each had its own stadhouder nominated from the ranks of the nobility by the central ruler. The Burgundian dukes, copying the monarchical institutions of France, but altering them to suit the circumstances of their northern State, endeavored to build up a central government, to establish a greater degree of community of interests, and thus to make more effective the collective State. In this they were aided by the economic forces of the time, the need of peace and protection. In 1463 Philip the Good created the States-General, an institution made up of delegates from the estates of each province, one that met almost every year, one that gave the prince an opportunity to meet the statesmen of his subjects face to face and to discuss with them the things of general import, one that gave the people a share in the general government, and one that proved a potent factor in welding into an organic unity the miscellaneous agglomeration of principalities. There was created also a council that had cognizance of political affairs and another council that formed a supreme court of justice with jurisdiction over the seventeen provinces. Charles V divided the political council into three councils; (1) the council of State, which had charge of political matters; (2) the privy council, which was principally administrative in function; and (3) the council of finance. The central court of justice, never acknowledged as the supreme court of appeal by all the provinces and so never a complete success, sat at Mechlin; and the three councils sat at Brussels, where, after 1531, the representative of the sovereign also resided, thus making it the capital of the collective State. But everywhere the ancient constitutions of the different States were left intact and the territorial autonomy was preserved. Each province retained its estates, the essential organ of its autonomy, and through that body exercised the right of voting the taxes. And with each of the provinces there rested the right to confirm or repudiate the action of its delegates to the States-General. Particularism, then, was by no means destroyed by the erection of a central government.

Under Charles V the Netherlands enjoyed great commercial prosperity. But beneath the surface there was an increasing discontent. The country had been persuaded to bear a larger proportionate share of taxation than any other part of the imperial possessions, and it was in consequence burdened with debt; Spanish garrisons in the various towns aroused the hatred of the populace; and the persecution of the Lutherans, Zwinglians, Calvinists and Anabaptists, while failing to effect the extinction of heresy, aggravated the general discontent. On October 25, 1555, Charles relinquished the government of the Netherlands to his son Philip II and left to him the legacy of accumulating dissatisfaction. The first four years of his reign were spent by Philip in the Netherlands, and in that time, although his financial and ecclesiastical policies, and the methods employed for their execution, were the same as those of his father, the dissatisfaction greatly increased. Philip, unlike his father, was unmistakably a foreigner in this northern State. To the several causes of revolt that were already silently at work before his accession to the throne there was added another and a more fundamental one — a deepening antipathy to the Spanish rule. In 1559 Philip left the Netherlands never to return. The regent to whom he confided the care of the country was his half-sister, Margaret of Parma, a woman of masculine character and no slight administrative ability, who had been born and brought up in the country. Secret instructions required her to continue the policy of religious persecution and to accept the advice of the council of State, the privy council, and the council of finance. Thus she was directed in all things by Philip and by the three men whom she had placed at the head of the councils — Berlaymont, Viglius, and Granvella (bishop of Arras and, later on, a member of the college of cardinals) of whom the latter, the virtual governor of the Netherlands, was by far the most important. The powerful and masterful ecclesiastic endeavored, but without avail, to mitigate the cruel policy of persecution upon which the absent king insisted. In the execution of that policy, and in the general conduct of the government, the local charters and privileges were often violated, the great nobles of the land were practically ignored, and the populace were made more dissatisfied than ever. Foremost among the nobles of the Netherlands were William of Nassau, Prince of Orange (1533–84), Lamoral, Count of Egmont (1522–68), and Philip, Count of Hoorne (1520–68). The first, later known as "William the Silent," because of his customary discreetness, was the most important of the three, being the heir of vast possessions in Germany and France as well as in the Netherlands, and, despite his youth, an experienced general and a skilful diplomat. Becoming aware about the time of Philip's departure for Spain of that monarch's intention of resorting to the use of fire and sword for the extinction of heresy in his realms he resolved to drive "this vermin of Spaniards" out of his country, and this despite the fact that he was himself a Catholic. The grievances of the country were made known to Philip by the States-General before he left the Netherlands. Fourteen months later the Spanish troops were withdrawn. But the causes of discontent were not removed. In some cases they were, indeed, increased. Taxation continued to be oppressive; the rigorous persecution of heresy, for which purpose the Inquisition had been established in the Netherlands, was carried on in violation of the provincial constitutions; and the papal bulls, issued at the instigation of Philip, that increased the number of bishoprics from three to seventeen also infringed upon the rights guaranteed to the people. The estrangement between Philip and his subjects in the Netherlands was growing; and its progress was not retarded by the marriage of William of Orange, soon after the death of his first wife, to the Protestant princess Anne, daughter and heiress of Maurice of Saxony. It was the mistaken belief of the malcontents that Cardinal Granvella was primarily responsible for many of the grievances; but as a matter of fact he favored a policy of moderation and in all repressive measures he was merely the reluctant instrument of Philip. Because of this belief the three men who were at the head of the nobility wrote twice to the king in 1563 requesting him to recall the cardinal; and in the same year Margaret, seeing that things were going from bad to worse, made a similar request. As a result of these communications Granvella was removed in the following year under the disguise of voluntary retirement. Five months later Philip issued an order for the enforcement of the Tridentine decrees in the Netherlands. The order aroused vigorous protest and Egmont was despatched as a special messenger to the king to request in plain and unmistakable terms a redress of grievances. But on the point of heresy Philip was inexorable; he insisted, after Egmont had returned home, upon the strict enforcement of the placards, or edicts, against heresy and the promulgation of the decrees of the Council of Trent. The mission was therefore a failure. With this decision of the king the die was cast. Revolt was made inevitable. It required no special gift of prophecy to enable William of Orange to predict that his countrymen would soon see "the beginning of a fine tragedy."

When Philip's decision became known lawless outbreaks took place among the indignant populace, many of the magistrates declined to enforce the edicts, and the lesser nobility began to join those of higher rank in opposition to the Spanish power,

# THE NETHERLANDS
## AT THE
## ABDICATION OF CHARLES V
### Scale of Miles

0  10  20  40  60  80  100

Spanish Netherlands

United Netherlands

Drenth was not admitted into the Dutch
Republic as a separate State until 1796

C.S. HAMMOND & CO., N.Y.

Longitude 4° East from 5° Greenwich

CHAP.
XXV

1564-67

Incipient
and Icon-
oclastic
Outbreak

going, indeed, much further than at that time the greater nobles
desired to go. The principles of the minor nobility were embodied in a document known as the " Compromise " which was
directed chiefly against the Inquisition and which was soon
signed by over two thousand people many of whom were Catholics. When some two hundred and fifty of the nobles presented to the regent a " request " that she should send an envoy
to the king to ask him to abolish the placards and the Inquisition, Berlaymont attempted to reassure her by describing them
contemptuously as *gueux,*— beggars. The name was accepted
by the confederates with enthusiasm and everywhere nobles,
burghers, and peasants wore the emblem of the beggar's wallet.
Foremost among the leaders of *les gueux* were Henry, Viscount
of Brederode, a Catholic, a man of many faults, bold and reckless, a spendthrift and a rake, but generous, kindly, and sincere;
Marnix of St. Aldegonde, a Calvinist, poet, orator, and diplomat, as well as a soldier; and Louis of Nassau, at this time
a Lutheran, *le bon chevalier,* a younger brother of William,
a brave and loyal man. Two months later the Marquis of
Berghen and the Baron of Montigny were despatched to Spain.
Seemingly they met with success, for although Philip definitely
refused to summon the States-General he agreed to withdraw
the Inquisition from the Netherlands, to include in a general
pardon all those approved by the regent, and to grant religious
tolerance as far as it was consistent with the maintenance of
Catholicism. But the king did not intend to keep a single one of
these promises. He sought only to postpone revolt until he
found himself in a position to crush all opposition to his will.
In the meantime the revolutionary movement had been growing ever more tumultuous. The arm of the law seemed paralyzed. Great numbers of religious refugees ventured to return;
and Calvinist and Anabaptist preachers attracted great crowds
to hear them. At last in 1566 the pent-up wrath of the populace
found vent in a series of deplorable iconoclastic outbreaks in
the towns, especially in Antwerp where the splendid cathedral
suffered irreparable injury. It was only the scum of the population that indulged in the wild debauch of pillage and destruction, but their deeds resulted disastrously to the Protestant cause
in the Netherlands. The more liberal Catholics, who had been
quite as ardent as the dissenters in their resistance to the Spanish oppression, were alienated by the desecration of their sanctu-
aries and withdrew from the revolt; and eventually, in the last
years of the century, there came about the separation of the
Catholic south from the Protestant north. Becoming aware

through his secret agents of Philip's intention to crush the opposition in the Netherlands and to punish the great nobles who were regarded as the instigators of the revolt, and failing to persuade Egmont and Hoorne to take up arms with him, William retired on April 22, 1567, with all his household to his ancestral castle in Germany. Exactly four months later the stern and dreaded duke of Alva entered Brussels, having brought with him into the Netherlands some eleven thousand Spanish, Italian and German troops, splendidly equipped and controlled with an iron discipline, and having in his possession commissions from the king that made him all powerful in both civil and military matters. Finding herself to be regent in name only Margaret resigned, and with the acceptance of her resignation there came the appointment of Alva to the office.

The gaunt and war-worn veteran who had never known defeat, fanatically devoted to his king and to Catholicism, proceeded to carry out his instructions to " arrest and bring to condign punishment the chief persons of the country who had shown themselves guilty during the late troubles." Egmont and Hoorne were lured to Brussels in 1567, suddenly seized and thrown into prison; and a tribunal with summary procedure popularly known as the " Council of Blood " was established. At the head of the court was the unscrupulous duke himself, and all the other members, including the infamous Juan de Vargas (who consented to serve), were merely his tools. Wholesale condemnations were made; and everywhere, with fagot and ax and gibbet, the public executioners were busily engaged in putting the heretics and rebels to death and in seizing their property. Confiscation rapidly impoverished the country and judicial murder stained it red with blood; and when at last the man who exceeded without remorse the cruelty of an age of cruelty resigned his office he made the boast that he had put to death 18,600 persons in addition to those who had perished in battle. William declined to appear before the arbitrary tribunal and caused three expeditions to be made against the Spanish forces. Only one of the invasions met with a temporary success; but Alva was so enraged that he confiscated William's property, sent Egmont and Hoorne to the block, and inflicted a crushing defeat upon the miscellaneous bands that Louis of Nassau had gathered about him. The two executions instead of over-awing the populace served only to increase their hatred of the Spanish tyranny; and the slaughter of seven thousand men served only to increase the determination of William to persevere. For the time being Alva was able to continue his work of putting an end to the political autonomy of the country and exterminating heresy. In order to meet his financial needs he proposed to levy three taxes, (1) a tax once for all of one per cent upon all property, (2) a tax of five per cent upon every sale or transfer of landed property, and (3) a tax of ten per cent upon every sale of every article of commerce. So ruinous would this burden have been and so brutal were the endeavors of Alva to enforce it that it met everywhere with vigorous opposition and he was forced to accept a compromise.

It was the men of the sea and not those of the land who were the first successfully to dispute the power of Alva and to begin the ending of his atrocities. In 1569 William gave letters of marque to some eighteen small vessels to prey upon the Spanish ships. The refugees and desperadoes who manned the irregular fleet, the "wild beggars of the sea," soon equaled the cruel deeds of the duke, and William found himself unable to control their fearful barbarities. Within a year the number of the ships had increased five-fold; and on April 1, 1572, they seized the port of Brill and ran up the flag that later on was to be the emblem of the Dutch Republic. In quick succession other ports were captured, Flushing, Delfshaven and Schiedam; and then, a thrill of hope running through the land, most of the important towns of the north declared for William. On July 15 delegates from eight towns met at Dort, unanimously declared William to be the Stadhouder of the northern provinces, and voted him a large sum of money for carrying on the war. But disasters were to follow. William entered the Netherlands from Germany with 20,000 men; but he made the great mistake of failing to relieve Mons, which, with French aid, his brother Louis had taken, and of then attacking Alva with the combined forces. The town was retaken by the Spanish troops; and then the south being cleared of the revolutionary armies, Alva sent his regiments into the north to wreak a terrible vengeance upon the revolted towns. For three days Mechlin was handed over to pillage, torture and murder, at the hands of the brutal soldiery; more barbarous still was the sack of Zutphen; and the little town of Naarden was reduced to ashes and almost its entire population was put to death. Then came the heroic defense of Haarlem. Almost surrounded by its shallow seas, in the midst of the dense fogs and the bitter cold of winter, the brave city resisted every attempt of the besieging Spaniards to storm and to undermine its walls. At last on July 11, 1573, after a siege of seven months, in which extreme heroism and ferocity had been displayed on both sides, the city was com-

Battles
on Sea
and Lan'

pelled to surrender and suffered the fate of a general massacre. Here, however, the triumph of the Spanish forces practically ended. They were defeated in their attempt to take Alkmaar; and in October the " beggars of the sea," destroyed the Spanish fleet and took its admiral prisoner. Inadequately supported by his sovereign and broken in heart, Alva, at his own request, was recalled by Philip, and so on December 18, 1573, the man with the heart of stone, who everywhere else had been a victor, left the land which for six years he had deluged with blood, baffled and defeated.

The successor of the pitiless duke was Don Luis Requesens, a man of milder manners, who endeavored to bring an end to the revolution by negotiation. William, however, insisted upon three things, religious freedom, the integrity of the old charters, and the withdrawal of the Spanish troops, which the king was unwilling to grant; and so the negotiations failed and the war continued. Middleburg was captured by the sea-beggars; but in the battle of Mook the brave and chivalrous Louis, " the Bayard of the Netherlands," lost his life. Leyden was besieged for nine months by a large force of Spaniards; but when the dykes were cut and the land was flooded with water the sea-beggars were able to sail in shallow barges to its rescue and the city was relieved. After a cessation of hostilities a conference was held at Breda; but owing to Philip's refusal to tolerate Calvinism it ended in failure. The death of Requesens threw the Spanish forces into confusion, in the midst of which the Dutch cause was advanced by the union of Holland and Zeeland, a federation that foreshadowed the union of all the northern States. Still further, but at an appalling cost, was the patriotic cause furthered by a terrible massacre at Antwerp. On November 4, 1576, the Spanish troops in that city, mutinous because of arrears of pay, seized and destroyed property of untold value, set fire to the finest buildings, ravished the women and tortured the men, and put six thousand men, women and children to death. This atrocious outbreak, known as "the Spanish Fury," made Antwerp "the most forlorn and desolate city of Christendom" and sent a thrill of horror throughout the Netherlands that for a time united the people despite their sundering antagonisms. A treaty known as the Pacification of Ghent established an alliance between the southern provinces and Holland and Zeeland, and bound them to unite in driving the foreigners out of the country and then to consider the religious problem at a meeting of the States-General. In the meantime all the placards and ordinances against heresy were to be suspended. Some military successes followed. Friesland and Groningen were regained from the Spaniards; and then, in January, 1577, the compact of Ghent received the indorsement of the people in the Union of Brussels, an agreement that was widely signed especially in the southern provinces. In the meantime there had arrived the new representative of Philip, the illegitimate son of Charles V, and therefore the half-brother of the king. Don John of Austria was a handsome and fascinating man, the hero of Lepanto, who had captured the sacred banner of the Prophet, and struck a telling blow at the supremacy of the Crescent. But until he had approved the compact between the provinces and sworn to respect the ancient characters the States-General declined to receive him as governor. Every way he turned "the impetuous and brilliant soldier found himself thwarted by the sleepless and indefatigable diplomatist." The favorable situation, however, was suddenly altered by the arrival in the Netherlands, with a force of 20,000 men of Alexander of Parma, a consummate military genius, and, with his patient, temperate and unscrupulous character, scarcely less able as a diplomat. At Gembloux, in 1578, he fell upon the federal army and utterly routed it. After the death of Don John, in the same year, the victorious commander was appointed regent. The new and artful representative of the king saw his opportunity in the reappearing and increasing differences between the north and the south, the Calvinists and the Catholics, and he was quick to seize it. In the following January he was able to bring about the Union of Arras between the provinces of Artois and Hainault and the towns of Lille, Douai, and Orchies for the protection of the Catholic interests in those districts. This southern compact was answered in less than a month by the Union of Utrecht in which the northern provinces of Holland, Zeeland, Utrecht, Gelderland, and Zutphen, banded themselves together against every foreign force sent to oppress them. Thus the impending cleavage between the north and south became a fact. The south resumed the Spanish yoke which it was to bear for yet two hundred years; while the north, although it still retained the allegiance to Spain, began the formation of the heroic little Dutch Republic.

To William it seemed that France was the most likely source of aid for the northern provinces and so he desired them to accept the Duke of Anjou, the heir to the French throne, as their titular sovereign. In the meantime Alexander of Parma, was winning successes in intrigue and war. He regained the support of the south almost completely; he captured the important

CHAP.
XXV

1579-84

The
French
Alliance
and the
Assassina-
tion of
William
the
Silent

town of Maestricht (the entrance to Germany) almost exterminating the population of the place in three days of pillage, outrage, and butchery; and he recovered Mechlin and Groningen. On March 15, 1581, William was proclaimed an outlaw and a reward of twenty-five thousand crowns and a patent of nobility was offered to whomsoever should deliver him to the king, dead or alive, or put an end to his life. Before long William replied to the Ban with his *Apologia* which refuted every charge made against him and leveled serious accusations against the king. Becoming more aggressive he brought about the abjuration of Philip's rule, on July 26, 1581, by Brabant, Flanders, Utrecht, Gelderland, Holland and Zeeland; and then he persuaded various of the provinces to accept Anjou as their sovereign. It was little aid the Dutch provinces received for the various titles they bestowed upon the false and ugly duke. Not satisfied with his nominal rule he determined to make himself the actual ruler by force. But the " French Fury," an attempt in 1583 to seize Antwerp, and with it William of Orange, was a failure, and five months later Anjou returned to France. At last, on July 10 of the following year, avarice and fanaticism had their way. William, after no less than five attempts had been made upon his life, was shot to death by Balthasar Gerard, a Burgundian whom he had just befriended. Thus passed away the noblest statesman of the sixteenth century, and one of the noblest rulers of all time. It is not possible to justify his every word and deed. But for his undaunted devotion in the face of every danger to the cause of his country's liberty and for his religious tolerance in which he was the pioneer among modern princes he deserves the lasting admiration of men. From the very beginning of his public career he aimed to secure for the Netherlands civic liberty and religious tolerance. This aim he kept always clearly in mind. At first he did not deem independence from Spain to be necessary to attain these desired ends. Only gradually did he perceive them to be inseparable from revolution. Then he desired to see the whole of the Low Countries included in the new State and he was convinced only at the last hour that such a dream was vain. Deficient in important respects both as a general and as a practical statesman he yet won all that could be won of the high aim he cherished in his heart by the almost superhuman tenacity with which he clung to it. The hour of his untimely death was indeed a dark one for his country. And yet his task was done. The strength of Spain was already sapped by the long and exhausting struggle, and four years later it was shattered by the defeat of the Armada.

His life was a series of failures. But out of those failures as the fruit of his imperturbable endurance and his steadfast devotion, there arose a singular triumph — the freedom of the land for which he had suffered and died.

The central government of the revolted provinces consisted of their States-General. Possessed of little power, and realizing its serious weakness and the perilous strait of the country, that body looked for aid to a foreign ruler. When negotiations with Henry III of France came to naught, Elizabeth of England was approached. Declining to accept the sovereignty of the Dutch provinces, that shifty and parsimonious princess contracted to maintain in the Netherlands 5,000 foot and 1,000 horse on condition of being repaid for the expense. In the midst of the haggling over the petty details of the bargain, Parma, after a six months' siege, captured Antwerp. Only after that event was the English force sent over. Its commander was the Earl of Leicester, the queen's favorite, who allowed himself, without consulting his sovereign, to be invested with almost supreme authority under the title of governor-general. Elizabeth had feared to commit herself too completely against Spain and so her cunning as well as her jealousy resulted in an outburst of anger against her "sweet Robin." As a consequence of the quarrel the suspicions of the Dutch regarding the intentions of Elizabeth were aroused. Leicester was no man to make the best of so difficult a situation. He could not speak the language of the country; he did not understand the people with whom he had to deal; and he was neither sagacious nor tactful. It was chiefly the governing classes who suspected the English motives; so Leicester turned for support to the people. In pursuance of his democratic policy he committed a number of egregious errors, deepening the many divisions of the loosely connected provinces. So in spite of the fact that Philip, bent upon his preparations for an invasion of England, failed to send efficient aid to Parma, the year 1586 was one of disaster for the patriotic cause. Free rein was given to the separatist forces; and the provinces became increasingly antagonistic to each other. Grave and Venloo were captured by the Spanish commander, and Deventer and Zutphen were surrendered to him. Later on he took the important seaport of Sluys. Then, broken in purse, in health, and in spirit, Leicester returned to England. It was in the hope that Spain's threatened attack upon England would thereby be averted, that Elizabeth had refrained from accepting the sovereignty of the northern provinces. The hope was vain. On May 30, 1588, the Armada sailed for the English Channel, but only to meet with a crushing defeat. In the following year a joint Dutch and English expedition to Portugal inflicted some damage upon Spanish shipping and indicated a *rapprochement* of the two countries whose interests were almost identical.

Olden-
Barneveld
and
Maurice
of Nassau

The destiny of the divided provinces was now in the hands of two men, a statesman and a soldier, each the necessary complement of the other. Johan van Olden-Barneveld (1547–1619), trained as a lawyer, had become the principal minister in the province of Holland and its chief spokesman in the States-General. He was a statesman of great ability, and he became the real founder of the Dutch Republic. Philip William, the oldest son of the martyred William, had been kidnapped in his boyhood by Philip II of Spain and brought up in Madrid. So his next oldest brother, Maurice of Nassau (1567–1625), a born soldier and a master of military tactics, was the captain-general and admiral of the Union as well as the stadhouder of every province except Friesland. Assisted by his cousin, William Louis of Nassau, Maurice effected radical reforms in the Dutch army; transforming, with better drill, better discipline, better arms, and regular pay, the motley mob of William's time into a fighting machine that could cope successfully with the Spaniards in the field. When these reforms were under way Maurice began the task of reducing the Spanish strongholds in the northern provinces. Early in 1590 Breda was taken by an ingenious surprise; in 1591 Zutphen, Deventer, Hulst, and Nymegen were captured; in 1592 Steenwyck and Koevorden surrendered; and in 1593 Geertruidenburg and Groningen were regained. Thus at the age of twenty-seven Maurice having practically driven the Spaniards from the Dutch provinces, had proved himself to be one of the ablest generals of his time. In the meantime, in 1592, Alexander of Parma had died. There came to the Netherlands in his place the archduke Ernest of Austria who in turn was succeeded by the archduke Albert of Austria. Some Spanish successes were followed in 1596 by a triple alliance between France, England, and the Dutch, in which the independence of the United Provinces was recognized by the allies. A long series of victories was achieved by Maurice in the following year; and then, in May, 1598, the southern provinces were bestowed by Philip as a separate State upon the archduke Albert, who, in the same year, married Isabella, Philip's eldest daughter. A desultory war between the southern and the northern State dragged out its weary length until 1609, when a truce of twelve years virtually recognized the independence of the latter.

The Dutch State was made up of seven provinces — Gelderland, Utrecht, Friesland, Overyssel, Groningen, Zeeland, and Holland. Drenth, because of its poverty and its sparse population, was not admitted into the union as a separate State until 1796. The long struggle had bound the people together, though many difficulties still remained; and with one will they set to work, eagerly and intelligently, with unexampled enterprise, to increase the industrial and commercial importance of their country. The generation of almost continuous warfare had by no means exhausted them. As fishers, shipbuilders, carriers, and traders, they made the sea their own. Every sea and every shore saw the sails of their ships — the Baltic, the Mediterranean, the Gold Coast of Africa, the East and West Indies, and even the coasts of far Cathay. Their weavers' looms were never idle; their universities became the chief centers of learning; and their printing-presses were the most important in Europe. Their scholars, as we shall see in our last chapter, were among the most distinguished of the later Renaissance. They preceded every other nation in political progress, for it was they who prepared the way for democracy.

CHAP.
XXV

1589-1609

The Dutch
Republic
and its
Accom-
plishments

# CHAPTER XXVI

## THE RELIGIOUS WARS IN FRANCE

1. France at the Outbreak of the Religious Wars.
2. The Provocations.
3. The Wars.

CHAP.
XXVI

1559

The Ambi-
tion of
Catherine
de' Medici

A T the outbreak of the religious wars in France that country was in a very disorganized condition. The maladministration of the government, the financial extortion of which it had been guilty, oppressed the lower classes and put them in a state of sore discontent, and all the severe measures to which Henry II had resorted had failed to check the spread of heresy. When that monarch died, his wife, Catherine de' Medici, became for the first time an important factor in the affairs of France. For a quarter of a century she had been neglected by her royal husband; but as soon as her son succeeded to the throne she began her attempts to make herself the actual ruler. She did not understand the people with whom her lot was cast; and she remained always an alien in their midst. True daughter of the Florentine despots, she looked at France through the eyes of an Italian prince of the Renaissance period. The State, so it seemed to her, existed for the benefit of its ruler; and power, an end in itself, was to be gained, regardless of legal or moral restraint, by any device that promised success. Her own personal advantage, or that of her children, was with her the mainspring of action. She could not understand men who were impelled by a fanaticism or a passion that balked not at self-sacrifice. It was a matter of indifference to her whether the men who served her ends were Catholics or Calvinists. She was tolerant, but it was the tolerance of indifference, and not that of a wide spiritual horizon. Her son, Francis II (1559–60), was a boy not yet sixteen, weak in mind and body. He was married to Mary Stuart, a beautiful and brilliant girl, niece of the duke of Guise and his brother Cardinal Lorraine. It was these powerful uncles of the queen who were to be the first obstacles in the path of Catherine. But there were policies as well as people that were to stand in the way of the fulfilment of her ambition.

Two faiths divided the land. The Catholics far outnumbered the Calvinists. But the Huguenots, as the latter were called, were by no means insignificant in number. By the middle of the sixteenth century they had, perhaps, somewhere between 300,000 and 400,000 members; and it is estimated that when the wars of religion broke out there were 1,500,000 of them. In spite of persecution, they were to be found in every province, particularly in the south; and in every class of society, even among the ecclesiastics, but chiefly among the working classes in the towns. Interwoven with these two faiths were several factions. One was grouped about the person of Anne de Montmorency, constable of France, an able general and an ambitious and cruel man. He had three nephews, the Chatillons, who were men of note and chief of whom was Gaspard de Coligny, the admiral. A second faction was gathered about the Guises. These powerful lords, whose home was in Lorraine, then not yet a part of France, were disliked both because they were strangers and because of their aggressive ambition. Francis, duke of Guise, had won a reputation as a successful soldier; and both he and his brother were possessed of a grasping temper. Charles, Cardinal of Lorraine, was a man of penetrating insight, eloquent, scholarly, avaricious, and unscrupulous. Their sister Mary had been married to James V of Scotland, and it was her daughter, Mary Stuart, who was the wife of the young king. A third faction had for its head Antoine de Bourbon, who, having married Jeanne d'Albret, the only child of the king of Navarre, had succeeded to that throne upon the death of his father-in-law. The little kingdom now consisted of only a few square miles on the northern slope of the Pyrénées, but its ruler was a sovereign monarch. Antoine did not cease to be a French nobleman when he became king of Navarre. He was the nearest blood relative to the French royal family. Naturally the direction of affairs during the youth of the king should have fallen to him, but this robust, affable and generous man was also vain, vacillating, and essentially weak in character. Catherine was sagacious enough to see that she could not clear the path in front of her of all three of these factions. So she threw in her lot with the Guises. But it was they and not she who assumed control of the national government. That government had become highly centralized. The feudal nobility had lost much of their former power; and the towns had also been deprived of the most important of the governmental privileges they once possessed.  But the nobility had by no means been reduced to impotence.  Owning great estates and living in fortified castles, they were the most powerful class in the kingdom; and they were eager to seize every opportunity to regain something of their former independence.  The administration of governmental affairs under Henry II had been wasteful and incompetent.  Existing taxes had been increased and new ones imposed.  In the twelve years of that monarch's reign more taxes were extorted from the people of France than in the preceding forty years.  Very naturally discontent was rife.

The control of the young king by the Guises and the usurpation of power by these hated " foreigners " was soon challenged. To the ranks of the Huguenots there were added nobles who were opposed to the power of the Guises and who wished to regain their feudal independence.  Thus religion and politics combined to produce the wars in France that were to last for almost half a century.  It was planned to seize Cardinal Lorraine and the duke of Guise, to obtain possession of the king, and then to assemble the States-General.  The " Tumult of Amboise " was a failure.  But the cruel punishment inflicted upon the conspirators served only to fan the flames of discontent.  There were frequent outbreaks of disorder.  Even in the court many approved of the attempt to suppress the tyranny of the Guises. Catherine, the queen-mother, was ill-pleased by their assumption of power that naturally belonged to her.  So when François Oliver, one of their followers who held the office of chancellor, died she was active in the appointment of Michel de l'Hôpital in his place.  A few weeks later, May, 1560, the edict of Romorantin was issued, restoring to the clergy the jurisdiction of religious affairs.  This did away with the summary procedure that had hitherto been employed with heretics.  A supplementary decree limited the action of bishops against religious dissenters to preachers and to those persons who permitted heretical meetings to be held in their houses.  The situation that resulted was favorable to the Huguenots.  So they grew in strength.  And the personal attack upon the Guises increased in vigor.  But those strongly entrenched nobles were not easily to be deprived of their ascendancy.  Louis, Prince of Condé, a younger brother of Antoine of Navarre, was arrested on the charge of being concerned in the outbreaks in southern France, tried and sentenced to death.  Only the death of the king prevented the execution of the sentence.

The new king, Charles IX (1560–74), was a child of ten. So the king of Navarre, the oldest and nearest prince of the blood, became regent. But for a time Catherine succeeded in making herself the real ruler. Throughout the land there was such an insistent demand for the summoning of the States-General to inquire into the affairs of State and Church, to redress the grievances of the nation, that, after an interval of eighty years, that body was convened once more. Three problems confronted the delegates assembled at Orleans in December, 1560, religion, the reform of the finances, and the reform of the courts of law. Without coming to any final conclusions the Estates were prorogued and did not meet again until August, 1561, at Pontoise. Just as the adjournment at Orleans took place a royal edict was issued providing for the cessation of all persecution for religion and the release of all who were imprisoned upon the charge of heresy. Thus encouraged, the Huguenots became insolent and defiant, many of their preachers flocked back to France from Geneva and Germany, congregations and meetings were held openly in many places, dangerous riots occurred in all parts of the country, and civil war seemed imminent. The sittings of the States-General at Pontoise failed to effect a satisfactory settlement of the secular problems; and the Colloquy of Poissy, held almost simultaneously at the instigation of Catherine, far from producing the desired religious unity, did not even conciliate the opposing sects, but proved instead to be "the watershed from which the two religions parted." Disappointed in her purpose of finding a common ground upon which the Catholics and Calvinists could agree, and failing also to arrange a compromise that would satisfy both sides, the queen-mother caused to be issued the provisional Edict of January (1562) which, awaiting the decisions of the Council of Trent, permitted the Huguenots to gather for worship in any place outside the walled towns. But even this degree of toleration proved impossible for the administration to carry out. For some time forces hostile to the insurrectionary heretics had been drawing together. The duke of Guise and the Constable Montmorency, heads of opposing factions, became reconciled to each other. To them was added St. André, one of the marshals of France, a tool of the Guises. This powerful triumvirate was joined later on by Antoine of Navarre, who, by various considerations, one of which was the promise to bestow upon him as a reward "the kingdom of Tunis," had been made "never so earnest on the Protestant side as he was now furious on the other." Opposed to these militant Catholics was a much weaker group, consisting of the courageous and fascinating Prince of Condé, brother of Navarre, and the three Chatillons.

nephews of the Constable, one of whom, as we have seen, was the masterful Coligny. Tumults and massacres continued to take place in various parts of the country, the most serious of which was a conflict at Vassy, on March 1, 1562, between armed retainers of the duke of Guise and a body of Huguenots who were conducting religious services in a barn. The massacre of sixty heretics and the wounding of many others so incensed the Protestants throughout France that it acted as the spark for which the fuel was waiting. Civil war was inevitable.

The First Religious War

In the first of the long series of religious wars (1562–63) the Huguenots secured aid from England, but it profited them little. Despite the presence of English troops, Rouen, which next to Paris was the most important city in France, was captured by the duke of Guise. Yet the loss of the town was not without its compensation. In the attack the king of Navarre received a mortal wound, and the leadership of his house devolved upon Condé and upon Antoine's son, a lad of nine, who in future years was to lead the Protestant cause. Then followed a desultory warfare in the south; while in the north was fought the battle of Dreux, in which the Huguenots were beaten. In February, 1563, the duke of Guise was assassinated by a fanatical Huguenot. The death of the Catholic leader so altered the condition of affairs that less than a month later the Pacification of Amboise was signed. The provisions of the edict, which permitted the Huguenots to worship in certain prescribed places, failed to satisfy either side, but under them peace was maintained for several years. In this interval of peace the country was virtually ruled by the learned, cultured, and tolerant chancellor, Michel de l'Hôpital, leader of the moderate Catholic party.

The Second Religious War

But despite the efforts of the wise and tolerant chancellor, theological acrimony continued to increase. Fearful, in the first place, that Spain and France might join forces to exterminate them and, later, that a body of Swiss troops employed to watch Alva's march from Savoy to the Netherlands was really intended to be used against them, the Huguenots, in September, 1567, attempted to seize the king at Meaux. The plot which failed to accomplish its purpose, opened the second war (1567–68). It was not only religious rancor that had fanned the smoldering fire into flame. Many of the Huguenot nobles were animated by political ambition; and the bourgeoisie were actuated by the desire to effect administrative and economic reform. The most important event in this second clash of arms was the battle of St. Denis, which, despite the overwhelming number of the Catholics, resulted somewhat to the advantage of the Huguenots.

And when the queen-mother and the chancellor, because of the mortal wounding of the constable, found their influence increased, it became possible in the following year, 1568, to issue the edict of Lonjumeau, which was in the main a confirmation of the edict that ended the first war.

As usual neither side was satisfied with the settlement. Indeed, the third war (1568-70) broke out in less than six months. This time it was the Catholics who opened hostilities. Condé and Coligny got wind of a plot to seize them and narrowly escaped to La Rochelle, the western stronghold of the Huguenots. The dismissal of L'Hôpital from office and the revocation of the edicts of toleration indicated that the Catholics intended to be more aggressive than before. In the battle of Jarnac, March, 1569, Condé was slain. He was succeeded as the leader of the Huguenot party by a boy of sixteen, Henry, son of Antoine of Navarre; and Coligny was made the commander-in-chief of their forces. More serious was the defeat sustained by the Huguenots in October at Moncontour. And yet in spite of their reverses the Peace of St. Germain, 1570, was more favorable to them than the edicts that had ended the previous wars. After ten years of internecine warfare both the government and the people of France desired peace. Only the ambition of the Guises and the interference of Spain in the affairs of France made the new cessation of hostilities of so short a duration.

In order to strengthen the position of France against Spain and to forward her own interests and those of her children Catherine planned to marry one of her sons, first the duke of Anjou and then the duke of Alençon, to Elizabeth of England, and to marry her daughter, Margaret of Valois, to Henry of Navarre. The first of these projected marriages came to naught; but on August 18, 1572, the second was performed. Many Huguenots had flocked to Paris to be there at the time of the nuptials. Not all of them were careful to avoid offending the intensely Catholic populace of Paris. And their exuberance of spirits probably made the political ascendancy of Coligny seem greater than was actually the case. That ascendancy aroused the jealous animosity of Catherine. Ever since the death of her husband she had sought to secure political control for herself by balancing one party against the other. By his ascension to power in the Huguenot party, and by his influence over the king, Coligny had upset that balance and had become an obstacle in her path. So she plotted his death. On August 22 an assassin fired upon the admiral, but succeeded only in inflicting a serious wound. The plot had resulted not in the removal of the enemy but only in making him more dangerous. Wild with rage and fear the queen-mother took council with the dukes of Guise and Anjou and with several others. The king was won over to the action upon which they determined. Long before the day broke on the feast of St. Bartholomew, August 24, the tocsin was sounded for a general massacre of the Huguenots. It is impossible to say how many were killed in Paris. The estimates range from one thousand to ten times that number. It seems to be well established that the massacre in the capital was unpremeditated, that it resulted from the momentary fear and the jealous passion of the queen-mother. But the subsequent provincial massacres were deliberately ordered in cold blood. The total number of victims, according to the computation of Sully, was seventy thousand; and ten thousand is the lowest estimate that has been made. The wholesale slaughter of the Huguenots by no means put an end to the difficulties of Catherine. " France," said Sully, " atoned for the massacre by twenty-six years of disaster, carnage, and horror. The Huguenots, it is true, had lost their leader; but they had a number of strongholds — Montauban in the south, Sancerre in central France, and La Rochelle in the west. It was the effort to take these and other citadels of Protestantism that precipitated the fourth war (1572–73). Twenty thousand lives were lost in the unsuccessful siege of La Rochelle. Peace was concluded at that place in June, 1573. Every individual was allowed to believe as he desired, but permission to hold public worship was granted only to La Rochelle, Nîmes, and Montauban. Later on the same privilege was extended to Sancerre. In spite of these provisions the war dragged on in the south. Weary of the continual warfare there was gradually formed among the moderate Catholics a new party known as the " Politiques." They were opposed to the aggressive Catholics, headed by the Guises, and entered into a working agreement with the Huguenots. Jealousy among the Catholic nobles was doubtless a factor in the formation of this new party, but its members were also imbued with a genuine desire to put an end to the long-continued religious warfare and its depopulation and impoverishment of the kingdom. " A man does not cease to be a citizen," they said, " because he is excommunicated." In the south the Huguenots themselves were much better organized than they had ever been before. At the end of 1573 they had formed a confederation that, under a written scheme of government, took charge of the war, regulated finances, administered civil affairs and provided for religious protection. Thus they formed a state within a state. In their ranks the bourgeoisie had

gained power, while the influence of the nobles had declined.
As a consequence republican ideas had become widespread among
them. These ideas found expression in many political pamphlets
of which one is the *Franco-Gallia* of François Hotman, who for
some years had lived in Geneva, and another is the *Vindiciæ
contra Tyrannos* of Duplessis-Mornay. It was under such conditions that the Huguenots put forth their most sweeping demands. They required from the king the unhindered exercise
of their religion throughout France, the maintenance at national
expense of Huguenot garrisons in every stronghold possessed
by them, and the cession of two fortresses in every province
in the kingdom as a security that the compact would be kept.
Catherine was furious at the demands of *ces miserables,* as she
dubbed them, and the unfavorable reception of the Huguenot
stipulations made inevitable another war.

At the beginning of the fifth war (1574–76) the Huguenots
met with some success in the west; but the two plots to remove
the duke of Alençon, the youngest son of Catherine, and the
young king of Navarre from the influence of the court failed.
The Huguenots and the Politiques both desired to see Alençon
recognized as the heir-presumptive to the throne in place of his
elder brother, the duke of Anjou, who had recently been elected
king of Poland and who was now in that distant and distracted
country. The death of Charles IX, May 30, 1574, and the
absence of Anjou, now become Henry III (1574–89), in Poland,
contributed to bring about a temporary cessation of the struggle.
Acting under the influence of his mother, who, now that her
favorite son had succeeded to the throne, hoped that, after all
opposition had been crushed, her influence would be supreme,
Henry declined to adopt the conciliatory policy towards the
Huguenots and Politiques that had been recommended to him.
This decision of the king turned the working agreement of the
moderate Catholics and the Protestants into a definite alliance.
The program of the combined parties consisted of full religious
tolerance, the cessation of the sale of offices, a reduction of taxes,
and the summoning of the States-General. The war, which in
the meantime had been dragging out its weary length, had now
to a large extent lost its religious character. It had become a
factional fight between Guise on the one hand and Francis, Duke
of Montmorency, on the other, between intolerance and political
corruption and tolerance and administrative reform. Such was
the situation when the king's younger brother, Alençon, who had
now become the duke of Anjou, and the king of Navarre succeeded in making their escape from the court. With the freedom

of these princes from surveillance the Huguenots and Politiques had decidedly the advantage, and so events soon led to the " Peace of Monsieur," May, 1576, so-called because of Anjou's activity in the matter, the title of Monsieur being always given to the eldest living brother of the king. The agreement gave to the Huguenots the best terms they had thus far secured. They were permitted to worship everywhere in France except within a short distance of Paris and their religion was not to disqualify them from holding office. As for political reform, it was decided to convoke the States-General.

The Sixth
Religious
War

The terms of the new peace aroused the indignation of the Catholics and accelerated the formation of provincial leagues among them which eventually coalesced into the general League that prolonged the warfare for yet another twenty years. Under the inspiration of the Guises the elections to the States-General resulted in the selection of deputies opposed to religious tolerance. When, therefore, the Estates were convoked at Blois they declared that only one religion should be permitted in France. Before this, the sixth war (1577) had broken out. The Huguenots lost La Charité and Brouage, the latter being one of their important places, and only the lack of unity among their opponents and the prevailing desire for peace enabled them to secure terms at Bergerac, September, 1577, scarcely less favorable than those they had obtained a year ago.

The Seventh Religious War

It is little wonder that the compact failed to give satisfaction to the Catholic zealots and to those who were utilizing the League to promote their own personal ends. Outbreaks occurred in different parts of the country. But the real cause of the seventh war (1580) was the dispute between the king and Henry of Navarre regarding the dower of the latter's wife. The war consisted only of spasmodic skirmishes and attacks upon places of minor importance and it was brought to an end in November by the peace signed at Fleix. Then followed five years of peace that was, however, by no means profound. They were years filled with discontent, intrigue, duels, assassinations, and general demoralization. The nobility gave free rein to their ambitions and their vices; the lower classes complained bitterly of their increasing burdens.

The
Eighth
Religious
War

In 1584 Anjou, the only remaining brother of Henry III, died. The king was childless and so Henry of Navarre became the heir-presumptive, and that prince, now that William of Orange was dead, was the most important of the military leaders of Protestantism in continental Europe. Opposed to Navarre was Henry of Guise who secured the support of the League, now in

the final stages of its organization, and who concluded at Joinville, January, 1585, an alliance with Spain against the Protestants and the Protestant heir.  Six months later the king came
to terms with the League at Nemours by which he agreed to all
its demands and abandoned the principle of toleration.  In conformity with the agreement an edict was issued by which the
Huguenots were outlawed.  Navarre made a forcible protest,
but without avail, and in September the Pope pronounced his
excommunication.  Before this the " War of the three Henries,"
the eighth war (1585–89), had begun.  Ostensibly it was a war
between Henry III and Henry of Guise against Henry of Navarre.  But the League was by no means a whole-hearted ally
of the royal party.  It had become impregnated with repub-
licanism, and many of its leaders, especially the Guises, had
their own interests to conserve.  The Huguenots were aided by
the Politiques and by the Duke of Montmorency, who was jealous of the Guises.  At first the tide of war went against the
Protestants and their allies, but the discords in the Catholic
ranks, the fretting of the king under the control of the League,
and the military skill of Navarre, gradually wrought a change.
After a number of successes in guerilla warfare the Protestant
leader won his first pitched battle at Coutras, 1587, where he
defeated a force twice as large as his own.  Shortly after, however, Guise defeated a German force that was marching to the
aid of Navarre.  Flushed with this success the leaders of the
League demanded of the king, who all along had doubted the
wisdom of the course he had been persuaded to pursue, that he
should dismiss from his presence all the persons of whom they
disapproved, that he should publish the Tridentine decrees in
France, and that he should confiscate the property of the Huguenots.  The king hesitated to comply with these radical demands;
and Guise, in defiance of the royal injunction, entered Paris.
Then the king ordered four thousand Swiss troops who were
stationed in the suburbs to enter the city.  The Parisians, who
were the most ardent supporters of the League, rushed to arms,
barricaded the streets, attacked the Swiss and compelled them
to capitulate.  Powerless to control the situation the king acceded to all the demands of the League, which had become an
*imperium in imperio,* and surrendered the conduct of the war to
its leader, the duke of Guise.  Some months later the king
deemed himself to be in a position to carry out a project he had
formed of getting rid of Guise.  On December 23, 1588, the
duke was assassinated and his brother, the Cardinal of Guise,
was arrested and on the next day executed.  The king's plan

to make himself supreme failed to effect its purpose. The
League rose in revolt, declared the crown to be elective, strengthened its hold upon Paris, and secured control of most of the
important towns in central and southern France. Catherine de'
Medici died in the midst of this tumult, January 5, 1589, worn
out in her endeavor to secure peace for the country of her
adoption. She had failed because the causes and the motives
which she had to deal with were beyond her experience and her
divination. The situation compelled the king to sign a truce
with Navarre. The Huguenots were not to be persecuted; they,
in their turn, were not to molest the Catholics; and Navarre
was to aid the king against the duke of Mayenne, the sole surviving brother of the duke of Guise. The royal forces thus
augmented took many towns and laid siege to Paris. But before the assault was delivered upon the capital a fanatic friar,
Jacques Clement, stabbed the king, who, two days later, August 2,
1589, after designating Navarre as his heir, died of the wound.

It was not an encouraging prospect that Henry IV (1589–
1610) now faced. Had he followed the advice given him to
become a Catholic it was probable that only the moderate Catholics would have flocked to his support, and he would certainly
have alienated himself from the Huguenots. So, for the present,
being guided very largely by policy, he decided not to abjure his
faith. Instead he issued a declaration recognizing Catholicism
as the religion of the realm, promising to grant to the Huguenots no further privileges than they already possessed, and stat-
ing his willingness to be instructed in the Catholic creed. The
declaration failed to rally the kingdom to his banner; and so,
feeling himself too weak to take and hold the capital, he moved
up into Normandy from whence the city drew its supplies.
Thither Mayenne, at the head of a far larger force, followed
him and thus the ninth war (1589–95) began. In the series of
engagements known as the battle of Arques, 1589, the advantage
lay with the new king; and in the following year, in the famous
battle of Ivry, although greatly outnumbered, he inflicted a severe defeat upon Mayenne. Then he laid siege to Paris. Becoming convinced that his acceptance of the Catholic religion
was the surest means of restoring peace to his distracted country
he abandoned the faith of his childhood and was received into
the Catholic fold at St. Denis, one of the suburbs of Paris.
Henry IV was not a man of impressive appearance. There was
about him a certain insignificance that hid the great leader from
casual eyes. He was a sensual man, this tireless, courageous
and skilful soldier, whose good-nature, unmistakable devotion

The Ninth
Religious
War

to his country, and biting wit, won friends for him everywhere. Lacking in deep-seated religious conviction, and having a considerable cynical element in his make-up, it may nevertheless be true that his saying " Paris was well worth a mass " had something of bitter regret in it as well as the light-hearted indifference to which it is usually attributed. In later years he seems to have grown attached to his new religion. All but the most bigoted members of the League and those nobles who, like Mayenne, were bent upon advancing their own personal interests, came over to him. Rouen, the last important city in the north, surrendered; and four days later, March 21, 1594, he entered Paris. The capital had not been given to him, he said, but had been bought " and at a goodly price."

It required more than the king's " conversion " to win the kingdom. Opposition, though greatly lessened by the abjuration of his old faith, was by no means extinct. Mayenne and the duke of Mercœur, among others, still held out. An attempt on the life of Henry by a pupil of the Jesuits (though these seem not to have been responsible for his deed) brought to a crisis the hostility that had long been growing against that Order and its members were expelled by the parlements of Paris, Rouen, and Dijon from their respective jurisdictions. With courage or with compromise, and with unfailing affability, Henry gradually won his way. Then, when he thought himself securely established he declared war upon Spain. Ever since he had inherited the crown he had been in reality at war with that country, for Spain had sent men and money to his opponents. Before the Spanish war (1595–98) had long been under way Burgundy was taken by the king. In the same year the Pope absolved Henry from every taint of heresy, and soon after Mayenne came over to the royal side and proved an able and loyal follower of his new master. Then the Spanish were beaten in northeastern France, and on May 2, 1598, peace was signed between the two countries at Vervins. A short time previous to the conclusion of peace Henry signed the famous Edict of Nantes, April 15, that codified and increased the rights previously granted to the Calvinists. Freedom to worship everywhere in private according to the rites of one's creed was granted, and freedom to worship in public in about two hundred towns and in two places in every *bailliage* and every *sénéchaussée* in the kingdom and in many castles of the Huguenot nobles, and no Calvinist was to be disturbed in any way because of his religion. Full civil rights and the protection of the law was extended to the Huguenots. They were once more declared eligible for all

The Spanish War and the Edict of Nantes

public offices; and they were permitted to hold their ecclesiastical assemblies. Two hundred towns were to remain in their control until 1607, their possession afterwards being extended to 1612, among them the redoutable strongholds of La Rochelle, Montauban, and Montpellier; and the State was to furnish funds for the maintenance of the garrisons and fortifications. Like most such agreements the Edict of Nantes was a compromise. It was by no means perfect. It had serious shortcomings and contained the seeds of discord. It extended tolerance to no other dissenting sect than Calvinism. Its provisions for local political liberty increased the decentralizing tendencies of the time. But it was perhaps as good an agreement as could be made under the circumstances. It brought peace to the unhappy land. At last the wild struggles of the protracted religious wars were over and there began that regeneration of France that made her the heiress of the attainments and civilization of Italy and the intellectual and artistic leader of Europe.

# CHAPTER XXVII

## PAPACY AND EMPIRE

1. The Two Medieval World-Powers in the Sixteenth Century.
2. Ferdinand of Hapsburg.
3. The Reforming Papacy.
4. Maximilian II.
5. Militant Catholicism in Germany.

THE Papacy and the Holy Roman Empire had been the two great world-powers all through the Middle Ages. In the sixteenth century they were eclipsed by the new nations. The Papacy had steadily declined in power from the day on which Boniface VIII was struck in the face by one of the emissaries of the king of France. Though it abated none of its great claims to authority over the State it found it politic to let them remain in abeyance. The Empire, too, had lost much of its power and prestige. The days of German expansion were long past. Steadily the imperial boundaries had retreated. The loss of the Burgundian and Italian domains was not significant of weakness, for they had always been alien possessions, foreign to the true purpose of the Empire. But the loss of the Swiss cantons and then that of the Dutch provinces were far more serious. Internally, too, affairs were not such as to make for the renewal of Germanic power. Potentially all the elements of power were there. Germany was the land of inventors and engineers. She had military strength and wealth of resources; and her capitalists were the richest and ablest of the century. But the political forces of the time were increasingly centrifugal. The territorial lords had passed too far beyond the position of the nobility in France and England and Spain to make it easy or, indeed, possible to reduce them to the position of mere barons or grandees. As a result the imperial diet was not a real parliament but instead an assembly of princes who were intent upon furthering the interests of their own houses, states, and class, and of municipal deputies who were bent upon advancing the welfare of their respective cities and of that of the bourgeoisie in general.

The gifted and gracious Maximilian I (1493–1519), over whose life so many German historians have loved to linger, had large dreams of reform, but his lack of perseverance and foresight, and the expenditure of his resources upon territorial expansion rather than upon internal reform permitted the particularistic forces to pursue their aims successfully.   Charles V (1520–56), too, had had his schemes for the unification of Germany, but they were postponed by the great ecclesiastical revolution and hampered by the encroachment of the Turks and the machinations of France and crippled by the papal distrust of his intentions.   For a moment, indeed, it seemed as though they would succeed.   In 1547, after the battle of Mühlberg, all Germany, with a few minor exceptions, seemed to lie at the Emperor's feet.   But his widely-scattered possessions and the multitudinous interests and affairs in which he was involved dissipated his energy and left the true interests of the Empire in an increasingly precarious condition.

Such was the Empire to which, upon the abdication of Charles, his younger brother, Ferdinand I (1556–64) succeeded.   The new Emperor's brief reign was occupied chiefly with an attempt to settle the religious differences of the Empire and in an endeavor to make a more vigorous attack upon the Turks.   In both efforts he was unsuccessful.   He was politic in mind, and just and tolerant in disposition.   It was his desire that substantial concessions should be made to the Protestants by the Council of Trent.   That desire was not fulfilled by the conciliar fathers; and Ferdinand's refusal to abrogate the ecclesiastical reservation of the Peace of Augsburg served still further to render futile his efforts to bring about a reconciliation.   There had been no permanent settlement between the two religions, but only a truce. The history of the Empire in the sixty-three years that elapsed between the Peace of Augsburg and the beginning of the Thirty Years' War may be summed up as a series of efforts on the part of Catholics and Protestants to achieve territorial predominance.

The Papacy, it will be remembered, had been obliged to relegate its policy of political expansion to the background, if not to abandon it altogether, and to occupy itself with the tasks of reforming the Church and combating heresy.   We have already noticed the reforming work of the first popes of the Catholic Reformation.   With the pontificate of Sixtus V (1585–90) we come to the most remarkable of all the pontiffs since the medieval age.   Like so many other great popes he rose from extreme poverty to the papal throne, by the strength of his intellect and the force of his character.   Very early he became a Franciscan friar and won celebrity first as a preacher and then as a university lecturer. He served for a time as inquisitor-general at Venice, took part in the debates of the Council of Trent, and was promoted to the cardinalate. When he assumed the duties of his highest office he found the affairs of the Papal States in a most deplorable condition. Learned in the canon law and in patriotic lore he was also a most able administrator. With relentless rigor, in little more than two years, he rid the Papal States almost completely of the hordes of brigands with which it had been infested, and he greatly curtailed the lingering feudal powers of the nobility. Then, with the same directness of procedure, he turned his attention to the work of putting the finances in order. The defective system that he found was not replaced with another, but it was improved and developed; and, as a result, in spite of his vast expenditures, the new pope became one of the richest rulers in Europe. Many public works were undertaken; roads were built, marshes drained, farms laid out, mills erected, old industries revived and new ones introduced, palaces and churches rebuilt and enlarged, the vast dome of St. Peter's almost completed and a great obelisk, that once had stood in the circus of Nero and had for long remained half buried, was erected in front of the cathedral there to testify to the victories of the Cross that was placed upon its summit. But in the mind of Sixtus there loomed two things as being greater deeds to do than these — the restoration to the ancient fold of the heretics and the driving back of the Turks beyond the eastern frontier of the Holy Land. Friar as he was, with a strain of the mystic in him, he dreamed of the conversion and coöperation of Elizabeth. It was an illusion in which he was encouraged by the Jesuits. His dream, however, did not dissuade him from promoting an attack upon England. In every possible way he furthered the great Spanish expedition against that country, and he attributed the destruction of the Armada very largely to Philip's delay that had permitted the English to perfect their preparations for defense. In order to carry out the canons and decrees of the Council of Trent it was necessary that the machinery of the papal administration should be improved. This was done by limiting the number of cardinals to seventy and dividing them into fifteen congregations each of which had its own special work, and by taking into the employ of the Papacy the ablest assistants that could be procured. Sixtus also directed an emendation of the Vulgate. And he was not slow to perceive the danger that might arise from the rapidly increasing power of the Jesuits, but his death prevented the carrying out of the radical changes in their constitutions that he contemplated. In the intricate relations that the circumstances of the time compelled him to enter into with the various political powers of Europe he was always animated by his central idea of inducing the Protestants to return to the fold they had forsaken. His pontificate was a brief one but it left traces of its aims and methods that have not yet disappeared.

The successor of Sixtus, Urban VII (1590), died eleven days after his election and before the ceremonies of his installation had been completed by the act of coronation. Brief, too, was the reign of the next pontiff, Gregory XIV (1590–91), who died ten months and ten days after his election. He was a man of blameless character who fasted twice each week, said mass every day, and devoted a considerable part of his time to prayer and to the reading of religious books. But, wholly subservient to the interests of Spain, he was utterly incompetent as an administrator and he left the Papal States once more afflicted with brigandage and suffering from famine. Still another short pontificate was that of Innocent IX (1591) between whose election and death only two months elapsed. It was the policy of Clement VIII (1592–1605) to bring about a *rapprochement* between France and the Papacy. He granted absolution to Henry IV, thus clearing the way for that monarch's legitimate inheritance of the throne; and he had much to do with the Peace of Vervins (1598) that made peace between France and Spain, the two powers upon which the welfare of Catholicism so largely depended. Gradually the Papacy was freed from the dictation of Spain and its policy made to rest upon a broader basis. It was then possible for the work of internal reform to proceed with less hindrance.

Ferdinand was succeeded in the imperial office by his eldest son Maximilian II (1564–76) much of whose early life had been spent in Spain. Possessed of an open mind and a friendly disposition, and, because of his sympathetic nature and varied experience, able to appreciate the desirable elements in each of the clashing forces of his conglomerate Empire, he became a popular ruler. In his youth he had doubtless learned something of Lutheranism, and political reasons led him to maintain friendly relations with several of the Protestant princes. Later on his association with Lutherans. and with men who had pronounced leanings towards Lutheranism, caused no little uneasiness to his father. But, although his religious views were colored with Lutheranism, he remained, nominally at least, an adherent of the ancestral Church, and his brief reign, overshadowed by the terror of the Turks and troubled with the religious and territorial rivalries of the time, was one in which militant Catholicism met with considerable success in Germany.

CHAP.
XXVII

1576-1612

The Neg-
lected Em-
pire

Despite Maximilian's intelligence and his desire to treat every religious party with tolerance it was no peaceful situation that he left to his son Rudolf II (1576–1612) who fell heir to all the sore perplexities of the distracted Empire. The religious peace of 1555 was proving more and more to be no peace at all. It lacked precision and so it was misinterpreted. It conflicted with personal interests and so it was ignored. Protestant princes continued their attacks upon Catholic property; and Catholic authorities placed before their Protestant subjects the alternatives of acceptance of the old faith or exile. There was no power sufficient to interpret the settlement and to enforce it. Germany was already drifting into the Thirty Years' War. When eleven years of age Rudolf, because of the ambition of his father that he should inherit the Spanish throne, had been sent to Spain to be educated and there he had lived for nine years. He was not without ability, but in character he resembled his uncle Philip II more than his father. Quiet and reserved he had acquired a reading knowledge of several languages and he was interested in all the arts and sciences. Gradually he became a great patron of artists and scholars, and he also became a notable collector. Then he began to neglect the affairs of state. After 1594 he did not attend a meeting of the imperial diet and three or four years later he exhibited great reluctance to transact the ordinary business of government. A series of valets gained ascendancy over him and so completely did he withdraw himself from the world that when the new century opened it became exceedingly difficult even for the highest officials to gain access to him. Rumors of madness spread abroad. All through his reign the border warfare with the Turks continued and a great disaster in which 50,000 imperial soldiers were killed was inflicted in 1596 upon the German forces. In the religious disputes Rudolf was a partisan of the Catholic cause, and despite insurrection, the Catholic predominance in Austria was restored. So impotent was his rule that he left the Empire in a condition bordering upon chaos.

The reign of Rudolf II coincided with the militant activity of Catholicism. The success of that activity was assisted, it will be remembered, by a widely prevalent feeling of panic. It was also furthered by the dissensions among the Protestants. Lutherans and Calvinists became ever more distrustful of each other and their distrust was fostered by the Catholics. According to the terms of the religious settlement of 1555 the only

CHAP.
XXVII

1576-1612

The Split
in Protes-
tantism

Protestants who were to profit by its provisions were those who subscribed to the Confession of Augsburg. But the Calvinists, who were excluded from the scope of the settlement, had increased in numbers within the borders of the Empire. They were to be found principally in the territory that intervenes between Switzerland and the Low Countries. One of the results of the battle of Mühlberg, as we have seen, was a new division of Saxony. The electoral title and a large part of the electoral lands passed from the Ernestine to the Albertine branch of the Saxon house. Ernestine Saxony was left a comparatively unimportant province. The first elector of Albertine Saxony was Maurice I (1547–53) of whom we have seen something in our study of Protestantism and the Balance of Power. He was succeeded by his brother Augustus I (1553–86) who increased the area of electoral Saxony and developed its resources. He was, however, a most intolerant Lutheran and he employed rigorous measures to extinguish Calvinism in his dominions. At the head of electoral Brandenburg at this time was Joachim II (1535–71) who had established a state church of his own very like the Church of England. He granted Lutheranism free entrance into his dominions; and he secularized Catholic bishoprics as a means of adding to his wealth and personal territory. His successor John George (1571–98) was a thorough-going Lutheran who heartily disliked Calvinism. On the other hand Frederick III (1559–76), elector Palatine, one of the most aggressive of the Protestant princes, was an ardent Calvinist; and, though his son and successor Louis VI (1576–83) was a Lutheran, his brother John Casimir, who from 1583 to 1592 acted as regent during the minority of his grandson Frederick IV (1583–1610), was an equally active supporter of Calvinism. Under Frederick III the so-called Heidelberg Catechism was put forth as the prescribed form of belief and worship for the Palatinate. In it the doctrine of the eucharist was formulated in accordance with the ideas of Calvin. This aroused the antagonism of Lutherans and Catholics alike. The Lutheran citizens of the electorate and some of the neighboring Lutheran princes protested vigorously but in vain. The breach between Lutheranism and Calvinism was made permanent and the Lutheran rulers became more determined than ever not to permit the heads of Calvinist States to be included in the scope of the Peace of Augsburg. Thus was the split in Protestantism made wider and the task of the Emperor Rudolf in furthering the cause of Catholicism made easier.

But Lutheranism itself, as we have seen in our study of the

sects to which the Protestant Revolution gave rise, was by no means united. Differences of opinion regarding dogma that had their origin in the ill-defined character of the Lutheran creed, in the idiosyncrasies of individual religious teachers, and in the personal preferences of rulers, began to crystallize into definite systems of belief between which enmity arose. The principal arena of the internal disputes of the Lutherans was the two Saxonies; and the chief disputants may be classed as Flacianists and Philippists. The former professed to stand by the teachings of Luther, while the latter claimed to represent the more conciliatory views of Melanchthon. Each party, however, much as the fact was disclaimed, had made changes in the views of its authority. The new University of Jena (1558) became the citadel of the Flacianists, while those of Wittenberg and Leipzig were the strongholds of the Philippists. The controversy between the two parties, which was exceedingly bitter, was accentuated by the political animosity that existed between the two Saxonies. One of the questions about which controversy raged was that of free will. Another was that of the Lord's Supper. The Flacianists favored the Lutheran doctrine that in the bread and wine the body and blood of Christ are present as heat is present in red-hot iron. Some of the Philippists leaned toward the Calvinist view that the bread and wine are never more than mere symbols of the body and blood, while others fully accepted that view. These latter from motives of expediency avoided making any open avowal of their Calvinism. They were known as Crypto-Calvinists. Later on, however, they became bolder and then they were cruelly persecuted. So rancorous were the disputes between the various Lutheran divisions that several of the princes, chief of whom was the elector Augustus of Albertine Saxony, began to take measures looking towards pacification and unity. In 1576 the *Torgau Book,* so called from the place of its composition, was issued. It is a body of doctrine to which it was hoped all Lutherans would subscribe. It was discussed in many ecclesiastical conventions, called for the purpose of considering it, but the result was far short of universal acceptance. The book was then revised in the following year by some theologians and in 1680 it was publicly announced. It became known as the *Concord Book.* The men who performed the task of recension deemed their work to be final. They declared it to be the true Lutheran doctrine. But while the *Formula of Concord* settled some of the old controversies it gave rise to others that were none the less serious and acrimonious. It seems, indeed, to have done more harm than good. Abuse descended almost to unplumbed depths and violent conflicts were of frequent occurrence.

While Protestantism in the Empire was thus distracted with internal dissensions Catholicism found the circumstances favorable for an effort to regain its lost territory. In this attempt the leadership was taken by Bavaria. Duke William IV (1508-50) obtained a considerable grant of power from the Pope over the bishoprics and monastic orders in the duchy and enacted repressive measures against the Protestants. In 1541 he invited the Jesuits into his dominion. And the University of Ingolstadt became their headquarters not only for Bavaria but also for all Germany. Albert V (1550-79), the most aggressive of all the Catholic princes in Germany, gave his sanction to the decrees of the Council of Trent and vigorously furthered the recently aroused militant activity of Catholicism. His son and successor William V (1579-97), surnamed the Pious, had been educated by the Jesuits and was one of their most ardent supporters. Chief of the Jesuit propagandists was Peter Canisius (1524-97), eloquent, prudent, and blameless of life. After ten years' work in Bavaria he was summoned by Ferdinand I to Vienna where he swayed vast audiences at his will and became the chief adviser in religious affairs of the Emperor. So aggressive was the spirit of the great Jesuit, so tactful were his measures and so indefatigable were his labors, that he is justly reckoned as being one of the most important forces in the rehabilitation of Catholicism in Germany. The restoration of Catholicism in Austria, begun under Ferdinand I, and continued somewhat hesitatingly under Maximilian II, was pushed by Rudolf II with great energy. The Catholic advance in Germany was naturally disputed wherever possible by the Protestants. The very ambiguous character of the Peace of Augsburg was the excuse if not the cause of many altercations. Every prince could determine the religion that should prevail in his principality. The same right was granted to the imperial towns. But every imperial town where in 1555 more than one religion was established had to maintain those religions in the same proportion as then prevailed. Such a provision was admirably calculated to create trouble. Out of it disputes arose in Aachen where the Lutherans and Calvinists demanded the right to exercise their religions. Their contentions were not decided until 1598 when all Protestant worship was abolished in Aachen by order of the Emperor. The provisions of the Peace of Augsburg were also involved in a struggle that arose for the possession of Cologne. In 1583 the Archbishop Gebhard married, and being loath to lose his see he attempted to Protestantize it.  Such an act was

of course a direct violation of the ecclesiastical reservation.  The
practical annulment of the provision in their favor was not
unwelcome to the Protestant princes, but, owing to the disputes
between the Lutherans and the Calvinists and between the Lutherans themselves, Gebhard failed to receive the combined Protestant support.  The warlike prelate was forced to flee into the
Netherlands, the diocese was speedily restored to the ancient faith,
and Ernest, a brother of the duke of Bavaria, was elected archbishop.  The recovery of this important province to Catholicism
had a decided effect upon the situation.  In 1585 three important
neighboring bishoprics, Münster, Paderborn, and Osnabrück,
were restored to Catholicism, and soon afterwards they were
followed by the smaller one of Minden.  Not so immediately
successful for the Catholics was the fight for Strasburg, a town
in which, according to the settlement of 1555, churches of the
old and new faiths were to be permitted, but in which the ancient worship in the Catholic churches had been suppressed.  An
eight months' war ended with the agreement to divide the diocese between a Protestant and a Catholic bishop until the dispute
should be finally decided in court.  At the compromise of
Hagenau in 1604 the Protestant bishop was bought out.  New
Catholic leaders appeared in the persons of a new duke of Bavaria, Maximilian I (1583–1651), and the archduke Ferdinand
of Styria who afterwards ascended the imperial throne.  Maximilian, who became known as " the Catholic," found the duchy
heavily burdened with debt and in a disorderly condition; but
a decade of his vigorous administration put the province into
such good shape as to enable him to take an effective part in
the great war of the next century.  He was devoted to the cause
of Catholicism because for long that cause was the traditional
policy of his dynasty and because he perceived that it coincided
with his political prosperity.  He was not only an excellent administrator, but also an accomplished statesman and a man of
fine courage.  Educated by the Jesuits in the University of
Ingolstadt, Ferdinand became the most vigorous of all the German princes in support of the aggressive Catholicism of the
time.  When he assumed the government of the archduchies of
Styria, Carinthia, and Carniola he suppressed the Protestant
worship and offered to his Protestant subjects the alternatives
of conversion or exile.

Such acts of aggression as we have noted on the part of both
Protestants and Catholics found their excuse if not their origin
in the exceedingly unsatisfactory character of the Peace of Augs-

burg. The conflict between the two camps could not find its
end in any such half-way measure. The whole period of the
Emperor Rudolf's reign was one in which the seeds of war were
germinating. The next century was to reap the harvest of
disaster.

Militant Catholicism achieved the most astonishing successes.
**The Re-
action in
Favor of
Catholi-
cism**
Much was accomplished by political and military measures. But
it was not chiefly to ordinances and to force of arms that these
successes were due, but to a great reaction of public opinion.
"During the first half century after the commencement of the
Reformation," says Macaulay, "the current of feeling in the
countries on this side of the Alps and of the Pyrénées ran im-
petuously towards the new doctrines. Then the tide turned,
and rushed as fiercely in the opposite direction. Neither during
the one period nor during the other did much depend upon the
event of battles or sieges. The Protestant movement was hardly
checked for an instant by the defeat at Mühlberg. The Catholic
reaction went on at full speed in spite of the destruction of the
Armada. It is difficult to say whether the violence of the first
blow or of the recoil was the greater. Fifty years after the
Lutheran separation, Catholicism could scarcely maintain itself
on the shores of the Mediterranean. A hundred years after the
separation, Protestantism could scarcely maintain itself on the
shores of the Baltic." After all due allowance has been made
for the rhetorical exaggeration of this passage the fact remains
that the situation at the end of the century was altogether unlike
that at the opening of the second quarter of the century. "Not
only was there at this time a much more intense zeal among the
Catholics than among the Protestants," continues Macaulay,
"but the whole zeal of the Catholics was directed against the
Protestants, while almost the whole zeal of the Protestants was
directed against each other. Within the Catholic Church there
were no serious disputes on points of doctrine. The decisions
of the Council of Trent were received . . . the whole force of
Rome was therefore effective for the purpose of carrying on the
war against the Reformation. On the other hand, the force
which ought to have fought the battle of the Reformation was
exhausted in civil conflict. While Jesuit preachers, Jesuit confessors, Jesuit teachers of youth, overspread Europe, eager to
expend every faculty of their minds and every drop of their
blood in the cause of their Church, Protestant doctors were con-
futing, and Protestant rulers were punishing, sectaries who were
just as good Protestants as themselves."

# CHAPTER XXVIII

## MAGYAR AND SLAV

1. The Eclipse of Hungary.
2. The Uniting and Dissolution of Poland.
3. The Rise of Russia.

L AST of the peoples whose political careers we are to notice are the Magyars and Slavs. It is merely as a matter of convenient arrangement that we are to deal with them in the same chapter and not because they are closely related to each other. There is, indeed, between them a greater difference than between German and French. They lived upon the confines of European civilization and so they have not figured very largely in our previous chapters.

The Magyars found themselves situated in a country of unusual geographical unity and great fertility, lying as it does within the immense curve of the Carpathians and having for its southern boundary the Danube and the Save. But dwelling as they did between the Byzantine and Germanic Empires they were subjected to many dangers. After a varied and turbulent history the thirteenth century witnessed their imminent relapse into barbarism. From that peril they were saved by two princes of the house of Anjou, Charles I (1310–42) and Louis I (1342–82), who led the Magyars back to civilization and won for their nation an important place in the affairs of Europe. But almost a generation before the death of Louis the Turks had set foot in Europe and begun their advance to the west. Three names stand out prominently in the resistance of Hungary to the Turks. The Emperor Sigismund, a brave soldier and a far-seeing statesman who from 1387 to 1437 was also king of Hungary, struggled valiantly against the oncoming of the Crescent throughout the half-century of his reign; and the famous warrior John Hunyady (1387–1456), who rose from the position of an obscure noble to be the leader of his nation, seemed at one time to be on the point of driving the Turks back across the Hellespont. No less famous was Matthias I (1458–90), a son of

Hunyady who ascended the throne, who made his country the most powerful in central Europe, and who if he did not threaten the position of the Turks as seriously as his father had done at least compelled them to retreat beyond the Balkans. It was after his death that the Turk became so great a terror to Christendom. The death of Matthias was followed by a relapse into medieval chaos. So terrible was the oppression of the peasantry that they rose in revolt. But although the half-clad and poorly armed countrymen, joined by the rabble of the towns, met with some successes they soon fell victims to the mail-clad nobles who punished them with fiendish ferocity. The suppression of the revolt did not put an end to the troubles of the time. The entire laboring class had been transformed into a force sullenly hostile to the selfish aristocracy and the whole atmosphere of the time was one of robbery, cruelty, and violent death. Every spark of patriotism had been extinguished. "If this realm could be saved at the expense of three florins," said the papal envoy, "there is not a man here willing to make the sacrifice." Little wonder that city after city fell into the hands of Solyman the Magnificent. In 1526 the hastily gathered forces of the Hungarians, so pitiful in their appearance that the sultan could not believe that they constituted the national army, were completely annihilated in the battle of Mohacs. When the Turks set out on their homeward march they took with them more than a hundred thousand captives and an enormous amount of spoil. One quarter of the country, wrote a contemporary, had been ruined as completely as if it had been subjected to a devastating flood. No longer could Hungary make the proud claim of being the "Buckler of Christendom."

But a worse disaster was to befall the unhappy country. There were two claimants for the throne, John Zapolya (1526–40) and the archduke Ferdinand of Austria, and, under the pretext of enforcing the contentions of the rivals, unscrupulous adventurers of every sort oppressed the peasants from one end of the land to the other. Rapine and robbery were every day affairs. Finally, in 1538, the two contestants agreed to divide between themselves that part of the country which was not in possession of the Turks. One-third of the land, the part adjoining Austria, was retained by Ferdinand, while the remaining two-thirds, of which the principal part was Transylvania, together with the title of king of Hungary, was kept by Zapolya. War broke out between Hungary and Austria upon the death of Zapolya and Solyman renewed his invasion. Peace was concluded by another division. This time Austria obtained a much larger share, securing thirty-five of the seventy-three counties. John Sigismund, the infant son of Zapolya, kept Transylvania and sixteen counties together with the title of prince; while the Turks acquired all the remainder of the country which included most of the central counties. This partition of Hungary continued until almost the end of the seventeenth century. The borders of the three divisions continually fluctuated, and Transylvania fell alternately under the influence of the Hapsburg and the Ottoman power.

We have seen something of the development of humanism in Poland and of the part which that border land played in the ecclesiastical revolution. At this point we are to deal with its political development and the changes effected by the militant Catholicism of the time. It was after a period of lawlessness and retrogression that Sigismund I (1506–48) came to the throne. On every side save only on the southwest where it touched the Carpathian mountains his country lacked the advantage of a natural boundary; and on all sides she was face to face with aggressive and hostile neighbors. Clearly, as the new king saw, there was great need of an effective army. But so indifferent were the privileged classes to the welfare of their country that a quarter of a century went by before Sigismund succeeded in getting something like a satisfactory increase and improvement of the military force, and even that step was gained only by the granting of impolitic compromises. It was not only the advancing Muscovite and Turk that threatened the peace of Poland. There were grave internal disturbances. Members of the nobility and the bourgeoisie had appropriated the humanism of the Renaissance with such avidity that it was said that " more Latinists were to be found in Poland than there used to be in Latium." But this appetite for the new learning could not be satisfied in the provincial schools of the country nor in the university of Cracow, the national capital, for those institutions were still committed to the scholasticism of a departed age. So they went abroad, especially to the schools of Germany. Many of them returned to propagate the conflicting creeds of the various Protestant churches; and the Anti-Trinitarians, as we have seen, gained a substantial following in the distracted country.

Sigismund II (1548–72) proved a sagacious director in this period of grave disturbances. To his initiative was due the acquisition of the Livonian provinces in 1561–2 and the welding together in 1569 of all the loosely related Polish possessions by the Union of Lublin. Sigismund, however, died childless, and with him the great Jagellon dynasty that for so long had guided with keen perception the destiny of this country so prone to anarchy. After an interregnum of a year Henry of Valois, Duke of Anjou, was elected king. But previously the Polish nobles had passed the " Henrican Articles " that made the monarchy but an empty name. No king thereafter was to be entrusted with any power beyond that of summoning the diet at will, leading the army, appointing to the chief military and ecclesiastical posts, and figuring in the public pageants and half-barbaric feasts. He had no voice in the choice of his successor, nor could he marry without the consent of the senate. Thus was the Polish monarchy completely transformed. Henry, instead of hesitating at the insulting terms, employed cajolery and corruption to obtain the crown under them; and, in the *Pacta Conventa,* signed other burdensome and humiliating conditions. Then, thirteen months after his election, he suddenly abandoned the Polish throne in order to secure that of France made vacant by the death of his brother. This trying period was followed by the brief but brilliant reign of Stephen (Báthory) I (1575–86), a gallant soldier who had seen much service in Transylvania, where, indeed, he had been elected prince, and a skilful diplomat. As soon as he was able Stephen turned his attention to the encroaching enemies from the east. Not content with defending the frontier he crossed it and marched far into the realms of Muscovy. For five months in 1581–82 his little army laid siege to the great and strongly fortified city of Pskov under conditions of arctic severity until Ivan the Terrible, fearing to lose the largest city in his Empire, ceded all of Livonia to the intrepid invader.

On the vast plain that stretches from the Dnieper to the Ural Mountains there lived a wild people, hunters, fishers and fugitive serfs, who because of their occupations and the necessity of defending themselves against the Tartars had acquired great strength and skill as horsemen and in the use of arms. They were known as Cossacks, a word meaning freebooter, strangely derived from their very enemies, the Tartars. Somewhere about the beginning of the sixteenth century they began to form themselves into a definite state. It was but a nebulous state, however, and its history, inextricably confused with legend, need not detain us. Stephen organized six thousand selected Cossacks into six regiments and confided to their care the defense of the eastern frontier. The Cossack community still continued its independent existence, and it was Stephen's intention to respect their independence as long as they performed the duty of protecting the frontier. But social, racial, and religious differences between the Poles and the Cossacks gave rise to many conflicts that culminated, in the fourth decade of the seventeenth century, in the abolition of the Cossack State.

It was in Stephen's reign that the Jesuits were established in Poland. Their schools and colleges were soon to be found in every part of the country, the most important center of their teaching being the University of Wilna. They penetrated even into Livonia, which had gone over to Protestantism almost entirely and two of their colleges were founded at Dorpat and Riga. The religious tolerance that formerly prevailed in Poland and made the country a refuge for the most radical thinkers of the religious revolution gradually disappeared. Calvinism was eliminated. Lutheranism was restricted, the oppression of the Greek Catholics greatly diminished their number, and Catholicism became thoroughly reinvigorated. The Jesuits in
Poland

In the mind of Stephen there was born the idea of uniting Poland, Muscovy and Transylvania into one compact State whose military power should eventually expel the Turks from Europe. But only the Jesuits were able to appreciate the significance of the plan, and the sudden death of the king prevented an attempt to realize it.

The election of Sigismund III (1587–1632), a son of John III of Sweden, was unfortunate in many respects. In the course of his long reign there came to Poland the opportunity of making herself the most effective nation in central Europe. The Muscovite power in the east suffered a serious set-back and Germany in the west was plunged into the horrors of the Thirty Years' War. But Sigismund was unequal to the situation. He failed to strengthen the country within its existing boundaries. His claim to the Swedish crown involved Poland in a series of wars from which she could hope to gain little and was certain to lose much. And this together with his other external interests, made still more difficult the task of reforming the deplorable Polish constitution which, as he well knew, was a most effective preventive of all measures looking to the permanent security and real greatness of the country. The constitution provided for an extreme condition of decentralization, whereas at the end of the sixteenth century it was clearly evident that the future belonged not to any feudal congeries of powers but to the strong, compact, and centralized monarchies. Chief of the Polish powers among whom the governmental power was distributed were the greater nobles, the lesser nobles (*Szlachta*) and the cities. At this time the *Szlachta* dominated the national diet. Narrow-minded and selfish beyond measure they were intensely hostile The Domination of
the
*Szlachta*

to anything that in the remotest degree resembled discipline. The dire needs of their nation left them unmoved. Money they would not vote, and service they would not volunteer. And the requirement of a unanimous vote in the diet made it possible for any one of them to veto any and every measure of reform. This *liberum veto* they regarded as one of their most valuable privileges, and even had not Sigismund been engrossed in so many external matters it would have been a very difficult task to have replaced it with the decision by a plurality of votes that he so much desired. Upon the rock of their opposition every attempt to reform the constitution was wrecked. Religious troubles hastened the decline. Sigismund, actuated by the Jesuits, was consistently opposed to every sect outside the Catholic pale. The Protestants were deprived of all their civil rights; and the Orthodox Greek Catholics who refused to follow the example of large numbers of their co-religionists in acknowledging the authority of the Pope incurred the bitter hatred of their erstwhile associates and were subjected to severe persecution. Thus it was that Poland fell irretrievably into a condition of political decrepitude.

In the forest land of Lake Ilmen, which lies between the easternmost arm of the Baltic Sea and the headwaters of the Dnieper River, there lived in the ninth century some Slav and Finnish tribes who were subjugated by Norsemen and who in time assimilated their conquerors. These Norsemen were known as Rus or Ros and it is from their name that the word Russia, which did not become the customary name for the new Empire until the eighteenth century, has been derived. Territorial expansion went on apace, until the Caspian Sea and the Ural Mountains were reached, with little regard to internal consolidation. The land of these " tall, white and crafty barbarians " was divided into many principalities, each ruled by its own prince, that were connected with each other only by slender ties. For several centuries innumerable struggles took place between the various divisions for leadership and for land. Several of the more important of the principalities, especially those of Moscow and of Novgorod, were still struggling for precedence in the middle of the thirteenth century when a great body of Tartars, " the terrible strangers whose origin no man knew," invaded the vast and thinly populated plains in the southeast of Muscovy and made a capital for themselves, which they called Sarai, on the lower Volga. For nearly three hundred years they held the Russians in sway. Their own State, or Khanate, was known as the Golden Horde. At last in 1380 internal dissensions among

**Muscovy
and the
Tartars**

them enabled a number of Russian princes to inflict a severe defeat upon them in the battle of Kulikoo. Then the work of consolidating the various principalities of the victors was carried well on towards completion by Dimitri Donskoi, but it remained for others to finish the work of creating the autocratic Empire of Muscovy.

First of all the three great rulers who together completed the policy of absorbing the principalities that still remained independent and of centralizing all governmental authority was Ivan III (1462–1505), surnamed the Great. Of the five principalities that were independent at the time of his accession he succeeded in subduing two; while his son Basil III (1505–33) incorporated the remaining three. The tasks that confronted Ivan IV (1533–84), known as the Terrible, were to prevent the revival of any of the extinct principalities and to establish an autocratic rule. The progress of gradual centralization that had been going on met with the sullen discontent of many of the nobles. Ivan was a child of three when his father died. The time seemed ripe for the recovery of lost power and during the government of the queen-mother and afterwards of first one faction of the nobles and then another the autocracy of the two preceding reigns began to disappear. But in 1547 the boy of seventeen had himself crowned, not merely as the grand-duke of Muscovy, but as the Tsar (supposed by some to be a corruption of the word Cæsar and declared by others to be an Asiatic title) of all Russia. The Golden Horde having become separated into several khanates, two of them, Kazan and Astrakhan, were annexed in 1552–54 by the young Tsar without much difficulty. But Ivan was not satisfied with expansion to the east. Like his predecessors he looked with longing eyes beyond the western border of his domains. There the Polish possessions stretched from the Baltic to the Black Sea barring the way to farther advance in that direction. The Polish kings were equally desirous of extending their territory to the east. It was, therefore, inevitable that conflicts should occur. Ivan the Terrible looked farther than any of his predecessors, who had desired merely to obtain a strip of Lithuania, and, in order to make it possible for his subjects to trade directly with western Europe, sought to secure a stretch of the Baltic coast. He knew that his country was closed to outside influences by vast intervening wastes on the east and by hostile and warring States on the west, he realized perhaps that it was powerless to develop unaided a satisfactory civilization, and he hoped in particular, as a result of direct trade with the west, to be able to equip his soldiers with the arms and ammunition of the modern nations. When in 1553 an English ship, endeavoring to reach China by the northeast passage, entered the White Sea, another route was called to his attention, and the English were granted the freedom of trading in the towns of Muscovy. Acting on this permission Anthony Jenkinson, an English sailor, merchant, and explorer, journeyed from London by way of Archangel, Novgorod, Astrakhan, and the Caspian Sea, to Bokhara, being the first Englishman to penetrate central Asia, and returned by the same route. It was a roundabout way, however, and closed for a considerable part of the year by ice and so Ivan still longed for a port on the Baltic. But war, alternately with one of his western neighbors and then another, Sweden, Livonia, Poland, and Denmark, that lasted intermittently until his death, failed to attain his object.

Ivan's
Character

The atrocities of Ivan have doubtless been exaggerated. But those that remain after all possible winnowing of legend and fact are quite sufficient to reveal a cruel and relentless character. Yet it was not the Russians who called him Terrible. By them he was styled *groznui,* a word that signifies the quality of being respectable and the fact of being respected. In that wild land, however, in those wild times, the ruler who was engrossed in the great task of fusing into one the score of peoples who owned his sway and of finding an outlet for them to the western ocean might conceivably resort to extreme measures without losing the approbation of the mass of his subjects. And the fact is that in spite of all his errors, vices, and crimes he never lost their support.

Feodor
Ivanovitch
and Boris
Godúnov

It was not in one life-time that the gigantic task the Russian Tsar had set himself could be accomplished. So when his weak if saintly son Feodor (1584–98) came to the throne it is scarcely a matter of surprise that the old elements of disorder and disintegration reasserted themselves. Fortunately, however, the brother-in-law of the new Tsar, Boris Godúnov, proved strong enough to keep the restless nobles in subjection. Godúnov completed the establishment of serfdom. The wide-stretching plains of Muscovy were very thinly populated and so the demand for agricultural laborers was greatly in excess of the supply. In the competition for laborers the large land-owners had a decided advantage over the small ones. It was proposed, therefore, that the laborers should be forbidden to move from one estate to another. This permanent attachment of the peasants to the land, accomplished in the time of the last of the dynasty that had ruled since the days of the Norsemen, put them under the

complete control of the men on whose estates they lived. Another innovation brought about by the active administrator was
the creation of the patriarchate. The highest ecclesiastical official in Muscovy up to this time was the metropolitan. Nominally he was subject to the jurisdiction of the patriarch of Constantinople who was the head of the Greek Church. But nearly
a century and a half ago Constantinople had fallen into the
hands of the Turks and since that time the Tsars had asserted
themselves to be the successors of the Byzantine Emperors. The
Eastern Church is not, like that of Rome, a monarchy endowed
with practically unlimited power. It is, instead, an oligarchy
of patriarchs in which each patriarch is supreme within his diocese and subject only to a general council. It seemed but natural,
therefore, that the church in Muscovy should be given a head of
its own with primary jurisdiction. To this establishment of a
new patriarchate the Eastern Orthodox Church gave its consent.
The patriarch of Constantinople raised the metropolitan bishop
of Muscovy to the patriarchal dignity and the act was subsequently approved by a general council of the Eastern Church.

So skilful had been Godúnov's conduct of the affairs of state
that when the Tsar died without a son to succeed him he was
chosen by a national assembly to be the next ruler. The reign
of Borris Godúnov (1598–1605) was brief, and because of the
opposition to him on the part of the great nobles it was less successful than his administration under Feodor. For almost two
decades the land was filled with mercenaries and marauders of
all sorts who pillaged at will and perpetrated the most frightful
atrocities. Not till the Romanov dynasty ascended the throne
in 1613 was peace restored to the robber-ridden and famine-
stricken country. And until the coming of Peter the Great this
land whose possibilities are still unplumbed, where medieval
pilgrims still trudge the highways, where the west with its
febrility gradually merges into the leisured east, remained in
almost utter ignorance of the civilization of Europe. The culture and the Christianity of Muscovy were both borrowed from
the corrupt and decrepit Eastern Empire. And when the culture
and the religion of the later Byzantine Empire are recalled to
mind the claim of the Tsars to be the successors of the Byzantine
rulers becomes most significant.

# CHAPTER XXIX

## THE REPUBLIC OF LETTERS

CHAP.
XXIX
——
1450-1600

The Universality
of the
Humanist
Genius

WHEN the Renaissance spread from Italy to the other countries of western Europe it resulted in time, despite all national differences, in the formation of a common culture, a general intellectual atmosphere, an international currency of ideas, for all the different countries. Political dissociation and political antagonism failed to prevent intellectual and artistic association and communion. The common interests of humanism became ever more subtle and pervasive. They broadened into common activities in letters, art, and science. The love of beauty and the search for truth answered to the need and echoed the desire of human life in every nation, no matter how sundered from its fellows by the estranging tide of clashing material interests. Political confederation lay far in the future, as it still does to-day, but Europe was united in a common enthusiasm for art and science, and in a common faith in the splendid future they were to bring to birth. In spite of all its wars and revolutions the sixteenth century witnessed the acme of the art of painting, and it is from the same period that we date the beginning of modern scientific and philosophical thought.

The Influence of
the Universities

The Latin tongue was still employed in the universities and it served to knit together natives of all lands and to render possible a European republic of letters. Humanism had greatly secularized the universities and it had been the paramount influence in the development of the secondary schools. The middle class it was that, in every country, profited chiefly by this broadening of academic education. So well did its members profit by their opportunities that, according to a French panegyrist, they surpassed the clergy in learning and the nobility in good manners; and so obvious was the importance of this new culture that far from despising the learning of the burghers, as at first they were wont to do, the nobles ended by sending their sons to their schools. Thus were the several classes in each of the various countries represented in the new republic.

The influence of the publishers in helping to establish this republic of letters should not pass unnoticed. After the invention of printing the work of writing a book and the business of producing it and placing it for sale upon the market came to be differentiated. In the process of becoming established as a separate class the publishers found that they needed men of letters as assistants. These men whose work it was to correct typographical errors, mistakes in grammar, and other shortcomings, were known as proofreaders. They were employed to estimate the value of the manuscripts submitted for publication, to give advice to their employers regarding the probable sale and intrinsic worth of literary productions. Thus they exercised a great influence in the civilization of the time. Leading men of letters were not reluctant to accept such positions. The publishers themselves did much to further the interests of the republic of letters. Aldo Manuzio (1450–1515), the founder of the Aldine press, made more secure the possessions of many masterpieces of Greek, Latin, and Italian literature and greatly extended their use by putting them in type. He chose Venice as the site of his press because it was a great distributing center; and the beauty of his type and paper surpassed that of any of his predecessors. So devoted was he to his work that he died a poor man, but he had "bequeathed Greek literature as an inalienable possession to the world." His son, Paolo Manuzio (1512–74), who, after an interval, carried on his work, found the list of Greek classics almost completely finished; so, being passionately devoted to Cicero, his principal publications were in the field of Latin letters. He left the work of his press to be carried on by his son, the younger Aldo Manuzio (1547–97) with whom the work of the famous press came to an end. Johannes Froben (1460?–1527) published many of Erasmus's works and his press made Basel the most important center of German printing and publication in the sixteenth century. After his death the work of his press was carried on by his son Jerome and by his son-in-law Nicolaus Episcopius.

The ideals and the work of the Ciceronians were also a factor in shaping the literary republic. All through the Middle Ages it was Cicero who had been the principal exemplar of the art of rhetoric, as Vergil was the leading name in Latin literature. In the period of the Renaissance his influence became paramount. "Father supreme of Roman eloquence," he was styled by Petrarch, who was enchanted with the linked smoothness long drawn out of his favorite author. Something of the influence of Cicero upon Italian men of letters from Petrarch to Bembo we have seen in our previous chapters that deal with literature. In the sixteenth century there had come to be a cult of Cicero, a servile imitation, which, in 1528, in his *Ciceronianus,* was cleverly caricatured and seriously refuted by Erasmus. The masterly exposition aroused a storm of opposition. Erasmus himself did not reply to any of the attacks of the extreme Ciceronians but others did. The battle of books continued beyond his death and did not come to an end until the first decade of the seventeenth century had been passed. The phrase-mongering of the Ciceronians was unfortunate in so far as it led men to devote their entire attention not to what an author had to say but to the manner in which he said it. Yet in so far as it helped to banish a barbarous Latinity and substitute in its place one of lucidity and elegance it performed a needed service.

Important, too, in the formation of the republic of letters was the influence of Erasmus that for an entire generation dominated the minds of men, whose Latin, devoid of pedantry and instinct with an incomparable linguistic feeling, was a world-tongue for the ideas and the sentiments of the time, and whose thought did so much to lead men into the modern world. We have already discussed the remedy that he had to offer for the settlement of the ecclesiastical abuses and theological differences of his time. It was but natural that this delicate, small, and sickly man, with the half-shut, blue, observing eyes, should rely so entirely upon words. But always he battled for the liberal ideas of the time. The joy of the emancipated intellect in its freedom irradiates his personality and shines through his wit and humor no less than through his scholarly and critical earnestness. The tide of enthusiasm for the new learning had already flowed into the principal countries of Europe and now it was finding its way into the most remote places. Much of the love of letters that had grown up in Germany, France, England, Spain and the Low Countries was the creation of Erasmus. We cannot measure his influence in the new republic, but we know it to have been vast.

The unfavorable results to letters that were the immediate outcome of the Lutheran schism, and the still more unfavorable results of the mutual antagonisms of the various Protestant churches and sects, have already been noticed. In Germany throughout the entire country, in Catholic and Protestant lands alike, there was a distinct intellectual retrogression. It seems

as if that land had exhausted itself in the efforts put forth during the great revolution.  In those years hope ran high and a
general soaring of the intellectual life had been expected.  That
hope was not fulfilled.  Instead, all the conditions of the times,
the petty squabbles of the period, weighed upon the intellectual
life.  The opening of the second half of the sixteenth century
saw the beginning of the rudest period in the social and literary
history of Germany.  The theological interests, which became
ever narrower and duller, killed every other form of intellectual
activity  There was a long pause in the progress of the German intellect.  The indestructible strength of that intellect revealed itself in only one thing, the development of the positive
sciences, in this period of decline.

If such had been the influence of the Protestant Revolution,
what was that of the Catholic Reformation?  It has been customary to describe the revival of the militant activity of the
Mother Church as being reactionary in character.  And such it
was in so far as it wished to restore to Catholicism its medieval
character and to make that Catholicism predominant in Europe.
But what was the influence of the movement upon letters and
upon art?  It has been the fashion to describe that influence as
wholly detrimental.  Such, however, was not the case.  In Spain,
it is true, the Inquisition, under the control of the State far
more than that of the Church, had a blighting effect upon
intellectual and artistic activity.  But the social and intellectual
decline of Italy was due in a large degree to secular causes.  The
interminable wars of the plundering French, Swiss, Germans and
Spaniards did much to despoil the peninsula of its bloom and
to impoverish the people.  Without the least desire to palliate
the crimes of the Inquisition or to condone the oppression of
the Index, it may be said that these and the other instruments
and forces of militant Catholicism, while they were antagonistic
to the philosophical thought of the time, had less to do with
the decline of art and literature in Italy than is generally assumed.  Militant Catholicism, though antagonistic to the thought
of a Bruno, whose philosophy we are soon to consider, was by
no means opposed to literature and art in the abstract.  The
militant movement of Catholicism was directed against the abuses
that existed within the Church, against Protestantism, and
against philosophic thought that seemed to deny its dogmas.
It was by no means directed against the Renaissance in its
artistic aspects.  The truth is that the artistic Renaissance died
a natural death.  Like all other similar outbursts of the human
spirit it was followed naturally by a period of the sere and

yellow leaf, a time of lassitude and decline. It seems to be a law in the economy of nature that a period of creative production leads to one of introspection and meditation. Militant Catholicism, then, did not attempt to stifle or to put back the artistic Renaissance. It rather appropriated the products of an epoch whose decline was due to internal conditions. The enthusiasm for art and literature was greater in Catholic than in Protestant countries. In every land that was invaded by Calvinism the appreciation of art declined, while the ideal of life in Catholic countries continued to be sensuous and æsthetic. The life and culture of the Catholic peoples was richer and more harmonious than that of the Protestants. "Enthusiasm for art and taste spread in proportion as the Counter-Reformation advances," says Gothein, "while in Protestant countries ecclesiastical and civil art alike fall into decay." The noble bearing and the careful calculation of appearance and deportment which were practised at the Catholic courts of the Romance countries, as distinguished from those of the Protestant lands, which for the time nearly all sank into rudeness of manners, were favorable to art. Yet the opposition of the Church to philosophic thought and scientific investigation had a most depressing and detrimental effect. The two were almost inseparably connected at that time. Speculation seemed to be opening its wings for a great flight. There was a noble loftiness of anticipation in the air. How glorious might have been its accomplishments had it been free to expend its zeal in the pursuit of truth!

The Growth of Criticism, of Specialization and of Science

The period of creative production in art in Italy was rapidly drawing to a close. Torquato Tasso was the only surviving genius in the realm of literature. In painting Veronese and Tintoretto represent the splendid color of the sunset. Cervantes and Shakespeare represent the acme of the creative period in Spain and England which naturally came later in those countries than in the land of its origin. An age of reflection was at hand. Humanity always needs time to digest and absorb the new materials that have been introduced into its life by such a period as that of the Renaissance. Criticism, speculation, and the development of science were the engrossing occupations of the members of the republic of letters and of art whose activities are now to be described.

Aristotelians and Anti-Aristotelians

First, then, we are to deal with those members of the republic who devoted their lives to philosophy. We shall find them divided into two schools. Every one, said Coleridge, is born a Platonist or an Aristotelian. The Aristotelians and their opponents formed the two philosophical camps of the time. The former regarded the universe as being limited in extent and as being created by God who stands apart from his work, transcending it, and regarding it as a potter regards the vessel he has turned upon his wheel. The Platonists of the time held that God is immanent in the universe; that nature is but the vesture of its creator. The former were legalists; the latter were mystics. We have seen something of the mysticism of the Florentine Academy. In the first part of the sixteenth century the Neo-Platonism of the Renaissance threatened to assume predominance in philosophic thought; but the second part witnessed a stiffening of the opposing thought into exclusive Aristotelianism and intolerant orthodoxy, a retrogression into medieval scholasticism. Platonism, like all mystic thought, influences only those particular minds that have an inward affinity to it. It leads easily to innovation and to heresy. Aristotelianism, as it was known at that time, lends itself to formal logic and to the schematization of theology. It had become the tyrant of souls. Numerous controversial writings flew back and forth between the two hostile camps, and academic disputations were held. But theologians of all the leading creeds lent their aid to the Aristotelians, whose views were so well-fitted to give systematic development and formal completion to the doctrines they regarded as incontestable, and therefore by the middle of the century the reaction in favor of scholasticism became everywhere complete. The most important of the Anti-Aristotelians in the latter part of the controversy was Pierre de la Ramée (1515–72), better known as Ramus, whom we paused to notice as one of the free-thinkers of the era of the Protestant Revolution. The son of a peasant, he had found an opportunity to satisfy his consuming thirst for knowledge when he became the servant of a student in the College of Navarre. After he had studied the Aristotelian logic for three and a half years he became convinced of its emptiness and uselessness. For a quarter of a century he was the most prominent teacher in the University of Paris. There, in that citadel of the Stagirite, he succeeded in breaking down the supremacy of the Aristotelianism of his day; and, although he perished as a consequence in the Massacre of St. Bartholomew, he gave rise to a movement that eventually permeated the entire republic of letters.

Born of the revival of science, and deeply imbued with Neo-Platonism, a new philosophy came into the world. One of the earliest of these thinkers was Girolamo Cardano (1501–76), to whose work in the development of mathematics we have already alluded. In two great works, *De Subtilitate Rerum* and *De*

Cardano

*Varietate Rerum,* he embodied the most advanced speculation of the unfolding science of the time that thus far had been made; and in the assertion that the inorganic as well as the organic realm is animated he dwelt upon a topic that still fascinates but eludes the world of science. It is true that in spite of his great ability and his unfailing industry he was more of an *ignis fatuus* than a steadfast light to his followers, leading them at times astray; and yet by insisting upon the necessity of observing the processes of nature he helped to give a new direction to philosophical thought.

**Telesio**

More important work than that of Cardano in the founding of a distinctive philosophy of nature was accomplished by Bernardino Telesio (1508–88), a vigorous opponent of Aristotelianism and one of the most widely educated scholars of the time. Born of a noble Neapolitan family he was the leader of a great movement in the south of Italy that aimed to substitute for authority and formal logic the principle of individual freedom and the process of experimentation. Of course exact individual observation of any considerable range in time or space was lacking as yet, and its procedure and apparatus were still in their infancy, so that the beginnings of the new philosophy of nature were very imperfect. And the ties that bound speculation to the thought of the ancient philosophers were still strong. But the principles of observation and induction were firmly grasped and so it was inevitable that philosophy should break with the past and spread its wings for a larger flight.

**Giordano Bruno**

With that knight-errant of thought Giordano Bruno (1548–1600) philosophy soared to great heights. Born at Nola, among whose inhabitants, it was said, distinct traces of the early Greek colonists of southern Italy were still discernible, he entered a Dominican convent from whose walls could be seen the gay life of Naples and all the glamour of its beautiful bay. The exact knowledge of Aristotle that he displayed in his later years leads one to think that he began life as an adherent of that thinker. The Dominicans swore by Aristotle, and in that very convent his great continuer, St. Thomas Aquinas, had lived and worked. But gradual change led Bruno into a philosophy of his own. He drank deep from the well of Neo-Platonism; and so thoroughly imbued was he with the scientific thought of his time that he became the first great philosopher of the Copernican theory of the world. " Noble Copernicus," he said, " whose monumental work set my mind in motion at an early age." Filled with many doubts, dissatisfied with the old astronomical theory of the universe and the monastic view of life, and threatened with first one inquisitorial process and then another, he fled from Naples to Rome, and, failing to find a harbor of refuge in the Holy City, he discarded his friar's robe and began those long wanderings of which we have but an imperfect record and that were to end only with his death. For sixteen years he traveled in Switzerland, France, England and Germany, feeling himself everywhere an exile, until his irresistible yearning for the land of his birth drove him back to Italy and his terrible doom. It was only that south-land, the district of his birth that lies between the fiery volcano of Vesuvius and the blue and smiling Mediterranean, of which he was so indigenous a product, that could understand him. His verses, his stupendous memory, his yearning, his sparkling wit, his virtuosity of conversation, his soaring imagination and his passionate feeling for beauty — all these opened to him the doors of many a courtly society, won for him the favor of kings, the admiration of great men, and the affection of women. But the stormy contrasts of his volcanic nature, his outbreaks of immeasurable conceit, his violent attacks upon literary opponents, and the constant outcroppings of that burlesque and buffoonery that is native to the Neapolitan, gave rise to frequent conflict and catastrophe. Superior to his contemporaries in reach of imagination and power of synthetic thought, he was a lonely man wherever he went. Yet if these wanderings brought only trouble and sorrow to the man they were filled with suggestion to the philosopher. The intolerance of all the leading churches of the time, personal experience of which was his in abundance, led him to believe that not one of them could raise life and society to that high level it ought to attain. He found them all opposed to the progress of science; each was as narrowly dogmatic as the other. The narrow Aristotelianism of the schools, the medieval astronomy, and the benumbing dogmas of every creed, these were the three oppressions that distressed him everywhere he went — at Rome, at Geneva, at Paris, at Oxford, and at Wittenberg. So he made war upon them. He was the first philosopher to cast them utterly aside. The two years that he spent in England form the zenith of his career. In that refined society in which he lived and moved, penetrated with the delicate aroma of the Italian Renaissance, he became for the first time his true self. There in the society of Sidney and of Shakespeare, in that brief space of time, he produced one after another the six philosophical masterpieces that have given to his name undying fame. His soaring thought broke through the fixed-star firmament and his philosophy is the first to include the full consequences of the Copernican system, the idea of the unity of the universe, the idea of the gradual development of the universe, and the idea of the immanence of God in the universe. His distinguishing faculty was imagination, and it was the imagination of a poet rather than that of a philosopher. His genius was essentially spontaneous. Prolonged and exact observation, patient and silent reflection, were not the processes he employed. He was daring rather than studious, a meteor rather than a star. But he was the first monistic philosopher of modern times and as such he was the forerunner of Spinoza. To-day a statue stands in Rome to mark the place where, because he declined to retract his thought, he was committed to the flames.

Militant Catholicism seems to have limited very greatly the contemporary influence of Bruno, though the fact that it was by no means entirely extinguished is proved by the affinity of the systems of later thinkers to his ideas. The time was ripe for new philosophic thought and so we find original thinkers in almost every land into which the revival of science and the renewed regard for Plato had won their way. Thomas Campanella (1568–1639), another poet-philosopher, began, quite in the spirit of Immanuel Kant, to doubt the reliability of the knowledge that man possesses. Such knowledge, he said, has been obtained solely through the senses which are limited in their range and which fail to report the things of the outside world without obscuring them. He therefore started with a keen analysis of the faculty of cognition. The germs of many of the thoughts that since his day have been fruitful in science and philosophy are to be found in his writings. He wandered restlessly from place to place and his teeming ideas never reached cohesion. But, by the magnetism of his noble personality and the stimulating character of his thought, everywhere he went he drew men towards him. The sum of his reasoning is that in the universe there is a law which, in conformity with reason, leads men in the true way of life. Christianity is in harmony with this law and therefore it is the true religion. In his " City of the Sun " he drew a picture, as Sir Thomas More in " Utopia " had drawn one before him, of an ideal state of society. His thought was too audacious for the ecclesiastical authorities and so he spent a quarter of a century in Neapolitan dungeons from which he was liberated only to die.

The greatest and most fundamental force in the movement of life that we call the Renaissance was the revival and intensification of individuality. In the writings of Michel Eyquem (1533–92), Seigneur de Montaigne, the autonomy of the human

*Campanella*

*Montaigne*

reason, the gospel of the freedom and self-sufficiency of the individual, finds its most impressive utterance. All through the long turmoil of the civil and religious wars of France he lived in his château, writing at his ease, up in the third story of the tower, those inimitable essays that win so readily not only the interest but also the affection of the reader. He may be said to have been the originator of the essay, and he it was who first revealed the real power of French prose. His essays give the impression at first of being the careless compositions of a profound but random thinker. And his own description of himself as a *nouvelle figure, un philosophe imprémédité et fortuit,* accords with that impression. But his neatly poised sentences are not the accidents of a moment. He had read widely and systematically in the philosophers of antiquity, he was gifted with a keen insight into human nature, his ideas of life were organically arranged and articulated and he expended no small amount of toil in the expression of what he had to say to men. From the Roman stoics he inherited the idea that a single law governs the universe, the law of nature, which includes in its dominion both the human and the divine. Wisdom, therefore, consists in living one's life in accordance with this law. It is a law that permits the widest emancipation of the individual. The literature of the revival and development of individuality increased greatly during the sixteenth century, and in the seventeenth it became a stream of amazing breadth. But in one sense it found its culmination in the essays of Montaigne who held that all the inclinations and passions of man can be controlled and directed by the inherent strength of his will. The stoic belief that virtue consists in living according to nature is the central idea of his philosophy, and he expressed and developed it more simply and soundly than any classic writer had ever done. Nature, he said, actuates us in the earliest years of our life. It is our duty to listen to her voice. She guides us by the impulse to seek joy. The passions are a legitimate part of any sound life. Without them a human soul would be as motionless as a ship upon a windless sea. All this is very far away from the lingering metaphysics of the Middle Ages and the ecclesiastical dogmas of the contemporary time. Montaigne has been described as essentially a skeptic. The description is unjust. He certainly was skeptical towards the metaphysics and the theologies of his age. But his assertion of the rational and moral autonomy of man is the very antithesis of the point of view of one whose general attitude towards life is skeptical. In this cardinal principle of his philosophy he gives expression to the entire humanistic sentiment of the age which reached its zenith in the second half of the sixteenth century. Yet there is much in his writings, the imperturbable and unaffected *joie de vivre,* the happy combination of a clear intellect and a cheerful heart, of his own individuality and of the spirits of the French nation. He was at one with the stoics of old in preferring to the feeling of compassion the vigorous, joyous, and fearless emotions. Regret and remorse he repudiated because the past has become a part of the general cohesion of the universe. But he differed from the stoics in finding the general law of the universe not in abstract principles, which he always regarded with suspicion, but in the harmony of our aims with the universe and their consequent regulation. Man should seek to live according to the universal law of nature, to preserve himself from danger, to fill his life with joy, to regulate his passions in their early stages while they are yet amenable to discipline, to shun melancholy, to heighten such gratifications as he permits himself by thoroughly chewing and digesting them, and never to allow any sentiment or passion to take complete possession of him. One may treasure health, wife, children, and wealth, but one must preserve an inner chamber for oneself into which one can retire with a sense of perfect freedom. " The happiness of life," he said, " depends upon the tranquility and contentment of a well-disciplined spirit, upon an inflexible will in a well-regulated soul." He was a follower of Socrates and Seneca ; but, because it was more far-reaching and touched to finer issues than that of the ancients, his assertion of the autonomy of the individual made him the precursor of Descartes.

The moral autonomy of man, the ability of man to regulate the proper conduct of his own life, and the independence of such autonomy of every theology, received expression at the hands of other thinkers. In the writings of Francis Bacon (1561–1626) it found a popular and powerful exposition. The English philosopher undertook to win for man dominion over the world of nature by obtaining a complete knowledge of natural law. Thus would he place in the hands of the emancipated individual a key that should unlock every riddle. Human thought, he insisted, is creative in its power; and by the power of the human will the general welfare of man may be realized. Slowly these two great forces would develop and replace the warlike and theological passions that had not yet relinquished their hold upon humanity. Thus from a practical point of view did he postulate the moral autonomy of man. His great work, the *Novum Organum,* is only a part of his vast and unfinished scheme for reorganizing the sciences and developing a method by which man could win for himself a complete knowledge of the law of nature and so direct with certainty his individual life and the conduct of society.

From the philosophers in the republic of letters we now pass to the philologians. For a long time classical studies had occupied the front rank in the activities of scholars. But in spite of their achievements those studies gradually lost the leading position in the world of letters and underwent a transformation. They became changed from humanism, which sought in the literature of antiquity the classical ideal of life, into philology, the new-born science of words. This change was accomplished most decisively in Holland where Huguenot scholars devoted themselves to philological studies with much zeal. But with this metamorphosis of the old humanism the servile imitation of the styles of classic authors, which was exemplified by the Ciceronians, passed into the background and was replaced by an effort to understand correctly the subject-matter of the ancient writers and to appropriate their culture. The philology of the second half of the sixteenth century, then, had for its aim interpretation. It was from this fact that it derived its value. Adrianus Turnebus (1512–65) was a French scholar who taught in the University of Toulouse and who then went to Paris where he devoted himself to textual criticism of Greek literature. He wrote philological commentaries on Æschylus, Sophocles, and other Greek authors, and made translations of several Greek writings into Latin and French. Conrad Gesner (1516–65), of Zürich, compiled a biographical and bibliographical dictionary of all the writers in Greek, Latin and Hebrew whose works were known to him. He also made a dictionary of classical and proper names, and made the first attempt towards the comparative study of language. Marc-Antoine Muret (1526–85), better known as Muretus, wâs a great French philologian who, in spite of a bad character, raised himself merely by writing good Latin from poverty almost to the cardinal's purple. His melodious cadences enchanted every ear. One of the Ciceronians who replied to the criticisms of Erasmus was Julius Cæsar Scaliger (1484–1558), an Italian who went to live in France. He wrote a book on the principles of the Latin language and another in which, almost for the first time in the modern era, an attempt was made to deal with the art of poetry in a systematic way. His son, Joseph Scaliger (1540–1609), the foremost scholar of his age, after making progress in textual criticism, measuring out the boundaries of the science and establishing its method, devoted himself to the study of ancient history and the subject-matter of classical writings. He was a great man who studied life as well as literature. "He did not beat about the bush like the rest," said one of his students at Geneva where for a time he lectured, "but explained his author." When he undertook the study of ancient history he was the first modern scholar to venture into that field and it was not until the nineteenth century that he found his first follower. In his time nothing was known of the civilizations beyond that of Greece. The Hebrew, the Syrian, the Egyptian and other early civilizations were unknown or ignored. Indeed the study of ancient history was discountenanced by the principle of Protestant exegesis that secular history should have no place in the interpretation of the Bible. But as Scaliger put aside the dilettantism of the Ciceronians, so did he go beyond the narrow limits of the sectarians and set himself to travel along the road to truth. For thirty years he carried on his studies in the milieu of the religious wars in France. Then he went to the University of Leyden, where he was held in the highest esteem, and with him he took to its new home in Holland the unfolding science of philology. Fourteen years before Scaliger went to the newly-founded university another great Latin scholar, Justus Lipsius, (1547–1606), had taken up his residence there, only to leave it, however, twelve years later to be received again into the Catholic fold. He was especially skilled in textual criticism and interpretation and his masterpiece is an edition of Tacitus which is based upon a very thorough knowledge of Roman history. Isaac Casaubon (1559–1614), the child of a Huguenot pastor who had fled to Geneva, was compelled to pursue his classical studies in that city where literary interest had become almost extinct. But he corresponded with other scholars and when Scaliger died he wrote of him as "the sweet patron" of his life. When the religious wars in France drew to their close he went to lecture on classical literature and history at Montpellier and afterwards at Paris. After the assassination of Henry IV he went to England. He edited a number of classical authors, and he lives for later centuries in his "Letters" and in a journal that he wrote in Latin.

We have seen something of the part played by the publishers in the creation of the republic of letters. We have now to deal with the activity of the leading printer-publishers in the literary world. A printer in the sixteenth century was of necessity a scholar, his business was recognized as a learned profession. In our own times the combination of the scholar and editor with the practical printer is comparatively rare. A printing establishment in the era of which we write was like a little college of learned men. It was able to direct and to assist in the work of literary production as well as to perform the mechanical details of the press. Such an establishment was that of the Estiennes which was founded by Henri Estienne (?–1520) in Paris. His son Robert Estienne (1503–59) was himself the author of a Latin dictionary that greatly surpassed any of its predecessors. Becoming involved in theological disputes with the Sorbonne he fled to Geneva; and so there came to be two Estienne presses, one in the capital of France and the other in the capital of Calvinism, each sending forth books simultaneously. His editions of the biblical writings constitute his most important work. They are of great typographical beauty, being printed in the most perfect and beautiful of all Greek types; and he was the first to print the New Testament with an accompanying critical apparatus. When Robert went to Geneva the printing establishment in Paris was carried on by his brother, Charles Estienne (1504?–6), who in his turn as a printer, was succeeded by Robert's eldest son, Henri Estienne (1531–98), the greatest scholar of the family. This second Henri continued the press at Geneva. Seldom has the cause of learning had a more devoted promoter. For more than a generation he labored as author, editor, and printer and gave to the world an enormous mass of work. Some of his views were objectionable to the Genevan consistory, and so he became a wanderer. Because of his poverty he was unable to use the best paper and ink and so the beauty of his books is due to the type. But it is for their scholarship rather than their appearance that his productions are noted. His principal works are a Greek dictionary and an *Apology for Herodotus*. In the Netherlands, too, where printing had been invented, the art was carried to a high degree of perfection. One of the most famous presses was that of Christophe Plantin (1514–89), a Frenchman who settled in Antwerp, and whose books are famous for their beauty and accuracy. But more noted was the press of the Elzevirs, founded in Leyden by Louis Elzevir (1540–1617) and continued by his sons, the most important products of which appeared in the seventeenth century.

The jurists, too, had their place in the republic of letters The scholars of the Renaissance had discovered the true text of Justinian's codification of the old Roman law; and even before that the study of the civil law of the Romans had begun to curtail the wide pretentions of the canon law of the Middle Ages and to reduce the Church not merely to a condition of

Spread and Influence of the Roman Law

equality with the State but to one that was distinctly subordinate. For this reason the legists had been encouraged by those kings who, like Philip IV, of France, were bent upon increasing their power at the expense of that of the ecclesiastics. The evident superiority of the Roman law to the common law and to feudal custom was another factor in the zeal with which men started to study it anew. So the Roman law made encroachments upon the indigenous law of France, Germany, the Netherlands and Spain. The primacy of theology as a study in the universities of those countries was displaced by jurisprudence. Bourgeois and even peasant students who fitted themselves for the work of jurists found important positions in the judicial, administrative, and legislative work of their countries. In France a new nobility, that of the robe, came into existence, obtained many privileges, and succeeded in making itself hereditary. In Spain, too, the entire class of municipal and State officials got itself ennobled. The jurists wrested for their profession the place of pride which the ecclesiastics had held for so many centuries. A better interpretation of the Roman law was gradually developed. Andrea Alciati (1492–1550), an Italian scholar who enjoyed the patronage of Francis I and taught at Bourges, was the leader in the reformation of jurisprudence in France. He employed history, the classical languages, and literature in the exposition of the civil law, and he made the teaching of law something of a science. The new jurisprudence also found its way into the universities of Orleans, Poitiers, Bordeaux, and Toulouse. At Toulouse, however, the citadel of medieval jurisprudence, Jean de Boyssone, a fine scholar whose name has slipped out of the pages of history, found grave obstacles in his way. Yet he succeeded in getting rid of the medieval impediment to the proper study of the Roman law. Other such teachers were André de Govea (1497–1548) at Bordeaux; François Duaren (1509–59), who held a professorship at Bourges; François Baudouin (1520–73), who taught at Paris and Strasburg; Jacques de Cujas (1520–90), who, by ignoring the incompetent commentators upon Roman law and devoting his attention to the law itself, gained a European reputation as a teacher in various French universities; François Hotman (1524–90), who conceived the thought of a national code of French law but whose espousal of the Huguenot cause made him a wanderer from place to place; and Hugo Donellus (1527–91), one of the greatest jurists of the epoch.

Still another group of scholars in the republic of letters was that of the publicists, the men who wrote upon national and international law. The Protestant Revolution had given rise to new political thought. In the opening years of the movement the question whether, because of religious opinion, extreme oppression by the State might be resisted by force had become a burning one. Luther held that every civil authority had a claim to unconditional obedience. He was temperamentally predisposed in favor of the established secular authority no matter how it had come into power. Tyranny, he declared, should be endured as a divine punishment of the sins of men. But it is difficult if not impossible to harmonize all of Luther's views, and it may be deducted from his writings that a contract exists between the prince and his subjects and that the people possess the right to resist oppression. Calvin, who also preached the doctrine of patient obedience to the magistrate, spoke very cautiously of resistance to godless attempts on the part of the ruler. But the circumstances of the time proved too strong for the temperamental preferences of the leading reformers. The century and a half that immediately followed the outbreak of the great revolt from Rome proved to be an extraordinary fertile and determinative period in the field of political thought. To the conclusions of the ancient world and those of the Middle Ages it added its own. So, with all their dislike of democracy, the reformers indirectly gave impetus to a movement very closely identified with representative and republican ideas. Humanism also contributed something to the new political thought of the time. It furnished critical comparisons of the contemporary with the classical world in which the freedom of the latter was extolled. Erasmus wrote on the folly of hereditary monarchy and the advantages of representative institutions; and in the writings of Sir Thomas More the idea of the equality of all citizens before the law is a basic principle. Thus there was formed a common opinion, of varied origin, opposed to the increasing absolutism of the time. In his *Discours de la servitude volontaire,* Étienne de la Boétie (1530–63) protested boldly against the monarchical theory. "Nature gave us all the same form and the whole earth to inhabit in common and thus quartered us in the same house," he said; "it is impossible to doubt that we are all free by nature; it is inconceivable that nature intended any of us to be slaves." Even more outspoken and certainly more original is the *Franco-Gallia* of François Hotman (1524–90), a work so far in advance of its age that it was looked upon with disfavor not only by the Catholics but also by the Huguenots in whose behalf it was written. Yet it was widely read. Driven from France by the Massacre of St. Bartholomew.

Hotman attempted to prove by history that the French monarchy was limited by the people and the Estates and that a constitution was legally established. The people, he held, were justified in rebelling whenever the contract between them and the prince was violated by the tyranny of the latter. In the *Vindiciæ contra Tyrannos,* written by Philippe du Plessis-Mornay (1549–1623), the development of modern constitutional law was continued. The constitutional contract, it holds, is the sole source of political organization and of law. Rebellion is justified whenever oppression results from the violation of the contract by the ruler. Down to the French Revolution this idea, expressed with great force and eloquence in this book of disputed authorship that was "fitted by its very faults to become the text-book of ordinary men," served as the basis of every theoretical and practical attempt to reform the political organization of the modern States. The Englishman John Poynet (1514?–56), or Ponet, bishop of Winchester, was one of the first modern advocates of the justifiability of tyrannicide. The Scottish humanist George Buchanan (1506–82), who spent much of his life in France, and who there embraced Calvinism, also proclaimed the doctrine that all political power emanates from the people, that every monarchy is limited by the contract under which it was established, and that the punishment of tyranny is permissible. When Henry of Navarre became the heir-presumptive to the throne of France the scene was suddenly changed. The Huguenots now became the advocates of legitimism and the Jesuit theorists and those of the Catholic League became the champions of the doctrine of resistance and tyrannicide. And the Catholic publicists, as befitted "the party of the Paris mob," outdid their Protestant predecessors and contemporaries in the democratic tendency of their writings. Amid the great mass of pamphlets to which the French wars of religion gave rise the *Satire Ménippée* (1593–94), written by several collaborators no one of whom was an author of importance, stands preëminent. It is a burlesque account of the proceedings of the States-General that met in 1593 for the purpose of furthering the aims of the League. Its biting satire upon the evils of the time, its exposition of the wrong-doings of the chief members of the League, and its concluding speech of noble eloquence, lead us to believe that its contemporaries were right when they said that it did more for Henry IV than all the other writings on his behalf. In the midst of all the opposing and struggling tendencies of the time there appeared Jean Bodin (1530–96) who with Grotius and Hobbes created a definite political science. And the greatest thinker of the three was undoubtedly Bodin. In his *Republic* he advocates with great learning and vigorous thought the theory of an absolute monarchy that shall respect freedom of conscience and strive to realize the welfare of the entire community, not any form of a monarchy but one in which the people obey the laws of the ruler and the ruler obeys the laws of nature. When the prince fails to observe the fundamental laws of nature the people are released from the duty of obedience. Bodin lived in the communion of the Catholic Church and he was attached to the court party. So doubtless his advocacy of a monarchy limited only by the laws of nature was put forward in opposition to the anti-monarchical ideas of the Huguenots. The germs of much of the subsequent development of political science are to be found in his work. Far more important than his conclusions was the scientific method he employed in arriving at them. The last of the publicists whom we shall notice is Richard Hooker (1553?-1600), whose *Laws of Ecclesiastical Polity,* with its clear and attractive style, did much to reveal the latent power of English prose. The book was designed to refute the attacks of the Puritans upon the customs and polity of the Anglican church, but its chief interest to-day lies not so much in its theological discussions as in its philosophical and political thought; in its exposition of the unity and comprehensive character of law, " whose seat is the bosom of God, whose voice is the harmony of the world," whose operation determines the life of the individual, the organization of society, the conduct of the State, and, indeed, all the phenomena of nature. Law, he held, is of two kinds: — natural law, which is eternal and unchanging; and positive law, which varies according to circumstances. It is upon laws of the latter class that, applied with reason and the light of experience, all governments are based. Every government derives its justification from the approval of the governed, given either directly by those who are at the time being governed, or indirectly by their ancestors. Thus did the gentle and gracious priest picture the universality of law. Much of his thought has lost the approbation of men, but his latent idea that government derives its sanction from the governed has developed into the fundamental principle of democracy.

Closely connected with the publicists were the historians. The writing of history had been undergoing a gradual development, though by no means a steady one, ever since the days of the slender annalists of the early Middle Ages. The Renaissance, as we have seen in our study of Machiavelli and Guicciardini, gave a distinct impetus to historiography. Classical examples of history writing were recovered, interest in the human past and intelligent curiosity in the present were aroused, the spirit and method and apparatus of criticism were all developed, the sense of literary style became keener and more general, and the invention of printing was an enormous advantage both to the historian and to his readers. The revival of individuality, the fundamental factor of the entire Renaissance movement, gave rise to numerous biographical and auto-biographical writings; and the revival of nationality was the cause of many an attempt to write a national history. Then came the Protestant Revolution and the answering outburst of militant Catholicism to give a special impulse to the activity of historians. The new theologies had to justify themselves historically; and, on the other hand, their historical claims had to be refuted. In Germany, the most notable historian was John Sleidan (1506–56), conscientious and cautious annalist of the religious revolution, whose great work, containing many important documents, remains one of the most valuable of the contemporary histories of its times. The writers of the *Magdeburg Centuries,* of whom the principal one was Matthias Flacius, gave to the world (1559–74) the first general ecclesiastical history written from a Protestant point of view. The reproach of revolutionary innovation made against the Protestants turned the attention of Flacius and his collaborators to the past. The centuriators endeavored to gather for the overthrow of the Catholic claims documentary proof of alterations that had been made in doctrine, ceremonies, and ecclesiastical polity. Written in the midst of the bitter controversies of the time the *Centuries* is nevertheless a scholarly work and it has been called " the first monument of modern historical research." With far greater resources at his command Cardinal Cæsar Baronius (1538–1607) the chief of the Vatican library, and the little army of scholars in the libraries of many lands whom he was able by his position to summon to his assistance, began a work in reply that took forty years to complete. The work of Baronius is defective, yet it greatly excelled any previous similar attempt. Such work as that of the centuriators and the librarian of the Vatican had for its impulse an avowedly polemical purpose; nevertheless the researches that it entailed bore fruit in the development of historical method. The necessity of consulting original sources gradually became evident. Collections of sources were made by a number of scholars. The *History of the Council of Trent* is the most important work of Fra Paolo Sarpi (1552–

1623) whom Gibbon called an "incomparable historian." It is informed by an undying hatred of the Papacy of his time, but it is notably accurate in detail and is brilliantly written. The conscientious and reliable work of Geronimo de Zurita (1512–80), as the official historian of Aragon, still has its worth for the student of Spanish history. Also important is the work of another Spanish writer, the Jesuit Juan de Mariana (1536–1624), deemed in his own time and country to be the "prince of historians." His work has been described in a later century by Ticknor, the historian of Spanish literature, as being "the most remarkable union of picturesque chronicling with sober history the world has ever seen." The merit of his style is beyond question, and his work, although it is defective and is not notable for critical sifting or analyzing of sources, is not without a considerable degree of accuracy and penetration. In France where constitutional law rather than theology engaged the attention of the historians, Claude Fauchet (1530–1601) made researches in the history of the Franks down to the beginning of the Capetian dynasty in which is displayed a mature and systematic mind. A far greater historian was Jacques de Thou (1553–1617) who undertook to write a history of his own times. His history, which deals with events from 1546 to 1607, consists of five parts. The fact that it is written in Latin shows that French had not yet won complete acceptance as a language fitted for a learned work. In the matter of style he was surpassed by many of his fellow countrymen but he is unequaled in breadth of view, ripeness of judgment and invincible sense of justice. With few exceptions his views have been confirmed by the historical research of our own time; and his own century regarded his history, which is by no means narrowly confined to political affairs, as something of a secular bible. In England historiography was represented by William Camden (1551–1623) who, in his *Britannia,* wrote in elegant Latin a survey of the British Isles, and in his *Annales* a history of the reign of Elizabeth. George Buchanan (1506–82), whom we have already noticed as a publicist, gained for Scotland the fame of possessing the best Latinist in contemporary Europe. His *Rerum Scoticarum Historia,* written to clear the history of his native country "of some English lies and Scottish vanity," is still of great value for the history of Scotland during the period known personally to its author.

Side by side with the historians there should be noted the memoir-writers whose work did not always rise to the dignity of history but who nevertheless oftentimes exhibited attractive literary qualities and who inaugurated a species of literature in which France remains unequaled and, indeed, unapproached. The French very early brought to a high degree of perfection their national art of writing lively and learned memoirs and witty biographical essays with sharp portrayal of character. More than the men of any other country they seem to have a predilection for confiding to print all they have seen or heard, felt or thought, dreamed or done. And, tumultuous as it was, the long period of the religious wars, so full of color and passion, was rich in these chatty and charming memoirs. A few of these writers we must stop to notice. The *Commentaires* of Blaise de Monluc (1503?–77), it is said, was described by Henry IV as the "soldier's Bible." Whether the saying attributed to the king be authentic or no, it is a fitting description of this engaging book which is generally acknowledged to be superior to all other similar works of the time. Monluc was a true Gascon. Ferocious and fanatical in the Catholic cause, he was at once vain and valiant, crafty and impetuous. He saw the humor of a situation or a saying with unfailing quickness; yet he was pitiless in the warfare upon Protestantism. His memoirs, dictated in his old age, reveal a ready command of language and they are full of vivid passages and striking images. François de la Noue (1531–91) was a Huguenot soldier whose memoirs are an impartial account of the wars in which he participated, who saw the humorous side of life, and whose style is virile, clear, and exact. Pierre de Bourdeilles (1540?–1614), better known as Brantôme from the abbey of which he was the lay abbot, was another vivacious reporter of experiences and persons. In his pages are reflected the love of display, the immorality, and the cruelty that characterized the French court of his time. Murder and adultery are reported by him with the same gusto and facility as any other exciting episode of the world's pageantry that so delighted him. His range was limited. Real greatness was beyond his understanding. Italy, too, made a notable contribution to the literature of reminiscence. The charm of a natural language, close akin to conversation, was not confined to France. The Italian goldsmith and sculptor Benvenuto Cellini (1500–70), whom we should have noticed as a master of his craft, wrote his celebrated autobiography which is still read in every civilized country. His energetic, egotistical, quarrelsome and vindictive character doubtless made him unbearable to most of those with whom he came into contact, but it made the story of his life full of movement and interest, and this, combined with the zest and vivacity of the improvised style and the passion for unreserved communication, make the book one of absorbing interest.

Here, too, there must be noticed the dawn of the newspaper. Peaceful intercourse between the various governments had gradually assumed stable forms. The papal curia, by virtue of its world-wide relations, was the first to establish an elaborate diplomatic correspondence. The civil States of Italy, because of their ramified commercial connections, had long been compelled to develop regular intercourse with other powers. With the opening of the sixteenth century Spain and France began the maintenance of permanent embassies at foreign courts. From this collecting of news by politicians, merchants, and scholars, there gradually developed the profession of journalists. The reading public had greatly increased, people were eager to get the " latest intelligence," and the invention of printing had made the necessary multiplication of copies a commercial possibility. Newsbooks preceded newspapers. It was probably in the Netherlands, about 1526, that a continuous series of news-pamphlets, which may be called the first newspaper, first started; but the first definite regular publication containing current news, started in 1615, was the *Frankfurter Journal.*

To the poets we must now turn our attention. There were still men of letters, especially in Italy, who had so far surrendered themselves to the study of antiquity that they repudiated personal inspiration and the direct observation of life and devoted themselves to the narrating in Latin verse of fabulous or historical subjects. But it is not with them that we shall spend our time, but rather with those men who were able to put the life they knew into poetry. Such a man was Torquato Tasso (1544–95) the last of the great cycle of the Italian poets of the Renaissance. For the first ten years of his life he lived in the fairy-like surroundings of the Bay of Naples whose languorous beauty found a responsive echo in the sensitive nature of the dreamy little child. There, too, he heard much of the piratical descents of the Turks upon the shores of Italy. His father was a poet and under his direction he made rapid progress in his studies. When his education was concluded he entered the service of the Cardinal Luigi d'Este at Ferrara. And he was not more than eighteen years of age when his *Rinaldo,* in which he submitted the romantic and desultory adventures of his hero to the rigid rules of the epic, won him an early celebrity. Amorous lyrics, too, he wrote, musical and touched with a languorous sensuality, limpid and caressing, such as suited the taste of the courtiers of his time. Handsome in person, elegant in manner, and accomplished in his profession, he had become a general

CHAP.
XXIX
———
1526-1615

The Dawn
of the
News-
paper

Tasso

favorite of the brilliant court at Ferrara. But his great work, the *Gerusalemme Liberata,* was still to be written. The recovery of Jerusalem, the crowning work of the crusades, afforded a story of true epic character; and the anxieties and fear caused by the encroachments of the Turks made it especially timely and popular. The plot is very simple, and it possesses that unity and logical connection of its component parts which Tasso deemed to be the first requisite of an epic. The main outline of the story recalls the *Iliad,* but the brilliant series of episodes remind one of the *Orlando Furioso.* The romantic and the classical elements are intermingled in the poem, but the latter is often submerged by the former; and it seems that a greater success would have been achieved had the poet abandoned his desire to write an epic and confined himself to a pure romance. For it is due to its lyrical and romantic elements rather than to its epic qualities that the poem retains its place in the affections of all lovers of Italian literature. Despite passages of a somewhat empty sonorousness, frequent stiffness, and a continued tension due to the endeavor to attain the majesty and splendor of the epic, the *Jerusalem* is the most truly popular of the great Italian poems. It is " pitched in a lower and a calmer key " than the *Orlando Furioso,* the rich imagination of Ariosto is replaced with a silvery delicacy of sentiment, but within its limits it moves gracefully and with dignity. Its fine description of battles, its moving melody, its tender gaiety, its sincere emotion, its nobility and above all its large humanity, give this swan-song of the Italian literature of its epoch a permanent human interest. The story of Tasso's insanity we have not space to tell. His life may be taken as an exemplification of the Renaissance — a smiling morn, a golden noon, the rich glow of the sunset, and then the chill of the approaching night. He lived, this precursor of modern romanticism, with its mysterious longings and vague shudderings at unknown perils, in the midst of an over-refined civilization and his delicate spirit was made sick with all the contradictions of the age.

From the days of that memorable invasion of Italy by Charles VIII there had been, it will be remembered, an increasing influence of Italian art and literature in the artistic activity of France. That influence, however, was, at this time, the influence of an era that was passing into the night, for that is the destiny of all such outbursts of the human spirit as the Renaissance. Tasso's song was lonely amid the host of men who strove to sing with the voices of Latin poets of a time long dead. But this influence of imitative writers who were preoccupied with style was not altogether amiss in the development of French literature. Style was a quality in which French verse was to seek. The group of poets who succeeded in giving style to French poetry is known as the Pleiad. It was not to Italy alone that they were indebted for their lesson. They learned much from the literature of Greece. The leader of the group was Pierre de Ronsard (1524–85) and his associates were Joachim du Bellay (1522–60), Remi Belleau (1526?–77), Jean Antoine de Baïf (1532–89), Jean Dorat (1501?–58), Pontius de Tyard (?–1605), and Étienne Jodelle (1532–73). In 1549 Du Bellay gave to the public a treatise defending the French language and demonstrating a way in which it could be made illustrious. Potentially, he said, it was as fine a medium of expression as the classic tongues; it needed only cultivation. The innovators met with no little opposition, but gradually they won the support of the literary persons of the day. Ronsard became the official poet of the court and secured a wide general popularity. It was the hymns of the "prince of poets," as he was called, that most pleased his contemporaries; but it is in his lovely songs, his beautiful sonnets, and his elegiac odes, full of a real love of fields and flowers and a tender regard for his fellow-men, exhaling a suave regret, expressed with flawless taste and skill, revealing the charm of music and of mood, that we of to-day find the chief attraction of the "first great master of French meter." Du Bellay, the author of the famous manifesto of the Pleiad, is more uniformly excellent than Ronsard, but he wrote far less, and he is inferior in technical skill and poetic vision. Tyard's work, strongly influenced by his Italian predecessors, is correct and monotonous, and he soon abandoned verse for theology and mathematics. Belleau displayed his love of the country with something of the true Vergilian spirit. Baïf was more of a scholar than a poet, but his verse reveals a lively fancy, grace and elegance. The verse of Dorat is insignificant; while Jodelle won for himself an important place in the development of the French drama. The best work of this group of poets is not translatable. Its tender grace and airy spirit are too elusive to be conveyed by any other medium than their own language. Its cool and silvery air, fragrant with the faint odors of the dawn, may be seen in the pictures that Corot loved to paint, its delicate distinction in those of Watteau. What was the effect of the new program for poetry that found its origin in the travelers' talk of a chance encounter between Ronsard and Du Bellay in a wayside tavern? It gave to French literature some of the refinement which hitherto it had lacked and it prepared the way

Camoens

for the perfection which was eventually to win for that literature the admiration of the literary world.

Portugal was represented among the poets by Luis vaz de
Camoens (1524-80), an untitled noble, who came under the influence of the Renaissance at the University of Coimbra where
he absorbed a mass of classical learning so completely that afterwards he was able to write his epic crowded with literary and
historical allusions in the far-off fortresses of Africa and Asia.
Exiled from the court of Lisbon because of his indiscretion he
became a soldier and served in Africa and India. It was probably on the voyage to India that he conceived the idea of his
maritime epic, the *Luciads*. After an absence of seventeen
years in the East he returned to Lisbon with the completed epic,
written in the intervals of a most checkered career, ready for
the press. The *Luciads* is the most successful attempt to write
a modern epic. It is prolix and frequently commonplace, but
is often touched with a real tenderness and at times it rises
to nobility. Camoens knew how to choose his material from
the history of his own country with an unerring eye for its tragic
moments. His epic transfigures the past of the land he loved,
and it breathes a stirring patriotism. So it has been a potent
factor not only in keeping alive the national feeling of the Portuguese but also in preserving the ties that bind Brazil to the
mother-country. Better examples of his genuine poetic power
are his sonnets and other poems of which he wrote a great
number. In them the tenderness and the melancholy that he
often felt receive a fitting expression. So well did he write
his own language that even to-day it is called "the language of
Camoens."

Spenser
and
Sidney

The poetry of the great Italians, of Boiardo, Ariosto, and
Tasso, found a worthy addition in the work of Edmund Spenser
(1552-99) which was, however, not merely imitative but born
of its author's own individual genius and filled with the English spirit. All the splendid pageantry of forests and castles
and caves with their knights, ladies, dragons, and enchanters,
the picturesque phantasmagoria of knight-errantry, is to be
found in the "Faerie Queene," sung with the exquisite melody
that gained for Spenser the fame of being the poets' poet and
steeped in the magic of a restful and dreamy felicity. The allegory that was demanded by his abstract and contemplative genius
and his predilection for Neo-Platonism is fortunately so unob-
trusive as to make it unlikely that it would ever have been discovered had he not himself called attention to it. The heroic
circumstances of the death of Sir Philip Sidney (1554-86) have

made his name familiar to every school-boy; but to the lovers of literature he is known as the first voice capable of soaring melody in the lyric choir of the Elizabethan age.

The birth of the modern drama brought a new set of men into the republic of letters. Two sources furnished suggestion for the play-wright of the time — the medieval and the classical drama. Italy, some of whose earlier dramatists we have already noticed, won no conspicuous success in the field of dramatic literature, but she gave to the world a new type in the form of the pastoral drama. Bucolic poetry had always been keenly enjoyed in Italy ever since the days of Boccaccio. Perhaps it was because of the strong contrast it afforded to their own lives that the idealized life of the shepherds, the portrayal of its traditional innocence and simplicity, appealed so unfailingly to the refined and corrupt courts of the peninsula; at least the recognition of a contrast, either explicit or implicit, between the simplicity of pastoral life and the complexity of the life of the court or the city is a constant element in the literature known as pastoral. This longing of the satiate soul to escape, if only in imagination and for a fleeting moment, from the world that is too much with us to a life of simplicity and innocence is expressed with idyllic sweetness in the writings of Theocritus and is given with greater and more poignant intensity in those of Tasso and Guarini. Indeed, Tasso in the simple and artless drama of *Aminta* produced the typical pastoral play. Full of tender images, roguish innocence and melodious verse, touched here and there with the profound melancholy of the waning Renaissance, its alluring simplicity concealing a most consummate art, it is one of the most beautiful flowers of Italian poetry. Ten years later one of Tasso's fellow-courtiers at Ferrara, Battista Guarini (1538–1612), paid him the compliment of imitation by writing *Il Pastor Fido*. Guarini was a clear-eyed man of considerable culture who was well aware of the true character of the society in which he lived and moved. " The court is a dead institution," he wrote; " it is a shadow not a substance in Italy to-day. Ours is an age of appearances, and we go a-masquerading." His play is far more complex in plot than the *Aminta;* indeed, so consummate is the ingenuity of the plot that it is not equaled by that of any preceding Italian play; and it combines the features of the lyrical eclogue, of tragedy, and of comedy; but it is almost entirely lacking in true dramatic feeling. At first its success as a play surpassed that of its immediate predecessor and it exercised a far greater influence upon the succeeding drama of Italy than did Tasso's " perfumed and delicate " play; but its essen-

The Dramatists

tially artificial character has left it stranded upon the shores of time while the poetry of the *Aminta* continues successfully to defy every change in taste. Guarini's ornaments are merely stage jewels; and the type of play itself is one that by its very nature was destined to early decadence. The work of his successors was given over to preciosities and affectations, an expression of the decline of Italian culture after a supreme and glorious age. In France the medieval drama gradually gave place to the modern because of the impact of the drama of classical antiquity and the Italian Renaissance. To Jodelle, one of the stars of the Pleiad, belongs the credit of having written both the first comedy and the first tragedy in French. But while French comedy soon became distinctly national in tone, tragedy had to wait until the seventeenth century for its real dawn in France. Spain would have nothing to do with translations of classical drama, and she interested herself but slightly in the contemporary theater of Italy. In consequence her writers undertook to represent her own life on the Spanish stage. They found a fitting leader in Lope de Vega (1562–1635), the number of whose plays makes the greatest demand upon our credulity. Eighteen hundred *comedias* and four hundred *autos sacramentales* are said to represent his total contribution to the stage. Whether these vast ascriptions be authentic or no the fact remains that he had the creative faculty in abounding measure. In his works are to be found either in developed form or in germ every subsequent quality and characteristic of the Spanish drama. In his time the native drama fulfilled all the conditions of a national art. It was born of a national passion for the stage, and it appealed to all classes of the people. The English, also, had the wisdom and the courage to be themselves on the stage, to cast the classical unities to the winds, and to make their own rules, much freer than those they discarded but none the less conducive to a glorious art. With but a scant development of the technic of playwriting and a slight improvement in the language of the drama as the only performance of his predecessors there burst upon the scene William Shakespeare (1564–1616), the greatest of all modern poets with a profound knowledge of man. No other writer has portrayed for us so many aspects of human nature or rendered for us so many moods and passions each with its own authentic accent. To him and to his numerous contemporaries is due the fact that the Elizabethan stage infinitely transcends that of any other country and any other time since the long departed days of "the glory that was Greece."

Last of the members of the republic of letters whom we shall deal with are the novelists. The rise of the novel and something of its development we have already noticed. With the death of Bandello the Italian novel began visibly to decline and nothing more of merit was produced in the peninsula in that line until the nineteenth century. France did not make a practice of novel-writing until the sixteenth century was well under way. The one French novelist of importance in the period with which we are dealing is Margaret of Angoulême (1492–1540) whom Michelet has happily styled "the amiable mother of the Renaissance." She set out to write a new *Decameron,* but only seventy-two stories were completed. It is thought that all the characters of the *Heptameron* represent real persons and it is certain that they illustrate the society of that day. The book is the most vivid portrayal that we have of the early French Renaissance, "of its social and intellectual atmosphere, of that curious mixture of coarseness and refinement, of cynicism and enthusiasm, of irreverence and piety, of delight in living and love of meditation on death which characterized that period of transition between the medieval and the modern world." The stories themselves are for the most part mediocre. By the middle of the sixteenth century Italian novels "as merry companions to shorten the tedious toil of weary ways" had become very popular in England. The bent of the literary genius of the time was towards the lyric and the drama; but Sidney's *Arcadia,* usually styled a pastoral novel, though in reality a "book of knightly deeds," may be mentioned to demonstrate the fact that the Elizabethans did not wholly neglect the prose story. Another species of the story of adventure, the picaresque novel, gained great favor especially in Spain. The picaroon story is the autobiographical narrative of a real or imaginative rogue who recites his robberies and depredations upon society with gusto and who exhibits a feeling of contempt for the public he has plundered. It may be found in undeveloped form in classical literature and in the *fableaux* of the Middle Ages, but it was in Spain that it received its final form. The first example of the *novela picaresca* is *La vida de Lazarillo de Tormes,* of uncertain authorship, that made its appearance about the middle of the sixteenth century. Many imitations were made of so popular a story, but it was not until the last year of the century that in the *Guzman de Alfarache* of Mateo Aleman (1547–1609?) its first serious rival appeared. This was quickly followed by a number of brilliant narratives in the same style and the picaresque literature rapidly won for itself a wide popularity not only in Spain but also in the other countries of western Europe. Romances of chivalry had long been popular in every European land. Especially popular in Spain was the story of *Amadis of Gaul* which was probably written in Castile about 1350; and many other stories of knight-errantry were written in imitation of it. These stories, like chivalry itself, degenerated into the most fantastic and tedious absurdities. One of the two chief theories about *Don Quixote,* the masterpiece, begotten in a jail, of Miguel de Cervantes Saavedra (1547-1616), which is the only product of Spanish literature that has won for itself the world's esteem, is that it was intended as a burlesque upon these romances of chivalry. The other is that it was intended as a satire upon human enthusiasm. Be these surmises as they may, it is not to either of these purposes, or even to its numerous adventures, that the book owes its wide popularity but to the true and sympathetic portrayal of its brave, humane and courteous hero, his shrewd and selfish yet wholly kindly and loyal servant, and all the minor characters, priests and innkeepers, hidalgos and beggars, tavern wenches and lady's maids, shepherds and barbers, muleteers and monks, and all the panorama of contemporary Spanish life unfolded in its teeming pages with penetrating insight and genial spirit. In Cervantes, said Victor Hugo, was the deep poetic spirit of the Renaissance. So full is his book of the milk of loving kindness that the simple human relations become more significant to us and we become more aware of the value of the words of our fellow-men and more responsive to the touch of their hands in our greetings and partings.

# CHAPTER XXX

## THE REPUBLIC OF THE ARTS

1. Architecture.
2. Sculpture.
3. Painting.
4. Music.
5. The End of the Century.

CHAP.
XXX

1540-80

The New
Classicism
in Archi-
tecture

FIRST among the artists whom we shall consider in our study of the republic of arts are the architects. We have noted the germs of decadence in the architectural work of Michelangelo. That decadence became more pronounced as the years unrolled. The chastity of the April of the Renaissance had passed away and the exuberance of its Indian summer was at hand. But there were some artists who resisted the tendency towards the florid and the ornate. Giacomo Barocchio (1507–75), sometimes called Barozzi da Vignola, who succeeded Michelangelo as the architect of St. Peter's, was a builder of wide knowledge and fine taste who, although he permitted himself to employ such devices as the broken pediment over door and window, did much to uphold the neo-classic style amid the increasing architectural excesses of the time. A still greater advocate of the neo-classic architecture of the earlier Renaissance was Andrea Palladio (1518–80) whose work in building is somewhat analogous to that of the Ciceronians in literature. So powerful was the influence that he exerted, by means of writings as well as architectural works, that the cold and calculated style which he fostered has received the name of Palladian. Yet the tyranny of his mathematical and correct uniformity, restrained and restful, but intolerant alike of diversity and spontaneity, was not without its value in a time when architecture was running to seed in the unchecked desire for novelty of design and luxuriance of decoration.

We have seen that the varying Italian interpretations of classic architecture made their way into France and, fused with the flamboyant Gothic of the end of the Middle Ages produced first a transitional style and afterwards a distinct Renaissance type informed with the national genius. But the architecture of the

CHAP.
XXX

1500-1600

Italian
Influence
in France

French Renaissance was not so distinctively national as it might have been had not the Italian influence, induced by sixty years of French military activity in the peninsula and supported by the great Medicean princess at the Parisian court, been prolonged. Among the French architects of the time were Pierre Lescot ( ?–1578), the designer of a part of the Louvre, who worked in close conjunction with Jean Goujon (1520?–66?), a sculptor who possessed the architectural sense in a high degree; Philibert de l'Orme ( ?–1570), who studied his art in Italy and strove to remove the lingering Gothic traces and to restore the style of Greece; and Jean Bullant (1513?–78), an artist of exceptional power and originality. French architecture, iike that of Italy, experienced a decline. It had depended very largely upon the patronage of the court and the taste of the later Valois kings tended towards extravagance. Then, too, the long anarchy of the religious wars was disastrous to almost every kind of art.

But it is to the degeneracy of Italian architecture, more important in itself and in its influence than that of France, that we must turn our attention. The exuberant ornamentation of buildings produced a fantastic style that is called " baroque," a term

derived from the Spanish word *barrueco* or *berrueco* which is the name given to an imperfectly rounded pearl. The baroque is sometimes called the *style jésuite,* but with injustice to the followers of Loyola. Long before the first Jesuit church was built in Italy examples of baroque exaggeration were to be found in more than one of the plastic arts in the peninsula. It is true the Jesuits were the leading patrons of the style in ecclesiastical buildings, but that was perhaps because they were building more churches at the time than was any other religious order. And the style was by no means confined to churches. It was adopted for secular buildings, both public and private, of every sort. It has been the fashion to condemn the baroque unsparingly. Every pediment was a paradox we are told, and every column a conceit. And we have just spoken of it as a degenerate style. Yet it was not without its merits. What produced this style whose embodiment one may see in the beautiful church of Santa Maria della Salute in Venice? Was it not a revolt against the cold and oftentimes clumsy classicism of Palladio and his contemporary purists? Baroque, it is true, could break every canon of the art and become bizarre, even delirious, almost beyond belief. Yet do we judge Gothic by its worst examples? Baroque had certain qualities of scale and composition that have too frequently been overlooked; it was not always insincere; and he who looks with eyes to see may behold in it much that is imaginative and not a little that is beautiful.

CHAP.
XXX

1550-1608

The
Transition
of Sculp-
ture to
the Sensa-
tional

Signs of decay were not wanting in the art of sculpture. The culture of the time which produced the Ciceronian literature induced the sculptor to neglect his own vision of the world and to work only in accordance with the accepted standards of classic beauty. So, instead of thinking, the sculpture of the later Renaissance merely adapted thought; and, instead of feeling, it was content to simulate the feeling of the classic age. The revelation of the individual, then, which is the most precious thing in art, was diminished. But on the other hand technical facility was greatly increased. There was nothing possible to the carver of stone which the sculptors at the end of the sixteenth century could not do. Indeed, the marble group known as the Rape of the Sabines is said to have been made by Giovanni da Bologna (1524–1608) to prove that the fragility of the stone placed no limit upon his technical skill. Yet wonderful as was that skill it produced for us figures that appeal to us only as poses and not as personages. When the century closed, the transition of sculpture to the sensational was almost complete. For the sake of surprise and wonder, truth was banished and in its place was substituted the display of a consummate technic, extravagant movement, and exaggerated conduct.

Painting on the other hand had found a new center in Venice where the cult of antiquity was not so controlling as at Florence and Rome and where rich impulses came from the prevalent desire to see, originally and independently, life and the world in which men live. And a new force, as it were, had come into existence to renew the vitality of painting. For the first time the full glory of color was being revealed by the Venetians. In the sumptuous art of Paolo Veronese (1528–88) the golden and magistral pageant of the city in the sea found a masterly expression. It is not form but color, miraculous, rich, smoldering, alternatingly gorgeous and tender according to the circumstances of light and shade, that gives to the cathedral of St. Mark its special beauty. So, too, is it color and not form that makes Venetian painting beautiful. The greatest master of color that Venice produced, the most glorious painter of her pageantry, was Veronese. In him we shall seek in vain for nobility of thought and for religious fervor, and seldom shall we find a touch of tender sentiment; but the life of the city impearled amid its ministering sea, its slender campanili, its glistening domes, the palaces that fringe its fantastic waterways, its processions and banquets, its pomp of color, the fullness of its splendor, all this and much more born of his own imagination he painted as no one else in the world has ever been able to paint.

**Tintoretto**

If profound imagination and spiritual insight are lacking in the work of Veronese they are surely present in that of Jacopo Robusti (1518–94) whom, because as a boy he helped his father in the work of dyeing silk, men have always called Tintoretto. On the wall of his studio, when still a youth, he wrote the words " the drawing of Michelangelo and the color of Titian " as the ideal to which he wished to attain. And the energy of the one and the color of the other of the two masters whom he most admired speak to us to-day from the great pictures that he painted. The range of Tintoretto's subjects is very wide. It includes themes from the classic past, the Christian story, and the life and personages of his own republic. All of these he treated in his own original way. Imagination, excelled only by that of Shakespeare, enabled him to penetrate to the heart of every subject that he selected, to picture almost every phase of human experience and to portray the many sides of its aspiration. His pictorial sense, and a masterly technic obtained by infinite painstaking, enabled him to obtain, with instantaneous touch and almost unapproachable precision, certain qualities of light and color charged, beyond that of any other artist, with the emotion of the subject, and to steep his figures in a poetry of atmosphere that gives to them life and meaning and imparts to his scenes their astonishing effect of reality.

Tintoretto was the last of all the supreme Italian painters. The art that followed him was but the bloom of a period of decay. Most of the great painters had left behind them a train of followers, servile imitators who were known as " mannerists "; but a reaction, in the form of eclectic schools, arose against the various mannerisms based upon the imitation of the works of single great painters. Chief and most influential of these schools was the academy at Bologna founded by Lodovico Caracci (1555–1619), whose two nephews, Agostino Caracci (1557–1602) and Annibale Caracci (1560–1609), were for a time associated with him. The principle that determined the proceeding of these eclectics, who forgot that " poems distilled from other poems pass away," was to copy from the work of each great master the quality that seemed most worthily to represent him and to combine these qualities in their own productions. The whole was to be at least as excellent as the sum of the component parts. It is quite evident from such a program as this that all spontaneity in painting had spent itself. But, although

**The Eclectic Painters**

it has been said that the only result of this attempt to resuscitate the dead was to kill the living, the work of the eclectics is not altogether without merit and significance.  Something they contributed to the technic of their art and they gave expression to the fervor of the first stage of militant Catholicism.  One of the most important followers of the Caracci was Zampieri Domenichino (1581–1641), whose work testifies to the sway that religion had resumed over the minds of the Italians.  After the death of Lodovico the school was led by Guido Reni (1575–1642) whose masterpiece, the fresco of Aurora, is so well-known by its reproductions, and whose work at its best has a soft charm of delicate color and graceful line.

In still another way did the reaction against the mannerists express itself.  Michel Angelo Caravaggio (1569–1609), and the realists who followed his lead, painted the baldest of transcripts from nature.  The principle of reproducing nature without modification was not without its attractive results as long as the subjects were the gamesters and bravi of the wayside taverns, but when it attempted religious figures it failed completely.  One other thing, an exaggerated chiaroscuro, characterized Caravaggio and his followers.  So theatrical became their contrasts of light and shadow, and so somber the colors they preferred, that they were known as the *Tenebrosi*.

These painters of the period of decline, especially the eclectics, became extremely popular in other countries than their own.  The art criticism of the two succeeding centuries is full of their praises.  Literature and art in Italy had spent their force and declined from the summits of poetry and inspiration to the depths of a facile skill that had nothing to say.  The motives that inspired the brush of Raphael and the pen of Ariosto were exhausted.  Painters and poets alike depend in great measure upon their epoch.  They give utterance to its thought and aspirations.  When these have been expressed a pause must come until a succeeding age has made its contribution in thought, emotion, and ideals, to the history of the world.  Art cannot anticipate these things.  And it requires a long time for human experience and aspiration to work out new thought, to develop new emotion, and to choose new ideals, for art to express.  Between the different periods of great creative activity, therefore, there will always be found times of reflection which may take the form of pedantry or of sound criticism.  So the decline of literature and painting must not be hastily attributed to the action of militant Catholicism.  That movement, beyond all doubt, was unfavorable to art in its purest forms; but it was by no means the sole or even the principal cause of the general decline. The simple truth is that the aloe had blossomed and the end had come.

Pales-
trina and
the Birth
of Modern
Music

But in this period of decline Italy had become the cradle of another art, even purer and nobler than those whose decadence we have just noted. Thus far music had made no notable progress, and it was especially backward in Italy. Not a single great composer appeared in the peninsula until the second half of the sixteenth century and most of the executants were men from beyond the Alps. The first form in which modern music began its development was that of the madrigal, a song written for three or more voices. The true madrigal may be said to have had its rise in Flanders, but the art of its composition did not reach its full maturity until it was transferred to Italy. In Rome the madrigal found many composers of distinction; in Venice and Florence it enjoyed great popularity; in Naples it had a brilliant period; and, though it failed to ingratiate itself into the favor of either the French or the Germans, it won for itself the affection of the English. The Church was in great need of this power to write harmonically and melodiously. She was in still greater need of the power and the desire to write in a true religious spirit. The mass, its poetic and dramatic situations entirely ignored, had become a performance of musical acrobatics in which the jigs and catches of the taverns, together with their words that were oftentimes licentious, had found a place. And so inappropriate and discordant was the instrumental accompaniment that the Council of Trent seriously thought of reverting to the stern and naked plain-song of the Middle Ages. The conciliar fathers, however, contented themselves with a resolution against the *mescolamento di sagro e profano* in the music of the mass; and in 1564 Pius IV created a commission of eight cardinals to carry out the resolution. Fortunately in the person of Giovanni Pier Luigi da Palestrina (1514?–94) there appeared the very man for the hour. After suffering the pangs of poverty and the bitterness of defeated hope he had been installed as *maestro di capella* in the church of Santa Maria Maggiore in Rome when two of the cardinals of the commission requested him to submit a musical setting of the mass. In response, so it is averred, Palestrina placed three masses in the hands of Cardinal Carlo Borromeo. The third mass, the ineffably beautiful *Missa Papæ Marcelli*, in which the words of the mass are most eloquently expressed, was sung in the Sistine Chapel before the enchanted pope, and soon " the whole of Italy welcomed it with a burst of passionate applause." All doubts were set at rest. Music, the most spiritual of all the arts, found its fitting place in the most solemn and majestic ritual that the world has known. It is not easy to reconcile the story of the submission of the three masses with the chronology of Palestrina's works, but there is no doubt that the Church was greatly aided by him in the task of improving the music of her services. The "Mass of Pope Marcellus" is perhaps Palestrina's greatest work, but he wrote at least ninety-four masses and many hymns. Among the former is the *Missa Brevis*, which is often sung to-day, and the beautiful *Assumpta est Maria in Cœlum;* while among the latter is the splendid *Surge. illuminare Jerusalem,* the sweet and tender *Peccantem me quotidie,* and the pathetic *Super flumine Babylonis.* Thus did a new and noble art arise and religion receive if not its most splendid music at least that which can rightly claim to be its most reverent and devout.

The modern mass was not the only music-form that had its beginning at this time. In Philip Neri's church at Rome, known as the Oratory, as well as in other churches, it was the custom to present from time to time one or other of the biblical stories with choruses, solos, and instrumental accompaniment. It became the endeavor to express more faithfully in the music the dramatic character of the words, and thus was developed the oratorio. Closely allied with the oratorio at this time was still another new music form, the opera, which is a secular drama set to music. The first distinct work of the new species was the *Euridice* of Jacopo Peri (1561–1609?), which is not without beauty and effectiveness in the new declamatory style. But opera had to wait for its first real master until Gluck began to compose in the eighteenth century.

*Birth of the Oratorio and the Opera*

Our study of the revival of science carried us to the end of our period and even beyond it, for Galileo did not die until almost the middle of the seventeenth century. Each of the sciences that we have noticed continued to progress, to become aware more definitely of its field, to make explorations in that field, and to perfect its procedure; and other sciences were being born. The progress of the sciences did much to spread the conviction that the human understanding is in itself sufficient to comprehend nature and to regulate the life of the individual and that of society. From the close of the sixteenth century there was an ever-increasing body of scholarly and cultivated men who based their thought and their daily life upon the autonomy of the human understanding. Thus did they disown the dominion of external authority and carry on in the realm of thought that

*Progress of the Sciences*

CHAP.
XXX

1550-1600

End of
the Six-
teenth
Century

revival of the individual which we have found to be the basic element of the Renaissance.

Our story comes to an end with the opening of the seventeenth century. It was an unsettled time. The opposing forces of human life, called into greater energy by the revival of nationality and that of individuality, had not found their resultant. Indeed, they have not done so yet; nor can any man say when that will be accomplished. It was a time of gusty and variable storms, rather than of winds that were setting steadily into accustomed directions. But in all this seething and clashing life there was at work quietly and unceasingly, as there is to-day, that most potent of all the forces of all the ages, aye, of life itself — the development of individuality.

**THE END**

# APPENDIX

# MEMBERS OF THE HOUSE OF HAPSBURG

The names of the emperors are printed in larger type

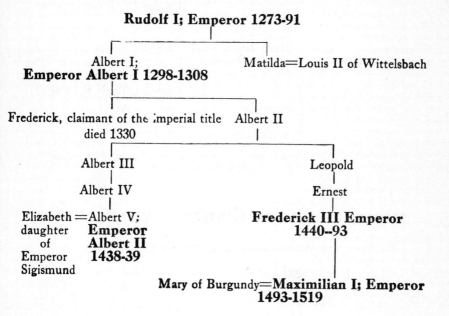

**Rudolf I; Emperor 1273-91**

Albert I;        Matilda=Louis II of Wittelsbach
**Emperor Albert I 1298-1308**

Frederick, claimant of the imperial title     Albert II
died 1330

Albert III                 Leopold

Albert IV                 Ernest

Elizabeth =Albert V;        **Frederick III Emperor**
daughter   **Emperor**               **1440--93**
of         **Albert II**
Emperor   **1438-39**
Sigismund

Mary of Burgundy=**Maximilian I; Emperor**
**1493-1519**

## MEMBERS OF THE HOUSE OF LUXEMBURG

Henry VII; Emperor 1308-13
|
John of Bohemia=Elizabeth,
daughter of Wenzel II of Bohemia
|
Charles IV; Emperor 1346-78
|

| Wencelaus; | Mary daughter of =Sigismund; King of Hungary; |
| Emperor 1378-1400 | Louis of Hungary        Emperor 1410-37 |
| | Elizabeth=Albert V of Hapsburg; |
| | Emperor Albert II 1438-39 |

## MEMBERS OF THE HOUSE OF WITTELSBACH

Otto I, first Wittelsbach duke of Bavaria; died 1183
|
Louis I; 1183-1231
|
Otto II; 1231-53
|
Louis II (1253-94)=Matilda, daughter of Emperor Rudolf I
|
Louis III, the Bavarian; Emperor Louis IV; 1314-47

# PRINCIPAL MEMBERS OF THE HOUSE OF ARAGON IN SICILY AND NAPLES

(The names of the Sicilian rulers are printed in larger type than the others)

**Peter I of Sicily and III of Aragon** (1282-85) = Constance; daughter of Manfred the illigetimate son of the Emperor Frederick II.

Eleanor, daughter of Charles II of Naples = **Frederick I of Sicily** (1296-1337)

**Peter II of Sicily** (1337-42)

**Frederick II of Sicily** (1355-77)

**James II** of Aragon and **Sicily** (1285-96)

Alfonso IV of Aragon

Peter IV of Aragon = Eleanor

**Louis I of Sicily** (1342-55)

**Martin** I of Aragon and **II of Sicily** (1409-10)

**Martin I** joint ruler of **Sicily** 1391-1402 with his wife = **Mary of Sicily** (1377-1402)

**Martin I** Sole Ruler of **Sicily** (1402-09)

John I of Castile = Eleanor

**Ferdinand I** of Aragon, **King of Sicily** (1410-16)

**Alfonso V**, the Magnanimous, King of Aragon and **Sicily** (1416-58) and Naples (1435-58)

**John II** of Aragon and **Sicily** (1458-79)

**Ferdinand** I of Aragon and **II of Sicily** (1479-1516) = Isabella of Castile

Ferdinand (Ferrante) I of Naples; illegitimate son of Alfonso, (1458-94)

Frederick (Federigo) I of Naples (1496-1501)

Alfonso II of Naples (1494-95)

**Ferdinand II** (Ferante) of Naples (1495-96)

*In 1502 as a result of the war alluded to in Chapter 10 Naples fell into the possession of Ferdinand of Spain*

## PRINCIPAL MEMBERS OF THE FIRST HOUSE OF ANJOU IN NAPLES AND HUNGARY

(The names of the Neapolitan rulers are printed in larger type than the others.)

**Charles I** of Anjou (1266-85) brother of Louis IX of France

**Charles II** (1285-1309) = Mary, daughter of Stephen IV King of Hungary

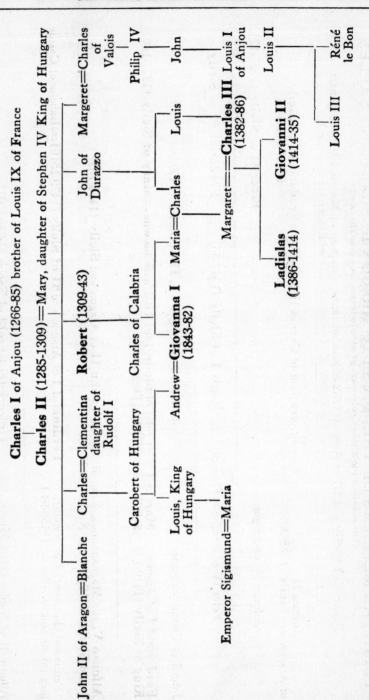

## PRINCIPAL MEMBERS
## OF THE HOUSE OF TRASTAMARA

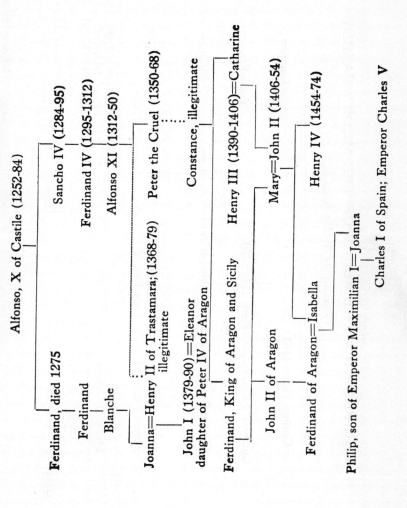

Alfonso, X of Castile (1252-84)

Ferdinand, died 1275

Ferdinand

Blanche

Sancho IV (1284-95)

Ferdinand IV (1295-1312)

Alfonso XI (1312-50)

Peter the Cruel (1350-68)

Constance, illegitimate

Joanna=Henry II of Trastamara; (1368-79)
illegitimate

John I (1379-90)=Eleanor
daughter of Peter IV of Aragon

Henry III (1390-1406)=Catharine

Mary=John II (1406-54)

Henry IV (1454-74)

Ferdinand, King of Aragon and Sicily

John II of Aragon

Ferdinand of Aragon=Isabella

Philip, son of Emperor Maximilian I=Joanna

Charles I of Spain; Emperor Charles V

# THE PRINCIPAL MEMBERS OF THE MEDICI FAMILY

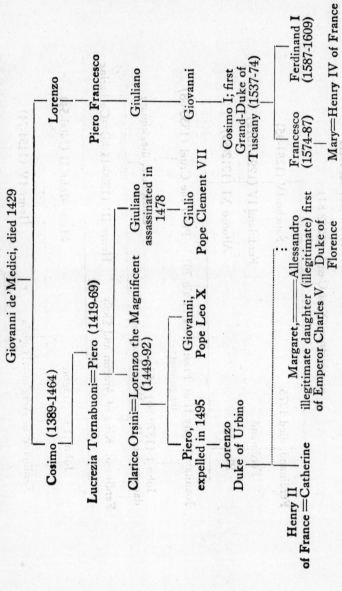

Giovanni de'Medici, died 1429

Cosimo (1389-1464)

Lorenzo

Lucrezia Tornabuoni=Piero (1419-69)

Piero Francesco

Clarice Orsini=Lorenzo the Magnificent (1449-92)

Giuliano assassinated in 1478

Giuliano

Piero, expelled in 1495

Giovanni, Pope Leo X

Giulio Pope Clement VII

Giovanni

Lorenzo Duke of Urbino

Margaret,——=Allessandro illegitimate daughter (illegitimate) first of Emperor Charles V Duke of Florence

Cosimo I; first Grand-Duke of Tuscany (1537-74)

Henry II of France=Catherine

Francesco (1574-87)

Ferdinand I (1587-1609)

Mary=Henry IV of France

# PRINCIPAL MEMBERS OF THE TWO SAXON HOUSES

Frederick I (1423-28); first Elector of Saxony

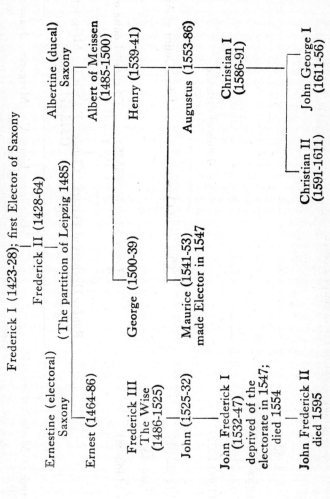

Frederick II (1428-64)

(The partition of Leipzig 1485)

Ernestine (electoral) Saxony          Albertine (ducal) Saxony

Ernest (1464-86)          Albert of Meissen (1485-1500)

Frederick III The Wise (1486-1525)     George (1500-39)     Henry (1539-41)

John (1525-32)     Maurice (1541-53) made Elector in 1547     Augustus (1553-86)

John Frederick I (1532-47) deprived of the electorate in 1547; died 1554     Christian I (1586-91)

John Frederick II died 1595     Christian II (1591-1611)     John George I (1611-56)

# PRINCIPAL MEMBERS OF THE HOUSE OF VALOIS

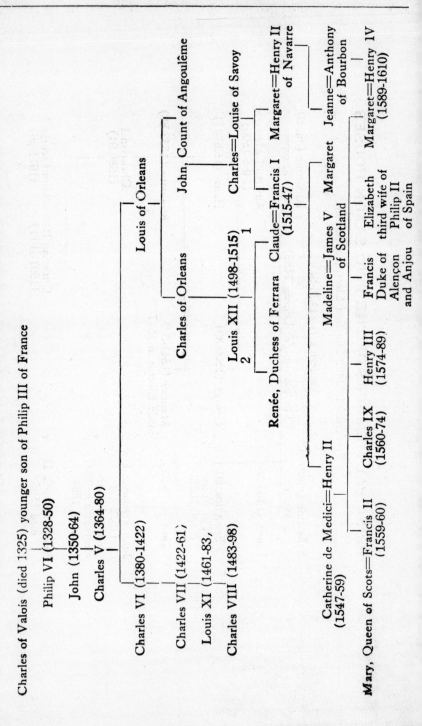

# PRINCIPAL MEMBERS OF THE HOUSE OF GUISE

René, Duke of Lorraine; died 1508

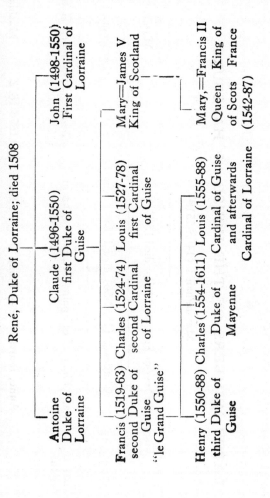

Antoine
Duke of
Lorraine

Claude (1496-1550)
first Duke of
Guise

John (1498-1550)
First Cardinal of
Lorraine

Francis (1519-63)
second Duke of
Guise
"le Grand Guise"

Charles (1524-74)
second Cardinal
of Lorraine

Louis (1527-78)
first Cardinal
of Guise

Mary═James V
King of Scotland

Henry (1550-88)
third Duke of
Guise

Charles (1554-1611)
Duke of
Mayenne

Louis (1555-88)
Cardinal of Guise
and afterwards
Cardinal of Lorraine

Mary,═Francis II
Queen   King of
of Scots   France
(1542-87)

# LATER MEMBERS OF THE HOUSE OF HAPSBURG

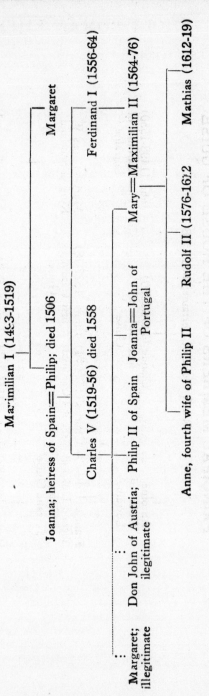

Maximilian I (1453-1519)

Margaret

Joanna; heiress of Spain=Philip; died 1506

Charles V (1519-56) died 1558

Ferdinand I (1556-64)

Philp II of Spain   Joanna=John of Portugal

Mary=Maximilian II (1564-76)

Don John of Austria; ilegitimate

Anne, fourth wife of Philip II   Rudolf II (1576-16)2   Mathias (1612-19)

Margaret; illegitimate

# HOLY ROMAN EMPERORS

Rudolf I (of Hapsburg) ; 1273–91.
Adolf I (of Nassau) ; 1292–98.
Albert I (of Hapsburg) ; 1298–1308.
Henry VII (of Luxemburg) ; 1308–13.
Louis IV (of Wittelsbach; the Bavarian) ; 1314–46.
*Frederick II (of Hapsburg), claimant of the imperial title;*
   1314–21.
Charles IV (of Luxemburg) ; 1346–78.
Wenceslaus (of Luxemburg) ; 1378–1400.
Rupert (of Wittelsbach) ; 1400–10.
Sigismund (of Luxemburg) ; 1410–37.
Albert II (of Hapsburg) ; 1438–39.
Frederick III (of Hapsburg) ; 1440–93.
Maximilian I (of Hapsburg) ; 1493–1519.
Charles V (of Hapsburg) ; 1519–56.
Ferdinand I (of Hapsburg) ; 1556–64.
Maximilian II (of Hapsburg) ; 1564–76.
Rudolf II (of Hapsburg) ; 1576–1612.
Mathias (of Hapsburg) ; 1612–19.

# LIST OF POPES

*(The schismatic Popes are printed in italics.)*

Gregory X (Teobaldo Visconti) ; 1271–76.
Innocent V (Petrus Tarentasia) ; 1276.
Adrian V (Ottobuono Fieschi) ; 1276.
John XXI (Petrus Juliani) ; 1276–77.
Nicholas III (Giovanni Gaetani Orsini) ; 1277–80.
Martin IV (Simon de Brie) ; 1281–85.
Honorius IV (Giacomo Savelli) ; 1285–87.
Nicholas IV (Girolamo Masci) ; 1288–92.
Celestine V (Pietro di Murrone) ; 1294.
Boniface VIII (Benedetto Gaetano) ; 1294–1303.
Benedict XI (Niccolo Boccasini) ; 1303–04.
Clement V (Bertrand de Goth) ; 1305–14.
John XXII (Jacques d'Euse) ; 1316–34.
Benedict XII (Jacques Fournier) ; 1334–42.
Clement VI (Pierre Roger) ; 1342–52.
Innocent VI (Étienne Aubert) ; 1352–62.
Urban V (Guillaume de Grimoard, or Grimaud de Beauvoir);
   1362–70.
Gregory XI (Pierre Roger de Beaufort) ; 1370–78.

### The Great Schism of the West

| Roman Popes | Avigonese Popes |
|---|---|

Urban VI (Bartolommeo Prignano) ; 1378–89.

Boniface IX (Piero Tomacelli) ; 1390–1404.

Innocent VII (Cosimo dei Migliorati) ; 1404–06.

Gregory XII (Angelo Corrario) ; 1406–09.

Alexander V (Pietro Philargi) ; 1409–10.

John XXIII (Baldassare Cossa) ; 1410–15.

Martin V (Odo Colonna) ; 1417–31.

Eugene IV (Gabriel Condulmieri) ; 1431–47.

*Clement VII (Roger of Geneva); 1378–94.*

*Benedict XIII (Peter de Luna); 1394–1424.*

*Clement VIII; 1424–29.*

*Benedict XIV; 1424.*

*Pope elected by the Council of Basel*

*Felix V (Amadeus, Duke of Savoy;) 1439–49.*

Nicholas V (Tommaso Parentucelli of Sarzana) ; 1447–55.
Calixtus III (Alfonso Borgia) ; 1455–58.
Pius II (Æneas Sylvius Piccolomini) ; 1458–64.
Paul II (Pietro Barbo) ; 1464–71.
Sixtus IV (Francesco della Rovere) ; 1471–84.
Innocent VIII (Giovanni Battista Cibò) ; 1484–92.
Alexander VI (Roderigo Borgia) ; 1492–1503.
Pius III (Francesco Todeschini Piccolomini) ; 1503.
Julius II (Juliano della Rovere) ; 1503–13.
Leo X (Giovanni de' Medici) ; 1513–21.
Adrian VI (Adrian Dedel) ; 1522–23.
Clement VII (Giulio de' Medici) ; 1523–34.
Paul III (Alessandro Farnese) ; 1534–49.
Julius III (Giammaria Ciocchi del Monte) ; 1550–55.
Marcellus II (Marcello Cervini degli Spannochi) ; 1555.
Paul IV (Giovanni Pietro Caraffa) ; 1555–59.
Pius IV (Giovanni Angelo Medici) ; 1559–65.
Pius V (Michele Ghisleri) ; 1566–72.
Gregory XIII (Ugo Buoncompagni) ; 1572–85.
Sixtus V (Felice Peretti) ; 1585–90.
Urban VII (Giambattista Castagna) ; 1590.
Gregory XIV (Niccolò Sfondrati) ; 1590–91.
Innocent IX (Giovanni Antonio Facchinetti) ; 1591.
Clement VIII (Ippolito Aldobrandini) ; 1592–1605.

# A LIST OF REFERENCES

## INTRODUCTORY NOTE

No attempt is made here to give an exhaustive bibliography of the original and derived sources of the period with which the present work deals. There is neither space nor necessity for such a bibliography between the covers of our book. The lack of space is evident to all who have an inkling of the vast literature that deals with the life of continental Europe and the European colonies in the three and a half centuries of the Renaissance and Reformation period; while the lack of necessity will be apparent when it is remembered that the book is addressed not to scholars engaged in research work, though the hope is expressed that it may be of occasional value even to them, but to the undergraduate student and to the general public. Only here and there, principally in the chapters that have to do with literature, are original sources given, those sources that speak to us of their own knowledge, that are for us the ultimate resort in the search for information. The college student and the general reader are more likely to need references to derived sources, those sources that are indebted to others for their knowledge; and it is, therefore, this class of sources that chiefly comprises our list of references.

It should not be understood that original sources are invariably superior to derived sources. An original source is trustworthy only in so far as its author knew the truth, was animated by the desire to tell the truth, and possessed the capacity to tell the truth. The best derived sources are based not merely upon one original source, but upon several or upon all of them that relate to the subject with which the derived source has to do. The value of a derived source, indeed, is determined by the extent of its use of original sources and by the competency of its study of them.

The bibliographies of the first three volumes of *The Cambridge Modern History,* those in the pertinent volumes of the *Histoire Générale* of Lavisse and Rambaud, and those appended to the pertinent articles in the *Encyclopædia Britannica,* though these last are often erratic and incomplete, are excellent guides to the original sources for the study of our period.

The encyclopedias are so comprehensive in their scope that they will be found to contain articles on almost every topic with which the book has to do, and so, with a few exceptions, they are named here once for all. The very brevity of their treatment of most of our topics and their inclusive character often make these articles the most desirable preliminary surveys and sometimes the most effective sum-

571

maries. Chief of the encyclopedias are, in English, the *Encyclopædia Britannica,* not without serious faults, but unrivaled in many important respects, and *The Catholic Encyclopædia,* an authoritative account of Catholicism in all its phases by eminent Catholic writers of many countries; in French, the *Dictionnaire Universel,* of Larousse, the *Nouveau Larousse Illustré,* and the *Grande Encyclopédie;* in German, Brockhaus's *Konversations Lexikon,* which, though its articles are often briefer than one wishes, is very dependable and is especially valuable as a source of information relating to German topics, the *Neues Konversations-Lexicon,* of Meyer, an admirable work closely following that of Brockhaus, and, more copious than either of these, Ersch and Gruber's *Allgemeine Encyklopädie der Wissenschaften und Künste,* Herzog-Hauck's *Realencyklopadie für Protestantische Theologie,* and Wetzer and Welte's *Kirchenlexikon;* in Italien, the *Nuova Enciclopedia Italiana;* in Spanish, the *Diccionario Enciclopedico Hispano-Americano;* in Scandinavian tongues, the *Nordisk Conversations-Lexicon,* and the *Svenskt Conversations-Lexicon;* and, in Russian, the masterly *Russkiy Entsiklopedicheskiy Slovar,* to which all the leading Russian scholars in letters and science have contributed. Encyclopedias have also been published in the Polish, Hungarian, Bohemian, and Rumanian languages.

It may be well to call attention here to the fact that the general histories, such as the *Histoire Générale,* of Lavisse and Rambaud, the *Cambridge Modern History,* and, when the last volume is published, the *Cambridge Medieval History,* contain matter that relates to every chapter of our book.

## CHAPTER I

### THE PAPACY

The twelfth chapter of Adams's *Civilization of the Middle Ages* forms an excellent introduction to this study; and good chapters are to be found in Pastor's *History of the Popes,* a learned and well-documented work, but unmistakably clerical in spirit; Creighton's *History of the Papacy,* attractively written, but touched here and there by an insular point of view; chapters eighteen, nineteen, and twenty of the second volume of Sedgwick's *Italy in the Thirteenth Century;* Medley's *Church and Empire;* Schaff's *History of the Christian Church;* and, fairly impartial, but incomplete as yet, Grisar's *Storia di Roma e dei Papi nel Medio Evo.*

More special works are Valois's *La crise religieuse du XV siècle;* Mollat's *Les Papes d'Avignon;* Valois's *Le Pape et le Concile;* Hallays's *Avignon et la Comtat-Venaissin;* Tosti's *History of Pope Boniface VIII,* the work of a scholarly Benedictine monk; Tosti's *Storia del Concilio di Costanza;* Gregorovius's *Rome in the Middle Ages,* an interesting work, rather spectacular at times, marred here and there by slight errors, but unusually valuable; Rocquain's *Le cour de Rome et l'esprit de réforme avant Luther;* Kitts's *In the Days of the Councils;* Kitts's *Pope John the Twenty-Third,* two books that may be cordially commended; Gardner's *Saint Catherine of Siena,* written by an English Catholic scholar who has made himself a master of the period, wholly delightful and dependable, it gives an impartial, minute, and orderly study of a difficult age; Ragg's

*Dante and His Italy;* Villari's *Medieval Italy;* Mackinnon's *History of Modern Liberty;* Lodge's *Close of the Middle Ages;* Drumann's *Bonifacius VIII;* Boutaric's *La France sous Philippe le Bel;* Döllinger's *Studies in European History,* the work of an independent Catholic scholar; Salembier's *The Great Schism of the West;* Robinson's *The End of the Middle Ages;* Wylie's *The Council of Constance;* Wylie's *England under Henry IV,* for the stirring chapters on the Schism and the Council of Pisa; Locke's *The Age of the Great Schism;* and, for the suppression of the Templars, Lea's *History of the Inquisition of the Middle Ages,* the most masterly treatment of its general subject, and, in several respects, the greatest contribution of America to historical writing.

## CHAPTER II

### POLITICAL AFFAIRS IN THE AGE OF THE RENAISSANCE

For the history of the Germanic Empire the best survey is Bryce's *Holy Roman Empire,* an interesting and accurate work in which the essential points are well emphasized. Other books are Lindner's *Deutsche Geschichte unter den Habsburgern und Luxemburgern;* Lindner's *Geschichte des deutschen Reiches unter König Wenzel;* Lorenz's *Untersuchungen zur Geschichte des 13. und 14. Jahrhundert;* Knüll's *Historische Geographie Deutschlands im Mittelalter;* and Henderson's *A Short History of Germany,* a book whose length belies its title and whose learning and literary style alike commend it. To these should be added the excellent biological articles in the *Allgemeine deutsche Biographie,* one of the finest works of its kind, in which the word *deutsche* is given an exceedingly broad interpretation, and the article on Occam in the corresponding British publication, *The Dictionary of National Biography.* Briefer studies are Lodge's *Close of the Middle Ages;* and Döllinger's *Studies in European History.* Pattison's *Leading Figures of European History* contains a chapter on Charles IV.

The only general history of Austria in English is Coxe's *History of the House of Austria,* and that is now superannuated. A recent book of considerable merit is Steed's *The Hapsburg Monarchy.* Leger's *History of Austria-Hungary* is translated from the French; Dopsch's *Forschungen zur inneren Geschichte Osterreichs* is still incomplete; and Drage's *Austria-Hungary* is a recent small book.

Of the books that have to do with the rise of the Swiss Confederation the best is Dierauer's *Geschichte der schweizerischen Eidgenossenschaft,* which, in considerable detail, gives the original and derived sources that are the bases of its statements. Other works are McCrackan's *The Rise of the Swiss Republic;* Van Muyden's *Histoire de la nation suisse;* Oechsli's *Die Anfänge der schweizerischen Eidgenossenschaft;* Rilliet's *Les origines de la confédération suisse;* Sutz's *Schweizer-Geschichte für das Volk erzählt,* which is popular in character; Gobat's *Histoire de la Suisse racontée au peuple;* and Vulliéty's *La Suisse à travers les âges,* a brief work, attractively written, that touches upon the economic and social history of the mountain democracy.

The best book on Bohemia in English is Lützow's *Bohemia;* and another is Gregor's *The Story of Bohemia.* For an intensive study of the early history of the country Bachmann's *Geschichte Böhmens,* which is pro-German in its sympathy, is indispensable. The three books by Denis (*Jean Hus; Fin de l'independence bohème;* and *La Bohême depuis la*

*Montagne blanche*) are comprehensive and scholarly, and they extend beyond the limits of our study.

The story of Bavaria may be traced in Riezler's *Geschichte Bayerns;* Brecher's *Darstellung der geschichtlichen Entwickelung des bayrischen Staatsgebiets;* and Heigel's *Die Wittelsbacher.* In Döllinger's *Studies in European History* there is a chapter devoted to the House of Wittelsbach. Important, too, is Riezler's *Die literarischen Widersacher der Päpste zur Zeit Ludwigs des Baiers.*

The affairs of other Germanic states may be studied in Hausser's *Geschichte der rheinischen Pfalz;* Droysen's *Geschichte der preussischen Politik;* in Prutz's *Preussische Geschichte;* Bornhak's *Preussische Staats- und Rechtsgeschichte,* especially valuable for constitutional matters; Stenzel and Berner's *Geschichte des preussischen Staats;* Böttiger's *Geschichte des Kurstaates und Königreichs Sachsen;* Sturmhöfel's *Geschichte der sächsischen Lände;* Jacobs's *Geschichte der Provinz Sachsen;* Heinemann's *Geschichte von Braunschweig und Hannover;* Blok's *History of the People of the Netherlands;* Putnam's *Alsace and Lorraine;* Barante's *Histoire des ducs de Bourgogne de la maison de Valois;* Barthold's *Geschichte der deutschen Städte;* Schlözer's *Die Hansa;* Danell's *Geschichte der deutschen Hanse;* Zimmern's *The Hansa Towns;* and, for the Vehmic courts, Lindner's *Die Veme.*

The literature of the Hundred Years' War is catalogued in Molinier's *Sources de l'histoire de France.* The war itself is dealt with in the following books: Lodge's *Close of the Middle Ages;* Vickers's *England in the Later Middle Ages;* Tout's *The History of England from the Accession of Richard II to the Death of Richard III;* Macdonald's *A History of France;* Lavisse's *L'Histoire de France,* one of the greatest productions of the brilliant French school of history, written by fifteen different authors; Luce's *Bertrand du Guesclin;* Luce's *La Jacquerie;* Luce's *La France pendant la guerre de Cent Ans;* Luce's *Jeanne d'Arc;* Anatole France's *Joan of Arc,* written with all the author's well known literary charm and skepticism of temperament; Lang's *The Maid of France,* a chivalrous and ardent defense of the deliverer of her country; Lowell's *Joan of Arc,* a scholarly and beautiful book, still the best life of the wonderful girl whose story it recounts; Richemond's *Jeanne d'Arc, d'apres les documents contemporains;* Hanotaux's *Jeanne d'Arc;* and Lea's *Inquisition of the Middle Ages,* in the third volume of which will be found a concise and vivid account of Joan's career. For the more advanced reader the great work of Quicherat, *Le Procès de Jeanne d'Arc,* which contains nearly all the original sources for the study of Joan, will be found indispensable. Important, also, is Marty's *L'Histoire de Jeanne d'Arc.*

For the story of the European invasions of the Turk and Mongol those who read German should consult Purgstall's *Geschichte des Osmanischen Reiches,* a monument of patient research, which, despite the fact that its first volume appeared almost a century ago, is still the standard work. Based upon Purgstall's great work are Creasy's *History of the Ottoman Turks;* and Lane-Poole's *Turkey.* Abdurrahman Sheref's *Tarikh-i-devlet-i-osmanié,* in Turkish, is said to be careful and impartial. Among other books that may be recommended are Miller's *The Balkans;* Remusat's *Relations politiques des princes chrétiens avec les empereurs mongols;* Remusat's *Nouveaux mélanges;* Remusat's *Mémoires sur plusieurs questions relatives à la géographie de l'Asie centrale;* Lane-

Poole's *The Mohammedan Dynasties;* Freeman's *The Ottoman Power in Europe;* Finlay's *The Byzantine and Greek Empires;* Finlay's *Greece and the Empire of Trebizond;* Grosvenor's *Constantinople;* Paparrigopoulo's *Histoire de la civilization hellénique;* Gregorovius's *Geschichte der Stadt Athen in Mittelalter;* Pears's *The Destruction of the Greek Empire;* Sturdza's *La terre et les races roumaines;* Xenopol's *Histoire des Roumains;* Szilágyi's *History of the Hungarian Nation,* the work of many collaborators, not written in English, as the title as given here would seem to indicate, but in Magyar; Leger's *History of Austria-Hungary,* translated from the French; Vámbéry's *Hungary in Ancient and Modern Times;* Acsády's *History of the Magyar Empire;* Knatchbull-Hugessen's *The Political Evolution of the Hungarian Nation;* Karamsin's *Histoire de l'empire russe,* translated from the Russian; Morfill's *Russia;* Rambaud's *History of Russia;* and Munro's *Rise of the Russian Empire.* The most important work in English on the Mongols is Howorth's *History of the Mongols from the ninth to the nineteenth Century.* Gibbon's *Decline and Fall of the Roman Empire* has masterly chapters dealing with this topic.

The break-up of Italy has been described in Sedgwick's *Italy in the Thirteenth Century;* Sedgwick's *A Short History of Italy;* Smeaton's *The Medici;* Cantu's *Storia degli Italiani;* Gregorovius's *History of Rome in the Middle Ages;* Balan's *Storia d'Italia;* Cipolla's *Storia delle Signorie Italiane;* Duffy's *Tuscan Republics;* Butler's *The Lombard Communes;* Villari's *Medieval Italy;* and Sismondi's *Italian Republics,* which has been completely recast and supplemented by Boulting. There are many books relating to single states and cities. See Bruni's *Historiarum Florentinarum Libri XII.;* Machiavelli's *Historie florentine;* Guicciardini's *Storia d'Italia;* Villari's *Machiavelli and his Times;* Capponi's *Storia di Firenze;* Perrens's *Histoire de Florence;* Gardner's *Florence;* Oliphant's *Makers of Florence;* Oliphant's *Makers of Venice;* Okey's *Venice;* Molmenti's *The Story of Venice;* Daru's *Storia della Republica di Venezia;* Hazlitt's *The Venetian Republic;* Thayer's *Short History of Venice;* Brown's *Venice;* Brown's *Studies in the History of Venice;* Kretschmer's *Geschichte von Venedig;* James's *Bologna;* Bréquigny's *Histoire des révolutions de Gênes;* Malleson's *Studies from Genoese History;* Carla's *Storia del regno della Due Sicilie;* Crawford's *Southern Italy and Sicily;* Verri's *Storia di Milano;* Malaguzzi's *Milano;* Ady's *History of Milan under the Sforza;* Noyes's *Milan;* Noyes's *Ferrara;* Symonds and Gordon's *Perugia;* Young's *Rome;* Wiel's *Verona;* and Gardner's *Siena.* To these may be added Browning's *Guelphs and Ghibellines;* Browning's *The Age of the Condottieri;* and Symon and Bensusan's *The Renaissance.*

The building of Spain may be studied in Altamira's *Historia de España;* La Fuente's *Estudios críticos;* Dozy's *Spanish Islam,* now happily available in an adequate English translation; Lane-Poole's *The Moors in Spain;* Scott's *History of the Moorish Empire in Europe;* and Hume's *Spain.* Of books relating to Portugal the following are recommended: Herculano's *Historia de Portugal;* Barros's *Historia da administraçado publica em Portugal;* Stephens's *Portugal;* MacMurdo's *History of Portugal;* and Schafer's *Geschichte von Portugal.*

## CHAPTER III

### THE REVIVAL OF THE NATION

The best exposition of nationality is Renan's essay *Qu'est-ce qu'-une nation?* And Mulford's *The Nation* will be found illuminating and inspiring. Suggestive passages will be found in Pollard's *Factors in Modern History;* and in Berger's *Die Kulturaufgaben der Reformation.* Chapter nine of Acton's *History of Freedom* is helpful; and several chapters in Dewe's *Psychology of Politics and History* bear upon the subject and are provocative of thought. See also the first two chapters in Van Dyke's *Age of the Renascence.* A brief but excellent survey of the rise of the principal modern nations is to be found in Wilson's *The State;* and more detailed accounts of the early history of the different nations that were in existence in the Renaissance period are to be gathered from the articles dealing with those countries in the encyclopedias, in the various national histories, and in the larger general histories.

## CHAPTER IV

### THE REVIVAL OF THE INDIVIDUAL

The pioneer book on this subject, and still one of the best, is Burckhardt's *The Civilization of the Period of the Renaissance in Italy.* A writer who has developed Burckhardt's germinal idea is Gebhart. See especially his *Les origines de la Renaissance en Italie,* his *Conteurs Florentines du Moyen Age,* and his *Les Jardins de l'Histoire.* A translation of a part of one of Gebhart's books that bears upon this subject is to be found in Munro and Sellery's *Medieval Civilization.* The first pages of Hudson's *Story of the Renaissance* and the first chapter of Mackinnon's *History of Modern Liberty* touch upon our topic; and much that is suggestive will be found in Symonds's *Age of the Despots;* Symonds's *The Revival of Learning;* Symonds's *The Fine Arts;* Voigt's *Die Wiederbelebung des classischen Alterthums;* Geiger's *Renaissance und Humanismus;* Körting's *Geschichte der Litteratur Italiens im Zeitalter der Renaissance;* Robinson and Rolfe's *Petrarch;* and Sedgwick's *Italy in the Thirteenth Century,* especially chapter eleven of the second volume. It would be well, also, to read Voysey's *Individuality;* and Holmes's thoughtful pamphlet *The Tarn and the Lake.*

The first great exponent of individuality among the political rulers at the end of the Middle Ages may be studied in Hampe's *Friedrich II;* and in Kington's *History of Frederic I.*

For the wandering scholars see Haezner's *Goliardendichtung und die Satire;* Spiegel's *Die Vaganten und ihr "Orden";* and Symonds's *Wine, Women, and Song.*

Provence and the Albigenses are well treated in De Manteyer's *La Provence du 1er à 12e siècle;* Mariéton's *La Terre provençale;* Schmidt's *Histoire de la Cathares ou Albigeois;* and Alphandéry's *Les idees morales chez les hétérodoxes latins au debut du XIIIe siècle.* And for the troubadours see Diez's (revised by Bartsch) *Leben und Werke der Troubadours;* and, by the same authors, *Die Poesie der Troubadours.* See also Meyer's *Les Derniers Troubadours de la Provence;* Appel's *Provenzalische chrestomathie;* Anglade's *Les Troubadours;* and Smith's *The Troubadours at Home.*

For the city republics and the despots see Boulting's edition of Sismondi's *History of the Italian Republics,* and Symonds's *Age of the Despots.*

## CHAPTER V

### THE REVIVAL OF LITERATURE

No other writer has so well demonstrated the reasons why Italy, and not France, became the birthplace of the Renaissance as Gebhart has done in his *Les origines de la Renaissance en Italie.*

Much that relates to the revival of literature is to be found in the general histories of the several countries in which that revival took place. There are many excellent books for the study of Italian literature and the revival of learning in Italy. The early volumes of the *Storia letteraria d' Italia scritta da una società di professori* are scholarly and interesting. They are Giussani's *Letteratura romana;* Novati's *Origini della lingua;* Zingarelli's *Dante;* Volpi's *Il Trecento;* and Rossi's *Il Quattrocento.* Of great interest and value is Monnier's *Le Quattrocento;* and a more recent book, written with unusual charm and insight, is Hauvette's *Littérature italienne.* Other recent books that may be recommended are Rossi's *Storia della letteratura italiana;* Flamini's *Compendio di storia della letteratura italiana.* Useful still are the two older histories of Italian literature by Giudici and by De Sanctis, the latter having a distinct literary value. In German there are the two works by Bartoli and Gaspary, a part of the former having been translated into English; and two later works are those by Wilse-Persopo and by Casini. In English there are three brief books; Garnett's *History of Italian Literature;* Castle's *Italian Literature;* and Everett's *The Italian Poets Since Dante.* The last of these is especially valuable because it contains verse translations and its literary criticisms succeed unusually well in revealing the characteristic qualities of the various writers with which it deals. A larger book in English is Symonds's *Italian Literature,* vivid and full of color, written by a gifted and ardent lover of beauty who devoted himself under difficult circumstances to an intensive study of the Renaissance. There are good chapters in Symon and Bensusan's *The Renaissance and its Makers;* and Whitcomb's *Source Book of the Italian Renaissance* is a useful body of translations from Italian writers of this time.

A complete edition of Dante's works has been published by the Oxford University Press, *Tutte le Opere di Dante Aligheri.* There are two excellent translations of the *Commedia* into English prose, one by Norton and the other by Tozer; and two translations into English blank verse, one by Cary and the other by Longfellow, are to be commended. The *Vita Nuova* has been done into English by Norton and by Rossetti; and the *De monarchia* has been translated into our tongue by Church, by Wicksteed, and by Henry. An admirable introduction to the study of the great poet is Church's *Dante and other Essays.* Excellent, too, are Gardner's *Dante;* Dinsmore's *Teachings of Dante;* Dinsmore's *Aids to the Study of Dante;* Symonds's *Introduction to the Study of Dante;* Scartazzini's *A Companion to Dante;* Gardner's *Dante's Ten Heavens;* Gardner's *Dante and the Mystics;* Harris's *Spiritual Sense of Dante's Divina Commedia;* Moore's *Studies in Dante,* three volumes of scholarly essays by the editor of the Oxford edition of Dante's works that will be found particularly helpful in difficult passages; Rossetti's *A Shadow of*

*Dante,* a fine analysis of the great epic, and a study of the poet's life, by the daughter of the English poet; Wyld's *The Dread Inferno,* despite the fact that it deals only with the first part of the *Commedia,* is an exceedingly helpful preface to the entire poem. One of the most penetrating studies of Dante is to be found in Gebhart's *Italie Mystique;* and the same author's *Les origines de la Renaissance en Italie* contains passages that relate to all the early Italian writers of note.

Of the books in foreign languages that relate to Petrarch those by Koerting, De Sade, Badelli, Fracassetti, Domenico Rossetti, Mezières, and De Nolhac will be found helpful. One of De Nolhac's books, *Petrarch and the Ancient World,* has been put into English. And in English there are, among others, Hollway-Calthrop's *Petrarch,* written with intimate knowledge of the subject and in a lucid and alluring style; Robinson and Rolfe's *Petrarch the first Modern Scholar and Man of Letters,* which gives a vivid presentation of the conditions of the period of the early Renaissance in Italy; and Jerrold's *Francesco Petrarca, Poet and Humanist.*

In Italian there are lives of Boccaccio by Tiraboschi, Mazzuchelli, and Baldelli. In German there is one by Landau, and a much better one by Koerting. And in English, in addition to Symonds's *Giovanni Boccaccio as Man and Author,* there is a very satisfactory one by Hutton. Not to be overlooked is a fine essay on Boccaccio by Ker, in *Studies in European Literature* (*The Taylorian Lectures, 1889–99*). His relation to the revival of letters, as well as that of Petrarch, is treated in Voigt's *Die Wiederbelebung des classischen Alterthums,* and in Sandys's *History of Classical Scholarship.* A dependable translation of *The Decameron* is that by John Payne.

The authoritative modern edition of Chaucer's works is that edited by Skeat and published by the Clarendon Press. In *The Modern Reader's Chaucer* the complete works of the poet have been put into modern English by Tatlock and MacKaye. The question as to what works may rightly be regarded as Chaucer's is discussed in *The Chaucer Canon* by Skeat. Helpful criticism of Chaucer's work are to be found in *The Cambridge History of English Literature;* in Newcomer's *English Literature,* an eloquent little book that, in itself, is a fine piece of literature; in *Chaucer,* an admirable primer by Pollard; and, at greater length, in Lounsbury's *Studies in Chaucer.* Coulton's *Chaucer and his England* is especially valuable as an exposition of the social conditions in England at the end of the fourteenth century.

The revival of learning can be studied in the book by Voigt whose title we have just given, and in his *Enea Silvio und sein Zeitalter;* and in English in Symonds's *The Revival of Learning;* in the first volume of *The Cambridge Modern History;* in Woodward's *Studies in Education during the age of the Renaissance;* and in the scholarly *History of Classical Scholarship* by Sandys.

The second creative period in Italian literature and the development of humanism are treated in the histories of Italian literature already mentioned. To these should be added the lives of Lorenzo de' Medici by Roscoe, Armstrong, and Horsburgh, the last of which is an exceptionally useful book; and Pattison's *Leading Figures in European History,* which contains an essay on Lorenzo. See also Ross's *Lives of the Medici from their Letters.* A biography of Pico della Mirandola was written by his nephew and translated into English by Sir Thomas More; it was reprinted in 1890 with a prefatory study by Rigg. The charming and illuminating study of the young philosopher in Pater's *Renaissance in Italy* should not be overlooked. Boulting's *Æneas Silvius* is a recent study of one of the humanist Popes; and still another good study of Æneas Silvius is Ady's *Pius II, the humanist Pope.* The other Popes who were patrons of art and letters can be studied in any of the general histories and in the histories of the Papacy already mentioned. The Italian poems of Poliziano have been edited by Carducci; and his writings in prose and in Greek and Latin have been edited by Del Lungo. Translations from his works are to be found in Symonds's *Sketches and Studies in Italy.* The political and social background of all this artistic and literary activity is set forth in *The Cambridge Modern History;* in Villari's *Machiavelli and his Times;* in Capponi's *Storia della Republica di Firenze;* in Perrens's *La civilization florentine;* in Janitschek's *Die Gesellschaft der Renaissance in Italien;* in Hyett's *Florence;* in Gebhart's *Florence;* and in the other histories of the various Italian towns.

Humanism beyond the Alps is treated in *The Cambridge Modern History.* Extracts from original sources are given in Whitcomb's *Source Book of the German Renaissance.*

## CHAPTER VI

### THE REVIVAL OF ART

The architecture of the early Renaissance in Italy is described in Hamlin's brief *History of Architecture;* in Sturgis's *History of Architecture;* in Simpson's *A History of Architectural Development;* and in the scholarly but unsympathetic *Character of Renaissance Architecture* by Moore. Suggestive snatches of information are to be found in Peabody's delightful book *An Architect's Sketch Book.* Of great importance, one is almost tempted to say indispensable, is the chapter on "The Rise of the Renaissance" in Phillipps's *The Works of Man,* an illuminating book. Of the monographs on the three leading architects of the early Italian Renaissance the following are commended: Von Fabriczy's *Filippo Brunelleschi;* Mancini's *Vita di Alberti;* and Semper's *Donato Bramante.*

Cox's *Old Masters and New* contains an essay on the sculptors of this time; and Freeman's *Italian Sculpture of the Renaissance* is well adapted for a preliminary study of the subject. Other books that deal with the revival of sculpture in Italy are Symonds's *The Fine Arts;* Waters's *Italian Sculptors;* Bode's *Florentine Sculptors of the Renaissance;* and Balcarres's *The Evolution of Italian Sculpture.* An excellent book, to which we shall refer later on with enthusiasm, *Mornings with Masters of Art,* by Powers, contains a fine chapter on Donatello and another on Ghiberti. Written with the suavity that is characteristic of his style, Pater has devoted a chapter to Luca della Robbia in his *Renaissance in Italy.* The following books relate to individual sculptors: Cornelius's *Jacopo della Quercia;* Balcarres's *Donatello;* Meyer's *Donatello,* translated from the German; Cruttwell's *Donatello;* Cruttwell's *Luca and Andrea della Robbia and their Successors;* Reymond's *Les della Robbia;* and Marquand's *Luca della Robbia,* a masterly work that supersedes everything else on the subject.

The revised edition of Bryan's *Dictionary of Painters and Engravers,* which, unfortunately, is devoid of references, contains brief biographies of the painters, and criticisms of their art, with whom we have to deal here and in our two subsequent chapters devoted to art. A great deal of our information about the lives of the early Italian artists is obtained from Vasari (1511-71), whose great work *Delle Vite de' più eccellenti pittori, scultori, ed architettori* was first published in 1550. Modern research has disproved many of his biographical details; and his criticisms, remarkable as they are for a man of his time, seem somewhat thin when compared with those of our own time; but, with all this, the work remains a classic that must be consulted in any thorough study of the art of the Renaissance in Italy. There is a recent translation into English by De Vere. A German edition, by Frey, with the original text annotated with characteristic German completeness, is in course of publication and promises to render all previous editions obsolete. The recent edition of Crowe and Cavalcaselle's *History of Painting in Italy* by Langton Douglas is inaccurate here and there, and it is rather too polemical, but it contains much information that is very useful. Venturi's *Storia dell' Arte Italiana* is uneven in merit but valuable. Michel's *Histoire de l' Art* is sympathetic and discriminating; Symonds is at his best in his volume on *The Fine Arts;* Taine's *Philosophy of Art in Italy* is subtle and suggestive as to the influence of environment upon art; and Powers's *Mornings with Masters of Art* is one of the very best books with which to begin the study of Italian painting. Berenson's three books, *Florentine Painters of the Renaissance, Central Italian Painters of the Renaissance,* and *Venetian Painters of the Renaissance,* are the work of an original mind. Caffin's *How to Study Pictures* is a popular and useful introductory study; and MacFall's *A History of Painting* is the best of the recent general histories of the subject. Cole's *Old Italian Masters,* illustrated with wood-cuts that give an unusually faithful idea of the original paintings in whose presence they were made, is also an admirable book to begin with. Not to be overlooked is Hirn's *The Sacred Shrine,* a study of the poetry and art of the Catholic Church, which, though it relates very largely to the Middle Ages, has much of value for the understanding of the period of the Renaissance and Reformation. For the beginnings of Italian art no better introduction can be found than Gebhart's charming *Les origines de la Renaissance en Italie;* and for the social background of the time Janitschek's *Die Gesellschaft der Renaissance in Italien und die Kunst* is useful. From the flood of monographs on the individual painters of our period the following are selected: Perkins's *Giotto;* Douglas's *Giotto;* Yriarte's *Tommaso dei Guidi* (Masaccio); Douglas's *Fra Angelico;* Strutt's *Filippo Lippi;* Kristeller's *Mantegna;* Horne's *Botticelli,* the most important book upon its subject; Gebhart's *Botticelli;* Binyon's admirable study *The Art of Botticelli;* Oppé's excellently written and finely illustrated *Botticelli;* Cruttwell's *Signorelli;* Davies's *Ghirlandaio;* Hauvette's *Ghirlandajo,* in French; Williamson's *Perugino;* and Hutton's *Cities of Umbria,* which contains good chapters upon Umbrian art and Perugino. Botticelli's passionless painting is the subject of one of Pater's languorous chapters.

## CHAPTER VII

### THE REVIVAL OF SCIENCE

The childish conception of science in medieval Christendom is portrayed in the books written on the subject in that period. One of these is the *De naturis rerum* of Alexander of Neckam (1157-1217), an English schoolman and man of science who probably compiled his work about 1180. The most famous encyclopedia of the Middle Ages is the *Speculum Majus* of Vincent of Beauvais (1190?-1264?), a great compendium of all the knowledge of the time, which consists of four parts, the last being quite evidently the work of a later writer. The first part, the *Speculum Naturale,* is a summary of all the natural history known to Latin Christendom about the middle of the thirteenth century; the second part, the *Speculum Doctrinale,* deals with the mechanic arts as well as with the philosophy, logic, mathematics and inorganic science of the time; while the third part, the *Speculum Historiale,* is, as the name implies, a " mirror " of history. Langlois, in *La Connaissance de la Nature et du Monde au Moyen Age,* has reprinted six medieval writings, most of which deal with the physical environment of man, that help to afford us an idea of the scientific knowledge current in the thirteenth century.

There are two excellent books in English from which one may gather the medieval point of view and learn the slow and painful steps by which men rose out of it into the freer and more truthful attitude of our own time. They are White's *History of the Warfare of Science with Theology in Christendom;* and Taylor's *The Medieval Mind.* Somewhat out of date, but still useful, is Draper's *History of the Intellectual Development of Europe;* and his *History of the Conflict between Religion and Science.* The medieval attitude is given an able exposition in Von Eicken's *Geschichte und System der mittelalterlichen Weltanschauung.* Other books that deal in a general way with our topic are Hudson's *The Story of the Renaissance;* Berger's *Die Kulturaufgaben der Reformation;* and Allbutt's *Science and Medieval Thought.*

For the restoration of Aristotle one may consult the first two chapters of Douglas's *Pietro Pomponazzi;* Valois's *Guillaume d' Auvergne;* Jourdain's *Excursions historiques et philosophiques à travers le moyen âge;* Renan's *Averroès et l'Averroïsme;* and De Boer's *History of Philosophy in Islam.* The recovery of some of the lost books of Aristotle and its effect upon the thought and science of the time may, of course, be studied in the histories of philosophy. Good general histories of philosophy are those by Erdmann, Ueberweg, and Windelband; and good histories of philosophy in the Middle Ages are those by Hauréau, Stöckl, and Werner. To these may be added the history of materialism by Lange. There is a brief essay on Lull in Gebhart's *La Vieille Eglise.*

For the revival of research and of criticism in philosophy one may go to the article on " Petrarch and the beginning of modern Science," in the first volume of *The Yale Review,* by George Burton Adams; and to that on " Des progrès des sciences historiques en France depuis le 16e siècle," by Monod, in the first volume of the *Revue Historique.* And there are passages relevant to the same subject in Von Wegele's *Geschichte der deutschen Historiographie,* and in Bernheim's *Lehrbuch der historischen Methode.* In Langlois's *Manuel de bibliographie historique* one will find a general survey of the whole apparatus of historical research.

Much that relates to the revival of science is to be found in Rashdall's *The Universities of Europe in the Middle Ages,* now unfortunately out of print; in Lecky's *History of the Rise and Influence of Rationalism in Europe;* in Whewell's *History of the Inductive Sciences;* in Maugain's *Etude sur l'évolution intellectuelle de l'Italie;* and in White's *History of the Warfare of Science with Theology.* The best history of mathematics is Cantor's *Vorlesungen über Geschichte der Mathematik;* and a briefer one is Ball's *A Short History of Mathematics*. On astronomy there are two books by Delambre, *Histoire de l'astronomie au moyen âge,* and *Histoire de l'astronomie moderne.* In German there are Mädler's *Geschichte der Himmelskunde;* and Wolf's *Geschichte der Astronomie.* While in English one may turn to Berry's *History of Astronomy.* Not to be overlooked is Fahie's *Galileo.* In other sciences there are Cajori's *History of Physics;* Kopp's *Geschichte der Chemie;* Ladenburg's *Entwicklungsgeschichte de Chemie;* Meyer's *History of Chemistry;* Carus's *Geschichte der Zoologie;* and Sachs's *History of Botany.* There is no satisfactory history of anatomy, but a fairly complete summary is to be found in the first volume of *The Reference Handbook of Medical Sciences* (New York; 1900); and to this should be added the opening pages of Roth's *Versalius.* Osler's *Michael Servetus* contains useful information and valuable illustrations. Baas's *History of Medicine* may be recommended; and there are others by Daremberg, Häser and Park.

No satisfactory general history of inventions has yet been written, but much may be learned from the articles on the various inventions in the encyclopedias and from those upon the inventors. The best work on the book-making of the Middle Ages is Wattenbach's *Das Schriftwesen im Mittelalter;* and for the changes incident to the invention of printing one should read the first volume of Kapp's *Geschichte des deutschen Buchhandels.* Other books in German that deal at length and in a trustworthy manner with the subject are Hartwig's *Festschrift sum fünfhundertjährigen Geburtstag von Johann Gutenberg;* Schwenke's *Untersuchungen zur Geschichte des ersten Buchdrucks;* Börckel's *Gutenberg;* and Börckel's *Gutenberg und seine berühmten Nachfolger in ersten Jahrhundert der Typographie.* The best English history of the art of printing is De Vinne's *The Invention of Printing;* and a briefer one is Hoe's *A Short History of the Printing Press.* An able and interesting work that deals with the whole subject of book-making at the time of our study is Putnam's *Books and their makers during the Middle Ages.*

## CHAPTER VIII

### THE REVIVAL OF CONSCIENCE

It would be well at the outset of this study to obtain as correct an understanding as possible of the schoolmen's notion of *conscientia* and of *synderesis.* Perhaps the most convenient modern discussion of these medieval ideas is to be found in Gass's *Die Lehre vom Gewissen,* and in his *Geschichte der Christlichen Ethik.* For the insistence of medieval authorities upon implicit faith, and for the beginnings of the gradual return to reliance upon conscience, Reuter's *Geschichte der religiosen Aufklarung im Mittelalter* is still of value; but Hoffmann's *Die Lehre von der Fides Implicita* is indispensable. An admirable introduction to the subject of our entire study is the chapter on "Reform before the Reformation" in Beard's eloquent *The Reformation of the Sixteenth Century.*

For the first group of critics, the Goliardi, see, first of all, the collection of some of their songs published under the title of *Carmina Burana,* and those of them that were translated into English by John Addington Symonds in his little volume *Wine, Women, and Song.* These wandering students have been dealt with at some length in Haezner's *Goliardendichtung und die Satire;* and in Spiegel's *Die Vaganten und ihr "Orden."*

The final chapter in Gebhart's illuminating *L'Italie Mystique* is a penetrating discussion of Dante's attitude toward the religious and ethical questions of the time. References to the writings of Dante, to those of Petrarch, to those of Boccaccio, and to those of Chaucer, and to writings about them, are given in our list of books for the chapter on the revival of literature. For Valla, the most systematic of all the critics, see Mancini's *Vita di Lorenzo Valla;* and Wolff's *Lorenzo Valla.* Much that is pertinent to our topic is to be found in the histories of philosophy and the histories of literature; and Owen's *The Skeptics of the Italian Renaissance* is particularly useful.

The monastic, papal, and conciliar reformers are treated in the church histories and in the histories of the Papacy, especially those by Creighton and Pastor. The articles on the individual reformers in the encyclopedias should be consulted. The councils are dealt with in Von Hefele's *Conciliengeschichte;* in Du Bose's *The Ecumenical Councils;* in Harnack's *History of Dogma;* and in Loofs's *Leitfaden der Dogmengeschichte.* And for the papal reformers see especially Rocquain's *La cour de Rome et l'esprit de réform avant Luther.*

For the biblical reformers one may read, in addition to the church histories, Ullmann's *Reformers before the Reformation;* and Hahn's *Geschichte der Ketzer im Mittelalter.* The Waldenses are treated in Schmidt's *Histoire des Cathares;* Dieckhoff's *Die Waldenser im Mittelalter;* Preger's *Beiträge zur Geschichte der Waldesier;* Cantù's *Gli Eretici in Italia;* Comba's *Storia della Riforma in Italia;* Tocco's *L'Eresia nel medio evo;* and in Lea's monumental *History of the Inquisition of the Middle Ages.* The best work on the followers of Wycliffe is Gairdner's *Lollardy and the Reformation in England.* For the individual biblical reformers see Lechler's *Johann von Wiclif;* the masterly study prefixed to Shirley's edition of the *Fasciculi Zizaniorum;* Trevelyan's *England in the Age of Wycliffe;* Loserth's *Hus and Wiclif;* Lützow's *The Life and Times of John Hus;* and Schaff's *John Hus.*

The mystics may be studied in the histories of philosophy, in the church histories, and in the histories of dogma. General works relating to them are Görres's *Die christliche Mystik;* Preger's *Geschichte der deutschen Mystiker;* Jones's *Studies in Mystical Religion;* Steiner's *Mystics of the Renaissance;* and Inge's *Christian Mysticism.* Joachim of Flora and *The Everlasting Gospel* have been described with great sympathy and notable synthetic power in Gebhart's *L'Italie Mystique;* and for additional reading one may turn to the essay by Renan on "Joachim de Flora et l'Évangile éternel" in his *Nouvelles études d'histoire religieuse;* to another by Fournier on "Joachim de Flora, ses doctrines, son influence" that, in 1900, was published in the *Revue des questiones historiques;* to the fourth and twenty-sixth chapters of Sedgwick's *Italy in the Thirteenth Century;* to Sabatier's *Franciscan Studies,* which has two chapters on the great Calabrian mystic; and also to the third volume of Lea's *Inquisition in the Middle Ages.* The mystical friars are described in Muzzey's scholarly little book *The Spiritual Franciscans.* For the German mystics see Landauer's *Meister Eckharts mystiche Schriften;* Delacroix's *Le Mysticisme spéculatif en Allemagne au XIVe siècle;* Bihlmeyer's *Deutsche Schriften* (by Suso); Preger's *Briefe Heinrich Susos;* Jäger's *Heinrich Seuse aus Schwaben;* the edition of Tauler's sermons for festivals by Hutton published under the title of *The Inner Way;* Schmidt's *Die Gottesfreunde;* Jundt's *Les amis de Dieu;* Altmeyer's *Les précurseurs de la Réforme aux Pays-Bas;* Maeterlinck's *Ruysbroek and the Mystics;* and

Underhill's *Ruysbroek.* There is a Catholic life of Thomas à Kempis by Cruise; and a recent Protestant one, *Thomas à Kempis, his Age and Book,* written with appreciation of the saintly recluse and his age, by Montmorency. There are many translations and editions of *The Imitation of Christ,* and, naturally, they vary very greatly in merit. A good one is that by Bigg, to which is prefixed an excellent introduction that has been reprinted in his *Wayside Sketches in Ecclesiastical History.* For the French mystics see Chevallier's *Histoire de Saint Bernard;* Eales's *Saint Bernard;* Storrs's *Bernard of Clairvaux;* D'Haussonville's *Saint Bernard;* Dupin's *Gersoniana,* which includes a life of the Parisian scholar, statesman, and mystic, and is prefixed to an edition of his works; Tschackert's *Peter von Ailli;* Salembier's *Petrus de Alliaco;* and De Wulf's *Histoire de la philosophie médiévale.* The English mystics may be studied in Inge's *Studies of English Mystics.* The subject of mysticism itself is well discussed in three books by Underhill, *Mysticism, Practical Mysticism,* and *The Mystic Way.* Boutroux's *Psychologie du Mysticisme* is very suggestive.

## CHAPTER IX

### THE AGE OF DISCOVERY

The first chapter of the first volume of *The Cambridge Modern History* is a detailed account of the geographical discoveries of the era of the Renaissance; and to the volume is appended a comprehensive bibliography of the subject. The other general histories, the histories of geography and of commerce, the histories of the countries that were discovered at this time, and the articles on the different continents and countries in the encyclopedias contain information relating to the age of discovery in convenient form. Among the more important books dealing with the subject are Beazley's *The Dawn of Modern Geography,* altogether the best work upon the subject; Brown's *The Story of Africa and its Explorers;* Payne's *History of the New World called America;* Beazley's *Prince Henry the Navigator;* Mees's *Henri le Navigateur;* Mees's *Histoire de la découverte des îles Açores;* Jayne's *Vasco da Gama and his Successors;* Ravenstein's *Vasco da Gama's First Voyage,* a translation into English, with notes, of a journal written by one of the great sailor's subordinates; *Calcoen [Calicut], a Dutch Narrative of the Second Voyage of Da Gama,* written by an unknown seaman of the voyage and translated into English; Stephens's *Life of Albuquerque;* Winsor's *Christopher Columbus;* Gaffarel's *Histoire de la découverte de l'Amerique;* Elton's *Career of Columbus;* Pattison's *Leading Figures in European History;* Thatcher's *Christopher Columbus;* Young's *Christopher Columbus and the New World of his Discovery;* Guillemard's *Life of Magellan;* Pigafetta's *Magellan's Voyage around the World,* translated and edited by Robertson; Hudson's *The Story of the Renaissance;* Symon and Bensusan's *The Renaissance;* Fiske's *The Discovery of America;* Helps's *The Spanish Conquest in America;* Kretschmer's *Die Entdeckung Amerikas;* and the twenty-fifth chapter of Walsh's *The Thirteenth Century.*

Accounts of journeys to the eastern lands by western travelers, among them Carpini and Rubruquis, are to be found in the publications of the Hakluyt Society. Richard Hakluyt (1553?–1616) was a British geographer who collected and published narratives of journeys and discoveries. The Society bearing his name was founded in 1846 for the purpose of printing rare and unpublished voyages and travels, and its publications, together with those it has "fathered," number more than one hundred and fifty volumes.

## CHAPTER X

### POLITICAL AFFAIRS AT THE OPENING OF THE PROTESTANT REVOLUTION

For Louis XI of France see Lavisse's *Histoire de France,* in which there is an admirable summary by Charles Petit-Dutaillis. See also Macdonald's *A History of France;* Charavay and Vaesen's *Lettres de Louis XI;* Willert's *The Reign of Louis XI;* and Hare's *The Life of Louis XI.*

The story of Charles the Bold is narrated in De Vausse's *Histoire des ducs de Bourgogne;* Fredericq's *Le rôle des ducs de Bourgogne dans les Pay-Bas;* De la Marche's *Mémoires;* Kirk's *Charles the Bold;* and Putnam's *Charles the Bold.*

The dreams and the deeds of the gifted Maximilian I are told in Watson's *Maximilian I;* Ulmann's *Kaiser Maximilian I;* Schulte's *Kaiser Maximilian I;* Hare's *Maximilian the Dreamer;* Kaser's *Deutsche Geschichte zur Zeit Maximilians I,* very useful for the social conditions of the Germanic lands at this time; and, in a brief but excellent manner, Von Bezold's *Staat und Gesellschaft des Reformationszeitalters.*

The building of Spain may be studied in Lafuente's history of Spain, edited by Valera; in Altamira's *Historia de España y de la civilización española;* in Prescott's *Ferdinand and Isabella;* and in De Nervo's *Isabella the Catholic,* which has been translated into English by Temple-West.

For the important Popes of this period see Pastor, Creighton, and Gregorovius; also Gregorovius's *Lucrezia Borgia;* and Villari's *Machiavelli.*

The first French invasion of Italy is described in Delaborde's *Expedition de Charles VIII en Italie;* and its significance is well stated in Robinson's *The End of the Middle Ages.* See also for all the topics of our chapter Lodge's *The Close of the Middle Ages;* and Johnson's *Europe in the Sixteenth Century.*

The political activity of Savonarola and his tragic end are dealt with in the histories of the Papacy. See also Pastor's *Zur Beurteilung Savonarolas;* Lucas's *Girolamo Savonarola;* and Schnitzer's *Quellen und Forschungen zur Geschichte Savonarolas.* Villari's *Studies* contains an essay on the reforming friar.

For Louis XII and his foreign and domestic policy turn to the chapter by Lemonnier on "Les Guerres d'Italie" in Lavisse; to Lacroix and Maulde-la-Clavière's *Louis XII;* and to Maulde-la-Clavière's *Les origines de la révolution française au commencement du 16ᵉ siècle.*

For France under Francis I, and, incidentally, that mirror of chivalry at its best, the Chevalier Bayard, *le chevalier sans peur et sans reproche,* see the general histories, Lavisse, and Macdonald, and also a biographical study of Francis I by Bourrilly in the fourth volume of the *Revue d'histoire moderne et contemporaine.*

Of general use for the topics of our chapter are the second and fifteenth chapters of Acton's *Historical Essays;* and several chapters of Symon and Bensusan's *Renaissance.*

## CHAPTER XI

### HUMANISM AND HERESY

The beginnings of English humanism are described in the second and third volumes of the monumental *Cambridge History of English Literature,* where exhaustive bibliographies will be found. Other histories of English literature are Courthope's *History of English Poetry;* Jusserand's *Literary History of the English People;* and Seccombe and Allen's *The Age of Shakespeare.* See also Einstein's *The Italian Renaissance in England,* a work of considerable charm as well as pronounced scholarship; Harrison's *Platonism in Elizabethan Poetry;* Lee's *Elizabethan Sonnets;* Herford's *Literary Relations of England and Germany in the Sixteenth Century;* Underhill's *Spanish Literature in the England of the Tudors;* Spingarn's *History of Literary Criticism in the Renaissance;* Sandys's *History of Classical Scholarship;* and Seebohm's *The Oxford Reformers.* To the leading English humanists (Grocyn, Linacre, Colet, and More) articles in *The Dictionary of National Biography* are devoted, each of which has a list of references. For More see the chapter that deals with him in Lee's *Great Englishmen of the Sixteenth Century;* and the two books by Bridgett and by Hutton, both of which bear the same title, *The Life and Writings of Sir Thomas More.* A fine chapter on "The Dawn of the English Renaissance" is to be found in Fisher's *History of England from the Accession of Henry VII to the Death of Henry VIII;* and the chapter on "The Birth of the Reformation" in Innes's *England under the Tudors* is pertinent. One should not overlook the gracious pages of Green, both in his longer and his shorter *History of the English People.*

An excellent introduction to the study of French humanism and its connections with heresy is the chapter by Buisson in the fourth volume of the *Histoire Générale.* See also the great history by Lavisse. Then turn to the article "De l'humanisme et de la reforme en France" by Henri Hauser in the sixty-fourth volume of the *Revue historique;* to the article by Paquier on "L'université de Paris et l'humanisme au début du 16e siècle" in the sixty-fourth and sixty-fifth volumes of the *Revue des questions historiques;* and to the article by Imbart de la Tour on "Renaissance et Réforme; la Religion des Humanistes" in the *Compte Rendu de l'Académie des Sciences Morales et Politiques,* June, 1914. Much valuable matter is to be found in Petit de Julleville's *Histoire de la langue et de la littérature françaises.* Briefer histories of French literature are Saintsbury's *A Short History of French Literature;* and Dowden's *French Literature.* Two admirable books by a master of the subject are Tilley's *Literature of the French Renaissance;* and his *Rabelais.* Gebhart's charming *Rabelais* contains a fine chapter on the religion of that original thinker; Stapfer's book on Rabelais is by no means antiquated; and one may turn to a number of valuable articles on the far-seeing Frenchman in the *Revue des études Rabelaisiennes* which first appeared in 1903; and also to the essay on Rabelais in Faguet's *Seizième Siècle.* Delaruelle's *Etudes sur l'humanisme* is a book of merit. For Dolet see the two books with the same title, *Etienne Dolet,* by Christie and Galtier, the first in English and the second in French. The opening chapters of Buisson's masterly monograph *Sébastien Castellion* and parts of Doumergue's great work on Calvin are of much importance in the study of French humanism.

The Spanish humanists are at least touched upon in the histories of

Spain already mentioned; and one may find something relating to them in the histories of Spanish literature, especially Ticknor's *History of Spanish Literature*. Briefer books are, in German, Baist's *Die Spanische Litteratur;* Becker's *Geschichte de Spanischen Literatur;* and Beer's *Spanische Literaturgeschichte;* in French, the slight *Précis d'histoire de la littérature espanole* by Mérimée; and, in English, Fitzmaurice-Kelly's *History of Spanish Literature* and his *Chapters on Spanish Literature*. Of books devoted to individual humanists there are, among others, Hefele's *Ximenez*, translated from the German; Boehmer's *Spanish Reformers;* Wiffen's *Life and Writings of Juan Valdés;* San Martin's *Louis Vives y la filosofia del renacimiento;* Woodward's *Studies in Education*, which is also useful for the study of German and English humanism; and Hoppe's *Die Psychologie von Juan Louis Vives*. With one or two slight exceptions all the Spanish humanists who were perceptibly inclined toward heresy are treated in Menendez-Pelayo's *Los Heterodoxos Españoles*. Of prime importance is Lea's *History of the Inquisition of Spain;* and not without value for our purpose is his *History of the Inquisition in the Spanish Dependencies;* while one may still turn with profit to his *Chapters from the religious history of Spain,* which was the forerunner of his greater book.

One may well begin the study of German humanism in histories that relate to the Empire at this time, two of which are Von Kraus's *Deutsche Geschichte im Ausgange des Mittelalters;* and Von Bezold's *Geschichte der deutschen Reformation*. Then it would be well to take up books that deal specifically with literary men and with literature; and to these Nollen's *A Chronological and Practical Bibliography of Modern German Literature* is a guide. One of the best of these is Geiger's *Renaissance und Humanismus in Italien und Deutschland;* and others are Hagen's *Deutschlands religiöse und literarische Verhältnisse im Reformationszeitalter;* Paulsen's *Geschichte des gelehrten Unterrichts;* Paulsen's *German Education, Past and Present;* and Borinski's *Geschichte der deutschen Literatur seit dem Ausgange des Mittelalters*. Of exceeding value are Berger's *Die Kulturaufgaben der Reformation,* and Dilthey's essays on *Weltanschauung und Analyse des Menschen seit Renaissance und Reformation,* now happily published in book form as the second volume of his *Gesammelte Schriften*. And, written in ingratiating style with fine sympathy and scholarship, one of the chapters in Beard's *Reformation of the Sixteenth Century* forms an admirable survey of the subject in English. Whitcomb's *Literary Source Book of the German Renaissance* will supply the student with translations into English from the writings of a number of the German humanists. Biographies of all the leading German humanists are to be found, of course, in the indispensable *Allgemeine Deutsche Biographie*. In Stokes's edition of the *Epistolae Obscurorum Virorum* the Latin text and a surprisingly good translation into English are given. See, too, with regard to these famous " letters " Brecht's *Die Verfasser der Epistolae Obscurorum Virorum*. Strauss's *Ulrich von Hutten,* translated from the German, may still be read with profit as well as pleasure. A briefer and more recent account is Deckert's *Ulrich von Huttens Leben und Wirken*. For the study of Erasmus a useful book is Meyer's *Etude critique sur les relations d'Erasme et de Luther*. One may find several of the books by the prince of humanists translated into English; and in Nichols's *The Epistles of Erasmus* some of his letters are done into our language. In the *Letters of Erasmus,* edited by Allen, all of the great humanist's letters that are to be obtained are in course of publication by the Oxford University Press. Books on Erasmus in English have been written by Froude,

Emerton, Allen, and Capey. In Hudson's *Story of the Renaissance* there are good pages for the study of humanism and its connections with heresy; and see, too, the introduction to Vedder's *Reformation in Germany*.

## CHAPTER XII

### THE GERMAN REVOLT FROM ROME

Of recent general histories in English of the Protestant Revolution, or, as it is more commonly called, the Protestant Reformation, the best is Lindsay's *A History of the Reformation;* and another good one is Vedder's *The Reformation in Germany*. Still another recent book is Plummer's *The Continental Reformation*. The first three volumes of *The Cambridge Modern History* relate to the subject, and in them may be found extensive bibliographies. The chapters that have to do with Luther, in the *Cambridge History*, are to be found in the second volume. They are the work of Professor Albert Frederick Pollard, of the University of London, one of the finest scholars working in the field of history to-day. Not to be overlooked is Von Ranke's *History of the Reformation,* the work of a pioneer in scientific history. Creighton's *History of the Papacy* has much to say of the German revolt. In English, too, are to be found translations of Pastor's *History of the Papacy,* not yet completed, the most scholarly presentation of the Catholic view of this much mooted movement; and Janssen's *History of the German People at the Close of the Middle Ages,* which abounds in information, and which, here and there, is cleverly polemical. Harnack's great *History of Dogma* may also be read in English; and there is an admirable survey, comprehensive in its scope and authentic in the mastery of its material, by Professor James Harvey Robinson in the eleventh edition of the *Britannica*. Among the older books in English one can do no better than to turn to Beard's eloquent and illuminating *The Reformation of the Sixteenth Century,* and to the excellent little *Era of the Protestant Revolution* by Seebohm. Of the many books in German the best introduction to the subject is Berger's *Die Kulturaufgaben der Reformation;* and a very satisfactory general history is Von Bezold's *Geschichte der deutschen Reformation*.

The best book in English that relates specifically to Luther is Beard's *Martin Luther,* of which, unfortunately, only the first volume was written; and the latest one, based very carefully upon the writings of the great heretical friar, is that by Preserved Smith, *The Life and Letters of Martin Luther*. Interesting and well illustrated is McGiffert's *Martin Luther*. The standard books in German are Köstlin's *Martin Luther, sein Leben und seine Schriften;* Kolde's *Martin Luther;* Boehmer's *Luther im Lichte der Neueren Forschungen;* Berger's *Martin Luther in kulturgeschichtlicher Darstellung,* only two volumes of which, bringing the story down to 1532, have as yet been published; and Friedrich von Bezold's able and interesting *Staat und Gesellschaft des Reformationszeitalters*. For a vigorous exposition of Luther and his work by a Catholic scholar see Denifle's *Luther und Lutherthum;* and see, too, Grisar's *Luther,* which has been translated into English. Luther's three great pamphlets of 1517-20 are to be found in English in Wace and Buchheim's *First Principles of the Reformation;* and other documents of the time are contained in Kidd's *Documents illustrative of the Continental Reformation;* and in Smith's *Luther's Correspondence and other Contemporary Letters*.

## CHAPTER XIII

### THE SOCIAL REVOLUTION

The social theories of the Waldenses are described in the works relating to these interesting heretics, such as Preger's *Beiträge zur Geschichte der Waldesier;* Comba's *Histoire des Vaudois d'Italie;* Tocco's *L'Eresia nel medio evo;* and Hahn's *Geschichte der neumanichäischen Ketzer.* See also Lea's *Inquisition of the Middle Ages.*

A good brief account of the English peasant revolt is to be found in Oman's *History of England from the Accession of Richard II to the Death of Richard III;* another in Vickers's *England in the Later Middle Ages;* and a fuller one in Oman's *The Great Revolt of 1381.* See also Réville's *Le Soulèvement des travailleurs d'Angleterre en 1381;* Trevelyan's *England in the Age of Wycliffe;* and the article by Cronin in the twenty-second volume of *The English Historical Review* on "The Twelve Conclusions of the Lollards."

The story of the social revolution in Germanic lands is given briefly in Von Bezold's *Geschichte der deutschen Reformation;* and in his *Staat und Gesellschaft des Reformationszeitalters;* and, at greater length, in Gothein's *Politische und religiöse Volksbewegungen vor der Reformation;* Zöllner's *Zur Vorgeschichte des Bauernkrieges;* Vogt's *Die Vorgeschichte des Bauernkrieges;* Zimmermann's *Geschichte des grossen Bauernkriegs;* Schapiro's *Social Reform and the Reformation;* Bax's *The Peasants' War in Germany;* Bax's *Social Side of the Reformation in Germany;* Bax's *German Society at the Close of the Middle Ages;* Kautsky's *Communism in Central Europe at the time of the Reformation.* See also for brief treatments of the subject Vedder's *Reformation in Germany;* and the second volume of *The Cambridge Modern History,* where, too, there is a bibliography.

Among the biographies that bear upon this study are Merx's *Thomas Münzer und Heinrich Pfeiffer;* Barge's *Andreas Bodenstein von Karlstadt;* Strauss's *Ulrich von Hutten;* and Deckert's *Ulrich von Huttens Leben und Wirken.*

The influence of the almanac-makers upon the social revolution may be studied in Friedrich's *Astrologie und Reformation.*

## CHAPTER XIV

### PROTESTANTISM AND THE BALANCE OF POWER

The general histories, the church histories, the histories of the Germanic Empire, and the histories of the Reformation, and the histories of France, enumerated in the references for the four chapters immediately preceding this one contain abundant information relating to this subject. A good brief book is Johnson's *Europe in the Sixteenth Century.* Among the books that relate more specifically to the topic are Robertson's *History of the Emperor Charles V,* a classic work, which should be supplemented by Armstrong's *The Emperor Charles V;* Mignet's *Rivalité de François I et de Charles-quint;* Coignet's *François I;* Paris's *Etudes sur François I;* De Meaux's *La réforme et la politique française en Europe;* and Maurenbrecher's *Karl V und die deutschen Protestanten.* Original sources relating to the growth and organization of Lutheranism are contained in Kidd's *Documents illustrative of the Continental Reformation.*

## CHAPTER XV

### THE SWISS REVOLT FROM ROME

One of the best recent general histories of Switzerland is Dierauer's *Geschichte der schweizerischen Eidgenossenschaft*, which, having reached the year 1648, is still in course of publication. Briefer books are Van Muyden's *Histoire de la nation suisse;* McCrackan's *The Rise of the Swiss Republic;* and Vulliéty's *La Suisse à travers les âges,* the last of which deals with the industrial and social aspects of the history of the country.

The *Zeitschrift für Schweizerische Kirchengeschichte* contains much material relating to the ecclesiastical history of the Confederation; and a book devoted to the subject is Ruchat's *Histoire de la Réformation de la Suisse.* The chapter devoted to the subject in the second volume of *The Cambridge Modern History* is disappointing, but there is a good bibliography appended. The second volume of Fleischlin's *Studien und Beiträge zur schweizerische Kirchengeschichte* comes down to 1520 and is written from a Catholic point of view; and another Catholic book is Mayer's *Das Conzil von Trent und die Gegenreformation in der Schweiz.* A Protestant book is Bloesch's *Geschichte der schweizerisch-reformierten Kirchen;* and another is Hadorn's *Kirchengeschichte der reformierten Schweiz.*

There are biographies of Zwingli by Hottinger, Christoffel, and Grob, translated into English; and one, *Huldreich Zwingli,* written in English by Jackson. The best exposition of Zwingli's religious views, as far as the knowledge of the present writer extends, is that to be found in the second volume of Dilthey's *Gesammelte Schriften,* a book that becomes increasingly valuable to us from now on to the last of our chapters. A body of Zwingli's writings translated into English will be found in Jackson's *Selected Works of Huldreich Zwingli;* and for other original source material see Kidd's *Documents illustrative of the Continental Reformation.*

## CHAPTER XVI

### THE FRENCH REVOLT FROM ROME

The pertinent chapters in Lavisse and Rambaud's *Histoire Générale,* in Lavisse's *Histoire de France;* and in Macdonald's *History of France,* may be recommended to the reader to begin with. In the first two of these books, as well as in the second volume of *The Cambridge Modern History,* and in Hauser's *Les Sources de l'Histoire de France,* extensive bibliographies of the subject will be found. The other general histories, the histories of France, and the ecclesiastical histories, that we have previously mentioned, deal with the subject; as does Jervis's *History of the Church of France.* And of books that deal only with the French revolt there are Hauser's *Etudes sur la Réforme Française;* Browning's *History of the Huguenots;* Smedley's *History of the Reformed Religion in rrance;* Baird's *The Rise of the Huguenots,* strongly biased in favor of the theological seceders; Puaux's *Histoire de la Réformation française;* Polenz's *Geschichte des französichen Calvinismus;* Imbart de la Tour's *Les origines de la Réforme;* and, most important of all, the *Bulletin de la societé d'histoire du protestantisme française.*

Biographies of some of the early French Protestants are to be found in

Bordier's revised, but incomplete, edition of Haag's *La France protestante*. Special biographical studies are the old one of Lefèvre of Etaples by Graf; Schmidt's *Etudes sur Farel;* Bevan's *William Farel;* Morley's *Clément Marot;* and the essay on Marot in Faguet's *Seizième Siècle*.

For Geneva use Roget's *Histoire du peuple de Genève;* Gaberel's *Histoire de l' église de Genève;* Borgeaud's *Histoire de l'université de Genève;* Denkinger's *Histoire populaire du canton de Genève;* Gautier's *Histoire de Genève;* Perrin's *Les Vieux Quartiers de Genève;* and the scholarly article, with numerous references in the footnotes, by Foster in the eighth volume of *The American Historical Review*.

The standard edition of Calvin's works is that by the five Strasburg scholars (Baum, Cunitz, Reuss, Lobstein, and Erichson) in fifty-nine volumes, the last of which contains a very full bibliography. Most of the writings have been published in English, at Edinburgh, by The Calvin Translation Society. And for other original sources see Kidd's *Documents illustrative of the Continental Reformation*. Three biographies of Calvin in English may be recommended. They are the one by Dyer; a more recent one, *John Calvin,* an admirable book, by Walker; and *John Calvin,* by Reyburn. In German there is Kampschulte's *Johann Calvin, seine Kirche und sein Staat in Genf,* a scholarly and fair work of considerable value. In French the outstanding work is Doumergue's great work, elaborately illustrated, *Jean Calvin; les hommes et les choses de son temps*. But the best study of his early years is still Lefranc's *La Jeunesse de Calvin*. Two excellent books on the government of Geneva during Calvin's régime are Choisy's *La Théocratie à Genève au temps de Calvin;* and his *L'Etat chrétien Calviniste à Genève au temps de Théodore de Bèze*. One of the best of the many articles on Calvin is that by Mark Pattison to be found in his *Essays* and also in the fifty-ninth volume of *The Living Age*. Another brief essay is that by Gebhart in his *La Vieille Eglise;* and still another is the one in Faguet's *Seizième Siècle*.

The copious literature relating to Servetus is listed quite fully in Linde's *Michael Servet*. And of books that deal with him as a religious thinker and as a man the following are recommended. In English, Willis's *Servetus and Calvin;* Porter's *Servetus and Calvin;* in German, Tollin's *Characterbild M. Servets;* and, in Spanish, the second volume of Menendez-Pelayo's *Los Heterodoxos Españoles*. For the great apostle of tolerance see Buisson's admirable monograph *Sébastien Castellion,* which contains a bibliography useful for our entire chapter; and Giran's *Sébastien Castellion et la Réforme Calviniste*.

## CHAPTER XVII

### REVOLT IN THE NORTH AND HERESY IN THE SOUTH

For a list of references for the first part of this study see the bibliography for the seventeenth chapter of the second volume of *The Cambridge Modern History;* and for one dealing with the second part see the bibliographies for the twelfth and eighteenth chapters of the same volume.

The revolt of Denmark from the ancestral Church may be traced in *Danmark's Riges Historie;* in Bain's *Scandinavia,* which, as the title implies, deals also with the other Scandinavian countries; in Weitemeyer's *Denmark;* and in Schäfer's *Geschichte von Dänemark*. In each of these books a bibliography will be found. For Norway see Wilson's *History of Church and State in Norway.* Something of our topic may be learned from Nyström's *Sveriges politiska historia;* and much more from Butler's *The Reformation in Sweden;* and from Watson's *The Swedish Revolution under Gustavus Vasa.* Original sources relating to Protestantism in Scandinavia are to be found in Kidd's *Documents illustrative of the Continental Reformation.*

Protestantism in Prussia may be studied in Prutz's *Preussische Geschichte;* in Lohmeyer's *Herzog Albrecht von Preussen;* and, to much better advantage, in Tschackert's *Herzog Albrect von Preussen als reformatorische Personlichkeit;* and in Plum's *The Teutonic Order and its Secularization.*

For the beginnings of Protestantism in the other Baltic lands see Schiemann's *Russland, Polen und Livland;* Seraphim's *Geschichte Livlands, Esthlands, und Kurlands;* Seraphim's *Geschichte von Livland;* and Schybergson's *Geschichte Finnlands.*

Something of the story of Protestantism in Poland and Lithuania may be gathered from Sokolowski's *History of Poland;* and Darowski's *Bona Sforza;* and much more may be learned in the *Historia reformationis polonicae* of Lubieniecius (Lubienski); in Krasinski's *Reformation in Poland;* in Dalton's *John a Lasco,* an English translation of the first part of a German book; in the article on Laski in *The Dictionary of National Biography;* in Pascal's *Jean de Lasco;* and in Bukowski's *History of the Reformation in Poland,* which is available only in Polish.

For Hungary see the references to histories of that country given in the list for our twenty-eighth chapter; and see also the references that relate to the Socini which are included in the list for chapter eighteen.

For the general attitude of Italy at the time of the Renaissance see Burckhardt's *History of the Civilization of the Renaissance in Italy;* the introduction to the fifth volume of the English translation of Pastor's *History of the Popes;* Owen's *Skeptics of the Italian Renaissance;* Voigt's *Die Wiederbelebung des classischen Alterthums;* Dejob's *La Foi Religieuse en Italie au Quatorzième Siècle;* and Barzelotti's *Italia mistica e Italia pagana.*

Bembo and the trend toward paganism may be studied in Casa's *Vita di Bembo;* and in the histories of Italian literature. For Pomponazzi and the trend toward rationalism see the histories of philosophy; Benn's *History of Rationalism;* and Douglas's *Philosophy and Psychology of Pietro Pomponazzi.*

The proceedings and influence of the Fifth Lateran Council and the reforms of Adrian VI are described in the church histories and the histories of the Popes, in Hefele-Hergenröther's *Conciliengeschichte,* and in Gregorovius's *Rome in the Middle Ages.*

In the ecclesiastical and papal histories one may study the beginnings of Catholic reform in Italy. For this, and for all the subsequent topics of our chapter, see the twelfth and the eighteenth chapters, with their bibliographies, of the second volume of *The Cambridge Modern History.* For the newer monastic orders see the articles on them, each with a list of references in Heimbucher's *Orden und Kongregationen;* in *The Catholic Encyclopædia;* and in Herzog-Hauck's *Realencyklopädie.* In the church and papal histories, too, one will find the story of the mediating reformers; and in such books as Maurenbrecher's *Die Katholische Reformation;* Braun's *Cardinal Gasparo Contarini;* and Pasolini's *Adriano VI.*

The out-cropping of Protestant ideas in Italy and their penetration into the peninsula from other lands may be studied in two old books, Gerdes's

*Specimen Italiae reformatae,* and M'Crie's *History of the progress and suppression of the Reformation in Italy,* that still have some value; and in such later books as Comba's *Storia della riforma in Italie;* Comba's *I nostri protestanti;* Cantù's *Gli Eretici d'Italia;* Jerrold's *Vittoria Colonna;* Hare's *Men and Women of the Italian Reformation;* and Lea's *History of the Inquisition in the Spanish Dependencies.* There is no satisfactory history of the revived Inquisition, nor can there be one until the archives of that terrible institution are opened to the historical scholar. But see Buschbell's *Reformation und Inquisition in Italien,* and the passages in Pastor's *History of the Popes* that relate to Paul III and Paul IV.

Nearly all the books relating to Spanish humanism mentioned in the references for our eleventh chapter will be found useful for the study of Spanish Protestantism. The greatest work on the subject is Lea's *History of the Inquisition of Spain;* but see also his *Chapters from the Religious History of Spain.* Interesting articles by Reinach on Lea's great work were published in 1906–08 in the *Revue Critique.* A far slighter book, but of some use in our present study, is Sabatini's *Torquemada and the Spanish Inquisition.* There are two slight but attractive essays on Saint Teresa in Gebhart's *La Vieille Eglise.* More important works on this great mystic are the *Life* edited by Graham; Whyte's *Santa Teresa;* Hello's *Studies in Saintship;* Joly's excellent *Saint Teresa;* and Colvill's *Saint Teresa of Spain.*

## CHAPTER XVIII

### THE RESULTS OF THE PROTESTANT REVOLUTION

Summaries of the results of the Revolution, differing from each other as widely as the points of view of their authors, are to be found in most of the church histories and in the histories of the Reformation. Of the latter, the more important recent ones are Lindsay's *History of the Reformation;* Von Bezold's *Geschichte der deutschen Reformation;* Troeltsch's *Protestantisches Christentum und Kirche der Neuzeit;* and, best of all for our present purpose, Beard's admirable book, *The Reformation of the Sixteenth Century in its Relation to Modern Thought and Knowledge.* See also the articles on the Reformation in the various encyclopedias. The social and economic results are clearly outlined in Seebohm's *The Era of the Protestant Revolution;* the place of the Revolution in the development of Christianity is satisfactorily indicated in Pünjer's *History of the Christian Philosophy of Religion;* and its part in the history of civilization is admirably set forth by Laurent in his *La Réforme,* which is one of the volumes of his *Etudes sur l'histoire de l'humanité.* Not to be overlooked is the brief but effective statement (pages 117–18) in Robinson's *The New History;* and also that (pages 121–26) in Hudson's *Story of the Renaissance.* There are, too, pertinent pages in Lecky's *Rationalism in Europe.* There is, of course, a great mass of literature from each of the two great camps of western Christendom upon this mooted subject. It may suffice to mention, from the Catholic side, Döllinger's *Die Reformation;* Balmès's *European Civilization; Protestantism and Catholicity Compared;* Janssen's *History of the German People at the End of the Middle Ages;* Baudrillart's *The Catholic Church, the Renaissance, and Protestantism;* and the fifth chapter of Acton's *History of Freedom;* and, from the Protestant side, Carlyle's essay on "The Hero as Priest" in his *Heroes and Hero-Worship;* and Mead's *Martin Luther.*

There is much thoughtful matter pertinent to our topic in the second book of Sabatier's *Religions of Authority and the Religion of the Spirit;* and a useful book is Pfleiderer's *The Development of Christianity.*

For the Bohemian Brothers, or, as their spiritual descendants are now called, the Moravian Brethren, see Gindely's *Geschichte der Bömischen-Brüder;* Gindely's *Quellen zur Geschichte der Böhmischen-Brüder;* Müller's *Zinzendorf als Erneurer der alten Brüder-Kirche;* Becker's *Zinzendorf und sein Christentum;* and Hutton's *History of the Moravian Church.*

Of the increasing number of books that relate to the Anabaptists, a set of men still much misunderstood, the following, of the more recent ones, are useful. Bax's *Rise and Fall of the Anabaptists;* Heath's *Anabaptism;* Keller's *Geschichte der Wiedertaüfer und ihres Reichs zu Münster;* Kerssenbroch's *Leben und Schriften,* edited by Detmer; Tumbült's *Die Wiedertaüfer;* Burrage's *The Anabaptists of the Sixteenth Century;* and Newman's *History of Anti-Pedobaptism.* In addition there are Merx's *Thomas Münzer und Heinrich Pfeiffer;* F. O. zur Linden's *Melchior Hofmann;* Loserth's *Balthasar Hübmayer;* Vedder's *Balthasar Hübmaier;* and Burckhardt's article on "Jan of Leyden" in his *Basler Biographien.*

The Anti-Trinitarians may be studied best in their writings and in the biographies of the leaders. The literature relating to Servetus is extensive. In addition to the books relating to him cited in the references for our sixteenth chapter, see Tollin's *Das Lehrsystem Michael Servets genetisch dargestellt.* Tollin has discussed, in at least forty magazine articles, almost every question connected with the ill-fated thinker; and his book is the best study of the theological speculations and conclusions of Servetus. For the Socini see Trechsel's *Die protestantischen Anti-Trinitarier vor Faustus Socin;* and Fock's *Der Socinianismus.* For the Anti-Trinitarians in general see Bonet-Maury's *Early Sources of English Unitarian Christianity,* translated into English; Sand's *Bibliotheca Anti-Trinitariorum;* and Allen's *Historical Sketch of the Unitarian Movement since the Reformation.*

For the schisms see Döllinger's and Pünjer's books already named; Dorner's *Geschichte der protestantischen Theologie;* Richard's *The Confessional History of the Lutheran Church;* and M'Giffert's *Protestant Thought before Kant,* a little book that will be found useful for several of our chapters.

The freethinkers are dealt with in the histories of philosophy; in Beard's *Reformation;* in Robertson's *Short History of Free Thought;* in Owen's *Evenings with the Skeptics;* in Owen's *Skeptics of the Italian Renaissance;* and in Owen's *Skeptics of the French Renaissance.* See also Morley's *Life of Agrippa;* Stoddart's *Life of Paracelsus;* Sudhoff's *Versuch einer Kritik der Echtheit der Paracelsischen Schriften;* the *Corpus Schwenckfeldianorum;* Tausch's *Sebastian Franck von Donauwörth und seine Lehrer;* and Graves's *Peter Ramus and the Educational Reform of the Sixteenth Century.*

The study of the history of tolerance, and of its champions, may be carried on in Ruffini's *Religious Liberty,* now happily translated into English, which has pages that bear in a helpful manner upon most of our remaining chapters; in the chapter entitled "On Persecution" in Lecky's *Rationalism;* in Creighton's *Persecution and Tolerance;* in Völker's *Toleranz und Intoleranz im Zeitalter der Reformation;* in Schaff's *History of the Christian Church* (6:50-86; 7:612-58, 687-712); in the chapters on "Reason and Liberty" and "The Sects of the Reformation" in Beard's *Reformation of the Sixteenth Century;* in Giran's *Sébastien Castellion et la Réforme Calviniste;* in Buisson's masterly *Sébastien Castellion,* which is of greatest value to us at this point of our study; and in the second volume of Dilthey's *Gesammelte Schriften,* which deals with the subject in an admirable manner. The eloquent French version of the remarkable little book *Traité des Hérétiques,* doubtless a collective work by Italian refugees, aided by several men of Teutonic race, at Basel, of whom Castellion, a Savoyard, was the most important, has recently been reprinted. Copies of the Latin original (1554) are extremely rare; and only three copies of the French version (1554) are known to be extant, and they are all in Swiss libraries. The book is indispensable in any serious history of civilization.

## CHAPTER XIX

### THE DEVELOPMENT OF LETTERS AND ART

For the development of literature during the disturbances of the Protestant Revolution see the histories of letters and of literature cited as references for our fifth chapter. In addition to them see Saintsbury's *The Earlier Renaissance;* Gardner's *Dukes and Poets in Ferrara,* in which historical accuracy and literary charm are pleasingly compounded; Gobineau's *Renaissance,* which has been translated into English; and chapter fourteen, with its bibliography, of the third volume of *The Cambridge Modern History.* Panizzi's edition of *Boiardo* contains all the important works of the poet; and in *Euphorion,* by Vernon Lee (Violet Paget's nom de plume), there is a notable essay on "The School of Boiardo." There are other essays in this suggestive but immature book that will be found of considerable value in the study of Italian social conditions and Italian art in the period of the Renaissance. Panizzi's edition of the *Orlando Furioso* is the most useful. See also W. Stewart Rose's translation of Ariosto's great poem; and Gardner's *Ariosto: the Prince of Court Poets,* a scholarly and sympathetic work that succeeds admirably in giving the spirit of the age; and the little essay on Ariosto in Gebhart's *De Panurge à Sancho Pança.* The more complete editions of Machiavelli's writings are those by Parenti and by Usigli. But see Burd's *Il Principe,* which contains an excellent introduction. The best biography of the great exponent of statecraft is Villari's *Machiavelli and His Times,* finely translated into English by the historian's wife, Linda White Villari. See also Morley's *Machiavelli;* the essay on Machiavelli in Gebhart's *La Renaissance Italienne;* and the notable passages relating to Machiavelli in the second volume of Dilthey's *Gesammelte Schriften.* Gherardi, a Florentine archivist, is engaged upon the first complete edition of Guicciardini's works. The best biography of the historian and statesman is Rossi's *Francesco Guicciardini.* For Leo X see Pastor's *History of the Popes;* Creighton's *History of the Papacy;* Gregorovius's *Rome in the Middle Ages;* Roscoe's *Life and Pontificate of Leo X,* a notable book in its time and still quite useful; and Vaughan's *The Medici Popes.* In the second volume of Casa's works will be found his *Vita di Bembo.* There are three biographical works relating to Sadoleto; one by Fiordibello, which is to be found in the Verona edition of the cardinal's works; Péricaud's *Fragments biographiques sur Jacob Sadolet;* and Joly's *Etudes sur Sadolet.* Bembo and Sadoleto are both dealt with in Sandys's *History of Classical Scholarship.* There is a recent translation, by Opdycke, of Castiglione's golden book *The Courtier.* See also Hare's *Courts and*

*Camps of the Italian Renaissance;* and Cartwright's *Baldassare Castiglione, the Perfect Courtier,* which has a good bibliography.

For the development of architecture see the references relating to that art given in the list of books for our sixth chapter.

The general books on sculpture listed in the references for the same chapter are useful for our present study. Add to them Symonds's *The Life of Michelangelo;* Mackowsky's excellent *Michelagniolo;* Gebhart's *Michel-Ange, sculpteur et peintre,* written with much of the charm and insight that characterize the books of this historian; Knapp's *Michelangelo;* and Davies's *Michangelo.*

For the painters of this period see the general histories of the art cited in the references for our sixth chapter; and also the following books. Fromentin's *The Masters of Past Time;* Gronau's *Leonardo da Vinci;* Berenson's *The Drawings of Florentine Painters;* the second edition of Solmi's *Leonardo;* the second edition of Séailles's *Leonardo da Vinci, l'artiste et le savant;* McCurdy's *Leonardo da Vinci,* a good brief book; McCurdy's *Leonardo da Vinci's Note-Books;* and Thiis's *Leonardo da Vinci,* unique in the difficult questions of attribution, but notable for its clarity of exposition and for a vivid portrayal of the personal and social background of Leonardo's early career. Pater's essay on Leonardo, which contains the famous interpretation of the Mona Lisa, is to be found in his *Renaissance.* Raphael is dealt with in Morelli's *Italian Masters;* in Berenson's *Central Italian Painters;* and in Oppé's *Raphael,* a useful monograph, well-illustrated. There is a brief biography of Andrea del Sarto in English by Guiness. For Correggio see Ricci's *Life and Times of Correggio;* Thode's *Correggio;* and Moore's *Correggio.* A fine exposition of the great contributions of Venice to the development of painting (the marvelous enrichment of coloring, and a broad and simple fashion of treating the landscape background) is to be found in Phillipps's *The Venetian School of Painting.* Meynell's *Giovanni Bellini* has quite a full set of reproductions of the pictures that are authentically attributed to this early Venetian painter. For Giorgione see Gronau's *Zorzon da Castelfranco;* Cook's *Giorgione;* and De Villard's *Giorgione da Castelfranco.* For Titian see Crowe and Cavalcaselle's *The Life and Times of Titian;* Gronau's *Titian,* translated from the German, the most important work on the painter; Phillipps's *The Earlier and Later Works of Titian;* and Ricketts's *Titian,* the most recent book on the subject, well-illustrated.

For the art of the Low Countries see Crowe and Cavalcaselle's *The Early Flemish Painters;* Wurzbach's *Niederländisches Künstler-Lexicon;* Weale's *John van Eyck;* Bode's *Studien zur geschichte der Holländischen Melerei;* and Harvard's *The Dutch School of Painting.* Ward's *The Architecture of the Renaissance in France* has a scholarly text and unusually serviceable illustrations. Lafenestre's *Jehan Fouquet* is a very satisfactory study of the most representative French painter of the fifteenth century; and admirably illustrated is Vitry and Briere's *Documents de la Sculpture française du Renaissance.*

The early history of German painting may be studied in Janitschek's *Geschichte der deutschen malerei.* Of the many books that relate to the great German painter, draughtsman, and engraver, see Cust's *Albrecht Dürer;* Knackfuss's *Dürer,* translated from the German; Zucker's *Albrecht Dürer;* and Wölfflin's *Die Kunst Albrecht Dürers,* an excellent monograph. And for Hans Holbein, the younger, see Knackfuss's *Holbein;* Davies's *Holbein;* and Woltmann's *Holbein und seine Zeit.*

## CHAPTER XX

### THE TURK, THE COMET, AND THE DEVIL

Many of the books relating to the Turk and Mongol in Europe cited in the references for our second chapter will be found useful for this present study of the continued advance of the Turk. To these may be added Pears's *The Destruction of the Greek Empire;* Lane-Poole's *Mohammedan Dynasties;* Butler's *The Arab Conquest of Egypt;* and Becker's *Beiträge zur Geschichte Agyptens.* For the maritime successes of the Turk see Lane-Poole's *Story of the Barbary Corsairs,* in which, and in the fourth and fifth volumes of Lavisse and Rambaud's *Histoire Générale,* will be found bibliographies of the subject. The Janizaries are described in Djévad Bey's *État militaire ottoman;* in Thuasne's *Djem-Sultan* the Turkish relations in these years with western powers are set forth; while in Ranke's *Die Osmanen und die spanische Monarchie,* in Eliot's admirable *Turkey in Europe,* and in Lybyer's *The Government of the Ottoman Empire in the time of Suleiman the Magnificent,* much may be learned of the Turkish administration.

Some information of the terror in Latin Christendom caused by the encroaching Turk may be gathered from Knolles's *Historie of the Turks,* and from the anonymous *Libellus de ritu et moribus Turcorum,* a little book, widely circulated in that day, one edition of which was prepared by Luther; but by far the best source of information is to be found in the news-letters, sermons, and other writings of the day, which are to be found not in books but in the great libraries.

The terror caused in the sixteenth century by celestial signs and wonders may at least be glimpsed in Friedrich's *Astrologie und Reformation;* in Lund's *Himmelsbild und Weltanschauung;* and in White's *History of the Warfare of Science with Theology in Christendom* (see the chapter entitled " From ' Signs and Wonders ' to Law in the Heavens "), where the footnotes give references to the contemporary comet literature.

For the study of the panic, created by the belief in the Devil and his alleged servants, the witches, that prevailed throughout Latin Christendom, and for the rise of the terrible witch persecution of the sixteenth century, use Roskoff's *Geschichte des Teufels;* Soldan and Heppe and Bauer's *Geschichte der Hexenprozesse,* whose wealth of illustrations in itself makes the book one of unusual value; Janssen's *History of the German People at the End of the Middle Ages;* Hansen's *Zauberwahn, Inquisition und Hexenprozess im Mittelalter;* Hansen's *Quellen und Untersuchungen;* and the second volume of Duhr's *Geschichte der Jesuiten in den Ländern Deutscher Zunge.* In English there are several chapters in Lecky's *Rationalism in Europe;* and others in White's *Warfare of Science;* Scott's *Letters on Demonology and Witchcraft;* Wright's *Narratives of Sorcery and Magic;* the little collection of extracts from original sources, edited by George Lincoln Burr, entitled "The Witch Persecutions," in the University of Pennsylvania series of *Translations and Reprints;* Burr's *The Fate of Dietrich Flade;* and Notestein's interesting and authentic *History of Witchcraft in England.*

## CHAPTER XXI

### THE RISE OF THE JESUITS

A great mass of original source material relating to the Society of Jesus and its early leaders, including the fundamental documents of the Order (its *Constitutiones* and *Decreta Congregationum Generalium,* its *Regulae,* and its *Rationes Studiorum*), is in course of publication. The volumes that have appeared are listed, for the most part, in the bibliographies appended to the articles on Ignatius Loyola and on the Society of Jesus in *The Catholic Encyclopædia* and in *The Encyclopædia Britannica.*

For the life of the founder of the Order see his autobiography, communicated to González de Camara, translated into English by Rix, and published under the title of *The Testament of Ignatius Loyola.* There is also another translation into English by O'Connor, entitled *The Autobiography of Ignatius Loyola.* Hundreds of biographies of Ignatius have been written. Perhaps next to the *Autobiography* in point of time is the *Vita Ignatii Loiolae* by Polanco, who, towards the end of Loyola's life, was the saint's secretary. It is to be found in the *Monumenta historica Societas Jesu,* which, as already stated, is now in course of publication. Ribadeneira, who in his youth was associated with Loyola, wrote a life of the great leader in Spanish. It has been translated into French, and edited by Clair, under the title of *La Vie de Saint Ignace.* Another early biography is that by Bartoli, written in Latin, of which the best modern edition, published under the title of *Histoire de Saint Ignace,* is that by Michel. Of the numerous lives written in later times the following are among the best. Genelli's *Das Leben des heiligen Ignatius von Loyola,* which has been translated into English; Henri Joli's *Saint Ignace de Loyola,* one of the best of the briefer books, which also has been done into English; and a recent one by Francis Thompson, the English poet, *Life of Saint Ignatius,* beautifully illustrated. See also Watrigant's interesting study *La genèse des exercices de Saint Ignace de Loyola.*

For the first associates of Ignatius, as well as for Ignatius himself, see the very useful and well-illustrated *Saint Ignatius and the Early Jesuits,* by Stewart Rose (*nom de plume* of Caroline Stewart Erskine); Pise's *The Founders of the Jesuits;* Taylor's *Loyola and Jesuitism in its Rudiments;* Coleridge's *The Life and Letters of Saint Francis Xavier;* Müller's *Les origines de la Compagnie de Jésus,* in which the author endeavors to establish a Mohammedan origin for many of Loyola's ideas; and the eloquent essay on "Ignatius Loyola and his Associates" by Sir James Stephen in his *Essays in Ecclesiastical Biography.*

The organization of the Order may best be studied in its fundamental documents, which we have already mentioned; and, after them, in the encyclopedia articles; in Cartwright's *The Jesuits, their Constitution and Teaching;* and in Heimbucher's *Die Orden und Kongregationen.* Its educational methods may be studied in Hughes's *Loyola and the Educational System of the Jesuits;* and in Schwickerath's *Jesuit Education.*

For the history of the Order one may select out of the great mass of literature on the subject the notable essay by Macaulay on Ranke's *History of the Popes;* the little book by Ward on *The Counter-Reformation;* the sixth chapter of Wishart's *Monks and Monasticism;* Symonds's *The Catholic Reaction,* written in a spirit of animosity; Philippson's *La contre-*

*révolution religieuse au 16ᵉ siècle;* Laurent's *Les guerres de religion,* a book that displays something of its author's fine synthetic power; Gothein's *Ignatius von Loyola und die Gegenreformation,* one of the very best books on the subject, and one which, as the title indicates, relates to most of our succeeding chapters; Böhmer's *Les Jésuites,* translated from the German into French by Monod, who has written an excellent introduction to the volume; Reusch's *Beiträge zur Geschichte der Jesuiten;* Taunton's *History of the Jesuits in England;* Brou's *Concerning Jesuits;* Tacchi-Venturi's *Storia della Compagnia di Gesù in Italia;* Duhr's scholarly and sincere *Geschichte der Jesuiten in den Ländern deutscher Zunge;* Droysen's *Geschichte der Gegenreformation;* Philippson's *West-Europa im Zeitalter von Philipp II;* Crétineau Joly's *Histoire de la Compagnie de Jésus;* Guettée's *Histoire des Jésuites;* Wolff's *Allgemeine Geschichte der Jesuiten;* Fouqueray's inclusive, credulous, and sharply partisan *Histoire de la Compagnie de Jésus en France;* and McCabe's *Candid History of the Jesuits.*

## CHAPTER XXII

### THE COUNCIL OF TRENT

The religious crisis at the middle of the sixteenth century may be studied in the church histories, the general histories, and the national histories, whose titles have already been given; and in such general works, given as references for the chapter immediately preceding this, as Gothein's *Ignatius von Loyola und die Gegenreformation.*

All the original sources for the history of the Council, ably edited, are in process of publication by the body of German Catholic scholars, organized in 1876, known as the Görres-Gesellschaft (Societas Goerresiana), named after the historian Johann Joseph von Görres. The great work is entitled *Concilium Tridentinum: diariorum, actorum, epistularum, tractatuum nova collectio.* There are older collections of sources, of course, but all of them are incomplete. They are listed in most of the encyclopedia articles on the subject, especially in the *Britannica.*

One of the standard histories of the Council is still "the brilliant old book of the Rome-hating Venetian statesman, Father Paul Sarpi," *Istoria del concilio tridentino,* "accessible to us in the quaint old English version of Brent"; and another is "its elaborate refutation," by the Jesuit priest and cardinal, Pallavicini, entitled *Istoria del concilio di Trento,* "enriched in its French translation by valuable additions." Following these it might be well to read Brischar's *Zur Beurteilung der Kontroversen zwischen Sarpi und Pallavicini.* A more general work, of which the third and fourth volumes relate to our subject, is Wessenberg's *Die grossen Kirchenversammlungen;* and in the third volume of Moeller's *Lehrbuch der Kirchengeschichte,* and the third volume of Hergenröther's *Handbuch der allegemeinen Kirchengeschichte* (the new edition of 1909, by Kirsch), general accounts of the Council and its work will be found. See also Dejob's *De l'influence du Concile de Trente;* and Döllinger's essay on the Council in his *Kleinere Schriften.* In English the best Catholic history of the Council, aside from the article in *The Catholic Encyclopædia,* is that by Waterford, which also contains an English translation of the Canons and Decrees of the Council. And in our own language one may read Bungener's *History of the Council of Trent,* translated from the French, and Froude's pungent *Lectures on the Council of Trent.*

Particular aspects of the Council are treated in Deslandres's *Le Concile de Trente, et la réforme du clergé;* in Korte's *Die Konzilspolitik Karls V;* in Kassowitz's *Die Reformvorschläge Ferdinands I;* in Hefner's *Entstehungsgeschichte des trienter Rechtfertigungsdekretes;* and in Prumbs's *Die Stellung des Trienterkonzils zu der Frage nach dem Wesen der heiligmachenden Gnade.*

For the Popes of the period see the ecclesiastical and papal histories, and add to them Duruy's *Le Cardinal Carlo Caraffa.*

For the *Index Librorum Prohibitorum* see Reusch's *Der Index der verbotenen Bücher,* in every respect the most important book on the subject; Arndt's *De Libris prohibitis commentarii;* Hilger's *Der Index der verbotenen Bücher;* Vermeersch's *De prohibitione et censura librorum;* Mendham's *Literary Policy of the Church of Rome;* Putnam's *The Censorship of the Church of Rome,* the largest book on the subject in English, based very largely upon Reusch, but lamentably inaccurate; and Betten's little book, *The Roman Index of Forbidden Books,* written for Catholic readers.

The *Catechism* of the Council of Trent, *Catechismus Romanus,* after the original Italian text was revised by Carlo Borromeo, was turned into elegant Latin by the famous humanists Julius Pogianus and Paulus Manutius; and, by command of Pius V, it was translated into Italian, French, German, and Polish. The first known English translation, by Jeremy Donovan, was published in 1829 at Dublin. A more elegant translation into English it that by Buckley, published in 1852 at London.

An article on the famous bull *In coena Domini* will be found in *The Catholic Encyclopædia* (7:717-18), to which several references are appended.

## CHAPTER XXIII

### THE TRIUMPH OF MILITANT CATHOLICISM

Many of the references given for the two chapters immediately preceding this will be found useful for the study we have now in hand. They will often be found far more useful than the more special references given here, and certainly they are more available. Not to be forgotten is the scholarly and stimulating *Staat und Gesellschaft des Zeitalters der Gegenreformation* by Gothein, which will be found useful for almost all our remaining chapters as well as for this one.

There is a contemporary life of Pius V, in the *Vitae et gestae summorum pontificum romanorum,* by Ciaconius. Mendham's *Life and Pontificate of Saint Pius V* is extremely controversial; Falloux's *Histoire de Saint Pie V* is highly eulogistic; while Hillger's *Die Wahl Pius V* is quite a well-balanced book. There is also an interesting article on this Pope in the forty-ninth volume of *The Dublin Review.*

For the work of Carlo Borromeo, cardinal and saint of the Catholic Church, see Giussano's *Life of Saint Carlo Borromeo,* one of the three lives written by contemporaries, translated into English; Canon Sylvain's *Histoire de Saint Charles Borromée;* and, more valuable than either of these, Cantono's *Un grande riformatore del secolo XVI.*

It might be well at this point to speak of the *Acta Sanctorum,* a great work that deals with the lives of men and women canonized by the Catholic

Church. It was begun in the first years of the seventeenth century. The first volume was edited by Father John van Bolland, of the Society of Jesus; and since then the collaborators have been known as the Bollandists. The idea of the work was first conceived by Heribert Rosweyde, who also was a Jesuit. The work now consists of more than three score volumes, and it is still incomplete.

The character and work of Gregory XIII may be studied in the contemporary biography by Cicarella, continuator of the gossipy and interesting Platina, in *De vitis pontiff. Rom.;* in the life by Ciaconius, which is to be found in the work by him already cited; in Ciappi's *Comp. dell' attioni e santa vita di Gregorio XIII;* in Bompiano's *Hist. pontificatus Gregorii XIII;* and in Maffei's *Annales Gregorii XIII.* For the correction of the calendar see the articles in the various encyclopedias under the heading " Calendar."

For the activity of the Jesuits in the various countries see the references already given on the history of their Order; and add to them Pollard's *The Jesuits in Poland;* Duhr's *Die Jesuiten an den deutschen Fürstenhofen;* Lohr's *Der Kampf um Paderborn;* Keller's *Die Gegenreformation in Westfalen und am Niederrhein;* and Astrain's *Historia de la Compañia de Tesús en la Asistencia de España.*

There is an article on the *Ratio Studiorum* in *The Catholic Encyclopædia* (12:654–57), very guarded in its statements, to which is appended a select bibliography.

There is no adequate work dealing with the revived Inquisition. Buschbell's *Reformation und Inquisition in Italien* has dealt with the beginnings of it in Italy. Ranke has touched upon it in his *History of the Popes.* Pastor has spoken about it in dealing with the lives of Paul III and Paul IV. And Fredericq is at work upon the history of the institution in the Netherlands. But it seems hopeless to expect a satisfactory general history of the subject until the Congregation of the Inquisition decides to give access to its records to competent scholars.

For the *Index,* in addition to the books cited in the references for our twenty-second chapter, see Reusch's *Die Indices librorum prohibitorum des 16. Jahrhunderts,* in which all the sixteenth century indexes have been collected into a single exhaustive volume.

## CHAPTER XXIV

### THE SPANISH SUPREMACY

Bibliographies are to be found in Hume's *Spain, its Greatness and Decay;* in his *The Spanish People;* in Armstrong's *The Emperor Charles V;* and in the second volume (chapter XV) and the third volume (chapter XV) of *The Cambridge Modern History.* Only a few of the more important sources, and certain studies not included in these bibliographies, will be given here.

Among the writings on general Spanish history by Spanish writers the *Estudios críticos* of Don Vicente de la Fuente, and Don Rafael Altamira's *Historia de España,* hold a distinguished place. A commendable book in French is Romey's *Histoire d'Espagne.*

For the Moors in Spain see Lea's *The Moriscos of Spain;* Lane-Poole's *The Moors in Spain;* Scott's *History of the Moorish Empire in Europe;* Dozy's *Spanish Islam,* now fortunately translated from the French; Dozy's *Histoire des Musulmans d'Espagne;* Codera's *Decadencia y desaparición de los Almoravides en España;* and Codera's *Estudios críticos de historia árabe española.*

The economic conditions of Spain are ably discussed in Bernays's article "Zur inneren Entwicklung Castiliens unter Karl V" in the first volume of the *Deutsche Zeitschrift für Geschichtswissenschaft.* The social conditions of the time are authoritatively and interestingly set forth by Morel-Fatio in his chapter on "L'Espagne du Don Quijote" in *Studies in European Literature (The Taylorian Lectures 1881-99)* ; in his *Etudes sur l'Espagne;* and in his *L'Espagne au XVIᵉ et XVIIᵉ Siècle,* a collection of historical and literary documents. See also Julio Puyol y Alonso's *Estado social que refleja 'El Quijote';* and Havelock Ellis's *The Soul of Spain,* a book of penetrating insight by a scholar unusually gifted and trained for such a study.

Of books that relate specially to Philip II see Forneron's *Histoire de Philippe II,* in which the personal equation is a disturbing element; Hume's *Philip II,* a fair-minded book, with a good bibliography, by a notable authority; Hume's *Two English Queens and Philip II,* written eleven years after the preceding book; De Córdoba's *Felipe II;* Clauzel's *Philippe II,* one of the best recent books that have to do with this somber sovereign; Bratli's *Philippe II, roi d'Espagne,* which contains a good survey of Spain in the middle of the sixteenth century; and the essay on Philip in Pattison's *Leading Figures in European History.* For the politics of Spain and the Papacy see Herre's *Papsttum und Papstwahl im Zeitalter Philipps II.* See also the English translation of Coloma's *Don Juan of Austria.*

## CHAPTER XXV

### THE REVOLT OF THE NETHERLANDS

Lists of references relating to the subject are to be found in Blok's *History of the People of the Netherlands;* in both volumes of Putnam's *William the Silent;* in Harrison's *William the Silent;* in Squire's *William the Silent;* and (for the sixth, seventh, and nineteenth chapters) in the third volume of *The Cambridge Modern History.*

Of derived sources one naturally thinks first of all of Motley's classic work *The Rise of the Dutch Republic,* of its continuation *The History of the United Netherlands,* and of *The Life and Death of John Barneveld;* but these works, eloquent and scholarly though they be, are colored with the pronounced views of their author and they must therefore be rectified by the work of more dispassionate writers. Four such historians and their works we have already named; and to them we may add Pirenne's *Histoire de Belgique;* Laurent's *Les guerres de religion;* Namèche's *Guillaume le Taciturne et la révolution des Pays-Bas;* Rachfahl's *Margaretha von Parma;* Stirling-Maxwell's *Don John of Austria;* and Gossart's *L'etablissement du Régime Espagnol dans les Pays-Bas et l'Insurrection,* the last of which, like the books by Pirenne and Blok, emphasizes the political rather than the religious causes of the revolt.

## CHAPTER XXVI

### THE RELIGIOUS WARS IN FRANCE

The literature of the subject is listed in Monod's *Bibliographie de l'histoire de France,* and in the bibliographies of Lavisse and Rambaud's

*Histoire Générale,* Lavisse's *Histoire de France,* the third and fourth volumes of Hauser's *Les Sources de l'histoire de France,* and the third volume of *The Cambridge Modern History.* Many of the abundant memoires of the time are included in great collections, and to these Franklin's *Les sources de l'histoire de France* furnishes a convenient key.

General descriptions of this tumultuous time are to be found in the histories already named; and in Macdonald's *History of France;* Armstrong's *The French Wars of Religion;* Baird's *The Rise of the Huguenots;* Baird's *The Huguenots and Henry of Navarre;* Thompson's *The Wars of Religion in France;* and Ranke's *Civil Wars and Monarchy in France,* translated from the German.

Among books dealing with aspects and personages of the time the following are useful. Sichel's *Catherine de' Medici and the French Reformation;* Forneron's *Les Guise et leur époque;* Decrue's *Anne, duc de Montmorency;* Marcks's *Gaspard von Coligny;* Whitehead's *Gaspard de Coligny;* Merki's *L'Admiral de Coligny;* Besant's *Gaspard de Coligny;* White's *The Massacre of Saint Bartholomew;* Atkinson's *Michel de l'Hospital;* and Willert's *Henry of Navarre.*

## CHAPTER XXVII

### PAPACY AND EMPIRE

For works that relate to the Empire see the *Quellenkunde der deutschen Geschichte* of Dahlmann-Waitz-Steindorff; Jastrow's *Jahresberichte der Geschichtswissenschaften;* and Loewe's *Bücherkunde der deutschen Geschichte.* See also the bibliography for the fifth and twenty-first chapters of the third volume of *The Cambridge Modern History;* and also the lists of references appended to the pertinent biographies in the *Allgemeine Deutsche Biographie.* Many of the general histories of Germany already enumerated will be found useful for this study. And to them should be added Ranke's *Zur deutschen Geschichte vom Religionsfrieden bis zum 30jahrigen Kriege;* Stubb's *Lectures on European History;* Kaser's *Deutsche Geschichte zur Zeit Maximilians I;* Scherg's *Ueber die religiose Entwicklung Kaiser Maximilians II;* Droysen's *Geschichte der Gegenreformation;* Ritter's *Der Augsburger Religionsfriede;* Wolf's *Der Augsburger Religionsfriede;* Von Bezold's *Staat und Gesellschaft des Reformationszeitalters,* and Gothein's *Staat und Gesellschaft des Zeitalters der Gegenreformation,* which will be found to be admirable summaries of the second and third periods of our book.

Books for the study of the reforming Papacy have been mentioned in preceding lists of references. They are, for the most part, church histories, histories of the Papacy, and histories of the Counter-Reformation or the Catholic Reaction. These should now be supplemented with the biographies of the Popes of this period and with other books that relate specially to them. Chapter thirteen of the third volume of *The Cambridge Modern History* is an excellent description of the character and work of Sixtus V, and a very complete bibliography is appended. See also Von Hübner's *Sixte-Quint,* which has been translated into English. It may be well to call attention once more to Von Ranke's masterly *History of the Popes* and to the suggestive and stimulating essay on it by Macaulay.

For the theological divisions among the Protestants see the list of books that relate to the schisms included in the references for our eighteenth chapter.

## CHAPTER XXVIII

### MAGYAR AND SLAV

The most important of the recent histories of Hungary in the Magyar or Hungarian language is the *History of the Hungarian Nation* by Szilágyì and many collaborators; and of considerable value is Acsády's *History of the Magyar Empire*. Szilágyì's *Hungarian Historical Biographies* is a dictionary of national biography, well illustrated, by many notable scholars. Of the books on Hungary in French one may read Sayous's *Histoire générale des Hongrois;* and Chélard's *La Hongrie millénaire*. In English there are Knatchbull-Hugessen's *The Political Evolution of the Hungarian Nation;* Andrássy's *The Development of Hungarian Constitutional Liberty,* translated from the French, more valuable for a later period than our own; and Vámbéry's *Origin of the Magyars,* the work of a Hungarian scholar who made himself famous as an Orientalist. Many of the books on Austria are useful for the study of Hungary, and of these Leger's *History of Austria-Hungary,* translated from the French, Huber's *Geschichte Oesterrichs,* and Drage's *Austria-Hungary,* may be mentioned.

For Transylvania (the name in German is Siebenbürgen) see Bielz's *Siebenbürgen.*

The histories of the Turks enumerated in the references for previous chapters and some of those contained in the bibliography for the fourth chapter of the third volume of *The Cambridge Modern History* will also be found serviceable for our present study.

For a bibliography of Poland see the one for the third chapter of the third volume of *The Cambridge Modern History.* Among the books in the language of the country are Szujski's monumental *History of Poland,* and Sokolowski's *Illustrated History of Poland.* In German there are Roepell and Caro's *Geschichte Polens,* and Schiemann's *Russland, Polen und Livland.* In French there is De Noailles's *Henri de Valois et la Pologne.* And in English there are Morfill's *Poland,* and Bain's *Slavonic Europe,* the latter of which is also useful for the other Slavonic countries.

A good bibliography of Russia is contained in the seventeenth volume of *The Times* edition (1907) of *The Historians' History of the World,* where also will be found considerable extracts from Russian works not elsewhere to be found in English. The two most important secondary histories of Russia are Karamzin's work, translated into French, and Soloviev's monumental work, which, though inferior to the former as literature, greatly surpasses it in authentic scholarship, but which, unfortunately, remains inaccessible to all of us who do not read Russian. Of the many other books that deal with the early history of the great empire these may be commended. Morfill's *Russia;* Morfill's *History of Russia,* which, however, begins only with the birth of Peter the Great; Munro's *Rise of the Russian Empire;* Rambaud's *History of Russia,* translated from the French; Schiemann's *Russland, Polen und Livland;* Waliszewski's *La Crise révolutionnaire;* and, for the relations of Russia with the Papacy, Pierling's *Russie et le Saint-Siège.* Of great value are the pertinent chapters in the *Histoire Générale* of Lavisse and Rambaud.

The publications of the Hakluyt Society, of which we have spoken previously, include accounts of the journeys of Chancellor, Jenkinson, Fletcher, and Horsey to these eastern lands and beyond them.

## CHAPTER XXIX

### THE REPUBLIC OF LETTERS

For general introductions to the study of the Republic of Letters and also to that of the Republic of Art see the passages relating to the intellectual tendency of the age in the first volume of Von Ranke's *History of the Popes;* Symond's two volumes on *The Catholic Reaction,* which are stamped with a vigorous anti-clerical spirit; and Gothein's *Staat und Gesellschaft des Zeitalters der Gegenreformation.*

The Ciceronians may be studied in Sandys's *History of Classical Scholarship;* in Hauvette's *Littérature italienne;* and in other histories of Italian literature. For the influence of Erasmus see, in addition to the lives of the great humanist mentioned in the references for our eleventh chapter, Dilthey's eloquent *Weltanschauung und Analyse des Menschen seit Renaissance und Reformation,* which constitutes the second volume of his *Gesammelte Schriften.* The results of the Lutheran schism and of the Protestant dissensions upon literature and art are nowhere stated better than in Beard's *The Reformation of the Sixteenth Century.* In Gothein's book, already mentioned, the results of the Catholic Reformation to letters and art are clearly set forth.

The philosophers are treated in a most satisfactory way in Dilthey's *Schriften* and in the various histories of philosophy. For Giordano Bruno see M'Intyre's *Giordano Bruno;* Owen's *Skeptics of the Italian Renaissance;* Adamson's *Development of Modern Philosophy;* Louis's *Giordano Bruno seine Weltanschauung und Lebensauffassung;* Reiner's *Giordano Bruno und seine Weltanschauung;* Gentile's *Bruno nella Storia della cultura;* and, of great value, Brinton and Davidson's *Giordano Bruno.* Carriere's *Philosophische Weltanschauung der Reformationszeit* deals with other thinkers of the time as well as with Bruno. For Montaigne see Bonnefon's *Montaigne, l'homme et l'œuvre;* Stapfer's *Montaigne,* a notable book; Sichel's *Michel de Montaigne;* Emerson's *Representative Men;* and Pater's graceful story *Gaston de Latour,* which remains unfinished. There is a reliable translation of Montaigne's *Essays* by Cotton and Hazlitt; and Waters has put *The Journal of Montaigne's Travels* into English in a very acceptable manner.

For the philologians, printer-publishers, jurists, and publicists, see the articles in the encyclopedias with their bibliographies, and see, too, the histories of literature and of the Roman Law. The second and the twenty-second chapters of the third volume of *The Cambridge Modern History,* together with their bibliographies, are both convenient and useful. There are, of course, special books that deal with these men, such as Brown's *George Buchanan, Humanist and Reformer,* of which the bibliographies will furnish information.

The historians, poets, dramatists, and novelists are to be studied in the histories of literature enumerated in the references for our fifth and nineteenth chapters and in Hannay's *The Later Renaissance.* Of books that deal with historians, special attention may be called to Courteault's *Blaise de Monluc,* an unusually scholarly book. For the poets the following books are recommended. Rosini's edition of Tasso's works. Boulting's *Tasso,* an excellent biography. For all the French writers included in our present study, see Petit de Julleville's *Histoire de la langue et de la littérature françaises,* whose chapters, written by different authors, are of unequal merit, and whose bibliographies are particularly valuable. The *Manual of*

*French Literature* by Brunetière, a critic of great learning and undaunted courage, whose intense convictions and smashing blows were directed against the trivial and the unreal in life and in literature, was done into English by Derechef. Tilley's *Literature of the French Renaissance* is an admirable book for our purpose. In the *Causeries du lundi,* a series of articles, afterwards reprinted in book form, that for three years appeared every Monday in the *Constitutionnel,* a Parisian publication, and in a previous set of essays called in their collected form *Critiques et portraits littéraires,* admirable studies are to be found of a number of the French writers of the sixteenth century by Sainte-Beuve, a critic of great gifts and conscientious industry. The *Life of Benvenuto Cellini* has been translated into English by Symonds; and also by Cust,— *The Memoirs of Benvenuto Cellini.* For the poets see Perdrizet's *Ronsard et la réforme;* Wyndham's graceful and dependable *Ronsard and La Pléiade;* Pater's essay on " Joachim du Bellay " in his *Renaissance;* the essay on " Ronsard," the one on " Du Bellay," and the one on " Montaigne," in Faguet's *Seizième Siècle;* Braga's *Camões, epoca e Vida;* Braga's *Camões e o Sentimento National;* Martin's *Camões e a Renascença em Portugal;* Burton's *Camoens;* Aubertin's translation into English of the *Lusiads;* Church's *Spenser;* Carpenter's *Guide to the Study of Spenser;* Fox Bourne's *A Memoir of Sir Philip Sidney;* Fox Bourne's *Life of Sir Philip Sidney;* and Symonds's *Sir Philip Sidney.*

For the dramatists, in addition to the histories of literature, see Creizenach's *Geschichte des neueren Dramas;* D'Ancona's *Origini del teatro italiano;* Lyonnet's *Le Théâtre en Espagne;* Fitzmaurice-Kelly's *Lope de Vega and the Spanish Drama;* Lyonnet's *Le Théâtre au Portugal;* Petit de Julleville's *Le théâtre en France depuis ses origines jusqu' à nos jours;* Rigal's *Le théâtre français avant le periode classique;* Roy's *Etudes sur la théâtre français du XV^e et du XVI^e siècle;* Ward's *History of English Dramatic Literature to the Death of Queen Anne;* Symonds's *Shakespere's Predecessors in the English Drama;* Baker's *The Development of Shakespeare as a Dramatist,* one of the most substantial and satisfying of the innumerable books upon the great play-writer; and Raleigh's *Shakespeare.*

The novelists may be studied in the histories of literature, in such books as Gebhart's *Conteurs du moyen âge;* Warren's *History of the Novel previous to the Seventeenth Century;* Bever and Sansot-Orland's *Œuvres galantes des conteurs italiens;* Raleigh's *The English Novel;* Menéndez y Pelayo's *Origines de la Novela,* one of the most remarkable contributions to the history of Spanish literature; and Jusserand's *The English Novel in the Time of Shakespeare.* In addition to these books that are devoted to this particular form of literature, there are, of course, books that relate specifically to individual novelists, such as Aspráiz's *Estudio historico-crítico sobre las Novelas ejemplares de Cervantes;* De Icaza's *Las Novelas ejemplares de Cervantes;* De Escovar's *Apuntes escenicos cervantinos;* and Fitzmaurice-Kelly's *The Life of Miguel de Cervantes Saavedra.* And there are many magazine articles and separate chapters in books, such as the three essays on " Don Quixote " and the one on " Camoens " in Gebhart's *De Panurge à Sancho Pança,* and the one on " Don Quixote " in his *La Renaissance Italienne,* that will be found useful. For the pastoral element in literature no better book can be found than Greg's *Pastoral Poetry and Pastoral Drama,* the product of exceptional learning, unusual delicacy of appreciation, and a grateful felicity of style. And for the picaresque novels Chandler's *Romances of Roguery;* Clarke's essay on " The Spanish Rogue Story " in *Studies in European Literature (The Taylorian Lectures*

*1889-99);* Schultheiss's *Der Schelmenroman der Spanier;* Garriga's *Estudio de la Novela picaresca;* Morel-Fatio's *Etudes sur l'Espagne;* and Chandler's *The Literature of Roguery.*

## CHAPTER XXX
### THE REPUBLIC OF THE ARTS

The study of the architecture of the sunset period of the Renaissance may be pursued to advantage in the general histories of the art given in the references for our sixth and nineteenth chapters, where also will be found the titles of books suitable for the study of the sculpture and painting of this period. And of books that relate exclusively to the architecture of this time the following are recommended. Fletcher's *Andrea Palladio;* Ricci's *Baroque Architecture and Sculpture in Italy,* profusely and admirably illustrated; Briggs's *In the Heel of Italy,* a charming description of this less-frequented part of the peninsula in which baroque architecture may be studied at its best, and a sympathetic appreciation of this florid style of building. But the best literature relating to this much berated style is to be found not in books but in the leading periodical architectural publications of Europe and America.

For the continuation of the study of Venetian painting no better books can be found than Phillipps's *The Venetian School of Painting;* Powers's *Mornings with Masters of Art;* Berenson's *Venetian Painters;* and Ruskin's *Stones of Venice,* the last of which is especially good for the study of Tintoretto.

There are biographies of Veronese (Paolo Caliari, or Paolo Cagliari) by Yriarte, Meisner, and Bell. For Tintoretto see Thode's *Tintoretto;* Holborn's *Jacopo Robusti;* and, best of all, handsomely illustrated, appreciative and authentic in its criticism, Phillipps's *Tintoretto.* The Carracci and their followers are adequately treated in Venturi's *I Carracci e la loro scuola.* See also Sweetser's *Guido Reni.*

The birth of the new art of music may be studied to advantage in various articles in Grove's *Dictionary of Music and Musicians,* especially in the article on Palestrina; in *The Oxford History of Music;* and in Eitner's *Quellenlexicon.* For the rise of the Oratorio see (20:161–64) the article in the *Britannica;* and the rise of the Opera (20:121–26) may be studied in the same volume.

# INDEX

# INDEX

611